W9-BVU-654

Dispersed Relations

Dispersed Relations

Americans and Canadians in Upper North America

Reginald C. Stuart

Woodrow Wilson Center Press
Washington, D.C.

The Johns Hopkins University Press
Baltimore

EDITORIAL OFFICES
Woodrow Wilson Center Press
Woodrow Wilson International Center for Scholars
One Woodrow Wilson Plaza
1300 Pennsylvania Avenue, N.W.
Washington, D.C. 20004-3027
Telephone: 202-691-4010
www.wilsoncenter.org

ORDER FROM
The Johns Hopkins University Press
Hampden Station
P.O. Box 50370
Baltimore, Maryland 21211
Telephone: 1-800-537-5487
www.press.jhu.edu/books/

Printed in the United States of America on acid-free paper ∞

2 4 6 8 9 7 5 3 1

Library of Congress Cataloging-in-Publication Data

Stuart, Reginald C.
Dispersed relations : Americans and Canadians in upper North America / Reginald C. Stuart.
p. cm.
Includes bibliographical references and index.
ISBN 978-0-8018-8785-7 (cloth : alk. paper)
1. United States—Relations—Canada. 2. Canada—Relations—United States. 3. National characteristics, American. 4. National characteristics, Canadian. 5. Transnationalism. I. Title.
E183.8C2S78 2007
327.73071—dc22

2007016402

The Woodrow Wilson International Center for Scholars, established by Congress in 1968 and headquartered in Washington, D.C., is a living national memorial to President Wilson. The Center's mission is to commemorate the ideals and concerns of Woodrow Wilson by providing a link between the worlds of ideas and policy, while fostering research, study, discussion and collaboration among a broad spectrum of individuals concerned with policy and scholarship in national and international affairs. Supported by public and private funds, the Center is a nonpartisan institution engaged in the study of national and world affairs. It establishes and maintains a neutral forum for free, open and informed dialogue. Conclusions or opinions expressed in Center publications and programs are those of the authors and speakers and do not necessarily reflect the views of the Center staff, fellows, trustees, advisory groups, or any individuals or organizations that provide financial support to the Center.

The Center is the publisher of *The Wilson Quarterly* and home of Woodrow Wilson Center Press, *dialogue* radio and television, and the monthly newsletter "Centerpoint." For more information about the Center's activities and publications, please visit us on the Web at www.wilsoncenter.org.

For Penni
and to the memory of John K. Mahon

Contents

Acknowledgments

No author can conduct a major project or write a book such as this without assistance and encouragement from a vast array of people. Over many years, I have been fortunate in the kindness of colleagues, friends, strangers who became friends, journalists, think-tank scholars, and officials in both Canada and the United States who gave freely of their time to talk about the themes that developed into this book. Even casual chats sparked ideas and confirmed or questioned a hypothesis or line of inquiry in a project that dealt with contemporary affairs and policy themes. This was new territory for a historian. Throughout, my Mount Saint Vincent University colleagues provided sounding boards for early phases of thought and development. The Mount granted sabbatical leaves, the university Senate Research Committee granted an award for a summer assistant and research travel at an early stage of the project, and the Deans' Travel Committee supported travel to enable me to give papers, sit on or organize panels, and attend colloquia. This activity generated many contacts, especially at the alternating U.S. and Canadian meetings of the Association for Canadian Studies in the United States, which draws an array of Canadian-U.S. specialists from a broad spectrum of institutions and backgrounds and has provided me with a rich resource in many ways.

I must collectively thank all the politicians, civil servants, and officials in both federal governments who gave of their time for conversations and suggestions as the project developed. The good offices of my member of Parliament, Geoff Regan, got me appointments with officials such as the onetime defense minister, David Pratt, and later a productive telephone conversation with John Manley. U.S. diplomatic officers were continuously generous with their time, and Leonard Hill, Steve Kashkett, Stephen Kelly, and Buck Shinkman stand out among many. In Washington, Terence Breese of the U.S. State Department welcomed me on several occasions, as did the staff at Canada's Embassy, particularly Dan Abele, Terri Colli, Ariel Delouya, Mike Dorey, and Colin Robertson, as well as the consul general in New York City, Pamela Wallin. Stephen Knowles, clerk of the Standing Committee on Foreign Affairs and International Trade, deserves a nod for asking me to brief the committee on its Halifax visit shortly after the events of September 11, 2001. This experience helped to pull me out of a purely academic project into contemporary policy issues.

Two institutions proved vital to the timely completion of this book: the Canada-U.S. Fulbright Foundation in Ottawa, and the Canada Institute at the Woodrow Wilson International Center for Scholars in Washington. At the first, Michael Hawes and his able staff offered encouragement and assistance in my bid for a Senior Scholars leave fellowship. My referees—Denis Stairs of Dalhousie University, Christopher Sands, then of the Center for Strategic and International Studies, and John H. Thompson of Duke University—supported my application, and our collective efforts were rewarded. I was awarded a five-month tenure as the Fulbright–Woodrow Wilson International Center for Scholars Chair in Canada-U.S. Relations. The Canada Institute's director, David Biette, a colleague for the award's tenure, and since, became a friend and companion at many of the endless talks, panels, speeches, roundtables, and less formal occasions to which a temporary Washington "insider" had access. Other Woodrow Wilson Center staff members, especially Lee Hamilton, the president and director, had a keen interest in United States–Canada affairs as well as my project and offered helpful suggestions in our conversations. Christopher Sands deserves more than a passing mention because of his encouragement and advice during final revisions of the manuscript. David and Chris remain valued mementoes of my Fulbright experience.

Others who deserve mention include Carl Ek of the Congressional Research Service and Dwight Mason of the Center for Strategic and International Studies, which hosts a steady schedule of events on Canadian-U.S. and international affairs. The Woodrow Wilson Center also provided a delightful and conscientious intern, Catherine Godbout. Many journalists spared time to talk with me, and I had opportunities to comment on cross-border affairs for the Canadian Broadcasting Corporation and other media organizations. Stephen Randall of the University of Calgary and Ronald Tallman of Roosevelt University in Chicago provided early venues for presenting my central ideas. As the chapter drafts came together, many colleagues and friends read and offered advice. David Biette, Jason Bristow, Brian Lee Crowley, Beth La Dow, Ted Magder, and Peter Mombourquette stand out among many. Also, I could not be more honored and pleased than to have the Woodrow Wilson Center Press and the Johns Hopkins University Press copublish this book. My appreciation goes to Joe Brinley, director of the Woodrow Wilson Center Press, to his able staff, and to the readers who guided me in shaping the manuscript into final form.

Last, and far, far from least, my companions at home were central. My Siamese cats always reminded me when I should take a break and admire or feed them. They also knew better than I did when it was time to call it a day. My wife Penni encouraged and supported me in countless ways, as she has over the years, took my absence for research and conferences in stride, and happily came on the Fulbright sojourn in Washington. Throughout, she has accepted my long periods of absorption, tattering newspapers and magazines, and, as someone of Upper North American heritage, provided a sounding board. She weathered the "obsessive compulsive" disorder writers both suffer from and need. And as a reader of final drafts, she saved me from small slips and was my "technical adviser" in the final editing. However solitary writers feel at times, they are never alone, and their final product is really a group endeavor.

Dispersed Relations

Prologue: The Upper North American Arena

Upper North American transnational relations are the arteries of what are usually called Canadian-American relations. This ostensibly binational relationship between two sovereign governments has in historical terms unfolded in cultural, social, economic, and political realms that have dispersed throughout space, time, and human activity.[1] Transnationalism renders problematical the border as a barrier or line that marks sharp differences, despite its political and at times economic significance. The barrier definition has, however, remained central in the histories of the two countries, and in studies of their formal relations, because ideological distinctions have seemed important to explain North American culture and society. Conventional wisdom about the cultural and social impact of borders notwithstanding, recent work suggests otherwise. Although the border marked distinct polities, the cultures, societies, and economies intertwined as a shared, transnational whole that Washington and Ottawa managed in an Upper North American arena.[2]

This book draws from many disciplines and a large literature to explore the Canadian-American relationship throughout four realms. Wide-angle historical narratives organize themselves primarily around political and economic themes, while social and cultural cases weave in and out, at times as almost asides from the central political-economic focus.[3] Social scientists generally take a comparative approach, whereas economists study systems of production, commerce, and consumption as well as government policies. Interdependence became the central theme after the 1988 Free Trade Agreement and 1994 North American Free Trade Agreement. Their focus was more on the business of transnational trade than on the integrated economic system long in place. Literary scholars examine themes and traditions in writers best known in their canons, and they find cross-border distinctions of tone, theme, and style.[4] Historical geographers generally ignore national political compartments. They favor the juxtaposition of cultural, social, economic, and political themes in landscapes.[5]

In the early 1990s, a small school of borderlands scholars developed theoretical foundations that they and others used to move into transnational studies. They respected the significance of borders, but they developed comparative and regional perspectives on migrations, institutions, and community development.[6] Transnationalism has emerged as the most recent perspective, and it interweaves cultural, social, and economic themes in analyzing large regions with geographic coherence, such as the Great Lakes Basin.[7] This work has attracted other writers, including historians, who have explored the idea of a greater North America that discounts political borders as significant dividing lines for understanding the larger context.[8] By contrast, nationalist Canadian scholars and writers have always praised the border as a guarantor of welcome differences.[9]

Canadian-American affairs as a field appeared in the 1920s as a subcategory of Anglo-American relations, and with considerable intellectual coherence. A binational group came to be known as the Carnegie scholars because of their funding source. Their historical context was the aftermath of World War I, which convinced them that the peaceful cross-border relationship for over a century stood in stark contrast to the European carnage they had just witnessed, although Upper North American bilateral comity still sat in a triangular framework with Great Britain because of the habits of mind Anglo-Saxonism gave to North American intellectuals. Most attention went to political and economic themes, and cross-border social mingling emerged as a special kind of North American migration. The Carnegie scholars also assumed a nation-state equality alongside a binational asymmetry.[10] They saw permeable borders while formal relations occurred only through accredited consuls and ministers in each other's major centers. Cultural and social interaction wove around, but seemed less important than, economic and political relations between the two states and peoples. Meanwhile, by the later 1930s, the United States came to matter for Canada above all other countries. From the U.S. side, a handful of Americans in Washington began to see Canadians as familiar, friendly, and not really foreign, a perspective that extended throughout the century. Some Canadians complained about this outlook, but arguably a vague and benign image is better than no image at all. On a personal level, by then the mass media allowed Americans and Canadians to follow one another's affairs and trends on a daily basis as people interrelated across the border with family, friends, associates, and strangers.[11]

Americans, meanwhile, saw the United States as sui generis, an exceptional nation for God's chosen people in a chosen land. Canadians (Quebecers and Acadians aside) saw themselves as British. By the 1950s, "British" became a heritage as immigration broadened Canadian society. Many who became interpreters of the national identity, however, believed that whatever Canadians might be, they were not Americans. This perspective obscured, and even ignored, the complex, diffuse, ever-changing, and dispersed Upper North American cultural and social interlinkages. It also drew on stereotypes and oversimplified images about cross-border relations.[12] Even historians who saw comparable themes such as westward expansion or a frontier experience took pains to explain that the border and different historical and social traditions created divergent cultural and social patterns.[13] An Upper North American perspective, therefore, acts as a corrective to this exaggerated influence of the political boundary, because millions of people in successive generations became stakeholders in Upper North America's transnational regions.[14]

This volume examines the cross-border relationship in cultural, social, economic, and political realms, and in that order. The Atlantic northeastern borderland, or Greater New England, suggests why.[15] The geographic and social intimacy of the region and its deep and intertwined history coexisted and wove into the cross-border historical experience. People with regional family and economic interests developed a stake in good political relations. Current and future scholars, analysts, and policymakers must also understand that regionalism aside, each realm has its own threads, logic, and impetus, and each intertwines with the others. Thus the political significance of any particular issue depends upon what we are talking about, and when. Too often, policymakers lack the historical understanding of what lies both behind and beneath economic and political affairs, or what social consequence a potential plan of action will have in Upper North America, including the prospect that local stakeholders will work to oppose, defeat, or thwart policies that work against their heritage and immediate interests. The book also explores how the four realms developed and interwove through time to get us where we are: members of a transnational culture, society, and economy who retain an identification with and allegiance to distinct national political systems and governments in Upper North America.

Inescapable fundamental forces shaped this historical development. Geography ordained that each country emerged largely isolated in northern

North America with the other as its most important neighbor by the later nineteenth century. Continental geographic features ran in north-south lines with east-west climatic zones. East-to-west distances and geographic barriers meant that Canadians and Americans in borderland regions became more familiar with their immediate northern or southern neighbors than with fellow citizens in the regions to either side. This proximity effect led newcomers and settlers to mingle on a continuous basis in transnational borderland regions. Currently, over 80 percent of Canadians live and work within 200 miles of the border in a region with nearby Americans, who make up perhaps 16 percent of the U.S. population. Zones of selected shared outlooks evolved. Canadians mingled and dealt with Americans on a personal basis far more than the reverse, but interaction in the transborder zones has been intense and continuous nonetheless.

Asymmetry has also typified this interrelationship. The U.S. and Canadian population ratios have been about 10 to 1, but gross domestic product ratios have been 13 or 14 to 1. In global political or military terms, the ratio has been 2,000 or 3,000 to 1. Upper North American transnational economic integration thus has made Washington's policies at any given time more significant for Canada than Ottawa's policies are for the United States. Washington also came to sit in a global cave of political winds by the 1940s, so while Ottawa and Canadians pay constant attention to the United States, Washington and Americans take only episodic interest in Canada. Many Canadians have wavered between being shocked, shocked that Americans pay so little attention to Canada and worrying, worrying that they might pay too much attention. Some have suffered from an anticipatory annexation syndrome that asserts distinctions and divergences (with or without differences) to buttress national sovereignty. The majority of Canadians, however, have consistently seen themselves as similar to Americans and have favored or accepted integrated economies alongside their distinct sovereignties. Consistently, Canadians as nationals and stakeholders in this transnational relationship have had more confidence in their identity than those who claim to speak for them.[16] Arguments that Canada would become a "fifty-first state" because of economic integration have arisen from ideological impulses and have served domestic partisan purposes rather than the cross-border interdependencies that so many Upper North American stakeholders have relied upon.[17]

Great events can, however, shake any matrix of outlooks and systems. The mechanical, electrical, and electronic revolutions in production, transportation, and communications provide examples aplenty, but over protracted periods of time. September 11, 2001, within months, by contrast, transformed debates over, but not the facts of, cross-border economic integration and interdependence. The Smart Border Accord that Ottawa and Washington signed was smart policy, but efforts to rationalize border management had been under way piecemeal for a decade, albeit without substantive overall change. September 11 focused everyone's mind wonderfully, but coordinating Upper North American stakeholder and political will remain difficult, because millions in open societies feel at risk with invisible-until-they-strike terrorists. Inertia and the defensive character of domestic partisan politics in both countries have also exerted their influence but have proven less potent than anticipated as regional stakeholders have asserted their interests and politicians have attempted to juggle interests and fears.[18]

This book explores the origins, evolution, and contemporary character of Upper North American interdependence and political independence. The cultural, social, economic, and political realms have developed varying degrees of integration over time, but all have made both countries and peoples more alike in a mutual diversity rather than turning Canada into a photocopy of the United States.[19] The political and economic realms have become the most visible, and in modern times how prime ministers and presidents have seemed to get along has been a barometer of the overall relationship in Canada, but never in the United States. The nations' chief executives have, however, been the core of an ever-expanding coaxial axis. The political realm has also had traditional linkages and agreements numbering in the thousands at all levels of government, and liaisons among law enforcement agencies such as the Federal Bureau of Investigation and the Royal Canadian Mounted Police. Asymmetry, distinct constitutional and political systems, global influence, and sovereignty assertion have underscored differences in this realm.

The economic realm has coequal status with politics, although asymmetry of attention ensures that Canadians are far more aware than Americans of cross-border problems and realities. The transnational Upper North American economy has become a mostly free market, although Canadians in the past expected and tolerated a greater level of government intervention in their cultural, social, and economic affairs than do Americans.[20] The historical record reveals how nearly two centuries of Upper North American economic development has produced a transnational integration and interdependence not well appreciated by the public in either country. Some Canadian commentators shudder at talk of a deep economic integration that already exists, although they are more concerned with the ramifications for national independence than the system itself. The economic realm has always been the most dynamic, occasionally volatile, and most dispersed. Millions in borderland regions and beyond often do not realize that they are stakeholders in the Upper North American economic system until Ottawa's or Washington's policies touch their particular sensibilities.

The focus on political and economic realms has distracted North Americans from the cultural and social realms. All social systems evolve, but migrants to North America have always found open conditions to recreate or build personal lives and communities, whether in rural or urban settings. The same ethnic groups landed and settled in both countries, including the French, although not blacks. More important, immigration scholars have tended to think in national contexts and for some time overlooked Upper North American ethnic patterns. This accounted in part for the multicultural mosaic–versus–melting pot clichés that Canadian commentators used to explain their cultural and social distinctiveness from the United States. In addition, transnational patterns of ethnic and racial prejudice developed. Americans and Canadians expected immigrants to conform to social, legal, and political systems based on Anglo-Saxon values, and to learn English as the working language. Apart from particular institutions, a broad consideration of transnational social relations can dissolve, or at least perforate, the border as a dividing line.

The cultural realm dispersed within a transnational North America that reached far south to include California, the southern plains, and even the Gulf Coast states. A range of large and small ideas about life has interlinked people in both countries through values, ideas, customs, and leisure interests. The creative arts have always been cosmopolitan, and so has popular culture. By the early twentieth century, North Americans shared a complex, dispersed, interwoven culture, whether among intellectual and social elites, ethnic and gender groups, or the broad population. Technological communications systems dispersed cultural genres to individual levels and assembled mass audiences. Political borders disappeared as diffuse cultural forms dispersed throughout North America to the extent that "California" bungalows acquired heritage status in Vancouver.[21]

The book begins with the cultural realm, moves through the social and economic realms, and ends with the political realm. Ottawa's and Washington's policies have been more shaped by than able to shape even the economies of the Upper North American transnational regions, let alone culture and society. Central governments enacted regulations to govern border crossers long after transnational patterns had developed, because dispersed political interrelationships developed as a consequence of patterns in the other three realms. This sequence displays the role that millions of stakeholders have always played in transnational Upper North American history. This has become clear even in the post–September 11, 2001, era. Federal politicians, officials, and bureaucrats who legally hold the initiative have faced opposition from dispersed but organized groups with a strong stake in open border access. Ottawa's strongest allies to maintain a border open to the efficient transit of people and goods are Upper North American borderlanders and interests dispersed throughout both countries. Thirty-eight of the fifty states have one or more provinces as their largest economic partner. Geography, proximity, and interdependence have limited all but draconian determination to stop up border traffic and transit in the name of security, which in democratic political systems builds upon the assembly of dispersed local interests that is impossible to apply.[22] As a result, in the early twenty-first century, everyone and no one manages transnational Upper North America. Circular debates over binational divergence or convergence that have so absorbed nationalist and partisan passions in Canada have found no useful answers to these questions.[23]

This volume synthesizes historical and contemporary themes into a paradigm that relates the impact of events on policymaking to explain the complex transnational relationship of Canada and the United States in Upper North America. Americans and Canadians are both North Americans more than they realize, or are willing to admit. Integration and interdependence exist in all realms. These points are essential, because in the post–September 11, 2001, era the two peoples and their governments are seeking to craft a future that balances security with the freedoms of millions of stakeholders who must live and work together in difficult times.

Part I

Cultural Realm

The British writer Matthew Arnold believed that being cultured meant a broad acquaintance with the best that had been known and said in the world. This defines culture as enduring ideas, artifacts, and images from the high philosophical and creative arts. But what about the ideas, artifacts, and images of daily life? What about popular or mass culture? What about those who preferred a velvet painting of a lagoon to a Renoir? Does a preference for Mozart over Elvis, or the reverse, suggest greater or lesser cultural sensitivity, or taste? As history evolves, so does culture, however defined. Do new creations blend with or replace parts of the previous generation's mosaic? Do moral, social, economic, or political judgments shape culture? Is culture democratic, or elitist? And who says so? Arnold's definition reassures elitist sensibilities, and elites often self-define and self-recruit for their inner circles. Surely, however, personal tastes from all social sectors must be involved in culture, whether broad or narrow, elite or plebeian. And what then does culture mean in such liberal democratic societies as in Upper North America? Whether unique or mass produced, any human creation has a cultural foundation. Insofar as any Upper North American culture is concerned, Walter Lippmann may have hit upon the most useful definition. Culture seemed to him "what people are interested in, their thoughts, their models, the books they read and the speeches they hear, their table talk, gossip, controversies, historical sense and scientific training, the values they appreciate, the quality of life they admire. All communities have a culture. It is the climate of their civilization."[1]

In historical as well as contemporary Upper North America, many local and regional communities overlap and intertwine to make up a transnational culture such as Canada and the United States share. This also sits within a broad Western European context, at first dominantly Anglo-Saxon, but increasingly eclectic as time passed. Upper North American societies in the U.S. or British/Canadian jurisdiction assembled from a wide range of societies and produced variegated cultural forms and styles. Successive immigrants arrived and mingled to become parts of a social conglomeration in Upper North America. Anglo-Saxon values of personal liberty, land freehold, representative politics, and constitutional systems defined political legitimacy and established laws that restrained conduct within federal structures. Comparable, albeit divergent, attitudes emerged about the state's role as a social and economic overseer. Cultural and social values and habits of daily living were sufficiently similar that people from one Upper North American jurisdiction or region could mingle in another. Anyone from a city or suburb in Upper North America generally feels unfamiliar but comfortable in another, not foreign in manner, speech, or behavior. Moreover, regional differences within each country often proved more significant than with neighbors in borderland regions. Albertans seemed "western" in Halifax, for example, just as Texans did in Boston or New York.

The Upper North American transnational culture comprises many common attitudes and values. People prize leisure, share passions for sports and games, read the same authors, and with some exceptions, speak the same language. Vacations and holidays recall a national founding, or veterans and war dead. Each country celebrates "Labor Day" to honor working people. Both observe Christian religious celebrations such as Christmas and Easter, and accept all others, although they do not have an official "holiday" status for workers. Upper North Americans celebrate mothers, fathers, and lovers with dedicated days. Comparative studies of cross-border values and institutions have taken two broad views of such cultural themes. Seymour Martin Lipset argued, for example, that the Canadian and U.S. cultures began from a common origin and with the American Revolution split onto tracks destined to run forever parallel. Many now argue that the Revolution was not as significant as Lipset supposed. Revisionists suggest that several transnational regions developed by the end of the nineteenth century, and both cultural and social outlooks ignored national boundaries in the Atlantic Northeast, Franco-America, and later the Great Lakes Basin, the upper Great Plains, and the Pacific Northwest. A growing body of scholarship on each region has shown how they became established and evolved as transnational entities where the border cleaved political and legal but not economic, social, or cultural realms.[2] Even when national economic policies sought to orient trade and commerce along interregional east-west lines, cultural and social outlooks and transnational regional interests sustained their own interlinkages. Successive immigrant groups to these regions rapidly absorbed the local habit of ignoring the border while they developed a political patriotism loyal to their respective nation-state.[3] These cultural themes and shared values informed social development in Upper North America and also shaped economic interests and political forms.

Upper North American asymmetry nevertheless convinced patriotic Canadian elites in modern times that their "national" culture needed protection. Otherwise, American values and forms would prevail, and when that happened, political independence would be gone. Even the shared language, let alone cultural values, was a hazard. The elites had political but not always social influence over other classes. Domestic legislation or border controls had limited influence over cultural transnationalism. Social and intellectual values interwove with cultural themes to create Upper North American norms. At the same time, the border mattered for political loyalty and identity, as polls over the past several decades have revealed. Canadian and American values and culture might be transnational, but their political identities were national.[4] Moreover, in social terms most Upper North Americans have come to see themselves as middle class and have defined social status by income, education, profession, and property. In their personal taste in music, literature, and entertainment, they have sorted into groups of consumers dispersed throughout Upper North America. Popular culture has become as cosmopolitan as high culture. Moreover, electronic communications systems have created endlessly malleable mass North American audiences.

Part I explores selected topics as case studies in Upper North American transnational cultural themes. Chapter 1 examines cultural identities to consider distinctions with and without differences to argue that Canadians and Americans have become Upper North Americans. Connected and shared cultural strands coexist with discrete political identities and divergent international outlooks. Chapter 2 examines North America's culture of the printed word by focusing on writers, readers, publishers, and how the magazine and book industries became entangled in clashes over Canada's modern identity, where the stakes were not cultural but political and economic. By the early twentieth century, the two countries had become arguably the most literate societies on earth because of their public education systems and institutions of higher learning. English was the common language, as the use of French withered in Franco-American regions. The largely market-driven freedom to write, publish, and read at will allowed Upper North

Americans to select what suited their interests and tastes. An asymmetry of opportunities drew many aspiring Canadian writers to the United States, either directly as residents or through publishers and book sales. Current large urban markets and publishing industries mean that writers, unless specialized in subject matter, work within an integrated North American literary industry. Chapter 3 probes the character of the transnational mass entertainment system that developed from the later nineteenth century to modern times. Entertainers exploited new communications to reach scattered yet ever-larger audiences. Canada's Anglo-elites disdained popular preferences for U.S. entertainment or religious revival styles, and some argued for Ottawa to restrict U.S. practitioners or their work, but millions of stakeholders in the transnational mass culture defeated such efforts. Shared ideas, values, and language enhanced the coincidence of proximity and the power of asymmetry to develop mass entertainment genres in transnational Upper North America.

Chapter 1

Cultural Identities

Andrew Kleinfeld, a U.S. Circuit Court of Appeals judge in Alaska, and his wife, Judith, had grown curious about the distinctions and differences between Canadians and Americans. So they visited nearby Hyder, Alaska, and its twin just across the border, Stewart, British Columbia. Each town had a hundred or so citizens, and this subarctic borderland area was facing hard economic times. Once-prosperous mining and resource industries had dried up. When the Kleinfelds arrived, however, appearances belied the reality. Stewart, on the one hand, was attractive and clean, with paved streets, well-kept homes and businesses, and a cozy bed-and-breakfast. Hyder, on the other hand, looked ramshackle, with dirt and gravel roads, and buildings and homes more in various states of disrepair than repair. A rough-hewn lodge and saloon offered the only accommodation. Hyder's nearly two dozen companies, meanwhile, bustled. New cars and trucks sat in driveways or outside the buildings. Most homes had satellite dishes. Local taxes were low. Stewart's few companies, by contrast, were shut up, for sale, or about to go under. The fewer cars were older and small. Local taxes were well above Hyder's rates. Had the Kleinfelds entered a land of Oz? No—and the explanation for the towns' contrasting conditions lay in the cultural values of the people in that remote transnational borderland.

An aggressive free market capitalism reigned in Hyder, where the Americans had a self-reliant, optimistic, can-do spirit. They cherished personal freedom first, community appearances second. A nonprofit organization managed local political affairs without a village council. The Kleinfelds looked again and decided that a statist mentality ruled in Stewart. It was first and foremost a bureaucratic municipality, thanks to grants from Victoria, the capital of British Columbia. The locals seemed content but lethargic, hesitant to try new ventures. Life was calm, but also flat. In Hyder, people relied on themselves, not government. The Kleinfelds appreciated Stewart's tranquillity, but they felt more at home in Hyder, with its frontier democratic spirit and tolerance for eccentricity. Clearly, the border divided more than two national jurisdictions. These were subjective impressions, however, and a more thorough analysis might have taken them in other directions.

Convergence and Asymmetry

To begin with, the United States and Canada are both transcontinental North American countries, with variegated societies, and about 80 percent urbanized. Hyder and Stewart were atypical when it came to how most North Americans lived. Each rural region, small town, city, suburb, or province and state can vary from others. Stewart and Truro, Nova Scotia, or Hyder and Hantsport, Maine, are a universe away from each other, although in the same country. Yet urban and suburban culture seem much the same everywhere in North America. When Kevin Newman left ABC studios in New York City and returned to Toronto, however, Canadians struck him as more competitive and bolder—in a word, more American—than seven years earlier when he left.[1]

Has a shared North American urban culture developed? If so, does a border exert a passive or active force to distinguish the peoples' values and identity? Do any distinctions betray stark differences, or variations on themes? What roles do locale, economic circumstances, social structures and attitudes, the size and organization of population clusters, or government play? How do Americans and Canadians see themselves in terms of one another? What cultural values do they share, or not? Canadians and Americans from all walks of life circulate freely in one another's country, commonly unrecognizable to locals, "stealth" foreigners with no clear accents to prick ears.[2] Canadian journalists in the United States such as Morley Safer and the late Peter Jennings sounded like Americans with a faint British accent, as does Robert MacNeil. Canadians cannot tell from her columns that Diane Francis, the *National Post* business writer, was born in the United States. Francis and Jennings both raised the cultural identity issue. He claimed that Canadians did not cross against red lights, but experience and observation suggest that pedestrians in both countries have similar habits. Canadian visitors to Washington or San Francisco might anticipate carnage as walkers head into four lanes of traffic-laden streets, but mishaps are rare. Another Jennings observation, that Canadians saw the world as it was while Americans saw the world as they wanted it to be, seems more appropriate. It may be more than a satirical comment that an American invented Monopoly during the Great Depression and that two Canadians invented Trivial Pursuit during the television age. At the same time, can Upper North American cultural identities be reduced to such levels? As David Frum noted, however, "To the consternation of some, the border between the U.S. and Canada is the most permeable in the world. And it's not just grain and capital and airplanes that cross it unimpeded, it's people. People who increasingly recognize themselves—in addition to their other national identities—as participants in a common North American culture."[3]

The Canadian comedian Rick Mercer seemed to expose cultural differences in his ambush television interviews with Americans, which were reminiscent of Art Linkletter's *People Are Funny.* Mercer elicited sympathetic reactions from polite American people who were innocently unaware of their northern neighbors' ways of life. Thus, they were not sure about Canada using a "twenty-four-hour clock" but were aghast that the mayor of Toronto had reinstated polar bear hunts in the downtown area. Canadian audiences howled at this April Fool's Day broadcast, which asserted the amusement, if not tyranny, of small differences. Canadians, eschewing American terms, pronunciations, and spelling, continue to use British forms, but less so over time. A lexicologist explained that such affectations reflected regionalism. If so, Upper North America was the context. Canadian speech patterns seem, to some Americans, reminiscent of Minnesota. If Canadians in the United States for any length of time picked up local inflections, did that make them quasi-American? Even Canadians sometimes admitted that the two countries were so alike that they should just unite and be done with it.[4] A vast surface of assumption concealed deep, diffuse, and contradictory views and values about Upper North American similarities and differences. Beyond that, which asserted differences are merely subjective, or chauvinistic, judgments? Such a serious matter surely demands more than anecdotal commentary, yet subjective perceptions more than research shape how Canadians and Americans think about their own identity and one another in Upper North America.

North American identities emerged from the eighteenth-century Colonial and nineteenth-century transcontinental experience. This process included a U.S. political identity forged in the Declaration of Independence and Revolutionary War, the formalization of a republican ideology in the Constitution of 1787 and the 1791 Bill of Rights, and the wrenching U.S.

Civil War sixty years later. The Frenchman Hector St. John de Crevecoeur sailed from France to the United States after 1783 to ask what was the American, this new man. He answered that Americans were a libertarian people distinct from European societies in the Old Regime, yet they were postcolonials with no national history. Canada had no dramatic founding moments, and no de Crevecoeur asking who they were. By Confederation in 1867, lettered Canadians in their own minds were British and not Americans. Confederation was a legislative act with British forms adapted to North American conditions, whereby Canada sat alone alongside a large and muscular United States. At the same time, Canadian provincials had interacted with Americans for nearly a century. Political institutions gave both countries stability as they absorbed immigrants into similarly multiethnic societies. Newcomers to the United States accepted tacitly, or later by oath and affirmation, the republican ethos by the mere act of settlement. Anybody could become an American, provided they accepted liberal egalitarianism, individualism, republicanism, and secular democracy along with fidelity to the Constitution. A betrayal of commitment to that political ideology branded the individual un-American, a concept with no synonym in Canada's vocabulary, where loyalty was to the Crown, Britain's monarch.[5]

The British-Canadian cultural identity evolved throughout ninety years in three locales—Upper and Lower Canada, and the Maritimes—with Franco–North Americans along the Saint Lawrence River and in New Brunswick. Each had regional cross-border linkages. The British North America Act of 1867 created a federal political entity but did not assert any national ideological affirmation, even though the nineteenth century was an age of nationalism in the Western world. The Franco–North American identity of the many French people who had migrated south into the United States by 1867 revolved around local communities, family, the Roman Catholic religion, heritage, and language. Those Franco-Americans in the United States lost their French over time, but they retained a sense of cultural commonality with their ethnic siblings in Quebec. The provinces had a British political identity, and local Anglo-elites stood on guard against cultural infection from the republican United States. Neither the descendants of the original French colonials nor the British provincials, not even those who arrived after 1815, saw themselves remade by the act of transplantation, as did immigrants to the United States. Franco–North Americans remained more suspicious of Anglo Upper Canada than their southern neighbors in the United States. In the Atlantic Northeast, Maritimers interacted with New Englanders and produced a transnational regional culture.[6] Great Britain became a homeland distant in time as well as space and culture to Canadians who became North Americans as generations passed.

Two visitors to Canada in the first decade of the twentieth century, one from England and the other from the United States, believed that to be the case. In 1902, the English journalist William Stead crossed the Atlantic to witness U.S. industrial power, which he saw as the engine for the "Americanization of the world." Canadians surprised him because they seemed far more American than English. Cross-border economic integration was in "full swing." As proof, Stead cited the Vanderbilt railroad interests in Nova Scotia coal, the Dominion Iron and Steel Company's U.S.-born president, and the subsidies Ottawa extended to U.S. investors:

> There is little or no difference in the social and political conditions of the settlers. . . . It was inevitable that this should be so. The United States is close at hand; the Canadians are American in their taste, and goods prepared for the American market find a ready sale across the frontier. It is a remarkable fact . . . that the Canadians, who are only 5,500,000 in number, buy more goods from the United States than are purchased by all the inhabitants of all the Central and South American Republics.[7]

The New Yorker Samuel E. Moffett pronounced as fact the Americanization of Canada in his book as well, finding what he wanted to see, but he wrote the first comprehensive account of dispersed cross-border relations in progress. On every hand, he saw a North American cultural identity that flowed from economic integration, communications systems, and tastes and habits, echoing the English academic Goldwyn Smith's observations that if the United States was not annexing Canada, it was certainly annexing Canadians. Urban newspapers resembled those in New York or Boston, complete with banner headlines, classified advertisements, and Sunday supplements. City life in Montreal and Toronto seemed much like that in Chicago or New York, with comparable ethnic mixtures and neighborhoods. Canadian views on social rank and wealth followed U.S., not British, norms. Democratic legislatures, representation by population adjusted at each census, a federal national structure, and the local focus of party politics also paralleled those in the United States:

> The conclusion to which all the converging lines of evidence unmistakably point is that the Americans and the English-speaking Canadians have been welded into one people. The French Canadians are of course

> different from both, but even in their case the international boundary is not a dividing line. But French Canada is merely a little island in the midst of a sea of English-speaking people, of diverse origins indeed, but unified by a common language, common institutions, and common habits of life. The English-speaking Canadians protest that they will never become Americans—they are already Americans without knowing it.[8]

Stead and Moffett both believed that transnational Upper North American cultural identities had appeared that separated the people from Britons and Europeans, but that did not make Canadians U.S. citizens in the making. Their political allegiance remained firm, although their individual and collective preferences and initiative reflected North American cultural themes. By the time both writers arrived in Canada, Ottawa had extended the limited independence Britain granted in Confederation. World War I later demonstrated that in political and patriotic terms Canadians remained British, but the brutal experience in Flanders Fields quickened Prime Minister Robert Borden's quest for Canada's full political autonomy as a sovereign nation.

An Upper North American Identity

In the 1920s, the sense of an Upper North American cultural identity appeared in a series of scholarly works that founded the field of Canada–United States studies. The Columbia University professor James T. Shotwell, director of the Economics and History Division of the Carnegie Endowment for International Peace and a veteran of Woodrow Wilson's "Inquiry" Group at Versailles, gathered academics who researched the two identities, their differences, and their interrelations in North America. They also established the default order of the realms in which the two nations' identities and relationship unfolded, beginning with politics as the compartment of national identity, moving into economics as the national engine, and lastly considering social and cultural themes. In all their work, Canada emerged as a North American nation interwoven with the United States.[9] These Carnegie scholars also established another theme: the asymmetry of cross-border attention in Upper North America. Canadians looked south far more often than Americans looked north, and though Canadians might be North Americans, their political identity and allegiance remained distinct.

Later Canadian nationalists picked up this point to argue that any distinctions not only amounted to real differences but also served as the stuff of a cultural identity.

Despite Canadian sacrifice and patriotism during World War I, the Ontarian Sir Robert Falconer stressed in the 1920s how North American Canadians had become, even the French in Quebec. Canadian intellectuals read such Progressive U.S. periodicals as E. L. Godkin's *The Nation,* as well as newspapers from major U.S. cities. People saw U.S. movies, and in Canada's "world of the average man," educational systems, organized labor, and community service clubs all copied U.S. examples. Canadians sought higher education at Harvard, Yale, Columbia, and Chicago universities. Their professions followed U.S., not British, pathways. As Falconer noted, "It will be observed by those who know both countries that the influence of the Americans upon the Canadians is greater among the average folk who meet one another in business and read ordinary newspapers, than it is in the intellectual circles and those who devote themselves to society."[10] He concluded that in Canada's democratic society, individuals had the initiative, and the habits of life and mind of ordinary people had transformed the country into a North American nation. The Nova Scotian Hugh MacLennan thought so when he landed in Halifax after being overseas during World War II. All around him, Haligonians read U.S. magazines, followed U.S. professional sports, and watched Hollywood movies. They felt more comfortable in the United States than in England, and MacLennan himself headed for New York to find work. A transnational North American identity had emerged, which he confirmed by marrying an American girl. Ontario's Robertson Davies, however, bitter about the Revolutionaries' expulsion of his loyalist ancestors, forever rued cross-border cultural intertwining.[11] Sentiment or conviction about cultural identities often depended upon personal perspective, and judgments said as much about the viewer as the viewed.

Modern U.S. analysts have reached similar conclusions. Seymour Martin Lipset argued that asymmetry explained why Canadians inevitably saw themselves in relation to Americans. The American Revolution cleaved British North Americans into radical Whig Republicans and conservative social Tories. These groups created the founding and enduring ideologies of both the United States and Canada. The individual commanded the state south of the border, but the state ruled people north of the border. The two nations' political credos—"Life, Liberty, and the Pursuit of Happiness," and "Peace, Order, and Good Government"—captured the dichotomy. For all that, shared cultural identities developed. Both people held communitarian social ideas, but they approached their societies differently. Both prized an educated populace and personal prosperity, but they differed over whether private or public enterprise should power the country's economic engine. Both held tolerant Christian social attitudes, but Americans steered toward, and Canadians veered away from, perfectionist religious doctrines. At the same time, shared cultural themes and parallels lay in how the English common law tradition checked government power and in constitutional guarantees for human and civil rights.

U.S. egalitarianism and Canadian elitism survived into modern times. In 1989, Lipset concluded, the United States was still Whig, Canada still Tory. Challengers eroded Lipset's pride of place in this debate and the significance of the border as a divider of Upper North American cultural identities.[12] A subtler sense of transnational Upper North American cultural regions emerged. Charles Doran favored psychological profiles over variations on themes. Americans, but not Canadians, disliked personal or social eccentricities, which contradicted both American individualism and Canadian communitarianism. Canadians respected authority, political centralism, and social hierarchy, whereas Americans challenged all three. Canadians also distrusted U.S. democratic and egalitarian ideals, lest these subvert Canada's social order. Doran concluded that "if an emotional bomb confronts the U.S.-Canada relationship, it is the problem of the Canadian identity and the way Americans respond to this identity. Anti-Americanism, when it is something more than a strategic political instrument is . . . directly a response to the American tendency to erase or subordinate the Canadian identity."[13]

Thus the Tory foundations for Canadian cultural distinctions from Americans were, in a word, overstated. After 1783, differences of identity rested on allegiance to the British Crown or the U.S. Constitution, not on ethnicity, language, social values or structure, or even economic systems. Most loyalist refugees remained the liberal individualists they had been in Pennsylvania or New York. Dissidents from republicanism became Federalists in the United States, while some drifted to the Atlantic provinces and Upper Canada after 1783. Acquaintances corresponded with one another. Connections survived or emerged between descendants, kinfolk, friends, and associates. Cultural identities were not nearly as clear as the political jurisdictions implied. A tangled web of values, attitudes, ideas, motivations, and behavior sprawled across the boundary. Even with homogeneous societies, generalizations do not come easily. How much more was that the case in

Upper North America in the decades after 1783? The War of 1812 severed many linkages, and the generation of the American Revolutionary era died off. At the same time, some provincials refused to swear loyalty to King George, just as many Americans near the border refused to wage war on their neighbors. Other provincials hoped to remain neutral, although any who openly supported U.S. forces went into exile. British officials and colonials in the war-burned Niagara Peninsula nursed anti-American (often described as anti-republican) resentments that sank into the emerging upper Canadian identity. Elites nursed such feelings through generations and shaped views of the United States later in the nineteenth century. In Lower Canada, the French disliked the British far more than Americans; and in the Atlantic Northeast, people still saw themselves as part of a Greater New England. It was unclear, however, both how widespread and far down into provincial societies elite dislike of the United States or suspicion of Americans extended. Many British immigrants to Canada after 1815 headed to the United States as soon as they could.[14] Provincial reform leaders in the 1820s and 1830s, such as William Lyon Mackenzie and Louis Joseph Papineau, adopted the rough-and-tumble democratic politics of their U.S. Jacksonian counterparts. Before 1867, "Clear Grits" preferred U.S. to British political forms, rejected England's union of church and state. Their cultural identities were Upper North American, not transatlantic, and even Canada's political system was a British-U.S. hybrid.[15]

Throughout the nineteenth century, Upper North American cultural identities diverged from transatlantic patterns and stood apart from southern U.S. society. Americans saw provincials as North American by location and heritage who, once they recognized the inherent virtue of republicanism, would freely join the United States. Franco-Americans chafed under British domination, and anti-British views animated many Americans. Jacksonian democrats thus cheered and supported the 1837 insurrections against Tory oligarchies in Upper and Lower Canada, and when the rebels failed, their leaders and those who fled across the border found sanctuary in the United States.[16]

Meanwhile, tens of thousands of ordinary Upper North Americans farmed, plied trades, and labored to earn their keep as the first phase of the Industrial Revolution began to transform the United States and, by virtue of proximity, British North America. The social cultures blended as the people mingled. Northeasterners developed a regional culture oriented toward forests and Atlantic waters. Upper North Americans in the Great Lakes Basin shared social values and prejudice against blacks, although a young Wilfrid

Laurier transferred his opposition to black slavery from Britain to the United States after Parliament abolished slavery in the Empire in 1833. Thousands of provincials later enlisted in the North's armies during the U.S. Civil War, some to support the Union, but more to uproot slavery. Personal freedom was, after all, an Upper North American value. So was prejudice against Roman Catholics and Jews. English Canadians also referred to Franco-Americans as a distinct "race," although they seem to have meant this in ethnic, linguistic, and religious terms. This was a far milder prejudice, however, than the vicious racism in the southern United States after 1865.

Shared cross-border culture and values continued to shape Upper North American identities. Many Canadians preferred U.S. ideas and models to those from Great Britain, as Stead and Moffet noted. In the early twentieth century, Anglo-Saxon unionists and anticapitalist Canadians formed cross-border intellectual and personal links with Americans such as Josiah Strong and Henry George, among other U.S. political philosophers, but rejected English and European socialism as appropriate for North America. Canadian newspapers, magazines, and books spread U.S. cultural and social ideas, and observers in the United States thought that Britain's withdrawal from North America after 1867 would only enhance the provincials' fundamentally North American identity.

Industrialization reshaped both economies and steadily transformed the lives of working- and middle-class people. At the same time, partisan politicians in Canada often exaggerated cross-border cultural differences both to win votes and assert their own nascent national identity. The British link with Canada encouraged an Imperial patriotism in the late nineteenth and early twentieth centuries, but it became progressively ritualistic as ever more diverse, complex, and dispersed cross-border cultural, social, and economic interlinkages bred North American commonalities. By the 1920s, the impact of World War I and the appearance of mass entertainment further emphasized how Upper North Americans had developed a transnational cultural outlook. Geography, proximity, and asymmetric economic entanglement limited the border's influence on cultural (although not political) identities. During the Great Depression after 1933, President Franklin D. Roosevelt's progressive social programs attracted wide Canadian attention, but no legislative imitations for several years.

World War II extended and further dispersed interlinkages in the realms, making Canada increasingly North American in cultural orientation and outlook as Britain and continental Europe destroyed themselves. An entire generation of Ottawa officials and Canadian leaders interacted with Americans in the Grand Alliance against Fascism, and thus they came to know and trust one another because of shared cultural values and Upper North American identities, a spirit that carried into the Cold War decades. The broad mass of Canadians and Americans distrusted communism and the Soviet Union. Upper North Americans became further intertwined in transnational cultural, social, economic, and even political realms, but they nurtured separate political identities. In the 1950s and 1960s, elite anti-Americanism failed to shape policy in Canada, although its themes permeated creative, and intellectual elements in academia and the media.[17] Many asserted values that seemed derived from what Sigmund Freud termed the narcissism, and anthropologists the tyranny, of small differences to stress how distinct Canadians and Americans were. Meanwhile, millions of ordinary and workaday Upper North Americans intermingled in a tapestry of entanglement held apart from political identities and loyalty. By 2000, this streak of Canadian narcissism sank to the level of commercial satire, as audiences in movie houses discovered. When projectors rolled, a diffident young man in a green plaid shirt recited a speech:

> I'm not a lumber jack, or a fur trader. And I don't live in an igloo, or eat blubber, or own a dog sled. And I don't know Jimmy, Sally or Suzie from Canada, although I am certain they are really really nice. I have a Prime Minister, not a President; I speak English and French, not American; and I pronounce it "about" not "a boot." I can proudly sew my country's flag on my backpack; and I believe in peacekeeping, not policing; diversity, not assimilation; and that the beaver is a proud and noble animal. A toque is a hat, a chesterfield is a couch, and it is pronounced "zed." Not "zee," "zed." Canada is the second largest land mass, first nation of hockey, and the best part of North America. My name is Joe and I am Canadian.[18]

Most Canadians believed, said, and did none of this. Such trivia meant more than the sum of their parts, however, for those Canadians insecure about their national identity next to the United States. The irony of it all, however, soon made "Joe's rant" a public joke. "Joe" Canuck, actor Jeff Douglas's character, shilled beer for Molson's, a Canadian brewery with a large North American market. Americans loved his mock-serious "we are not Americans" theme, although Douglas himself soon headed for Hollywood to pursue his acting career.[19] While analysts and scholars parsed, probed, debated the "rant" as though it were part of a Heritage Canada cultural offensive, ordinary Canadians went about their affairs as Upper North Americans. Nationalists cheered, and interest groups called for greater support for the Canadian Broadcasting Corporation (CBC) after Ottawa's funding cuts. The director of the Washington Council of Hemispheric Affairs applauded Canadians for defending their country and identity, and a Buffalo reporter insisted that Americans really wanted to be like Joe, polite and not opinionated. Rising laughter, meanwhile, overthrew the tyranny of small differences and transformed earnest debate about Canada's cultural identity in North America into an exercise in trivial pursuit, because the two peoples shared a popular culture.[20]

This process had begun during the 1920s, when middle-class mass consumer spending started to transform Upper North America into a transnational market. Canadians adopted the U.S. poet Clement Moore's Santa Claus personification of Saint Nicholas, and advertisers used his image in the North American commercialization of Christmas. Coca-Cola portrayed Santa in Canadian and U.S. magazines pausing to refresh himself. Crossword puzzles and contract bridge became popular North American pastimes. Such trends accelerated, and in 1967 the organizers of the nationalistic Montreal Expo '67 world's fair eschewed the modesty often associated with the Canadian identity to create a patriotic event reminiscent of U.S. Fourth of July celebrations. Vancouver's 1986 Expo hired American marketers to attract U.S. tourists, and they took the same approach. Molson's breweries created a "Canadian" brand, not to express national identity but to carve out an image in the crowded U.S. beer market. In 2005, however, Molson's merged with Colorado's Coors company. U.S. advertising firms adapted the we-are-not-Americans cliché to snare Canadian attention as dispersed cross-border commercial interlinkages exploited cultural identity themes in Upper North America.[21] So the narcissism and tyranny of small differences lost their utility to distinguish the Canadian from the U.S. cultural identity. The failure of ideological nationalism to establish a distinct Canadian mass culture had become apparent.

Nationalists nevertheless savored a few small triumphs. A 1960s campaign to stop hiring U.S. academics to teach in Canadian universities, lest the national identity be diluted, survived as hiring-preference legislation. Ottawa's support for the arts and cultural industries, and protection of a limited number of domestically published magazines, also received nationalist applause. But values and identities became increasingly transnational in Upper North America. One nationalist finally explored the European roots of Canada's cultural identity as a counterweight to U.S. influence so Canadians could understand what kind of North Americans they had become. A few Americans even thought Canadians were pushy about their cultural identity, another sign of their North Americanization.[22] Polls revealed that Canadians had acquired a cultural confidence as North Americans in the latter decades of the twentieth century. Andrew Coyne noted, "Far from safeguarding our independence, Canadian nationalism has made us almost wholly psychologically dependent on the United States, mixing equal parts of envy of American achievement, fear of American influence, and smug contempt for American values, real or imagined, but always measuring ourselves, for good or ill, by the American example."[23] Therein lay the real significance for Canadians of how the Upper North American identities interwove, shared cultural values and outlooks, yet retained their singularities. Even the handful who continued to lament and fear the virus of next-door U.S. nationalism admitted that the asserted distinctions between the two identities had become less relevant than they once believed.[24]

Cultural Convergence and Identity Divergence

Patriotic and political distinctions aside, but not discounted, the fault line for North American cultural identities never coincided with the political boundary between Canada and the United States. North American communities of habits, interests, and tastes defied compartmentalization. Transnational, regional, and local cultural identities overlapped and coexisted with the increasingly diversified mass consumer culture of movies, clothing brands, chain restaurants, personal goods, and music in Upper North America. Neither Canadians' nor Americans' cultural identity derived from their government's policies or jurisdictions. The misleading red state / blue state cultural explanation of the 2004 U.S. national election results, and Canadian instincts to identify themselves as blue staters (to U.S. amusement) exposed the fallacy of relying on political boundaries to contain or exclude cultural identities.

Lyndon Johnson once referred to cross-border disputes as akin to the problems in a small town where the locals disagree a good deal but remain the same people for all that. Thus *Washington Post* correspondents assigned to Canada at first saw themselves in a parallel universe. A New Yorker in the Maritimes took local criticisms of the United States to heart, then realized that Canadians shared with Americans the same cultural virtues, flaws, and faults. So what remained? In large measure, North American identities became less cultural than social, and even more political because of divergent policies. The differences that mattered were how those outlooks worked through the two political systems while cultural themes played out in public life.[25]

The real distinctions in Upper North American cultural identities lay in the two constitutional jurisdictions, political systems, and partisan ideologies. Miscues and confusion arose because Canadians had no image among ordinary Americans, apart from a narrow belt of borderland communities, cross-border groups that worked together, specialists who followed Canadian affairs, and friends and relations in close contact. The U.S. media only reported domestic Canadian issues when they intersected with Washington's policies or domestic U.S. social concerns. Geography, proximity, asymmetry, and the panoramic windows Canadians had on the United States gave them ever-changing pieces of an unmade mental jigsaw puzzle. Canadians also believed that they understood the U.S. cultural identity, but they rarely ventured beyond assumptions, clichés, and the 300-channel media system devoted to entertainment and profit they absorbed that made them all Upper North Americans.

When an issue truly central to Canada's cultural identity in Upper North America aroused U.S. interests, Americans paid close attention. The possibility of Canada's fragmentation in the 1970s recalled not the Declaration of Independence and the right of revolution but the horrors of secession and civil war. René Levesque, Quebec's first separatist leader, missed that point entirely, as did Lucien Bouchard in the 1990s. Beyond that, U.S. correspondents reported on economic, political, and diplomatic events, but they wrote few cultural or social stories beyond human interest tales connected with Canadians. After the events of September 11, 2001, polls reported that most Americans and half of Canadians saw themselves as "essentially" or "mainly" one people. Nationalists drew the wrong conclusions when they insisted that Canadians had lost their cultural identity because they missed the transnational Upper North American identity that was separate from national political allegiances. That was why a *Washington Post* correspondent suddenly understood the truth of Robertson Davies's remark that Canada was not a country its people loved but one they worried about.[26] Ordinary Canadians proved more confident about their cultural identity in North America than intellectuals, professional nationalists, or policymaking elites. As polls probed more deeply for national values, the clearer that became. Whereas national views on the place of religion in politics differed sharply, for example, opinion on abortion rights, immigrant quotas, gun control, and the family revealed cross-border patterns. More than three-quarters of

Canadians believed their cultural identity lay within North America, and they denied that not being Americans had anything to do with it.[27]

Meanwhile, Canadians who saw their identity in ideological terms warred in Canada's media about how national cultural identity could be based on prejudice and bile. "Anti-Americanism was never either benign or worthy," academic Robert Fulford noted, "but now it is worse than that—it is a betrayal of our own national virtues." And the historians Jack Granatstein and Norman Hillmer observed that "if anything has come out of the week since the terrorist attacks, it's the revelation of the dark muddles that animate popular thinking and beliefs—muddles that are created and fostered by a small army of what can only be described as ideological cranks."[28] Once President George W. Bush launched the attack in Afghanistan to destroy al Qaeda, Canadian nationalists denounced support for Washington on grounds of morality and cultural identity.[29] Political ideology and identity also fused in Canadians' unwilling to sacrifice individual interests to a common purpose they rejected on principle. Even those political currents, however, ignored the boundary between the two countries.[30] Cultural identities seemed in flux, but in the charged post–September 11 era, people were uncertain about the future. It seemed that Canadian and American cultural identities in Upper North American now differed in two ways. First, religious belief and practice played a large and important role in the lives of young Americans, and far less so for young Canadians. Second, Canadians accepted Ottawa's large role in their lives, whereas Americans remained suspicious about Washington.

As developments in the social and economic realms revealed, however, those cultural views defied reality. In the early twenty-first century, ordinary Canadians, more than their American counterparts, no longer compared elements of their cultural identity with their neighbors, and seemed not, except in moments of political stress, to deny their North American identities. Stephen LeDrew, when president of Canada's Liberal Party, remarked, "Our history, culture, our very fiber proves us to be different from the United States, but we are also markedly similar in outlook, aspirations and tastes." Former United Nations ambassador Yves Fortier argued that Canada's nationalists, who insisted on distinctions from Americans, betrayed naïveté and mistrusted their compatriots. Canadians were North Americans, he continued, and supported Washington's war against terrorists because of shared values such as pluralism, secularism, and democracy.[31]

The cultural identity of Canadian civic nationalism sat inside a federal, pluralist state that usually had broad support (or at least acceptance) for its domestic and foreign policies. Upper North American cultural identities evolved, however, so Canadians redefined themselves over time. Many discovered that they were North American as well as Canadian. The historian John H. Thompson found that living in the United States chaffed his cultural identity, but he also saw how "Canadians have used the United States as an ideological reference point, as an 'other' against which to construct a Canadian identity." This had always been in a North American context, and he urged Canadians to "stop imagining that our American neighbours really have a single, dominant national identity and an uncontested national history either." Richard Gwyn, after a lengthy sabbatical in his native England, returned with fresh perspectives on the cultural identity question. Canadians seemed to him, after a time away, more North American than before. Similarities aside, he found that they now placed greater emphasis on individualism and entrepreneurship, which contradicted many of their self-declared distinctions. Canadians also carried an assortment of perspectives that contradicted their cultural assertions. Gwyn argued that identity politics had faded in Canada, and he thought Canadians were more like Americans than before. He also thought that individualism no longer sat at the core of the U.S. cultural identity. He might also have asked, given late-twentieth-century demographic changes in Canada, what the Anglo-Canadian cultural identity would mean to immigrants from the West Indies or the Middle East. The loyalist myth was only a textbook footnote for British Columbians and Albertans. Canadians seemed to have discovered themselves as North Americans who differed from those living in the United States in degree but not kind.[32]

The history of Upper North American cultural identities calls to mind a kaleidoscope, a sealed cardboard or plastic tube with mirrors and a small heap of colored glass inside. Look through the peephole, point the other end with its opaque plastic stopper at a light, and rotate the tube. Ever-shifting patterns form. Hold up another kaleidoscope and turn them simultaneously. Differences in the patterns blur in the eye and the mind, just as the jumbled crystals of Upper North American cultural values and characteristics have throughout history. The patterns shift, always resemble one another, but are never twice the same. The Kleinfelds sensed this reality on their study tour of Hyder, Alaska, and Stewart, British Columbia. Some distinctions in the cross-border cultural identities reveal substantive distinctions, and many do not. It takes a steady eye and steely gaze to recognize what matters, what does not, and when, because cultural identities remain moving targets in transnational Upper North America.

Chapter 2

Print and Culture

Richard Siklos thought he had tumbled down Alice's rabbit hole when Ottawa's heritage minister, Sheila Copps, insisted that any writing or any printed word in Canada was ipso facto a piece of national culture. Furthermore, U.S. influence had to be kept out of the country or its identity was doomed. Reportedly, she had once berated Americans at a Canadian Embassy gathering in Washington because the United States did not have a Cabinet secretary devoted to culture. Siklos, a Canadian himself, thought such rants were just nonsense, and impossible to translate into policy. In New York, where he sat through her speech, global cultural currents blew in, swirled together, and thrived. The idea that political boundaries could contain, let alone define, culture seemed absurd. Of course he knew that Copps wanted policy protection for particular cultural producers, so the whole issue was more about special interests and politics than culture anyway.[1]

The Industrial Revolution, urbanization, growing middle-class wealth, and literacy combined by the beginning of the twentieth century to erode the isolation of people and communities in Upper North America. In a few hours steam-powered and then electrically powered rotogravure presses could print thousands of copies of books and magazines with illustrations on cheap paper made with wood pulp. Legions of aspiring writers, editors, and publishers produced and sold papers, magazines, and books to ever wider readerships. New North American consumer societies consumed printed words along with all other mass-produced cultural items. In North America, this revolution first took hold in major cities—New York, Chicago, Boston, and less so in Toronto, although that center had readers aplenty. Samuel Moffett noted many U.S. newspapers for sale there, and in Montreal for the English-speaking community. Canadians from Vancouver to Halifax could on any given day pick up editions from nearby U.S. centers as information dispersed among Upper North Americans. Wire services carried overseas news on intercontinental cables, and once in North America zipped to centers all over the continent. Books took longer to produce but also found wide readerships. North American newspapers and magazines also looked much the same, wherever they were published. Banner headlines, pictures, common internal organizational patterns, and mixtures of reporting, commentary, and reviews captured the attention and imaginations of readers and writers alike. Aspiring provincial writers had few opportunities to publish anywhere in Canada, so many converged on New York and Chicago, where jobs at newspapers, magazines, and publishing houses were to be had for support while they wrote by night or as reporters. National boundaries were irrelevant to them as they dispersed into the Upper North American literary world.[2]

Literary Upper North America

In restricted ways, this Upper North American literary world began even before the War of 1812. News traveled slowly in a four-mile-an-hour world where literacy was limited, so people in small borderland settlements such as Kingston, Upper Canada, took what they could get from word of mouth and other publications, mostly from the United States.[3] Before the age of copyright, publishers in borderland towns stole shamelessly from one another and printed editions that had a long shelf life in recirculation. By the 1860s, hundreds of newspapers were published in the United States, but the provinces had only 23, and 123 by 1900. The telegraph sped up the passage of information while railroads sped up the delivery of papers and magazines. Canadian editors adopted U.S. innovations in layout, design, and management, and John Ross Robertson of the Toronto *Telegram* shamelessly pirated U.S. dime novels as a profitable sideline. Paper maker John Riordan imported printing machines from New York and modeled his *Mail* on New York newspapers. He acquired the rights to Associated Press copy in the 1870s. By 1893, 33 Canadian papers drew from the United Press, and 14 from the Associated Press. The Canadian Press was formed in 1903 to distribute European news off the transatlantic cable. By 1905, postal services in both countries offered newspapers free delivery in rural areas. By 1912, imported U.S. and British periodicals outsold domestic publications ten to one in Canada, and spreading literacy created new markets of clerks, factory workers, and domestics. Publishers of periodicals and books alike became capitalistic organizations that competed in a free market for writers and readers—as also did the Hearst and Canadian Southam newspaper chains. They all followed the same procedures in their publication and distribution methods. The difference was that U.S. publishers saw Canada as an extension of their domestic market, whereas the reverse was never true. Daily editions in both countries boasted banner headlines, photographs, editorials, and news from international to local levels. Women's and sports sections, and leisure activities such as crossword puzzles and comic strips, typified weekend editions by World War I. Syndicated U.S. columnists found North American readerships and offered advice for the lovelorn as well as comments on the political and social affairs of the day.

The dispersed culture of print in newspapers and other publications became omnipresent in Upper North American lives by the 1920s, although writers in Quebec served only their own linguistic markets. The millions of Franco-Americans in the United States had mostly lost their language by then and were focused on local communities. Immigrant groups published newspapers in their own language in cosmopolitan cities such as Chicago, Montreal, New York, and San Francisco. Canadian papers carried U.S. news, but the reverse was rare. The asymmetrical North American reading markets gave U.S. publishers economies of scale their Canadian counterparts could not match, but the striking feature of North American print culture in any form was its geographic dispersal. After 1900, Canadian and U.S. newspapers developed largely within regional markets, although major papers came to be seen as "national." The border mattered for political news, but not for international affairs, entertainment, or business and financial matters. The nature of the markets, not the location of a press, determined the patterns of distribution.[4]

A comparable historical evolution occurred in Upper North American book publishing. One of Canada's earliest writers, Susanna Moodie, was published in the United States because London or Edinburgh publishers showed no interest in colonial authors and Canada itself had no publishers at the time. Later in the nineteenth century, Toronto publishers rejected Lucy Maud Montgomery's *Anne of Green Gables* story, but Macmillan of New York accepted it and in time enabled Montgomery to become a popular and successful writer with a lucrative copyright that extended long after her death. After World War I, Canada's North American orientation began to outweigh British links and sensibilities. The Ontario literary establishment often disdained domestic writers such as Morley Callaghan for being

"American" because he wrote about ordinary people in urban settings.[5] Furthermore, writing often intended as high culture became popular in mass markets because readers appreciated strong characters and stories. Beginning in the 1920s, radio, movies, and later television created ever more dispersed North American audiences for writers in all genres. Canadian elites and cultural nationalists renovated their rhetoric over time, but not their view that writing was a mere entertainment unless it contributed to what they defined as culture.

Many Canadian writers in this era found markets in the United States. Because no domestic comic book industry existed, Joe Shuster and his partner marketed his "Superman" creation in New York and created a U.S. patriotic icon. Toronto publishers rejected the journalist Lionel Shapiro's writing because he sought a popular rather than an Anglo-elite readership. A U.S. publisher accepted his work, so he migrated south and enjoyed a comfortable writing career after work as a combat reporter during World War II. Many such cases arose because asymmetry, proximity, and the commercial orientation of U.S. publishers alerted them to markets, not the national origin of a writer. Conversely, the U.S.-born poet Carol Shields moved to Canada but acquired a North American reputation for her short stories. Shared values, traits, and interests meant that readers in both countries readily understood writers from either and responded in the same way to good prose in various genres as well as general fiction and poetry.[6]

By the 1930s, an asymmetrical interdependence had developed for English-language writing in North America. Canadian novelists and short story writers still had only small readerships at home, so many sought U.S. agents and publishing houses. Those who gained publication often found wider markets and favorable reviews from U.S. critics. They also earned better incomes, and this prompted John Metcalf, the editor of a small press in Erin, Ontario, to note that the reputations of well-known Canadian writers soared at home only after U.S. editors and reviewers praised and promoted their work. Kenneth Harvey worried about the fate of domestic writers in such an Upper North American environment, because Canadian booksellers knew that established authors sold much better than lesser-known domestic writers. He believed that Canadian writers could not survive without government subsidies and protection if they reached only domestic readers. "Show a little pride for God's sake," Harvey wrote. "Buy CanLit. Get those damn Yankee books out of my country. But in the meantime, someone find me a U.S. publisher."[7] Recently, U.S. television talk show hosts such as

Oprah Winfrey have furthered many literary fortunes through prime-time interviews in which she endorsed their books. Her name had such influence among women readers that publishers in both countries sleuthed her guest lists so they could rush extra copies to bookstores ahead of broadcast times if their writer was scheduled to appear.

Writers wither without readers, recognition, and incomes. A shared language, common taste in literary genres, cross-border literary and topical interests—all created a dispersed North American book market by the later twentieth century. Margaret Atwood often winced at mass literary tastes, and what she saw as the U.S. cultural domination in Canada. But her own books sold better and earned wide recognition in such tangible ways as visiting professorships and sales to movie makers in the United States. The novels of Atwood and Robertson Davies entered the Western literary canon taught in university English departments, and the authors' national origins were secondary to intellectual and aesthetic considerations.

Writers from both countries often wove U.S. and Canadian themes into their work, as though North America were a single cultural arena. Howard Norman taught writing in the city of Washington but set his novels in Canada because he saw a not-quite America tinged by exoticism that offered an outside point of view to comment on U.S. themes. Clark Blaise once lived in Florida, where life in rural regions evoked his early life in Canada. John Irving wove borderland themes into his novels. Genre writers transplanted easily. Detective, romance, and science fiction fans cared nothing for an author's nationality. The South Carolinian William Gibson arrived in Vancouver during the 1960s and became one of North America's leading science fiction writers. Montreal cemeteries inspired the horror writer Nancy Kilpatrick, and the forensic anthropologist Kathy Reichs also used Montreal with its North American French culture as an exotic background.[8]

Many Canadian writers who migrated south of the border had similar experiences. Ross Macdonald wove Canadian references into his southern California mysteries. Bruce McCall worked and prospered in Detroit advertising, then wrote and illustrated for *The New Yorker* and *Vanity Fair.* Robert MacNeil pursued a journalism career in London, New York, and Washington, then cofounded the U.S. Public Broadcasting System's evening *News Hour.* Canadian themes were woven through his nonfiction and fiction. Canadian writers who could not get a domestic publisher often turned to Boston or New York and got into print.[9] All saw themselves as transnational intellectual practitioners, not as nationalists.

Transnational Print Culture

Upper North American habits of mind, English as the shared working language, and the many commonalities of the two societies over time established the infrastructure and patterns of a transnational print culture. At any level of readership interest, the two literary cultures betrayed variations on North American themes. The border mattered most, however, to those with Anglo-elite sensibilities. Such intellectuals viewed the mass market itself with suspicion and scorn on the grounds that those who wrote for the masses practiced commercialism, not culture. Only masterworks from those who wrote the best that had been thought and said, in Matthew Arnold's phrase, could uplift and distinguish a society, and North American intellectual elites agreed.[10]

Most authors, however, needed markets to make a living. Intellectuals and writers in universities, or in Montreal, Toronto, and to a lesser degree in other cities, balanced North American and national sensibilities with counterparts in Boston and New York while they plied their trades in the transnational culture and commerce of words. During World War II, balance-of-payments problems and shortages of raw materials, rather than cultural policy, forced Ottawa to ban the importation of a wide spectrum of consumer goods from the United States, including comic books and pulp genre magazines, where writers focused on action, adventure, romance, and mystery genres. In this case, a market existed without writers, so short-lived comic and pulp publications appeared in Canada that blended U.S. styles and themes with domestic content. A few publishers survived on such magazines as *Factual Detective Stories,* and illustrators even created a few comic books, usually in black and white. "Johnny Canuck," the defender of a "Canadian Way" that seemed North American, was perhaps the best known. In 1945, these controls ended and the cross-border commerce of print culture with the United States resumed. The rise of cheap paperback publications and television doomed the Upper North American market for pulp magazines, but boys and girls in secondary schools read U.S.-produced magazines, comics, secondhand pulps, and paperbacks that at least honed their reading skills. Canadian boys who at one time would read and collect British Imperial adventure stories by G. A. Henty and H. Rider Haggard turned to Edgar Rice Burroughs's *Tarzan* and *John Carter* stories, Tom Corbett, Space Cadet, and the Hardy Boys and Tom Swift series from Edward Stratemeyer's prolific U.S. publishing house. Girls had only the Bobbsey Twins and Nancy Drew, but many teenagers with a literary bent read Ray Bradbury and other U.S. authors. School libraries stocked a variety of these stories, which knit young Canadians into the U.S. world of books and magazines.[11]

Academic and Anglo-intellectual elites ignored popular genres, but they dominated Vincent Massey's 1949–51 Royal Commission on National Development in the Arts, Letters, and Sciences, which deliberately excluded and ignored popular and mass market writers and readers.[12] The Massey Commission and Ottawa's policies therefore had a limited impact at best on public reading habits. Policymakers could only focus on writers and publishers, not markets, because readers decided what they would borrow or buy based on taste and interest. U.S. publishers continued to see Canada as an important next-door market, and Canadian publishers now attempted to export or seek U.S. rights to reach the large American readership. Upper North America remained a transnational literary market, but after 1945 Ottawa enacted an ever more complex set of regulations with the declared aim of protecting national cultural identity. The effect was to distribute subsidies to domestic writers and publishers, but that did little to shape public reading tastes. Recycled rhetoric about the perils of Americanization convinced public advocacy groups, intellectuals, and domestic publishers but did not serve the mass of Canadian readers one way or another. Ottawa policymakers accepted elite arguments that protective legislation would vouchsafe a domestic literary culture. All it accomplished, however, was to support a handful of writers and publishers.[13] At the same time, change was afoot. Dispersed cross-border social and cultural interaction drew U.S. literary practitioners and practices to Canada. The development of a transnational Upper North American print culture confounded those who expected legislation to stem the cross-border commerce of print in the name of national identity. In the end, it seemed that all Ottawa politicians and policymakers had done was to disguise protectionism for a favored few in the cladding of a national cultural interest to defy the United States and gain domestic political favor.

North America's transnational print culture world had in any event long subverted what Canada's Anglo-elites and their Ottawa sympathizers sought to achieve. The New York literary agents Stanley and Nancy Colbert, for example, moved to Toronto in the mid-1970s and set themselves up in business. They went after clients who were writers in the writing business rather than in academic cultural creation. They soon signed up John Fraser and Timothy Findley—writers with high profiles in Canada—and negotiated more lucrative contracts, larger advances, international rights, and wider distribution for them than domestic publishers had ever granted. Domestic publishers disliked the Colberts' U.S. origins and aggressive American ways, but free market dynamics worked their way into the sheltered world of Canadian publishing. The Colberts also established their own publishing house and challenged domestic legislation that governed foreign ownership in cultural industries. A four-year Investment Canada probe exonerated them precisely because they developed, published, and promoted Canadian authors in ways the old system had failed to do. The Colberts also became 5 percent owners of the Canadian part of Rupert Murdoch's 1989 merger of the U.S.-based Harper & Row and the Canadian/British William Collins into HarperCollins. They then weathered another outcry from domestic publishers and prospered until they retired back in the United States.[14]

Meanwhile, more Canadian writers looked south to widen their readerships and incomes. Children's literature writers found success but faced a new kind of dilemma. With nearly 70 percent of their sales in the United States, American-English spellings and U.S. references crept into their books. Critics claimed that this was incremental Americanization and would retard the development of Canadian children's national identity. The publishers replied that without U.S. sales, they could not remain in business at all because Canada had too small a market to support them. Was it more important to educate children along particular guidelines and then go out of business or to use the transnational market to accomplish their goals? In the end, the market argument won the day.[15]

Upper North American corporate changes in the 1990s also reshaped the culture of print. The U.S. media giant Gulf & Western bought Paramount in 1992, and by default Ginn Publishing, Paramount's small Canadian subsidiary. Ottawa legislation dictated that the government must purchase Ginn to prevent foreign ownership of a cultural industry. This was all well and good but severed Ginn from its sources of supply and distribution, so the company went bankrupt. Ottawa had lost $10 million (Canadian) with nothing to show for it. The 1988 Free Trade Agreement (FTA) allowed Paramount to sue for this loss because Ottawa had expropriated their assets. Knee deep in a small briar patch, Ottawa settled out of court and wrote off another loss. The logic of commerce defied nationalist ideological assertions, and every such expense was money that Ottawa could not put into social or some other services. The owner of the publisher McClelland & Stewart attempted to evade this conundrum when in the summer of 2000 he donated his 75 percent of the company's shares (the domestic subsidiary of U.S. Random House held the rest) to the University of Toronto. Independently, Doubleday's Canadian subsidiary merged with Random House, and the new company's sales were twice those of its largest Canadian-owned rival. Whether this game of musical publishing houses was about philanthropy, the culture of print, or profits, other publishers feared the competition. Once again, commentators reported how public money had drained into partial state ownership of a money-losing private commercial publisher.[16] Then Stoddart declared bankruptcy, which exposed a rattletrap publisher that had served neither writers nor readers, neither booksellers nor Canadian culture—indeed, no interest anyone could name. All that remained were piles of unpaid bills from all Ottawa's cash and credit. The government sensibly refused to run Stoddart as a crown corporation, so writers were set adrift, creditors wrote off bad debts, and the company died with scarcely a whimper.[17]

The limits of the state's role in the print and culture mix had become apparent, but politicians and bureaucrats seem not to have grasped this point. And no one even attempted to explain how this served Canada's cultural interests—or even what they were any more. The market in North America's cross-border commerce of print had always been dispersed and uncertain. Even in provinces where departments of education hired writers to produce textbooks for captive markets, they required a long life span (meanwhile, the texts went out of date) to repay the investment from annual budgets. And short of censorship, governments could not control private reading habits.

In the 1960s, readers still patronized small bookshops. Such Canadian shops absorbed some 40 percent of U.S. foreign book sales. Book-of-the-month clubs survived as a species of subscription service—increasingly genre-based in history, science fiction, or mystery—and undercut retail shops through bulk buying and a list of subscribers predisposed to purchase books. But these clubs fell on hard times as Upper North American postal rates rose and book marketing methods changed. In the 1980s, U.S. entrepreneurs created national chains, then built what became known as megastores, such as Barnes & Noble and Borders, located throughout metropolitan areas, but mostly in large shopping centers. These stores carried recorded music, posters, and videos, and they sold memberships that offered discounts, mail-order service, and regular fliers that featured new titles and special sales. They also offered a social as well as literary experience. Consumers browsed in open spaces and read until closing time. Young readers' sections had staff that doubled as in-house babysitters. These stores also booked authors on speaking tours to talk about and sign their latest works. Though these megastores were initially located in the United States but not in Canada, the proximity of Canadians and their cross-border shopping habits drew them in on day and weekend trips. From 1991 to 1994, independent book stores in Upper North America lost market share while megastores acquired 40 percent of all sales and created a cultural controversy in both countries.[18]

Megastores and Magazines

The megastore marketers' controversial relationship with culture and books hit home in Canada when Ottawa's foreign ownership laws forced the British-owned W. H. Smith bookstore chain to sell out in 1994. The Toronto entrepreneur Larry Stevenson bought Smith and merged it with Coles bookstores to form Chapters. He also took legal action to block Barnes & Noble and Borders from opening Canadian branches. Chapters stores appeared from Halifax to Vancouver and soon controlled 40 percent of Canada's book market. Many local bookstores found themselves unable to compete with mass book merchandisers. Vancouver's Duthie Books, for example, long beloved among local bibliophiles, succumbed to the remorseless pressure from megastores with the power to lower prices on best sellers and almost any title.

Then U.S.-based Borders and Heather Riesman's Toronto-based Indigo Books essayed a transnational merger in 1997. Chapters' Stevenson complained to Ottawa's Investment Review Board (IRB) that this breached Canadian law. He used the cultural protection argument that U.S. managers would ignore Canadian authors and the national identity would suffer. This was all in the interests of fiscal success, not patriotism, because any Canadian bookseller relied on the integrated Upper North American market. In this case, the IRB supported Stevenson. Borders folded its tent. Advocacy groups and protectionists waved the victory banner of Canadian culture against wicked commercial greed while Indigo bought or built more stores to compete with Chapters.[19]

Meanwhile, the Seattle-based Web book retailer Amazon.com also served a transnational book market. In an Internet boom reminiscent of the Great Bull Market prior to the Crash of 1929, Amazon's share prices spiraled, with many Canadians among its 17 million customers. Chapters set up its own Web site while Amazon hired Frank McKenna, a former New Brunswick premier and future Ottawa ambassador to the United States, to lobby the IRB for permission to establish Canadian call and distribution centers.[20] It was déjà vu all over again, as Yogi Berra once remarked in another context, and a further round of domestic debate about cultural Americanization erupted. Amazon next cosponsored the TV program *Books in Canada,* advertised Canadian books in the United States, and arranged for Vancouver's Raincoast Books to distribute Amazon's sales. Canada Post handled deliveries. Amazon also established Amazon.ca, with Ottawa's approval.[21] Private enterprise was now in firm control of the dispersed transnational mass book supply business in Upper North America.

Magazines followed a similar historical evolution. In the 1880s, they provided a major market for writers and a business opportunity that echoed the way newspapers had become mass consumption commodities. At the same time, they served readerships in a broad range of markets, from general news to highly specialized and refined interests. U.S. publishers treated Canada as an extension of their domestic market, and after the 1890s they hired many Canadian editors and writers who had headed south to find work. By the 1920s, U.S. magazine imports became an issue in Canada's culture identity politics, where they remained for the rest of the century. Only a few score U.S. magazine titles came north, but their North American circulation rose to 202 million by 1929 and 240 million in 1939, fell during World War II, rebounded to 385 million in 1948, and reached 392 million a decade later.[22]

As the North American market leveled off, magazines proliferated to reach ever narrower readerships. The emergence of mass entertainment in radio and the movies led to niche magazines about celebrities and the film world. Crime, romance, science fiction, horror, and other genre magazines on cheap paper became known collectively as "pulps" and found a steady market for their editions. In Canada, *The Busy Man's Magazine* (*Maclean's* forerunner) appeared in 1894 with Ontario as its principal market. Others soon appeared, and in 1919 a number of editors formed the Canadian National Newspaper and Periodicals Association, then in 1920 the Magazine Publishers Association. In 1926, Canadian magazines competed with 300 U.S. periodicals selling 50 million issues a year (eight times the domestic Canadian sales), including the *Saturday Evening Post, Ladies' Home Journal, Pictorial Review,* and *McCall's Magazine.* The total circulation of those four magazines was double the four best-selling Canadian domestics—*Maclean's Magazine, Canadian Home Journal, Saturday Night,* and *Canadian Magazine.* The Magazine Publishers Association lobbied Ottawa for protection and subsidies, pioneering morality, patriotism, and national culture as arguments for why Ottawa should give fiscal support to private interests. The association also denounced licentious U.S. "pulp" magazines and insisted that Canadians should read only morally uplifting material to foster national unity and culture. Although J. B. Maclean pled impending bankruptcy, he shortly founded several new and successful periodicals in addition to his flagship *MacLean's.* This inaugural debate over North American magazines was about profits and protection, despite the moralistic and patriotic arguments Maclean and others used to gather a coalition of union leaders, printers, and other groups to support their lobby in Ottawa.[23]

The Magazine Publishers Association and its supporters relied heavily on moralistic and patriotic arguments, and even ideological anti-Americanism. Some speakers, such as the university professor who insisted that his colleagues all agreed with him, really only represented themselves. Even the association represented only 11 of Canada's 1,500 publishers. The president of the Trades and Labor Congress argued that jobs were at risk if U.S. magazines kept coming, but he wanted exemptions for trade union, fraternal society, and technical periodicals because there were no domestic equivalents. R. J. Deachman, by contrast, insisted that Canada had to open itself to the world. If morality was in peril, legislate censorship. Besides, he argued, patriotism and national unity had increased all the while Canadians bought and read U.S. magazines. Drawbacks and subsidies could deal with the economic issues. Readers were a free market and would deal with questions of quality by their choice of purchase. Finally, the Canadian Wholesale Newsdealers Association argued that its members would suffer if Ottawa barred U.S. magazines. The debate pitted elitist protectionism to preserve Canada as a British country against liberal, free market arguments that saw Canada as a North American nation. In 1928 Ottawa legislated, but only drawbacks on imported supplies and materials, and in 1931 the government set a tariff on imported magazines. U.S. periodical circulation fell by 60 percent over the next six years, largely from the Great Depression's impact on private discretionary spending and the protective tariffs both countries maintained. A 1935 Ottawa-Washington trade agreement removed most tariffs, and economic recovery caused U.S. magazine sales in Canada to rise from $2 to $6.5 million (Canadian) by 1939. During World War II, both governments curtailed magazine publication, and Ottawa barred those politicians deemed libelous or salacious. In 1949 that included U.S. crime comics, but not comic strips in newspapers. A few lonely voices, such as the B.C. Conservative E. Davie Fulton, branded comics tools of U.S. imperialism, but by 1950 all were in free circulation once again in Canada.[24] As Britain's cultural influence faded into a heritage, Canadians saw their print culture as North American. Proximity, asymmetry, and Britain's collapse after 1945 furthered Canada's long process of economic and cultural reorientation into the North American context. Canadian readers viewed magazines and books as consumer products to suit personal taste and interest. By the early 1950s, U.S. publishers supplied 80 percent of Canada's magazine market.

Intellectuals and Anglo-elites meanwhile asserted a political influence out of proportion to their numbers in the 1950s and 1960s. Various advocacy groups urged Ottawa to enact protection against U.S. magazines and books.[25] In response, Louis St. Laurent's Liberal government levied a 20 percent tax on advertising revenues earned by what were called split-run magazines. Split runs were U.S. produced and published, then reprinted in Canada with token domestic content, but with all the advertisements that could be sold. Canadian costs involved administration and distribution, so split-run magazines proved profitable for U.S. publishers, such as the influential Henry Luce. He lobbied members of Congress, and even President Dwight Eisenhower, to get the Canadian tax removed. Washington trade officials not only agreed for domestic political reasons but also to deny other countries a precedent to protect their own domestic markets and disadvantage U.S. export interests. This dispute over cross-border print culture inflamed partisan politics in both capitals, and magazines became a lightning rod for a variety of reasons that never arose in the diplomatic discussions. U.S. officials insisted that Ottawa's magazine tax could potentially compromise all Canadian relations with the United States, and they found an unlikely ally in John Diefenbaker, Canada's Conservative leader, who was eager to defeat the Liberals. Diefenbaker exploited anti-Americanism for votes during his 1957 campaign, but once in power he promptly repealed the magazine tax.

Print culture lobbies responded. The Canadian Periodical Press Association and publishers, especially Maclean-Hunter, insisted that new split-run magazines were waiting to invade Canada and bury domestic periodicals. Such hyperbole became standard fare over the next forty years, always mounted with indignation and emotion but no evidence. The shared Upper North American popular culture had created the transnational print market, but only the most popular U.S. magazines, such as *Time,* could justify split-run production. *Newsweek* and *National Geographic* tested that market in the 1980s, but they gave up because circulation never offset costs. This distinction between a split run and regular run was clear to experts, lobbyists, and officials in Ottawa but not to the reading public, so all U.S. magazines got tarred with the same nationalist rhetoric. A Royal Commission on Publications recommended a protective tax and regulatory measures, which the *Calgary Herald* and *Winnipeg Free Press* opposed. U.S. diplomats added that such discriminatory duties violated provisions of the General Agreement on Tariffs and Trade that banned protectionism. Washington also argued freedom of speech. A rattled Diefenbaker government shelved the issue, then lost the 1963 general election. As before in disputes over the dispersed cross-border commerce of words and print, the rhetoric and debates in political and intellectual circles were about everything except Canada's cultural identity.

The new Liberal prime minister, Lester Pearson, dealt with President Lyndon Johnson who, like all experienced Washington politicians of this era, knew that if Henry Luce was upset, everybody would suffer. Johnson accepted Ottawa legislation to exempt *Time* and *Reader's Digest* from protectionist regulations. Cultural nationalists vowed to fight another day. Meanwhile, the mass of Canadians, who had neither been consulted nor polled about their reading habits, continued to buy according to taste and interest. Magazine circulation and sales increased as U.S. and Canadian magazines refined their research and served growing numbers of niche markets. A magazine trade deficit of $219 million (Canadian) in 1979 rose to $271 million two years later. Split runs constituted under 8 percent of periodical imports while nearly 33 million copies of U.S. magazines circulated annually to 80 percent of Canada's population. Combined, they provided more than 68 percent of the U.S. industry's income from foreign sales. Foreign or Canadian adaptations of foreign magazines constituted 71 percent of all periodicals in circulation, although the sales of the Canadianized *Time, Reader's Digest,* and *TV Guide* amounted to half of even domestically printed magazines. Cross-border economic integration accelerated after the FTA and then the North American Free Trade Agreement (NAFTA), which further limited domestic advertising sales for magazines in the North American market. Finally, many Canadian advertising firms were branches or partners of U.S. agencies.[26] At no time did the discussions grapple with the point made by Raymond Williams: that culture, print or otherwise, was merely "a given people's particular set of preferences, predispositions, attitudes, goals, a particular way of perceiving, feeling, thinking and reacting to objective reality." Canada's cultural nationalists and policymakers preferred ideological arguments to mask a clash of self-interests and consulted only advocacy groups. This approach misled and isolated policymakers when the magazine issue resurfaced a few years later.[27]

Practitioners and professionals in the integrated transnational magazine industry treated Upper North America as a unit while pursuing their careers. For example, Bonnie Fuller quit law school in Toronto to edit *Flare,* a local fashion magazine. Success there led to the editorship of *Young Miss.* Next, she launched the U.S. edition of *Marie Claire,* a French fashion magazine. Helen Gurley Brown picked her to edit *Cosmopolitan* when Brown retired. Fuller next shifted to *Glamour,* and from there launched a bid to take over *Harper's Bazaar.* That failed, and she went into a professional tailspin, landing at the *National Enquirer,* where she resurrected her talent for creating fluff with depth and making money.[28] Paul Tough entered Columbia University's journalism program, quit to write for *Harper's,* and was published in *Esquire, The New Yorker,* and other magazines. An eclectic empathy with people led him to create *This American Life* for National Public Radio in Chicago. Next, *Saturday Night*'s publishers drew him north to rescue Canada's ailing, but honored magazine, but he found no market to support it.[29] This Upper North American arena for writers, editors, and magazines responded to the tastes of millions of readers in both countries. Even if few Canadian magazines found markets in the United States, Canadian journalists found jobs, because common Upper North American cultural themes meant that what worked in one market usually worked in the other. This was, after all, about commerce, not national cultural identities.

Canada's domestic publishers and cultural nationalists, meanwhile, took whatever solace was available. Protectionism survived in postal subsidies for domestic but not foreign (i.e., U.S.) magazines, mandatory reviews for any foreign (U.S.) attempt to invest in domestic publishing or book selling, and income tax regulations that lowered exemptions when Canadians advertised in U.S. split runs. Finally, Ottawa put tariffs and special excise and service taxes in place to deter new split-run initiatives. Despite the rhetoric that peppered public debates, these measures made little difference to the Upper North American mass periodical market. Scholarly and literary publications, true Canadian culture magazines, limped along on puny subscription lists, meager support from university or government grants, and rare over-the-counter sales. Other solvent periodicals served specialized or niche markets, such as associations of nurses, truck drivers, and dental technicians. Finally, Upper North America's magazines survived as affiliates or subsidiaries of transnational media conglomerates.[30]

Canadians integrated into the North American magazine market in other ways during the 1990s. They edited *Harper's Bazaar,* launched *Spy* magazine, and took over *Vanity Fair.* John Cruikshank's editorial career spanned the *Vancouver Sun,* the *Globe and Mail,* and the *Chicago Sun-Times.*[31] Torontonians Laas Turnbull and Andrew Heintzman created *Shift,* about entertainment, media, and technology in North America's "digital culture." They then created *Shift* TV, opened a New York office, and organized for the San Francisco and Seattle markets—but overreached. U.S. readers had over 5,000 magazines to choose from each month, so when Turnbull and Heintzman failed to find U.S. partners, they retreated to Montreal's Multi-Vision Publishing, which produced in-store magazines for Shoppers Drug Mart and other clients. Free market forces, not politics or the border, governed the integrated Upper North American magazine market.[32] Furthermore, the idea of a cultural product had fragmented into diverse genre and other categories that were both focused and cosmopolitan, to the point that in the early twenty-first century many publishers and editors no longer needed a mass North American market, just a niche big enough to balance their books.[33]

The magazine issue retained its power to spark an Ottawa-Washington crisis if the right combination of interests, rhetoric, politicians, and coincidences collided. In 1993 Investment Canada allowed U.S. Time Warner to publish a split-run edition of *Sports Illustrated,* but two years later Ottawa legislated to stop such ventures and imposed an 80 percent tax on its advertising revenue. *Sports Illustrated*'s split-run edition shut down after twenty-eight issues, but Time Warner executives and Washington officials saw the broader issue of a precedent for international trade.[34] Mickey Kantor, the U.S. trade representative, a Cabinet-level position in Washington, notified Ottawa, then challenged the legislation before the World Trade Organization (WTO) as discrimination of trade. Washington won both preliminary and final judgments, then appeal/counterappeal judgments in 1997–98. The WTO judged magazines a product, subject to trade rather than cultural regulations, and ordered Ottawa to get rid of its excise tax, income tax rules, and postal subsidies because they violated WTO rules. The tariff and postal subsidies disappeared, but cultural nationalists—along with Maclean-Hunter and Telemedia, which faced new competition—cried foul. Split-run magazines would smother Canada's stories and voices, Heritage Minister Copps insisted, and claimed that even as she spoke, split-run hordes were gathered near the border ready to scorch Canada's cultural earth.[35] The majority government promptly legislated.

The new law read that advertisers in split runs aimed solely at Canadian readers would be charged in criminal court. If convicted, fines would begin at $250,000. Opinion in Canada was sharply divided on this measure, and

U.S. ambassador Gordon Giffin denounced it as a transparent recast of what the WTO had just rejected. He noted that NAFTA authorized retaliation in such circumstances proportionate to U.S. losses from the new legislation. Asymmetry gave Washington the bigger battalions and flexibility, while Ottawa had fewer options and resources, and hence greater vulnerability. Washington also conducted its campaign in full public glare, so the Canadian media, ever suspicious of Ottawa, dissected every rumor and every comment, proposal, point, and counterpoint made by Copps, Trade Minister Sergio Marchi, and other officials. The media also put Canada's magazine industry under a microscope and reporters exposed how little of what Maclean-Hunter and Copps claimed was really at risk. The *Washington Post* and *New York Times* reported the story in detail and other U.S. papers followed events closely, so negotiating positions appeared daily on front pages. Ottawa had political fights on several fronts: domestic public relations; splits in party ranks; the official opposition; U.S. negotiators who had firm White House support; and U.S. interests such as Disney and Microsoft keen to keep Canada's market open. Giffin held regular news conferences to denounce Copps, saying that she refused to return his telephone calls and had snubbed Washington with her international cultural network conference, which seemed to his administration to constitute a protectionist alliance against the United States. Marchi knew a cross-border battle over magazines was all but suicidal. A mortal blow struck Ottawa when the WTO's year-end trade review report noted that "Canada has yet to find a tenable balance between its international commitments and its perceived need to promote its cultural identity in an increasingly borderless market."[36]

The Great Magazine War absorbed ever-more-senior Ottawa officials as talks shifted from the quicksands of print culture onto hard political ground. Support for "Bad" Copps, as she later styled herself, melted along with the snows. Giffin, Charlene Barshevsky, the new U.S. trade representative, and President Bill Clinton held the high cards. Canadian commentators concluded that Ottawa had coddled Maclean-Hunter and Telemedia, both of which relied more on government protection than their own productivity. Cabinet dissension deepened.[37] When Bill Merkin, a senior U.S. official, suggested that Canadian plastics, steel, and textile exports might face retaliation, Copps's constituency support ducked for cover because her Hamilton riding had large steel plants integrated into the Upper North American economy. The mention of plastics companies referred to Marchi's Toronto riding. Montreal clothiers then found out that they might suffer for the sake of already subsidized English-language magazines. Canada's media dismissed Maclean-Hunter's claims of impending disaster and reported that negotiators were now haggling over profits, advertising space and costs, revenues, and other matters related to percentages of editorial content in any future U.S. split-run magazines. The Ottawa-Washington conversation was now about horse trading, and when Ottawa hinted at subsidies, Maclean-Hunter and the other publishers balked. What would happen to their editorial independence? Budget priorities could change, and they could not stand on potentially shifting ground.[38] The final agreement allowed both sides to declare victory. Bill C-55 became law but was never proclaimed, and therefore was effectively null, so Washington accepted the "Agreement on Periodicals."[39]

Ottawa's rhetoric aside, it had been clear throughout that Canadian publishers, like their U.S. counterparts, ran private industries and printed publications for sale. Magazines were products, and Upper North American economic integration meant that any salable product was de facto commercial. Some of Canada's editors and publishers went none too gently into that new dawn, but they had little choice. Perhaps the greatest advance came in the separation of protectionist rhetoric and illusion from commercial reality. U.S. periodicals had 80 percent of newsstand space, and half of all sales in Canada. The mass of readers had voted their tastes all along. Furthermore, from 1991 to 1997, sales of Canadian-produced periodicals declined by more than 10 percent and annual circulation fell by just over 6 percent, but profits rose by 350 percent.[40]

Meanwhile, the integrated cross-border commerce of print remained open along its customary asymmetrical lines. If U.S. magazines came north, *Hockey News* and *Shift* went south. So did *Harrowsmith,* a Canadian consumer magazine that went split run in the U.S. market, partly financed by Ottawa's excise tax that protectionists insisted was only to deflect domestic U.S. competitors. Canada's children's magazines, *Owl* and *Chickadee,* flourished in the United States. When Hearst Magazines considered split runs of *Cosmopolitan* and *Good Housekeeping,* it promised to use local staff people and production materials. This was about jobs, not culture or identity. Bill C-55 moldered in limbo while Ottawa granted Heritage Canada $150 million (about 5 percent of the magazine industry's annual revenue) as a three-year subsidy to support Canadian content. Meanwhile, domestic mergers occurred, as when *Canadian Geographic* bought *Equinox,* a failing competitor. Local advertising supported urban magazines such as *Toronto Life, Ottawa City Magazine,* and *Where in Halifax?*[41] Ottawa's fund mostly subsidized small-circulation magazines in niche markets, and political favorites, such as Rogers Communication, already a profitable company. French-language magazines in Quebec got more than 20 percent of the annual grants, even though none faced the slightest likelihood of U.S. split-run competition. Officials later tacitly confessed that their rhetoric had been smoke and mirrors, and postal and editorial subsidies. The few split runs that did arrive, such as *People* (U.S.) and *Maxim* (British), had little impact on the distribution of Canadian advertising dollars.[42]

Policymakers seemed after that to distinguish mass from restricted, service, or niche markets for Upper North America's print culture. And periodicals evolved. Self-declared rebels against middle-class values had founded "underground" newspapers and magazines in the 1960s, such as New York's *The Village Voice* and Vancouver's *Georgia Strait.* Over time, they became commercial. In 1999, the Canadian Imperial Bank of Commerce bought *The Village Voice,* which attracted new generations of young people involved in punk rock, raves, and drug gatherings and had money behind them, publishers who gloried in the label "Punk capitalists." *Playback* covered Canada's domestic film production and broadcast industries. *Kidscreen* served toy makers, the fast food industry, and television producers. *Boards* reported international theatrical production. All were Canadian owned with primary markets in the United States and outside North America. So were manufacturing and service company magazines that disguised their products with "lifestyle" themes, such as *Space* for Ikea furniture, *Famous* for Famous Players theaters, and *Joe* for Starbucks. The Imperial Tobacco Company, forbidden by law to advertise in Canada, published *Pursuit,* an imitation of *Real Edge,* both of which targeted young male smokers. At the other end of the Upper North American demographic spectrum, the Canadian Association for Retired Persons published *50 Plus,* in which investment counselors and travel agents advertised for well-to-do clients among senior citizens.[43] These publications typified the new periodicals that emerged in North America's cross-border commerce of print in the early twenty-first century.

Ottawa's assumed policy linkage between culture and the printed word ended. Canadian writers aimed for different markets, and the magazine world had left the 1950s and 1960s behind. Political generations changed. The Canadian Radio and Telecommunications Commission threw up its hands over any attempt to regulate Canadian content on the Internet, although the Web carried countless virtual magazines such as *eCompany Now* and *Business 2.0* that also issued print versions. When anyone with a computer could create or print an online magazine, how could regulations about

Canadian content or advertising levels be monitored, let alone enforced? How could culture as identity be distinguished from culture as commerce? The link between products and cultural identity became ever more tenuous.[44] The Great Magazine War's greatest legacy, however, lay in the exposure of how Ottawa ideologues and politicians ignored evidence, public tastes, and even political logic, and pandered to companies that did not need protection. As for the subsidy fund, the Treasury Board emptied and shut it down in 2003 as unnecessary.

Meanwhile, periodicals evolved to hold on to readers and compete with Internet magazines. Editors knew that *Maclean's* had to be more than merely Canadian to retain or attract new readers. One analyst noted that news magazines were all attempting to reinvent themselves, but magazines went through cycles, as had *Saturday Night*. Many publications in both countries disappeared because they fell out of fashion.[45] Mass taste in magazines and other consumer products was evanescent. The argument that Canada's identity would collapse under U.S. pressure without protection became a straw man without stuffing. In 1999, *Maclean's* annual poll revealed that, respectively, 49 and 71 percent of the Canadians and Americans surveyed believed that they shared an Upper North American mass culture, but not political or ideological values.[46] The two realms were largely independent, in both the public mind and policy circles. Printed culture and commerce survived as partners without Ottawa's protection and subsidies, and the sky had not fallen after all.

Chapter 3

Mass Entertainment

When Elvis Presley, the King, the greatest mass entertainer of his time in every available medium, swept up teenagers in the 1950s, Frank McEnany was an eager convert. He worshiped Elvis, whether seeing him in live performance at Toronto's Maple Leaf Gardens or when impersonating him by night in the garage at home. Then he grew up, wrote plays, and settled in Collingwood, Ontario. In 1994, the local mayor began an annual Elvis convention, with Elvis impersonators, to attract tourists. The ersatz Elvises arrived afoot, motorized, even by parachute. McEnany was hooked all over again, and before long stood in line with other Elvis pilgrims to tour Graceland.[1] McEnany was also a case study in how North American mass entertainment swept up Canadians and Americans alike as stakeholders in modern popular culture. Millions of ordinary people for over a century knew what they liked and formed transnational clusters of interest and taste as proximity, asymmetry, and the themes of modern transportation and communications interwove Upper North Americans. In their leisure hours, people chose their own forms of relaxation and amusement, which developed into a mass entertainment system.

From Popular Culture to Mass Entertainment

Upper North American mass entertainment emerged in the late nineteenth century from various forms of popular performances. The railroad and telegraph sped heavy transport and communications by the 1860s that bound provinces and states into an Upper North American network. This was vital infrastructure for the development of mass entertainment because it allowed the rapid movement of performers to scattered, but in total large potential audiences. The telegraph, and later the telephone, allowed booking agents and impresarios in a variety of centers along rail lines to schedule a series of performances. The separate audiences, when combined, constituted a mass that saw the same performers and acts, albeit at different times and in dispersed venues at stops on the circuit where each repeated performance seemed fresh to each new audience. These audiences gathered in saloons, concert halls, vaudeville houses, or more formal theaters, and rapid technological change in the early twentieth century allowed that generation and their children to form mass audiences for live performances, radio broadcasts, and motion pictures. Songs, skits, dances, and jokes, whether live or recorded, became products for consumption. Mass entertainment therefore began and remained a free market phenomenon. By 1910, the wind-up phonograph was on the market, and four years later RCA Victor and Columbia produced a half million discs a year for customers to play in their homes.

Proximity made Canada's provinces an extension of northeastern and northwestern entertainment markets. A shared heritage and culture created a common sense about what was funny or tragic, mediocre or bravura. Particularly popular performers became "stars," earned top billing in vaudeville houses, and made a good living from their talent. Furthermore, Canadian performers headed south as much as Americans came north. Talent, not national origin or citizenship, mattered.[2] And stage personality, as much as the performance, connected stars with their followings. Canadians and Americans took pride in the accomplishments of "their own," but responded on aesthetic rather than patriotic grounds as the Upper North American world of cross-border mass entertainment emerged, often through generations of performers. And interests passed through succeeding generations, so mass entertainment, while it began in the United States, became transnational about the same time.[3]

It all began when circuses entrained on tour. For sheltered arenas, they used large portable tents devised during the U.S. Civil War. P. T. Barnum attracted huge crowds in Brooklyn in 1873 when he entrained for stops in New England and eastern Canada. The Ringling Brothers, Barnum's rival, traveled separately until the two companies merged. In all, some forty circuses traveled Upper North American circuits in summer seasons in the 1890s and 1900s.[4] Rising costs, falling profits, and a new form of traveling entertainment, vaudeville, both replaced circuses and absorbed many of their clown and animal acts. Vaudeville Managers of America incorporated in Albany, New York, in November 1894, and signed up rosters of performers to market in theaters, opera houses, and music halls along rail lines in the United States and Canada. Other agencies soon appeared in Chicago and San Francisco. Acrobats, magicians, comedians, dancers, singers, and performing animals made up most of the acts. Less experienced performers went out on small town circuits, and once they became popular, competed for lucrative bookings in major cities, especially New York, with its Broadway houses and specially built vaudeville palaces.[5]

From the 1890s to the 1920s, vaudevillians toured a crowded eastern circuit from New York and Chicago bases. A western tour ranged from Seattle to Vancouver, and then to Calgary, Moose Jaw, Winnipeg, and Minneapolis. U.S. performers dubbed Canada the "Death Trail" because of the cold, but local audiences loved American performers such as Fred Allen, Jimmy Durante, and Groucho Marx. Bob Hope appeared in Toronto in 1929, when many vaudeville performers had begun to move onto radio because their reputations created audiences for this new mass entertainment medium. Hope soon followed them.[6]

Many Canadians became vaudeville stars. Marie Dressler acted on stage, then in movies, and won the first two Academy Awards for best actress. Eva Tanguey from Marbleton, Quebec, made a fortune with a risqué act, settled in New York City, lost her money in the 1929 stock market crash, and married among other men a member of Henry Ford's family. Few Canadian companies toured the United States, although The Dumbbells, an all-male veterans troupe that entertained troops during World War I, was an exception. The Canadian stage actor Raymond Massey, brother to Ottawa's first ambassador in Washington, quit England in the 1930s for the United States and worked in radio and the movies, even starring as U.S. historical figures John Brown and Abraham Lincoln. In the 1950s, Stratford Theatre Festival actors—such as Christopher Plummer, Lorne Greene, and William Shatner—moved into U.S. stage, television, and movie work. Montreal's Cirque de Soleil troupe gained North American attention at the 1980 Los Angeles Arts Festival, then landed a twelve-year contract at the Treasure Island Hotel in Las Vegas and became a global as well as North American entertainment phenomenon. A handful of impresarios, touting Toronto as Canada's New York, developed and staged touring musicals. Performers always had eyes on New York, the heart of live performance and many Canadians took up U.S. residence to break into Broadway and Off-Broadway productions.[7] Garth Dabrinsky's 1990s Livent productions for Ford theaters in Toronto, Vancouver, and New York offered modern versions of this form of Upper

North American mass entertainment. He mounted *Ragtime, Sunset Boulevard,* Leonard Bernstein's *Candide,* and Jerome Kern's *Showboat* on Canadian as well as U.S. circuits. Livent lost money heavily in 1997 and 1998 and then collapsed under fraud investigations.[8] Vaudeville, however, had set the pattern, not just for live performers on tour but also for the successive generations of Canadians and Americans merging into Upper North America's transnational mass entertainment system.

Motion pictures developed while vaudeville moved toward its peak, and they later replaced touring live acts with touring reels of film. Thomas Alva Edison's first peep show films appeared in 1894. Movie houses opened when practical projectors were developed, six years later. Vaudeville theaters put up screens to keep customers coming. By 1910, most cities had several storefront movie houses that showed films produced mostly in New Jersey and New York. French and British films were also screened in Canada during the silent era, but World War I destroyed the nascent European film industry. American producers, such as William Fox and Adolph Zukor, developed longer films, then called features.[9] Canadians joined Americans in this pioneering age. Florence Lawrence from Ontario starred in Biograph films from 1905 to 1914. So did Gladys Smith, but then a Famous Players publicist anointed her Mary Pickford, "America's Sweetheart," because of her sunny presence and work raising money for U.S. troops during World War I. Canadian directors included the Ontario-born Keystone Kops creator Mack Sennett. Jack Warner and Louis B. Mayer became studio magnates, and a host of other directors, graphic artists, technicians, and production people, both Canadian and American, trekked to California in the 1920s to become part of Hollywood's founding generation.

Movies shaped social fads and fancies, and U.S. films dominated North American screens through innovations such as sound, then color, and then the studio star system. Women in Toronto and Vancouver alike swooned over Rudolph Valentino and mourned his premature death. When Clark Gable bared his chest in *It Happened One Night,* undershirt sales dropped in both countries. When Marlene Dietrich sported slacks on screen, she turned them into a fashion rage throughout Upper North America. A new generation of Canadian actors such as Norma Shearer, Walter Houston, and Deanna Durbin worked in Hollywood.[10] Producers made films in genres such as crime and detective, horror, fantasy, and westerns popular on radio and in magazines. Meanwhile, theater venues were transformed. Marcus Loew had set the standard in New York in 1905. He reasoned that ordinary people sought to escape their drab lives while they were entertained. Loew built a palace with thick carpets, velvet curtains, boxed seats, chandeliers, and staff that treated patrons as though they were royalty. When vaudeville died, Loew's became a movie palace, and entrepreneurs reproduced the artistic styles of the day, such as Art Deco.[11]

In terms of content, Canadian nationalists in the 1920s recoiled at the mania over U.S. movies. Money not only left the country, but young people, "rather than drinking in Canadian and British ideals, is imbibing American ideals; in fact, the influx is looked upon in the nature of a sort of unconscious but insidious propaganda." British Board of Trade president Philip Cunliffe-Lister and Anglophile patriotic organizations such as the Imperial Order of the Daughters of the Empire warned that the national identity would die unless Ottawa protected British films. It was too late. In terms of mass entertainment, Canadians had reoriented themselves as Upper North Americans. English-speaking audiences voted with their admissions and identified increasingly with Americans rather than their British cousins. Hollywood also controlled Canadian screens. A subsidiary of Famous Players appeared in 1920, and Hollywood producers established the Motion Picture Distributors and Exhibitors of Canada (MPDE), which became an unofficial lobby for U.S. studios. Paramount Pictures soon surpassed Famous Players as the largest chain in Canada. Political efforts in Ontario (1931), British Columbia (1932), and Alberta (1933) to get British films onto Canadian screens failed because the MPDE swiftly mobilized public opinion, which had an immediate impact on local politicians.[12]

The movie business became the core of North America's mass entertainment system because it drew performers and audiences from all other genres. The media converged as movie magazines marketed stars and their films, planting stories and advertisements in newspapers to gain publicity. Radio announcers interviewed stars and narrated the Academy Awards. Generations of Canadian hopefuls trekked to California because proximity, asymmetry, the center of film-making gravity, and the lure of money made Hollywood the center of North America's mass entertainment system. A shared language, cultural and social values, literary heritage, and even outlooks on world affairs combined Canadians and Americans into a mass audience. Only Quebecers needed subtitles. Hollywood's glamour, wealth, and earning power also generated political support in Washington. These forces and the costs of production foreclosed a feature film industry in Canada. John Grierson advised Ottawa to forget the mass entertainment market and develop a niche in documentaries. The 1934 National Film Act thus focused on training filmmakers and documentary production in a National Film Board. Even then, skilled illustrators and animators left for Hollywood. During World War II, North Americans continued their patronage of movie houses, which ran newsreels on national and international affairs before the main features. In 1947, Ottawa faced a severe dollar shortage that curbed film imports, but the U.S. Motion Pictures Export Association responded immediately, holding out financial and other incentives, such as putting Canadian place names in films to maintain Canada as Hollywood's only active export market for several years. Canadian ambassador Lester Pearson understood how Upper North Americans were all stakeholders in the U.S. film industry:

> We have a common heritage in democratic ideals. We have a common language, common social customs, and in general a common culture. No better illustration of the general and constant commerce between our two countries can be found than that provided by our own domestic market. There is no quota for American films shown in Canada. Every theatre in Canada shows them and the documentaries of our government-sponsored National Film Board are widely shown in your country.

In the 1950s, Hollywood also drew a younger generation, the North American teenage market, into downtown, suburban, and drive-in cinemas. Young people had money to spend on entertainment in the prosperous 1950s, and movies featured teenage heroes and heroines as well as rock-and-roll stars such as Elvis.[13]

Commercial radio ran as a parallel mass entertainment medium to movies. The first North American radio broadcasts occurred in 1920, at XWA in Montreal and KDKA in Pittsburgh. Radio reached mass listeners once technology extended broadcast ranges and designers created cheap and easy-to-use receiving sets in small boxes with speakers. In 1924, the U.S. Department of Commerce listed 101 radio frequencies and set six aside for Canada. Entrepreneurs instantly overwhelmed this allocation. By 1925, Canada had 90 stations, all much weaker than the hundreds of U.S. broadcasters. Most Canadians, their population scattered along a 5,000-mile band from one coast to the other, could not pick up domestic stations except near large cities, but at night they tuned in strong U.S. stations. Transcontinental private networks formed first in the United States, and by 1929 Canadian stations bought 80 percent of their programs from the United States. Americans had spent $3.4 billion (U.S.) on radio sets by then, and Canadians only a fraction of that figure. The U.S. free market system ensured that radio would be commercial, as it was for a decade in Canada as well. Advertisements aired by the later 1920s, and marketers sought consumers among the invisible mass of listeners. Broadcasters learned that housewives tuned in during the day, so household products makers sponsored dramatic serials, quickly dubbed "soap operas," to capture audiences and potential customers. Musical and variety shows aired in the evenings, when families tended to be together. In Halifax, the first children's show consisted of an announcer reading comic strips from Boston newspapers. Ottawa established some control through the Radio Acts of 1912 and 1927, which set up the Federal Radio Commission. Washington created the Federal Communications Commission in 1934, which supervised a free-market system under private ownership.[14] Station managers hired performers to woo listeners and sell commercials.

Meanwhile, Canadians trickled into this U.S. system. The struggling Ontario orchestra leader Guy Lombardo got his musicians a job at a Cleveland radio station, used his popularity there to move to Chicago, and then landed in New York and Upper North American stardom. His Royal Canadians at the Waldorf-Astoria hotel brought in countless New Year's Eves on annual broadcasts. In 1928, several Canadian station owners joined the U.S. Columbia Broadcasting System (CBS) to import shows that would attract listeners and expand their markets for the sale of advertisements. Hamilton's CKOC imported *The Shadow* to make money. Proximity and improved receiving sets allowed more Canadians to pick up signals from U.S. cities, and they heard former vaudeville stars, such as Edgar Bergen and Jack Benny, on weekly shows that sustained their popularity in the new mass communications market. *Amos 'n' Andy* became the most popular radio program in Upper North America in the 1930s.[15]

During the 1920s, Ottawa had left radio to free market forces, although it required stations to broadcast a quota of Canadian-produced hours. When Ottawa delegates traveled to Washington in 1929 as part of the U.S. Department of Commerce review of frequency allocations, they blanched at the political and economic power of private broadcast corporations. The U.S. invasion of the airwaves, however popular among Canadians, seemed an electronic version of Manifest Destiny. Senior Anglophile bureaucrats admired British ways, so the Aird Royal Commission of 1929 on the future management of Canadian radio recommended that Ottawa acquire a monopoly over radio as London had done with the British Broadcasting Corporation (BBC). Transcontinental distances, asymmetry, and U.S. proximity defeated that plan, but Prime Minister R. B. Bennett and the Liberal leader William Lyon Mackenzie King both saw how President Franklin Delano Roosevelt had spread his national popularity over radio with fireside chats, interviews, and regular addresses to all Americans. The Canadian leaders believed a national radio system would enhance Ottawa's presence and reach. The U.S. example, politics, and elitism thus shaped the Canadian Radio Broadcasting Corporation (later the CBC) in 1933 as a government-funded and -managed national radio system.[16] Two broadcast streams operated in Canada as a result, but with federal support, the CBC did not need to be managed as a business.

North American conditions and interrelated cultures meant that however national in scale it became, the CBC could never become a monopoly as the BBC had. For entertainment, Upper North Americans tuned in to Cecil B. DeMille's *Radio Theater;* to *Inner Sanctum,* where Raymond Massey's chilling laugh opened each program; and to *My Friend Irma.* The characters on *Ma Perkins, Big Sister,* and other U.S. soap operas also became Canadian favorites. Former vaudevillians Fred Allen and Jack Benny amused listeners in both countries. Orson Welles's 1938 Halloween eve Mercury Theater production of H. G. Wells's *War of the Worlds* sparked alarm in both countries, and panic in the New York–New Jersey area. Young listeners tuned in for the *Lone Ranger* and his trusty sidekick Tonto, while their parents preferred Bing Crosby and Mantovani. Throughout, Quebec remained a closed French island in North America's English-speaking sea. Early television mimicked the public/private radio patterns in each country, but not until after World War II. Throughout the 1950s, producers adapted radio dramas, soap operas, westerns, mysteries, and comedies to the small screen.[17]

Radio slumped when television rose in mass popularity, but it revived with a vengeance in the 1950s, when Alan Freed in New York became the first of thousands of disc jockeys who, by force of their own personality and rock-and-roll music, became celebrities with mass teenage audiences. They became an important consumer group in North America's mass entertainment market. One-song, 45-rpm records and then long-playing albums aired on the radio and were sold in stores. Promoters took rock-and-roll groups on tour in a manner reminiscent of vaudeville. They visited radio stations and drew fans to personal appearances at concerts.

Technological advances accelerated this radio revival when the Japanese firm Sony created transistorized receivers small enough to fit into automobile dashboards, purses, and pockets. Mass production and marketing reduced prices, and broad-based postwar prosperity allowed even marginally employed teenagers to buy personal radios. Many middle- and working-class households by 1960 had several radios, TV sets, and phonographs that played all forms of post-1945 mass entertainment.[18] Teenagers everywhere had, or knew someone who had, a radio as a sidekick for quiet listening, dates, and parties. They gathered in dispersed, invisible, small groups at the same time and thus constituted a mass market. TV broadcast mass entertainment over the airwaves, as radio had, and later through microwave and satellite cable systems. Variety programs such as Ed Sullivan's vaudeville-like revue of dancers, comedians, and popular singers drew masses of viewers on Sunday evenings. By the 1960s, millions of all ages paid in time and money as eager stakeholders in Upper North American mass entertainment.[19]

Canada's elites and intellectuals, rarely in touch with ordinary people, let alone teenagers in or outside their own homes, missed the cultural and social significance of this mass entertainment market that fed into the integrating Upper North American economy. While technology reinforced transnational cultural forces and spread popular tastes to create mass audiences from individuals and small groups, the elites lobbied and persuaded Ottawa to create a Royal Commission on the Arts to defend Canadian culture. From 1949 to 1951, Vincent Massey and his equally Anglophile elite commissioners held hearings and collected opinion and evidence but ignored popular tastes to recommend that Ottawa fund the high arts in Canada and develop an elite culture to counter United States–based North American mass entertainment. Louis St. Laurent's government duly funded the Canada Council, university programs, and other institutions, but the plan never had a prayer of success. U.S. dominance of Upper North American mass entertainment continued. A perhaps apocryphal story circulated that illustrated part of the problem these elites encountered. One academic asked another why he worried because Canada had no soap operas. After all, soap operas were junk. Of course soap operas were junk, the first replied, but an independent Canada should have its own junk. Throughout, elite advocates and policymakers discounted the tastes of work-a-day people who exercised their freedom to be entertained as they chose. Even CBC cultural mavens appreciated Hollywood films. Clyde Gilmour's choices for best movie, actor, producer, and director in 1950 and 1960 were all from U.S. productions.[20]

U.S. intellectual and cultural elite commentators shared their Canadian counterparts' disdain for mass entertainment. Dwight Macdonald in New York, for example, believed that Hollywood films and popular genre writers debased U.S. values. If Soviet leaders saw the Russian masses as an ideological construct, U.S. entertainment leaders saw the Americans as mass consumers. The free market forced taste down to its lowest common denominator, wringing out all cultural merit. Macdonald decried the tyranny of commerce over high art in the United States, much as the Massey Commission had for Canada. Both overlooked that mass entertainers tapped popular sensibilities, interests, and tastes. And while critics praised the cosmopolitanism of high culture, they ignored the cosmopolitanism of mass entertainment. Elitism and ideology had a higher call on their judgment than evidence and democratic sensibilities. So shared values and ideas about entertainment combined Canadians and Americans as individuals, small groups, and large audiences into stakeholders as well as critics in Upper North American mass entertainment.[21]

Transnational movie markets survived Hollywood's seismic changes during the 1950s. Antitrust judgments led Congress to break up the studio system that had monopolized filmmaking since the 1920s. Finance, production, ownership, distribution, and screening all became separate operations. At the same time, television emerged as a new mass market for theatrical and original films. European studios recovered from postwar destruction, and niche markets arose, such as from Quebec's secular Quiet Revolution, which provided a provincial market for Francophone cultural products. Independent filmmakers drew talent from Hollywood, while North American social change and a growing university student population chose art house films over mass market productions. The patrons for North America's mass entertainment fragmented, then regrouped in smaller cross-border audiences with special interests, whether they sat before large or small screens. Ottawa's 1967 Canada Film Development Corporation (CFDC) advanced money and credit to domestic production companies in anticipation of repayment from exhibition revenues. Those never appeared, so CFDC became a de facto film council. The cost of feature films frightened Ottawa officials, however, because millions evaporated in production. Moreover, proximity and private enterprise continued to exert their power. The CFDC could not afford to produce feature films, so Ottawa shifted to a policy of tax credits for cultural production. Telefilm Canada's few productions absorbed a lot of money but drew tiny audiences. Ottawa's enthusiasm faded along with Telefilm budgets over four decades while cross-border mass entertainment movies drew huge audiences and profits. Moreover, Ottawa's bureaucratic approach to the creative arts drove many Canadian filmmakers to the United States. Norman Jewison, David Cronenberg, and Ivan Reitman became successful Hollywood and independent producers and directors. Technicians and aspiring actors honed their skills in local or domestic Canadian productions to build résumés, then decamped for Hollywood. Famous Players and Cineplex Odeon controlled thousands of movie screens, and Gulf and Western's influence, not Canadian lobbyists, shaped the Free Trade Agreement's cultural clauses.

Problems of Integrated Entertainment

Proximity and asymmetry demanded mass entertainment entrepreneurs serve a mass North American market. Hollywood's legendary ability to spend led state, provincial, and municipal governments in both countries to set up film offices and attract production companies on location. Entrepreneurs built sound stages in Vancouver and Halifax, universities and colleges funded film programs, and graduates found work in the North American mass entertainment industry.[22] As far as locations went, in make-believe film worlds, anywhere could be anywhere. Toronto stood in for New York or Chicago, Alberta for Kansas, and Vancouver for Los Angeles. Currency differentials in the 1980s and 1990s drew U.S. production companies north for Canada's scenery, where they also found skilled technicians and government tax incentives. The historical patterns of Upper North American mass entertainment persisted, and they even intensified when computers became crucial for special effects. Canadian college programs supplied a pool of talent there, and the more accomplished artists headed south to work for Lucasfilms Industrial Light and Magic, on the Star Wars films, *Jurassic Park,* and series TV. A North American animation community of supply and demand for mass entertainment production emerged, and freelance specialists worked several projects for a single market.[23]

The real distinctions among the various films produced for the now-integrated North American movie world lay in the producer's intent. Atom Egoyan's *The Sweet Hereafter* aimed for, but did not reach, a mass audience. Yet the part-Canadian *The English Patient,* one of the best films of 1997, did. Timing and the quality of production had to match public tastes because market size mattered, and North American mass entertainment audiences poured millions onto box office counters. In 1998, for example, Canadian films drew $10.5 of $423 million (Canadian) of all Canadian box office revenues, and that proportion declined in later years. Canadian film exhibitors, meanwhile, paid the U.S. Motion Picture Association $5.97 billion (U.S.) for their films shown in Canada in the same year.[24] Nationalists bemoaned Canadians' refusal to see their "own" films, but the vast majority of North Americans went to movies for entertainment, not to express patriotism. The cross-border asymmetry of financial resources and audiences meant that no Canadian filmmaker could produce for the mass North American market without U.S. partners, and without them, lacked the resources to produce films at all. That was why as early as 1983 Los Angeles became the fourth-largest "Canadian" city by population because of all the expatriates in the U.S. film industry. By contrast, in 1999 Vancouver was North America's third-largest production center after Los Angeles and New York City.[25]

In some ways, the border did matter. Relative currency values and income tax differentials created marginal competitive advantages. Both factors contributed between 1978 and 2000 to the increase of U.S. film and television spending in Canada from $12 million to $1.18 billion (U.S.). When U.S. actors struck in 2000, many union members headed north or south across the border to take jobs.[26] California and Washington politicians complained about "runaway" productions to Canada that drew money from local and national economies. That worried B.C. film officials, but political rhetoric was one thing, the realities of power another, and the high stakes in North America's dispersed and interdependent mass entertainment industry a third.[27] These variables interwove with movie making, and the television industry, the third mass entertainment medium that interwove Americans and Canadians in Upper North America.

Regular TV broadcasts began in 1936 to limited markets in New York City. Three years later, David Sarnoff organized the National Broadcasting Corporation (NBC) as a commercial television system, but development stopped during World War II. It resumed after 1945, when Americans owned fewer than 8,000 sets. A year later, 60,000 sets had been sold, two-thirds of them in New York, the corporate and broadcasting headquarters for radio and TV networks. By 1948, 100 stations broadcast national news, public affairs, and entertainment programming to 30 million sets. Ottawa approved TV broadcasting in 1949, but Parliament held private broadcasters back so that the CBC could develop production capacities. By 1952, the CBC had built stations from Halifax to Vancouver, but it broadcast only a few hours each day. Private TV stations were also ready and could broadcast U.S. programs, provided they carried ten and a half hours of CBC material each week. Given Canadian demographic distribution in the borderland zone, most could view U.S. channels drawn in by rooftop antennas, or even set-top systems dubbed "rabbit ears." Canadians' postwar prosperity generated sales of 3 million sets during the first three months of 1950, and 7 million by 1953. In 1957, Ottawa's Fowler Commission confirmed Canada's public/private broadcasting mixture. Despite a discussion about trying to bar U.S. signals, politicians realized that the voters would rebel against any such ban. By 1960, 94 percent of Canadians owned TV sets, a higher ratio than had telephones. Forty years later, 98 percent of all North American homes had at least one TV, and many had three or four. News and public affairs blurred into entertainment with domestic talk and commentary programs, but most entertainment was U.S. produced, so Canadians became integrated into Upper North American mass entertainment in this medium even faster than with radio during the 1920s.[28]

The volume and extent of U.S. production and audience favorites held Canadians into this system throughout the post-1945 era. *Gunsmoke* ran for two decades, *Ed Sullivan* for twenty-three years, and *Bonanza* for fourteen years. *Father Knows Best,* adapted from radio, *The Donna Reed Show,* and *Ozzie and Harriet* ran a decade each and created for all suburban North Americans a stereotyped ideal of family structure and values. Walt Disney, a favorite source of mass family entertainment from his early animated films such as *Fantasia,* built mass North American audiences through his movie and TV program productions, children's books, and comics spun from the films, and from the Disney theme parks in Anaheim, California, and Orlando, Florida.[29] Canadians moved into the United States to work in TV production from the 1950s on. The CBC cancelled Monty Hall's *Let's Make a Deal,* even though he drew audiences, so Hall decamped for New York. He sold the program to networks, hosted 4,700 episodes to mass North American audiences, and retired a wealthy U.S. citizen and Upper North American celebrity. CBC bureaucrats wanted Alex Trebek's *Jeopardy,* but not Trebek himself. He too left for the United States and made himself a wealthy star in North American mass entertainment. Production centers lay in New York and Los Angeles, where rewards for the successful were greatest, and Canadians had limited opportunities and incomes at home. Even actors with moderate talents could, with hard work, an agent, and luck, make from three to ten times the money available in Toronto. The stage actors Lorne Greene and William Shatner, for example, became mass entertainment celebrities through their lead roles in the long-running *Bonanza* and *Star Trek* series. Forty years after *Star Trek* first aired, the latest generation of fans gathered in conventions from all professional and social backgrounds, in many countries, connected by their devotion to a fictitious future.[30]

Ottawa legislated a formula for Canadian content (known as cancon), which the Canadian Radio-television and Telecommunications Commission (CRTC) was to apply to domestic mass media broadcasts and to cable TV companies. These limits applied to satellite TV services as well, but many subscribers were able to watch all the U.S. mass entertainment productions they wanted. Audience demand for U.S. shows remained high, and during their broadcasts cancon ensured spots for local advertisers. The fees collected went into domestic production. As for programming, demand in Canada far outstripped production capacities. Private networks and stations, the CBC included, sent scouts and journalists to Los Angeles to grapple with publicity agents and production companies to book series programs at Hollywood's spring fairs. Satellite relays, meanwhile, multiplied niche channels, such as for golf, nature, and history, that carried many of the same programs, whether U.S. or Canadian based. Cancon had come to focus on domestic industrial, but not cultural, protection. In the 1987 Free Trade Agreement negotiations, Gordon Ritchie recalled that his cultural advisers were a Quebec filmmaker and a rock music composer. They wanted their version of the status quo—free Canadian access to the U.S. market but limited U.S. access to the Canadian market. Domestic entertainment lobbyists just wanted more money, while the CRTC and cable companies talked about cultural identity. Ritchie hoped that the use of U.S. TV satellites, dubbed "Death Stars," would show how little interest Canadian viewers had in this incestuous and mendacious circle of cultural self-servers.[31]

Cross-border mass entertainment in the early twentieth-first century rests on the cultural commonalities and shared methods of creation, production, exhibition, and consumption. U.S. media programs resembled split-run magazines because studios sold Canadian rights to their programs below cost to hold a market. Meanwhile, the CRTC repeatedly failed to reach its audience targets for domestic productions. Between 1960 and 1997, viewers watching domestically produced Canadian programs rose by one-sixteenth, from 32 to 34 percent. Cancon seemed a Byzantine bureaucratic burden that made production for Canada's small domestic market more, not less, difficult, because it forced Canadian filmmakers to find U.S. partners. The CRTC limited the numbers of U.S. channels and set quotas for domestic cable companies. These policies transferred revenue to support domestic production but had little impact on what Canadians watched once the news hours had ended.[32]

Domestic producers had also by 1994 become the world's second largest TV film exporters (after the United States), but largely within North America. Production exports between 1996 and 2000 rose 61 percent, and 94 percent of that went to the United States. The English language encouraged a symbiotic production system. For example, Disney Productions and a Toronto company produced *Road to Avonlea,* based on Lucy Maud Montgomery's *Anne of Green Gables* stories. That became a seven-year series, the most successful cross-border collaboration ever. It drew millions of Upper North American viewers, dollars, and many artistic awards. The producer, Kevin Sullivan, confessed that he learned not just how to make movies but also how to produce for the North American market. Lion's Gate films, Alliance-Atlantis, and Paragon became binational production and distribution companies from Canadian locations. Alliance produced TV romances in partnership with Harlequin's stable of U.S. and Canadian writers, all of which eluded Ottawa's gaze. Economic shifts within the industry shaped this process, but it remained in scope and operation an Upper North American mass entertainment system.[33]

Technology and Transnational Patterns

New communications technologies reinforced this transnational system and distributed ever more diverse material to ever more fragmented markets. When Ottawa lowered barriers to foreign investment in 1984, transnational corporate integration in mass entertainment accelerated. North Americans wanted cheap rates as communications blended with entertainment. The CRTC's fingers slipped from the domestic telecommunications market, and Republican members of Congress openly resented the election of Canadians to seats on the Internet Corporation for Assigned Names and Numbers. Throughout, however, the real initiative lay with millions of stakeholders. North American mass entertainment accelerated transnational cultural and economic intertwining, as the personal computer and the Internet demonstrated.[34] By 1999, the World Wide Web interconnected hundreds of millions of people and organizations onto a mass, albeit atomized, network of active and passive users and sites throughout the world.

Mass entertainment products became available anytime all the time for these global mass audiences of scattered individuals. The line between reality and entertainment blurred.[35] TV broadcasters showed movies, shows about movies, and movies such as *The Truman Show* that dealt with the social impact of television. Production companies put projects on Web sites to attract the millions who searched for new movies. Asymmetrical cultural interdependence deepened while Upper North Americans integrated seamlessly as mass entertainment producers, performers, and consumers. Nationality mattered far less than talent and competence. Mass entertainment was about the production, the performance, and the audience, not national cultural identity.[36]

The Internet also democratized a system that had begun as a closed preserve of U.S. military and intelligence services and academics. A buccaneering free market mentality prevailed as Web sites multiplied and millions of homes became interlinked. William Craig of Toronto, a former CRTC broadcast analyst, glimpsed opportunity and launched iCrave TV to resell entertainment and advertisements to North American Internet users. Broadcast and entertainment companies a decade before had barred Canadian cable owners from doing just that with microwave technology, and U.S. media organizations sued to recover profits from pilfered signals. They shut iCrave TV down because commercial rights prevailed in court over free market champions. At the same time, asymmetry mattered less on the Internet than in other mass entertainment media because national boundaries had disappeared.[37]

Polls through the latter decades of the twentieth century suggested that Canadians had strengthened their sense of identity despite a century of integrating transnational mass entertainment in Upper North America.[38] They also watched about 30 percent less television than Americans, and some variations in taste appeared. In the fall 1999 TV season, for example, the networks swiftly cancelled *Action,* a comedy about a reptilian Hollywood producer, when U.S. audiences tuned out. Canadians appreciated its sardonic humor, however, and watched several cycles of all seven episodes that reran only on Canadian channels. Canadians also stuck with *The X-Files,* a glacial saga about aliens taking over the earth, and *The Simpsons,* until both built audiences in the larger U.S. market. Furthermore, Canadians watched *The West Wing* and *L.A. Doctors* more loyally and in greater relative numbers than Americans. Conversely, they only gradually accepted those great U.S. favorites, morning newsmagazines and late night talk shows. Nationalists insisted that Canadians had higher-toned taste than Americans, but after watching domestic local news, they turned to U.S. international and public affairs programs and network offerings, sampling from the entertainment bazaar all the channels offered.[39]

Canadians also merged into the Upper North American celebrity world. Late-nineteenth-century periodical editors discovered that circulation increased when pictures of prominent personalities from various walks of life appeared on the covers. By the 1920s, professional sports figures such as "Babe" Ruth and Jack Dempsey, or a genuine hero of the air age, Charles A. Lindbergh, had achieved celebrity status. Then celebrities began to be famous for being famous, rather than for their accomplishments. With skilled management, mere publicity created celebrities, as Hollywood studios and press agents discovered. In mass marketed movies, audiences sustained the celebrity status of stars such as Mary Pickford, Douglas Fairbanks, and Marlene Dietrich. A celebrity's star power often increased after death, as Rudolph Valentino's and Elvis Presley's posthumous legends showed. After 1922, more than half of U.S. and Canadian celebrities were entertainers and sports figures, commodities in the dispersed transnational mass entertainment market. National origin or talent mattered far less than audience appeal. *People* magazine regularly announced those who had in the editors' judgment "arrived," and the *National Inquirer* mocked has-been celebrities with unflattering photos.[40]

Ambitious Canadian entertainers have always eyed the United States. Only there might they become stars and convince other Canadians that they were true celebrities. *Maclean's* magazine in 1990 polled Canadians to see which of six show business celebrities women and men would respectively choose to be marooned with. Tom Cruise and Michelle Pfeiffer headed the list.[41] In Los Angeles, stars' handprints in cement occupied part of a Hollywood Boulevard sidewalk in front of Grauman's Chinese Theater. In 1998, Toronto arts and entertainment leaders created a similar "Walk of Fame." Chosen celebrities had maple leaf plaques set in a theater district sidewalk. The criteria went beyond mere box-office appeal, board members insisted. Accomplished people from any endeavor qualified, so the long-retired skater Barbara Ann Scott, the race car driver Jacques Villeneuve, and the ballerina Karen Kain had plaques set alongside those for Jim Carrey, Christopher Plummer, and Norman Jewison. Canada's Global TV network began the *Star!* channel in 1999, which drew half its programs from the U.S. E! Network. Mass entertainment fans watched both, and *Access Hollywood,* to follow film celebrities.[42]

Asymmetrical interdependence characterized the Upper North American mass entertainment media, but every genre had prominent Canadians. Country music maker Hank Snow never forgot his Canadian roots for all his fame with Nashville's Grand Ole Opry. Neither did Percy Faith after moving to California. Some, such as the teen heartthrob singer Paul Anka, seemed to have no regrets about departing. The folk singers Gordon Lightfoot and Joni Mitchell found that their genre had unlimited potential in the

1960s because they fit with U.S. traditions and such singers as Arlo and Woody Guthrie, Pete Seeger and Bob Dylan. Lightfoot, however, rejected the CRTC's program to support songwriters, singers, groups, and bands. "Well, the CRTC did absolutely nothing for me, I didn't want it, I didn't need it, absolutely nothing . . . and I don't like it. They can ruin you, man. Canadian content is fine if you're not doing well. But I'm in the music business and I have a huge American audience. I'm going to do Carnegie Hall for the second time. I like to record down there, but I like to live up here." Every new generation of pop singer sank into this transnational world of mass entertainment.[43]

Comedians have been part of Upper North American mass entertainment since vaudeville, and in some respects only the media have changed. Successful early comedians moved from the stage into radio and the movies, and some lasted into the television age. Humor on one level is intensely personal, yet the cultural values and tastes of Americans and Canadians derived from and fed into a shared heritage and experience that comedians used to reach mass audiences in both countries. The Canadian Mack Sennett's slapstick "Keystone Cops" films convulsed North Americans, as did the American Buster Keaton and the Englishman Charlie Chaplin. Standup vaudevillians such as George Burns and Gracie Allen, Jack Benny, and Bob Hope, and even Edgar Bergen and his puppet characters Charlie McCarthy and Mortimer Snerd (how could anyone tell if ventriloquism worked on radio?), attracted mass audiences. Stan Laurel and Oliver Hardy, the Marx Brothers, and Bud Abbott and Lou Costello's vaudeville routines shifted into movies that survived into the 1950s in TV reruns and beyond in the mass market digital video disc industry. Johnny Wayne and Frank Shuster had an extended career on CBC Television, but they reached transnational mass market stardom through sixty-seven appearances on Ed Sullivan's variety show.[44]

Canadian comedians believed that they had an instinctive sense of what made Americans laugh because they had seen so much U.S. television comedy as youngsters. In the 1994–95 season, five of the twenty most-watched TV shows were U.S. and Canadian comedies, but more than 90 percent of those were filmed in the United States. Canada offered a small market in this genre, as it did in all other forms of entertainment. Even so, aspiring comics honed their skills in local clubs, at standup festivals, or in small theaters in all Upper North American cities. Some moved from being cast members on *Saturday Night Live* or *SCTV* onto the bigger U.S. stage.[45] A few, such as Leslie Nielsen, came late to mass entertainment comedy, but he had an early role as a star ship captain in *Forbidden Planet* that some believed inspired William Shatner as *Star Trek*'s Captain James T. Kirk. Canadian venues were often a training ground for the transnational mass entertainment world, and those who became Upper North American stars never lost their home-country audiences.[46]

Twenty-first-century mass entertainment wears a thousand faces, each with its own history, and tourism has become part of it all. Proximity and demographic distribution drew visitors from each country across the border in the hundreds of thousands annually. In 1999, Canada earned some $50 billion from mass tourism, and provincial departments and entrepreneurs worked to attract visitors and keep them amused while they stayed. Shared cultural and social patterns made such transitions easy because of the common language, except in Quebec, but people there worked hard to attract U.S. tourists as well. The events of September 11, 2001, however, constricted both ground and air travel in North America. Established patterns rebounded, but recent border security measures and passport requirements have discouraged the casual crossings of old.[47] More significantly, the nationalist argument that North American mass entertainment would subvert culture has largely disappeared from public discourse in Canada. Upper North Americans moved into an age of brands that apply in mass entertainment as much as for merchandising commodities and consumer goods.

Moreover, Canadians seem secure in their cultural identity within Upper North America and see themselves as producers, consumers, and stakeholders in a transnational Upper North America mass entertainment system. This even embraces museums and art galleries. Although symbols of national high culture, they have adopted the techniques of mass entertainment to attract patrons.[48] When cross-border debates arise in policy circles and between Ottawa and Washington, cultural support groups such as Friends of the CBC, academics, intellectuals, and others work from ideological premises that often disregard public interests and taste. The broad mass of North Americans, however, accept the free market logic of transnational mass entertainment and see even formal cultural institutions in that way. That is why, when Ottawa and Washington officials argued positions over such matters in political relations, they often just talked past one another and attempted to protect special, not public, interests and taste.[49]

Upper North American mass entertainment embraces many genres and media, and stakeholders in this realm include consumers as well as producers. This realm also rivals the North American economy in its cross-border integration and asymmetrically interdependent character. It shapes currents in the social realm as Canadians and Americans mingle to pursue careers or to join audiences for productions and performances. North American mass entertainment rests upon a common working language and shared values and sensibilities. In 2006, this transnational realm included millions of Upper North Americans who are stakeholders, whether as producers or consumers, of mass entertainment.[50] In an age of instant satellite communications and entertainment available anytime and anywhere, it is instructive to recall how when P. T. Barnum first booked his circus on the northern railroad network to find new audiences in the Dominion of Canada, he founded Upper North American mass entertainment at the same time.

Part II

Social Realm

The novelist Robertson Davies once observed that Canadians more worry about than love their country, although he may have exaggerated to create a quip. Even so, many at a 2004 Toronto conference seemed to agree when they argued that economic integration forecast eventual political amalgamation with the United States. That argument baffled the *Washington Post* correspondent Steven Pearlstein because Canadians seemed socially more like Americans than otherwise, and certainly not like the Europeans some claimed as their nearest social kin.[1] A list of controversial social issues in either country could apply to the other, and domestic opinion customarily broke out in similar ways. Values seemed much the same, especially in the Upper North American borderland zone where most Canadians and many Americans lived. Both peoples were democratic, optimistic, individualistic, and community minded. Even in health care, majorities believed that whatever form policies took, government was obligated to provide benefits.[2]

The social realm is amorphous, however, because of its complexity. This part of the book examines three topics: Upper North American mingling, attitudes, and approaches to the management of common social themes. Both Canadian and American societies assembled and interwove on the Upper North American stage throughout two centuries. Successive immigrant groups arrived from Europe and Asia, formed, reformed, and interacted in constant flux, much as they chose. Even when Congress enacted legislation to control U.S. immigration, Canadians were exempt until 1931, and while the border's jurisdictional authority fell on migrants, that had little affect on shared attitudes and outlooks. In the 2004 U.S. presidential election, some Canadians called themselves "blue staters" to assert a social and ideological kinship with liberal Democrats over social policy. "Red state" Republicans were antagonists. But every province and state had "blue" and "red" camps. Such judgments described social tendencies, not watertight compartments.

Upper North American social attitudes offer fewer sharp distinctions than might be supposed. The two peoples sort into transnational sectarian patterns, for example, with strong adherents to their faiths in both countries. For such people, however, Americans attended religious services three or four times more often than their Canadian counterparts. At the same time, strong believers in both countries were equally likely to vote for socially conservative political candidates. Moreover, all Upper North Americans supported religious freedom and tolerance. Racial and ethnic prejudice and tolerance existed in similar patterns in both countries. Controversial social issues, such as same-sex marriage, evoked comparably strong opinions in both countries, although the politics and legislation fell out differently. Ottawa had defined marriage as between a man and a woman some years before congressional Republicans called for a constitutional amendment to enshrine the same principle in the United States. Social opinions divided much the same in both countries, although rates of political activism differed. The political arenas for social action also varied. Each nation's constitution divided powers between federal and state or provincial governments, but politics and policy results emerged and were applied in different ways. Meanwhile, the sides in the debates in Canada and the United States had largely identical perspectives in cultural and social terms.[3]

Americans and Canadians have become so socially and intellectually similar that most can move from one to the other country and feel socially welcome and comfortable, always finding like-minded friends or coworkers who share views on social and political issues. Statistically, the two peoples seem much the same. Life expectancy and age distribution rates have in recent decades been close. About 80 percent of the population is Christian. Crime rates are comparable, except that U.S. homicide rates have been as much as five times higher.[4] Settler groups included many Western European peoples, but were dominantly British, with French and blacks from western Africa the major early ethnic distinctions, and Hispanics as the most recent U.S. distinction. Quebec's Upper North American diaspora created a Franco-American population, although after a few generations those living in the United States lost their French language. The United States was more ethnically variegated than Canada until recently, and in both cases, immigrants had to adapt to prevailing social and political patterns and learn enough English to get by. Despite Canada's claims to bilingualism, the 2000 census revealed that more Canadians spoke a Chinese dialect than French, which had declined over the previous decade. Spanish has become the major U.S. second language and provoked debates about English as the U.S. national language. Upper North American cities now reveal regional, not national, variations. Where "melting pot" and "multicultural mosaic" clichés rhetorically once distinguished the two countries, diversity now characterizes both societies. Some Americans, with an eye on the Quebec issue in Canada, even wonder if ethnic and linguistic pluralism might erode national unity.[5]

Upper North American cultural and social attitudes and institutions sprawl over the political boundary in regional patterns. Both legal systems have Anglo-Saxon roots with regional variations, the French Civil Code in Canada and Louisiana, and Spanish practices in the U.S. Southwest. Both political systems reflect shared social foundations and values such as democracy, representative and responsible government, the rule of law, and independent judiciaries. The state subsidizes public education up to graduate and professional levels, and standards are so similar that graduates can work throughout Upper North America.[6]

Part II explores selected themes to suggest how Canadians and Americans in Upper North America share transnational social issues but in some cases have developed divergent national legislation to manage them. Chapter 4 explains how immigrant and later generation peoples intermingled as Upper North Americans down to contemporary times. A common language facilitated mingling, with more movement south than north, but created Upper North American patterns. Social migration was no zero-sum game, where the balance of movement reflects a gain or loss. Mingling produced successive generations of stakeholders in borderland areas for an open Upper North America. Chapter 5 analyzes the social foundations of negative ideological and political attitudes that Canadians and Americans developed about one another. Canada's anti-Americanism has no U.S. counterpart, although during the past decade some negative political attitudes have emerged from conservative circles that formed new patterns. At the same time, these seem to have arisen in the context of disagreement about domestic and international policies, rather than from social roots. Chapter 6 explores several common issues that play out in dissimilar ways because of the two nations' different constitutional and political systems but reveal Upper North American patterns that spill across national boundaries.[7] These and other social themes link with threads from the cultural realm, reflecting the constants of geography, proximity, and asymmetry. In combination, the elements of the cultural and social realms help to explain the dynamics of transnational economic affairs in Upper North America and the Ottawa-Washington political relationship that has emerged over the past century.

Chapter 4

North American Mingling

Before the events of September 11, 2001, Upper North Americans thought next to nothing about crossing the international border between their countries to mingle for work, shopping, or vacations. "Snowbirds" headed south to escape winter's icy blasts, and Americans went north to escape summer's heat. A complex of industries facilitated this temporary social mingling. Travel agents, tax advisers, and publishers offered advice and directions. The Canadian and American automobile associations and other organizations lobbied on behalf of their members. Transnational patterns ran in north-south lines, but Quebecers congregated in particular areas—Old Orchard Beach, Maine, in the 1920s, and more recently parts of south Florida, where more French than English or Spanish could be heard once tourist season came. That was an exception to how the shared cultural values and habits of the two people, especially their common English language, made each other's country only slightly foreign, quite friendly, near, and inexpensive. Upper North American mingling included all the interests and activities that people pursued, whether for education, work, or amusement. Transportation networks carried large numbers of Canadians deep into the United States, while few Americans went north beyond that populated band of Canada within 100 miles of the border. And after the 1920s, widespread automobile ownership created highly dispersed patterns on the ever-increasing road network that overlay both countries.[1]

Several themes stood out in the history of this process. First, shared cultural and social values and habits eased the transition for those on the move. Second, proximity rendered travel times brief. Third, movement from north to south far exceeded the reverse. Fourth, "mingling" or "intermingling" seems a more appropriate description of the process and its results than "immigration" or "emigration." Fifth, transit of the Upper North American border, however many people were involved, had with few exceptions no impact on the ethnic pluralism that came to characterize both countries. Sixth and last, the mingling began when the United States achieved sovereign independence in the 1783 Treaty of Paris that laid out the future boundary with the remnants of British North America.

Historical Themes and Patterns

Western Europeans, mostly British and French peoples, and native tribes constituted the early population of Upper North America. The colonial imperial wars shaped the social landscape of eastern North America. New Englanders and the British deported long-settled Acadians from the Atlantic Northeast in 1755 to Quebec, New England, Louisiana, and France (a few). After the British capture of Quebec in 1759, London controlled the Roman Catholic French society along the Saint Lawrence River and established indirect rule over Canadian "habitants," who essentially were peasants descended from French immigrants, under close control of the Roman Catholic Church, working land owned by seigneurs.

The Acadians in the Atlantic provinces had a different historical image, which New England poet Henry Wadsworth Longfellow immortalized in his telling of the tragedy *Evangeline,* whose statue stands outside a stone church in Grand Pré, Nova Scotia, where the British collected Acadians for deportation in 1755.[2] In the 1760s, several thousand settlers and land speculators from Massachusetts and other colonies migrated to southern Nova Scotia, founded towns and villages, and created a socially homogeneous Greater New England that extended west into the Champlain Valley.[3] For a brief historical hour, British North America covered the eastern part of the continent from Hudson's Bay to Spanish Florida and west to the Mississippi River.

The American Revolution and War of Independence split the British Empire and created thousands of refugees, dubbed Loyalists, who mostly dispersed north to the remaining British-controlled territory following the Treaty of Paris. Coastal New Englander loyalists, after a stop at Castine, which rumor falsely let them believe would be British territory, crossed the Saint Croix River to Saint Andrews and settled along the valley. Farther west, frontier families occupied the Niagara Peninsula. Sir Guy Carleton's Royal Navy vessels shipped most of the Loyalists from New York City, where they had collected during the war, to Nova Scotian ports, especially Halifax, and along the Bay of Fundy shores. From there, they established communities in the Saint John River Valley and founded the province of New Brunswick. Meanwhile, their agents lobbied London for reparations and land in what remained of British North America. Moreover, some 80,000 to 100,000 blacks fled slavery, landing in Halifax, Shelburne, and other places. Some 1,500 free blacks founded Birchtown, across an inlet from Shelburne, where prejudice and competition for labor sparked North America's first race riot. Whites and blacks alike found Nova Scotia's climate bitter and unproductive. In 1792, 1,500 Nova Scotia blacks migrated to Sierra Leone. Whites, meanwhile, moved up the Saint Lawrence River to Upper Canada lands. In come cases, a few Loyalists even returned to their former communities in the United States once local bitterness faded.[4]

After 1783, the border was a line on maps of uncharted and unknown territory, neither surveyed nor marked for decades, but British North Americans and U.S. citizens still shared cultural values, social attitudes and systems, and the English language. Those transnational factors facilitated mingling in the borderland region. The political character of two sovereignties diverged, but socially not as sharply as the revolutionary schism suggested, despite Upper North American elite tendencies to see monarchism and republicanism as ideological opposites. Both saw the French in Lower Canada as foreign, even a separate race, because of language, religion, the power of the church, local laws, and the seigneurial system. The broadly British Upper North Americans lived in similar ways and circumstances with similar ideas about politics and the place of organized religion, in sum, as variations on North American social themes with an unmarked, open border between them. Businessmen and families alike intermingled freely in Upper North America in search of opportunities, or to unite with kinfolk. Migration in the sense of moving from one political jurisdiction to another occurred, but that process was so frequent and in such dispersed patterns that mingling seems more descriptive. Such relocation could be temporary, to visit family or associates; semipermanent, for seasonal jobs in forests or on the sea; or permanent, to take up land for homesteads.

This intermingling became a habit of Upper North American borderland life rather than a formal relocation to the territory of a foreign power with a change of allegiance and citizenship, despite the clear political differences between monarchically governed British provinces and the republican United States.[5] This Upper North American social experience contrasted with that of millions of immigrants to North America in the nineteenth and twentieth centuries who came for a refuge and to find opportunities. They experienced a cultural and social transplanting, adapted, and learned enough of a foreign language to make their way in unfamiliar social and political conditions. The images of the two countries also differed for Europeans. The United States offered political and religious freedom, vast tracts of land, and economic opportunity. British North America was still British, and thus was not attractive to Irish immigrants, for example, who sought escape from British overlords.

In Upper North America, shared waterways and wilderness roads interlinked borderland settlements, which developed local barter and commercial systems. Long-distance travel was difficult, slow, and awkward for bulky goods except on lakes and deep rivers. The canal era after the 1820s interlaced river and lake ports in Upper North America, but railroads created the overland transnational transportation system that made possible the intermingling of goods and people who moved to find work, land, a better climate, or form business associations. North-to-south movement was always greater than the reverse, because the United States offered more opportunities, especially for work, than the provinces. New Brunswick and Quebec woodsmen moved seasonally into Maine, New Hampshire, and later Michigan and Minnesota forests. There, distance imposed a permanent relocation. Neither U.S. nor British regulations limited such mingling on either a temporary or permanent basis. Atlantic northeastern seamen and fishermen moved to New England ports, and landless French-Canadian habitants escaped the seigneurial system, found land and jobs in adjacent states, and created Franco–North American communities throughout the Northeast.[6]

The numbers of people on the move and mingling even in the 1790s are impressive, given travel conditions and the tyranny of geography and climate. Some 15,000 Vermonters and New Hampshirites moved into the Eastern Townships of Lower Canada to take up British land offered on easy terms. U.S. civil unrest in Shays' Rebellion of 1786, the Whiskey Rebellion of 1794, and local discontent with post-Revolutionary conditions elsewhere generated a handful of refugees who fled north to British territory. Moravian missionaries feared that local frontiersmen would slaughter their Indian charges, and they led a small exodus to safety in the Thames Valley. Another 50,000 people from the north country migrated to parts of Upper Canada to farm and reunite with their kinfolk. The result was a mingled social and economic borderland. The U.S. migrants swore allegiance to King George as required, but British officials feared their numbers. They might rebel, or, if Anglo-U.S. relations deteriorated into war, reinforce invading U.S. armies. Social and political outlooks also sprawled across the border. New England and New York Federalists shared conservative ideas about the better sort as natural rulers to maintain social order, for example. When the War of 1812 broke out, many Upper Canadians, whether of loyalist or other background, avoided militia service. Some enlisted to defend their lands and fought against former countrymen, while others aided the U.S. invaders. Most, however, ducked for cover. Saint Croix Valley settlers insisted that the war was none of their affair and continued their mingled lives in this isolated borderland region. British naval officers brought a new group of migrants to Nova Scotia in the form of some 2,000 slaves liberated from Chesapeake Bay plantations.[7] After 1815, Upper North American bitterness faded quickly. New generations of borderlanders practiced regional migratory mingling as new states such as Indiana, Ohio, and Michigan emerged and developed. The social institution of slavery remained legal in the British Empire until 1833, although Upper Canada's legislature enacted gradual emancipation laws, as did many northern states, which reflected shared Upper North American moral and social values.[8]

After 1815, London sponsored settlers to the provinces (principally Upper Canada) to increase the population as a foundation for the militia. Between 1820 and 1865, however, some three-quarters of these migrants and provincials, numbering 3.5 million, headed south over the open border to resettle in the United States. Furthermore, between a quarter and a third of the French in Lower Canada, upward of another million people, migrated south to mingle with Americans in upper New England. Land, which they could not own under the seigneurial system, drew them. More than 150 Roman Catholic parishes appeared in upper New England in coming decades and formed a regional network that sprawled across the international border. Social interaction continued, but slowed after 1854 when the government of the United Canadas abolished the seigneurial system. By then, however, a permanent Upper North American Franco-American society had been established. By then as well, the early Industrial Revolution in New England had lured French and Upper Canadians to fill jobs in textile and lumber mills and construction, as well as to labor on farms. The Upper North American borderland pulsed with social and economic migrants and minglers, but anti-British feeling in the northern states meant that this mingling was mostly one way. Few Americans, apart from traders or entrepreneurs, moved onto British territory throughout this period.

At the same time, this sense of the British provinces as "foreign" generated a new form of temporary mingling. Some Americans in the upper states were curious about their British and French neighbors who gained attention in local newspapers and literary periodicals. U.S. travelers walked, rode, and sailed in a thin but steady stream of tourists, temporary minglers on what came to be known as the "Great Northern Tour." By the 1850s, seasonal routes ran from Niagara Falls down Lake Ontario and the Saint Lawrence River to Montreal and Quebec City. Yankee tourists came for the sights, natural wonders such as Niagara and Montmorency Falls, old regime architecture and churches in Montreal and Quebec, British redcoats and fortifications, and the habitants in their villages and peasant garb. American anti-Catholicism emerged in travelers' accounts. The habitants, on the one hand, seemed an alien people, under church control, unable to speak English. Upper Canadians, on the other hand, seemed a variant of U.S. yeoman farmers, progressive and productive, and convinced some who recorded their journey that Upper North American values and societies were so much alike that the two peoples would soon merge by mutual consent. Northeastern provincials received fewer U.S. visitors, but those who came thought of them as like New Englanders: poor, but hardy and industrious.[9] Social similarities and the broadly shared English language eased this mingling without migration in Upper North America.

Upper Canada's conservative ruling oligarchy, the Family Compact, and its Lower Canada counterpart, the Chateau Clique, disdained and feared U.S. social and political ideas. Many Upper Canadians, however, adopted such U.S. innovations as publicly supported schools, and political reformers such as Alexander Gourlay and William Lyon Mackenzie adapted U.S. republican ideas in their democratic protests. Lower Canadian reform leaders, principally Louis-Joseph Papineau, argued for republicanism to end British domination of the French. The Upper and Lower Canadian rebellions of 1837 failed, but survivors found a ready social refuge in next-door states. U.S. and British political developments also spawned sporadic social migrations that furthered cross-border mingling. After Britain abolished slavery in 1833, the tiny provincial population of aging blacks became a free, albeit scarcely equal, people. Meanwhile, free blacks and escaped slaves founded settlements in Upper Canada. The abolitionist William Lloyd Garrison visited one near Malden, on the provincial side of the Detroit River. Black slaves in the U.S. South imagined Canada as a "Canaan" in poetry and song. A few who fled slavery or were smuggled north on the Underground Railroad made it as far as a provincial refuge. Overall, in the 1840s, 40,000 lived in Upper Canada in what they saw as a temporary relocation. This migration quickened after Congress passed a stringent Fugitive Slave Law in the Compromise of 1850. On the Pacific Coast, 400 free blacks migrated to British Vancouver Island to escape California's discriminatory laws. A Colored Wesleyan church of some 100 members met in Toronto by 1850 and survived until 1875. Blacks already living in, or who migrated to, the provinces did not mingle socially because of white prejudice and discrimination, and most refugees returned to the United States during and after the U.S. Civil War. Blacks in Ontario after 1867 lived in near-ghettoes, shunned, dependent victims of the racism that accompanied Upper North American mingling.[10]

The borderlands unfolded across the continent and provided regional arenas in which social mingling evolved. Travel was easier north-south than east-west, even after the 1850s, when the northeastern railroad and telegraph grid were in place. Bulky cargoes still moved on water by sail and steam, and provincials and Americans conducted business, traveled, visited friends and relatives, and transplanted themselves. A sparse far western mingling began in the 1840s when U.S. missionaries, entrepreneurs, and overland migrants settled in the lower Columbia River and Willamette River valleys. Hudson's Bay Company employees around Fort Vancouver on the Columbia River's north bank withdrew to Victoria, on Vancouver Island, just before the 1846 Oregon Treaty extended the 49th Parallel as the border to Pacific waters. After the 1849 California gold rush, miners fanned out in the western mountain ranges, and in 1858 some 40,000 to 50,000 pushed up the Fraser River in British Columbia. British officials feared a U.S. conquest by default, but the miners were after gold, not land, and promptly decamped when the diggings played out.

In the Great Lakes Basin borderland after 1861, the U.S. Civil War generated new forms of political, if not social, mingling. Provincials closely followed news of secession and the outbreak of the war in U.S. newspapers. They also debated the virtues of both the North's and the South's arguments, and the war's progress. Most provincials shared northern social views about slavery, and though often motivated by bonuses and dreams of adventure, perhaps as many as 50,000 provincials, both French and English, enlisted to wear Union blue and defeat the Confederacy. Proximity and ease of access also transformed the provinces into a political refuge for Union deserters and Confederate agents, or prisoners of war who escaped northern camps. Spies from both sides in the war played cat and mouse with provincial police agents sent out by John A. Macdonald. Most plots came to little, but one gang rode from Montreal to Saint Albans, Vermont, in 1864, robbed the banks, and scampered back across the line ahead of a hard-riding posse. Washington waited for British officials to act, but when a Montreal court released the raiders, Secretary of State William Henry Seward threatened a passport requirement for all provincials. Macdonald regained Seward's confidence with more vigorous police action. Agents shadowed and reported on Confederates, and Seward relented. The social character of Upper North American mingling changed during the war years, but resumed its old patterns after the Confederate surrender at Appomattox. Many of the provincials in Union ranks, however, including Franco-Americans, remained in the United States.[11]

Transnational Migrations

Upper North American mingling patterns after 1865 began to operate on a transcontinental scale. In 1869, the Union Pacific Railroad linked California with the Midwest and East in the United States. Other rail lines, including the Canadian Pacific, crossed the northern Great Plains in the next decades and sent spurs north and south that created a borderland network. After Confederation in 1867, a deep depression in the Atlantic provinces sparked an exodus. Young single men and women responded to well-known opportunities in New England and worked on the sea, in factories, and in other occupations. U.S. economic expansion and demands for labor had a similar effect in Ontario and Quebec. Canadians abandoned farms and debts for jobs, resettling or mingling socially in towns and cities. Quebecers mingled in Franco–Upper North America, and most migrants and minglers did not venture below the borderland tier of states. Eastern Ontarians, for example, moved to Waterville, New York, where they fit into the local society and took up a variety of jobs in railroad car production and other occupations. After Macdonald's National Policy raised tariffs and prices, Canadians headed to Great Plains states to work and take up land. They also mingled with Americans from Boston to Detroit. In Chicago, the large numbers of resettled provincials initially formed expatriate associations and printed their own newspapers, but the common English language and similar cultural and social values and outlooks rapidly dissolved their sense of an expatriate Canadian identity. They assimilated into U.S. society, took up the same range of jobs Americans did, and sank easily into local life. Quebecers blended into established Franco-American enclaves in New England, where French-language newspapers appeared. They maintained Upper North American linkages when hundreds of delegates attended assemblies of the Saint Jean Baptiste Society in Montreal (1874), Quebec City (1880), Cohoes, New York (1882), and Nashua, New Hampshire (1892). Language and religion kept Franco-Americans close-knit. In northern Maine, however, social pressures, class consciousness, and English education systems first diluted and then smothered their use of French. Still, they retained the "Canuck" moniker, maintained social contacts with relatives in Quebec, and spoke in a French-accented English.[12]

In the later nineteenth century, millions of European migrants headed for North America, drawn by the political and economic freedoms and opportunities the United States offered. Many also landed in Canada, and the demographic and ethnic social patterns of Montreal and Toronto compared on a smaller scale to the patterns of New York and Chicago. Pacific rim and South Asian peoples landed in West Coast centers from San Francisco to Vancouver. Social outlooks and ethnic patterns there ran in north-south lines, and prejudice forced Asians to form isolated settlements on the social margins. U.S. entrepreneurs and businessmen appeared in Upper North American cities, but by 1914 only Toronto and Montreal could be called industrial centers, ethnically diverse with large workforces and social conditions comparable to Chicago or Boston.[13] Asymmetries of opportunity, productivity, and dreams of success propelled cross-border as well as international migration into the Upper North American borderlands, and deeper into the United States. Immigrants and long-settled people alike sought those opportunities, but the Upper North Americans had an easier resettlement because of their shared culture and language, and similar social systems.

Upper North American patterns on the Great Plains looked much the same, but with an agrarian theme and sparser population. During Canada's 1880–1910 prairie boom, many Americans headed north for land. Macdonald's Royal North West Mounted Police (RNWMP), a quasi-military constabulary, and fewer hostile tribes on the Canadian side of the border made the prairies safer than northern plains states. In the 1870s, RNWMP officers cleared U.S. Whisky and Indian traders out of Fort Whoop Up near the Montana border. They also kept watch on Chief Sitting Bull, who led his Sioux over the "medicine line" for sanctuary to escape U.S. columns eager for revenge over the massacre of Colonel George Custer's command at the Battle of the Little Big Horn in 1876. Ottawa denied the Sioux rations but allowed them to camp and hunt. Five years later, near starvation forced them south again.[14] Farmers and cattlemen drifted up and down the transnational Great Plains from the 1870s through to the 1920s, often in response to climate changes. In 1887, a few Mormon families from Utah and Idaho entered southeastern British Columbia and founded closed settlements that survived into modern times.[15] Between 1896 and 1914, drought and depression drove 162,000 farmers from Minnesota, North Dakota, and Montana to western Canadian provinces, but many returned when hard times seemed to follow them. During World War I, groups of Jews and nearly 2,000 Hutterites fled nativist prejudice in the Dakotas for the quieter prairie provinces.[16]

Mingling was diverse in both directions and jurisdictions, because people shifted repeatedly and the plains seemed to become culturally and socially a shared region. For a time, about one-third of all Canadian prairie residents were U.S. born. Ottawa sent agents south to recruit farmers from mid- and central western states such as Nebraska and Oklahoma. The agents persuaded expatriate Canadians to return, but few Americans did, in part because the agents on Ottawa's order turned away blacks. Shared cultural and social attitudes, family ties, friendships, and community spirit encouraged residents in borderland zones along the jurisdictional boundary to mingle. Shared social celebrations of each nation's independence day had livestock trading, horse races, picnics, and baseball games. As settlements grew, local commercial patterns emerged, and people gathered to exchange books and help on building projects. When automobiles arrived, local gasoline stations on one side or the other served car owners within the region. Doctors ministered to patients on both sides of the border. Upper North American plains people furthered their shared social identity as a result. Pursuit of opportunities combined with asymmetry to shape statistical patterns. By 1900, about 11 percent of foreign nationals in the United States were Canadian born and under 2 percent of the smaller Canadian population was U.S. born.[17]

North-to-south migration and mingling always outnumbered the reverse flows. Between 1820 and 1865, 3.4 million provincials, three times as many English as French, migrated to the United States. Between 1840 and 1900, over half a million Quebecers who could find no job or only marginal employment at home left to work in Massachusetts, New York, and Michigan in construction booms, as factory hands, and as house servants. They constituted 20 percent of local populations in mill towns such as Fall River, Massachusetts, and Manchester, New Hampshire. Domestic economic depressions and news of labor shortages in the United States drew nearly half a million Atlantic Canadians to Massachusetts and similar numbers of Ontarians to New York, Great Lakes Basin states, and Minnesota. The English/French ratio was roughly 2 to 1. Single young women took positions as housekeepers, nurses, and teachers. They usually settled permanently and married partners with the same language and religion. As a result, English speakers ranged more widely and deeply into U.S. society than Franco-Americans, who mostly remained in the upper northeastern states. Men who acquired an education or experience in business became lawyers, clergymen, professors, and entrepreneurs. An 1890s *Who's Who in America* listed 245 English and French Canadians prominent in U.S. industry and the higher professions.[18] Once they became so established, they tended not to return. In 1900, by contrast, only 127,000 Americans lived in Canada, but they constituted 19 percent of the foreign born.[19]

Upper North American mingling ebbed and flowed with economic cycles, but rapid northeastern U.S. industrialization notwithstanding, over half the Canadians on the move filled planting and harvest jobs. Washington did not develop bureaucratic management of immigrants until the 1890s, but it paid little attention to the northern border with Canada except to collect statistics. Meanwhile, the people on both sides of the border treated neighboring states and provinces as social and economic regions where they could find seasonal or permanent work and settle. By then, water and rail transportation systems interlinked the scattered components of the North American forest industry, which relied on migratory labor to hew, process, and distribute their production into widely dispersed markets. Americans and Canadians constituted a single labor force that developed Upper North America's integrating economic system.[20] A transnational ethnic mosaic also resulted, and family members in subsequent generations remained in communication and visited for social reasons, stakeholders in an open border.

Travel and upper-middle-class tourism remained a temporary way for Americans to mingle in the provinces throughout this era. Asymmetry in the northeastern population and larger wealthy classes made U.S. visitors increasingly common in various parts of Canada. Ontario and Quebec were favorite destinations, and by 1900 many wealthy and even patrician U.S. families moved up the Greater New England coast to build summer homes or fishing lodges. The islands and shores in Passamaquoddy Bay gathered part-time residents, and the Roosevelt family compound appeared on Campobello Island, New Brunswick, in the 1880s. Niagara Falls became a tourist and newlywed retreat. William Howard Taft made annual summer visits to a small village in Quebec where he played the role of patriarch and became popular with local people. He acquired a narrowly based but warm view of Canada from that experience. Provincial governments began to advertise their natural assets to attract more American visitors. New Brunswick and Nova Scotia built roads, and the Canadian Pacific Railway developed a series of elegant resort hotels from the Algonquin in Saint Andrews through Banff Springs and on to the Empress in Victoria to draw U.S. tourists.

During the 1920s, proliferating automobile use furthered borderland mingling as middle- and even working-class tourism appeared. After Prohibition began in the United States, Americans drove north to Canada on weekend tippling tours. Yachtsmen sailed coastal and inland waters to visit, sojourn, and participate in regattas and races. Amateur, and later professional, sportsmen and teams went on tours while entertainers worked vaudeville circuits.[21] In the 1930s, New Englanders who bought land and built summer homes along Nova Scotia's South Shore developed the village of Chester into a resort town. San Francisco families summered in Victoria and along the British Columbia coast northwest of Vancouver. Cultural and social themes blended in Upper North American mingling, and in turn spilled into the economic realm. All borderland regions seethed with people on the move by the early twentieth century, as statistical tallies revealed. U.S. Bureau of Immigration and Customs records confirmed that in the Great Lakes–Saint Lawrence River region more mingling than migration occurred. Many single French women, for example, moved repeatedly among branches of their extended families dispersed throughout Quebec and New England.[22] Ontarians followed similar patterns, but once they left, Maritimers tended not to return to their perpetually depressed homelands.

Shifts in social policy reshaped these patterns. After 1905, U.S. politicians and nativists became concerned about European immigrants arriving in vast numbers at Ellis Island. Many seemed to have dangerous socialist or anarchist ideas. Border Patrol and Immigration officials also kept watch for Europeans who landed in Montreal and attempted to enter the United States from Canada. Canadians still entered freely, but U.S. officers questioned them more closely than before. After the guns of August opened fire in 1914, immigration from Europe dried up. Britain's Lord Grey noted how the lights winked out all over Europe, but he overlooked how they remained ablaze in the neutral United States, where war orders from Britain and France sparked an industrial boom. Ontarians and Quebecers headed south for jobs, and to evade military service as news of casualties on the Western Front's charnel house began to appear in local newspapers. A total of 86,000 entered in 1914, and in 1917 the count reached 105,000. Canada's conscription crisis produced draft evaders until the armistice of November 11, 1918.

Upper North American economic rhythms interwove and remained a factor that shaped transnational migration patterns. After 1919, a postwar depression struck both countries, but the United States recovered two years before Canada did, where hard times lingered until 1923. The U.S. boom thus drew another million unemployed Canadians south. Meanwhile, the Nativist bloc in Congress surged. Politicians feared that European millions would once again clamor for admission. These concerns arose in Canada as well, and politicians in both countries held anti-Semitic, anti-Bolshevik, and anti-Catholic as well as anti-ethnic nativist outlooks. U.S. Immigration and Naturalization acts in 1921 (amended in 1924) reduced the influx. These acts set annual quotas based on percentages of a nationality's population in the 1900 census. Canadians were exempt, but many agreed with their neighbors' nativist views. Ontario Orangemen opposed Roman Catholic and Eastern Orthodox immigrants, and anyone who might hold socialist ideas. These conservatives allied with the American Protective Association, a prominent nativist group centered in Minnesota. Suspicion of foreigners spread across the prairie provinces to British Columbia in patriotic organizations of the day such as the Canadian Legion, Native Sons of Canada, and even an Alberta branch of the second Ku Klux Klan. All wrapped themselves in the British flag to draw political support and ban the immigration of peoples they saw as foreign to North America. The Canadian Klan also opposed black migrants coming from the United States and lobbied to bar Poles, Slovaks, and Hungarians who turned toward Canada when the United States refused them entry. Such cultural, social, and ideological themes intertwined to limit Upper North American mingling in the interwar years.

Meanwhile, the Great Depression slowed transatlantic migration, and as the U.S. quota system and Nazi and Fascist movements gained power and publicity, nativist groups lost their social appeal. Anti-Semitism still shaped social attitudes in both countries, even toward refugees on the run from Germany's Nazi government after 1933. Prime Minister Mackenzie King, when asked how many Jews Canada should accept, reportedly replied none was too many. The fear of left-radicalism and anti-Semitism mingled in Upper North American cultural and social attitudes to shape western Canada's Social Credit movement from the 1930s to the 1950s.[23]

U.S. immigration quotas did not apply to Canadians until 1931. Canada's poorer economy generated fewer opportunities, and many jobs offered lower wages than in the United States, so after 1919 southward migration resumed. Those Canadian immigrants with professional credentials and university degrees took teaching and other positions and mingled culturally and socially with Americans while retaining their national sensibilities, as the Canadians among the Carnegie scholars illustrated. Between 1919 and 1926, 11 percent of the University of Toronto's graduates headed to the United States, as did 15 and 36 percent, respectively, of all graduates from the University of Western Ontario and Acadia University. Most never returned. The working man's brawn drain was mostly over, but a brain drain replaced it. By 1927, some 600 Canadians worked in U.S. universities—a small number, but a harbinger of future patterns. The migration and mingling was not all north to south. By 1931, some 345,000 Americans resided permanently in Canada, and 10 percent of the total population was U.S. born. Cross-border commuting also emerged where urban regions straddled the border, such as for Ontarians who lived in Windsor but worked in Detroit. A cultural and social mingling of show business talent occurred, as when Mary Pickford (nee Gladys Smith) moved south to enter the rising mass entertainment industry. U.S. census takers in 1930 reported some 1.3 million resident Canadians, equivalent to 12 percent of the country's population at the time. The Great Depression and drought of the 1930s struck both countries simultaneously, and Canadians who headed through designated ports in search of jobs faced immigration officers who turned them back if they lacked the means to support themselves. Between 1932 and 1939, these policies blocked over 100,000 Canadians and reduced southward migration by over 80 percent.

After September 1939, however, labor demands rose when war erupted again in Europe while Washington maintained a limited neutrality. After the Japanese attack on Pearl Harbor, December 7, 1941, North America's economic depression evaporated and the northern border reopened. U.S. industry needed workers, and Canadians who went south earned more than they could at home. Migration rose to 10,000 a year, but with a focus on those educated and skilled in scientific and technical fields, and they remained in the United States after 1945. By contrast, few Americans moved north. U.S.-born residents and citizens, 5 percent of Canada's population around 1912, declined to about 3 percent by 1940, and 2 percent by 2000.[24] Economic variations throughout the twentieth century had been the principal force behind Upper North American migration and mingling. At the same time, Americans and Canadians mingled temporarily on business and for pleasure on millions of brief trips and sojourns. Tourism generated a growing service and support industry, whose owners became stakeholders in Upper North American freedom of movement. The American and Canadian automobile associations affiliated in the 1930s to serve a North American clientele, advise travelers and visitors about immigration and residency laws, hand out annual editions of road atlases and guide books, and arrange tours and package vacations for members.

Modern Mingling

Short-term cultural and modern mingling expanded when mass marketing and personal shopping patterns emerged in Upper North America during the 1950s. Often, such mingling interwove with travel and tourism by the members of the increasingly motorized middle and working classes, who drove to or toured regional Upper North American borderlands on family vacations. British Columbians explored the Pacific Coast states but rarely ventured farther east than western Alberta or Montana. Ontario license plates were common in New York and New England but rare in Vancouver. Quebecers headed into New York, Vermont, and for the coast of Maine. Nova Scotians mingled with New Englanders, often kinfolk, who hosted one another on exchange visits. The family camping boom of the 1950s and 1960s dispersed this tourist mingling further. The better heeled bought Airstream trailers to tow, and later recreational vehicles that amounted to motorized motel suites. Personal mobility increased, and Canadians headed into the Sunbelt states from California to Florida. Those with higher disposable incomes flew to vacation spots for short-term sojourns. Upper North American shopping trips increased in the 1970s due to proximity, asymmetry of consumer products, price differentials, and the relative spending power of the Canadian dollar and U.S. dollar. Entrepreneurs built shopping malls near border crossings, such as at Rouses Point, New York, and Bellingham, Washington. Bus tours ran from Halifax to Bangor, and later from parts of the United States to the gigantic Edmonton Mall.

Little of this kind of cross-border travel led to migration, yet millions of ordinary Americans and Canadians joined the corporate and other stakeholders who supported ease of access. Between 1990 and 1992, the numbers of Canadians returning from trips to the United States rose from 14.2 to 17.8 million. A steadily depreciating Canadian dollar in the 1990s, however, curtailed shopping expeditions, tourism, and winter sojourns from

Canada to the United States nearly 50 percent by 1998. Even so, by 2005, an estimated 5 million U.S. residents had Canadian origins, while between 500,000 and 800,000 U.S.-born Americans lived in Canada.[25]

The mingling ratios of the Upper North American society had been stable for some time. Moreover, each country had assembled a multicultural mosaic, but until after World War II Canada had fewer ethnic tessera than the U.S. prototype. Canadian nationalists nevertheless asserted in the late 1960s with little reflection and less investigation that Canada's multicultural mosaic had always been kinder, gentler, and more welcoming than the U.S. melting pot. This was fiction, as historians and social scientists had long known. Racial attitudes toward blacks seem to have been much the same in both countries, although Canada had no equivalent to the toxic legacy of slavery and racism in the United States. A trickle of black migrants to the north created a socially isolated black population. During World War I, blacks from the West Indies arrived to work in menial positions in Canadian cities and on railroads, where white union officials ensured that they remained in the lowest wage strata. When black workers unionized, they did so to pursue racial and civil rights as much as better wages and benefits. This Upper North American experience persisted into the 1950s and 1960s. Blacks in Toronto allied with the Jewish Labour committee to pursue civil rights along with improved working conditions and wages. U.S. civil rights groups of the 1960s lent Canadian blacks moral and organizational support. Leaders in Halifax saw themselves squarely within a North American, as well as local and national, campaigns for equality. They drew inspiration and support from leaders such as Martin Luther King, Jr. and others in the National Association for the Advancement of Colored People. Shared patterns of racial and religious prejudices had, after all, always characterized social patterns in Upper North America.[26]

Anglo-Canadians and Americans discriminated on racial and religious grounds against Asians as well as other groups because a similar cultural and social intolerance and prejudice infected both societies. Canada's 1882 Chinese Exclusion Act and later head tax offers a poignant example. Anti-Chinese riots erupted in Bellingham, Vancouver, Seattle, and other West Coast cities and towns in the early twentieth century. Prejudice against the Japanese shaped local politics in British Columbia, Washington, and California. Discriminatory laws restricted land ownership and other social rights. Resentment of local Japanese increased after Japan invaded China and seized Manchuria in 1931. U.S. and Canadian missionaries wrote to their home societies to lobby Washington and Ottawa to oppose Japan's policies. After the Pearl Harbor attack, anger and fear interwove with prejudice and politics to produce Japanese internment from British Columbia to California. State, provincial, and federal police and troops rounded up the Japanese and transported them to concentration camps in barren interior regions. Church and civil groups protested and worked for their release, although internments ended only after the Pacific war was over. Many Japanese renounced Canadian citizenship in disgust and returned to their homeland after 1945, but found themselves treated as foreigners because many spoke only English. The Japanese experience in the United States was similar, but once moved away from the West Coast, they found little prejudice. Most Americans farther east treated them as just another immigrant group.[27]

Both the British/Canadian and U.S. governments always expected immigrants to conform to their constitutional and political regimes, legal systems, and social norms and behavior. In Canada, "nationality" referred to French and English, and Canadians were British subjects until Parliament passed Canada's first nationality bill in 1946. English was the language of public affairs, and in the United States the "melting pot" implied a national ideological and political cohesion based on the principles of democracy, republican government, and the ideals and aspirations expressed in U.S. founding documents: the Declaration of Independence; the Constitution of the United States; the Bill of Rights. By the later nineteenth century, most northern U.S. cities contained comparable ethnic mosaics to those found in Montreal, Toronto, and Vancouver. Furthermore, Canada did not have a common language. Lord Durham's 1840 Report after the provincial rebellions of 1837 described Upper and Lower Canadians as two nations (French and English) warring in the bosom of a single state. Canada was hardly a single state, but Durham proposed French assimilation in a united Canada, not a two-tile social and linguistic mosaic. Assimilation failed, and what came to be called the two solitudes emerged as a major and parallel social component in Canada by the 1920s. By then, Jewish peoples had settled in Montreal, but they faced discrimination from French and English alike. A French Roman Catholic society persisted in Quebec, whose people culturally and socially, if not linguistically by this time, had more in common with Franco-Americans across the border than with Ontarians or Atlantic Canadians. Comparable patterns of ethnic, racial, and linguistic prejudice existed throughout Upper North America, and that is precisely the point.

Moreover, the U.S. Constitution had the Bill of Rights, and Canada had no equivalent until legislation by John Diefenbaker's Conservative government in the 1960s. No constitutional provisions appeared until repatriation by the Constitution Act of 1982 appended a Charter of Rights and Freedoms. That also made Canada's supreme court the final authority with jurisdiction over what could be called Canada's social compact, as the U.S. Supreme Court had been since the early nineteenth century. Upper North American multicultural mingling therefore evolved within and between these distinct political and constitutional frameworks, although with singular implications for those who settled in Quebec. In the United States, the same ideological and social ideals applied in all jurisdictions, if not equally to all people. The point is that the melting pot–versus–mosaic dichotomy misrepresented the historical and contemporary realities of the culturally and socially multiethnic Upper North American societies. By 2005, the mosaic / melting pot clichés had rhetorical, ideological, and political utility for some Canadians but concealed the interwoven historical story as well as contemporary similarities of the two societies.

In modern times, Upper North American migration and mingling quickened during World War II and just after in the thousands of officials, specialists, and military personnel who worked in Washington and Ottawa, in defense industries, or on the Manhattan Project. Many Canadians who moved to the United States during the war remained there, and more arrived with the rapid transition to the Cold War because of its demands for advanced research and industrial specialists. A wartime north-to-south brain drain and high-skills migration replaced the former generations of casual and permanent labor, but with no south-to-north counterpart. Many Canadians who moved to the United States achieved high reputations and influence, such as the economists John Kenneth Galbraith of Harvard University and Robert Mundell of Columbia University. Both advised U.S. presidents on economic policy. The paucity of university graduate positions in Canada before the 1960s meant that Canadians with advanced degrees had to find work in the United States. Between 1951 and 1955, the Upper North American free market for skills and education sent 66,000 Canadian university graduates and 20 percent of all engineering graduates to U.S. positions in scientific and technical organizations, medicine, engineering, and advanced research. Countless other Canadians developed careers in entertainment, publishing, and industry. Between 1945 and 1960, 78,000 Americans migrated north to live, but 300,000 Canadians passed them going the other way. Canada's university expansion of the 1960s and 1970s served Ottawa's nationalist policies, and the ambitions of baby boomers and their children, but had to offer tax incentives to U.S. academics to fill vacancies when the provinces opened new campuses. For a time during the 1970s,

California university graduates constituted virtually the entire Psychology and Business Administration departments of the University of British Columbia. U.S.-trained anthropologists, political scientists, and sociologists made up Simon Fraser University's departments, and this pattern occurred all across Canada, even at the new University of Prince Edward Island. Business schools imported the Harvard case-study method. This cultural and intellectual mingling became a limited social migration, although it spawned a backlash. For example, Robin Mathews of Carleton University denounced U.S. scholars as socially subversive by default, if not intent, unwitting agents of Washington imperialism. Anti-Americanism fueled such charges, because Oxford and Cambridge professors in a previous era had championed British, not Canadian, ideals. This tempest, after an acrimonious debate, produced the field of Canadian studies and preferential hiring practices, thanks to Ottawa's financial and legislative support.[28]

Quebecers, meanwhile, had for over a century mingled in Upper North America, linked through time by cultural and social heritage and family connections. Most in the United States had lost their French language but retained their religion, even through the anti-Catholicism of the 1920s. After the 1960s "Quiet Revolution," young Quebecers developed a cross-border, but not pan-Canadian, outlook. True, life in the United States threatened them with linguistic assimilation. But like so many, they saw education and work there as an opportunity to improve their English and pursue career opportunities. They become one more "ethnic" group in American terms who contributed to an internal debate on Crevecoeur's old question: What then is the American, this new man?[29]

Washington officials had less interest in such debates than managing North American mingling. By the 1960s, Congress stipulated a ceiling of 120,000 Western Hemisphere immigrants with a maximum of 20,000 annually from any one country, and it set priorities. First, physicians, scientists, engineers, and skilled workers could fill any shortages, which favored Canadians by proximity, language, known academic standards, and shared cultural and social mores. Second, any would-be entrant to the United States with a job offer was welcomed. Third, others could apply, but without any guarantee of admission. Continuous shortages in advanced technological and scientific fields meant that numerical ceilings in the first two categories were honored more in the breach than the observance. Canadians also stretched and evaded these restrictions, changing careers to migrate and mingle in the North American market for highly educated, skilled, and accomplished professionals. Even with a combination of inflation and recession in 1975, just over 11,000 Canadian emigrants entered the United States, the lowest number since 1945.[30]

The Vietnam War and U.S. social turmoil during the 1960s slowed Canadian migration and mingling. They also spurred young Americans toward Canada to escape the draft as the U.S. Selective Service system reached more deeply into society. First a trickle and then a spate of young, at times idealistic, Americans found a northern sanctuary. They soon saw Canada as a poorer, slower version of the United States with the same language, popular culture, social systems, and habits of life. A total of 15,000 arrived in 1965, a 30 percent rise in U.S. immigrants over the previous year. Between 1965 and 1976, American arrivals outnumbered Canadians heading south for the only time since the Loyalist exodus after the American Revolution. Estimates of U.S. draft evaders, antiwar protestors, and military deserters ranged from just over 15 to 60 percent of the decade's 200,000 U.S. immigrants, most of whom had not come to mingle with Canadians. Ottawa's 1967 reforms favored them because they were young, educated, and fluent in English. Once settled, they "North Americanized" Canadian universities with U.S. civil disobedience methods, such as teach-ins, sit-ins, and protest marches. In many ways, they acted as though they were still in the United States.

Canadians, however, proved far less anti-American than the American newcomers anticipated, seeing the newcomers as little more than opportunistic outsiders. The mayors of Montreal, Toronto, and Vancouver even suggested using the War Measures Act to bar U.S. radicals and draft evaders. Meanwhile, a few Canadians headed south to serve in branches of the U.S. armed forces and fight in Vietnam. Many who survived remained in the United States because military service gave them the immediate right to become citizens. After the war petered out, most U.S. refugees became invisible minglers. War-frayed sensibilities eased, and after 1976 President Jimmy Carter issued an amnesty, so many drifted back to their former homes in the United States. When Ottawa declared its own amnesty on these illegal immigrants, roughly 30,000 came forward and became legal residents and then citizens. Some, such as the sociologist John Hagan and the film critic and journalist Jay Scott, acquired an Upper North American outlook on themselves and their careers.[31]

The flow of Canadian migrants and minglers to the United States, meanwhile, remained steady after 1965, between 10,000 and 15,000 people annually. The 1988 Free Trade Agreement (FTA) expanded binational labor markets, and in 1994 the North American Free Trade Agreement (NAFTA) authorized year-long, annually renewable TN-1 work visas for up to five years. This encouraged mingling based on personal free market value with a bias toward educated and skilled Upper North Americans. Canadian journalists, scientists, academics, and creative artists who could document their accomplishments and value to the United States could apply directly for citizenship. As Upper North American economic interdependence deepened, Canadians and Americans mingled in senior financial, high-technology, and entertainment sectors. Many became citizens and explained that U.S. opportunities and cultural and social as well as geographic proximity made migration irresistible. Such people chased opportunities as virtual Upper North American citizens in a transnational arena. Perhaps, if the nineteenth-century New York *Tribune* editor Horace Greeley were resurrected in Toronto, he might advise "go south young Canuck, go south." One case of the intricate ramifications of this social intermingling came to light on September 11, 2001. Detroit's health care system almost collapsed when security measures jammed up the Ambassador Bridge because thousands of physicians, specialists, nurses, and aides could not cross to work from their Windsor homes.[32]

Strict security after September 11 created a political firestorm when Washington granted border officers discretionary power to determine how long visiting Canadians could remain in the United States and the automatic six-month grace period on any visa came to an end. The Canadian Snowbird Association, whose members owned property in Florida and other southern states, and spent billions during their winter sojourns, organized political opposition and marches on Congress while Ottawa protested at official levels. The House of Representatives Small Business Committee called public hearings that recommended leniency for snowbirds. Department of Homeland Security Secretary Tom Ridge personally assured Deputy Prime Minister John Manley that Canadians would be exempt from the proposed thirty-day visa limits. U.S. Immigration Commissioner James Ziglar promised the Snowbird Association president that her members would be free to come and go as always. This illustrated the latent political power that large numbers of mingling social stakeholders could exert on Upper North American policymaking, even under emergency circumstances.[33]

Contemporary Upper North American mingling occurs in widely dispersed formal and informal patterns. The shared cultural and social values and language that ease a migrant or temporary mingler into the other society in person operate just as effectively by telephone or e-mail, or in Web site chat rooms. Professionals mingle at conferences with colleagues and associates, uncover and pursue interests or opportunities north or south across the border. People meet and marry. Canadians or Americans with reputations in their fields often receive job offers from organizations in the other country, and young people mingle for their educations. Even those who do not physically cross the border become de facto Upper North Americans through economic integration and mass entertainment. And unlike immigrants from a truly foreign country, when cross-border minglers unpack they are already culturally and socially adjusted to their new circumstances. Considerable public discussion in Canada during the 1990s "brain drain" exposed the tyranny of marginal differences that argued the superiority of life in one or the other country. Cavils about costs of living, crime rates, school quality, and health care were minor concerns to would-be and decided Upper North American minglers. One newcomer in New York was surprised to find a Canadian Women's Club that had been founded eighty years earlier and still had a long, active membership list.[34]

Asymmetry of employment and other opportunities historically made the United States more attractive for Canadians than the reverse. North-south versus south-north migration ratios in modern times have been 2 to 1 for natural scientists and university professors, 6 to 1 for engineers and managers, 15 to 1 for computer scientists, and between 15 and 20 to 1 for health care professionals, physicians, and nurses.[35] Between 1986 and 1995, 9,000 managers, 5,900 medical professionals, 3,300 engineers, 2,275 teachers with advanced degrees, and 20 percent of Canada's graduating classes in these fields found jobs in the United States. North America had always been a free-market for the ambitious and skilled in either country. By 1997, 20 percent of Canada's 1995 medical graduates had departed south. The overall increase of highly educated and skilled Canadian minglers in the United States between 1986 and 1997 rose from 17,000 to 98,000. Some 20 percent of engineering and computer science graduates left each year. U.S. universities recruited Canadian students directly from high schools. Some New York colleges served a clientele largely from Ontario. In 1997, 5,000 professionals and managers entered the United States on permanent visas, and an additional 16,450 went under extendable NAFTA TN-1 visas. This modern Upper North American mingling was the latest phase of a talent shuffle that began during World War II.[36] Overall, however, Canadians taking up jobs in the United States outnumbered the reverse by 10 to 1, an inversion of the population ratios.[37] Washington's greater attention to security after September 11, 2001, clogged border entry ports and generated frustration among regular minglers, but it failed to disrupt the patterns.[38]

Modern Upper North American mingling has largely paralleled the economic integration and interdependence that accelerated after the FTA and NAFTA. Moreover, Canadians remained among the three largest groups of migrants in various states. This ran from just over 41 percent in Maine to 2 percent in Arizona. Such figures also revealed new geographic dispersal patterns. Formerly, the borderland states had shown the greatest increase in numbers of Canadians. Now Canadians mostly headed for the middle and southern states. Texas and Oklahoma had risen over 135 percent, New Mexico over 100 percent, and Colorado, Nevada, North and South Carolina, Tennessee, and Texas from 66 to 88 percent through 2003.[39] These shifts reflected economic change and professional employment patterns. During President George W. Bush's 2004 bid for a second term, for example, some of his detractors declared they would move to "blue-state" Canada in protest. Ottawa's Immigration Department Web site had over 115,000 "hits" just after election day, 10,000 daily for the next week or so, and then less than normal interest. Partisan sympathies had not generated a political sorting by jurisdiction after the American Revolution, let alone in modern times. Meanwhile, the flow of professional minglers in search of temporary or permanent opportunities continued in established channels.[40]

Geography, proximity, and asymmetry have allowed people with shared cultural and social attitudes, and mixtures of ethnicity, language, and religions, to disperse geographically and politically in Upper North America for more than two centuries. Central governments took jurisdictional control of this migration and mingling only in the early twentieth century, when the patterns were in place. A shared working language and comparable social systems eased relocation, often making it seem easier, given regional outlooks, to move on north-south rather than east-west lines. Quebecers and Hispanics were exceptions to these principles. The former had become rooted in the northeastern locales, and Hispanics, while distributed broadly, were dominantly in the southern tier of states. Proximity and familiarity with this Upper North American region generated convictions and expectations among the people that they were stakeholders in a transnational arena, and actors in a shared social and economic, but not common political, drama. A lack or surfeit of opportunities in one jurisdiction or the other and open or easily scaled borders spurred a regional borderland mingling that became a continuing feature of Upper North American life.

Chapter 5

Negative Vibrations

Fall 2003: A Canadian mob of anti–Iraq War demonstrators hounded terrified U.S. pee-wee hockey players out of Montreal because the Stars and Stripes was emblazoned on their bus. February 2004: With the U.S. general elections under way, a *Maclean's* cover read "Canadians to Bush: We Hope You Lose, Eh?" March 2004: The audience at a Montreal high school's multicultural festival booed a U.S. teenager carrying her country's flag until she fled the stage in tears. September 2004: Jean Bevan of Halifax told off a stranger who objected to a U.S. flag decal on her rear car window.[1]

Although some commentators passed such incidents off because of Canadian opposition to the U.S. invasion of Iraq and dislike of President George W. Bush, such anger and vitriol reflected more than policy disagreements. In social terms, do Canadians and Americans see double images of one another when they gaze across the border? Is the border a social two-way mirror? This cross-border discourse over Washington's policies, bafflement among Americans, and anger from many Canadians over Washington and Ottawa policies around the March 2003 U.S. invasion of Iraq and the confused morass of its aftermath seemed mild compared with the venomous debates in other parts of the world—Anti-Americanism "lite," we might say of the Canadian version. The blizzard of opinion polls that smothered each country consistently revealed, however, that the two peoples still regularly and persistently called one another best friends.[2]

Cross-border political judgments and social perceptions seemed to occupy separate compartments in Canadian and American thinking. Even the antagonism of a particular president and prime minister seemed to be personally, not socially, rooted. Furthermore, Canadians who took exception to aspects of U.S. culture and society knew that their own values were much the same, with shaded distinctions rather than stark differences. In many ways, politics and public moods aside, the two peoples were virtually interchangeable. So the vitriol and smug moralism, the episodic lament or rending of garments over Canada's fate as a North American country next to the United States, seemed not only fatuous but also futile.

Origins of Suspicion

Where, why, and how such negative vibrations arose and wafted north or south nonetheless tells us about why each people tends to respond to the other as it does. Furthermore, when divisive issues such as the Iraq War do infect public discourse, a parallel internal debate erupts within each society while policymakers dispute the national ramifications. At the same time, asymmetry, proximity, and interdependence have produced a fixed collective stare south compared with episodic glances north, and the internal character of U.S. society has shifted, in both demographic and distributional terms. The passage of time and the change from large-scale migration and mingling to sojourning, socializing, and secondment have all tended to fray social linkages that the two peoples developed up to the World War II era. Much of the commentary in Canada, and its absence in the United States, about people in the other jurisdiction identifies them as less Upper North Americans than another people with the same language and familiar faces.

This cultural and social familiarity has led commentators, politicians, officials, and citizens to struggle with how Canadians' anti-Americanism can be reconciled with their received ideas about how the two societies relate. The customary (and somewhat ritual) images of neighbors and best friends have not produced the patience and understanding in recent years that it once did. Whether the issues are related to trade in softwood lumber or global crises, debates and divergences have been sharper than might have been the case a decade or two ago. Canadian anti-Americanism has recently even evoked a spasmodic U.S. counterpart, so negative vibrations now go in both directions. Social change as well as international differences have eroded the sense of a stake that each people had in the other's foreign policies in the post–Cold War era. The origins, development, and character of these negative cross-border vibrations that vex and confuse policymakers, commentators, and citizens alike need to be understood.[3] The two-way mirror of the border still exists, but new generations now peer through.

The first negative images appeared (or were later so judged) during the

American Revolutionary War and War of 1812, from 1775 to 1815. The Revolution was also a civil war in British North America that produced social dislocation, refugees, and lingering bitterness, as civil wars always do. It seemed that republican Whig Patriots and monarchist Tory Loyalists split into two distinct ideological, social, and political peoples. The French in what became Lower Canada constituted a remnant of habitants and seigneurs in villages with a Roman Catholic religious hierarchy alien to the Anglo–North Americans of the age. So the French sat to one side in this paradigm. Though seemingly anti-American in political terms, the English-speaking Loyalists segregated themselves to the west in what soon became Upper Canada to distinguish their province from the French Catholic habitants of Lower Canada along the Saint Lawrence River. Anglo-elites in Upper Canada saw the United States' emergence as a sharp fork in the historical road. They insisted upon the social (and hence ideological and political) distinctions that provided the foundation for an anti-American British North America. This outlook, observers concluded, carried through Confederation in 1867 to become part of the subsequent Canadian national identity.[4]

Recent scholarship has revised this received image of loyalists. They were socially as well as politically caught in the middle of a civil war, forced out of farms and local communities because they refused to support the Patriot cause championed by a local faction or because they depended upon Britain in one way or another. A civil war resulted, and it raged within the overall provincial rebellion and republican revolution. Loyalists were refugees, by force or choice, and after 1783 they quietly mingled in upper northeastern North America. They were Anglo–North Americans in their culture, social attitudes, and even political behavior once resettled. British officials noted how American these Loyalists seemed, although provincial elites insisted on the superiority of the monarchy and British ideals. Allegiance to the central U.S. government during the first decades was often equally tenuous. Some loyalists returned to their former homes in the United States after local bitterness about "Tories" faded. Others in the provinces who reestablished contact with former friends, neighbors, or business associates were less British than North Americans, as Royal officials discovered. Those loyalists who returned to England, moreover, lived isolated lives in an alien society. People in the Upper North American borderlands, furthermore, moved to gain available land and commercial or employment opportunities regardless of the jurisdiction. The social fluidity of the borderlands and the nature of life in wilderness Upper North America confounded the efforts of officials such as John Graves Simcoe to transform the settlements into a British society in North America. Provincial Anglo-elites denounced U.S. republican democracy as mob rule, but New England Federalists betrayed much the same matrix of cultural, social, ideological, and partisan politics as the first party system emerged in the 1790s and 1800s. Many provincials saw the War of 1812 as a quarrel of governments, not peoples. Settlers in the Saint Croix Valley declared local neutrality. Upper North American social linkages formed throughout the Colonial era survived the furnace of war and revolution but faded as that generation died off.[5]

After 1815, Americans who looked or visited north distinguished between provincials and their London overlords. Whatever their views on the future of the United States, both Americans and provincials accepted the division of North America into two jurisdictions. Despite trumped-up fears among provincial elites and retroactively applied memories of aggression, little evidence emerged to argue a sustained or episodic U.S. interest in annexation—notwithstanding partisan rhetoric on the hustings, in Congress, or newspapers to the contrary. In the Jacksonian era of the late 1820s through the 1830s, Whig/Tory partisan labels resurfaced in U.S. politics for internal reasons. Meanwhile, North Americans migrated and mingled with one another for economic and social reasons, and they began to see themselves as much the same kind of people.

French migrants from Lower Canada formed Franco-American societies in the United States that maintained regular interaction across the border. U.S. citizens who visited the provinces saw locals as almost Americans, which in part was what they wanted to see. But political systems and loyalties aside, both became increasingly Upper North American as the generations passed.[6] After 1815, members of Upper Canada's Family Compact—such as John Strachan, John Beverly Robinson, and G. H. Markland—denounced U.S. aggression against their "country" in the late war. But throughout, many provincials remained close to former friends, neighbors, and associates. Negative vibrations emerged mostly from provincial elites, and in the United States such views focused on British policies and officials, not provincials.

After 1815, social and commercial migration and mingling resumed, and with Indian power broken in the northwestern United States, settlers followed geographic lines below the Great Lakes. The British provinces by then had little available arable land, although U.S. entrepreneurs saw opportunities beckon. Upper Canada was politically unattractive, however, and the Family Compact and Chateau Clique of British officials, seigneurs, and clerics resisted local pressures for democratization, which they portrayed as an Americanization that would doom British rule. Negative vibrations simmered among social and political elites as they invoked partly contrived historical memories of defense against U.S. "Manifest Destiny," while London and Washington compromised on boundary and economic matters in North America.[7]

When Baptist and Methodist preachers moved into provincial frontier regions, Anglican clerics denounced their leveling religious doctrines as evidence of U.S. political designs. But these preachers were part of North American frontier social development, not agents of Washington. And however effective provincial and Canadian leaders thought denunciation of the United States was for their domestic authority, such views had little effect on ordinary provincials. Democratic-republican political ideas reinforced such political reformers throughout the 1820s and 1830s as Robert Gourlay and William Lyon Mackenzie in Upper Canada, and Louis Joseph Papineau in Lower Canada. They adopted and promoted the ideas and methods of Jacksonian Democracy to balance British, clerical, and seigneurial social and political control.

Domestic social and political forces produced Upper and Lower Canadian rebellions in 1837. Americans in upstate Vermont, New York, and far-northern Michigan sympathized with and supported the provincials with money, arms, and volunteers for filibuster raids when British forces chased the rebels over the U.S. border, which acted as a two-way Upper North American political safety valve. U.S. filibuster leaders such as Rensselaer Van Rensselaer of Albany put themselves outside the law of either land when they marched north, however, and President Martin Van Buren ordered General Winfield Scott to disarm borderland Americans who plotted assaults on British territory to keep the Anglo-U.S. peace. Refugee rebels and local U.S. volunteers nevertheless organized filibuster expeditions. In 1839, U.S. marshals and troops blocked reinforcements to a force that crossed the Saint Lawrence River and attacked Prescott. Provincial militia and British troops dealt with the filibusters, and the U.S. authorities arrested the Americans who returned while the routed rebels became political refugees. These abortive rebellions stoked later Canadian anti-Americanism, however, and like the War of 1812, survived as a legend and legacy of U.S. aggression against provincials who created the country of Canada.[8]

Americans revealed little interest in British territory through this era. The U.S. secretary of the interior dispatched a secret agent to the far northwest in the early 1840s to report on what value British Columbia might have for the United States, because talks over extending the 49th Parallel boundary to the Pacific Coast had already begun. The report showed little agricultural land, so agrarian settlement was unlikely to flourish, and the United States already had a Pacific port in Puget Sound much more attractive than Burrard Inlet. During the U.S. Civil War, provincial Confederationists trumped up prejudice and warned that Canada's political union was essential for defense against Washington's possible territorial aggression. This appeal to domestic fears helped to revive a flagging movement, but when the Dominion of Canada appeared in 1867, American observers saw little more than fellow North Americans severing Old World ties. The *New York Times* only ventured that future economic integration might eventually produce political union.

For their part, conservative Anglo-elites bristled over what they suspected was Washington's collusion with Fenian raiders between 1867 and 1871. As the Treaty of Washington negotiations revealed, however, the ruling Republicans in Washington were not annexationists, despite their anger toward Great Britain. Canadian Anglo-elites nevertheless established anti-Americanism as a partisan device to stir public opinion and attract support in the polls. They accepted the Roman Catholic Church in Quebec for similar reasons, although there was no established church elsewhere in Canada. Confederation also established a nonsectarian educational system alongside this separation of church and state that mirrored an important component of the U.S. ideology.[9]

After 1867, Americans resumed leisure travel north and still saw Canada as a North American country, despite its British-oriented Anglophile elites. At the same time, Ontario politicians applied partisan anti-Americanism in new circumstances. Cartoonists limned negative vibrations in the form of a reedy, lascivious Brother Jonathan who leered at a young, innocent Miss Canada ripe for the plucking, socially at least, who had to depend upon a matronly Britannia for protection. Only Britain could shield Canada from U.S. rapacity. Prime Minister Sir John A. Macdonald juggled the Dominion's politics with British patriotism and the Imperial link at election times while he chased cooperation and reciprocal trade agreements with Washington. In 1890, the aging warhorse Macdonald and his Tories successfully demonized Wilfrid Laurier and the Liberals as in bed with the Yankee interests that had bought him off to add Canada to the U.S. Empire. Conservative cartoonists portrayed leering Liberals and cash-laden U.S. politicians conspiring in backrooms to destroy Canada's British heritage. This was fiction. When Macdonald vilified reciprocal trade with the United States, he contradicted his own past policies. These negative vibrations were intended for domestic consumption only, and they became a partisan staple at election times.[10] The effect of anti-Americanism on the outcome of such campaigns has, however, never been measured. Anti-Americanism was easier to assert than prove as a link with voting behavior when a variety of local and regional issues and attitudes always determined the electoral results that put one or the other party in power.

Negative vibrations and arrant anti-Americanism erupted with a vengeance in the Canadian election of 1911, mostly in Ontario. President William Howard Taft and Prime Minister Sir Wilfrid Laurier agreed after indirect private talks to establish reciprocity with concurrent executive agreements. Conservative leader Robert Borden raised no objections until a handful of Toronto businessmen who opposed reciprocity as contrary to their interests spurred him into action. Opposition in Parliament led Laurier to call an election. Coincidentally, the speaker of the U.S. House of Representatives responded to the proposal with the hope that this would lead to the Stars and Stripes flying clear up to the North Pole. Conservatives howled and stoked a vicious, scathing, partisan-motivated anti-American campaign where reciprocity became a symbol rather than a policy issue. Conservatives knew that lower U.S. tariffs were coming anyway. Laurier and the Liberals lost, and Borden took power. Taft and the Republicans blanched at the negative campaign and anti-American furor. Canada seemed far more British than—as they had supposed—North American.[11] As before, these intense negative vibrations were about domestic politics, not U.S. ambitions or intentions. The Liberals lost for a variety of social, economic, and political reasons.

This election, however, proved to be a midwife to a future rule of Canadian politics. Prime ministers, regardless of party, risked a partisan tar-and-feather job on the hustings if they appeared too friendly with U.S. presidents, and too eager to make cross-border bargains with Washington. Meanwhile, a cultural and social anti-Americanism arose in Quebec in the early part of the twentieth century. A clique of Roman Catholic clergy and intellectuals feared the growing impact of modern social and material ideas emanating from the United States. William Stead and Samuel Moffett observed this "Americanization" in Canada, and it was true, but not as the antagonists insisted. U.S. society was the vanguard of modernization for its time. Moreover, Quebec church and political leaders knew only too well that hundreds of thousands of ordinary Quebecers had steadily decamped for the northeastern states. If more left, or U.S. cultural and social ideas spread further in Quebec itself, they feared the doom of their traditional society. Less anti-American than antimodern, this opposition flailed at forces and currents far beyond the power of anyone to control, given the perils of geography, proximity, asymmetry, and social development in North America. Whether clerics or not, Quebec conservatives resented and opposed the secular and material modernization associated with the United States as a social menace.[12]

Nationalism and Policy Differences

World War I began shortly after the anti-American uproar of 1911. Many Canadian leaders grew disillusioned about the Empire when Britain seemed to falter on the Western Front and casualties mounted. That and Borden's own nationalism pushed him onto a divergent historical path from London's control, and the wide support for his campaign to gain Canada greater international autonomy vindicated his views. Cross-border commerce quickened after 1914, and many Canadians spent time among Americans and in Washington, more after Woodrow Wilson led the United States into the war in 1917. Domestic businessmen such as William Lyon Mackenzie King saw U.S. energy and power firsthand while domestic social and political ideas diverged from those of Britain. French Canadians soured further on Britain, and most Anglo-Canadians made a social transition toward being Upper North Americans with a British heritage as migration patterns changed. In addition, a new generation of university educated intellectuals emerged after 1918, and many perforce entered U.S. graduate programs. Once they received their advanced degrees, they taught in U.S. universities because Canada offered few such opportunities. The brain drain phase of cross-border social mingling had begun.

Throughout, Borden pressed London for full national autonomy and eyed a formal Washington-Ottawa relationship. Except for resentment that the United States had sat out much of the war to make money instead of fighting the just cause in Europe, negative vibrations sank to low levels. Mass automobile ownership stimulated borderland social and commercial mingling. U.S. newspapers and magazines had circulated in Canada for over two decades but became increasingly popular during the 1920s. The rise of electronic media encouraged Anglo-Canadians and even French Canadians to see themselves within a North American society.[13] Intellectuals and politicians nurtured negative vibrations toward the United States, but ordinary Canadians spent their money and time on what pleased them. Ordinary Americans also drove north during the U.S. Prohibition years to tipple. While the two peoples mingled socially, they also became more alike. The social interweaving of Americans and Canadians (Quebecers included) in Upper North America accelerated during the 1920s, and negative vibrations eased in both countries. The sense of a broad social stake in the cross-border relationship and continuous interaction created largely benign mutual social attitudes.

Anglophile elites, however, continued to treasure the British link as part of their social identity. Members of the University of Toronto, the Canadian League of Nations Society, the Association of Canadian Clubs, and the Canadian Institute of International Affairs denounced cultural and social Americanization and argued for institutional cultural and social defenses. Graham Spry advocated his Canadian Radio Broadcasting Corporation (later the CBC) proposal for an Ottawa-run national radio system modeled on the BBC. Canadian listeners, however, had already become part of the free-market-based North American audience. Spry's pro-British/anti-American argument resonated with those in power but washed over most Canadians:

> The Canadian Radio League is really based upon a two-fold foundation, distaste for commercialism, and apprehension of Americanization—an apprehension which has given Canada, I may add, many of the most progressive economic and constitutional changes in our history. Indeed, if the fear of the United States did not exist, it would be necessary, like Voltaire's God, to invent it.[14]

Supporters of a National Film Board wielded similarly anti-American views of U.S. cultural and social influence on Canada and wanted quotas for British films, but they had limited success. They never shaped popular tastes, but after 1945, they supported Vincent Massey, a former governor-general and ambassador in Washington, when he led the 1949–52 Royal Commission on the Arts. The report of the commission was more non- than anti-American, but Canadian high culture practitioners' dislike of and disdain for U.S. cultural and social patterns were clear.[15]

When Canada went to war in September 1939, the public once again resented U.S. neutrality, but it directed this attitude toward Washington politics rather than Americans as a people. After the Japanese attack on Pearl Harbor created the Grand Alliance, Washington and Ottawa worked together with camaraderie. After 1945, senior Ottawa bureaucrats such as C. D. Howe and Brooke Claxton, and diplomats such as Lester B. Pearson, found that their Washington counterparts could be somewhat overbearing, but all had favorable views of Americans and the United States. The reliance on U.S. nuclear deterrent forces accelerated Ottawa's inclination to use multilateral agencies as a balance to U.S. power. Throughout this era, however, Pearson and others sustained a broad-minded and charitable view of Washington's aims and intentions, and both peoples saw one another as friends and allies. Anti-Americanism found little political expression in Canada except among nationalist intellectuals until John Diefenbaker became leader of the Conservative Party, and then prime minister in 1957. He nursed nostalgia for the British Empire, but his prickly and defensive personality reacted to President John F. Kennedy, in an archetype of how the personal can become political. He disliked, envied, and disdained Kennedy as an arrogant upstart, lectured his own Cabinet on the president's faults, exploited public unease over nuclear weapons, and denounced the Liberal leader Pearson as a "Yankee lover."

When Pearson won a minority in 1963, Diefenbaker insisted that Washington had engineered his victory.[16] A few but not all members of his Cabinet, such as the pacifist-inclined Howard Green, agreed, but where and how Diefenbaker's anti-Americanism reflected or shaped public opinion remains hazy at best. Which social groups, factions, interests, or regions held similar views, and how did such ideas mix with the more mundane and pragmatic issues that shape voting behavior at the polls? No one yet knows. Popular electoral decisions arise from a mélange of interests, although one clue to the tenor of Canadian opinion about the United States appeared from young Americans who took refuge in Canada during the Vietnam War era of the late 1960s and early 1970s. Many were disappointed that, whatever policies Ottawa followed, ordinary Canadians were so un-anti-American.[17]

Negative vibrations about the United States bubbled into hostility in Canada's intellectual elites, but they lacked a broad social foundation or influence beyond their own circles. Scholars, commentators, nationalists, and socialist gadflies during the 1950s and 1960s prided themselves on anti-American attitudes. The historian and professional Tory Donald Creighton sneered at Americans as plebeian, Manifest Destiny Rotarians, claiming he never met one he liked. The Anglophile economists George Grant and Harold Innis opposed any cross-border interlinkage—real, alleged, or imagined—as a betrayal of Canada's destiny. Frank Underhill, tongue somewhat in cheek, wrote that the Canadian was "the first anti-American, the model anti-American, the archetypal anti-American, the ideal anti-American as he exists in the mind of God," in part to mock those around him who felt that way.[18]

As the aging Anglophile elitist generation faded, however, academics and intellectuals adopted a rhetoric that mixed leftist cultural, social, and ideological anti-Americanism. Many entered politics in the New Democratic Party (NDP) to shape public policy, but they had little influence because the party never held power. They wrote manifestos, articles, and books, founded magazines, and gave interviews to any reporter with poised pencil or microphone. And other themes always appeared. Stephen Clarkson and Philip Resnick disliked U.S. and any other free market capitalism. So did James Laxer and Mel Watkins of the NDP—which they decided was too moderate, so they formed their own splinter group. They insisted on Canadian content in school and university texts, the media, literature, and films to expunge all trace of Americanization. They called for Canadian studies programs and opposed U.S. educated faculty for fear that they would Americanize Canada's youth. In 1969. a faculty member at Vancouver's Simon Fraser University told Michael Fellman, fresh from California, to go back where he had come from. James Steele and Robin Mathews objected to American professors teaching at Carleton University, and when labeled as anti-American, they insisted that they were pro-Canadian, which given their tone seemed to many a distinction without a difference. Americans who came north found occasional animus, but they settled into life as they would have done in the United States. No U.S. counterpart to this anti-Americanism existed. Canada had no comparable profile south of the border, and while Canadians in the United States worried about being drafted, they also blended into U.S. life for study and work.[19] Cross-border negative vibrations in the 1960s and 1970s rarely reflected any more than transitory social and political attitudes, and usually fed upon disagreement over particular Washington policies. Meanwhile, high culture practitioners nursed a snobbish skepticism about the United States.

The historical evolution of liberalism in Canada offered some clues to understand such negative vibrations, and even anti-Americanism. In the later nineteenth century, entrepreneurs, corporate leaders, landowners, professional men, officials, and the politicians who represented them sorted into business-oriented and welfare-oriented wings in the early Liberal and Conservative parties, while Canada's commercial, industrial, and fiscal interests shifted from transatlantic into north-south channels. Business Liberals sought open U.S. markets, access to capital, and opportunities to generate personal and national wealth. They also sought trade policies with the United States that combined access, security, and low tariffs. Welfare liberals, by contrast, harbored Anglophile suspicions of U.S. expansion and feared that economic relations with the United States would lead to political integration, and thus cultural and social absorption. Their protectionist policies were to deflect U.S. influence and secure a distinct national society. These two views cohabited within both the Liberal and Conservative parties. Partisanship and interests also separated them from ostensibly natural allies, as happened with the Conservatives in 1911. From the 1920s through the 1950s, business liberals had the upper hand in the Liberal Party, supporting William Lyon Mackenzie King, Louis St. Laurent, and then Lester Pearson. Just after World War II, business Liberals rejected Washington's offer of a free trade agreement, not from any animus toward the United States, but because it might hand Conservatives an anti-American ace for the next election. The partisan potential of anti-Americanism then trumped policy and even ideological consistency with the 1935 trade agreement and the post–World War II General Agreement on Tariffs and Trade. In both those cases, the importance of freer trade for national interests, and world economic reconstruction, soothed any partisan qualms.[20]

Great Britain's economic collapse and refusal to transform the Commonwealth into a trading bloc after 1945 created further dilemmas for these Anglo-oriented business liberals, because Canada had become economically isolated in North America next to the United States. At the same time, private sector producers and consumers gained ever greater leverage in both economies. Ottawa's only feasible policy option thus encouraged cross-border economic integration and interdependence. By the 1960s, welfare liberals such as Walter Gordon argued that Canada had merely exchanged economic masters, and George Grant published his lament that the Canadian nation had been stillborn. Pearson's successor, Pierre Elliott Trudeau, bundled the two liberal streams with 1960s social nationalism and mused about deflecting cross-border economic integration, but he only pressed for policy-based anti-Americanism in a National Energy Policy and Foreign Investment Review Agency. The National Energy Policy in particular angered U.S. interests and Ronald Reagan's Republican administration. It also alienated domestic business and western interests. Washington pressured Ottawa to protect U.S. interests, while business liberals in both Canadian parties recoiled from ideological and interest-based anti-Americanism. Many business liberals supported the Conservative Brian Mulroney, who once elected generated positive vibrations toward Washington, reversed Trudeau's policies, and concluded the Free Trade Agreement (FTA).

Positive and negative vibrations about the United States, meanwhile, tussled within business and welfare liberal camps within both major parties.[21] During the 1992 election campaign, the Liberal leader Jean Chrétien resurrected anti-American rhetoric over the North American Free Trade Agreement (NAFTA). President Bill Clinton and many Canadian business leaders were relieved when, as prime minister, Chrétien signed on. He had been far less anti-NAFTA than the campaign suggested, but in office he balanced the substance of business liberalism with the rhetoric of welfare liberalism so he could deny being cozy with Washington. In the spring of 2000, however, he hinted that the next election might champion Liberal values against Americanization, but he failed to explain what he meant and never had the opportunity to follow through. A few Liberals still rued NAFTA, and would have preferred Ottawa to be more active in the economy, but growth in trade and prosperity, debt reduction, and Ottawa's need to spend on social policies produced further economic integration and interdependence.[22]

Ideology, Partisanship, and Policy

The ideological, nationalistic, partisan, and policy-oriented varieties of anti-Americanism rose from their shallow graves during the 2000 U.S. presidential election. The CBC humorist Rick Mercer ambushed the Republican nominee, George W. Bush, with the fiction that Prime Minister "Jean Poutine" had just endorsed the Texan. Bush appreciated that, and Canadians chuckled. Ottawa's ambassador in Washington, Raymond Chrétien (the prime minister's nephew), meanwhile suggested that Canadians traditionally felt more comfortable with Democrats than Republicans. This offended Republicans and Bush's close supporters. Canadian opinion generally sided with the Democrats, however—and after a protracted spectacle of recounts, court challenges, and arguments, capped by a U.S. Supreme Court decision, Canadians (like U.S. Democrats), concluded that Bush was an illegitimate president. After public anxiety that Bush had broken a nonexistent "tradition" by visiting the Mexican president before the Canadian prime minister, little more than the ever-present subterranean discontent about being in North America with the United States might have ensued.

On September 11, 2001, however, al Qaeda agents hijacked several transcontinental passenger jets as they left eastern U.S. airports, then flew them into New York City's World Trade Center towers, the Pentagon's east face, and a Pennsylvania field. Several thousand people died, and continuous TV coverage seared the horror of those events into the minds of all who saw them. This tragedy also elevated security to the first consideration in U.S. politics and Washington policymaking. In Canada, the events of September 11 not only evoked a torrent of human sympathy for the United States and Americans but also exhumed from the social graveyard a virulent, vocal, ideological, policy-oriented anti-Americanism that made "negative" seem a downright positive descriptor.

For a moment, Canadians clearly felt close to Americans. Thousands gathered spontaneously on Parliament Hill, overwhelming U.S. ambassador Paul Cellucci with their humanity. Polls exposed a widespread sense that the two countries' interests and values were either identical or "mostly the same." A large minority foresaw accelerated economic cooperation, and perhaps even a form of political integration. Simultaneously, ideological and policy-oriented anti-Americanism surged and exposed social divisions in Canada. Many Canadians seemed to believe that the United States, through its Middle East policies and support of Israel, had provoked al Qaeda's attack. A columnist watched the first World Trade Center tower collapse on television, and someone nearby reportedly said, "Well, that's what the Americans get for poking their noses into everyone's affairs." A U.S. journalist invited onto CBC Toronto's *Counterspin* was shocked and awed as both hosts and audience condemned U.S. international interests and Washington policies. Others insisted that the United States was a global menace, warmongering, violent. Any such commentary in the electronic or print media was rebroadcast and republished, crept onto the Internet, and aired on U.S. cable TV. Letters to editors from Americans living in Canada now complained bitterly about the prejudice Canadians had shown toward them and their country over many years. They had believed in Canadian tolerance, but experience and the reaction to the events of September 11 shattered their illusions.[23] Beneath these negative vibrations lay a deep and thinly veiled antagonism—even hate. The United States, its policies and politicians, and even all Americans, were tarred by this surge of bile and prejudice.

Canadian commentators grappled with these attitudes. Robert Fulford argued that the "persistent strain" of anti-Americanism in the national psyche was the only prejudice "accepted almost universally in Canada, tolerated in university classrooms and at dinner parties where racism and homophobia are considered shameful." Others called Canadians hypocritical to enjoy U.S. mass entertainment, wear Calvin Klein jeans, shop at Wal-Mart, and head for Disney World with their children, yet condemn the people who created all those pleasures. J. L. Granatstein and Norman Hillmer wondered how a self-professedly tolerant people could nurse such intolerance. Ottawa's one-time Washington ambassador, Allan Gotlieb, offered three observations. First, such people spoke as though in a confidential discussion, oblivious that in the global age no statement could be private. Second, the anti-Americans had no national vision or positive sense of purpose to offer. Third, they seemed to Gotlieb little more than smug hecklers who employed tangled logic, ignorance, prejudice, even bigotry.[24] Such analysis did little to assuage Americans on either side of the border who recoiled at the venom of people they saw as friends and were aghast to hear it in such awful circumstances.

In the political world, meanwhile, policymakers tackled their threatened interests. Washington worked to secure its borders while Ottawa's Liberal government focused on keeping crossing ports open for the flow of goods and people. Ottawa also mobilized some of what military resources it had available to support President Bush's Operation Enduring Freedom against Afghanistan's Taliban government, which had harbored al Qaeda and its leader, Osama bin Laden. Ottawa politicians supported the Afghanistan foray, but policy-oriented and personal anti-Americanism continued, notably among Liberal members of Parliament. Bonnie Brown of Toronto, for example, seemed annoyed over what Canada had been compelled to do, and she asked where the payoff was. In May 2002, U.S. pilots mistakenly bombed Canadian troops. It is no solace to those who lose loved ones to say that such things happen in war, and Ambassador Cellucci telephoned Ottawa at once to inform Chrétien. The next day Secretary of Defense Donald Rumsfeld apologized to Canada at a Pentagon briefing and Bush called Chrétien. U.S. diplomats in Canada visited the victims' families and attended services while Congress passed resolutions of sympathy. Media and political statements meanwhile condemned Washington and the United States, and polls revealed that large numbers of Canadians still believed global U.S. policy had caused al Qaeda's attack on September 11. Chrétien himself almost said as much in an interview broadcast on the event's first anniversary. He offended many in both countries, but especially Bush, his senior officials, and members of Congress.[25]

September 11 had pried open Canada's Pandora box of anti-Americanism. Many Canadians, commentators, and editors vented an ideological and political anti-Americanism that had no proximate cause and expressed a simmering dislike of the United States and all things American. Public and media anger flared again when Bush announced a National Security Strategy that asserted a right of preemptive rather than just preventive military action, and incidentally listed Canada among the countries that shared U.S. values. Members of Parliament continued their comments. Chrétien remained silent, but that implied the anti-Americans spoke for all Liberals.[26] Then his press officer, Francine Ducros, referred to Bush as a "moron" in a room full of journalists at a Prague conference. Many concluded that such a view was common among Chrétien's political intimates or it would never have been so casually voiced. This episode went global within a few days. Throughout the coming weeks, U.S. talk radio and TV shows, including CNN's then-popular *Crossfire,* featured the Ducros gaffe for days. Deputy Prime Minister John Manley, among others, warned with little effect that smug moralism about the United States and President Bush were self-defeating and would damage national interests.[27]

Anti-Americanism washed through the Liberal Party, which had always claimed to represent all Canadians. Individual parliamentarians vented animus as though nobody except their domestic constituents was listening. For example, an Ontario member of Parliament, Carolyn Parrish, condemned Bush's policies, then muttered, "Damn Americans. I hate those bastards," into microphones outside the House of Commons chamber. North America's twenty-four-hour news cycle made this a transnational story. Constituents, business leaders, and ordinary Canadians openly condemned her, but after a formal expression of regret and letter of apology to Ambassador Cellucci, she carried on. U.S. observers saw Parrish as part of the Chrétien government, although Canadians from Victoria to Halifax denounced her and themselves apologized to U.S. consular offices. Only then did the Liberals desert her.[28]

By early 2003, Ottawa knew that President Bush would send U.S. forces into Iraq on his ill-fated quest to remake Middle East politics. Bush-centered anti-Americanism swelled in Parliament, led mostly by southern Ontario and Ottawa-Toronto corridor politicians such as Parrish, Brown, John Bryden, and John Godfrey. They denounced the president as a warmonger and front for U.S. oil interests, among other charges.[29] Individual Americans also suffered generalized and personal barbs—and they were "invisible" foreigners because locals usually mistook them for Canadians and felt free to express an epithet or animus against Bush, the United States, and its people. Nora Jacobson had moved north to what she saw as a socially more tolerant land, but instead lived with "a powerful anti-Americanism that pervades many aspects of [Canadian] life." Siri Agrell found that when Canadians discovered he was American, all they wanted to talk about was how much they hated George Bush.[30] Washington officials resented the Liberal government's vocal and pointed refusal to join the U.S.–led coalition against Saddam Hussein's regime. Canadian military personnel assigned to North American Aerospace Defense headquarters, the Pentagon, and other U.S. facilities found themselves barred from offices and duties because, in this instance, they were not allies. Ambassador Cellucci rebuked Ottawa's decision, and Canadian "Friends of America" rallied in Toronto and Alberta. Premier Ralph Klein of Alberta publicly supported Washington, and Canadian businessmen headed south to mend fences.[31]

The public tone of Washington-Ottawa relations deteriorated. U.S. television and radio commentators objected to this political anti-Americanism, to insults to their president and to Republicans, and they rebuked Canadians for their morally superior airs. This tone added to the stridency and strains, all exacerbated by U.S. anxiety over the war in Iraq, where Americans were in harm's way.[32] U.S. news centers reported the existence of terrorist cells in Montreal and Toronto, and condemned Ottawa's immigrant and refugee policies in the ensuing weeks. Incessant news cycles meant that public, and even many private, discussions drew instant audiences. CNN's Robert Novak doubted that the United States could trust its "shifty" northern neighbor. Many Americans shared his judgment, and Chrétien's request that Liberals restrain their rhetoric seemed more pro forma than mea culpa because he continued to scold Bush. Washington soon just ignored Ottawa.[33] A *National Review* cover labeled the Royal Canadian Mounted Police "wimps," and inside Jonah Goldberg skewered Canada's reflexive social and political anti-Americanism. The expatriate David Frum suggested why President Bush could have omitted Canada as an ally in his speech to Congress after September 11:

> Was the Pentagon annoyed that Canada had not matched British and Australian offers of military assistance? Had Americans at last reacted against the lax refugee laws that had made Canada a haven for Islamic terrorists? The answer was yes, yes and yes-and-no. Canada was not omitted to send some elliptical message. Canada was omitted because it is easy to forget friends whose governments give you no cause to remember them.[34]

American commentators saw Canadian anti-Americanism in black-and-white terms, resenting slurs against their president, their country, and themselves. For the first time, negative vibrations north of the border had evoked a response in kind, and U.S. officials who dealt with their counterparts in Canada privately noted how anti-Americanism had begun to affect the working relationship. Whenever Washington representatives made a suggestion, their Ottawa counterparts suspected a hidden agenda. As secretary of state, Dean Rusk had understood this Canadian tendency in the 1960s. If in a press conference with his counterpart, Paul Martin Sr., Rusk always let Martin speak first. He might or might not agree on any given point, but he knew that Martin would perforce disagree with almost everything if Rusk spoke first. Ottawa officials and politicians also resisted or opposed U.S. proposals because they feared appearing weak to their political constituencies. Over time, the cumulative effect of these negative vibrations thickened, turning into a slow-setting glue poured into the cross-border policy engine's gearbox. Negative vibrations formed a background force, not a spasm, in the binational relationship.[35]

Circumstances might explain why this situation arose when it did. To be sure, Canada's negative vibrations had an impact because they were so public. Furthermore, the "Special Relationship" of the post-1945 era faded when the Pearson generation left public life. The momentum of social and political bonds formed during World War II and the Cold War carried Ottawa and Washington through policy disputes and personal clashes without residual animus. This was not the case by the 1990s, however, so negative vibrations reverberated with greater force than in the past. A few American journalists began to voice an embryonic anti-Canadianism, based in part on Ottawa's social policies, as reflected by Patrick Buchanan's "Soviet Canuckistan" remarks. Jonah Goldberg wondered why Canadians were so obsessed with the United States and its policies. He said that they acted like university students, who allowed passion and ego to trump facts and reason to protect their inferiority complex. They were also just negative, with no positive international vision except the United Nations. Chrétien all but stated that Washington had brought the September 11 tragedy on itself. Ottawa claimed to be an ally but refused to act like one. So why trust Canada? "Now don't get me wrong—I like Canadians. They are often among the nicest and most decent people you'd ever want to meet. They just don't live in a normal country."[36]

To be sure, Canadian anti-Americanism did seem "lite" compared with that in other countries. The demonstrations and marches that occurred were peaceful, polite, and nothing like those in Europe, where riots, police, tear gas, and casualties ensued. But Canadians seemed unable to distinguish disagreements over policy from social generalizations. Even the World Socialist Web site separated opposition to Washington from "vulgar anti-Americanism. . . . There are after all, two Americas . . . of Bush, Clinton and the other scoundrels, and another America, of its working people."[37] Canada's anti-Americanism often resembled a common room debate, with trumped-up anger, such as that expressed by the former Liberal foreign affairs minister Lloyd Axworthy. He stood on multilateralism and Canada's peacekeeping traditions to denounce, for example, Washington's Cuba policies, its refusal to sign the Ottawa Treaty on land mines, and its failure to embrace the International War Crimes Court or to endorse the Kyoto Accord. Ottawa must reject strategic and political integration with Washington, or it would be a mere "deputy sheriff" at George Bush's beck and call. Axworthy also insisted that "hatred of the values and principles of what they saw as a corrupt, secular, insensitive and dominant ruling global system" with the United States at its heart had driven al Qaeda to attack New York and Washington.[38] His anti-Americanism drew upon cultural and social generalizations phrased in a language of accusation, denunciation, and distemper that asserted Ottawa knew better how to manage global affairs. Given Washington's reaction, this amounted to no more than heckling from the bleachers.

Canadians and Americans intermingled in cultural, social, and economic terms in myriad ways every day, all this rancor notwithstanding. Millions of stakeholders enforced normality, despite congested borders and anguished headlines. Economic and social liberals in all parties and many walks of life in Canada took a realist view of the conduct of foreign policy and stressed national interests over moralism. Business organizations and think tanks such as the Institute for Research on Public Policy, the Fraser Institute, the C. D. Howe Institute, and other centers for international and military affairs at universities in Calgary, Vancouver, and Halifax all stressed pragmatism as the appropriate foundation for policymaking to serve Canadian society. A complex North American debate within each country thus combined with cross-border perceptions and misperceptions.[39] At the Chicago Council on Foreign Relations, Prime Minister Chrétien created new strains when he lectured Bush to act through the United Nations and added that the world did not trust Washington anymore. He made no comment when a Cabinet minister called the president a failed statesman, which official Washington took as a government view because they understood ministerial solidarity in parliamentary systems.[40] Chrétien criticized a president on U.S. soil to worse than no effect. Anti-Americanism cost Ottawa the ability even to be heard, let alone heeded. Meanwhile, a motley Greek chorus of ideological anti-Americanists carped and chided from the shadows. Judy Rebick and Maude Barlow rallied antiwar activists. Mel Hurtig and Stephen Clarkson resurrected personal causes and bemoaned cross-border economic integration.[41] The social underpinnings of this anti-Americanism were on the political left, among idealists and intellectuals, geographically in Ontario and part of British Columbia. Few negative vibrations emerged from the Atlantic and Great Plains provinces. Quebecers, broadly pacifist about foreign military ventures, opposed any part for Ottawa in the Iraq War but remained broadly pro-American.[42]

The frequent polls taken in modern social and political life can refine judgments about these negative cross-border vibrations in recent years. The public tended to separate views of the Bush administration, Washington policies, and Americans as a people. Many Canadians supported the war in Iraq, and business leaders—mindful of the interdependent economics—saw generalized anti-Americanism as contrary to national interests. Attitudes among ethnic and other social groups, however, lay submerged in the aggregate results pollsters reported. It was not at all clear, for example, that ethnic or immigrant social groups diverged from the broad mass of the Canadian population. It had been evident since the Boer War, however, that Quebecers (leaders and otherwise) opposed Canadian support for British imperial and international conflicts, which generated the Conscription Crisis in 1917, produced Ottawa's reliance on volunteers during World War II, and (apart from peacekeeping) opposed policies that might send Quebecers into danger outside the national borders.[43]

These patterns made up a North American patchwork quilt, rather than a cross-border divergence. Much negative attention focused on President Bush, while positive views about the United States and Americans remained strong. As the Iraq War ground on, ruffled sensibilities from the early period of decision and action, when Washington expected Ottawa's moral if not military support, smoothed.[44] U.S. commentators for conservative magazines, talk shows (Fox News), and Web logs generated negative vibrations and collected "strings" of opinions that tended to condemn Ottawa's policies but not Canadians in general. Patrick Buchanan focused on border security, and along with many Americans he saw Ottawa's immigration policies as a danger for U.S. security. "I think that . . . Canada is somewhat lackadaisical about internal security," he said. "That Canada is a friendly country. But the Canadians, somewhat like the French, like to take a stand opposite the United States, simply to demonstrate their independence." He also told Canadians not to be "thin skinned." Just give Americans a "hard time right back, we understand that."

Throughout, Americans separated policy clashes from a benign view of Canada and its people. Granted, TV pundits baited to draw audiences, as when Michael Savage labeled Canada "America Junior," and Tucker Carlson chuckled that "without the U.S., Canada is essentially Honduras, but colder and less interesting," and "irrelevance must be such a burden." When Paul Martin refused to support Ballistic Missile Defense in early 2005, he and his government, not Canadians in general, drew fire from below the border.[45] The *Weekly Standard,* a conservative magazine not much known in Canada, captured the spirit of U.S. chiding on the cover: "Welcome to Canada: The Great White Waste of Time," with "Bush-hating expats! Multicultural mealy mouths! Molson-drinking Zamboni drivers! Gordon Lightfoot lovers!" The author Matt Labash conducted much of his research in British Columbia and dismissed Canadians' "nails-on-the-blackboard nationalism." He noted, "You can tell a lot about a nation's mediocrity index by learning they invented synchronized swimming. Even more by the fact they're proud of it." He also saluted Canada's "greatest (only?) contribution to world cuisine, Tim Hortons donuts, which is owned by the American fast-food behemoth Wendy's."[46] In contrast to the bile common to Canadian anti-Americans, U.S. anti-Canadianism was satirical at worst.

Any vestigial illusions about a "special" Canada–United States relationship remained a speck in history's rearview mirror. A veteran observer in New York noted that Canada's U.S. enemies varied with the issue, party, outlook, location, and level of government. All were moving targets with shifting alliances. Agreement or disagreement on one issue rarely affected the others.[47] The Liberal use of anti-Americanism for partisan advantage in Canada's 2005–6 election sparked swift retorts from the U.S. ambassador, but the voters paid little attention to either side. Commentators in both countries condemned Paul Martin, and some U.S. journalists wrote up his loss at the polls as a defeat for anti-Americanism itself.[48] Subsidence of Canadian anti-Americanism was just that. Any reports of its death remained much exaggerated, although the cultural and social varieties inhabit left-wing national politics in the NDP and Liberal parties, as well as intellectuals, and commentators. Such awkward, if not always negative, vibrations will continue to shape cross-border policies and personality clashes between Canadian and U.S. politicians.[49] Equally important, as the 2005–6 election confirmed, the perpetual media news in the wired age meant that anyone can eavesdrop on almost anyone else at any time, and keep recordings. For example, although there was a judicial publication ban on details of a scandal related to Ottawa's largesse toward Quebec after the last vote on separatism, details of the testimony appeared on a U.S. Web log devoted to freedom of speech and were immediately dispersed from there.[50] The action-reaction rhythm of negative vibrations undercut their domestic partisan utility and effect and exposed the ideological groups that gave them voice.

Within Canada, the interminable, circular domestic debate about social identity vis-à-vis Americans continued. Now it was in the light of day, and when it shaped Ottawa's policy, U.S. commentators and officials could retaliate in kind. Anti-Americanism still resonated in cross-border affairs, but now to less than no effect. Sending independent or negative vibrations was one thing; encouraging them as a foundation for social or political cross-border relations was quite another. Canadian commentators often lamented that Americans ignored them. That was always untrue, but if after September 11, 2001, negative vibrations and anti-Americanism continued to guide Ottawa's policies, being ignored might have become preferable to being scorned as an inconsequential, will-of-the-wisp country Washington looked right through.[51]

Chapter 6

Transnational Societies

Bob MacCready shuddered over the world his grandchildren would grow up in and decided that the time had come to take action. So he contacted organizations that shared his views opposing gay marriage, such as the Knights of Columbus in Connecticut and Focus on the Family in Colorado, and exercised his sense of social responsibility to speak out on the issues that concerned him. Then he turned to politicians, both members of Congress in Washington and members of Parliament in Ottawa, because he was one person among millions of Upper North American families aware that contemporary social issues had spread beyond national borders.

MacCready lived in the western United States, and his grandchildren were with their parents in London, Ontario. His moral fears over the legalization of gay marriage reflected a transnational concern in both countries. Focus on the Family and the Knights of Columbus both have Canadian branches. Americans who shared his views on this issue bought full-page advertisements in Canadian newspapers opposing gay marriage. Meanwhile, campaigns for the legalization of gay marriage were equally transnational. U.S. couples even talked about migrating to Canada, and some headed across the border and took vows in Toronto churches.[1] In Upper North America, the border had no impact on such social attitudes, movements, or behavior because people sorted out over issues, not nationality. Canadians and Americans shared cultural values and social systems in ways that reduced the border to irrelevance. As a result, transnational lobbies worked on both national governments. The border divided constitutional and legal regimes, but not the social issues courts had to rule upon.[2]

Foundations and Permutations

The U.S. Progressive intellectual Randolph Bourne coined "transnational" in 1916. He had come to see national boundaries as culturally and socially porous, even though he recognized that historians had "a civic mission to teach citizens the past in national-centered narratives."[3] In the early twentieth century, Canada's Anglo-elites stressed how the British Imperial heritage stood separate from the U.S. experience, but social mores migrated in the minds and knapsacks of North America's mingling peoples. The policy environments were discrete, with distinct legislative and judicial systems in federal political structures. The French Civil Code in Quebec and Louisiana apart, English common and statute law formed the foundation for decisions up to supreme court levels. Social groups within national jurisdictions used a host of transnational legal values and principles, as well as decisions rendered in each other's courts. Both judiciaries derived from British principles of independence from partisan politics. Politics nevertheless is omnipresent in democratic societies. In the United States, judges are elected in many municipalities, counties, and states. The Senate Judiciary Committee reviews, and even interrogates, nominees to U.S. federal courts and the Supreme Court, and ideological differences can erupt and spill into the public domain, as the furor over Robert Bork's nomination and failure at confirmation hearings showed. In Canada, by contrast, Supreme Court nominees have been affirmed in camera, although recently candidates have met parliamentary committees before an expected confirmation in Parliament. Moreover, Crown prosecutors and state district attorneys play the same legal role, but the latter are elected and often have political ambitions, as Eliot Spritzer of New York revealed in 2006 when his success as a prosecutor built a political profile and base that took him to the governor's mansion in Albany. Canadian prosecutors, by contrast, work largely sheltered from the media, and hence from public gaze.

Upper North American social activists have also cited individual as well as group rights in their arguments. The U.S. Bill of Rights became part of the Constitution in 1791, and Supreme Court decisions over time placed such rights at the center of national life. The British North America Act of 1867 stressed community within the rule of law as a deliberate contrast to U.S. individualism, but this distinction became blurred over time. Provinces enacted civil rights legislation, but Ottawa only did so during John Diefenbaker's 1960s' government. Canada's equivalent to the U.S. Bill of Rights

(1790), the Charter of Rights and Freedoms, appeared in the Constitution Act of 1982. Because of that, Canadian Supreme Court justices, who already consulted U.S. case law, paid even more attention.[4]

In both societies, public trials historically exhibited the impartial rendering of justice. And in modern times, a free press in both the United States and Canada has covered legal matters and trials of every description. At times, reporters and analysts—especially in sensational cases such as the 1932 U.S. Lindbergh baby kidnapping and Canada's Paul Bernardo murder trial—shaped public opinion about guilt versus innocence. Modern mass entertainment productions about lawyers and trials have, moreover, also blurred the distinction between fictitious and real courtroom dramas in public minds, and the distinctions between the two Upper North American legal systems—a peril of proximity, it seems. Many Canadians believe they have "Miranda Rights," for example. These rights, which came from U.S. jurisprudence, require arresting officers to read a person's rights before he or she is taken into custody. In Canada, officers must also read suspects their rights, but they can make the arrest first. Besides, U.S. Supreme Court decisions do not apply to Canadian law. Proximity has, however, eroded perceptions, and even national legal autonomy. In Canada, judges may ban media reporting of testimony, as in the Bernardo trial. In this case, however, proximity defeated the intent, because U.S. reporters in Buffalo sniffed a good story, drove up to Toronto, and then published stories in their own newspapers. Copies of these papers circulated almost instantly in southern Ontario, confounding Canadian law as far as the public was concerned. Quebec justice John Gomery had a similar experience with his 2005 order of silence over hearings into the misuse of federal funds and corruption charges. An American free speech champion attended the hearings and posted reports on his Web log. The details circulated instantly in Upper North America and confounded Gomery's effort to control his proceedings.[5]

The power of proximity to shape Upper North American social and legal patterns appeared in the early nineteenth century as comparative themes emerged. The British Parliament abolished slavery in the Empire in 1833, which meant that fugitive U.S. slaves were automatically free once they reached provincial soil. A few managed to do so. Most arrivals were free blacks from northern states who feared recapture. Slaveholders determined to defend their institution and recover escapees petitioned U.S. courts to extradite runaways. British-appointed judges in Upper Canada refused, but one came close to granting extradition where the slaveholder argued that the runaway had committed a crime while escaping. After Confederation,

Ottawa enacted its own extradition legislation that covered all crimes punishable by two or more years in jail. U.S. criminals on the lam faced arrest, and Dominion courts dealt regularly with extradition cases. Criminal law fell under federal jurisdiction in Canada but state jurisdiction in the United States. Capital crimes often carried a death penalty, which existed in both countries until 1962, when Parliament abolished executions temporarily, and entirely in 1976. Since then, Canadian courts have not automatically granted extradition to the United States if the accused faced potential execution, and Ottawa has lobbied Washington and state governments to protect Canadians convicted of capital cases in U.S. jurisdictions. Recently, when capital cases involving Canadians have arisen, state prosecutors have waived the death penalty so that extradition and trial could proceed.[6]

Other cross-border cooperative linkages have also emerged. In 1999, the Cross Border Crime Forum established Integrated Border Enforcement Teams of officers from various agencies—such as the Federal Bureau of Investigation, Royal Canadian Mounted Police, and Border Patrol—and twenty-three of these teams currently work in designated borderland zones. The U.S. Secret Service and Bureau of Alcohol, Tobacco, Firearms, and Explosives have liaison offices in Ottawa and other Canadian cities for cooperation over cross-border money laundering, fraud, drug smuggling, and organized crime.[7] Agents have jointly probed extremists, such as the Heritage Front and white-supremacist and anti-Semitic cells. U.S. and Canadian agencies have also cooperated to infiltrate small Ku Klux Klan groups in British Columbia's Lower Mainland and Toronto.[8]

The complex historical evolution of Protestant religious movements reveals comparable patterns. For instance, Henry Alline's Nova Scotia revival was the last phase of the colonial New Light movement of the 1740s. The French diaspora from Lower Canada (later Quebec) spread the Roman Catholic Church through Upper New England and wherever Franco-Americans settled. Methodist and Baptist churches in northern U.S. states sent circuit-riding preachers to proselytize and organize frontier revivals in Upper Canada after the War of 1812, much to the distress of conservative Anglican clerics.[9] Religious and social patterns interwove in Upper North America as immigrants from Europe and Asia arrived with their faiths and established social religious enclaves in multiethnic and multisectarian Upper North America. Internal schisms had already complicated this process. As early as the 1840s, Mormons sent missionaries to England to proselytize for colonists in their Great Salt Lake wilderness Zion, and from there they planted colonies as far north as Alberta and eastern British Columbia.

Irish and Italian migrants reinforced Catholicism in eastern Upper North American cities. In the late nineteenth century, German Lutherans and Jews from several Central and Eastern European countries landed in North America, settling in Montreal and Toronto as well as New York and Chicago. Transnational anti-Semitism and anti-Catholicism already existed in Upper North America, and nativist prejudice targeted new religious sects, such as Shinto, Buddhism, and Sikhism, that appeared in Pacific Coast regions because of Asian immigration. By the early twenty-first century, Upper North America contained a dispersed multisectarian conglomeration drawn from a global hinterland in its own socially complex transnational regions.

Upper North American multicultural transnationalism varied among regions that straddled or abutted the border. The southern United States remained biracial until recent decades and Quebec remained dominantly French, albeit with transnational heritage sectors in neighboring states where Franco-Americans spoke English. Early generations of sociologists, however, saw all immigrant groups in national compartments. In Canada, attention focused on the French/English divide of Quebec and Ontario, often termed a "race" question, but not race as Americans in the South used the term. Lord Durham's 1840 report argued for French assimilation to solve British North America's "racial" question, in large measure because Anglo-Saxon ethnic prejudice mirrored U.S. outlooks on foreign peoples. Anti-Semitism characterized social relations in Montreal and Toronto, for example. Canadians simply thought themselves biethnic until 1964, when a Manitoba member of the Ottawa Senate noted the amalgam of non-English/non-French peoples that appeared in post-1945 immigration.[10] He, too, overlooked the fact that various Asian people had been part of West Coast society since the late nineteenth century. A Royal Commission on Bilingualism and Biculturalism issued its report in 1965, but six years passed before Prime Minister Pierre Trudeau declared Canada a multicultural country. Parliament passed a Multicultural and Citizenship Act that equated naturalized and native-born Canadians in 1988, six years after the Charter of Rights and Freedoms was enshrined as part of Canada's Constitution. Canadian nationalists, meanwhile, celebrated their tolerant multicultural mosaic as proof of cultural and social divergence from U.S. norms, especially what seemed the socially conformist melting pot. Yet the social reality, as comparative sociologists have uncovered, was far different. The evidence suggests that this asserted distinction was an example of how anti-American outlooks and ideological preferences have triumphed over social reality in Upper North America.[11]

Patterns of Prejudice

The comparative attitudes toward and treatment of blacks offer a case study in such misinterpretations of social reality. Without question, blacks in the United States lived through generations of brutal slavery and bitter segregation interwoven with a racial violence largely absent from the Canadian experience. Racial prejudice was, however, a shared and common social flaw. In Lower Canada, a Loyalist colonel kept about thirty slaves at Saint-Armand-Station until 1833, when the British Parliament abolished slavery in the Empire. Blacks remained in the area, and local lore holds that their remains still lie beneath a landmark locally known as "Nigger Rock."

Black refugees from borderland states, but only a few from the deep South, fled to Upper Canada in the 1840s and 1850s to elude slave catchers, but they still found racial and social discrimination. California blacks petitioned Queen Victoria for land on Vancouver Island to escape white prejudice, but after resettlement they found hardship, neglect, and prejudice as real there as anything they had faced before. They returned to California. Free blacks in Halifax attended church services, but they were customarily segregated in upper-story galleries referred to as "Nigger Heaven," a term later applied to segregated balconies in theaters and cinemas. Abraham Lincoln ended slavery in the Confederacy as a war measure, which effectively doomed it as a national institution. Congress passed full abolition after the war and extended citizenship and the Bill of Rights to blacks in the Thirteenth through Fifteenth amendments to the Constitution.

During that period, most blacks in Upper Canada returned to their former locales in the United States and to their kinfolk. Prejudice against blacks in Toronto and Montreal after 1867, however, confined them to the lowest social and poorest economic groups. In the early twentieth century, Canadian railway unions relegated blacks to menial jobs as sleeping car porters and kitchen help to preserve the more prestigious and better-paying positions for their white members.[12] In the 1940s in Dresden, Ontario, a handful of blacks descended from refugee slaves attended local schools and patronized shops, but whites barred them from social clubs and cafes. The Black National Unity Association integrated Dresden in the middle 1950s with help from the Canadian Jewish Labor Committee, whose members understood the impact of prejudice on people's lives. Whites in Priceville, northwest of Toronto, attempted to erase blacks' heritage by plowing over their cemetery. A local civic group recovered the lost tombstones and rededicated the plot in 1990. In the 1950s, movie houses in Halifax had segregated seating for blacks, who lived on the social as well as physical margins of city life. In the 1960s, the city expropriated and razed a poor, mostly black area called "Africville" to serve the ambitions of real estate developers. A forced diaspora to the city's outskirts ensued, although many former Africville residents were later relocated to inner-city public housing projects akin to those in U.S. cities. In the 1980s, two decades after the U.S. civil rights movement, local groups publicized this injustice and urged redress. City officials offered little more than ex post facto apologies.[13] Transnational black history in Upper North America diverged between the United States and Canada in some important respects but not in others, because white prejudice remained a powerful force through to modern times.

Immigrant groups coming to Upper North America fared better, but only in recent decades have they intermingled in Canadian society in a way that approached the claims of multiculturalism. A *Heritage Minute* CBC film marks the role Chinese coolie labor played in Canadian Pacific Railroad construction through the Rocky Mountains. Workers had to blast tunnels from the rock, and after an explosion, a white boss sends a coolie underground to set off the next charge. Another blast, and workers clearly fear the worst. But the coolie, powder blackened and tattered, survives. Yet hundreds of others did not, as the vignette points out. Coolies were expendable to the railway builders in the United States and Canada, who imported them to work as indentured, forced labor and then cast the survivors off to eke out lives as best they could. White North Americans saw all Chinese, and all Asians for that matter, as inassimilable heathens and a threat to local labor because they worked for so little. Anti-Chinese labor and race riots broke out in early Vancouver and in U.S. West Coast cities. Ottawa charged Chinese immigrants a $500 head tax once railroad construction ended, and in 1923 legislation excluded them from Canada altogether. Parliament repealed this act in 1947, but it took until 2006 for Ottawa to issue a formal apology and offer compensation to the handful of survivors and widows.

West Coast Upper North Americans did not want Japanese settlers, either. In 1900, President Theodore Roosevelt forced a "Gentleman's Agreement" on Japan to limit passports to migrants, and Ottawa followed this example in the Hayashi-Lemieux agreement of 1908. In 1905, a Japanese and Korean Exclusion League appeared in West Coast states, and San Francisco segregated Asians in schools. In Vancouver, the Asiatic Exclusion League organized a riot in 1907. California's 1913 Alien Land Law barred all Asians from owning property. Local racism led to the social segregation of Japanese settlers in Washington State and along the B.C. coast, where they built communities and eked out lives in forced isolation from white society.

South Asian people met a similar reception. In 1907, Bellingham whites rioted against Hindus. In May 1914, the Japanese steamer *Komagata Maru* dropped anchor in Vancouver Harbor, crammed with Sikh migrants. Vancouver whites nearly rioted to prevent them from landing. The Sikhs lived aboard the *Maru* for nearly two months while Ottawa dithered, and then ordered a naval vessel to escort the still-loaded vessel into international waters and send it back to Asia.[14]

By the 1930s, from half to three-quarters of Canada's Japanese were native born or naturalized citizens but were still shunned by whites. Upper North American West Coast hatred and prejudice deepened when Imperial Japan launched its war in China in 1931. After the Pearl Harbor attack of December 7, 1941, fear and racism spurred popular demands from San Diego to Vancouver to force Japanese Americans and Canadians into detention centers, then internment camps far from the coast. The authorities confiscated their land and possessions. They lost everything, though Ottawa passed a repatriation policy in 1945 when the Pacific war ended. Those who went "home" to Japan found themselves treated as cultural foreigners and some later returned to Canada. Only in the late twentieth century did survivors', descendants', and civil rights groups extract official apologies and compensation from Washington and Ottawa.[15] Prejudice, segregation, and racial violence were transnational forces in Upper North America in the late nineteenth and early twentieth centuries.

The modern black experience offers another example of transnational prejudice in Upper North America. The Ku Klux Klan revived in northern states such as Indiana in the 1920s, where local groups mixed nativism, racism, and religious prejudice to target Catholics, Jews, immigrants, and blacks. Klan branches formed in Ontario, Saskatchewan, Alberta, and British Columbia. In Quebec and Ontario in the 1920s and 1930s, anti-Semitism was a powerful force behind Ottawa's refusal to accept Jewish refugees from Nazi Germany before World War II. Parliament passed multiculturalism and employment equity programs in the mid–twentieth century, but after several decades, observers concluded that they had not produced the social equality Canadians claimed distinguished them from Americans. In both countries, civil rights organizations became public consciences for such groups with Ottawa and Washington, and publicized discrimination to compel redress. Upper North American multicultural mosaics followed convergent transnational patterns, not divergent national patterns. In both countries, the dark sides of discrimination, prejudice, racism, and even violence yielded only in modern times to tolerance or recompense.[16]

Social and Political Reforms

Social reform movements in Upper North America sought legal change, and so they appear rather more divergent, at least in terms of their lobbying, which focused on state, provincial, and national governments. The Anti-Saloon League in the late nineteenth and early twentieth centuries was nonetheless transnational. During the U.S. Progressive era in the early twentieth century, the league and its allies fought for Prohibition and succeeded with the Nineteenth Amendment to the U.S. Constitution, and the Volstead Act that enforced it. In Canada, provinces controlled alcohol production and sales. In Quebec, the Roman Catholic Church ensured that the provincial legislature never banned alcohol. Production continued, but under close government scrutiny. In other provinces, legislatures enacted paternalistic and coercive liquor regimes as much for the revenue as to exert social control.

The U.S. Prohibition era began in January 1920 and at once became transnational in Upper North America. Proximity, middle-class prosperity, and the automobile gave drinkers from the northern states a next-door source of liquor over newly built road networks in the borderlands. People went to Canada for evening or weekend drinking sprees. Canadian entrepreneurs built "hotels" near the border that sold more liquor than rooms to U.S. visitors. Winnipeg entrepreneurs advertised snowballs and highballs to attract conventions. Montreal distillers tried to fill a suddenly bottomless Upper North American market, and smugglers carried large liquor consignments to meet U.S. demand. Fast motorboats moved shipments over the Great Lakes and borderland rivers as well as through coastal and international waters. Despite political pressure from Washington, customs officials in Ottawa only delayed clearances of liquor cargoes to U.S. destinations, and some accepted bribes to ensure prompt shipment. In 1928, President Herbert Hoover threatened to order thousands of agents onto the border unless Ottawa stopped these exports. R. B. Bennett's government refused to become an arm of U.S. federal law enforcement agencies, but in 1930 William Lyon Mackenzie King's Liberal government agreed to ban liquor exports. That had little effect, and smuggling continued. Transnational social habits and a sense of individual entitlement to drink what they pleased meant that Upper North Americans transformed U.S. Prohibition into a transnational social policy failure. In the 1932 U.S. general election, Franklin D. Roosevelt promised to end Prohibition if elected, and after his victory the new Democratic Congress and the required three-quarters of the state governments swiftly passed the constitutional amendment. Social-policy-inspired Prohibition was over, and the transnational liquor trade blended into Upper North American commercial relations.[17]

Women who pursued civil rights and feminists on a quest for moral and social equality formed parallel political movements in the United States and Canada, in part because the two political and legal systems worked in different ways. Throughout, they drew moral support from one another as stakeholders in each other's success. Women in Wyoming and other parts of the U.S. West had the state franchise beginning in the 1880s, but Upper North America's first national suffrage occurred after several years of protest when Sir Robert Borden's Ottawa government granted women the vote for 1918 federal elections, in part for partisan reasons. The United States ratified a constitutional amendment for women's suffrage in 1920. The provincial franchise appeared in rapid succession as local Victorian patriarchy faded, although in Quebec the Catholic Church delayed women's voting rights until 1940. Labor demands during World War II pulled North American women into a wide range of social roles and established the foundations for the second, morally based wave of modern feminism that pursued equal employment opportunities as well as social and political status. Retrenchment occurred when veterans returned to civilian life and took up jobs guaranteed for them. These women's movements worked within each national jurisdiction, although results appeared virtually simultaneously because activists organized under umbrella organizations such as the U.S. National Organization of Women (1960) and the Canadian National Action Committee on the Status of Women (1971). They sought comparable and collective, rather than individual, rights of equity in jobs, status, education, pay, and child care.[18] Some activists called for abortion rights, which proved socially inflammatory in both countries because of shared, albeit controversial, religious and social values, and conservative Christian churchgoers opposed secular social views in both countries.

Several U.S. states repealed abortion laws in the 1960s. The 1973 Supreme Court *Roe v. Wade* decision (which hinged upon the right of privacy) overrode remaining state prohibitions. Polls showed that North American majorities viewed abortion as a special rather than a broad political interest.

By the 1990s and early 2000s, controversy over abortion had faded in Canada but continued in the United States. Every spring in Washington, national groups that support and oppose abortion gather and march down Constitution Avenue from the White House to the Capitol. Each side heckles the other in this public theater. Much interest focused on Justice John Roberts's 2005 nomination as chief justice of the U.S. Supreme Court, but he assuaged critics with his view that *Roe v. Wade* was settled law. In Canada, Dr. Henry Morgenthaler opened a series of abortion clinics under the 1982 Charter of Rights and Freedoms. After initial protests, the issue faded from Canadian public view. Transnational cultural and socioeconomic themes had generated transnational results within separate national political systems.[19]

A related transborder social theme arose in adoption. Provincial and state laws governed this practice, which remained largely out of the media and hence public gaze in Upper North America. In Quebec, church-run orphanages traditionally placed babies with Catholic families in New England states. In other provinces, social agencies arranged for the adoption of white babies from Canadian unwed mothers by U.S. families. In the Atlantic provinces, the "Ideal Maternity Home" ran a commercial system from New Brunswick and Nova Scotia into northeastern states through Saint John, Montreal, and Toronto. Once public welfare officials uncovered this clandestine cross-border free market operation, they closed it down.[20]

Urban and suburban social patterns became transnational in Upper North America, but because of income levels and demographic asymmetry this became more obvious in the period after 1945. Population growth and urbanization transformed cities by the early twentieth century, and both work and living places initially went vertical as crowded urban business cores and walking-distance residential neighborhoods both acquired clusters of high buildings. The horizontal dimension of suburban towns where middle-class workers commuted on trolleys evolved from the central cores. Montreal, Toronto, and Vancouver followed the patterns New York, Chicago, and San Francisco had established. After 1910, automobiles and buses operated on transit routes that proliferated into increasingly complex road patterns. Canadian cities grew more slowly than their U.S. counterparts, and for decades only Montreal and Toronto had more than a million inhabitants. The United States, with ten times the population, had more than two dozen cities of such size by 1920. In the post–World War II era, rising wages coincided with lowered costs of living. Members of the emerging mass consumer society used cars as the common form of transport by the 1950s, and multilane thoroughfares interlinked suburban towns and urban cores, with

Los Angeles as the prototype. Individually mobile middle- and working-class people moved out as real estate developers bought up farmland to convert into suburbs. The same mixture of brands and models of sedans, station wagons, vans, and small trucks from Detroit and Windsor plants, and later foreign makers as well, crowded roads, driveways, and parking lots. Over 90 percent of the people in these transnational urban and suburban sites traveled by car. By the 1970s, North American cities were virtually interchangeable in social living habits and patterns. In 1900 more than half of all North Americans lived in small towns and rural areas, and by 2000 less than a fifth did.[21]

Mobility and the mass consumer culture shaped North American shopping patterns. A few suburban shopping malls, versions of nineteenth-century urban arcades, appeared in the 1930s, but by 2006 malls smothered both moderate-sized and small cities and towns. Retail shops in downtown cores lost customers as people patronized large malls in expanding suburbs, where they had multiple stores in retail villages. Municipal governments began to capitalize on rising property values while they coped with social congestion. In the 1980s and 1990s, well-heeled professionals rejected commuting for residential and service clusters near their work. These "edge cities" appeared around airports, light industrial areas, even major shopping centers.

Throughout, Upper North America life and work reflected shared social ideas and patterns that made Canadians and Americans indistinguishable in their daily work and living habits by the early twenty-first century.[22] Only remote, low-population regions escaped this transformation. Canadians believed that their cities were cleaner and better managed than U.S. counterparts, but David Crombie, president of the Canadian Urban Institute and ex-mayor of Toronto, noted that those cities had declined in livability later than, but in similar ways to, U.S. urban centers. He also noted that old industrial centers once thought ruined, such as Cincinnati and Pittsburgh, had transformed themselves as tourism and convention destinations.[23]

The emergence of public social services also followed transnational patterns in Upper North America, despite divergent ideological foundations and different political structures. Before the 1930s, states, provinces, private charities, and cities funded social services, but the Great Depression overwhelmed them. The bundle of policies and institutions created by Franklin D. Roosevelt's New Deal programs assisted millions of Americans, established the Social Security system, and reshaped attitudes about government's responsibility and role that have survived into the twenty-first century. Ottawa essayed a version of this system, but later and in a more piecemeal fashion. In effect, the two countries developed alternate ways of dealing with the same problems while they instilled a shared sense of individual entitlement. In public health care, policymakers and analysts have pondered if the two systems reflected stark ideological, or liberal-democratic, social management distinctions because of divergent U.S. free market and Canadian communitarian values. In Canada, proponents of centralization emphasized this divergence to score domestic ideological or partisan points, but they slighted the parallels and similarities of the social welfare systems in both Upper North American nations.[24] For example, in recent years the United States has spent more per capita on health services than Canada, and about 30 percent of Canadian spending has gone to private providers of one kind or another. Though these programs diverge administratively, the evidence reveals common Upper North American patterns and outcomes.

The U.S. Social Security Act of 1935 created a nationwide, uniform social support system. But federal and state social programs interwove to create a patchwork during the following decade. Harry Truman, Roosevelt's successor, signed a national health insurance program. A Democratic Congress failed to pass a comprehensive federal system in 1949, but it enacted limited health plans for Social Security recipients in defined groups, such as senior citizens and federal employees. Medicare and Medicaid appeared in 1965 to supplement Social Security benefits with fiscal transfers to the states that provided income assistance. During the Cold War, Republicans wooed conservative voters when they denounced broad programs as socialist, or even communist, in nature. U.S. medical associations lobbied members of Congress to support selective and voluntary rather than national programs, framing professional self-interest in ideological terms. The U.S. political system made broad-based social-democratic legislation difficult to enact because stable, majority political blocs were hard to assemble and maintain, party discipline notwithstanding. The politics of Congress allows small groups and tenacious lobbies to block legislative efforts more effectively than loosely knit coalitions can promote them. Other factors also entered such equations. For example, organized labor opposed national health benefit programs because the unions wanted issues to bargain with employers. U.S. auto makers expanded their plants in Canada in part to reduce the effects of such bargaining and their own costs in light of Canadian social policies. Federal-state conflict also complicated the political process.

So Washington's piecemeal and dispersed health care system, once in place, became unmovable for a host of reasons.[25]

Divergent federal-subfederal political relations, regional interests, and political systems produced two national social systems that amounted to variations within the Upper North American context. In 1932, Canadian farm and labor groups in the West founded the Cooperative Commonwealth Federation out of frustration over Ottawa's failure to respond to their social problems during the Great Depression. This set western and eastern-based politicians at arm's length in some respects, but western provinces also needed money from Ottawa because until the energy boom developed in the 1980s and 1990s, they lacked the tax base to fund social services. Organized labor, less able to bargain social benefits from employers than its U.S. counterpart, wanted provincial and federal social support. In 1940, Prime Minister William Lyon Mackenzie King's Liberal government released a Royal Commission report on dominion-provincial relations recommending that Ottawa partially fund health care benefits. The Cooperative Commonwealth Federation, meanwhile, called for full national health insurance, which three-quarters of Canadians supported by 1942. King and the Liberals feared the impact of these forces on the next election, so they struck a social security committee in 1943. Five years later, legislation appeared and Ottawa signed agreements with the provinces. Federal transfer monies would support existing health programs and hospital construction. In 1956, Ottawa established a 50/50 percent cost-sharing hospital program. Ontario, the province with the greatest federal electoral strength, forced Ottawa to underwrite its provincial hospital insurance program, and soon all the provinces claimed to be parts of the national system. In 1961, the Saskatchewan populist John Diefenbaker's Conservative government established Canada's health care program in its modern form.[26]

This federal-provincial system was less national than ten similar provincial systems with Ottawa as an exchequer, monitor, and regulator. When some physicians began to bill patients for services, a 1984 Canadian Health Act held back payments to provinces that allowed such extra billing. This episode reinforced the myth of a national health care system, which was a myth because Ottawa managed and funded provincial systems under provincial control with a provincial budget that paid for designated services. Individuals and employers purchased additional health service coverage from private companies for a personal, or employment, fringe benefit. As costs rose for medical and health care of any kind, Canadians paid out of their pockets for about one-third of the services they received. Throughout, medical practitioners were free agents, relocating as they chose within a province, Canada, or Upper North America. Moreover, Washington and Ottawa faced identical problems: aging populations, rising demands for health care services, increased costs, deficits and debt, and administrative inefficiencies. Ottawa transferred funds in annual blocks, and the wrangle and rhetoric about the "national" system through the later decades of the twentieth century camouflaged disputes about costs and who would pay. Quebec allowed a private system for patients with means, which Ottawa ignored for political reasons. But when Alberta attempted private clinics, Ottawa threatened to withhold transfer monies. Regional and partisan politics shaped this national debate, as did free market forces. Meanwhile, Canadians who could not wait paid U.S. centers for faster personal treatment.[27]

Rhetoric, ideology, and belief in the border as a social policy container drew a veil over the common Upper North American character of the two national health care systems. U.S. policymakers and many Americans admired the idea of universal heath care but shuddered at its costs. Meanwhile, higher levels of subsidy only heightened the public sense of entitlement and further strained budgets. So the U.S. focus remained on specific groups: the elderly, poor people, children, and veterans. Canadians attempted to sustain both the illusion and form of a national and universal health care system. Transnational Upper North American cultural and social factors, especially language and professional mingling within a borderless marketplace, created mobile pools of medical staff members. U.S. observers who saw Canada's system as state supported overlooked its free market components. Canadians who criticized the U.S. system overlooked its state-supported components. The border acted as a psychological and ideological veil, while politics muddied both domestic and cross-border debates about health care reform. By 2006, politicians in each country selected for praise or condemnation aspects of the other system that played to their domestic constituencies.[28]

On a corporate level, Upper North American partnerships emerged. Canadian firms began to offer services in U.S. health care markets, while U.S. organizations offered services in Canada through subsidiaries where provincial systems did not cover what patients needed. Jurisdictional paradoxes emerged. An Ontario specialist could not practice in Quebec but could open a clinic in Plattsburgh, New York, and then see Quebec patients who drove down from Montreal for quicker service than was available in their own city and province. Toronto's private King's Health Centre clinic placed patients in U.S. facilities, while politicians and the media debated costs, budgets, and patient waiting times but ignored the transnational patterns.[29] B.C. researchers ran organ transplant data through computers and mapped optimum locations for such operations based on population size, needs, and the quality of facilities. The results showed that between 1990 and 1996, U.S. sites performed safer transplants than any Canadian center. Increased border-crossing security after the events of September 11, 2001, complicated these patterns, but the Atlantic Health Sciences Corporation and Eastern Maine Health Care shared human and other resources to serve rural areas with low populations. New Brunswick for a time licensed U.S. doctors to treat Canadians near the border because of the distances to provincial medical centers. In 1998, provincial officials sent Canadians to U.S. centers for treatment, and from 1999 to 2002 Ontario spent $67.4 million (Canadian), British Columbia $21.2 million, and Quebec $25 million for radiation and cancer treatments in the United States. New companies, such as Alberta's PPI Financial Group, offered U.S. health care programs to Canadians. Ottawa officials blustered and threatened while the small pool of stakeholders in informal transnational health care grew.[30]

Some cross-border social patterns, by contrast, have a recent genesis. The sale and consumption of prescription drugs generated thousands of stakeholders in each country in the first years of the twenty-first century and even suggested a pattern of economic and jurisdictional integration. The U.S. Food and Drug Administration (FDA) and Health Canada's Patented Medicines Prices Review Board oversaw the test and approval process, and they rarely disagreed about the safety of any pharmaceuticals offered for sale. In the United States, they sold in a free market. In Canada, Ottawa purchased for the domestic market and received bulk discounts. That, and the often higher purchasing value of the U.S. dollar, meant that any given prescription was likely far cheaper in Canada than in the United States. U.S. seniors discovered this while shopping for prescriptions over the Internet and from Canadian contacts. If they lived in a borderland region, they drove in person or organized weekend bus tours to purchase prescriptions. By law, only Canadian doctors could prescribe pharmaceuticals sold in Canada, so Quebec agencies arranged for provincial pharmacies to accept prescriptions from Vermont physicians. Sales to Americans increased and because 2000 was a U.S. election year, Republicans wanted Ottawa to raise prices. Seniors, meanwhile, lobbied for exemption from laws that banned traveling abroad to purchase prescriptions, and a bloc in Congress urged Medicare to create a prescription benefit.[31] Canadian pharmacy advertising reached ever-wider U.S. markets, and those pharmacies developed new marketing methods as a de facto transnational prescription system emerged.

Politics brought this mélange into the open when Vermont's governor, Howard Dean, urged his people to join the United Health Alliance's "Medicine Assist" to order pharmaceuticals from Ontario and Manitoba. The U.S. Coalition for Better Medicine argued that lower prices would forestall future life-saving drugs because pharmaceutical companies would cut back on research.[32] A Washington-Ottawa problem arose when the Mediplan Pharmacy opened in Minnedosa, Manitoba, 125 miles west of Winnipeg, and sold medicines over its Web site. U.S. orders generated 300 shipments daily, and Mediplan opened its own post office. Senior U.S. senators responded to pleas from elderly constituents and sponsored a bill to remove all restrictions on reimporting pharmaceuticals from Canada. Meanwhile, law suits filed in Florida and other states prevented local doctors from signing prescriptions and sending medical files to Canadian physicians. The Alliance for Retired American Seniors organized more border state bus tours, and southern Californians even chartered a train that rolled north to British Columbia with great fanfare and publicity. Puget Sound ferries carried seniors from Seattle to Victoria on prescription excursions, with a Butchardt Gardens tour on the side. Between 2002 and 2003, sales into the United States rose 321 percent in British Columbia, 316 percent in Alberta and Saskatchewan, 227 percent in Manitoba, and 80 percent in Ontario and New Brunswick, but decreased 33 percent in Quebec. U.S. city and state governments enabled this transnational system with Internet links, communication lines, and contracts with Canadian pharmacies for employee prescriptions. Almost a billion U.S. dollars went north, which increased Washington's balance-of-payments problems.[33]

The transnational pharmaceutical trade reflected social needs and created antagonistic self-interested camps within each jurisdiction. Some in Canada warned that this asymmetry could create potential shortages. U.S. pharmaceutical companies lobbied the FDA to bar imports and urged Congress and the White House to challenge foreign price control systems. The pharmaceutical giant Pfizer cut off sales to Canada to create political pressure that would sustain its profits, but pharmacists and U.S. patient rights groups urged the 10 million Americans who bought prescriptions from Canada directly or over the Internet to fight back through their representatives. Officials in Ottawa and Washington agreed to collaborate on regulations while public and private groups squared off in the United States.[34] A CBS *60 Minutes* segment that reran several times strongly suggested that pharmaceutical companies were profiteers. U.S. senators attacked the FDA, and John Kerry, the Democratic 2004 presidential nominee, promised full access to Canadian pharmacies if he won that November. Senators also balked at President George W. Bush's nominee to head Medicare and Medicaid because he had opposed prescription purchases from Canada. The governor of New Hampshire bought Canadian pharmaceuticals over the Internet and put the link on his state's official Web site.[35] By then, Internet pharmacies that sold primarily to U.S. customers operated in seven provinces. The Canadian dollar's rise against the U.S. dollar slowed sales, but state and city governments soon endorsed cross-border purchases to reduce their costs.[36]

Public pressure in several states attacked the levels of regulatory power designed to maintain two separate national pharmaceutical markets. Ottawa said it would restrict prescription exports when that served the national interest, and in 2005 Congress tabled legislation to allow imports from Canada. The episode faded from public attention, but it demonstrated that in Upper North America proximity, shared values and language, market forces, and the assertion of stakeholders acting in a mass had the power largely to defy the border's jurisdictional significance. This shaped Upper North American economic and political relations, domestic policies, and domestic partisan politics. Meanwhile, FDA and U.S. Customs officers turned blind eyes.[37] In 2006, FDA and Health Canada negotiated joint reviews of new pharmaceuticals for faster approval than maintaining two separate systems would allow. Mass stakeholders in the transnational prescription affair had forced administrative reforms and Washington-Ottawa cooperation.[38]

Illegal drug traffic generated greater cross-border cooperation as well, although for entirely different reasons. The United States provided a major market for such drugs, and proximity allowed smugglers to land illicit cargoes in Canada because surveillance seemed less stringent. Furthermore, once in Canada, the 5,000-mile borderline offered several points of access for smugglers. Between 1978 and 1993, Canadian authorities intercepted over 225 tons of hashish and marijuana headed for the West Coast of British Columbia alone, mostly for reexport to the U.S. market. Officials judged that this might have constituted 10 percent of the total attempted during that period. After the events of September 11, 2001, Washington increased offshore and ocean surveillance, inspected suspicious containers when they landed in North American ports, and reinforced the northern border. Seizures reduced drug traffic, but British Columbia's domestic underground marijuana production increased to compensate. Ottawa's planned decriminalization for possession of small amounts of marijuana for medicinal purposes aroused alarm in U.S. political and enforcement circles.[39] Frequent border crossers feared further congestion from drug inspections on top of the already enhanced security after September 11, 2001. U.S. politicians also argued that Canadian drug laws were too liberal and threatened U.S. interests. Washington officials opposed easing laws on the possession of small amounts of drugs, and they asserted that Ottawa had a moral obligation to protect its neighbor.[40] This transnational social issue folded into Washington's efforts to manage the northern border as a security line. Some Canadian commentators and politicians argued that this revealed Canadian virtues and rejected U.S. suggestions about how Ottawa should manage internal Canadian affairs.

The Ottawa and Washington positions on national social differences reversed over firearms smuggled into Canada and sold to urban gang members and organized criminals. Public discussion of firearms in Canada played into domestic stereotypes of the United States as a violent and fear-based society obsessed with arming itself. When handguns and automatic weapons turned up in criminals' hands in Toronto, some argued that Canada had somehow been Americanized. The historical record showed some social and jurisdictional differences, but also variations on transnational themes. Firearms had been a social necessity throughout the colonial era for hunting and community as well as personal defense. As provinces matured, officials and elected assemblies drew up militia legislation, and when the United States appeared in 1783, those who separated into Loyalist and U.S. political streams held the same views about personal firearm ownership. No British equivalent existed to the Second Amendment of the U.S. Constitution, although this amendment actually rested on English Whig theories about the need for an armed populace to guard against an overbearing central government, a political theme of the American Revolutionary era. The individual right to gun ownership had a moral and social purpose. Provincial firearms ownership legislation favored the better-to-do, and Royal governments stockpiled weapons under close guard to arm militias in case they were needed to repel invaders or restore civil order. Armed militias and regulars routed the rebels of 1837–39 in Upper and Lower Canada, restored order in Montreal's 1879 Orange Day rioting, and reinforced the Royal North West Mounted Police sent to suppress Louis Riel's Northwest Rebellion of 1885. The better to do among Canadians owned personal firearms throughout, but by the early twentieth century provincial and federal laws required citizens to obtain police permits to keep or carry handguns. Authorities also confiscated firearms from ethnic groups during wartime and seized registered weapons and other possessions from interned Japanese residents when the Pacific theater of World War II opened. After 1945, Ottawa repealed registration laws for rifles and shotguns, but not automatic firearms. When the separatist Front de la Liberation du Quebec sparked the October crisis of 1970, public and political pressure arose for more restrictive firearms laws.

In the United States, no federal or state laws restricted firearms ownership, but local ordinances applied. The Second Amendment provided continued constitutional protection for firearms ownership on philosophical and legal levels. After the War of 1812–15, the regular U.S. army was distributed in frontier garrisons. Organized territories as well as states replicated the militia system, with governors serving as constitutional commanders-in-chief to call troops out for community defense or aid civil authority if social upheavals occurred. Farmers, ranchers, and citizens in towns and cities also generally owned firearms. Soldiers mustered out after the U.S. Civil War kept their rifles and pistols, and the mass production of all such weapons and fixed ammunition made them cheaper, easier to use, and more reliable and widely available than in the past. Criminal elements as well as law-abiding citizens had access to firearms, and nineteenth-century cities all had armed criminal gangs and footpads. Urban police increasingly carried handguns and kept shotguns and rifles in their precinct houses. Gun makers marketed their products to homeowners fearful of burglars or assailants.

This period, it seems, is where Canada and the United States diverged. Practical, rather than moral forces were at play. No mass production arms industry developed in Canada, so firearms had to be imported and were expensive. Provincial legislatures gave justices of the peace authority to hand down six-month jail terms to anyone discovered with a handgun who could not convince the court that they faced assault against their lives or property. After 1892, laws forced gun merchants to keep records of all handgun sales along with the buyer's name. Under the Articles of Confederation, Ottawa controlled criminal law, which centralized firearms control in contrast to the patchwork of U.S. state and municipal oversight. This division of legal authority in the two federal systems seems a crucial distinction. In modern times, Congress has often discussed gun-control legislation, but incidents generated greater local than national concern. A gun industry lobby developed that argued against federal gun-control laws. Even when enacted, such laws have had term limits and faced court challenges. They fell into federal-state conflicts and withered when the social immediacy of what gave rise to the legislation faded from the public mind, as Congress's Brady Bill, enacted after an attempted assassination of President Ronald Reagan left one of his aides, Jim Brady, paralyzed from a gun injury. Many saw this divergence in moralistic terms, but it had deeper roots in social and political values. The U.S. Constitution enshrined individual rights and freedoms, whereas the British North America Act established community rights and the state to oversee national life.[41] Overall, personal ownership of firearms, especially handguns, had far less social credibility and sanction in Canada than in the United States.

This combination of historical, constitutional, and ideological factors also gained the United States a reputation as a society where visitors would never know who might have a firearm with them. Some states, such as Missouri, issued licenses for people to carry concealed weapons, whereas others did not. No state bans them outright. Mass entertainment genres feature and even confirm the wisdom of having a handgun for the right of self-defense and to take vengeance for personal wrongs inflicted. That said, much folklore seems to inform Canadian views of U.S. gun ownership and the social as well as legal and political foundations for attitudes about and the use of firearms. Divergent attitudes toward and differing legislation on an individual's liberty to own a firearm was clear enough, but it remained a largely unexplored subject in comparative North American social history. At the same time, anecdotes abound. A Canadian consul general would often contrive to ask at his Los Angeles receptions how many guests had brought their guns with them. It was legal to do so, and a majority of hands usually went up. He then asked why, because Beverly Hills was among the safest neighborhoods in the United States. The answers were variations of "You never know," "You cannot be too careful," or "Just in case." A Canadian woman moved to New York City, and a new friend in the expatriate community urged her to buy a handgun. People needed them, she insisted. Why? Well, because New York is a dangerous place.[42]

Sensational firearms murders occurred in recent years in both countries, with comparable moral and social reactions, but the different constitutional and legal frameworks as well as historical backgrounds shaped the aftermaths. On December 6, 1989, a troubled young man used a semiautomatic rifle and shot several women (fourteen died) in the classrooms and common areas of the University of Montreal's engineering school. Shocked Canadians pressed Ottawa, already at work on a federal firearms registry program, to quicken the pace. In the United States in April 1999, two equally disturbed young men carried firearms into Columbine High School in Littleton, Colorado, and shot several students and teachers in a cold-blooded manner that evoked transnational horror. Canadians who thought their country morally superior in this respect faced a similar event at W. R. Myers High School in Taber, Alberta, where a young man deliberately shot and killed a classmate. After initial reporting, the Canadian media fixed upon what seemed rising firearm use in street crime, robberies, especially between narcotics trade rivals. A cross-border smuggling trade in handguns and assault firearms emerged. Between 1990 and 2002, gun homicides in Toronto rose from 16 to 56 percent of the total. Federal and urban officials exploited this traffic for political purposes, but accredited Federal Bureau of Investigation and Bureau of Alcohol, Tobacco, Firearms, and Explosives agents worked with Ottawa's National Weapons Enforcement Support Team to manage this smuggling as best they could.[43] Canadians applauded Michael Moore's *Bowling for Columbine* pseudo-documentary for its apparent confirmation that the U.S. gun culture rested on a fear-based society. Perhaps Canadians were more trusting, as Moore asserted, but such arguments are easier to assert than prove, and Moore's goals were ideological and partisan within the U.S. context.[44]

On moral and social levels, Canadians and Americans seem to agree about personal firearms. But bodies of opinion do not begin and end at the border. The U.S. antigun lobby cites Canada as an ocean of enlightenment, while some Canadians support the U.S. approach. The Canadian Wildlife Federation led opposition to Bill C-51, the national gun registration law. They invited the actor Charlton Heston, then president of the National Rifle Association (NRA), to speak at their convention. He argued with some foundation that both peoples shared values of self-reliance, independence, individual freedom, and a reliance on firearms in rural regions. The NRA aroused opposition in both countries, however, when Heston and others added that North American values included a historical right to own and use firearms.[45] Social attitudes on gun ownership betrayed transnational patterns with national social variations and legislative regimes.

Gay rights offers the most recent case study in the transnational character of social issues in Upper North America. In the nineteenth and twentieth centuries, in British, provincial, and U.S. society, being homosexual was broadly considered a shame that dared not show its face. Attitudes have eased in recent decades. Gay groups have pursued civil and legal rights in a manner reminiscent of other social activists in democratic societies. Meanwhile, churches have struggled with how to treat both gay parishioners and clerics. Scandals about priests and choirboys led to lawsuits and court settlements. Both tarnished the reputation of, and impoverished, the Roman Catholic Church, in both countries. A New Jersey court struck down a ban on gay Boy Scout leaders as a violation of human rights. The Boy Scouts of America, with United Methodist Church support, petitioned the U.S. Supreme Court to support its ban on homosexual leaders. The Boy Scouts of Canada accepted gay leaders, although the Baden-Powell Scouts' Association of Canada retained inherited Victorian values of manliness and banned them from the organization. Elizabeth Birch, a young Canadian lesbian with strong free market views, headed Washington's Human Rights Campaign, a gay organization, and managed the Recording Industry Association's lobby. Conservatives condemned them as gays and for their association with Democratic President Bill Clinton. Party labels meant little, because Log Cabin Republicans was a gay group. In 1996, Congress passed a Defense of Marriage Act, as Parliament had, but in 2005, Parliament also recognized gay marriages in federal law.[46]

A popular Upper North America view that Canada was more liberal than the United States seemed confirmed when then-governor-general Adrienne Clarkson officially congratulated gay couples at Toronto's Metropolitan Community Church. The president of the Canadian Council of Catholic Bishops reproached her, however, and an Ontario government minister refused to recognize the unions. The provincial Superior Court later ruled that "the dignity of persons in same-sex relationships is violated by the exclusion of same-sex couples from the institution of marriage," which courts in British Columbia, Quebec, and Nova Scotia, but not in Alberta, upheld. Opinion in western Canada's "Bible Belt" south of Calgary and in British Columbia's Fraser Valley echoed conservative U.S. views, although eleven states recognized gay civil unions and the Massachusetts Supreme Court endorsed gay marriage in 2004. A Republican effort to initiate a constitutional amendment banning gay marriage died in Congress and ballot initiatives over the issue had various results in the 2006 U.S. midterm elections, although many states sanctioned gay civil unions in law. Meanwhile, in social terms, Americans generally saw Canada as a kind of neighboring state with different customs and laws.[47] Moreover, urban regions in both countries were more socially liberal than rural areas, and cultural and social attitudes interwove throughout Upper North America, although an important philosophical divergence remained. Gays argued in the United States for individual rights and in Canada for social equality.[48]

The border has proven permeable to mores and attitudes that produced parallel and similar social reforms through time. Shared democratic and human rights, faith in the rule of law, individualism flowing from constitutional provisions, balanced individual and community outlooks, and broad tolerance have produced two remarkably similar societies where themes and issues have transnational characteristics. Ideas about social justice have transferred easily from one national context to the other.[49] Transnational Upper North American social patterns have rested on the shared language and mores in systems where stakeholders have pursued change to reflect their preferences. Rhetorical differentiation aside, social themes in Upper North American history have reflected variations on themes, not national divergence.

Part III

Economic Realm

A casual glance at the U.S. and Canadian economies suggests a case study in asymmetry. A closer examination reveals a case study in integrated interdependence. In some cases, we also should speak of a transnational Upper North American economy rather than two intertwined national systems. Still, the comparative ratios are distracting. The ratios for gross domestic product are 12 to 1 or more. Transnational commerce generates nearly half of Canada's gross domestic product, but only 4 percent for the United States. At the same time, California and Texas have one or more of the provinces as their principal economic partners. Overall, thirty-nine states do more business with Canada than any other jurisdiction, country, or state. That means millions of U.S. companies, workers, and citizens, not to mention government revenues, depend upon these interdependent economies. Many companies in the two countries now less create goods and services to sell to each other than make things together and sell everywhere in the transnational marketplace. The Canadian-American Chamber of Commerce and the Canadian-American Business Council are two among many such associations that monitor and intercede with governments to promote this shared system.[1] To adapt an old General Motors slogan, what is good for transnational business is good for Upper North America.

Policymakers in the 1950s and 1960s who sought to balance public and private interests in cross-border trade and investment thought in terms of national jurisdictions with balance sheets rather than the progressive synergism that intertwined Upper North America. Furthermore, this was a two-century-old historical process that had evolved through successive and overlapping phases of the mercantile, industrial, and technological revolutions that began in the eighteenth century. Nation-states defended and policed their commercial monopolies in closed systems, but in Upper North America, tariff regimes notwithstanding, barriers began to be perforated in the early nineteenth century. Geography, the natural distribution of arable land and resources, waterways, and open boundaries thwarted government controls. This percolated in time to all realms of Upper North America. Entrepreneurs and their markets asserted from below an open economic system on the governments that claimed sovereign authority.[2] As populations grew and spread in Upper North American borderlands, stakeholders created elements of first local, then regional, and finally overall transnational economies before national systems appeared. Central governments in the age of Adam Smith encouraged such development and attempted, often without success, to tax the movement of goods. Growth in Upper North America produced in time cooperation on several levels, as in efforts to manage Great Lakes fisheries and water resources in the late nineteenth and early twentieth centuries.[3] When the Singer Sewing Machine Company built branch plants in Canada, it created one company in two places as capital, production, and markets interwove. Alcoa created Alcan to serve U.S. and Canadian consumers, and Upper North American strategic and economic interests in the Shipshaw hydroelectric project on the Saguenay River.[4] Ottawa and Washington comanaged ocean resources, and advocacy groups fought to control pollution or for other social causes in Upper North America.

The economic realm embraces highly dispersed threads that developed from and continued to interweave with themes from the cultural and social realms. Shared values and habits created similar societies with comparable needs and wants. The transnational economy interacted with the Upper North American political realm. Governments historically intended international borders to divide and protect zones of control, but they found in Upper North America that geography and proximity created interwoven systems. Even early differences in outlook about management, with free market private enterprise at one end of the spectrum and state-managed economies at the other, over time blended into a mixed approach in both countries. This shaped the economic engine of dispersed relations that became the most powerful private force in Upper North American affairs. In the wake of the events of September 11, 2001, Washington found that whatever economic advantages accrued from the North American Free Trade Agreement (NAFTA) over its southern border with Mexico, the social issue of illegal immigration has at least equal status with security to shape policy in that direction. To the north, commercial and fiscal interests balanced the security imperative because dispersed stakeholders in both countries have relied upon and insisted that the border remain open to the commerce that feeds the integrated and interdependent transnational economy.[5]

Part III focuses on three broad topics to explain this realm. Chapter 7 explores the development of consumption economies that reflect the interplay of central political and free market impulses. Borderland settlers built social and economic regions from the Atlantic littoral through the Great Lakes Basin to the Pacific Coast. Components of a mass production and marketing system in Upper North America evolved in each region, and though transnational in nature, they were also central to each country's prosperity. Compatible cultural and social values and systems have facilitated these developments to the point where in the early twenty-first century Upper North Americans jointly manage a transnational and largely free market system.

Chapter 8 examines trade and commerce. This captures public, media, and political attention in both governments, which use NAFTA as a synonym for the overall economic relationship. The asymmetry-of-attention principle has fixed the Canadian far more than the American public mind on these interlinkages, except in the borderland tier of states. Producers, marketers, and consumers depend upon an interdependent system that was widely taken for granted before the events of September 11 injected momentary paralysis at border crossing ports. Current debates over how to secure and develop a transnational system that is so beneficial to so many stakeholders go to the heart of political dispersed relations, because of the nature and number of large groups with power that insisted upon a free-flowing system. Private advocacy and research organizations in both countries have produced a torrent of proposals from narrow to wide scale, and short to long term. Ideas about how to reconcile the conflicting and perpetual goals of security and prosperity currently rest within the 2005 Security and Prosperity Partnership.

Chapter 9 explains fiscal integration, the most recent yet most extended Upper North American economic theme. Banking and financial institutions primarily served domestic markets until the mid–twentieth century while commercial interdependence thickened. Fiscal integration unfolded rapidly, however, in the wake of the 1988 Free Trade Agreement and NAFTA in the middle 1990s as domestic legislation encouraged transnational banking, investment, and other financial services. U.S. Citicorp, American Express, the Royal Bank of Canada, and the Bank of Montreal all became Upper North American companies as a result. Other fiscal services, such as insurance companies and investment, developed extensive cross-border partnerships.

Ottawa even recently abandoned a strict limit on Canadians' freedom to invest in U.S. securities and stocks in tax-sheltered retirement accounts. This and other developments have confirmed that a continental fiscal system has emerged where policy questions and proposals focus on concurrent standards. Here, too, shared cultural values interwove among social themes dispersed into personal as well as corporate fiscal action to broaden this Upper North American system.

Chapter 7

Markets and Consumers

When the journalist Milo Cernetig investigated foreign images of Canada, he grasped why exporters had failed to move much beyond their next-door U.S. customers. It was all about image. In the global marketplace, people bought brands, not from countries. So when a prime minister's Team Canada flight landed and business leaders and officials pressed the flesh with their Chinese or Brazilian counterparts, they did more to develop their own domestic political images than open new markets. Cernetig did some surveys of his own to find out more. He talked to a Filipina about Canada, and all she knew was trees and snow. A Chinese thought of seal oil, an aphrodisiac in his culture. Peasants said Boeing, Coca-Cola, General Motors, and Microsoft. Even in England, Canada's "mother" country, pub patrons called out wheat and hockey sticks. One had heard of Nortel, but said it was a U.S. firm. Brands identified a country, not the products, and whereas U.S. mass marketers had transformed their country into a branded nation, Canadians had not even begun to do so.[1]

At a commercial level, brands were common in Upper North America. A Hollywood film, Brooks Brothers suit, or Coke created images for consumers. Brands captured cultural and social themes. In the 1950s, older Canadians spoke reverentially about British goods, woolens for example, to express loyalty to heritage. But by then U.S. brands had replaced British fealty as a factor for the mass of Canadian consumers, who had in any event bought U.S. brands for decades. Advertisements in magazines or on television, and even over the radio, sparked snappy images, social occasions where people enjoyed themselves. The brand idea spread in Canadian society even into that most staid institution, the bank. Solid brass doors kept shiny and heavy walnut and marble interiors vanished. When the Royal

Bank of Canada and Bank of Montreal entered the U.S. market, they developed new images, logos, and stylized monograms that used their initials: RBC and BMO. They mass marketed images: informality; warmth; security; happiness. Financial services, like soft drinks after all, required a share of Upper North America's transnational mass markets to prosper. Other Canadian businesses adapted in similar ways when they moved into the U.S. marketplace, where even a marginal competitive advantage gave marketers an advantage because brands stuck in consumers minds.

Merchandising and Mass Markets

The search for mass consumers as markets became a central theme in North America by the late nineteenth century. Fifty years earlier, personal income levels and the distribution of wealth limited the quantities of merchandise that could be sold. Textile mills in New England and elsewhere produced bolts of cotton and wool cloth, but tailors and dressmakers fit the better to do, and ordinary people made their own clothes. The U.S. Civil War created a mass market for ready-made clothing and footwear in the Union armies. The principle Eli Whitney developed in machine tools to mass produce firearms was transferred to other products, such as clothing, household furniture, and pocket watches. The factory machines and supply systems developed for Washington's war worked just as well for civilian markets after 1865. Tailors, seamstresses, and housewives had only to adjust garments to fit consumers. Shoes could be made en masse for left and right feet and in many sizes. These U.S. goods crept north, along the same Upper North American transportation channels that carried raw materials and other commodities to develop markets in Canada's much smaller population centers. For northern mass producers and marketers, Canada was closer than many parts of the United States.

Transportation systems enhanced the geographic proximity of the U.S. Northeast and the provinces. On lakes and major rivers, steam- and sail-powered vessels and ferries increasingly ran on regular schedules. The first provincial railroad, out of Montreal in 1836, formed an Upper North American linkage with Island Pond in eastern Vermont, then the ice-free ports of Portland and Boston. From there, people and goods could travel over the increasingly complex northeastern railroad grid. By 1853, the Grand Trunk line linked Chicago and the U.S. heartland through Upper Canada, the only route until through rail lines appeared below the Great Lakes Basin. These trains had adjustable bogies for different gauges, but before long all North American railroads had a standard gauge to facilitate commerce. In 1854, John Roebling's suspension bridge, the first designed to do so, carried trains from Buffalo to Toronto over the Niagara Gorge. A decade later, travelers and freight rolled over the Saint Lawrence River on a casement bridge that offered a through line from New York City to Montreal. After 1865, rail lines poked onto the Great Plains, and transcontinental transportation emerged by 1869 in the United States, and 1885 in Canada, with an interwoven pattern of cross-border grids along the way.[2] Trains and ships carried people, commodities, and consumer goods to urban distribution centers, where they transferred onto horse- and mule-drawn wagons to reach the dispersed and fragmented components that made up North America's transnational mass markets. Sir John A. Macdonald's National Policy created a protective tariff that persuaded U.S. companies to invest in branch plants if they wanted to be competitive in Canadian markets. The plants also employed young Canadian men and women, but millions of others headed south for opportunities because the U.S. demand for workers seemed insatiable and expanding in the late nineteenth century.[3]

The National Policy nevertheless facilitated transnational marketing and mass consumerism in Upper North America. The U.S. Singer Sewing Machine Company manufactured 700,000 machines annually by 1871, and plants in Toronto and Montreal covered the Canadian market, where Singer became a brand synonymous with sewing, so that consumers later used the brand name as a generic noun for all such machines. Other U.S. companies planted branches to build combines, and later household appliances and automobiles. After the electrical phase of the Industrial Revolution moved from producing power in large-scale plants to small-scale machinery, General Electric supplied a mass transnational market with an increasing variety of machines. High wages had come with this industrialization, which increased what consumers could purchase for personal use. The assembly of many individual sales over time created wide markets and founded the mass consumer age.

The Upper North American mass market and consumer system was in place by 1910. It employed millions of workers and supplied an increasing variety of goods to more millions of customers. All thus became stakeholders in transnational commerce. The largely unregulated environment of the times encouraged salesmen to compete for and snare consumers. Canadian manufacturers had a reputation for careful operation, but small and fragmented markets were scattered across the continent. Proximity encouraged north-south or east-west links. A few Ontario entrepreneurs planted branches in Buffalo and Boston, tokens of an early asymmetrical interdependence, but these undercapitalized concerns usually collapsed during economic slumps, when U.S. firms bought them up. Throughout, consumers in Canada purchased U.S. as well as British products, and looked south for suppliers and markets. They also absorbed U.S. innovations as businessmen cultivated customers in what became a northern extension of their domestic market.

This process rested on shared and parallel cultural values and social systems. By 1900, both societies acquired such innovations as mass circulation daily newspapers and regular magazines that reached large readerships and developed the consumer society through advertisements. U.S. and Canadian marketers, after an experimental stage, used radio as a commercial system in Upper North America by the later 1920s. Entertainment itself became a mass marketed commodity, whether on stage or screen. Marketing to masses of consumers demanded bureaucratic and managerial innovations, departments devoted to sales and promotion, for example. General stores in small towns had a larger range of goods to deal with, and while specialty shops remained in cities, department stores revolutionized mass merchandising. Entrepreneurs such as Marshall Field in Chicago and John Wanamaker in Philadelphia built shopping palaces with ornate facades and interiors and legions of shop girls to serve masses of customers. They advertised in the large urban dailies and invented enticements such as exchanges for faulty merchandise, money-back guarantees, and credit and installment buying to hold customers. They also sent traveling salesmen to small towns and rural areas.

The Chicago merchant Aaron Montgomery Ward got his start as a traveling salesman in the later 1860s, but he abandoned the usual practice of carrying trunks loaded with samples in favor of notices and order forms mailed in advance to his scattered customers. He found that method efficient and, more important, he provided committed buyers with quicker service. He also won exclusive contracts to supply the Patrons of Husbandry, the Grange, which had hundreds of branches in many states and provinces. In 1872, he opened a mail-order-only business and pioneered the catalog with drawings (later photographs) of his complete range of merchandise. Other North American department store owners, such as Sears and Roebuck and Timothy Eaton, followed suit. All constructed mass markets from scattered and far-flung consumers along with shoppers in dense urban areas. In the process they all welded city, town, and country into a dispersed North American mass market. Shipping companies such as American Express delivered parcels to scattered consumers, and department stores established regional distribution centers. The U.S. and Canadian governments facilitated this process in the early twentieth century with free rural mail delivery. Down-market chain stores appeared in urban and small town settings. F. W. Woolworth, Kresge, Metropolitan, H. L. Green's, and Lewis K. Liggett's drugstores dotted North America under the generic title of five and ten cent stores. By 1900 Woolworth had over sixty shops in Upper North America with small items, such as needles and thread, for as little as a penny each.[4] The economic impact of World War I on Britain furthered the Upper North American transnational mass merchandising system developed over the previous half century.

Mass merchandising also reshaped all Upper North American cities in much the same way. Downtown shopping cores acquired several department stores and numerous specialty shops and other services within easy walking distance. Trolleys and motor buses provided transportation to outlying residential areas, and as the numbers of cars increased, so did paved streets and roads. Combined, these created a mass merchandising pattern that survived into the middle twentieth century.[5] To move their merchandise, entrepreneurs invented fresh techniques, such as opening specials, guaranteed prices, and savings coupons printed in newspapers or distributed by mass mailing. Department stores offered reduced-price sales for cash and provided services such as restaurants and baby-sitting rooms.[6] Consumers and merchandisers became symbiotic partners and remained that way as Upper North America's urban-suburban geography changed from the 1940s through the 1980s. Mass marketers adapted, opened branches, and fought for marginal competitive advantages. And always they looked for innovations that could become new merchandise.

Improvements to Thomas Alva Edison's wind-up phonograph (invented in 1877), for example, came from electrification and small electric motors, vacuum tubes, and sound amplifiers. Because enough people could afford them, a mass market developed. Continuous improvement and economies of scale reduced prices, and the recording and radio industries complemented each other by creating demand. Economic ups and downs aside, by the 1950s a transnational mass market existed. Other technical improvements in recording and playing, such as tapes, and then cassettes, expanded markets. George Eastman's box camera with celluloid film appeared in 1888 and reached a mass market almost at once through department stores and catalog sales. Kodak sold not just a gadget but also memories of special occasions or candid family scenes, a remembrance of children for parents. Buyers could take pictures on vacation and mail in the exposed film for development and enlargements. Mass-produced typewriters revolutionized record keeping and business correspondence but also became a personal consumer product. Sam McLaughlin, a Canadian auto maker, imported British-developed Canada Dry ginger ale and built bottling plants to create a mass market in Upper North America. Undercapitalization forced the McLaughlins to sell to U.S. interests, so Canada Dry became a U.S. company, but kept its brand name. Laura Secord chocolates sold better in U.S. than Canadian markets, despite the heritage brand name. The U.S. company prospered and became part owner of the Fanny Farmer grocery store chain, which North Americanized a Canadian heroine from the War of 1812. Electrical motors became smaller and more efficient, powering a variety of household appliances from mixers to washing machines. General Electric and other brands competed for transnational market shares with these items and advertised in Canadian and U.S. magazines to reach a mass of consumers. By the 1930s, Canadians could purchase Johnson electric floor polishers and branch-plant manufactured linoleum to keep polished. Commercial radio offered personalities from other media a mass entertainment market and new sources of income. Bob Hope became the "Pepsodent Kid," and Jack Benny welcomed listeners with "Jell-O everybody." Entertainers made themselves into brands. During U.S. Prohibition, Montreal distillers such as Hiram Walker and Seagram's became household names in the United States. They used profits from smuggled liquor to establish branch plants and serve the mass market others had created for them.[7]

Cars, Wars, and Middle Classes

Automobiles became central to transnational mass marketing in Upper North America, both as products and for personal transportation. Pioneers in the 1890s experimented with steam, electricity from batteries, and internal combustion engines to power a variety of prototype vehicles that were fragile and unreliable, with few spare parts or roads to run on. Technical advances accumulated, improved reliability, and the mass-produced internal combustion engine symbolized the modern Industrial Revolution. By 1914, Canadians produced some thirty-two different cars. By the 1920s, most were gone, victims of Henry Ford's assembly system in Dearborn, Michigan. He revolutionized mass production and, once he learned from his prototypes, marketed the simple, reliable, versatile, cheap-to-repair Model T in rural as well as urban markets.

Ford had a democratic and egalitarian cast of mind. He saw ordinary people as buyers and accepted small profits to create a mass market. He also made his cars as good as they needed to be, rather than fit for royalty, to reach his market. Personally and by association, Ford put North Americans on wheels en masse. Canadian car makers, by contrast, had set high profit margins, but they thought in terms of small markets and could not build a sufficient base of consumers to survive. The Dodge brothers of Windsor, Ontario, moved across the Detroit River to develop in the U.S. market, then sold out to Walter P. Chrysler. By the end of World War I, a variety of motor vehicles shared city streets with pedestrians, trolleys, trams, riders, and horse-drawn wagons. Mass-produced automobiles also needed parts, and Ford's assembly line produced plenty of spares. Auto service and repair became a mass service industry in itself and generated other businesses such as filling stations and used car lots.

The mass marketed automobile stimulated public services and bureaucratic government in Upper North America. Dirt roads proved a hazard, and improvements led to various surfaces. The most durable was concrete, and forms of tarmacadam balanced cost and efficiency. The construction of roads and bridges stimulated cement, steel, and construction companies as they bid for contracts. Provinces built highways south to link up with U.S. routes and provide access for visitors and transport. Standard numbering systems appeared, and publishers prepared road maps for sale in gas stations. With those, drivers could navigate a city, state, or province, and even the continent. Increasing numbers of paved roads and highway facilities encouraged more automobile sales. Millions drove for work and enjoyment, because cars democratized North American tourism. Dealers sold cars on installment plans, and manufacturers created finance departments that rivaled banks as lending institutions to the masses. State and provincial agencies issued driver's permits and registered cars and trucks for fees to keep track of them. By 1929, millions of automobiles were registered in Upper North America; and by the 1950s, vehicles combined drove over a trillion miles a year.[8]

Improved materials, technological innovations, and more efficient production techniques made motor vehicles ever more reliable, powerful, and comfortable. Specialized trucks hauled larger loads for manufacturing, service, and other consumer industries. U.S. car companies built more branch plants in western Ontario towns and cities to hurdle Ottawa's tariff and gain access to British export markets under Imperial preference arrangements. Ontario was the only large Canadian market, but railroads carried vehicles east and west for sale in all the provinces. Canada's GM sold 9,915 units in 1916, 22,000 in 1920, and 75,000 by 1928. Americans and Canadians had throughout the 1920s the first and second most personally registered vehicles in the world. Corporate consolidation into General Motors and Chrysler occurred, but Ford remained family owned. This transnational industry's thousands of workers organized into binational unions. Manufacturing plants for specialized parts appeared around Detroit and Windsor. Akron focused on tire production, serving North American markets. Cars and trucks consumed gasoline, oil, tires, spare parts, and the labor to repair and keep them running. Car dealers accepted used vehicles as down payments on newer or more expensive models, then resold the trade-ins. This practice dispersed cars more widely into Upper North American society. Filling stations soon offered repair services. Motels and roadside diners served travelers. State and provincial policymakers attempted to shape these changes, and by the late 1920s grasped how the auto industry had become central to the North American mass consumer phenomenon. Cars shaped social life, work habits, and leisure. They allowed people to venture afield from their neighborhoods, and in many respects automobiles combined the realms of dispersed relations for millions of Upper North Americans.

For one thing, because of proximity and demographic distribution, cars drew Canadians and Americans into each others' countries, initially in borderland regions, but farther afield over time. Continental distances made car travel easier north-south than east-west, and auto tourism developed. In the Atlantic Northeast, Nova Scotia created parks and campgrounds and advertised itself in U.S. newspapers as a rustic vacation spot. Ferries linked Portland, Maine, with Yarmouth, Nova Scotia, and crude roads wound through New Brunswick from improvised crossing ports. Other ferries took auto tourists to Prince Edward Island. Cars and trucks on the move ended the isolation of small towns, and local entrepreneurs built inns, motels, and cafes that offered services and provided seasonal employment for locals.[9] Canada's Automobile Chamber of Commerce and Automobile Association appeared in 1932 and affiliated with their U.S. counterparts. These organizations published maps and guidebooks as tourism by car became commonplace. They also lobbied governments to support better roads and fair treatment for drivers. In 1933, nearly 9 million Americans drove north across the line, while over 1 million Canadians headed into various parts of the United States. Americans and Canadians also mingled in dispersed and random, albeit temporary, patterns while they drove. After the 1929 Great Crash and following Depression, the market for cars slowed, but so many were on the road that driving remained the principal form of personal transport. In both countries, some drivers in dust bowl regions motored west to find work. Meanwhile, trucks carried ever greater amounts of goods, often in specialized containers, from production to consumption centers.

After World War I, mass marketing had saturated middle-class markets by the later 1920s, and the lull in sales contributed to the October 1929 Great Stock Market Crash on "Black Friday." The hardships of the Depression era were seared into the consciousness of all North Americans but had no long-term impact on mass marketing for consumers. And innovations arrived. For example, the first supermarket opened as a bargain food and supply store in an abandoned New Jersey auto plant. It offered low prices and customers waited on themselves, paid cash, and toted their groceries and items home in their cars. That also eliminated the costs of delivery. The supermarket was, in effect, a department store for food and small household items. Freezers kept food deliveries fresh in supermarkets for several days, and home refrigerators preserved the merchandise buyers brought home. Even ice boxes kept food fresh for a day or so and reduced weekly shopping trips.

The Depression shrank personal discretionary spending, but innovators created new products with potential mass appeal. Elizabeth Arden, and later Mary Kay Ash, developed personal beauty products sold through networks of entrepreneurs who recruited and trained sales agents in small towns and cities. They in turn constructed local markets of friends, neighbors, and relatives. A new form of mass marketing to consumers spread throughout North America as independent local supermarkets linked into chains. Head offices purchased in bulk and distributed to keep prices low, themselves becoming large, mass marketing businesses. By the 1940s and 1950s, A&P dominated the eastern United States, and Safeway the West Coast as far north as British Columbia. Food merchants, such as butchers, bakers, and produce sellers, evolved into specialty shops and had to remain open longer hours to stay in business.[10]

Mass consumer economies recovered in the later 1930s, and when World War II broke out in September 1939, industrial demand increased. Wartime conditions reduced discretionary spending but produced full employment in Upper North America. Millions of men and women entered the armed and other government services, and the war expanded both prosperity and unsatisfied demands in Upper North America. Canada benefited from Franklin Roosevelt's Lend-Lease Program, but consumer inventories shrank. Automobiles, gasoline, and many other mass marketed goods were in short supply. Savings rose, and pent-up demand produced a boom in consumer and other types of spending as World War II reached its end and Upper North American industries retooled for peacetime production, expecting millions of veterans to return and resume their lives.

Mass marketing and consumption resumed almost at once. The United States and Canada had the only intact industrial and domestic infrastructures in the world for several years. Western Europe was largely bankrupt and in rubble. Congress passed the Marshall Plan in 1947 to provide reconstruction funds, which were to be spent in the United States, but Ottawa gained the right to U.S. dollar credits to sustain its economy, and hence Upper North American commerce. Washington understood that a severe cash shortage in its only active market would have meant a tax on imports, almost all of which came from the United States.

By the early 1950s, the first members of the postwar baby boom were growing up, creating mass markets for a range of goods, and the North American auto industry was offering an ever wider array of increasingly powerful, sophisticated, and comfortable cars. Canadians had lower income levels but still constituted an important and affluent market. For two decades, Upper North Americans drove, serviced, repaired, and replaced vehicles from their transnational industry in Ontario and neighboring states across the Detroit River and Lake Erie.[11] When European and Japanese auto industries recovered in the 1960s, it took another decade before they could challenge North American vehicles in the world's richest consumer market.

Upper North Americans shared a mass marketing and consumer system after 1945 and doubled their personal consumption by 1950. Demographic redistribution created large housing tracts that sprawled on the outskirts of all major cities and became principal components in mass consumerism. Young families purchased cars, furniture, and an array of appliances, such as clothes washers and dryers, freezers, and stereo and television sets for home entertainment. Apparel emerged as a mass consumer industry. U.S. investment and credit financed half of Canada's manufacturing (including most of its auto industry) and two-thirds of its oil, pharmaceutical, and pulp and paper production. Nationalists, many from Anglophile and leftist perspectives, rejected U.S. capitalism and resented Britain's decline. To them, Canada had become an economic colony of the United States, and its cultural and social independence were in peril.[12] For the most part, however, academics debated these issues among themselves, although Walter Gordon's Royal Commission on Canada's Economic Prospects also denounced U.S. ownership and urged protective legislation. The mass of Canadians, however, lived the same kinds of lives with the same tastes for the same array of consumer goods as their U.S. counterparts. They continued to purchase, outright or on installment plans, the products they wanted. Gordon became minister of finance but found his nationalist program unworkable because of Canada's asymmetrical interdependence with the United States.[13]

Washington policymakers furthered Upper North American interdependence when President Lyndon Johnson and Prime Minister Lester Pearson signed the Auto Pact in 1965. This established the transnational manufacture of automobiles as a borderless industry for marketing in Upper North America's consumer economy. The pact generally fulfilled policymakers' expectations. Auto making soon generated 4 percent of each country's gross domestic product and employed 1.5 million workers in high-paying jobs. Asian and European auto makers penetrated North America's mass market with their own branch plants by the 1980s, but they always opposed the pact, which was folded into the 1988 Free Trade Agreement (FTA) and then into the 1994 North American Free Trade Agreement (NAFTA). In 2001, the World Trade Organization ruled that the pact was an export subsidy system, and because it had long served its purpose, Ottawa and Washington allowed it to expire without protest.[14]

The events of September 11, 2001, demonstrated the vulnerabilities of transnational industries dependent upon rapid border transit. Washington's defensive reflexes and focus on secure borders as good as shut them down for a brief time, and congestion at Upper North America's busiest entry port over the Ambassador Bridge transformed the Detroit-Windsor area into a massive parking lot. Officials worked to keep the just-in-time movement of assemblies on which the system relied in motion, but the mass marketing of vehicles to consumers had largely reached its saturation point in Upper North America. Car ownership was more than one per person in the United States, and about two vehicles to three persons in Canada, ratios unchanged since 1990. Additional financial shocks to the big auto makers a few years later suggested more forcefully that the day of the car as the core of North American mass market consumerism had reached, perhaps even passed, its zenith.[15] Mass marketing and consumerism, meanwhile, evolved an endless variety of products for millions of consumers, and when it came to travel, aircraft, after an uncertain start, became part of Upper North America's mass market.

Powered flight lagged automobiles as a practicable transportation method, but aircraft gained in lift and load capacity, reliability, and range because of technological changes during and just after World War I. Veteran fliers in North America turned to civil aviation, although aircraft seemed a novelty without practical application. In March 1919, William Boeing, a Seattle seaplane builder, sent one of his aircraft to a Vancouver exhibition as a novelty to please a wartime friend. That plane returned with a sack of mail, and within a decade postal flights ran between major Canadian and U.S. cities. Charles Lindbergh's transatlantic 1927 flight sparked imaginations about long-distance travel, and engineering advances led to Juan Trippe's Pan American clippers, big flying boats with transoceanic range that did not need expensive landing fields. Avionics developments accumulated, and World War II produced yet larger aircraft, again with improved load, reliability, speed, range, and safety. Government officials, corporate executives, and aviation pioneers were the principal consumers of air travel because the cost to individual passengers limited regular flying to those with high incomes or institutional budgets. Mass market consumer aviation emerged in the 1950s from a combination of jet engines and large-capacity aircraft that lowered costs to consumers. In an era of expanding transnational business and rising incomes, middle-class, and then working-class, people could afford to fly for work, or to vacation destinations. Four Washington-Ottawa agreements between 1966 and 1984 confirmed air travel as a mass transport system within Upper North America. Annual passenger flights rose into the millions of consumers while Ottawa and Washington subsidized this mass transportation industry through airport and weather services. Airlines began to pay for these in the 1980s, when Washington deregulated toward a free market commercial aviation system. Ottawa continued to mix public and private enterprise, but it soon followed the U.S. lead in deregulating commercial aviation. Each country was the other's largest market by 1990, when 13 million people flew on cross-border flights. Officials in Ottawa and Washington negotiated an Open Skies accord in 1995 to disperse a now broadly deregulated transnational market. Passenger traffic increased at many airports. Vancouver, for example, boasted a 23 percent rise in one year.[16]

Americans hewed more closely to free market ideals than Canadians, but cost alone convinced Ottawa that airlines were commercial, not state, enterprises. Skilled personnel, especially pilots and senior managers, moved within a transnational industry. During the 1990s, an American headed Air Canada and a Canadian ran American Airlines. Interest arose in cabotage, which meant that each country would treat the other's airlines as domestic within what had become a continental air space.[17] The events of September 11, 2001, took a toll on expectations here as they had in Upper North American automobile production, when al Qaeda terrorists seized control of loaded jetliners and transformed them into cruise missiles against U.S. landmarks. For several days afterward, only military aircraft flew in North American air space. When commercial travel resumed, ticket sales plummeted. People were terrified to fly. Washington assigned armed sky marshals to domestic flights as much to reassure passengers as to discourage further hijacking. After initial reluctance on political grounds, Ottawa did the same so that Canadian aircraft could land at the U.S. airports that sent and received most of the cross-border traffic. In early 2005, Ottawa moved quietly toward an open transnational free market system as bankruptcies threatened many major airlines. Formal negotiations also began to manage Upper North American air travel and increase markets for carriers in both countries.[18]

The automobile and aircraft industries developed mass markets for several reasons. First, North American distances and dispersed populations among the regions demanded time for travel and the means to do it. Second, Upper North Americans shared cultural and social attitudes about acquiring and spending wealth, or at least their incomes. Third, leisure as well as work time and travel became consumption commodities. Fourth, personal and corporate wealth was well distributed geographically and among people. Mass markets for transportation and industrial innovation reduced costs and opened travel for work, family, and pleasure to millions of North Americans who came to treat their vacations as a time to consume.[19]

When Washington financed the U.S. Interstate freeway complex of the 1950s as a defense project, Congress knew that it would be a mostly mass travel and commercial system. Furthermore, Canadians gained easy access to the Interstate network from all major crossing points. En route, well-appointed chain hotels and restaurants replaced old roadside motels and local diners, often in stopover villages a few hours drive apart. Canadian highways went south before they went east and west to link up with U.S. roads. Millions of Upper North Americans took to the roads each summer to visit family and attractions such as Disneyland and Banff and Yellowstone parks. Bus tours hauled millions of seniors. State and provincial governments built welcome centers with services, brochures, advisers, maps, and discount coupons. Canadian tourist promoters bought full Sunday ad supplements in the *New York Times* and other major U.S. newspapers to draw skiers north during the winter. "Snowbirds," retired Canadians and Americans, headed south in the tens of thousands to winter in warm climates. By 2001, North Americans made over 20 million personal travel trips annually. These numbers fell dramatically after September 11, but a year later mass leisure consumption had returned to the levels of just before the al Qaeda attack.[20] Marketing travel and tours became parts of dispersed, mass North American consumption.

Leisure and New Technologies

The mass marketing and consumption of personal goods and leisure time close to home came to characterize the Upper North American experience throughout the twentieth century. The variety of manufactured goods and services for mass consumption by the 1950s appeared in shopping malls and complexes outside downtown cores that had previously served consumers in North America. Upper North American malls echoed historical prototypes such as the Palais Royale in pre-Revolutionary Paris, and London's Burlington Arcade of 1819. In liberal democratic societies, however, malls were for the masses. The mall and the automobile intertwined, because road systems gave drivers infinitely variable route patterns as populations sprawled around cities.[21] Clusters of shops, offices, apartments, recreation facilities, and garden centers appeared in Baltimore in 1896, in Lake Forest, Illinois, in 1916, and in Kansas City in 1922. As New York grew, flagship stores in Manhattan built suburban branches as free-standing facilities until the Great Depression and World War II curtailed personal shopping as a mass activity. By 1946, only eight malls served U.S. consumers, and Canada had none. Before long, however, shopping centers / malls appeared in suburbs where land was cheap and taxes low, and where thousands of mobile customers lived in nearby housing developments. Many malls were simple plazas with a supermarket and some small service shops. All proliferated and expanded as suburban populations increased.

Provinces, states, and cities subsidized drivers in the 1950s with tax money that went into roads and highway complexes to ease commuting. In densely populated and sprawling areas, such as Los Angeles and Toronto, multilane expressways led to the same patterns of mass suburban living and consumption in both countries. Park Royal, Canada's first mall, opened in West Vancouver in 1957, when the International Council of Shopping Centers was founded. Malls grew, adding one or more department stores, chain outlet shops, cafes, services such as banks and insurance companies, and dental and medical clinics by the 1980s. North America's first "megamall," in Edmonton, Alberta, was built from 1981 through 1985. It boasted hundreds of shops, hotels to attract conventions, an indoor beach, and the usual diversity, but many more, of individual shops, eateries, and entertainment facilities to attract masses of consumers. The Edmonton mall, like the Mall of America in Minnesota, became a tourist destination. Malls and chain stores came to typify mass marketing to consumers, and cross-border asymmetry meant that the U.S. impact on Canada was proportionately greater in the volume of merchandise, brands, tastes, and outlooks than the reverse. But the historical process was transnational. In Canada between 1945 and 1975, the number of stores in malls tripled, from 6,580 to 18,500. In 1956, Canada had 27 malls with 16 stores or more, and 6 with over 30 outlets. By 1973, those numbers were 247 and 101, respectively. The United States had over fifteen times as many in both categories, a number proportionate to the 15 to 1 economic and 10 to 1 population ratios. By 2006, Upper North America had 500,000 malls.[22]

The mass consumer goods and services for sale were also brands. All household or personal-use appliances, automobiles, clothing, electronic equipment, movies, luggage, and personal services carried brand names and packaging. They carried the same guarantees, whether bought in Miami or Halifax, Chicago or Vancouver. And branded, centrally serviced credit and bank cards facilitated mass consumption in Upper North America. These began as gasoline company and department store charge cards to capture repeat customers. Diner's Club was the first general purpose card. Within a few years, bank and finance company cards created VISA and MasterCard as franchise names and enrolled a number of institutional partners to market their cards among the masses as part of consumerism. By the 1990s, the Internet interlinked banking and finance systems so cards could be verified electronically anywhere in North America or overseas. By 2007, Upper North America's mass consumer market operated as a transnational system. Free market forces drove the chain of brand conception, development, production, distribution, and consumption. A supporting array of advertisements seemed ever present in magazines and newspapers, on radio and television, on billboards and at local malls, and on the Internet. Mass marketing campaigns for new products and services appeared simultaneously. In the 1960s Quebecers, whose society had stood aloof from modernization, joined transnational marketing and consumption as part of the Quiet Revolution that reduced the power of the church and conservative elites. The FTA and NAFTA further transformed the binational management of branded transnational commerce, expanding the variety, origin, volume, and flow of branded goods within the system of mass marketing and consumption.

Mass markets and consumerism accelerated North American social mingling in the 1980s. Cross-border shopping was far more north to south than the reverse, for several reasons. Prices were lower, as were consumption taxes; the selection of brand name merchandise was greater; and U.S. marketers in borderland regions knew that 80 percent of Canadians lived within 100 miles of the border. U.S. retail competition for mass market sales had created price advantages that offset the currency differential between the Canadian and U.S. dollars for the buyers. Canadians could fill up with gas and had a large range of restaurants to choose from. In the Saint Croix Valley or along the Quebec-Vermont border, such trips took only a few minutes. Quebecers headed for Plattsburgh and Winnipeggers headed for Fargo, North Dakota. U.S. entrepreneurs built factory outlet malls with deep discounts on household items and clothing near the border to attract Canadian consumers. Malls and the goods they offered became interchangeable with one another, as their configuration, array of shops, and merchandise revealed.

When the Canadian dollar, or "loonie," declined against the U.S. dollar, or "greenback," throughout the 1990s, the marginal advantages of price, taxes, and duties, but not selection, slowed cross-border mass consumer traffic. But U.S. retailers brought their brand-name stores and merchandise north to compete directly with Canadian stores. In 2000, the head of one such U.S. branch won an award as "Distinguished Canadian Retailer" of the year for drawing in $260 billion in sales.[23] U.S. clothing chains such as The Gap and Old Navy appeared in malls all over Canada. So did lingerie and shoe stores, and fast food and chain restaurants. Thirty years earlier, Canadians who had not been to the United States could only wonder what McDonald's was like, although most cities had small drive-in restaurants such as Vancouver's White Spot chain. During the 1980s, fast-food consumerism spread from sea to shining sea in big cities and small towns. Great was the excitement when McDonald's opened in Charlottetown, Prince Edward Island, and its characteristic golden arches dotted northern landscapes and cities with their blend of mass entertainment, consumerism, and eating out.[24]

U.S. marketing innovations—such as discounts, coupons, and no-frills, help-yourself-from-a-pile-of-merchandise, warehouse-sized big-box stores —embodied transnational marketing for mass consumers in Upper North America. The discount chain Wal-Mart invaded Canadian towns and cities in 1994 when it bought out failing Woolco, the last incarnation of F. W. Woolworth's, a small-merchandise chain almost a century old. Commentators and intellectual elites cried the havoc of Americanization, but the mass of urban and rural Canadians wanted bargains, as they had for a century. Wal-Mart included McDonald's outlets to encourage family shopping and wooed vacationers in motor homes with free overnight parking and other services. This transnational pattern widened when Home Depot, the giant U.S. home renovation chain, opened in Canada and forced domestic competitors to improve their management and operations. Venerable Canadian department stores failed because they failed to adapt. Eaton's, a century-old merchandising name in Canada since the 1880s with both urban locations and suburban stores in malls, toppled into bankruptcy from poor management. Sears had been a U.S.-owned chain in Canada since the 1950s, and it survived, but the historic Hudson's Bay Company, a symbol of Canada's northern character and development, suffered the same self-inflicted fate to a southern U.S. entrepreneur named Jerry Zucker. In this Darwinian merchandising jungle, the collapse of Eaton's and Hudson's Bay and Wal-Mart's triumphs surprised no observers. Canada had 10 percent of Upper North America's consumers. The rest were in the United States, and Americans had higher disposable incomes than Canadians. Well-heeled shoppers were equally transnational in their spending habits, but for merchandisers it was all about the mass market.[25]

Shoppers prowled suburban malls and big-box centers in the millions. Throughout the 1990s, downtown retail sales declined 26 percent in Toronto, about the same in Montreal, and 38 percent in Edmonton. Shopping had also become a form of mass entertainment, and malls provided a wide range of shops and services—have a hair trim, get your shoes resoled, grab a snack, catch a movie.[26] Coffee house and restaurant chains also covered Upper North America and made travel predictable. People on the move could find a Red Lobster restaurant or quaff their favorite beers anywhere. The corporate decision to merge Molson's and Coors breweries happened long after both had become transnational brands.[27] Mass marketers had convinced North Americans that the merchandise for sale was better than its price tag, although much of that was illusory, sleight of hand in the shopping carnival, where taste and preference, along with price, drew in the millions of customers.

While U.S. merchandisers headed north, hopeful Canadian entrepreneurs sallied into the transnational market from the other direction. Mass media and entertainment had shaped Upper North American tastes and practices for decades, but Canadians who thought to attract U.S. consumers often misread the market. However much Canadians believe they know and understand Americans, subtle moral and social distinctions lurk beneath the surface of everyday life. For example, Americans were fierce competitors, demanding consumers, and played mass marketing as a zero-sum game. They tested sales techniques, abandoned what failed to produce quick results, and then tried another approach. They fought with imagination and tenacity for marginal advantages. Canadians were less aggressive, less ready to experiment or adapt. U.S. advertising shouted, where Canadian advertising often suggested, the virtues of a product or service. Americans were restless bargain hunters, so stores offset low markups with volume and focused on brands rather than products, whereas Canadians saw merchandising in general terms. Americans analyzed regional and local markets, adapted methods and style, and accepted low profits to build a clientele. Canadians were less aggressive in all those terms. The accumulation of small distinctions with differences meant that about half the Canadian forays south failed. U.S. success rates to the north were perhaps half again as high. The successful Canada-wide electronics chain Future Shop, Birks and other jewelers, and Canadian fashion stores also failed in the United States because of limited financial support and a refusal to rely on mass sales to offset slim profit margins. Canadians went into a mass merchandising environment ten times larger than their domestic consumer market with greater regional and ethnic variations.[28] So they pulled back, some to remain, others to regroup.

Successful Canadian marketers in the United States studied and learned which brands sold where, and to whom. Consulting groups advised them, and as FTA and NAFTA tariff reductions took effect in the 1990s, transnational mass marketing became easier. Montreal clothiers became principal suppliers of wool fabrics in the U.S. market, and their American competitors complained about being put out of business. Birks Jewelers and Future Shop did better on their second attempts. Irving Oil of New Brunswick prospered in Maine with a series of filling stations with corner stores. They marketed convenience and Irving as a brand. Danier leather goods became a successful brand in North America's most competitive mass clothing market, New York City. So did Club Monaco because of its brand and logo. Roots leisure wear became a brand when it outfitted the 2001 Canadian Winter Olympics team in Salt Lake City and gained two weeks of round-the-clock global publicity as athletes paraded and competed in their monogrammed warm-up and competition garb. Roots sales in Aspen, Beverly Hills, and even Detroit rose and stayed up long after the Olympics faded from TV screens.[29] These stories were a few among many little-noted Canadian triumphs in transnational mass market consumerism. In 1999, a Toronto advertising firm won a contract with Cincinnati Bell Wireless because it had learned how to market to Americans, not just sell itself. Proximity and acumen made Quebecers better mass marketers in the United States than in France, language notwithstanding.[30]

The Internet emerged as a marketing medium, and merchandisers moved into a virtual and infinite cyberspace mall. Millions of shoppers never left their homes, but dispersed as they were in time and space, constituted ever-shifting mass transnational markets in a global bazaar. Search programs gathered Web sites around topics and themes in moments to suit general or special interests. Consumers browsed, placed orders, typed in credit card numbers, printed the receipt, and waited for the merchandise to arrive courtesy of express delivery. Themes from the cultural and social realms emerged in attitudes toward the Internet as a marketing medium. Canadian Internet entrepreneurs needed venture capital to develop their ideas, but domestic lending institutions wanted collateral, which the mostly young businesspeople did not have. Thus many headed for U.S. money markets, where ideas could spark credit and funds, or to work in U.S. high-technology centers such as Seattle and Silicon Valley. Established brand names, such as L. L. Bean outdoor clothing and Lee Valley, a specialty tools merchandiser, combined catalog and Internet marketing to create a mass consumer market. Because any Web site could be anywhere, "national" customers no longer existed. Merchandisers and marketers could assemble a mass of consumers scattered all over the globe.[31]

Internet companies' Web sites were basically media and earned income from advertising. The mass sale of computers for personal, educational, and corporate use gave them a wide range of visitors. The fight for a market share of users reminded some commentators of early railroad days in the nineteenth century, when competing lines often drove one another into bankruptcy with ever lower prices to ship goods and ride. Casualties and debris, not to mention money, vanished into this virtual marketplace, and entrepreneurial also-rans limped off to die in the cyberspace graveyard.[32] In 1998, the U.S. Web portal Yahoo drew 100 times more hits than Canoe, Canada's leader. A total of 5 percent of Canadian shoppers, compared with 11 percent of U.S. shoppers, placed online orders. U.S. sites were first on the Internet and developed techniques that drew 60 percent of Canadian online spending. When the loonie lost value against the greenback in the 1990s, U.S. sites lowered prices to compensate. Though personal cross-border shopping by Canadians declined, their online shopping and sales rose. Consumers shared the transactional costs of this marketing system in delivery and customs fees but could escape local consumption taxes. Upper North American corporate acquisitions and mergers reflected the production and facility side of mass market consumerism. In the 1990s, Canadian firms spent $165 million (U.S.) on European acquisitions, down from $1.05 billion the year before, and Canadian Pacific Hotels allied with U.S. firms to move into mass market tourism in global markets.[33] Canadian life insurance companies, nursing home chains, telecommunications firms, and entertainment producers focused, instead of on global mass marketing, on cross-border markets, which were large enough to produce profits for them.[34] This development revealed distinctions between the two peoples. Canadian marketers hesitated to invest in Web sites, and they scrimped on the level of service offered to Internet buyers, unlike their U.S. competitors. Canadians also hesitated to divulge credit card information, whereas Americans did not. Internet customers in both countries initially worried about credit card security, but U.S. fears faded faster. Being latecomers to Internet mass marketing became a temporary advantage for Canadians, however, because they began to sell merchandise and services online to attract consumers about the time the recession began to lift.[35]

By the early twentieth-first century, Upper North America contained a sprawling and fragmented mass market of dispersed consumer groups. Cross-border mergers continued, and middle and upper managers mingled in transnational marketing. During the 1990s recession, the loonie fell against the greenback, but that made Canadian goods, services, and companies more attractive to U.S. entrepreneurs because their currency bought more, just as near par between the two currencies had the reverse effect by 2006. Mass merchandising takeovers in Canada doubled in value during the first nine months of 1999, and the U.S.-based Polo Ralph Lauren bought out Club Monaco, in one example. Patriotism vanished as a factor in Canadian mass market thinking, and regional patterns emerged. Quebecers shopped in provincially based stores, but western Canadians preferred U.S. merchandisers. Lower disposable incomes also made Canadians bargain hunters, as Wal-Mart's success revealed, while successful domestic mass marketers looked to the United States for future growth.[36] A few nationalists decried 1999 as a year of "hollowing out" because the depreciated loonie exposed domestic firms to "foreign" (i.e., U.S.) takeovers and experienced senior managers and professionals relocated.[37] Ottawa's 1999 statistics showed that "foreign" (mostly U.S.) companies controlled 31 percent of domestic operating revenues and more than 22 percent of assets, an increase over the previous year. Those companies grew faster than domestic competitors, however, in part because they were export oriented. In 1999, U.S. buyers put down $25 billion (U.S.) for 127 Canadian companies.

Had Canada's national soul been sold for a mess of mass merchandising pottage? Laments generally ignored what bankruptcies or failures might have meant in social dislocation, or job and economic losses, to Canadian communities. As economic nationalists had done since the 1950s, however, Peter C. Newman blamed Ottawa and implied that economic and corporate interlinkage would produce political integration.[38] No historical or contemporary evidence supported such a hypothesis, and no formal expression of interest in political union for economic reasons had arisen in Canada since the Montreal Annexation Manifesto of 1849.

Proximity and asymmetry encouraged shared cultural and social values and attitudes to disperse into an Upper North American mass merchandising and consumption system that grew increasingly prosperous over time. U.S., and later Canadian, manufacturers and merchandisers succeeded by serving mass domestic markets in Upper North America, however valuable foreign trade might be. Upper North America's scale and the success of both peoples created this transnational mass market. By 2007, it seemed that Ottawa's efforts to open global markets relied upon entrepreneurs and merchandisers to cultivate mass markets with brands and services, rather than mere agreements with other governments.[39] Globalization offered potential mass markets on a scale not conceived before, but Upper North America still constituted the most likely and most easily served market because cultural values and social systems, not to mention language, meant that Canadians and Americans did not see one another as foreign. Support services such as credit card and delivery companies were interlinked. The postal system was reliable and safe. All companies operated within the same business culture, as the idea of a North American Competition Commission to monitor mergers and maintain a free market context suggested.[40] The accumulated cultural, social, and other themes in the realms of dispersed relations encouraged and furthered Upper North American transnational mass marketing and consumerism from the nineteenth through the twenty-first centuries. Various interlinkages reinforced one another, but social and national political identities remained distinct. If this process was Americanization, as some critics asserted, it was Upper North Americanization, not a zero-sum game where one country's advantage was the other's loss, and it had no impact on the national identities of either people.

Chapter 8

Upper North American Commerce

"U.S. Senator Plays Hard Ball over Softwood" and "Montana Senator in B.C. Coal Mine Dust-Up." These headlines painted Max Baucus from Montana as a Washington politician Canadians loved to hate. His belligerent rhetoric into any live microphone made good copy as he waved off a string of North American Free Trade Agreement (NAFTA) and World Trade Organization (WTO) decisions that favored Canada's position on transborder softwood lumber disputes, and backed appeals and counterappeals that frustrated Ottawa and ran up enormous legal bills. He showed up unannounced at a coal project hearing in British Columbia's East Caetano region. He caused pandemonium when he insisted that the provincial government in Victoria had issued permits to rake in easy money and fund Vancouver's Winter Olympics while ignoring the poisons that headed downstream into his state of Montana. Baucus's fingernails-across-a-blackboard public style symbolized how U.S. politicians could exploit troubles in cross-border commerce for domestic advantage—but also how interdependent the regional components of the two national economies had become.[1]

To anyone who looked around in 2006, Upper North America's resources, countless organizations, workers, and markets had intertwined into a transnational system that supported millions of North American stakeholders and generated billions in private income and public revenue dollars for all levels of society and government. An elaborate secondary system of organizations brokered and hauled these goods, and all relied on think tanks to analyze problems and on lobbies to shape policy from municipal to federal levels and to reduce bureaucratic friction on the movement of goods and services from production through distribution to consumers. Canada had become the largest foreign exporter to thirty-nine of the fifty states and the largest importer from almost all of them. Its trade with Texas alone had risen to above $15 billion annually, and the entire two-way exchange hovered around $800 billion by 2006. When diplomats from the Canadian embassy's Advocacy Secretariat called at congressional offices, including Baucus's, they left charts, maps, and leaflets that capsuled how transborder commerce served U.S. constituencies.[2]

The energy sector was a case in point. In 2006 nearly 90 percent of U.S. natural gas imports, over 20 percent of the coal, and about 18 percent of the oil came from Canada. Power generation in both countries fed into shared regional grids. A cascade of systems failures in August 2003 blacked out the entire Northeast, all of Ontario, and states from Ohio to the Atlantic shore. Millions headed home on foot, jammed the Brooklyn Bridge, and after sundown sweltered in the silent dark. Satellite photographs at night showed an irregular black blotch akin to a vast inlet, girt on three sides by the lights of an industrial civilization. Unknown numbers of Upper North American industrial and service workers went on furlough until the power grid was restored. The events of September 11, 2001, had stalled dispersed transnational automobile production when Washington intensified security at the major highway ports. The economic system congealed, and companies lost millions of dollars an hour. During the blackout, it shut down entirely. Politicians and officials pointed fingers in all directions, but once the grid was restored, they focused on how to prevent a recurrence. The asymmetry-of-attention principle meant that Canadians far more than Americans (at least those below the borderland tier of states) understood that they were immediate and dependent stakeholders in transnational commerce and how such problems shaped the cross-border political relationship.

Extensive and expensive Ottawa-Washington commercial disputes touch thousands, and occasionally millions, of Upper North American stakeholders. Bellicose headlines and rhetoric about trade wars might persuade a stranger to North America that armored columns had mustered on the Great Plains to fight out a resolution. Officials in both governments correctly note, however, that 95 percent of the time 95 percent of all Upper North American commerce works smoothly to all stakeholders' mutual advantage. Ottawa and Washington in recent years have settled a salmon quota dispute in the Pacific Northwest by delegating decisionmaking to the provincial and state governments involved. Other disputes dissolved after negotiation or decisions under NAFTA and WTO systems for resolution. Washington and Ottawa accepted most such decisions, but from time to time the accumulated welter of domestic laws and regulations and domestic political interests have frustrated expectations and spilled into the courts and headlines.[3]

Origins of Interdependence

The foundations of this modern Upper North American commerce appeared even before Great Britain won control of eastern North America from Florida to Hudson's Bay, and west to the eastern Mississippi Valley in 1763. Trade routes for open and covert trade developed in and around settled Atlantic northeastern regions, and as part of the Great Lakes Basin's interior fur trade. The collective North American mercantile spirit bristled over regulations and centralized controls, a theme in the American Revolution and War of Independence that sorted Anglo North Americans into two political jurisdictions but had little effect on their free market commercial attitudes. Personal connections and economic needs soon generated mutual trade in such commodities as fish, furs, timber, grains, and imported finished goods. In the 1790s, migrants in the upper Champlain Valley and New York moved to work land on offer in Upper Canada. Montreal became the entrepôt for settlers and communities north of Albany, where John Jacob Astor built the Upper North American fur business that made him the first U.S. millionaire. Borderlanders defied Treasury Secretary Alexander Hamilton's effort to apply U.S. laws and collect trade duties, one of the few sources of income for governments of the day. Thomas Jefferson's quixotic 1807–9 Embargo to change British policies toward U.S. maritime interests only spurred borderland smugglers to greater efforts. Locals pursued illegal trade all through the War of 1812–15, and Americans exchanged beef on the hoof and other foodstuffs for British gold. When U.S. armies gathered near British territory, commissary agents could not feed them. Atlantic northeastern traders and merchants in Nova Scotia and Maine also ignored the war as much as they could to maintain their business connections.[4]

After 1815, immigrants dispersed through the Great Lakes Basin borderland, and Upper North American commerce formed increasingly complex patterns. Settlers and entrepreneurs mingled in Upper Canada and new states in the Old Northwest, such as Michigan and Ohio, as well as in established parts of New York and Pennsylvania. Regular shipping routes developed on lakes, but entrepreneurs built canals to improve borderland transportation. The Erie Canal from Albany opened to Buffalo in 1821 and expanded Upper North American commercial interests while it served farming areas around Lake Erie. Canals improved the Oswego and other rivers in the transportation revolution that served all of eastern Upper North America. Provincials and Americans settled, mingled, and did business, and by 1826 U.S. members of Congress concluded that this north country commerce had more value and future than the British West Indies markets they had long coveted. In 1827, fifty-three U.S. and several provincial vessels, both sail and steam powered, carried commodities and merchandise around the Great Lakes Basin. U.S. entrepreneurs invested in the provinces through this era, founding iron works in Gosfield Township in 1831 and the Eddy Match Company on the Ottawa River rapids in the 1850s. In 1836, the first provincial railway linked Montreal to Island Pond, Vermont, and Portland, Maine. Urban centers along these transportation routes—such as Buffalo, Montreal, and Chicago—by the 1860s served transnational as well as national and transatlantic commerce. Customs agents and consuls recorded a complex, ever more dispersed, diversified, and interlinked commerce as population growth stimulated Upper North American development. The first U.S. consul in the provinces appeared in Halifax in 1827. Others followed, and by 1860 a consul general in Montreal loosely oversaw a string of consuls from Halifax to Victoria, on the Pacific Coast. Commodities, goods, and people moved over the Upper North American transportation system of railroads and vessels. Cultural forces, the English language, commercial organization and management, legal systems, and social mingling facilitated this transnational development. Communications dispersed through the mail, then in newspapers that circulated, and finally on telegraph wires strung alongside railroad tracks.[5]

Both illegal trade and legal trade have always intertwined in Upper North America. In the 1800s, the U.S. Treasury sent undercover agents to track down smugglers that cost Washington revenue. These officers chased rumors, but borderlanders misled and defied them with conspiracies of silence. Local law officers proved reluctant at best to assist federal officials. Smugglers and their cohorts intimidated, threatened, and sprang suspects from jail. Even when trials occurred, local juries often ignored the evidence and acquitted the accused out of hand. Meanwhile, Britain shed its efforts to monopolize provincial grain when Parliament took a leap of faith and abolished the Corn Laws in 1846. Montreal merchants who had lost their protected British markets clamored for free trade with the United States, and they even urged political union in the Annexation Manifesto of 1849. U.S. interests fought to open Upper North American trade as well. The New Brunswick–born U.S. consul in Saint John, Israel Andrews, waged a one-man crusade for cross-border reciprocity with anyone who would listen, up to and including U.S. secretary of state William R. Marcy. Andrews lobbied provincial and U.S. politicians and businessmen. The Elgin-Marcy, or Reciprocity, Treaty of 1854 emerged as the first Anglo-American trade agreement focused on Upper North American affairs. Andrews lobbied U.S. senators and provincial legislators alike to ratify the treaty, believing that Upper North Americans shared a common destiny and that economic interlinkage would eventually produce a single country.

The Reciprocity Treaty was the first legislated and ratified effort to manage Upper North American commerce in the borderland regions. Nova Scotia coal went on the free list for New England markets, as did Pennsylvania coal for the Canadas. Timber floated down the Saint John River through both jurisdictions en route to the sea for export, but it now paid no duties. Half of all provincial exports soon headed south. Observers referred to a commercial continentalism, but provincials separated their economic interests and political allegiance. Politicians in both jurisdictions subsequently debated who had won or lost more from the Reciprocity Treaty, but businessmen and commercial journalists praised it.[6] Any trade arrangement creates winners and losers, but the treaty may also have helped to synchronize Upper North American business cycles. The depression of 1857 had a transborder impact, but U.S. demand for livestock and commodities rose sharply when the U.S. Civil War erupted.

Britain's proclamation of neutrality in April 1861 angered Republican politicians, who thought in economic nationalist terms and insisted that provincials had exploited the United States under the Reciprocity Treaty. Provincial supplies served Union needs, although after the South surrendered, Republican majorities cancelled reciprocity in 1866. An Upper North American coalition of business interests and politicians worked in vain to restore reciprocity under the treaty. But proximity, the early stages of the Industrial Revolution in the United States, and Upper North American interests sustained a growing trade and commerce that served hundreds of entrepreneurs. Thousands of producers and consumers relied on this increasingly complex transnational system. Improved transportation and economic services, such as credit systems and finance, supported these interlinked commercial activities. Prime Minister John A. Macdonald lowered Canadian tariffs in 1866, and Ontario and Quebec business interests persuaded politicians to promote a transcontinental railroad after Canada acquired Rupert's Land. They hoped to capture commodities and future markets for a national economy that would generate grand financial rewards.

A new region of the Upper North American commercial system had already appeared along the Pacific Coast by then. San Francisco supplied settlements in Oregon and Washington Territory in the 1850s, and farther north at Victoria on Vancouver Island. California miners came and went through the B.C. gold rush spasm along the Fraser River, but the Pacific Northwest's commercial character developed once settlers moved into the Puget Sound littoral, and San Juan and Vancouver islands. The Union and Central Pacific Railroads linked San Francisco with Saint Louis and the eastern United States in 1869 while the Canadian Pacific Railway (CPR) crept across the rugged Shield region north of Lake Superior. The CPR reached Vancouver in 1885, well after branch lines had come to northern Washington Territory.

On the Great Plains, the Red River Valley linked Metis and British settlements into an embryonic Upper North American region with Minnesota centers that had rail connections with Chicago. As prairie settlements spread, grain found export markets over U.S. railways before the CPR arrived.[7] In 1874, Ottawa proposed to stimulate transborder commerce with tariffs that favored U.S. over British goods. Both Washington and London rejected that idea, but it reflected how the Upper North American commercial system had begun to challenge Canada's transatlantic linkage with Britain. Ontario and Quebec business interests wanted Canada's industrial heartland in their provinces. Both Americans and Canadians saw railroads as developmental rather than service systems. They were mistaken. Upper North American stakeholders thought in transnational, not national, commercial patterns. Railroads and lake or river shipping facilitated and served markets, but they could not create production. Ottawa politicians, like their Washington counterparts in the 1850s, served special interests, and their schemes led to bankruptcies and the Pacific Scandal of 1873. The U.S. Upper Midwest became a regional heartland with Chicago as its hub, and the CPR linked into U.S. railroads to connect with a port to the oceans far closer than Toronto or Montreal. By the 1870s and 1880s, geography and proximity established north-south linkages that frustrated the transcontinental ambitions of central Canadian politicians. Meanwhile, Canada's source of funds and credit began its long shift from London to Chicago and New York.[8]

Ottawa's National Policy not only protected Eastern business interests; it also encouraged Upper North American commercial interdependence. High tariff barriers against U.S. manufactured products in the last quarter of the nineteenth century lured U.S. companies to build branches. Singer Manufacturing, International Harvester, National Cash Register, and Westinghouse all established plants in Ontario and Quebec to serve small markets there, and they hired local workers. This process only slowed the drain of Canadians to find jobs and other opportunities in the United States, because Canada's industrial base remained too small to absorb a growing population. The Great Lakes Basin transportation system and absence of immigration controls allowed Canadians easy access to a large market of seasonal and permanent U.S. jobs. Upper North American entrepreneurs both raised capital in New York and Chicago. U.S. businessmen of the time also developed in Canada what Secretary of State John Hay would later term the Open Door Policy in Latin America and Asia.[9] Domestic political interests in an open Upper North America encouraged economic development, but the ambitions and interests of entrepreneurs, producers, and consumers in the Great Lakes Basin and other borderland regions proved decisive in the long run.

Woods industries offer an example. Chemical treatment of wood pulp replaced rags as the basic raw material for paper by the 1890s. U.S. timber concerns worked stands of trees in states such as Minnesota and Michigan, and then in Quebec and Ontario. Mills appeared and railroads carried pulp wood south for northeastern markets. Later, investors built paper plants near the sources of supply and created another Upper North American industry. Steam, then electric high-speed printers and presses, produced millions of editions and magazines that reached expanding markets of urban and rural readers. Bureaucratic management in private and public organizations created another market for paper used for correspondence and records. Corporate reorganization followed. On the Pacific Coast, a San Francisco company bought the Lebanon Paper Company of Oregon, then acquired forest rights and built pulp mills as far north as Ocean Falls on the British Columbia coast. These operations consolidated into the Crown Zellerbach empire, which sold its products in coastal paper markets as far south as Los Angeles. In 1913, Congress removed duties on wood imports from Canada, and the Upper North American wood trade diversified and flourished through the 1920s until the Great Depression struck. World War II revived the U.S. market, and large lumber shipments once more headed south from British Columbia, Alberta, and the eastern provinces. Transnational acquisitions and mergers created other cross-border concerns up through modern times, such as when U.S. Weyerhaeuser bought British Columbia's MacMillan-Bloedel Company, International Paper and the Louisiana-Pacific Corporation acquired Canadian holdings, and British Columbia's West Fraser Timber Company bought a Seattle firm. An interdependent North American forest industry emerged over time that changed in response to markets, technological developments, private management, and national policies.[10] Domestic interests that sought protection for one reason or another could disrupt the operations of any Upper North American commercial system, but the underlying cultural, social, and economic forces nevertheless remained in place.

Politicians in both countries tended to focus on their constituencies and often lost sight of the larger context within which Upper North Americans worked. They also exploited themes from the cultural and social realms for partisan expediency, as the history of Canadian anti-Americanism revealed. Ontario and Quebec exploited such prejudices in their bid for power, and by the 1890s even private interests had come to appreciate how popular political fears might be manipulated. In the 1890 election, for example, Wilfrid Laurier's Liberals promoted reciprocity with the United States as their principal goal if put in power. Macdonald had sought reciprocity for decades, but without a blush wrapped himself in the Union Jack and claimed Laurier and the Liberals were in cahoots with Americans to sell Canada's British birthright to the United States. Power, not commerce, was at stake, but larger forces than political constituencies shaped the growing interdependence of the Upper North American economies. Legislation such as British Imperial Preference policies temporarily increased commodity and goods exports across the Atlantic from Canada, and trade with the United States eased between 1869 and 1899. But imports from the United States soon rose from 43 to almost 60 percent of Canada's totals, while those from Britain fell by more than half, from 56 to about 25 percent.[11] In 1910, the Republican president William Howard Taft offered now–prime minister Laurier a reciprocity arrangement. He proposed concurrent legislation to put it into effect. They agreed that treaties had inherent political difficulties, but each controlled legislative majorities so the matter could easily be settled.

Several political factors explained Taft's proposal. First, the Payne-Aldrich Tariff had raised U.S. rates, and Department of Commerce officials feared that Ottawa might retaliate on pulp and paper. If it did, powerful New York publishing interests might turn against the Republicans in the 1912 elections. Second, officials of the State and Commerce departments believed that the United States was the dominant force in an emerging Upper North American economic system. Canada, as a partner or satellite, would serve U.S. commercial interests because reciprocity would further the Open Door Policy's long-term objectives. Finally, Taft had a sentimental side. Villagers near his Quebec summer home always treated him like a father figure, generating his warm feelings toward Canada. The discussions produced bills, duly tabled, and Republicans voted reciprocity through both houses of Congress with large majorities.[12]

All indications suggested easy passage in Parliament, because Laurier's Liberals had a majority as well. When the prime minister tabled the reciprocity bill in 1911, the Conservatives raised no serious objections. A group of Toronto businessmen meanwhile decided that reciprocity threatened their domestic markets, but they couched their arguments in anti-American language. They knew U.S. tariffs would fall anyway and open markets for them, but they pushed Robert Borden and the Conservatives to oppose reciprocity to protect themselves in Ontario. While these discussions occurred, Champ Clark, the speaker of the U.S. House of Representatives, vocally supported reciprocity and remarked that it might lead to the Stars and Stripes snapping in the breeze all the way to the North Pole. Conservatives immediately cried that it was all about U.S. annexation, a false charge repeated in the Canadian press from sea to sea.

The outcry made Laurier hesitate, and the reciprocity bill stalled. Taft was astonished when Laurier next called a general election. The Liberals lost, but interests and market forces ensured that Upper North American economic interlinkages would keep progressing anyway. The election was more about the business of politics than the business of business, because once Prime Minister Borden was in office, he reassured Wall Street bankers that their money was safe in Canada, and the economic relationship continued. Patriotism in the pursuit of power was no vice in either country. Proximity, which nurtured shared cultural, social, and especially economic interests, strengthened the internal North American leg of the North Atlantic Triangle while the transatlantic leg progressively atrophied.[13]

From North Atlantic Triangle to Upper North America

World War I began a few years later, accelerating Upper North American economic integration and weakening Canada's transatlantic links with Britain. Washington declared neutrality in August 1914, but U.S. industry filled war orders, provided credits, and made loans to belligerents, and some of the resulting traffic came through Canada. U.S. firms founded new branch plants, and companies sold tons of war goods sent in allied convoys to British and European ports. The United States became a full belligerent in April 1917, and both Upper North American and transatlantic commerce quickened. U.S. officials, industrialists, and bankers believed that the war would deepen Canada's integration with the North American economic sphere, and they judged correctly. The range of commodities, products, and borderland routes of trade all diversified, and Canada's industrial modernization accelerated. By 1918, even commodity exports to Britain only slightly exceeded in value those going to the United States. More important, the economic impact of four grinding years of industrialized total war pushed Britain toward the impoverishment World War II would complete. By default, this ensured Canada's commercial integration with the United States.

After hostilities ended in 1919, postwar depressions settled onto Upper North America while the economies adjusted to peacetime conditions. The U.S. depression ended in 1921, but Canada's lasted for two more years. The protectionist U.S. Fordney-McCumber Tariff raised export costs, but that had little effect on the flow of Upper North American commerce. When Canada's economy recovered, the domestic middle class shared in the prosperity of the Roaring Twenties. A wide array of new U.S. consumer goods emerged from electrification, such as radios and toasters, and they all came onto the Canadian market. U.S. and branch plant cars and trucks crowded city streets and country roads, part of Upper North America's economic transformation into a market-driven system. Ottawa also welcomed new U.S. investment, which rose into the billions of dollars and built automobile plants in Ontario and pulpwood mills in Quebec. Upper North American economic integration continued, creating the world's largest bilateral trade relationship.[14]

The Great Crash in the New York Stock Market in October 1929 and the Great Depression that followed paradoxically wounded the transborder economy, but not Upper North American integration, because it devastated all Western economies. Canada's 1929 exports went in rough thirds to the United States, Britain, and other countries. Washington's protectionist U.S. Smoot-Hawley Tariff of 1930 slowed exports to the south while the Depression settled onto North America, but U.S. imports held at over 60 percent of Canada's totals. Geography, proximity, and the already interrelated threads of the two economies sustained these trends. Canada gained full sovereign powers in 1931, and the Imperial Economic Conference in Ottawa a year later failed to resurrect transatlantic trade. U.S. firms meanwhile revived branch plant building in Canada. In 1935, after protracted Ottawa-Washington discussions, President Franklin Roosevelt and Prime Minister William Lyon Mackenzie King concluded a trade agreement that lowered tariffs and put all Upper North American commerce on a "most-favored-nation" basis. Domestic producers who feared U.S. competition adjusted, while Anglophile Conservatives maintained in an ill-founded forecast that they could resurrect British Canada.[15]

European international politics fractured, while the Upper North American economy began to recover through the later 1930s. Nazi Germany launched World War II on September 1, 1939. The conflict swiftly engulfed other European powers and cut off the commerce both North American countries had developed there. President Franklin Roosevelt, still fearful of the isolationists' political power in Congress, hinted at future changes and sidled toward a tacit alliance with Britain and Canada, especially after France surrendered to Germany in May 1940. Canada and the United States both supplied war orders to Britain, but those became mostly self-financed as London ran out of cash and credits, which had a greater fiscal impact on Canada than the United States. Congress accepted Roosevelt's Lend-Lease Program, and Upper North American commerce surged. Ottawa incurred a rising trade deficit with the United States, but Mackenzie King's government refused Lend-Lease aid. In the 1941 Hyde Park Agreement, however, he tacitly accepted the United States as Canada's principal economic partner. That December, full U.S. belligerency expanded war-related trade and deepened commercial and economic integration with Canada. Binational agencies coordinated tariff-exempt war materials. Canada had no surpluses to offset its deficit with the United States, but by 1945 it had built a stronger and more diversified economy than in prewar years, while the book value of cross-border commerce soared. World War II thus affirmed and furthered Upper North American economic integration and interdependence.[16]

In 1945, Washington led the Geneva talks that produced the ill-fated International Trade Organization. Further discussions produced the General Agreement on Tariffs and Trade, and Ottawa hoped this organization would endure, restore international commerce, and offset integrated dependence on the United States. Congress, meanwhile, provided $300 million to help balance Canada's trade books. Ottawa officials next persuaded their wartime Washington colleagues to convince President Harry Truman that European recipients of Marshall Plan aid should be able to spend some of that credit in Canada. Otherwise, Ottawa would have to place a levy on U.S. imports. Truman and Congress agreed, because they saw such a concession as in their own and North America's interest, and they defended their decision to skeptics among U.S. commentators and the public. Senior Ottawa officials secretly suggested further economic integration with the United States when London decided against transforming the Commonwealth into a trading bloc. Income and other taxes, on consumption, had more than offset the government revenues derived from tariffs, so such a decision was easier to make than a decade before. However profitable to economic interests in both countries, deeper entanglement with the United States seemed unlikely. In 1948, Ottawa and Washington negotiated and almost formed a customs union, but Mackenzie King feared the Conservatives would lead an anti-American public backlash against his Liberals if he went ahead. So, while this was largely unknown at the time, the potential vagaries of partisan politics at that time foreclosed further steps in Upper North American economic integration, which was well advanced in industrial, fiscal, and commercial sectors in any event.

In the early Cold War years, U.S. investments developed Canada's strategic raw materials, especially uranium. Cultural and social similarities facilitated the shared Upper North American consumer boom from postwar middle- and working-class prosperity in both countries. Patterns of living and consumption became much the same, and the series of bilateral defense production sharing agreements and the construction of early warning lines in northern Canada as the Cold War unfolded created an asymmetrical, but real, Upper North American military-industrial complex. Meanwhile, transatlantic economic ties withered, and Britain increasingly became a historical "mother country" in economic as well as cultural and social ways as the character of immigration to Canada changed after 1945.[17] World War II had confirmed and accelerated Upper North American economic integration in all sectors as the countries became each other's principal commercial partners in a world that then had no alternatives. Canada's export/import ratios with the United States rose to the range of 85 and 75 percent for the rest of the century. Across the Atlantic, Western European countries organized a regional coal and steel group. Over time, this evolved into a stronger and more comprehensive trading bloc and then toward the more politically based European Union free trade system, which spelled the end of Canada's special economic link with Great Britain. The EU then developed common tariffs against all outsiders, such as Canada and the United States.

Economic nationalists in the later 1950s insisted that Ottawa had to redeem Canada from its economic dependence upon the United States or lose its political sovereignty. They urged the federal government adopt quasi-socialist policies to achieve those ends and often punctuated their arguments with anti-American rhetoric echoed by leftist political groups and media commentators.[18] But business leaders, particularly those in the auto industry, worked for further cross-border commercial integration. These two bodies of opinion makers were the contemporary incarnations of business and welfare liberals from the late nineteenth century. The major auto makers first lobbied and then worked with Ottawa officials in Lester Pearson's government to create a North American automobile industry rather than maintain two national systems. These efforts culminated in the January 1965 Auto Pact. Canada gained guaranteed shares of production and sales in the United States while both vehicles and components moved tariff free. An interdependent industry emerged, and the pact largely accomplished what its framers had hoped, although political negotiations might have stalled but for agreement among the industry's leaders. The pact managed an industry that constituted a major portion of North America's economic whole, but it needed to become more efficient. The larger market framework encouraged that, and it also provided a model and stepping stone to the Free Trade Agreement (FTA) and NAFTA two decades later.[19]

Energy sources were central to Upper North American industrial and trade agreements and traffic through the post-1945 era. U.S. money and expertise had pioneered early Canadian oil industries around Sarnia, Ontario, and Leduc, Alberta. Other developments for the U.S. market meant that by the 1950s Canada supplied nearly 40 percent of all U.S. energy consumption. The 1958–59 Borden Commission on energy exports relied upon U.S. advice to shape Prime Minister John Diefenbaker's 1961 policy. By 1969, President Richard M. Nixon's planners counted Canadian energy reserves as part of U.S. domestic capacity. Ottawa developed the trans-Canada pipeline to ship energy supplies to Ontario and Quebec, but also for sale in eastern U.S. markets. This liberated central Canada from Middle Eastern oil sent by pipeline from Portland, Maine. North American energy patterns went far beyond regional dependencies (insofar as reserves were concerned) into a near symmetrical interdependence. Shared oversight evolved when binational companies emerged. Washington seated an Alberta delegate on the U.S. Energy Council, which oversaw North American supplies and usage. Washington officials treated Canadian oil reserves and those who managed them as North American resources. Perspectives varied according to the political vantage point, because Ottawa deemed energy sources a national asset but Albertans insisted that, constitutionally, they were a provincial rather than a federal resource. In 2004, the Alberta premier agreed to set up a provincial office in the Washington Embassy Secretariat that had been established to lobby U.S. officials and Congress. On Canada Day two years later, Alberta mounted a fair on Washington's Mall, where the rest of

Canada was notably absent from the festivities. Throughout, Alberta's agents dealt directly with the U.S. administration. By then, Vice President Dick Cheney had twice visited the Alberta tar sands project. In all cases, energy producers, consumers, and regulators thought in terms of Upper North American regional markets.[20]

Upper North American electrical generation had foreshadowed this pattern from its earliest appearance. The technology that allowed long-range transmission did not emerge until the 1920s, but the 1903 Niagara Falls project served nearby domestic markets in both countries. By the middle 1930s, U.S. officials foresaw electricity shortages in the thickly settled Northeast for both consumer and industrial needs. More important, they anticipated that the United States would enter the expected war in Europe and would require massive amounts of electricity for both domestic consumption and aircraft manufacture because it involved so much aluminum. Ottawa minister C. D. Howe collaborated with members of Roosevelt's administration, and a cross-border regional industrial and electrical system based at the Shipshaw project on Quebec's Saguenay River emerged. U.S. money and expertise developed facilities that interwove the domestic and foreign policies of both countries in a way later Ottawa foreign policy analysts would call "intermestic."[21]

The 1964 Columbia River Treaty created similar circumstances in the Pacific Northwest. In some respects, it was a "Victoria-Washington Treaty," because B.C. premier W. A. C. Bennett cited provincial constitutional authority over resources to face down Diefenbaker's government and build the project with Washington State and Oregon. B.C. electric power went as far south as northern California in coming years. Quebec premier Robert Bourassa raised New York money for the massive James Bay hydroelectric project, which was only feasible with the transnational North American Northeast as its market. By the 1980s, a binational North American Electric Reliability Council oversaw a continental assembly of electrical regions where clusters of states and provinces shared oversight. The great blackout of August 2003 began in an Ohio plant and cascaded through the interdependent regional system.

After the great blackout, once internal and cross-border political finger pointing faded, the two national governments created a binational panel that worked with regional and local officials to reform the integrated system. Ottawa and Washington agreed, but Canadians who opposed energy exports to the south did not understand the systems' interdependency, nor that their usage ranked above that of Americans on the global energy user scale. The interwoven and integrated regional electrical systems underscored NAFTA's emphasis on services. In terms of planning, Alberta's deregulation studies and policies drew on California and Pennsylvania as well as provincial experience.[22] Throughout, Upper North American commentators and officials understood both the interdependency of this power generation and distribution network and the need for binational cooperation and oversight to effect change, as the aftermath of the 2003 blackout demonstrated.[23] At the same time, Ottawa and Washington moved toward a more comprehensive system of oversight than had existed. As in so many other ways, Upper North American commerce, whatever the commodity or service, had become about shared production to serve shared and common purposes, even if the relative values in and out appeared on annual trade reports as national deficits or surpluses.

Free Trade Era

NAFTA's framers and negotiators saw their goals in different ways, but the agreement became in operation about the management of a dispersed and interwoven three-country economic system, although the northern component far outweighed the southern section. In NAFTA, Ottawa and Washington granted each other joint supervision (along with states and provinces) of their dispersed cultural, social, and economic integration and interdependence. Some Canadian and U.S. commentators and politicians concerned about domestic employment levels decried a loss of sovereignty in both countries, but centralized control over economic affairs ebbed as Upper North American interdependence rolled on. By the 1970s, Upper North American economic integration persuaded Pierre Trudeau's Liberal government that Canada had three options: encourage; discourage; or offset that integration with other links. Ottawa dallied with but never seriously pursued the third option in any concerted way. By then, the European Community had become its own bloc, and no other markets existed to offset the United States for Canadian commodity producers or consumers.[24] Nationalists argued for state-centered policies, but the National Energy Program (NEP), Foreign Investment Review Agency (FIRA), and Canadian Development Corporation failed to live up to their expectations. FIRA was a regulatory body set up primarily to limit U.S. investment, but Wall Street was the major source of Canadian capital. The NEP needed continued increases in the global price of oil, but they fell instead, after Ottawa had expropriated U.S. energy operations in Alberta at vast fiscal and political expense. Together, the three programs created massive debts and alienated the domestic business community, U.S. interests, Washington, and, most important for domestic politics, Alberta. The NEP spawned Reform, a western populist party, and discredited Canadian nationalists who still nursed anti-American grievances. NEP also demonstrated the limits of Ottawa's power in a federal system.[25]

Meanwhile, Donald MacDonald's Royal Commission argued that comprehensive free trade with the United States, the first option, was the most feasible strategy for national economic development after all. Wall Street already supplied most of Canada's capital and credits; but without investor confidence, interest rates would rise. Trudeau quit politics, and an election put the Conservative Party in power. The new prime minister, Brian Mulroney, took up the pursuit of an Upper North American commercial agreement that became the FTA. In the United States, the FTA aroused little political interest except among protectionists, conservatives nervous about trade deficits, and labor groups fearful of job losses. In Canada, the FTA generated a furious national debate and became the principal issue in the 1988 election. After a campaign whose ideological anti-Americanism generated much rhetoric, voters returned Mulroney to power and President Ronald Reagan's Republican congressional majorities enacted the FTA after intense Canadian lobbying and political maneuvering in both capitals.[26]

The FTA had a thousand authors because of the myriad special and political interests that besieged the negotiators' ears, and the final document read that way. It also had an institutional structure with a secretariat and, at Ottawa's insistence, an adjudication system to resolve disputes. Tariffs declined according to a progressive schedule, but Congress and Parliament retained the right to use countervailing duties if they suspected the other party of unfair domestic subsidies. The FTA had a limited ability to offset Upper North American economic and political asymmetry. That very asymmetry, along with domestic ideological and economic fears, kept opposition alive. Ottawa and Canadian opinion groups were far more skeptical than Washington and U.S. groups about the FTA. It thus linked the opposites of free markets and protectionism. Furthermore, Canadians feared job losses more than Americans. An early 1990s depression related to the collapse of stock values in communications technologies evoked "we told you so" cries, but analysts and commentators all agreed that the FTA could not control global or continental investment or economic cycles.[27]

Meanwhile, Mexico City and Washington began free trade talks, and Ottawa, after some hesitation given the bruising domestic political battle over the FTA, joined in. Better a troika, Mulroney's government reasoned, than leave Washington to play the smaller, separated partners against each other. The 1992 debate over NAFTA was more controversial in the United States than Canada. The Texas billionaire Ross Perot claimed that he could hear a "giant sucking sound" as NAFTA siphoned U.S. jobs into Mexico. He bankrolled a Reform Party and ran for president with opposition to NAFTA as his principal plank. But the Democrat Bill Clinton won, while Canadians also went to the polls. The Liberals reduced the Conservative Party from a majority to two seats. Clinton and his advisers wondered if the new Liberal prime minister, Jean Chrétien, would sign NAFTA, given the anti-American rhetoric of his campaign. But Clinton discovered that in Canada, as in the United States, elections were about the business of politics, not the business of business. Chrétien signed.

Upper North American economic integration quickened after, and partly as a consequence of, NAFTA. Between 1989 and 1994, Canada's trade with the rest of North America rose by 75 percent, but with the rest of the world only by 10 percent. Canadians by then invested more per capita in the United States than Americans did in Canada. NAFTA extended regional interdependencies, and economic interlinkages dispersed farther and deeper into U.S. states. By 2006, thirty-nine states had some part of Canada as their largest trading partner and dispersed Upper North American commerce reached $1 billion a day as traffic clogged border crossing points. Borderland provinces and states began to deal with each other directly and created state-provincial agreements and regional associations. Concurrent licensing and other reforms soon allowed truckers from either country to carry loads in both directions. NAFTA's prime facie success led U.S. ambassador Gordon Giffin to express Washington's potential interest in a "NAFTA Plus," further evolution of the agreement, and much conference and editorial attention was devoted to this both before and after the events of September 11, 2001. Washington's fixation on border security clashed with Ottawa's concern for economic access, but steady consultations, studies, and agreements such as the Smart Border Plan emphasized NAFTA's management role while serving domestic political interests in each country. By 2006, enhanced border surveillance and inspection increased the costs of transporting goods for cross-border markets but had no impact on the volume of trade. Simply put, whatever vestigial regret and opposition existed in either country, Upper North America's dispersed, integrated, and interdependent economic system had become a vital binational interest.[28]

The institutional structure of this dispersed Upper North American economic system included a Free Trade Commission, a Secretariat, a North American Development Bank, and a Border Environment Cooperation Commission. A phalanx of other cross-border organizations operated in the public, private, and nongovernmental sectors. Officials and corporate leaders met continuously with their counterparts, while an array of professional organizations held annual conferences with politicians and leading Ottawa and Washington administrators. Information flowed, even swamping policy analysts and commentators who followed transnational trade operations. NAFTA tribunals resolved most disputes in an evenhanded, unbiased way, although some became the subject of protracted and expensive appeals and counterappeals that often involved the WTO. Media attention ensured that this legal maneuvering occurred in the light of day, and the asymmetry of attention principle led some Canadians to question the overall value of NAFTA. But such public doubts had no impact on policy in Ottawa.

For the most part, unless domestic political interests wielded political power in Washington and/or Ottawa, this resolution process reflected Upper North American shared cultural and social values, mores, and respect for due process. Litigation lingered where domestic interests had wealthy and politically powerful forces behind them. In those cases, the principle of asymmetry meant that for Canadians, U.S. special interests and Washington became the villain of the matter. Even so, a decade of experience convinced most observers that though NAFTA had been oversold and falsely vilified, it worked to mutual advantage.

Upper North American economic integration and interdependence thus progressed.[29] At the same time, the FTA and NAFTA had created management regimes for a process that had been under way for over a century. In 1870, 29 percent of Canada's trade was Upper North American. By 1950, that portion reached 50 percent. After 1999, it fluctuated between 80 and 85 percent and showed no signs of decline over the next seven years. NAFTA also strengthened Upper North American production and markets while the EU solidified. Canadian exports to the EU fell by two-thirds between 1971 and 1996, and trade with all of Asia remained flat at about 4 percent, the level over the past two decades. Upper North American commercial integration and interdependence deepened and dispersed as service industries such as advertising, banking, and insurance saw their north-south business double.

By 2006, Upper North America had millions of stakeholders in a system that had become part of their daily expectations and support. The cross-border alliance in the Upper North American borderland that succeeded in stalling Section 110 of the Illegal Immigrant Reform and Immigrant Responsibility Act suggested how those shared cultural, social, and economic interests could come together in a shared policy position on border management. Upper North American integration built as much in those collective personal ways as it did on commercial interests of profit, growth, and loss. Upper North America had become in some ways its own domestic (or intermestic) sphere, and that was how Canada's Embassy staff in Washington portrayed the relationship in their maps and charts for advocacy work with Congress.[30]

Throughout, the border continued in some respects as a line of Upper North American divergences. A 12 percent rise in U.S. disposable incomes through the 1990s, for example, compared with a 5 percent decline in Canada. U.S. stock market values rose 340 versus 95 percent for Canada throughout the same period. Some economic models posited that trade should decrease with distance, yet some provinces traded less with nearby states and more with one another. Were national linkages more powerful than cross-border pulls? The answer is unclear, because all provinces traded with an array of states. New Brunswick and British Columbia, respectively, had Maine and Washington State as their leading export/import partners. Alberta's principal partners were Texas and Ohio, and Nova Scotia's were Texas and Massachusetts.[31] Canada's productivity and standard of living meanwhile continued to lag against those of the United States, as they always had. Moreover, Upper North American commerce improved, but it did not equalize conditions in the provinces and states involved. Some Canadian producers exceeded U.S. productivity in metals, wood products, and printing and publishing but lagged in retail, finance and real estate services, and electronics.[32]

Overall, integrated and interdependent Upper North American commerce remained the same smorgasbord as ever, and while Canada lagged the United States in several economic indicators, NAFTA improved each indicator within its national context. Patterns remained fluid in the free market North American context. The asymmetry-of-attention principle led Canadian commentators to focus on commercial problems such as softwood lumber and the beef trade rather than the 95 percent of trade that worked smoothly. It also seemed that while Washington's security concerns complicated commerce after September 11, 2001, better systems and management reduced the frequency and extent of disruption.

Conversely, disputes such as softwood lumber that NAFTA failed to resolve infected and soured Ottawa-Washington political relations, in part because many Canadian politicians and commentators made them metaphors for overall relations. In 1999, U.S. Trade Representative Charlene Barshevsky criticized Canadian pharmaceutical patent laws that restrained U.S. companies and Ontario regulations that inconvenienced Minnesota sport fishermen. Maine Senator Susan Collins complained about Prince Edward Island's fish plant subsidies. Canadians resented what seemed to be U.S. interference in purely domestic affairs.[33] Ottawa grumbled when border officials confiscated bird seed made from hemp, an illegal substance under U.S. law, and that appliance and bingo card makers sold their goods below cost to undercut domestic Canadian competition. Ottawa and Washington each complained about the other's sugar policies, but they stood together over foreign-made steel entering North American markets. Both countries maintained protective agricultural legislation that dated from the Great Depression. Domestic U.S. politics made the 1920 Jones act that limited shipbuilding to domestic yards unassailable through NAFTA. Competition between wheat growers across the border from one another pitted political interests in a conflict that would cost more than any short-term gains for either party. Over time, a domestic sense of entitlement, and hence a political interest, remained entrenched whether times were good or bad. Most such disputes produced hearings, appeals, and then counterappeals, often moving on to the WTO. Whether adjudicated within Upper North America or by international bodies, such disputes guaranteed international trade lawyers near-permanent careers.[34] Washington, Ottawa, and the NAFTA Secretariat could not control the domestic politics of special interests that had the ability to embroil both governments in seemingly interminable transnational and international legal disputes. At least the "war" casualties were in budget lines, not lives.

Disputes over resources associated with a national sense of a birthright in either country posed particular problems for negotiation and adjustment. Water was a potent example with a deep history, easily shared as a medium of transportation, but less so as a commodity, or for the resources it contained. An 1892 joint commission to manage fisheries and pollution in the Great Lakes ran aground on politics in that transnational basin but laid foundations for the Boundary Waters Treaty and the International Joint Commission (IJC) of 1909. The IJC remained in operation, studied disputes under its jurisdiction, and recommended joint policies to Ottawa and Washington. For example, it oversaw hydroelectric projects and the Saint Lawrence Seaway that opened in 1959. Five years later, President Lyndon

Johnson and Prime Minister Lester Pearson signed a treaty to manage the seaway's watershed. U.S. interests also devised proposals to gain access to freshwater from Canada. One idea involved a dam on James Bay with giant flumes to channel freshwater south of the border. Less fanciful was California's Sun Belt Water Contract with the B.C. government. Ottawa cancelled the agreement unilaterally, and Sun Belt won a settlement under NAFTA's Chapter 11 that protected contracts from ex post facto regulations. The Nova Group in Sault Sainte Marie, Ontario, and the McCurdy Group in Newfoundland that essayed commercial arrangements with U.S. partners failed for similar reasons. Recent interest in Great Lakes water as a commodity to ease arid conditions in the Southwest, conversely, aroused emotional opposition. Entrepreneurs, officials, and politicians failed to convince the Council of Great Lakes Governors, which included the Ontario and Quebec premiers. The council banned exports and requested protective binational legislation. The IJC agreed, but policy to manage Great Lakes and other freshwater supplies remains in dispute.[35]

An Upper North American furor over the beef trade had its historical origins in the western Great Plains ranching industry of the 1880s. A regional borderland culture and society developed that extended from Alberta to Texas, and herds mingled until border controls appeared in the 1910s.[36] By the 1990s, a transnational Great Plains beef industry had developed. Abattoirs and meat packing and processing plants mostly closed down in Canada but expanded in the United States. Demographic asymmetry meant far larger markets there, and hence lower processing and shipping costs. A total of 90 percent of Canadian beef headed south, and from there to foreign markets in an interdependent Upper North American system. When Bovine spongiform encephalopathy, or "Mad Cow" disease, appeared, the U.S. Department of Agriculture (USDA) closed the border to Canadian beef for fear of an epidemic. Popular, scientific, economic, political, and bureaucratic forces combined into a maelstrom of argument and ill feelings that defied swift or clear resolution. Regional political pressures focused on both Ottawa and Washington in a protracted and well-publicized dispute that spilled through election cycles. Negotiations produced an agreement, and the USDA reopened the border. The protectionist Montana Ranchers-Cattlemen Action Legal Fund convinced a local federal judge to sustain the ban on Canadian beef, but the Washington-Ottawa agreement obliged the USDA to pursue the case on appeal. It won a dismissal from the Ninth Circuit Court of Appeals in July 2005.[37] Ironically, by then, the Upper North American beef industry had reverted to two domestic components.

Had the softwood lumber dispute been easy, as a Canadian official involved in the FTA negotiations noted, they would have settled it. NAFTA negotiators also set it aside, but they came to a separate limited-term agreement that was renewed in 1996. When that was about to expire in 2002, both sides let it lapse. NAFTA's managerial magic had limits, but in effect its regulations applied. The public debate was over protectionism and allegedly illegal subsidies, with powerful domestic political interests behind each side. The dispute worked through NAFTA and WTO resolution systems, but domestic U.S. interests had sufficient political power in Washington to prevent a settlement. Asymmetry also persuaded American officials that they would win a negotiated settlement because of superior bargaining abilities, and they believed that a separate agreement would protect both their domestic interests and the Upper North American economic management system. Ottawa favored binding adjudication to balance U.S. power.

The protracted stalemate over softwood lumber demonstrated how cultural and social values and attitudes shaped not just economic outlooks and interests but also Washington's and Ottawa's political behavior. Meanwhile, they seconded the management of Upper North American lumber commerce to international lawyers. Canadian public opinion interpreted the matter as a metaphor for the entire binational relationship. Moreover, domestic interests in both countries exploited the matter at election time to gain votes, and the Liberal Party exploited anti-Americanism and the dislike of George W. Bush's administration in a failed bid for reelection in early 2006. Throughout, both federal governments wrangled state, provincial, corporate, consumer, and lobby interests to move in the same direction. Washington State, Georgia, Idaho, and Montana politicians and interests had rejected any negative NAFTA or WTO judgments, appeals, counterappeals, or submissions. In British Columbia and Ontario, interests and governments had done the same. The issue moved politically beyond its place in Upper North American commerce. The annual value of the softwood business in 2000 was about $10 billion, less than a week's worth of the two nations' total annual trade. But interests in both countries treated the dispute as a zero-sum game.[38]

Opponents and allies, meanwhile, formed cross-border coalitions. The U.S. National Association of Home Builders, lumber buyer groups, and American Consumers for Affordable Homes fought the U.S. Coalition for Fair Lumber Imports in the media, with local politicians, and in Capitol Hill offices. The Montreal Free Trade Lumber Council financed American consumer groups, while U.S. lumber companies supported the coalition.[39] The

Canadian media vilified all prominent U.S. personalities, especially Max Baucus and President Bush. The dispute also revealed Canadian misapprehension about the U.S. political system. Presidents cannot command Congress as prime ministers with majorities can Parliament. Conversely, Ottawa lobby groups do not have anything like the sustained power of lobbies in Washington. Frustrations and rhetoric spilled onto front pages. A B.C. company sued Ottawa for breaching NAFTA obligations and called President Bush "gutless. " Senator Baucus labeled B.C. policies "Stalinist."[40] Impasse and insults waxed and waned while negotiators worked. In early 2006, Canada's Conservative Party won a minority government and shortly announced that Ottawa and Washington had arranged a deal that had been close for some time. Stephen Harper, the new prime minister, took advantage of the timing to take political credit.[41] Even then, the complexity and mixture of interests involved meant that this settlement was by no means final. The softwood lumber issue remains a case study in the way a serious cross-border commercial dispute can ramify into the cultural, social, economic, and political realms of dispersed relations.

Any formal trade agreement had limitations for the management of commercial relations through time because of how global, transnational, and national conditions changed. Whatever rulings emerged from panels or WTO appeals, the costs of legal action were roughly equal—but not the national bank accounts.[42] Even so, domestic politics and affairs left Ottawa officials with no choice but to proceed as best they could. Agreements such as NAFTA and institutions such as the WTO had limitations because concerted sovereign interests could assert themselves at any time in transnational disputes. NAFTA also contained controversial provisions, such as Chapter 11, which allowed private companies to sue for loss if either government violated regulations. A B.C. funeral operator lost his suit in Mississippi's supreme court over a state decision that he alleged had driven his company into bankruptcy. The U.S. United Parcel Service won against Ottawa on charges of monopoly practices and subsidies to Canada Post's courier companies. Ohio-based S. D. Myers won a substantial award from Ottawa after Canada's environment minister banned exports of polychlorinated biphenyls solely to favor a domestic company. Some Canadian nationalists feared that NAFTA had become a supergovernment, and "Public Citizen," a Washington based anti-free-trade group, argued that Chapter 11 claims would erode domestic courts' authority.[43] Many, such as the Chrétien adviser David Zussman, believed that "the reality of economic integration is outstripping the ability of government . . . to understand the trends or to shape the challenges of North American integration." George Haynal, a former chair of the Canada–United States Partnership, urged integrated Upper North American policies and procedures.

Neither country nor its economy could escape the other, and by 2006 it seemed clear that the two sovereign entities jointly managed Upper North America's free market.[44] Integration had evolved into selected interdependency, and public support for NAFTA remained high. Divergent attitudes remained, however, because Canadians saw disputes as symptoms of the overall relationship, whereas Americans saw them as business and political issues. This remained true despite strains after the events of September 11, 2001, that imposed U.S. geostrategic outlooks on Upper North America. The objective then became to balance security and market access to sustain the transnational economic system. Much attention also focused on NAFTA's evolution, a theme that ran through reports from the American Assembly and the Council on Foreign Relations in 2004. These reports fed into the Security and Prosperity Partnership, to which NAFTA leaders agreed in March 2005.[45] Stakeholders in the myriad interdependent parts of the interdependent economies generated ever greater collective influence in Washington and Ottawa to resolve problems, avoid self-defeating retaliation, and reduce barriers to the transit of goods and people.[46] The significance of global politics and the war on terror notwithstanding, domestic politics still shaped policy. The interdependent Upper North American economy had enormous momentum and embraced millions of stakeholders in three, not just two, countries. Despite the apparent policy status quo of the 2005 Security and Prosperity Partnership, conversations about a customs union and other future evolutionary stages of integrated and interdependent Upper North American commerce continued, although under increasing strain from the ever more complex and stringent border security system that unfolded after September 11, 2001.[47]

Chapter 9

Fiscal Integration

Bank of Canada governor David Dodge credited Ottawa's economic management for the 2004 rise of the Canadian dollar, dubbed the "loonie," against the U.S. dollar, or "greenback." The ratio of the two dollars, however, reflected more the greenback's decline in global fiscal markets than Canadian performance or policies. Two years earlier, the loonie wallowed at close to a 40 percent discount. Then Dodge thought perhaps it was time to create a single Upper North American currency, which would have meant the greenback, if Washington agreed. Other economists thought that if Upper North American economic integration continued, Ottawa might as well declare the U.S. dollar Canada's national currency and be done with it.[1]

A currency has both practical and symbolic qualities. On the practical side, the dollar is a medium of exchange, a way to quantify the absolute or relative value of merchandise or property. It is also a bookkeeping entry. Currency's symbolic quality relates to national sovereignty, can be a source of patriotic pride (or shame), and has national images and slogans stamped on coins or printed on notes. For Canadians, the loonie also symbolized fiscal independence from Americans, and both people were conservative about changing their currency. When Republicans proposed that Ronald Reagan should replace Thomas Jefferson on the U.S. nickel, a chorus shouted them down and Jefferson remained where he was. In terms of their relative value, the two dollars danced a pas de deux throughout the twentieth century. Asymmetry and proximity steadily integrated Upper North American fiscal markets and commerce while Canada remained, in economic terms, a small country. If Ottawa decided to protect the loonie's value against the greenback, it could spend all its cash reserves and then some without nudging the differential in any noticeable way.[2] Dodge, however, conjured the illusion of monetary sovereignty, with interest rates set for national needs, although the Bank of Canada's official rates tended to follow Washington's Federal Reserve Bank rate. Still, in the 1990s, the one-dollar or two-dollar question, apart from monetary convenience, revealed the intertwined and interdependent economic history of Upper North America.

Fiscal Relations Develop

This story began in the late eighteenth and early nineteenth centuries, after U.S. independence established the two Upper North American jurisdictions. In the Great Lakes Basin and Atlantic Northeast borderland regions, local settler economies operated on the basis of barter, credits, and promissory notes. Several currencies appeared in various places, but the British pound was the official provincial currency. North Americans preferred Spanish milled silver dollars because they held value and could not be shaved. Both had been legal tender in British North America since1763. After 1783, the American Revolution left the states saddled with unpayable debts until the government of the Constitution became the national fiscal policymaker. In the rest of British North America, provincial merchants used the Loyalist-imported York (for New York) rating, which set one Spanish dollar equal to the value of eight British shillings. In the 1790s, the U.S. Congress accepted Secretary of State Thomas Jefferson's recommendation for a decimal dollar system and chartered the First Bank of the United States (BUS). The BUS printed interest-bearing promissory notes as a national currency. In borderland regions, meanwhile, locals continued to barter, but merchants with established contacts in major centers such as Montreal, New York, Albany, and Boston wrote bills of exchange with trusted partners to do business.

The War of 1812 complicated but did not halt such transactions, and more complex Upper North American fiscal interlinkages developed after 1815. U.S. capital underwrote the Bank of Montreal in 1820, and that bank had an agent in New York three years later. U.S. investors also bankrolled the provincial entrepreneurs who developed the Ottawa Valley's timber resources. Various promissory notes circulated in Upper North America, most with decimal and dollar denominations. Little legislation in either jurisdiction governed this informal system. The BUS survived into the 1820s, but as domestic U.S. politics evolved, Democratic Party propaganda transformed it into an aristocratic institution, symbolized by haughty Nicholas Biddle, the BUS president. President Andrew Jackson detested Biddle and in 1832 put federal funds in state banks, which killed the BUS. Local banks in the states and provinces, meanwhile, used dollar denominations that circulated freely in the Upper North American borderlands. London often disallowed provincial currency, but that made no difference locally.

Many banks in both jurisdictions collapsed during the panic and depression of 1837–41. Lord Durham's 1840 Report united Upper and Lower Canada into a single province, and Francis Hicks, inspector general from 1848 to 1851, then prime minister to 1854, established a decimal dollar that served Upper North Americans as a medium of exchange. They were by then stakeholders in a regional economy that overlay two jurisdictions. In 1853, London accepted pounds and dollars as legal currency in the provinces. The 1854 Reciprocity Treaty, which Hicks strongly supported, led to Canada's formal adoption of a decimal dollar in 1858. The other provinces followed suit between 1860 and 1871. The Ottawa government had full internal fiscal powers after 1867 and decreed that new Dominion banks would be federally chartered. A Uniform Currency Act confirmed Canada's decimal dollar, with notes partially backed by gold. These were legal tender in all British North America and facilitated Upper North American commerce.[3]

The 1861–65 Civil War in the United States forced fiscal reforms because the scale and cost of the campaigns brought Abraham Lincoln's government near bankruptcy by 1862. Congress's Legal Tender Act nationalized currency in dollar Treasury notes called "greenbacks" to combat counterfeiting, a familiar fate for printed notes in this age. The common decimal system facilitated brisk cross-border wartime commerce, and provincials did business in greenbacks, despite their 60 percent inflation rate by July 1864, when Washington went off a gold standard. By then, a third of all paper money was bogus, so Congress created the Treasury Department's Secret Service to hunt counterfeiters. Congress also banned state banknotes, although many—such as the New York Mechanics National Bank in 1865 and the First National Gold Bank of San Francisco in 1870—put out limited-issue notes for local use. The U.S. Treasury also exchanged silver-backed Certificates for silver dollars in 1878 but converted back to a gold standard the next year.

Upper North American fiscal interlinkages continued, and Montreal and New York banks exchanged dollars at near-par based on market values of gold. Ottawa now minted its own coins and gradually repatriated British coinage to London.[4] Each country's currency continued to rest on gold's market price, so compatible systems facilitated trade, commerce, and fiscal convertibility throughout Upper North America. In the 1870s, Canada drew investment and current account capital from two directions, east from London and north from northern U.S. banks. London supplied some capital needs, although proximity, Upper North American economic development, and convertible currencies meant that Dominion investment houses also looked south to New York. The Quebec government floated a loan there in 1879. Canadians by then also looked to Chicago banks because the population and economies had grown in the Great Lakes Basin. In 1900, Canada drew 85 percent of its capital from Britain versus 13 percent from the United States, but World War I's financial impact changed that pattern.

Before 1914, both Upper North American governments reshaped their banking systems. The United States gradually centralized control over banks following financial panics in 1893 and 1907. In 1913, Congress created the Federal Reserve Bank to regulate money supplies, credit, currency, and interest rates. When Canada entered World War I in August 1914, Ottawa suspended gold conversion for its dollar and maintained parity with the greenback. It then printed banknotes to pay for the war effort, which inflated Canada's currency values. Ottawa throughout remained the lender of last resort, but it granted banks limited authority to issue their own notes to depositors. President Woodrow Wilson took the United States into war in April 1917, but U.S. belligerency was too brief to produce much inflation, so by 1918 the Canadian dollar had declined against the greenback, and fell another 15 percent by 1920. In the 1920s, Upper North American capital flows outweighed transatlantic movement. New York became Canada's fiscal center, where Canadian businessmen increasingly did business. Regional patterns continued around Chicago, and on the West Coast around San Francisco. Major Canadian and U.S. banks also sent agents to the other's business centers. Ottawa returned to a gold standard in 1926, and the two dollars exchanged at par. When Ottawa abandoned the gold standard in 1931 as the Great Depression deepened, however, Canada's dollar value declined against the greenback. U.S. investment in Canada meanwhile rose to just over $4 billion (U.S.) by 1930, and, the Great Crash notwithstanding, declined only slightly by 1936.[5] Five Canadian banks had U.S. branches by then, and by law the majority of any national bank's board of directors had to be British subjects. This effectively kept U.S. banks and branches out of Canada. British investment to Canada during this same period rose from $1 billion to $2.75 billion but declined again by 1936. Canadian investment in the United States, meanwhile, reached $1 billion by 1930, and higher after 1936. Investment to Britain through the same period declined by 30 percent.

Political pressure from Congress, meanwhile, had reformed U.S. banking. A legend arose during the Great Crash and subsequent collapse of many U.S. banks that they could not give depositors their cash because managers had transferred these deposits to redeem investments. Many in Congress believed this, and the Glass-Steagall Act was designed to separate financial services and prevent any recurrence. The act passed narrowly in 1933. Banks were separated into investment or commercial institutions.[6] Despite its narrow margin of passage, the Glass-Steagall Act remained in force. U.S. retail banks also remained state, not federally, chartered as in Canada, and the loonie and greenback traded at near par.

In 1934, Ottawa fixed its dollar a penny or so below the U.S. dollar (until 1947) and created the Bank of Canada as an analogue to the U.S. Federal Reserve. Because of the inflationary experience of World War I, many Canadians moved their money into U.S. banks for safekeeping during World War II. The Canadian and U.S. dollars were within a few cents of each other, and the United States remained on a gold standard. When the war ended, U.S. industrial and financial institutions were intact and sound, whereas Canada's small industrial and financial sectors were in a shaky condition, and only the United States had the fiscal reserves and ability to help. Ottawa and Washington were both in firm control of their banks and currencies, however, and New York became an unofficial market for the Canadian dollar, which was devalued nearly 10 percent against the U.S. dollar under the floating exchange system. Ottawa's currency reserves were also low, despite the wartime influx of U.S. dollars from the Alaska Highway project and other American spending.

By 1947, Canada also had a severe U.S. dollar shortage, which generated a balance-of-payments crisis with the United States because of the asymmetry of Upper North American commerce and fiscal holdings. World War II accelerated those trends and focused fiscal and economic activity onto military affairs in all three countries. The war's scale, destruction, and duration virtually bankrupted Great Britain by 1945, so Ottawa had to rely on the United States because Canada's small economy could not survive on its own. From Washington's perspective, Canada was part of a North American system, and that inclined U.S. policymakers and politicians to be sympathetic about Ottawa's fiscal needs. After Canadian representations, officials in Harry Truman's administration convinced Congress that Ottawa's lack of currency reserves and trade deficit with the United States threatened to foreclose an important U.S. market. Congress agreed that Marshall Plan dollars sent to Europe could be spent in Canada under specified restrictions, and their arrival eased Canada's balance-of-payment problem.

Binational Fiscal Interlinkages

Europe's wartime economic and political destruction also left Canada alone in North America with the United States, which furthered Upper North American fiscal integration. By 1957, the United States supplied 57 and 85 percent of Canada's total and direct investment. Britain had almost vanished from the charts. U.S. direct investment soon rose sixfold, to $113 billion (U.S.), and stock-market investment rose by a multiple of fourteen. Comparable investments from Canada to U.S. markets rose, respectively, thirty-eight and twenty-two times to levels of $76 billion and $44 billion (Canadian). Upper North American suburban and consumer growth expanded capital flows and furthered fiscal integration through investments, credit, sales, and dividends as Canadians en masse became cultural, social, and fiscal North Americans in the 1950s. The Auto Pact, energy trade, the Free Trade Agreement (FTA), and the North American Free Trade Agreement (NAFTA) shook loose many restraints on cross-border fiscal affairs.

From 1991 to 1996, direct U.S. investments, loans, and deposits to Canada rose respectively by 42, 132, and 157 percent. None of this was Washington's deliberate policy. The world wars and U.S. growth combined with Europe's prostration exaggerated the forces of proximity and asymmetry. Canada was now fiscally Upper North American. Canadian investment increases were equally dramatic, however, and per capita far more Canadian money went south than U.S. investment came north.[7] Geography, proximity, asymmetrical interdependence, and the absence of any alternative made millions of Canadians and Americans stakeholders in their Upper North American fiscal system. This accelerating economic integration alarmed nationalists such as George Grant and Walter Gordon, who became minister of finance in Lester Pearson's government. As policy developed, however, pragmatism trumped ideology.[8]

The Canadian and U.S. dollars exchanged at par until 1962. Then John Diefenbaker's Conservative government devalued and fixed Canada's dollar at 71/2 percent below the U.S. dollar and weathered outrage from a public that expected equivalency. Pearson's Liberal government floated the dollar to escape inflationary pressures that the Vietnam War had injected into the U.S. economy, while nationalists on Canada's ideological left such as Mel Watkins called for a policy of fiscal independence. Pearson and his successor Pierre Trudeau, however, maintained Upper North American commercial connections to sustain Canadian prosperity. In 1970, a severe trade deficit and balance-of-payments crisis, principally with Japan, led Richard Nixon's administration to take the U.S. dollar off the gold standard and institute financial controls. When Canadian officials called Treasury Secretary John Connally about this to complain, he bluntly replied it applied to them the same as everyone else. Ottawa thus faced another balance-of-payments crisis with the United States, and Trudeau headed for Washington to confer directly with Nixon. He discovered that the White House agreed with Connally that Canada was a small part of the overall problem. Further discussion brought the two administrations to an accommodation on their fiscal relations. Throughout, the purchasing power of Canada's dollar was a direct result of its value relative to the U.S. dollar.[9]

Throughout the 1970s and early 1980s, Upper North American economic integration and interdependence continued, but whatever fluctuations the U.S. dollar endured on global money markets, the Canadian dollar sagged against the only currency that truly mattered, the greenback. Eventually, that gap would fuel the domestic debate over a common currency. For the moment, attention fell on commerce, and as the Macdonald Commission had reported, any expectation that Ottawa could prevent, let alone reverse, Upper North American commercial and fiscal integration and interdependence with the United States vanished except for ideological critics. Trudeau's later nationalist policies sapped Ottawa's solvency and sparked a political crisis with Washington that turned out his tired government at the next election.[10]

Brian Mulroney and the Conservatives worked to restore a positive tone in the political realm and negotiated a commercial agreement with Washington. Europe had become a trade bloc with common external tariffs, and Canada's only feasible economic and fiscal ally, the United States, was also its only neighbor.[11] Interlinkages in the cultural, social, and political realms eased the Mulroney government's decision to propose a free trade arrangement, and after acrimonious legislative haggling that lasted until the eleventh hour, President Ronald Reagan signed the FTA in a Rose Garden ceremony on September 28, 1988. In fiscal terms, banking and investment houses had already increasingly intertwined across the political border. Close personal relations also existed among senior members of the private sector, and special agencies, such as the North American Securities Administration Association in Washington, that represented and assisted Ottawa with U.S. governments about securities regulation. In short, many conduits of an Upper North American fiscal network were already in place, which eased decisions at the center of the two governments. Ottawa's principal problems lay within its domestic political constituencies. During the FTA negotiations, asymmetry of attention meant that Canadians became involved at the public as well as interest-group levels, but Americans did not at a public level, though members of Congress had serious concerns. U.S. election cycles were fixed and turned on domestic and foreign issues. In Canada, fiscal matters were largely ignored, buried beneath the more volatile questions of identity and the still widespread view that overall economic integration with the United States would produce an eventual political amalgamation. Before long, however, discussions in the early 1990s folded the FTA into NAFTA in 1994 in a trilateral accord that included Mexico.[12]

In fiscal terms, the currency gap was the major concern among Canadian economists and officials. The question of Canada's ability to compete economically on Upper North American and international levels remained open. The media reported daily how the asymmetry of opportunities and rewards drew ambitious, talented, and educated Canadians south. NAFTA provisions eased this selective brain drain, which was less significant in and of itself than for the symbolism of a developed country unable to retain its best and brightest people. The Royal Bank of Canada (RBC) economist John McCallum noted that point, and he wondered if Canada would matter by 2010. Forecasts suggested that a policy status quo would leave federal and provincial governments with ever less working capital for their programs. He called for a thoroughgoing market-driven business culture that implied further Upper North American interlinkages. He also separated fiscal from cultural and social themes, although these informed and spurred discussion within the economic and political realms. Meanwhile, government agencies and think tanks such as the C. D. Howe and Fraser institutes echoed his arguments and issued detailed studies to urge further economic integration.[13]

Canadian banks, meanwhile, pursued their own transnational strategies. Despite their historically minor role in the United States, their transformation into Upper North American institutions began in 1984 when the Bank of Montreal (BMO) president, William Mulholland, persuaded his board to buy the Harris Bank in Chicago on the rationale that in terms of market potential, Chicago equaled Ontario. The BMO's foray also fit with U.S. domestic banking reforms. Globalization, the FTA, and NAFTA had all nudged Washington to alter U.S. financial regulations. Congress ended restrictions on interstate banking and allowed banks, brokerage and securities firms, and insurance companies to merge. American Express, Chase Manhattan, Wells Fargo, and Citicorp began to operate as national financial institutions in an economy fifteen times larger than Canada's with a well-established global presence and influence. Their wealth, efficiency, and array of services eclipsed anything Canadian banks could offer, but the BMO and others further dispersed into U.S. markets and accelerated Upper North American fiscal integration throughout the 1990s. In the United States, transnational political thinking and demographic shifts strengthened domestic support for banking reforms in rural areas, small towns, and suburban regions that largely erased opposition to fiscal and economic integration and interdependence in Upper North America.[14]

Ottawa bureaucrats also wanted to close the productivity gap between Canada and the United States. The gross domestic product ratio of 12 to 1 in favor of the United States in the 1980s had become 14 to 1 by 1999. Particular sectors more than the general trend troubled Canadian observers. The Internet commerce ratio was 15 to 1, Internet employment 16 to 1, electronic industries 38 to 1, and software and Web site development 100 to 1. Traditional Canadian manufacturing had fallen from a high of 80 percent to the 60 percent range of U.S. levels. The U.S. economy had modernized, but Canada's had stagnated. Overall productivity remained at 85 percent of U.S. levels throughout the 1990s, and other factors troubled Canadian economists.[15] Ottawa's accumulated debt and deficits, a fall in interest rates, and lower prices for commodities combined to depress the loonie, by now the common term for Canada's dollar, against the greenback. Federal and provincial debts, except for Alberta's because of its energy boom, increased, as did annual deficits. The *Wall Street Journal* added insult to injury when it dubbed Canada an honorary member of the developing world, and New York lenders pressed for reforms or suggested that Ottawa would pay higher interest rates on loans and credits.

After the 1992 Canadian election, the new Liberal government enacted domestic fiscal reforms. It cut transfer payments to provinces and met Wall Street's concerns. To greater effect, Ottawa paid down debts and cut spending. The loonie continued toward its nadir of a nearly 40 cent deficit against the greenback, and at that point Canada's leading economists, Richard Harris and Thomas Courchene among them, argued for pegging the two currencies at the same valuation and negotiating a shared currency. Reuven

Brenner, tongue in cheek, warned that such a policy would expose national economic mismanagement and produce unemployment among monetary specialists and central bank bureaucrats, not to mention delegations to the International Monetary Fund.[16] Some suggested "North American monetary unit" or the Latinesque "amero" as the name for a new common currency. The Canadian Nobel laureate Robert Mundell, who had advised Ronald Reagan's administrations and the European Community on monetary policy, knew that national sensibilities, and hence domestic politics, would block all efforts to establish a shared currency, whatever interest Washington displayed in the idea, and thus far it had shown none at all.

Furthermore, Upper North American integration could, however, push Ottawa to cede monetary sovereignty, but the European Union experience had shown that need not affect political independence. Upper North American economic and fiscal interdependence and integration meanwhile continued to grow, although each slip of the loonie against the greenback evoked fresh media rhetoric—apocalyptic or Olympian, depending on perspective and the relative values.[17] Withal, the loonie remained a fiscal and political symbol, albeit one that implied low productivity, high interest rates, low investment returns, and high tax rates. The border seemed to separate a limping economy from a thriving one, because the United States remained the inevitable yardstick for measuring Canada's national economic and fiscal health.[18] Fiscal integration had already created a virtual Upper North American system, which was not always apparent without a close study of financial reports. Different management styles masked shared fiscal attitudes and values. Cultural and social commonalities—such as educational programs and standards, legal systems, corporate organization, and proximity—allowed Canadians and Americans to work interchangeably in the branch offices and headquarters of binational fiscal organizations. Stock market expansion in the 1990s drew millions of medium-sized and small stakeholders in both countries into fiscal integration, just as the Internet did for investment research and transactions. As brokers competed for clients, fees declined and investment became a mass market for consumers in Upper North America. Canadian fund managers evaded Ottawa's limits on foreign investment in tax sheltered retirement programs with what were called "clone" accounts.[19] Officials of both the Montreal and the Toronto stock exchanges wanted binational partnerships to form regional clusters in this increasingly shared market, and the New York Stock Exchange president anticipated that all NAFTA countries would in time interlink for Internet trading. In the summer of 2000, the New York–based technology exchange

NASDAQ opened a Montreal office with costs and transactions in U.S. dollars. Any company that listed had to meet U.S. regulations. An elliptical courtship began between officials of the Toronto and New York stock exchanges, although any eventual marriage seemed some years off.[20] U.S. and Canadian business firms engaged in a flurry of mergers and purchases and, asymmetry aside, Canadians were active suitors. Their transactions outnumbered U.S. initiated mergers 265 to 170 between 1994 and 1999. Canadian companies also spent 28 percent more than U.S. firms in cross-border acquisitions. Furthermore, many Canadian high-technology companies now listed first offers in New York, not in Toronto or Montreal.[21]

By the early twenty-first century, investment market U.S. dollarization seemed well under way. Ontario, with one-third of Canada's population, had become an annex of the U.S. economy with 90 percent of its exports bound for U.S. markets. Paradoxically, public opinion surveys, increasingly central in Upper North America's followership politics, reported that while only 37 percent of Canadians wanted closer economic ties with the United States or supported a common currency, commercial and fiscal integration continued apace with no active public or political opposition. A majority in western Canada even wanted to scrap the loonie. U.S. policymakers took little heed of these domestic debates on their northern flank, although a U.S. Senate report endorsed the idea of a single Western Hemisphere currency. Senator Connie Mack of Florida encouraged Latin American countries about this idea, and Canada, if it wanted, could also join. He meant that Ottawa was free to peg the loonie to the greenback.[22]

The Jean Chrétien government, meanwhile, left the loonie afloat and built up trade surpluses. This policy favored exporters over consumers because shared cultural and social values, attitudes, and styles of living, as well as proximity, familiarity, and established connections, meant that three-quarters of Canadian purchases came from the United States. Whatever the relative currency values, Upper North America had become a single consumer market. Meanwhile, the loonie remained for both commentators and the public a symbol of national identity and independence that defied economic theories and practice, although fiscal and overall economic integration continued.[23] The euro's success (and Britain's adherence to the pound) showed that while a currency of value and account could become a currency of everyday exchange, emotional attachment to tradition remained. The lagging loonie was at a discount on national economic sovereignty, but many transnational institutions in multiple jurisdictions that de facto were working on fiscal integration only loosely fell under Ottawa's control. The public debate was about identity and politics, while asymmetrical fiscal integration continued. The interrelated and interdependent complexities of this process defied simple characterization.

By the late 1990s, several alternatives to the loonie/greenback dilemma had emerged, but there was no clear sense of what policy would develop. Some eschewed policy altogether—ignore the differential and let free market forces restore the loonie or allow U.S. dollarization by default. Others argued for pegging the loonie and greenback at the same value in each jurisdiction and treating them as a single currency insofar as global markets were concerned. A few suggested that Ottawa negotiate a shared dollar or adopt the greenback. That would make Canada a component in a United States–centered Upper North American fiscal system.[24]

Most Canadians and Americans ignored all this discussion, which appeared in the financial sections of Canadian newspapers but barely at all in the U.S. media. On a pragmatic level, Canadians felt better off if the loonie bought more in the United States on a given day, just as Americans felt better off if the greenback bought more in Canada. Business operators adjusted to differentials and assumed that better times would follow bad. U.S. tourist operators in Florida, meanwhile, accepted loonies at par to hold their clients. As a result, the recession that struck North America in the winter of 2000–1 had a greater impact on cross-border spending patterns than relative currency values.[25]

The loonie's low value against the greenback continued to disturb Canadians. Ottawa hinted that currency traders were at fault and launched a public relations campaign to bolster public confidence, but this had no effect on the loonie/greenback ratio. Officials pointed out that the greenback had fallen on global markets. That offered little solace, and given Upper North American fiscal and economic integration, the value of the euro, yen, or pound against the loonie was irrelevant. The European Union was Canada's second-largest trading partner, with 4 percent of total values. Canadians also invested more in the United States per capita than Americans did in Canada, where over 90 percent of foreign direct investment came from U.S. sources. A 2005 Statistics Canada report showed that foreign control of domestic assets amounted to more than $1 trillion (Canadian), and 62 percent of that came from U.S. investors.[26] Furthermore, for all this mania over the two countries' currencies, few noted that transnational banking operations had become a significant force in Upper North American fiscal integration.

In the spring of 1998, first the RBC and BMO, and then the Canadian Imperial Bank of Commerce (CIBC) and Toronto Dominion (TD), posted banns for corporate nuptials. They campaigned for public support and Ottawa's approval, arguing that if united they could protect Canada from foreign (i.e., U.S.) competition and improve the country's international position. If Ottawa denied the mergers, however, the banks argued that they would be unable to compete in international markets and could become vulnerable to foreign (i.e., U.S.) takeovers. Moreover, Toronto could well become a regional, not a national, banking center. Observers noted that these arguments were designed for domestic consumption and went on to mock big, rich Canadian banks with high profits getting bigger and richer by picking the wallets of ordinary Canadians. Populist, partisan, and political bias underlay much of this commentary. Finance Minister Paul Martin made a show of deliberation, then forbade the mergers, a decision derived more from public opinion than Upper North American policymaking. Canadian banking officials, meanwhile, had accelerated their North American development, which Ottawa paradoxically supported, and even facilitated, with revised foreign ownership rules that allowed U.S. banks to move into the Canadian market.[27] New York's American Express Company established the Amex Bank of Canada. Chase Manhattan, First Boston, the Mellon Bank, and J. P. Morgan opened Canadian branches and marketed financial services such as credit cards, loans, and investment, but not retail services for depositors.

The development of Upper North American fiscal integration changed domestic Canadian banking in two ways. First, U.S. banks established a strong corporate presence and operations in Canada, where they competed in regional and national markets from the Atlantic Northeast to the Pacific Northwest. Second, senior officials in Canada's banks concluded that Ottawa was more concerned about domestic politics than their future, so they implemented plans to develop the U.S. market.[28] Banks from both countries thus became transnational through partnership and purchase strategies. Canadian bank officials now emphasized their North American operations at annual meetings and in speeches, press releases, and publications. The BMO's Harris Bank, the seventh-largest foreign-owned bank in the United States, acquired new partners in a southern belt from Arizona to Florida to serve Canadian retirees and business interests. By 2000, more than half of the BMO's income was in the U.S. market. This played asymmetry for advantage, just as Canada's car and parts makers had done after the Auto Pact. The BMO also bought a Chicago discount brokerage firm, and then a New York financial services bank and investment advisory firm in Silicon Valley.[29] The RBC followed a similar strategy, investing in America Online for

Internet banking. RBC president John Cleghorn proclaimed that the RBC was North American, and it formed Internet partnerships with an Atlanta bank and a New York securities firm. The purchase of Centura Bank in Rocky Mount, North Carolina, established a regional base for the large merchant banking market in the U.S. Southeast and combined various financial services under one corporate roof. By 2006, the RBC boasted seamless cross-border services, and almost 18 percent of its employees were in the United States.[30]

Other Canadian banks followed the BMO's and RBC's lead. TD purchased New York City's Waterhouse operation, the third-largest U.S. discount broker, with more than 4,000 branches. Next, TD formed a partnership with the huge U.S. retailer Wal-Mart, which put branches in Wal-Mart stores in dozens of small U.S. communities.[31] CIBC negotiated affiliations in New York, Atlanta, Los Angeles, and San Francisco. Once the U.S. Federal Reserve approved the purchase of a small Chicago bank, the CIBC opened under its own name. Next, it convinced Winn-Dixie supermarkets in southern states, and Safeway in California, to set up machine kiosks linked to call centers. In 2000, CIBC announced a Madison Avenue office tower to show its "strong commitment to New York City." Canadian Internet banking services ran into difficulty, however, because, while Americans trusted the Internet more than Canadians for consumer shopping, the reverse was true when it came to personal banking. At the retail level, competition was also much higher than Canadian banks were accustomed to, with hundreds of banks at work in any given area. In 2004, Standard & Poor's found that the big Canadian banks in the United States were also less efficient than their U.S. counterparts, which had consolidated through mergers from twenty-five to a handful and become more productive and profitable in the process, especially in regional markets.[32] Overall, Upper North American banking convergence worked on four market levels: local, regional, national, and transnational.

Cultural and social integration as well as asymmetrical economic integration and interdependence lay beneath the evolution of Upper North American fiscal integration. Nuances existed among various regions, but in the cultural and social realms, Canadians and Americans interacted seamlessly with one another. NAFTA also eased the transition. Success gradually shifted the banks' financial centers of gravity, and though officials encountered variations in cultural and social attitudes between deceptively similar peoples, commonalities and familiar social and business systems eased adaptation. In 2006, TD hired the former Canadian ambassador to the

United States, Frank McKenna, who had many contacts among U.S. political and corporate elites. U.S. banks also exploited niche opportunities in Canada.[33] Banks and other financial service organizations migrated and mingled institutionally much as people and entrepreneurs had done, and they created millions of new stakeholders in dispersed relations in the process. When Ottawa rejected new domestic merger proposals, Canadian analysts dismissed what they termed small thinking from a bygone age. If the RBC or TD could not offer automobile lease financing or insurance, for example, U.S. companies would step in, and the profits would flow to U.S. rather than Canadian shareholders. Moreover, as U.S. banks merged and grew, their counterparts in Canada slid down the global ranking scale and became potential prey to takeovers.[34] Could Toronto- or Montreal-based banks and security companies compete against U.S. banks as their principal domestic, let alone international, rivals? Citigroup, for example, had assets of nearly $5 trillion (U.S.), more than the combined assets of Canada's five largest banks. Canadian companies also now are regularly listed on the New York Stock Exchange and/or NASDAQ. Two-thirds of domestic mergers in 2000 were of U.S. companies in Canada, and the top ten investment firms were half United States–owned. When Ottawa's 2005 budget removed all limits on foreign investment in Canada's tax-sheltered retirement programs, some feared that loonies would pour into U.S. investment houses and Canada would lose analysts, fund managers, and brokers.[35]

Washington policymakers had favored domestic U.S. bank mergers to reduce the large number of small institutions. When the Bank of America and Fleet Boston Financial merged, the scale of the resulting firm spurred Canadian banks to renew merger efforts in Ottawa. The Canadians also called for an open fiscal border to attract European as well as U.S. interests—in effect, globalize. Those that adopted a free market mentality had already done well, despite the recent recession, thanks to their new holdings and a tougher U.S. management style.[36] An unexpected but limited government intrusion into North American banks ensued after the events of September 11, 2001, as federal agents hunted for assets that al Qaeda and other terrorist groups might have buried in Upper North American institutions. Though transnational trade suffered delays and added costs from enhanced security at entry ports, fiscal integration operations continued through electronic networks, which are largely independent of physical movement. Little noticed during all this, the Bank of America moved into Canada and CIBC acquired rights to issue American Express Cards in

Canada's domestic market.[37] Upper North American fiscal integration remained a work in progress.

Once established in the United States, Canadian banks were national institutions in a North American context, just as Citicorp was in Canada. Throughout the 1990s, when the Federal Reserve posted new interest rates, the Bank of Canada had paused and then followed suit. If Federal Reserve chair Alan Greenspan sniffed a recession and suggested lower rates, both banks made much the same announcements in succession. Critics claimed that Ottawa was letting the United States set domestic policy, so the Bank of Canada issued fixed dates for rate announcements, supposedly to demonstrate its independent decisionmaking but actually more to focus media attention on Ottawa. U.S. interest rates remained significant, however, because many Canadian foreign debts were in greenbacks and interest payments rose and fell with the two currencies' interwoven course. Asymmetrical economic integration also meant that even if domestic Canadian conditions did not necessarily warrant shifting interests rates, Ottawa had to follow fiscal suit, especially if U.S. inflation rose.[38]

The loonie/greenback ratio had other ramifications. Throughout the 1990s, Canadians spent heavily on cross-border shopping, although the recession and low-value loonie nearly halved day trips. U.S. travelers brought more greenbacks into Canada, however—from $6.9 to $8.6 billion (U.S.) between 1998 and 1999—because Canada was a bargain. Some Americans even sent their children to Canadian universities because already-lower relative tuition levels declined.[39] Nationalists again feared creeping Americanization, but the Consumer Price Index revealed only small fluctuations. Debt servicing went up for the Halifax Bridge Commission, whose payments were calibrated in U.S. currency. Finally, Canada's export growth owed more to U.S. abilities to buy than to the falling loonie, and Canadian currency depreciation exposed domestic firms to U.S. buyouts. The evolution of Upper North American fiscal integration thus looped back into the loonie/greenback differential because devaluation by default reduced domestic prosperity. Critics condemned Ottawa's failure to adopt U.S. policies, lower taxes, reduce regulations, and ease protectionism for the estimated 40 percent of private companies that relied on government subsidies. Ottawa politicians would not, however, abandon state-centered policies that protected constituency interests any more than would their counterparts in Washington.[40] Economists knew that while the loonie would never match the greenback on a global scale, Canadians would retain it for emotional, psychological, sentimental, and political rather than fiscal reasons, as a Bank of Canada investigation confirmed.[41] Moreover, other transnational economic developments overtook and submerged the currency issue, so larger questions waited in the wings of the public policy stage. For example, how would a customs union, or the "NAFTA Plus" the New York Council on Foreign Relations suggested in 2005, affect currency differentials? The issue ramified widely while cross-border fiscal integration continued.[42]

Official Washington, apart from analysts and Treasury Department officials responsible for Canada policy, paid little attention. U.S. economists knew that the weak loonie earned Ottawa a high trade surplus from exports to the United States. Partially market-driven dollarization evolved once the FTA was in place for the convenience of binational accounting, but U.S. economic difficulties depressed the greenback through 2006. The forces of asymmetrical fiscal integration remained in effect because of the transnational economy.[43] Meanwhile, ever more Upper North Americans became stakeholders in this transnational economic system and adjusted to currency fluctuations. To keep or gain customers, tourist operators often accepted the other country's dollar at par or a discount/premium according to posted rates. Major league sports organizations paid athletes in greenbacks. That, along with small spectator markets, drove some Canadian teams to the United States. Canadians seeking capital in high-technology fields drew from U.S. investors or offered shares on NASDAQ, but not the Toronto Stock Exchange. Boston's John Hancock Bank offered longer terms and better rates to Atlantic Canadian entrepreneurs than would Canadian banks. U.S. film stars in Canadian-made movies received salaries in U.S. dollars.[44]

The loonie/greenback debate of the 1990s opened a window onto the complex permutations of Upper North American fiscal integration after the inception of the FTA and NAFTA. Individuals and organizations acquired greater scope and freedom to shape conditions while dispersed fiscal forces intermingled the two peoples as free market actors. Throughout, Canadians measured their material well-being in terms of the greenback and the living standard of Americans. Canadians looked out; Americans rarely looked in. The realities of domestic political life meant that Ottawa politicians retained their atavistic reflexes about sovereignty vis-à-vis the United States. But as asymmetrical fiscal integration continued, Washington and Ottawa both relaxed controls over financial industries. Ironically, deeper cross-border fiscal integration could well stimulate Canada's domestic economy. Eased foreign ownership restrictions beyond NAFTA stipulations could draw more capital to Canada from Wall Street. The business organization Industry

Canada argued for a reformed fiscal regime that included lower corporate tax rates and incentives to modernize. That implied greater acceptance of free market values, so money making became a public good instead of a private vice. Finally, the tacit became overt. Proximity and asymmetry offered benefits, and the United States held the only economic (if not cultural or social) benchmarks that mattered.[45] Commentators on the political left saw these developments as a compromise of sovereign economic independence and continued to insist that cross-border fiscal and economic integration would ultimately produce political absorption into the United States. This debate played out in ever narrower circles, however, and was divorced from policymaking.[46] Both Liberal policymakers such as John Manley and the Conservative politicians who formed a minority government in Ottawa in January 2006 urged domestic tax reforms to reflect free market thinking.[47]

Free market champions in Canada still felt as though they were pushing string uphill. Inherited cultural and social fears entangled with anti-American rhetoric often nudged discussion into cross-border comparisons of attitudes and values with ritual assertions of sovereignty. Ottawa's claims about the free market notwithstanding, Canadians overall retained faith in their governments as economic managers. Delegates to an Ottawa-sponsored "Culture of Opportunity" asked why Americans saw tycoons as leaders while Canadians saw them as plutocrats. No clear answer emerged, but a U.S. guest, the economist Lester Thurow, argued that "what you need is leaders, not debate." An observer noted:

> If there is a single defining difference between Canadians and Americans it is not higher tax rates or lower productivity results, it is our continuing capacity not only to accept but also to celebrate mediocrity. With government of any stripe, we are all too willing to agree. In debate, we applaud the banal. In business we support second best.[48]

Political circumstances as well as ideology shaped such views. Democratic politicians everywhere tend to respond to their constituents and keep moist fingers in the air. The two most important and influential political regions in Canada, Ontario and Quebec—with Alberta and British Columbia in the West forming a close third—determined which party would take power in any particular government. Indeed, the balances of strength in the 2006 vote suggested that an era of future minority governments might have emerged. The longtime historical habit of reliance on the liberal state in Canada meant that social welfare and liberal business camps existed in both the major parties. Old bromides may have rung hollow in the early twenty-first century, but they sparked reflexive ideological tics at election time.[49] Brian Mulroney rode the neoconservative hurricane of the 1980s that propelled Margaret Thatcher and Ronald Reagan into power as free market reformers, but that economic philosophy sank more deeply and widely into their home political ground than it did in Canada. NAFTA's dispute settlement mechanism and the World Trade Organization comforted Canadians more than the prospects of greater wealth excited them. Private enterprise pursued Upper North American and fiscal integration and interdependence in tandem with a cultural economic conservatism. U.S. auto companies invested in Canada because of the Auto Pact, but relative productivity aside, Canada's health care system meant that they did not have to bargain with union negotiators over expensive benefits. Canadian voters in provinces that needed fiscal support retained a high tolerance for paternalism and transfer payments from Ottawa. Fiscal forces, meanwhile, reinforced and accelerated transnational free market integration.[50]

Fiscal Integration Matures

The cultural and ideological currents at play affected investment returns. Between 1950 and 1999, for example, $100 (Canadian) broadly invested in U.S. stocks would have become $65,256, compared with $16,507 if in Canadian stocks. Average returns diverged sharply after the early 1980s as comparative taxation increasingly favored Americans and the loonie declined against the greenback. This divergence affected ever greater numbers of Canadian investors and generated a scattered but potentially powerful lobby of clients and investment firms. Banks and trust companies pressed to end limitations on investment in tax-sheltered registered retirement savings plans (individual retirement accounts, in U.S. terminology). Furthermore, securities investment stimulated job creation, and commentators cited differences to show why Canada had lower overall economic activity and higher unemployment rates than the United States. Proportionately, far more Canadian than American investors were involved in transnational fiscal integration, and snowbirds who wintered in the southern United States constituted a strong lobby through alliances with U.S. groups. The U.S. Securities and Exchange Commission (SEC), as well as Canadian provincial securities commissions, granted Canadian institutions the authority to manage retirement funds for these part-time residents from north of the border to keep them coming.[51]

During the 1990s, the personal computer revolution and the burgeoning Internet created new virtual and actual dimensions for Upper North American fiscal integration. Would-be inventors and investors found Canadian banks, tax laws, and fiscally conservative attitudes restrictive. Americans were more eager for speculative high-technology investments and more comfortable with bright young men and women in jeans and sneakers managing high-technology industries. U.S. banks and investment companies were also more receptive than their Canadian counterparts to new ideas and more willing to take risks. So the Toronto stockbroker Gerry Goldberg took his clients to New York, where he got e-business proposals onto the NASDAQ exchange. Mark Schwartz represented Canadian companies from an office in Washington to escape federal and provincial controls in Canada. Even domestic bankers advised technology clients to head south. This trend added to the 13 percent of publicly traded Canadian companies that reported U.S. earnings in 1999. Some opened "headquarters" offices in New York to list on NASDAQ but left all other operations in Canada. High-technology startups tripled the value of Canadian companies trading on U.S. exchanges to about $175 billion (U.S.) between 1990 and 1998.[52]

Capital shifted within this Upper North American system for the same reasons it went anywhere: security, returns, and short- and long-term profits. U.S. taxation rates were higher, but so were earnings. Moreover, investment made in Canada was often de facto made in the United States because of so many binational organizations and so much cross-border interdependence. This convinced the U.S. financial watchdog Standard & Poor's to open a Toronto office in 1993 and compete directly with Ontario's Dominion Bond Rating and Quebec's Canadian Bond Rating services. NAFTA had put all regulatory institutions into a North American context. Borders ceased to be jurisdictional barriers, and the asymmetry of opportunities and fiscal resources emphasized U.S. advantages as freer markets developed. So when Standard & Poor's and Moody's reminded Ottawa and provincial governments in the early 1990s that deficits and debts meant higher interest rates, politicians took notice. Fiscal integration produced restraint, and tax surpluses paid down Ottawa and provincial debts throughout the later 1990s.[53]

Political borders were perforated because the ideology of state sovereignty had little place and less utility in dispersed Upper North American fiscal relations and selected interdependent integration by the early twenty-first century. Canadian investors, both large and small, paid just as much attention, if not more, to Washington than to Ottawa, sending more money south when U.S. interest rates rose and less when they fell. U.S. markets wavered and slumped in early 2001, and values fell simultaneously in Canada. From early 2002, interest rates in both countries sat at historic lows, until in 2006 the cross-border fiscal fandango went into its next round. Surveys revealed popular confidence in both nations' central banks to manage fiscal affairs. Polls also identified problems about tax rates and venture capital funds that might discourage U.S. investors from risking their money in Canada.[54]

In the modern era of Upper North American fiscal integration, regulatory agencies adopted shared perspectives to guard investors against such predatory practices as price manipulation and insider trading that periodically shook investor and public confidence.[55] Anomalies arose now and then, but stakeholders tended to correct these as they occurred. In 1998, the SEC reviewed a binational agreement on cross-border investments and reclassified Canada as a foreign country. Canadian officials were shocked, and the New York investment executive Leonard Quigley responded:

> Paul Martin should get on the phone and call Larry Summers, the U.S. Secretary of the Treasury, and say, "Look, your bureaucrats are proposing to treat Canadians the same as Germans and Japanese and the French on securities matters. But you don't treat them the same on the Open Skies Agreement, you don't treat them the same on the Free Trade Agreement, you don't treat them the same on NAFTA. Why the hell do you have to treat them the same on Securities?"[56]

Whoever called whomever, the SEC shortly restored Canada to its old category of "not foreign," in effect a component of the U.S. market. Quigley's reaction revealed that along with asymmetry and integration, Upper North American interdependence was simply assumed by Americans who were involved in it.

Major scandals affected concurrent securities markets in the same way. The Enron investigation, scandals, trials, and sentencing illustrated how divergent corporate cultures and oversight could convergence in other ways. "Enron" became a scarlet banner on U.S. front pages and prime-time TV newscasts, where prosecutors in New York and other states made highly publicized arrests, jailed and indicted suspects, and prepared and prosecuted cases where large financial and other penalties fell on those found guilty. U.S. regulators all the while scrambled to hold public confidence.[57] Subsequent U.S. regulatory reforms consolidated in the Sarbanes-Oxley (SOX) Act, which President George W. Bush signed into law in 2002. Canadian companies on the New York and NASDAQ exchanges faced two overseers, and senior corporate officers were henceforth personally accountable for their subordinates' proven malfeasance. Anyone doing business in the United States, as thousands of Canadians did, was subject to those laws, but Upper North American corporate and fiscal integration sent SOX's reach into Canada's provincial and federal jurisdictions. Ottawa remained silent, but the BMO and Canadian organizations that were listed on the New York exchanges complied with SOX. In Canada, the Toronto Stock Exchange president disputed the Ontario Securities Commission's authority. The SEC accepted Canada's stock and debt offering documents as equivalent to U.S. filings, but Ottawa had little success corralling the herd of provincial stock exchange cats for common oversight. Meanwhile, firms doing transnational business felt the impact of Enron and SOX.[58] This legislation improved investor confidence and perhaps quickened progress toward the creation of a Canadian national securities regulator over separate provincial bodies.[59] Fiscal integration had become a central component of Upper North America's economy, and the two systems had in many ways become a single entity.

Part IV

Political Realm

Stephen Harper took office as prime minister of Canada in early 2006 after a bruising and protracted campaign where the Ottawa-Washington political relationship had both an overt and an implied impact on the outcome. Harper had pledged improved relations with the United States if he won, as had Brian Mulroney after a deterioration in Washington-Ottawa affairs in the early 1980s, and Paul Martin after the Jean Chrétien / George W. Bush estrangement. The two governments would differ on many issues, Harper noted, but he intended to maintain a civil tone and work to solve problems. In Washington, U.S. conservatives had sotto voce rooted for him. In ideological and political terms, they saw a fellow traveler elevated to high office when the results came in on election day, and they cheered, softly. When Michael Wilson, Harper's choice as ambassador to the United States, arrived in Washington, President Bush accepted his credentials almost at once, a certain sign of pleasure at the change of government in Ottawa.[1] Early president–prime minister conversations and public appearances revealed a welcome change in demeanor, although the interplay of domestic politics and future issues would shape how it progressed.

At least in a symbolic way, the two chief executives gathered threads from the cultural, social, economic, and political realms into agendas for their relationship. The political realm in modern times has become simultaneously a business meeting, a public morality play, an asymmetrical partnership, and a perpetual courtship conducted to avoid the altar. Canada's media often wields clichés such as "best friends," "allies," and "family" about Upper North Americans, or false dichotomies about the chief executives, such as "too cozy" or "aloof," to characterize their relationship. The clichés convey sentimentalized or nostalgic connotations, but they conceal much more. Yes, Upper North Americans share the most intertwined, intimate, interdependent, and profitable binational relationship in the world. Millions of individuals are both observers and stakeholders in how the president–prime minister axis interlinks and manages all aspects and layers of dispersed political relations.

Even the most experienced traveler through this dense policy jungle can become entangled and lose his or her way, but analysts and observers have developed a good sense of it. The Carnegie scholars first parsed Canada–United States relations as a discrete subject and sketched enduring themes and issues. Many others built on their foundations. This book has gathered and sorted the themes and details into cultural, social, economic, and political realms to explore how Upper North Americans have interrelated over time. The realms are best understood in a progressive order that begins with cultural foundations, moves through social systems, dissects the integrated and interdependent economies, and analyzes the political realm that gathers and manages threads and themes from the previous three.[2] The political is the most visible realm to the public and commentators, but Canadian-American relations go far beyond elected or appointed senior officials. Executive officers and departments have the ability to apply friction, or accelerate initiatives and action in any of the realms, although their power to reshape fundamentals is limited at best. Often, policymakers are as much victims as managers, and rarely masters of the realms. The two political systems are more alike than they seem at first glance. Both evolved from British forms and heritage with the same values of personal freedom, democracy, and the rule of law. Asymmetry and the visible structures of government suggest distinctions, but both are more alike than a first glance suggests. One major ostensible divergence could disappear in a whimper if Britain's monarchy ever dissolved.[3] In political behavior, conservatives in both countries have held similar views about comparable issues but have acted on them in different ways. Overall, the two liberal democratic societies have defined their liberalism and practiced their democracy differently in their jurisdictions.[4]

The term "border" has multiple meanings, depending upon which realm is under consideration. A border in Upper North America seems best defined as an agreed-upon international boundary within a shared zone where the dynamics of the cultural, social, and economic realms play out. A familiar international apparatus of embassies, consulates, and other accredited offices and officials in the capitals and major centers serve those who have formal business in either country. The events of September 11, 2001, redefined the border as a defensive barricade for Washington, but Ottawa saw only a new barrier to travel and commerce. Policymakers and officials from many agencies in both countries cooperated to ensure the transit of people and goods, and as they did redefined Upper North America's relationship. Ottawa officials and Canadians have long believed that Washington persistently ignored them, but distraction is a more accurate term. The United States became a global colossus with interests everywhere. Canada was the quiet next-door regional power that went about its business.[5]

Canadians occasionally still sigh about a vanished "special relationship" that somehow escaped. But it was never an Upper North American captive, only the product of how a particular generation in the political realm worked together from the 1940s to the 1970s. When that generation faded from public life, so did the dynamics they generated in the political management of the relationship. Their successors rose, worked, and passed through a different historical era, which dissolved in the 1990s when they too became elder statesmen. Throughout, Washington officials and policy analysts always paid far more attention to Canada than Canadians suspected. This took institutional form when the Woodrow Wilson International Center for Scholars established its Canada Institute to explore the relationship through scholars in residence and policy-oriented events both in Washington and major centers in both countries.[6] This was tangible, visible attention, even influential for policymakers, as are the *Washington Post* and *New York Times* correspondents periodically assigned to reside in Toronto and file regular stories deemed of interest to U.S. readers. Agents from many Washington bureaus and departments worked on assignments throughout Canada, and in far greater numbers after September 11, 2001. Politicians from every jurisdiction met in various forums, such as the Interparliamentary Group, to discuss problems and devise shared or concurrent policy solutions. True, in the White House, that euphemism for the vast executive branch of the U.S. government, a benign indifference about Canada often sat in the minds of presidential policy advisers. At the same time, they were there to manage crises, and Canada never was one. Furthermore, every pair of presidents and prime ministers had to learn anew how to interrelate, and neither could rely on the clichés expressed in first meetings as a substitute for active management of Upper North America's problems.[7]

Part IV explores the history and contemporary condition of central themes in the political realm. Chapter 10 traces the evolution of security, or defense, from the late eighteenth century onward.[8] London officials believed by the 1870s that the United States would secure North America, and hence the provinces, to secure itself. The only threat to British interests was possible annexation, either by design or accident. The last British garrison left Halifax in 1906, but after 1867 troops had been steadily withdrawn. London's international attention shifted east toward the Empire and European balance-of-power politics. The long rapprochement with Washington in effect left Canada, a self-governing dominion though not a fully sovereign country, to deal with the United States, for a time with help from Britain's Washington Embassy. The security relationship evolved from the Upper North American location and was formalized in pacts such as the Ogdensburg Agreement, the North Atlantic Treaty Organization, and the North American Aerospace Defense Command, which in 2006 included a maritime component. The definition of security shifted when threats to the United States, and hence North America, came not from nation-states or the Soviet bloc and nuclear weapons but from ideological and political groups in failed nation-states or entities that never truly were nation-states. One such group launched the events of September 11, 2001, which reshaped how Upper North American affairs would be managed for the foreseeable future.

Chapter 11 views border history as the evolution of the joint management that facilitated Upper North American cultural, social, and economic interrelationships. In modern times, this management became progressively complex and bureaucratic, but passive except during times of externally imposed political crises. Even then, border management continued to ensure access as Washington and Ottawa balanced interests, sovereignty, and security. Border officials, who were mostly concerned with people and goods in transit, assumed that the vast majority of border crossers were peaceful and benign, if not always honest about what they were up to. Border management was for most of the twentieth century little more than shared policing to deter, thwart, or nab miscreants who smuggled illicit goods or themselves. By the 1990s, traffic congestion drew political attention to the border because the press of vehicles and goods had degraded border communities and crossing stations. It all became increasingly costly to manage. Ottawa and Washington agencies coped with these problems, but the political will to apply greater resources flagged. After September 11, 2001, however, a sharp distinction in perception emerged. Washington's security focus dominated border policies, while Ottawa's economic focus forced accommodation for continued access to the U.S. market.

Chapter 12 analyzes the Ottawa-Washington coaxial axis, which is far greater than any given pair of presidents and prime ministers. All government departments at all levels have interacted continuously around a chief executives' core. Even by 1900, Britain's Washington Embassy could not manage Upper North American issues. The coaxial axis gained more threads during the world wars and the Cold War decades. After 1945, political relations spread into multilateral organizations, where Americans and Canadians worked in ad hoc groups on global security and social issues. Even if a given president–prime minister pair became dysfunctional, inertia and the myriad interlinkages around them sustained political relations until new chief executives took office.

Chapter 10

North American Security

By late 2005, President George W. Bush and his close advisers were convinced that Prime Minister Paul Martin would sign Canada onto the Ballistic Missile Defense (BMD) program. Martin's minority government had amended North American Aerospace Defense (NORAD) to accommodate BMD, renewed the Binational Planning Group on maritime cooperation for continental security, and agreed to other military cooperation measures to handle emergencies in Upper North America. Washington saw BMD in its own terms, however, and failed to weigh the symbolic and ideological impulses that shaped Ottawa's domestic political needs. For example, polls showed 30 percent of Quebecers wanted to eliminate the national armed forces, so it was not surprising that opinion there opposed BMD.[1]

Moreover, Bush's unpopularity in Canada meant that it was politically dangerous for a minority government prime minister to seem Washington's willing partner in any respect. When Martin announced the rejection of BMD, however, he insisted that Washington needed Ottawa's permission to shoot down any incoming missile in Canadian airspace. That remark dumbfounded Frank McKenna, Martin's ambassador in Washington, and U.S. officials. Secretary of State Condoleezza Rice cancelled her Ottawa visit. In an ironic symmetry, anti-Canada editorials and articles rippled through the U.S. media, excoriating Martin and the Liberals, just as anti-U.S. opinion in Canada speared Bush and the Republicans.[2]

Meanwhile, the dispersed security relationship continued to develop below the media radar. Canada's Border Services Agency worked closely with the U.S. Homeland Security Department. Thousands of telephone calls and e-mails flashed back and forth daily between U.S. and Canadian officials. Canadian personnel went on and off shift at NORAD headquarters in

Cheyenne Mountain, Colorado. Fundamentally, the Monroe Doctrine's thesis applied. Any threat or attack against the United States would provoke Washington to secure North America to protect itself. Ottawa would be consulted, but it had no veto over Washington's decisions. Even so, the politics of Upper North American affairs included the appearance as well as the actuality of active cooperation, even if Bush had opined in a conversation with Martin that a future administration might ask why U.S. taxpayers' money secured Canada while Ottawa kept its own military budgets low. The North Atlantic Treaty Organization (NATO) had made the same point for years, so the freeloader label had a lot of evidence and history behind it.[3]

Historical Roots

The Upper North American security theme has deep historical roots. It began after the 1783 Treaty of Paris that divided an independent United States from the remnants of British North America, which included a large number of subject French habitants. England retained control of its fur trading posts on U.S. territory, which many Americans saw as bases for inciting natives against settlers that dispersed into the borderlands of northern New England and New York in the 1790s. The potential for a clash led George Washington's government to dispatch John Jay to London, and in 1794 the treaty that bore his name settled commercial and other points still in dispute.[4]

The wars of the French Revolution, meanwhile, generated more Anglo–United States differences, especially over maritime issues, and eventually led to the War of 1812. This conflict was the American theater of Britain's Napoleonic wars, and James Madison's government confronted paradoxical strategic circumstances in its effort to secure national interests. British naval superiority meant that Washington could only retaliate to press London by attacking the British territory within reach—the North American provinces. English and provincial military authorities, as well as later provincial students of the war, believed the invading U.S. armies were agents of conquest. Hypothetically, if U.S. armies had taken and held strategic parts of Upper and Lower Canada, such as the Niagara region, Montreal, and Quebec City, Washington might well have demanded to keep the provinces as hard-won spoils of war. Stalemate in the north balanced British control of the coasts, however, and the Treaty of Ghent, signed on Christmas Eve, 1814, restored the territorial status quo ante bellum. It also devoted half its articles to the future boundary survey. Upper North American security in the coming decades thus rested on an Anglo-American international rapprochement.

Neither Washington nor London viewed a paper peace as sufficient unto itself for the Upper North American borderlands. The boundary survey got under way in 1816. In 1817, the Rush-Bagot Agreement limited armed vessels on the upper and lower Great Lakes to one cannon each. Next, the Convention of 1818 projected the jurisdictional border beyond the Great Lakes along the 49th Parallel of latitude from the Northwest Angle of Lake of the Woods to the Rocky Mountains. In the next decades, London also kept British troops in garrisons, built a series of fortifications from Halifax to Malden, and dug canals along the Ottawa and Saint Lawrence rivers. The Rideau Canal linked Bytown (Ottawa) with eastern Lake Ontario at Kingston. Work finished on the last citadel, massive Fort Henry, in the early 1840s. Washington decreased funds for northern forts and barracks, in part because internal migration patterns drew political attention and resources to western military posts. Congress also funded a series of casemented coastal forts from Maine to Florida to oppose any future British naval incursions. By the 1840s, most U.S. borderland posts were down at the heels, and the small garrisons spent more time socializing with than glaring at their British counterparts. Meanwhile, Upper North Americans intermingled, traded, developed transportation systems, and shared all the elements of a common culture, with some ethnic and linguistic exceptions. The transnational societies that developed in the borderlands contained stakeholders in the London-Washington rapprochement that built through the nineteenth century.[5]

This rapprochement tempered reactions to short-lived provincial rebellions in Upper and Lower Canada from 1837 to 1839. William Lyon Mackenzie, a republican who admired U.S. democratic practices, organized his followers to unseat by force the ruling Family Compact of Anglophile elites. In Lower Canada, Louis Joseph Papineau had similar plans for the Chateau Clique to overthrow English overlords, reduce the Roman Catholic Church's power, and transform habitants from seigneurial serfdom into North American yeoman farmers. The rebellions failed, but proximity to the border led to a next-door sanctuary with sympathy from republican Americans in borderland towns and villages from Vermont to Michigan. Mackenzie's band stopped on Navy Island in the Niagara River to recruit, regroup, and make another attempt. During the winter of 1837–38, sympathetic Americans in the border states donated money, weapons, and volunteered as filibusters organized in Hunters' Lodges to support their fellow republicans and unseat the English King. State authorities hesitated to act in an election year, but President Martin Van Buren in Washington dispatched General Winfield Scott with a handful of officers (more regulars followed) to quell unrest in the borderlands and forestall an Anglo-American clash. Scott asserted Washington's authority, faced down local zealots, and seized their weapons. He delayed and broke up filibuster bands if they marched north and quashed a security crisis neither London nor Washington wanted. Upper Canadian rebels and their filibuster allies sallied across the Saint Lawrence River near Prescott, but British and provincial militia bottled them up in a stone windmill. After taking casualties, the rebels surrendered. Van Buren waited while British courts tried and sent a few provincial and U.S. ringleaders into a dreary exile on Van Dieman's Land, a remote island prison off the coast of Australia. Others, such as Mackenzie, lived out their lives in the United States.

Another contretemps developed in 1859. U.S. and British settlers shared San Juan Island in northern Puget Sound on the far west coast, where the boundary had not yet been surveyed and marked. A U.S. farmer shot a British pig; tempers flared; militia, troops, and naval forces gathered; and an aging Scott replayed his border peacemaker role and subdued the bloodless (in human terms) San Juan "Pig War."[6]

The 1861–65 U.S. Civil War also threatened borderland security and offered more opportunities for an Anglo-U.S. clash. To begin with, Abraham Lincoln's government resented a British declaration of neutrality that implied recognition of the rebel Confederacy. Second, Captain John Wilkes of the Union warship *San Jacinto* stopped a British steamer on the high seas and removed Confederate emissaries bound for London. War rhetoric circulated, then subsided. Third, the Confederacy purchased vessels from British shipyards, then outfitted them as warships. The *Alabama* proved the most notorious as a U.S. commerce raider and sank much of the U.S. Pacific whaling fleet. Postwar U.S. claims, Canadians feared, might persuade London to cede British North America in settlement. Fourth, Confederate sympathizers hijacked a steamer in the Bay of Fundy, an act of piracy in international law, and Union navy vessels pursued them into Nova Scotia waters. Then local courts allowed those brought to trial in Halifax to escape.

Fifth, and most dangerous for Upper North American security, Confederate escapees from Northern prisons fled into Canada where rebel spies schemed against Union territory. Britain was legally bound to stop any forays, and John A. Macdonald's detectives thwarted some plans, but a raid from Montreal on Saint Alban's Banks in 1864, and a British judge's release of the raiders after their arrest in Montreal, with their loot, outraged Lincoln's administration. Secretary of State William Henry Seward closed the border, demanded foreigners henceforth carry passports, and threatened to abrogate the Rush-Bagot Agreement. Washington's policies prompted the Canadian and British governments to break up Confederate organizations, seize their property, and expel them into the United States. Seward next stated that the upper border was under control, and Washington lifted the passport law. After the war ended, however, mustered-out Irish veterans joined Fenian leaders from Ireland, who planned to foment an Anglo-U.S. war by invading the provinces to gain Irish home rule. U.S. forces at Fenian staging areas observed the filibuster expeditions, but when provincial militia threw them back, federal officers seized weapons, arrested the leaders, and disbanded the rank and file. In the remote Red River Valley borderland, a U.S. army officer led a column onto Canadian territory in pursuit of a Fenian party headed to reinforce the Riel Rebellion of 1871. During Anglo-American diplomatic talks, Secretary of State Hamilton Fish made it clear that Canada could join the United States if it wished, but Washington, after haggling over details, settled all borderland issues and accepted Prime Minister Macdonald's signature on the Treaty of Washington as Canada's representative. This tacitly acknowledged the new Dominion.[7]

The London-Washington rapprochement continued, and Whitehall reduced its Canadian garrisons, but Anglo-Conservatives such as George Taylor Denison did not trust the Americans. His garrison mentality convinced him that only Imperial protection could secure Canada's independence in North America. The Clear Grits (Liberals)—such as George Brown, Edward Blake, and Wilfrid Laurier—understood his views but disagreed about security policy. London neither could nor would secure Canada against the United States, but Washington would by default secure Canada against any external enemy.[8] Macdonald further understood that Ottawa had to maintain its own internal and border security as a preemptive strategy against U.S. help if domestic order deteriorated, as it had during the Fenian troubles and on the Great Plains. Washington had, after all, threatened France to end its ill-fated Mexican imperium founded during the Civil War, and cited the Monroe Doctrine. Incidents on the distant and open Great Plains borderland might draw U.S. troops onto Canadian soil in hot pursuit if Ottawa did not establish its authority in the West. Northern plains tribes treated the border as a "medicine line" that would protect them from U.S. troops. Macdonald's Royal North West Mounted Police thus both policed and managed security on Canada's plains to preempt any U.S. incursions, as when

Sitting Bull's Sioux fled north after the 1876 Battle of the Little Big Horn. That aside, North American matters were one thing, and potential external threats another. Prime Minister Wilfrid Laurier reminded a British official fresh from England and eager to build up Canada's militia as a defense against attack that Ottawa did not need to incur such expenses because Washington would defend all of North America to protect itself.

Between 1867 and 1914, border security, apart from plains tribes, was of marginal concern in Washington, and London drew down its remaining garrisons in Canada. As U.S. interests shifted into the Caribbean and the Pacific in the 1890s, Washington built a modern, albeit modest by European standards, ironclad ocean navy. An Anglo-American war scare during the 1893 Venezuelan Boundary Crisis was little more than a newspaper spasm in the deepening Washington-London rapprochement. When the British built fortifications at Esquimalt, British Columbia, in 1897, a U.S. officer in mufti reconnoitred, then reassured his Washington superiors those were defensive works only. U.S. policymakers, politicians, and writers saw Canada as part of North America, and by 1912, U.S. War Department planners assumed that Washington would be responsible for all of North America's security if any foreign threats appeared.[9]

Canada's conservative Anglophile elites meanwhile kept faith with Britain for security and became staunch supporters of the Empire throughout this era. Ottawa dispatched *Voyageur* volunteers to move supplies and troops up the Nile to relieve the Mahdi's siege of Khartoum in 1885. Quebec politicians, however, opposed sending Canadian troops on Imperial campaigns and were adamant against support for what they saw as Britain's war of suppression against the Boers in South Africa from 1899 to 1902. Anglo-Canadians, meanwhile, raised money, formed volunteer units such as Lord Strathcona's Horse, and cheered Britain on as loyal members of the Empire. During World War I, Anglo-Canadians again volunteered to serve Britain, but when mass casualties on the Western Front led Ottawa to invoke conscription, Quebec balked and created a constitutional crisis. For Quebecers, security meant within North America, not overseas.[10]

Twentieth-Century Wars

During World War I, English Canadians resented Washington's neutrality in what they saw as a clash of values with the German empire. Between 1914 and 1917, however, Americans trickled north to enlist in Canadian battalions, while Canadians headed south to avoid enlistment, find work, and later to evade conscription. Washington agents watched, and occasionally arrested, resident Germans who acted against Canada. World War I also produced a new threat to North American security, brought home when the United States was still neutral. A German submarine, the U-53, surfaced just off Rhode Island's U.S. Navy base, undetected until that moment, in a dramatic demonstration of Germany's technical capacities. U.S. and German officers dined together, and the U-53 departed. Before long, within full view of observers on shore, it sank several British vessels beyond the international limit. Canadians had a fresh reason for anger at Washington.

Ambiguity shrouded Upper North American security relations, however, because even before President Woodrow Wilson asked Congress to vote the United States as an associate ally in April 1917, senior Ottawa officials dealt directly with Washington counterparts. Sir George Foster, head of Canada's War Trade Board, set up offices in the U.S. capital, and by November 1917 the Imperial Munitions Board was working with the U.S. Ordnance Department. In 1918, Munitions Minister J. W. Flavelle dealt more closely with his U.S. than British counterpart. Upper North American security cooperation also extended to operations. Nine U.S. Navy ships, two seaplane squadrons, and several submarine chasers worked under Royal Canadian Navy (RCN) command on western North Atlantic patrols.[11] And when Prime Minister Robert Borden and President Wilson were at Versailles in 1919, they felt themselves North Americans among Europeans.

Canadians sidled closer to American outlooks on European great power politics and potential conflict in the 1920s. In part this rested on social ideas and economic and political interests. Many in Canada as well as the United States believed that isolation from European great power politics was an appropriate strategy to achieve North American security.[12] London notified Ottawa to stand ready to fight if Britain and Turkey came to blows in the 1922 Chanak Crisis, but Ottawa refused to oblige. In 1923, Ottawa and Washington jointly opposed renewal of the 1905 British alliance with Japan. A potential Japanese-U.S. conflict in the western Pacific, if Japan remained allied with Britain, would put Canada and the United States technically at war, an unthinkable prospect. London agreed, allowed the alliance to lapse, and weathered the anger of Japanese leaders. After the Statute of Westminster in 1931, Ottawa developed its own foreign and security policies with one eye on London and the other on Washington. Both governments distrusted Bolshevik Russia and the Stalinist Soviet Union, and they grew alarmed over reports from Protestant missionaries in China who wanted Western countries to oppose Japan's invasion of Manchuria in 1931. Upper North American opinion also decried Japan's 1932 creation of the puppet state Manchukuo, and the brutal war Tokyo waged deep into China after 1937. Ottawa and Washington were officially neutral during the 1936–39 Spanish Civil War, although U.S. and Canadian volunteers formed the Abraham Lincoln and Louis Joseph Papineau brigades respectively to fight against General Francisco Franco's fascist forces.

As Far Eastern and European events in the later 1930s eroded North American isolationism, James T. Shotwell and Washington's Carnegie Endowment for International Peace sponsored cross-border conferences with delegates drawn from both countries. They discussed shared foreign policy perspectives and interests alternately at Queen's and Saint Lawrence universities in Kingston, Ontario, and Canton, New York, from 1935 through 1941. Officials and senior academics explored the shared cultural values, social systems, economic interests, and political structures that to them united Upper North Americans. In 1939 and 1941, the delegates focused on North American security. John W. Dafoe, editor of the *Winnipeg Free Press,* believed the border had become irrelevant to Canadian and U.S. opinion on a possible war with Germany. Isolationists, collectivists, imperialists, and independents could be found in both countries, and that revealed a North American matrix, rather than distinct national perspectives, on domestic and international security policy.[13]

In 1938, Prime Minister William Lyon Mackenzie King arranged for Queen's University to grant President Franklin D. Roosevelt an honorary degree. Roosevelt's speech emphasized that the United States would not stand idly by if Canada were threatened by an outside power. He meant Germany, and external affairs officer Hume Wrong concluded that the United States would secure Canada if war erupted in Europe and Britain fell. Technical advances in naval and air power reaffirmed for U.S. military and political planners that North American security was indivisible, notwithstanding the border. Each country was a strategic extension of the other, as senior U.S. and Canadian military and diplomatic officers agreed during confidential talks. Ottawa entered World War II a week after Britain declared hostilities on Nazi Germany in September 1939. Roosevelt interwove U.S. isolationism with a biased neutrality that sidled toward a tacit agreement with Canada, and then toward belligerency after France capitulated to Germany in May 1940. North American officials also knew that the more resources Ottawa sent to a Britain possibly on the brink of collapse, the more dependent Canada became upon Washington. U.S. forces, meanwhile, took control of Greenland after Denmark fell under German occupation to secure strategic minerals and deny Axis forces bases that could threaten transatlantic shipping lanes.[14]

Roosevelt, King, and their senior political and military officers continued to confer on security planning and met at Ogdensburg, New York, in August 1940. After a brief consultation, they announced the Permanent Joint Board on Defense (PJBD) to advise Ottawa and Washington on common strategic and military policies. Senior U.S. officers wanted immediate command of all North American forces. Roosevelt and King agreed that could happen, but only when an Axis invasion became imminent, because asymmetry of power dictated that Washington had to assume operational control. At Hyde Park in 1941, King and Roosevelt interwove Upper North American security and economic policies. The British would be able to purchase war materials in Canada under Lend-Lease, which deepened Upper North American economic integration. Winston Churchill harrumphed that Canada had ducked for cover with Washington, which to a degree was true, but the Atlantic separated cultural, social, economic, and political-strategic linkages and goals. If Britain fell to Nazi occupation, Canada had only the United States for protection in North America. U.S. Coast Guard vessels, meanwhile, sent maritime intelligence to all North American coastal stations, and after discussions, Ottawa established the Clayton Knight Committee in Washington. This "private" organization recruited (with Washington's tacit connivance) volunteer U.S. pilots and crews for Commonwealth air forces, even though the United States was still officially neutral. By the fall of 1941, the U.S. Naval Command controlled RCN vessels in international Atlantic waters and had built facilities at Argentia, Newfoundland, acquired as part of the 1940 Destroyers for Bases deal. Senior officers also aligned Western Atlantic operations.

After Japan attacked Pearl Harbor on December 7, 1941, the United States entered World War II. RCN vessels escorted merchant shipping between Boston and New York. In May 1943, the RCN took command of the northwest Atlantic, which included U.S. Navy vessels assigned to those waters. Ottawa and Washington formed the joint "Devil's Brigade" to eject Japanese forces that occupied the Aleutian Islands, although they decamped before North American troops could move against them. The brigade served as a unified Canadian-American force for the rest of the war, notably in the Italian campaign. The PJBD recommended the Alaska Highway, which had long been discussed by U.S. and Canadian officials, as an overland link for U.S. territory separated from the lower states by British Columbia. Ottawa agreed, at least in part because it could not secure its Pacific Northwest territory or coastal waters. Throughout the war, the United States built bases and other installations on Canadian soil with Ottawa's permission. This "friendly invasion" brought export credits, greenbacks, jobs into local communities, and left infrastructure such as roads and other facilities for later civilian use.[15]

Upper North Americans in coastal regions during World War II developed a shared sense of vulnerability because both Germany and Japan operated submarines near their shores and in large inlets. U-boats exacted a jarring toll on Atlantic coastal shipping, even penetrated the Saint Lawrence River, and sank several merchant and other vessels, including an RCN warship. Others set up automatic weather stations, such as a site in Labrador that still worked in the 1980s when scholars in Ottawa's historical section tracked it down from a study of U-boat logs. Japanese submarines off British Columbia and Washington State occasionally shelled lighthouses with their deck guns, and released balloon-borne weapons into the winds. Canadians and Americans collaborated in Washington on a variety of military and civilian boards, the secret Manhattan Project, and in theater command and combat. Binational industrial and engineering organizations developed uranium mining and hydroelectric facilities that powered large parts of the northeast industrial heartland, with its vast aluminum plants that supplied Upper North American aircraft factories. Canadians sometimes bristled at the brash, overconfident, rich Yanks; but in the cultural, social, and economic realms, World War II furthered Canada's development as an asymmetrically interdependent Upper North American country. It was also clearly a junior member of the Grand Alliance, King's linchpin rhetoric aside. President Franklin D. Roosevelt dealt directly with Churchill on all important matters, to the point where Lester Pearson feared Canada would be squeezed, first between Britain and the United States, then out of Grand Alliance consultations altogether. He was mistaken on both counts. World War II ruined Britain but gave Ottawa an international presence through the support of its Upper North American and North Atlantic allies.[16]

As the ash-coated Axis rubble cooled throughout 1945, the forces of geography, proximity, and asymmetry muted somewhat because Canada stood as Washington's strongest conventional ally, asymmetry notwithstanding. The RCN was for a time the world's fourth-largest fighting navy. Ottawa reduced its army to a core and sustained the Royal Canadian Air Force. In the political realm, meanwhile, Ottawa's leading policymakers and politicians were, to borrow U.S. Secretary of State Dean Acheson's memorable memoir title, present at the creation of the postwar international system. They helped to found the United Nations, the International Monetary Fund, the General Agreement on Tariffs and Trade, other agencies, and the International Civil Aviation Organization with its headquarters in Montreal.

All this activity stimulated Ottawa's global political presence, stature, and prestige as ideas about defense and preparedness with their military connotations blurred into the broader concept of security. Washington officials often suspected that Ottawa was longer on rhetoric than action, but they saw Canada as a cultural, social, and economic partner as well as political and security ally. The Cold War shattered hopes of one world under the United Nations, and the Soviet-Western confrontation redefined global politics in the early 1950s. Ottawa shared Washington's alarm about such Soviet actions as the 1948 Prague coup and the Berlin Blockade, and officials in both capitals took similar positions in informal talks with the Brussels Pact nations to assuage European fears about an Upper North American isolationist resurgence, especially in the United States. Washington and Ottawa agreed about the Atlantic Charter, although Pearson had hoped cultural and social articles would soften the political and security focus Washington insisted upon. In April 1949, both Upper North American nations signed on to NATO—their first shared entangling military alliance.[17]

NATO embodied concepts of deterrence, balance of power, and security through civilian, military, and government intelligence agencies. That was particularly true in Upper North America, where elements from the transnational realms flowed into security planning and operations. Upper North American collaboration intensified when Ottawa shared Soviet spy and defector Igor Gouzenko with Washington and became part of the Anglo-American intelligence group. After President Harry Truman's Doctrine and George Kennan's strategic suggestions about how to handle the Soviet Union became the core of U.S. strategy, Canadian officials and politicians hesitated over Washington's containment policy. Kennan himself paid a quiet visit to Ottawa, explained what it was all about, and gained the confidence and support of Prime Minister Louis St. Laurent's government. More and more Americans and Canadians collaborated and shared security responsibilities in an ever-thickening Ottawa-Washington political coaxial axis. Cultural themes, a shared language, democratic values and the rule of law, social outlooks that included a shared love of baseball, and personal as well as political relationships cemented Upper North American security policy. The World War II experience and early Cold War created Canada's "special relationship" with the United States. Shared attitudes and policies about Upper North American security imparted an impetus to postwar political affairs. Officials and politicians came and went from each other's capital, understood each other's domestic conditions, and seemed eager to help.

Canada's low cash reserves after World War II provided an example of how that relationship worked throughout this era. The United States was the only functioning trade partner, and no markets yet existed that could offset the apparent dependency. A large trade deficit had built up with Washington, and Ottawa officials informed their U.S. colleagues that the fiscal crisis would force new export taxes and limit imports. Interests in both countries would suffer. Truman's administration understood, and while it rallied congressional and public support for the European reconstruction program that became known as the Marshall Plan, it also persuaded Congress to amend the legislation so Marshall Plan dollar credits that rebuilt Europe could be spent in Canada. As a result, Ottawa averted its fiscal crisis, sustained Upper North American commerce, and opened new markets.

Meanwhile, atomic weapons delivered by long-range bombers became the principal strike and retaliatory forces of the United States and the Soviet Union. The Soviets would have to fly a Great Circle route to attack the United States, and that made Canada's northern real estate a vital Upper North American strategic asset. After consultations, Washington funded and built cross-continent early warning radar networks and air bases in the north for advanced warning, weather forecasting, and interceptor bases. As this system became operational, Pearson and others in Ottawa had to remind Secretary of State Acheson that those bases were not on U.S. territory, so for any visit, he had to request permission through Canada's Washington Embassy. Acheson grumbled but complied. Upper North American military interoperability deepened throughout the 1950s, and Ottawa and Washington institutionalized their asymmetrical security alliance.[18]

NATO rested on several shared assumptions that all signatories supported. First, the United States was indispensable for any agreement that involved combined military organization. Second, Washington and Ottawa officials had confidence in one another from their experience as staunch and reliable allies. Third, the multiplying strands of the political coaxial axis furthered cross-border security operations in part because both rested on shared cultural, social, and economic foundations and interests. The Upper North American peoples and their governments were joint security stakeholders. A given president–prime minister pair might clash, and even become personally dysfunctional, but the interwoven strands around the core of the coaxial axis would keep it all in operation. Fourth, defense production sharing and other agreements reinforced the interdependent economic linkages. Fifth, domestic cross-border interests supported coordinated transnational policies. Sixth and last, several security groups formed within the coaxial axis. Ottawa and Washington established a Joint Industrial Mobilization Committee, for example, and C. D. Howe recruited businessmen with cross-border experience to expedite the committee's operations.

The Upper North American security relationship adjusted to emergencies during the post-1945 era. The asymmetry of fiscal and military resources meant that Ottawa could not spend on the scale Washington expected during the Korean War of 1950–54, for example. When Acheson complained about Canada's token commitment, Pearson noted that Ottawa had sent three destroyers, not the one Acheson claimed. The U.S. secretary of state conceded that Ottawa had indeed sent three tokens, not one. Ottawa also sent 25,000 soldiers and a Royal Canadian Air Force transport squadron. Meanwhile, asymmetry notwithstanding, by 1954 Upper North American military production trade was virtually equal in both directions, and after 1959 Canada's sales to the United States rose over 2.5 times to reach $254.3 million (Canadian). Ottawa gained more than income from Defense Production Sharing because these programs supported a more advanced technological infrastructure than Canada could have achieved on its own. When Prime Minister John Diefenbaker cancelled the domestic Avro Arrow project, nationalists blamed Washington pressure, but costs, Canada's small markets, and Ottawa policies lay behind that decision. At the same time, Canadian scientists and technicians promptly found work on U.S. aviation and space programs and many remained in the United States. To compensate for Canada's air defense forces, Washington offered Diefenbaker Bomarc antiaircraft missiles with nuclear warheads.[19] Ottawa also balanced multilateral agencies with North American security agreements.

By the middle 1960s, global political and strategic complexities had blurred the Cold War's earlier clarity, and domestic reactions to nuclear weapons generated elements of security divergence. The U.S. commitment to North American defense to secure itself meanwhile allowed Ottawa to transfer funds from military budgets to social programs. Ottawa also, with reference to Pearson's policy triumph in the Suez Crisis of 1956, emphasized international peacekeeping, but that served Cold War alliance interests more than the peacekeeping legend suggested. For example, the original mission in Suez in 1956 was as much to keep London and Washington from a major clash over Cold War policy as to separate Egypt and Israel. That anticipated Arab-Israeli war erupted anyway a few years later, but the delay dissolved the potential for crisis in the Western Alliance. Similarly, when Canada sent forces to Cyprus, Ottawa helped to forestall a possible political crisis between two NATO members, Greece and Turkey, that might even have led to bloodshed because hostile Greek and Turkish Cypriots intermingled on their island and a civil war was in the offing. Meanwhile, mostly beneath media notice, U.S. and Canadian forces interwove training, equipment, operations, and at senior levels of command as the price for Ottawa's role above its military capacities at policy discussions over North American security. Political and military engagement also softened political reactions to the certainty that the United States would do what it saw fit to secure itself in the North American strategic arena. The emergence and evolution of NORAD followed that same logic.

The 1957 NORAD agreement became the core of North American air security with surveillance and warning systems that evolved through bomber, intercontinental missile, and post–Cold War eras. Geography alone determined the linkage. Ontario and Quebec were parts of the North American heartland. Vancouver was alongside Puget Sound U.S. naval bases. Nuclear weapons would not discriminate, and real fear existed that they might be used. Cold War asymmetrical interdependence built upon the cross-border trust the PJBD had engendered. Congress paid 90 percent of NORAD's costs for facilities, created jobs in Canada, and installed advanced technical equipment and U.S. personnel at the Pine Tree, Mid-Canada, and Distant Early Warning line bases. It also gave Canada an asymmetrical presence, but command equity at NORAD's Cheyenne Mountain headquarters and other bases. President Dwight Eisenhower meanwhile convinced Congress to build the Saint Lawrence Seaway to secure the transport of strategic materials, but the seaway also served transnational private interests in the borderland region.[20]

During the October 1962 Cuban Missile Crisis, those security linkages ignored Prime Minister Diefenbaker's dysfunctional personal relationship with President John F. Kennedy. Washington proved the presence of Soviet missiles in Cuba before the UN General Assembly, but Diefenbaker refused to accept Washington's lead on a blockade and alert Canada's forces to U.S. levels, as NORAD and NATO obliged him to do. His Cabinet fragmented. Defense Minister Douglass Harkness and senior Canadian officers placed their commands on full alert anyway. Furthermore, on his own recognizance, Canadian rear admiral Kenneth Dyer deployed two dozen warships and several dozen aircraft out of Halifax to patrol for Soviet submarines and guard Upper North America's north Atlantic flank. That released USN vessels to confront Soviet ships en route for Cuba. The crisis ended, but it produced the only Canadian national election where security may have been politically decisive. Pearson and the Liberals took office and accepted nuclear warheads for the Bomarc missiles. Ottawa never mounted those warheads, so they sat in storage, as did U.S. nuclear mines at Goose Bay. This made Canada a de facto temporary nuclear power. Meanwhile, Ottawa's defense spending between 1963 and 1971 fell from 22 to 13 percent of the federal budget. Ottawa funded Canadian forces to purchase political credit in NATO and NORAD while it milked security budgets to cover domestic social programs.[21]

Washington's control of North American security produced a latent tension in the political realm of dispersed relations. U.S. administrations tolerated Ottawa's political reluctance to bear burdens or pay prices for North American security, but resented its argument to repeal the first-use doctrine of nuclear weapons after the Cold War ended. Throughout the political realm, Washington had come to see any moral stand Ottawa took as a ploy for favorable domestic press commentary to please Canadian anti-Americans and peace activists.[22] A 1987 Ottawa foreign policy White Paper spoke about reclaiming control in Arctic waters, perhaps with nuclear submarines for under-ice surveillance. This was fantasy. Ottawa funded only a few more overflights. Shortly before the Berlin Wall came down in 1989, however, Prime Minister Mulroney faced a dilemma when Ronald Reagan's administration proposed the Strategic Defense Initiative (SDI). Canadian commentators mocked SDI as "Star Wars," after a popular space opera movie about intergalactic conflict, and many now resented Washington's assumption that U.S. defense policy by default covered all of North America.[23]

For his part, Mulroney skipped a deft three-step. Step one, the Conservative caucus declined President Reagan's invitation. Step two, before he announced that, Mulroney telephoned Reagan to convey the decision. Reagan was disappointed, but he understood Mulroney's political situation and appreciated the courtesy. Step three, Mulroney allowed Canadian firms to bid on U.S. SDI contracts under cross-border defense production-sharing agreements. A pragmatic approach often interwove with domestic politics when moral conflicts surfaced about security during the Cold War era. Ottawa had, for example, de facto simultaneously supported the U.S. Nike Zeus antimissile while supporting nuclear disarmament. Ottawa regularly renewed NORAD, yet it stood morally opposed to the militarization of space, which now held satellite detection systems that benefited Ottawa. Canada also supported the U.S. National Aeronautics and Space Administration's shuttle program that flew military as well as civilian missions. And Ottawa did not join the U.S. Space Command, even though it was housed at NORAD headquarters and the same general commanded both agencies.[24]

The cross-border imperatives of shared North American security often ran afoul of Canadian domestic political exigencies, but circumstances and particular president–prime minister dynamics determined how such dichotomies shaped the public Washington-Ottawa relationship. Senior Canadian officials feared being left out of any phase of planning and operations that served Upper North American, not just U.S., security objectives. Ottawa officials and politicians balanced private support and public distance from Washington on domestically controversial issues to remain at the planning table, yet not appear too close to Washington's policy. Then, in 1989, the Cold War ended with a whimper when Moscow stumbled, the Warsaw Pact crumbled, and the Soviet Union fell apart. The foundation of global politics for a half century evaporated. Apart from managing the denouement of a world struggle, Washington policymakers feared that a regime or organization hostile to the United States or the West could still acquire atomic weapons to threaten North American security, or U.S. interests in other parts of the world. Such themes became plot material for international espionage thrillers, but often entangled with the politics of nonstate groups propelled by hatred of the United States. That was why Reagan's SDI project evolved into the Ballistic Missile Defense project of the 1990s as the Canadian and U.S. roles in global politics entered a post–Cold War world.[25]

Washington reshaped its strategic thinking more than Ottawa did, although both declared a peace dividend and reduced military budgets. Vastly greater U.S. resources allowed the Defense Department to embark on technological innovations to enhance military power, whereas Ottawa merely shifted the money into other budgets. Public opinion in both countries also began to see armed conflicts as overseas—in Africa, the Middle East, the Persian Gulf, or southern Asia—where they would not affect North American social, economic, or political interests.

Unconventional Insecurity

Ottawa and Washington renewed NORAD in 1991, and U.S. satellite surveillance assisted Coast Guard and police operations against drug and people smugglers, new threats to Upper North American security. Ottawa also sustained the partnership in North America to give its dwindling forces experience with U.S. units and benefit from agreements on planning, training, and operations. Congress funded the North Warning system for advanced missile detection and Canadian firms won contracts under the Defense Production Sharing agreement, which furthered cross-border high-technology integration. Ottawa also insisted that U.S. industries invest in Canada to be eligible for contracts, but Jean Chrétien's Liberal government subscribed to an emerging European emphasis on multilateralism to balance the now-enormous U.S. political and military power in global affairs. The extensive and sophisticated U.S. scientific, technical, and production facilities were beyond the capacity of any other power, and its military spending exceeded that of the next twenty-five countries combined.[26]

The American Assembly of Columbia University and New York's Council on Foreign Relations, and Toronto's York University Centre for International and Strategic Studies, produced divergent visions as analysts rethought their respective national security strategies in the post–Cold War age. Americans saw their country as the paramount political, military, and economic force on the planet, but now without a strategic focus. They sought a new core around which to build global and hence North American security policy. Even the definition of war had changed in the 1980s and 1990s. Once a formally declared legal condition of military conflict between sovereign states, war had become any form of organized armed violence with political or ideological goals. This fragmentation and dispersal of operations meant that security spread into domestic cultural, social, and economic realms in Upper North America, and that affected the core and many strands of the Washington-Ottawa coaxial axis. Furthermore, a new era had arrived. Security was no longer North American, but global and intertwined with domestic spheres.[27]

Canadian analysts, by contrast, focused on collective action in multilateral institutions. A loosely defined human security also became a counterbalance to U.S. international policies. This professed strategic outlook embodied the ideological and policy themes of anti-Americanism that came to characterize Ottawa's politics and policy in the 1990s. U.S. analysts spoke of peacemaking, creating the conditions for human security in failed countries that disintegrated or lacked stable governments. Canadian commentators talked only of peacekeeping, which presumed a political arrangement between organized antagonists that required a neutral third party to monitor and report on them.[28] Ottawa and Washington diverged over the foundations, causes, and management of instability in Africa and the Middle East, but they agreed about the chaotic, violent situation after Yugoslavia's disintegration. But officials in both countries underestimated how such forces could affect North American security.[29]

U.S. ambassador Gordon Giffin argued in early 1999 that Upper North American security rested on common values and economic prosperity, but military forces remained necessary because peace and security could not be assured. Canadian solicitor general Lawrence MacAulay's statement on security listed criminal activity, terrorists, nuclear weapons, and environmental hazards as North America's major security threats. New policies had to combine civil and military agencies, police, intelligence, emergency preparedness teams, and traditional armed forces. A former U.S. deputy assistant secretary of state for international law enforcement made that case to the Canadian Council for International Peace and Security. Western states needed to align themselves, promoting free markets, political stability, and economic opportunity. The Internet was vulnerable to "hackers" who stole data or embedded viruses that ruined or clogged networks, as a Montreal teenager proved when he penetrated the Department of Defense system.[30] When sensitive U.S. military technology turned up in a third country and agents traced the leak to Canada, State Department officials claimed Ottawa had failed to follow security protocols. They announced that they intended to exclude all Canadian aerospace and satellite companies from future technology transfers. Foreign minister Lloyd Axworthy grumbled about U.S. heavy-handedness, then headed for Washington. U.S. officials were blunt. Security was primary. Axworthy understood that if they saw Ottawa as unreliable, he could stand on principle and lose projects worth annually $5 billion—or he could compromise. He compromised. Ottawa and Washington also developed a harmonized export permit system within a North American security perimeter whenever technology went to a third party.[31]

Ottawa accepted the interdependence of North American security and domestic economic interests that de facto gave Washington the power to set policy. Ottawa put $10 million into the Boeing Company, and an additional $150 million went to Washington so that Canadian firms could bid on contracts for the prototype of a new fighter aircraft. General Motors of Canada later won a multi-billion-dollar contract to build light combat vehicles for the U.S. Army, and Canadian Aviation Electronics sold a flight simulator to train U.S. attack helicopter combat crews. Ottawa also overrode British Columbia's objections to U.S. underwater weapons testing on Vancouver Island's east coast.[32] Asymmetry of power and interdependent interests compelled Ottawa to meet Washington's standards to show it was a serious security partner.

Washington nevertheless remained skeptical about Ottawa's immigration and refugee policies. One of the 1992 World Trade Center bombers had entered New York over the northern border. And shortly before Millennium Eve, Border Patrol agents in Washington State on the Olympic Peninsula arrested Ahmed Ressam when he drove off a ferry from Vancouver Island. His rented car had a trunk full of explosive materials, and he planned to blow up the Los Angeles airport. Ressam had lived underground in Montreal's ethnic communities, eluded Ottawa authorities, and had twice left and returned to Canada undetected, once from an al Qaeda training camp. U.S. alarm grew after CBS's *60 Minutes* and PBS programs on Canadian immigration problems reran several times. U.S. officials and politicians had little confidence in Ottawa's policies, in part because Canada's Security and Intelligence Service listed fifty domestic ethnic groups with links to international terrorist organizations. Multiculturalism seemed to imperil Upper North America, and this point surfaced repeatedly in political relations between Washington and Ottawa whenever alerts, or even rumors about terrorists, arose.[33]

A divergence of views therefore emerged over the events of September 11, 2001. Canadians saw it as a horrible tragedy, but Americans saw it as an act of war. The "war on terror," or World War IV, as some came to call it, shifted immediately to the core of U.S. policymaking in Upper North America as well as overseas. NATO invoked its charter article that declared an attack on one member was an attack on all. That included Canada. The Bush administration formed a coalition and sent forces into Afghanistan to oust the Taliban government that refused to hand over al Qaeda's leader, Osama bin Laden, the mastermind behind September 11. Border security in Upper North America increased and threatened Canadian social and economic access to the United States. In Ottawa, the threat to Upper North American economic integration and interdependency focused Cabinet and other minds instantly. Canadian troops joined the NATO-sanctioned offensive against the Taliban, but a friendly-fire episode embittered domestic public opinion over Bush's policies. Canadians, meanwhile, clung to their self-image as a benign and tolerant people as a shield against Islamic extremists. They also condemned Bush's National Security Policy of preemptive and preventive war to defend U.S. interests. The security partnership creaked while officials focused on border management to sustain the integrated and interdependent economy.[34]

When, in March 2003, Bush ordered the invasion of Iraq, the Washington-Ottawa coaxial axis core shuddered and all but died. Prime Minister Chrétien condemned the attack, and anti-Americanism raged in Parliament and among Canadian commentators. Officials on both sides reshaped Upper North American security policies, but Bush cancelled a planned Ottawa visit and ignored the Chrétien government. In late 2003, Paul Martin became prime minister and began to work to reopen security relations with the White House. He even formed a Cabinet committee on U.S. relations. A rhetoric of renewal circulated, especially in interviews about the security relationship with Washington.[35] The interlinkages among the realms, proximity, asymmetry, and interdependence shaped unfolding ideas among Upper North Americans, who adjusted to a new kind of warfare against globally mobile insurgents with no fixed political or territorial address. Left-leaning domestic politicians and Canadian public opinion focused on Bush, U.S. policies, and terrorists in a cyclical cause-effect argument that recalled the theory of unintended consequences familiar in covert operations. If only the Americans had not done "x," many argued, then September 11 would not have happened.[36]

This ex post facto analysis seemed morally satisfying to some, but it offered no guidance for what to do next, which is what policymakers must consider. More important for Upper North American relations, Washington officials and analysts concluded that Ottawa had stalled and postured to curry favor among Canadian voters. Pressure to reform Canadian immigration policies and support border security produced what seemed a grudging reaction. None of the hijackers had entered the United States from Canada, but in the climate of alarm and fear it seemed as if Canadians could hardly remember what Americans could not forget. Washington's all-embracing definition of security blanketed North America. Ottawa did move to secure Canada's seaports and keep NORAD working. Satellite surveillance, maritime patrols, and immigration and intelligence reforms combined with close border management to fashion an incremental continental perimeter. Security demanded ever more information, and Washington pressed to share lists of terrorist suspects, screen air passengers and baggage, and reform refugee and immigration policies. Nationalists, some members of Parliament, and civil liberties groups opposed such changes and again embroidered their statements with anti-American and anti-Bush rhetoric. The Canadian public was far less fearful of a terrorist assault than were Americans, but more concerned about security than the nationalist groups believed, as Ambassador Paul Cellucci argued, and the polls supported his contentions. Ottawa became a willing, even eager collaborator on border security because it was clear that Washington's standards would apply.[37]

Incremental assembly of the North American security perimeter continued. Both governments enacted complex internal policies over domestic objections. Deputy Prime Minister John Manley worked with Secretary of Homeland Security Tom Ridge as disparate policies coalesced into coordinated programs.[38] Concurrent security legislation soon governed all border crossing points, hundreds of seaports and lake ports, and airports. The borderlands' sheer physical scale and social and economic complexity made full enforcement impossible. Officials focused on isolating and reducing risk as their primary objective.[39] Nationalists feared that Canada's sovereignty would fade as a result, but consultations and agreement occurred at all stages. In 2002, Canadian and U.S. officials established a binational planning group on maritime and land threats to North America at NORAD headquarters. The group shared intelligence, designed joint training programs, drafted contingency plans, and worked toward what some termed a "Naval NORAD" included in the renewed 2006 document.[40]

Ottawa and Washington now had managed to construct an Upper North American security and political perimeter, although the ideologically charged "p" word rarely slipped from Ottawa lips. Canada remained a sovereign equal with the United States, but a strategic and operational inferior, if not subordinate. The Pentagon's global strategic revision of 2002 redrew its operational sector boundaries. The Northern Command (NORTHCOM) now covered all of North America. Senior Canadian officers had been part of the discussions, and NORAD's commander also had charge of northcom. This embodied principles that strategic planners had worked from for over century, a contemporary manifestation of Sir Wilfrid Laurier's remark to the British official. Washington would secure North America to secure the United States. The minor media and political tempest over northcom subsided quickly, and Ottawa continued to manage integrated security through cross-border liaison, with an emphasis on NORAD.[41]

North American security required coordinated intelligence, strategies, and systems linked into global surveillance to manage commercial traffic. More than 15 million containers moved daily through a half-dozen major ports and dispersed into North America. Security increased at seaports, with fences, surveillance cameras, more staff, and new detection equipment. Ottawa and Washington also exchanged customs officers in major seaports for better intelligence on incoming cargoes. For a time, the U.S. Coast Guard patrolled Canadian as well as U.S. waters.[42] Ottawa also joined the

International Maritime Organization to intercept suspect vessels on the high seas, and a Canada-U.S. Military Planning Group at NORAD headquarters developed security protocols for electrical grids and communications. Combined Upper North American forces for maritime operations trained together.[43] The asymmetry of resources and motivation by default made Ottawa a dependent partner in North American security, but better a willing accomplice with a voice and presence than defiance that would certainly leave Upper North American security entirely under Washington's control.

Cross-border liaison among domestic security agencies intensified. The Federal Bureau of Investigation (FBI), Secret Service, Drug Enforcement Administration, and Bureau of Alcohol, Tobacco, and Firearms, and Explosives expanded liaison in Canada, and the New York Police Department sent detectives to Toronto. For a time, Ottawa assigned armed sky marshals on designated flights—to Washington, for example—and submitted passenger lists for the FBI to check against its files.[44] Many Canadians saw Americans as fearful and alarmist, but at institutional and operational levels, security personnel, armed forces, coast guards, and officers in customs and other border and enforcement agencies developed deep personal trust and confidence in one another. This could at times override the instinct to obey their political superiors' orders, as the Ahmed Ressam case in Canada illustrated. Washington remained skeptical about Ottawa's internal security efforts because the legend of the porous northern border remained alive in U.S. minds. Cultural, ideological, and policy anti-Americanism had also degraded Canada's public image in Washington and in particular among conservative politicians in an election year. The Canadian tendency to portray President Bush and his advisers such as Vice President Dick Cheney and Defense Secretary Donald Rumsfeld as incompetents or malevolent imperialists did little to change Washington's image. Even additional military spending in 2005 only marginally eased the view that Canada was a security freeloader. Meanwhile, the Royal Canadian Mounted Police, FBI, and other intelligence and law enforcement agencies trusted those they worked with and their counterpart agencies.[45] An argument might be made that the special relationship had not died but had been reborn at operational levels.[46] On policy levels in Ottawa and Washington, U.S. officials and senior political leaders were pleased with the renovated NORAD as an institutional core for future North American security that included a joint planning group and maritime component.[47]

Canadian attitudes betrayed some shift in July 2005, when terrorist suicide bombers, all British citizens and immigrants, struck London's transport system and left many grisly casualties. Voters who gave the Conservative Party a minority in the 2005–6 election also partly voted their security concerns. Prime Minister Stephen Harper's first foreign trip, to Canadian troops in Afghanistan, drew positive comment in both countries.[48] The Harper government further increased military spending to bolster domestic and U.S. confidence, and Canadians began to accept the idea that their troops were peacemakers in combined military and civil operations, rather than the UN peacekeepers of popular legend.[49] The June 2006 arrest of several young Canadian immigrants deemed to be on the brink of taking terrorist action against Toronto and Ottawa also shifted domestic and U.S. opinions.[50] Washington officials were quick to praise Ottawa as a willing and capable collaborator rather than a reluctant accomplice in Upper North American security, which countered the inflammatory remarks made by some members of Congress.[51]

Asymmetry and proximity governed the post–September 11 revision of attitudes and policies in Canada about security against terrorists, even over the likelihood of such assaults and casualties within the country. A transnational debate about the relative strength of security and civil rights had emerged. Those who treasured the cultural, social, and legal tenets of liberal democratic societies tussled with fears about enemies that might be among them. A global political transition was in full flight. The state-centered model of international affairs and security that emerged in the mid–sixteenth century had crumbled. One point persisted, however, because Washington would, as James Monroe implied in his 1823 doctrine, take the steps it saw fit to secure North America on its own recognizance. In the end, Canadians and Americans could not escape geography, proximity, or asymmetry in their shared Upper North America. The danger by 2007 was that U.S. politicians would wield the sheer power Washington could bring to bear to create marginal relative degrees of security at the expense of the interlinked Upper North American culture, society, and economy.

Chapter 11

Border Management

In social and economic realms, Upper North Americans intermingled in sustained and interwoven patterns. Early settlements thickened and provided production and markets for regional transnational commerce in the Great Lakes Basin. Around half of Canada's population in time lived there, with equal numbers of Americans in adjacent states in constant personal and corporate interaction and interdependence. The events of September 11, 2001, jolted Upper North Americans and assailed their sense of ease athwart the boundary when Washington accelerated tough border management on the U.S. side as a campaign front in its war on terror.

To make some sense of September 11's impact on the border, two reporters, Don Martin of Canada's *National Post* and Jerry Seper of the *Washington Times,* drove along the line. Their concerns differed. Martin sought out ordinary people from the Saint Croix Valley that divided New Brunswick from Maine, to isolated Point Roberts, a U.S. appendage below the B.C. lower mainland where that part of the border was a mile in length. Seper sought out U.S. border agents. They both found frustrated drivers with deadlines, local people bewildered by what had happened, lines of trucks and cars, and fears more terrorists might be there. Most of all, border agents coped with mountains of paper. In between, Martin and Seper drove through rural and wilderness regions under open skies, often alone. The people in small towns, hamlets, and rural areas lived in a world gone awry, forced to dig out or acquire identification for border agents they had known for years. By the early twenty-first century, some 200 million people crossed the border every year, and a laden truck every two seconds, most of them through a half-dozen of the 150 official border ports. Conventional criminal work was daunting enough. U.S. agents seized 14 tons of marijuana in 2002, perhaps 10 percent of the total smuggled. They had made 140,000 arrests for illegal entry and other infractions over the previous decade. On a human level, ordinary people suffered disruption and drew unwelcome attention from border officials. In the winter, Canadians on Campobello Island could not reach New Brunswick's mainland except through Lubec, Maine. They now ran a double gauntlet of officers who applied the letter of the law and all directives. Children from Point Roberts commuted to school in upper Washington State, a two-hour bus drive away. They faced the same thing. At some ports, assigned U.S. army reservists belied the "undefended border" cliché. The two reporters captured national outlooks on all this. Martin lamented the eclipse of innocence about Upper North American life on the border. Seper accepted the new reality and saw the border as a defensive barrier for national security.[1]

Political and military emergencies had disrupted the border in the past, such as during the U.S. Civil War and Fenian troubles, and the two world wars, but never like this. Generations of peaceful transit by the 1990s accumulated into a view that the border might be a jurisdictional boundary but did not need much by way of management. The social and commercial need for easy transit seemed paramount, and the paperwork was a nuisance, although perhaps necessary to collect fees or meet treaty agreements. In Upper North America's increasingly integrated and interdependent world, an informal popular consensus developed that the border was just a nuisance. But definitions of the border varied with the viewer. Officials saw a jurisdictional marker, a sovereignty to be protected. Borderlanders saw little more than a municipal boundary in a zone they felt free to roam at will. Journalists and politicians often boasted about the undefended border between friends. Canadian nationalists saw a barricade against cultural, social, and political infection from the aggressive and imperial world power just downstairs.[2] Washington's fear about security smothered such views after September 11, 2001. The border became a defensive bulwark where travelers had to prove their identities and innocent intentions. Lamentations and wounded feelings spilled into editorials, articles, speeches, and casual conversation. Throughout, people failed to grasp that management had always been a central concern along the Upper North American border.

Border Management Emerges

The 1783 Treaty of Paris described the general location of the new border between the United States and the northern rump of British North America.

The area was all open to the few people moving through the wilderness. Settlers and Indians, most of whom looked to British officials for protection, clashed, alarming policymakers in London and Philadelphia, the temporary U.S. capital. The 1794 Jay Treaty averted a potential frontier war and authorized a formal boundary survey, but nothing happened at first, and the War of 1812 foreclosed action on that project. The negotiators who wrote the Treaty of Ghent in 1814 to end that war devoted half their articles to how that survey would take place so that London and Washington could jointly manage the shared border between their territories. Two commissioners and their assistants met at the loyalist town of Saint Andrews, New Brunswick, in 1816. They agreed to defer decisions about problematic matters—such as jurisdiction over the welter of the Passamaquoddy Bay islands and the disputed area of northwestern Maine and New Brunswick—to London and Washington for settlement. They then led the survey party up the Saint Croix River, fixed locations, drew maps, cleared a swath, and built cairns as markers.

Meanwhile, another sign of the long Anglo-U.S. rapprochement getting under way in Upper North America appeared in the 1817 Rush Bagot Agreement, which limited armed naval vessels on the Great Lakes. The Convention of 1818 (renewed in 1828) set down the border from Lake of the Woods' northwest angle to the Great Divide of the Rockies as the 49th Parallel. The surveyors meanwhile reached the northeastern highlands, worked south to the 45th Parallel, then west to the Saint Lawrence River, roughly at present-day Cornwall. They headed upstream, wove through the Thousand Islands region, and drew a straight line along Lake Ontario to the Niagara River, which formed the boundary as far as Lake Erie. Another sail and paddle among islands got them to the Detroit River, then Lake Huron. They marked out maps, and Canada got all the islands there except Drummond. Past the Long Sault, they made for Lake Superior's shore. Isle Royale went to the United States. Their last leg was overland to the northwest angle of Lake of the Woods.

The surveyed border ran through areas sparsely populated, if at all. Settlers and local entrepreneurs and businessmen paid no heed to this imaginary line until disputes arose, which came once people moved into an area and laid conflicting claims. In 1835, for example, a handful of English-speaking settlers in Lower Canada and upper New Hampshire declared their own independent Republic of Indian Stream. The line ran through the erstwhile republic, but it fell apart from internal squabbling four years later. New Brunswick and Maine loggers, and hence British and Maine authorities, disputed jurisdiction when upper Aroostook Valley timber became a commercial prize. This spawned the so-called Aroostook war, but the only casualties occurred in a tavern brawl. U.S. secretary of state Daniel Webster paid off Maine to avert Senate opposition to his 1842 treaty with Lord Ashburton that partitioned the disputed territory. Great Britain then ceded its claims to the United States Indian Stream territory and Rouses's Point on the northwest shore of Lake Champlain. When surveyors found U.S. Fort Montgomery to be on British soil, Washington abandoned it. After 1818, the Oregon Territory was under joint jurisdiction. Throughout, apart from occasional customs posts (which smugglers in the borderlands bypassed or ignored), Washington and London exerted minimal border management control.

Settlement began in the Pacific Northwest borderland in the 1830s and 1840s, when overlanders from Midwestern states trekked the Oregon Trail and took up homesteads in the Willamette Valley, whose river drained north to the Columbia. Across that river, the Hudson's Bay Company had built Fort Vancouver as a commercial and political settlement, but the chief factor, John McLoughlin, knew that the arrival of U.S. settlers would give Washington claim over the territory. The company removed to southern Vancouver Island, and northern expansionists in Congress called to annex all the Oregon territory to the line of old Russian claims, British Columbia's current northern boundary. In Washington, sectionalism and politics in the 1844 elections kept James K. Polk's administration focused on Texas and hence Mexico. Polk negotiated with London over Oregon, waged war with Mexico, and acquired by 1848 what became the U.S. Southwest. The 1846 Oregon Treaty extended the 1818 line to the Gulf of Georgia shore and from there among the Gulf Islands out the Strait of Juan de Fuca into the Pacific. Arbitration after the 1871 Treaty of Washington resolved a disputed passage. The U.S. War Department put up small posts in Washington Territory at Bellingham, at Port Townsend on the Olympic Peninsula, at Colville in the interior, and on San Juan Island to watch local Indians, not to defend against the British. Washington had abandoned them all by 1893. Point Roberts was overlooked because nobody lived in the area.

The official boundary makers, meanwhile, found the going much easier once out of the tangled ground around Lake of the Woods. They had a fixed parallel of latitude and few topographical features to obstruct their march. "Rugged" was a mild term for the ground they had to cover from the eastern slopes of the Rockies to the Pacific Coast. Steep mountain ranges and narrow valleys all ran north-south. In coastal regions, the few settlers and those who worked forests and the sea already exploited resources. The realms of dispersed relations unfolded there as in other Upper North American borderlands. Discussions over the Alaska–British Columbia border had barely begun when gold strikes in the Yukon drew a flood of miners and disputes arose over where the boundary would run in the tangle of northwest coastal islands and inlets. Juneau was already a U.S. frontier settlement, so that claim seemed firm. Ottawa dispatched the Royal North West Mounted Police (RNWMP) and militia to co-manage the Yukon/Alaska border with U.S. regulars, while the mostly American miners headed for the Klondike during the 1898 gold rush. The 1903 Alaska Panhandle boundary commission included three Americans, two Canadians, and a British judge. President Theodore Roosevelt insisted on the U.S. claim, and with London's approval, the British delegate voted against the Canadian position. Both Ottawa and Washington now knew Canada was on its asymmetrical own with the United States in North America. The survey continued, and the final line ran straight north to the Arctic Ocean. The marked border ran from monument number 1 on Dochet Island in the Saint Croix River to monument number 141 at the 141st meridian of longitude on the Arctic shore.[3] Washington and Ottawa now co-managed a border that ran from sea to sea to sea.

The modern cliché of the undefended border was historically almost correct. After 1783, British officials maintained small detachments near principal crossing points and built blockhouses and defensive works such as Fort Niagara and Fort George on the north side of the Niagara River. Low Fort Lennox squatted on Isle-aux-Noix, where the Richelieu River met Lake Champlain. The construction dates of U.S. military posts after 1815 show how Congress's attention turned west and southwest after 1820. By 1841, small garrisons sat near the border in Fort Wayne and Fort Porter at, respectively, Detroit and Buffalo. U.S. soldiers did routine duties, occasionally aided local civil power, and fought boredom. The British took border management more seriously with their fortresses and supporting works, but by the 1850s, this concern tapered off because asymmetry made the border indefensible. Border management from the beginning was largely a bureaucratic affair through the long Anglo-U.S. rapprochement. First U.S. and British, then Canadian, agents collected customs duties and chased smugglers while migrants and travelers passed freely back and forth. Tension arose during the U.S. Civil War after the Confederate raid on Saint Alban's Banks and Secretary of State William H. Seward's threats of border closure. John A. Macdonald's government managed matters from the Canadian side, and the crisis passed.[4]

The Fenian raids onto Canadian soil from 1866 through 1871 momentarily compromised bilateral border management. From Macdonald's perspective, Irish voting strength in the northern states suggested that Washington might take revenge by proxy for Britain's wartime policies that seemed to favor the Confederacy. Secretary of State Seward, however, assured provincial envoy Alexander Galt that Andrew Johnson's administration would respect and enforce U.S. neutrality. In April 1866, U.S. troops disarmed small Fenian bands at Saint Albans, Vermont, and Eastport, Maine, before they could launch their assaults. Johnson had indeed proclaimed neutrality as promised, and he now ordered U.S. troops to seize weapons and supplies and to block further forays. In the Far West, Fenian William B. O'Donoughue marched from Minnesota toward the Red River Colony in 1871 to support Louis Riel's rebellion. It was all over by the time O'Donoughue arrived, but before long a detachment of U.S. regulars appeared and arrested him, on Canadian soil.

On one level, all was well that ended well, but Macdonald and Canadian politicians feared future repetition of this kind of U.S. help that treated Canada as an extension of U.S. territory. The RNWMP became a plains constabulary and border management force in Canada's West.[5] U.S. troops built Fort Assiniboine near the Alberta border to guard against the return of Sitting Bull's Sioux from sanctuary in British territory. The garrison went on alert during the 1885 Northwest Rebellion in case the Cree allied with Louis Riel's Metis headed into the United States. Canadian militia and the RNWMP quelled the uprising and captured Riel, and then Ottawa tried and executed him.[6] About that time, Sitting Bull and his people returned south across the line where the U.S. cavalry escorted them onto a reservation.

Themes from all four realms of dispersed relations interwove with border management throughout, and in the later nineteenth century reflected the North Atlantic Anglo-Saxon comity based on heritage, language, and institutions that Andrew Carnegie, Samuel Moffett, Goldwyn Smith, and even Theodore Roosevelt mused about. Many prominent Americans saw Canada in cultural and economic, but not political, terms. By the 1890s, strong evidence of Upper North American economic integration convinced Commerce, State, and Treasury department officials that Canada sat within a U.S.-dominated North American sphere of interest, although shared waterways created their own problems. Great Lakes pollution and conflict over fish stocks in the 1890s spawned a two-man binational commission that recommended joint watershed management. Jurisdictional and political complexity blocked that, but by 1909 officials and politicians in both countries supported the Boundary Waters Treaty, and the International Joint Commission henceforth oversaw border issues as they arose. The long rapprochement also encouraged settlement of Anglo-American issues, such as the 1910 Passamaquoddy Bay treaty that finally fixed and surveyed the boundary line among the bay's many islands. Some territorial items were never closed, such as Canada's claims over Northwest passage channels, which remain in contention, and a few unimportant islands.[7]

Ottawa and Washington became comanagers of their shared border after 1867. A handful of agents were assigned to the principal crossing points, including where railroad lines crossed and ferries or steamships landed. Legislation directed them to inspect goods and collect duties. Ottawa and Washington took control over immigration in 1867 and 1891, respectively. Congress standardized a welter of state laws, and after 1905 both Canadian and U.S. Border Patrol agents watched for foreign anarchists and kept track of who crossed the line in both directions. Canadian citizens and residents still passed freely, even though Congress enacted restrictive immigration acts in 1921 and 1924 that established an immigrant quota system. This did not apply to Canadians, who followed inherited habits of moving south in hard times to find work. The fiscal impact of the Great Depression on state governments after 1929, however, prompted Congress to classify Canada as a British nation in 1931, which meant prospective immigrants had to apply for admission according to quota laws. Canadian travelers passed freely, although congressional and public fears through the 1930s about communist social and economic ideas prompted U.S. officials to treat all immigrants as potential security hazards. After 1939, U.S. border officers recorded and fingerprinted noncitizens who entered the United States during World War II. Washington required Canadians to have passports, which were British-issued because Ottawa did not print Canadian passports (which described the bearers as British subjects) until 1947.

Dispersed Mobility and Other Complications

The automobile revolution of the early twentieth century complicated Upper North American border management more than any other modern development. Train or steamship passengers arrived on fixed routes, regular schedules, and in groups. Cars and trucks appeared any time of day or night, over an ever more dispersed borderland road network, alone, or a few people at a time. In 1903, a Detroit-Windsor group that styled itself the "International Committee" discussed cross-river car traffic beyond ferries. A regional referendum carried by a ratio of 8 to 1, and ground breaking for the

Ambassador Bridge occurred in 1927. The span opened two years later, with customs booths at each end. When traffic increased, Washington funded larger facilities and increased the staff. In 1913, a dirt-surfaced Pacific Highway ran beside railroad tracks that linked Vancouver and Seattle. When traffic became congested, Washington authorized a Customs House at Douglas, a small hamlet just inland.

Ten years later, cars rolled on a cement highway and pulled under a large covered shed in Blaine to serve growing cross-border automobile and truck traffic. Each new entry port needed customs and immigration personnel, booths, and lanes. The Peace Bridge between Niagara Falls and Buffalo opened in 1930, and before long 4 million cars and 20 million people had crossed in both directions. Traffic increased at all road ports along the 5,000-mile border, and each port had a customs station, parking lots, and storage sheds, common sights along the Upper North American borderline.[8] Eventually, state and provincial as well as federal governments funded and managed the approaches and facilities. Lonely roads might have only a sign to show travelers had entered the other country. It was up to them to report to a border officer at the first hamlet they reached. Officers were stationed in towns athwart the border, as along the Quebec/Vermont line that ran down main streets, and separated library stacks from the front desk. Schools could sit on one side of the border, their pupils on the other. Border management was informal in such circumstances because local officials came from the communities and knew the people. As this system became more bureaucratic, officers rotated in and out on tours of duty, and this depersonalized border crossing for local people accustomed to informal interaction with neighbors.

By the 1920s, border management of auto traffic had settled into routines and highways or dirt roads went to most of the crossing ports. The three-quarters of Canadians who lived within 100 miles of the border had easy access to the United States, and while Americans came north for business or pleasure, traffic quickened during U.S. Prohibition. Alcoholic drinks remained legal in Canada, and entrepreneurs from British Columbia to New Brunswick opened roadhouses, inns, hotels, and other drinking establishments to serve mobile American patrons. In the 1920s, hospitality became one of Canada's three largest industries, and Americans were almost the only customers. U.S. border agents faced new difficulties and dangers when armed smugglers moved consignments of liquor and beer by road or over water channels into the United States, usually in the dead of night. Neither federal nor state enforcement agencies could cope with this traffic. President Herbert Hoover threatened to put ten thousand agents on the U.S. side of the line if Ottawa did not curb the traffic, but the victory of Franklin D. Roosevelt and the Democrats in the 1932 election ended Prohibition. The liquor issue vanished as a border management problem. At the same time, the Great Depression reduced cross-border traffic over the Ambassador Bridge and all other ports. Hard times faded in the later 1930s, and traffic rebounded.

During World War II, border officers restricted private transit, which reduced car traffic by 24 percent, but truck haulage increased sharply. By 1945, more than 1 million vehicles rolled over the Ambassador Bridge alone as transnational war production quickened industrial integration around Lake Erie and the Detroit River. After 1945, Ottawa and Washington, often under pressure from borderland states, provinces, and municipalities, increased budgets to expand roads and facilities. By 1965, over 50 million people had crossed the Ambassador Bridge, and congestion demanded added staff, booths, and inspection yards for loaded trucks. Such expansions were large capital projects, so construction and renovations became continuous and put federal monies into local economies. So did the growing border staffs, as transnational commerce grew. In the 1950s and 1960s, provincial governments along the transcontinental line improved roads and built expressways to link with the U.S. Interstate highways. In 1985, 34 million U.S. residents entered Canada, while 37 million Canadian crossings went in the other direction, which, given the 10 to 1 population ratio in favor of the United States, demonstrated far greater Canadian border travel. Railroads declined as bulk shippers for a time, but truck transport increased. So did congestion. The Free Trade Agreement (FTA) and the North American Free Trade Agreement (NAFTA) doubled commercial truck traffic in the 1990s as the integrated and interdependent economies developed just-in-time manufacturing methods. The result always seemed to be more vehicles on the roads and longer waits, especially at morning and evening rush hours.[9]

The numbers staggered imaginations. By 1999, staff from more than sixty Ottawa and Washington agencies handed roughly 100 million crossings a year. A total of 30,000 vehicles a day crossed the Ambassador Bridge between Windsor and Detroit alone, and each person had to be processed individually. Bureaucratic innovations such as preclearances for commuters and shippers and electronic filing eased some of the paperwork. Even so, that year the U.S. Immigration and Naturalization Service (INS) alone filled out 11.5 million pieces of paper to record the millions of entrants to the

United States. The value of goods in transit approached an annual total of $1.8 trillion (U.S.) by 2005. In some congested borderland regions, people lived on one side of the line and worked on the other. Millions of people in Upper North American regions became commuters, visitors, shoppers, conference goers, or tourists. All relied on (and grumbled about) the ability of Ottawa and Washington to manage their transit efficiently, but waits of an hour or more became common. In 2001, the journalist Bill Cameron surveyed overrun facilities, understaffed posts, and frustration at major Ontario crossings and recommended that Washington and Ottawa just "blow it up."[10] He meant figuratively, of course, that the border should be open, with no inspections at all. However, the Ottawa and Washington governments were not even close to a discussion about, let alone plan and adopt, an open border or customs union.

By 2000, Ottawa and Washington managed hundreds of major and minor land crossing points, and hundreds more on sea, lake, and river coasts. Officers in airports processed thousands of travelers daily. But state, provincial, and municipal governments, as well as organizations that represented transnational commercial interests, often had better perspectives on border management issues than federal officials. Individual processing might improve marginally, but traffic and bureaucratic congestion still cost millions of dollars an hour. The preferred solutions began with more ports and highways. The Council of Maritime Premiers and New England Governors, for example, urged bigger transportation corridors to link regional rail and truck traffic to northeastern markets.[11] Ontario premiers maintained that the Great Lakes states were their most important economic partners. Quebec politicians said the same things about New York and New England. Premier-governor relationships thus became as important in those regions as president–prime minister linkages, and often the federal governments became an antagonist for local and regional interests. Ironically, border management problems encouraged cross-border regional solidarities. Nongovernmental organizations—such as the Canada–United States Border Net Alliance, the Canadian-American Chamber of Commerce, and the Golden Horseshoe Educational Alliance—lobbied all government levels to improve management and speed traffic flow. In the Pacific Northwest, trade and public interest groups, along with state and provincial officials, saw themselves as "citizens" of the binational Cascadia, living along its "Main Street," B.C. Highway 99 and U.S. Interstate 5.[12]

Asymmetry of awareness meant that most Canadians, but generally only Americans in the borderland tier of states, experienced these conditions on a regular basis. In the course of a week, all Canadian media down to local levels reported border congestion, delays, and management problems. Only U.S. towns and cities close to the border on major routes carried comparable stories, and then fewer of them. And within each country, divergent conclusions about border management emerged. Producers, consumers, transportation workers, and business interests favored open borders for more efficient transit. Cultural and ideological nationalists in Canada favored restrictions to preserve "sovereignty." But borderland stakeholders steadily gained political ground in this modern echo of business versus welfare liberalism. They proved instrumental in a series of conferences, seminars, publications, and meetings about improved border management throughout the 1990s.

President Bill Clinton and Prime Minister John Chrétien signed an Accord on Our Shared Borders on February 25, 1995, and many Ottawa policymakers praised the steady transnational economic integration. The U.S. executive director of the Can-Am Border Trade Alliance thought administrative reforms could solve the problems, but others called for more binational initiatives, such as prearrival processing, special clearances for frequent travelers, wider use of the "Smart Pass" pilot project for Pacific Northwest commuters, and the "Canpass" for truckers. The Eastern Border Transportation Coalition wanted fully open borders by 2012. Some forecast an Upper North American economic region. Border management seemed in rapid evolution, but U.S. politicians and officials still emphasized security.[13]

Border management also emerged as a theme at the Canada–United States Cross Border Crime Forum in 1997. Some delegates focused on international criminal activities, such as money laundering, abducted children, and drug and weapons smuggling. All Ottawa and Washington law enforcement agencies had liaisons with counterparts across the line. Other agencies focused on transportation, shared physical facilities at crossing points, and integrated groups of U.S. and Canadian customs officers.[14] The Integrated Border Enforcement Teams proved their value to both governments, and the agents who worked on the teams in effect became unified to the point that they had a trust in one another equal to, or perhaps greater than, the trust they placed in their national superiors.[15]

In 1999, Ottawa and Washington signed the Canada United States Partnership to improve collaboration and plan comprehensive and harmonized bilateral border management. A Vancouver conference gathered academics and delegates from all levels of government in both countries and the private sector for "Rethinking the Line: The Canada-U.S. Border." Several conclusions emerged. First, political border management responded to social and economic themes in every nook and cranny of Upper North American relations in all realms, and it always lagged conditions. Second, the momentum of the interrelationships, agreements, and cooperation in all Upper North American realms meant that governments could respond to and steer this process, but only stop it with draconian assertions of power. Third, ever more detailed bureaucratic operations appeared because security concerns foreclosed any relaxation of controls.[16]

Business, academic, and policy groups advanced schemes to manage the increasing economic integration and human interaction in Upper North America in the 1990s. A multinational European Union model did not seem to fit asymmetrical and binational North America, even though congestion, close inspections, and clearances wore down border personnel, those crossing, and aging infrastructures. All overwhelmed the ability of border managers, who coped with millions of crossings a month. Preclearances eased some congestion, and the conditions illustrated how asymmetrical interdependence had blurred, if not erased, the usual distinction between international and domestic policy in Upper North America.[17] The bureaucratic term "intermestic" captured this blurring of policy distinctions. By the spring of 2001, any reform had a thousand authors. Below the borderline states, however, the media and public opinion betrayed limited understanding of border conditions, although economic integration and interdependence dispersed ever deeper into the United States. When the word "border" occurred in national U.S. news reports, however, most people thought it meant with Mexico. Canadian snowbirds and tourists in both countries were equally concerned about efficient border transit and consulted U.S. Embassy and consular Web sites that showed border waiting times for shippers and travelers alike.[18]

Millions of Upper North American stakeholders who lived transnational lives struggled in this swamp of seemingly unmanageable congestion. Students in southern Ontario commuted to upstate New York universities and colleges. Thousands of Detroit health care professionals commuted from Windsor over the clogged Ambassador Bridge. Northern Washington State became a suburb of greater Vancouver as high-technology workers commuted on Cascadia's "Main Street" from as far away as Portland. Bob Bailey of PAC-Sierra in Burnaby, Michael Abrams, a drug company chief executive in Langley, B.C., and Ron Dixon, who worked in downtown Vancouver, had, with 35,000 others, a "Smart Pass." Once approved, drivers received a windshield sticker and dedicated lane through the sprawling Peace Arch plazas. Such bureaucratic innovations made border crossing seem almost a virtual experience.[19]

Concern grew in Washington over border security in the 1990s, however—as Donald Chatwin, who drove between Abbotsford, British Columbia, and Bellingham on his Smart Pass for several years, discovered in the summer of 1998. INS officers interrogated him for five hours; ruled that his visa did not describe his work; and photographed, fingerprinted, and barred him from entering the United States for five years. Other border commuters suffered the same treatment. They complained, and then they hired lawyers with support from the American Immigration Law Foundation and filed class-action lawsuits under FTA and NAFTA articles.

Divergent Objectives

Border management's fine-grinding machinery ground on, but the divergence between Canada's concern for access and the United States' concern for security widened as officials and politicians responded to threats from nonstate militant groups and terrorists, such as those who carried out the 1992 World Trade Center bombing. Some had entered New York from Canada, and that knowledge made Washington officials unsympathetic to Ottawa's pleas for easier border transit. U.S. representative Lamar Smith of Texas insisted that Ottawa's refugee, immigration, border control, and enforcement policies were lax and put Americans at risk. Southern state politicians across the Mexican border were concerned about illegal immigrants as well, and a coalition emerged. In 1996, Congress passed the Illegal Immigrant Reform and Immigrant Responsibility Act. Section 110 of this act required that all visiting foreigners have a visa, leave on the departure date, and surrender their documents. The limited number of Upper North American crossings meant that border ports would congeal with traffic. The millions of Canadians who entered the United States daily, some several times a day, would need a visa for each trip after September 30, 1998. Canadians considered free entry a virtual birthright, an entitlement to come and go without let or hindrance, and Ottawa reacted.[20]

Ambassador Raymond Chrétien and his staff lobbied the White House, State Department, and any and all representatives, senators, and their staff within reach of a telephone, pager, e-mail, or personal encounter to have Canadians declared exempt. They created their own bloc of border-state representatives, senators, governors, and state politicians whose constituents wanted open, not closed, borders with Canada. Executives and union leaders in the integrated cross-border auto industry added their support, along with local chambers of commerce, tourism associations, shopping mall owners, and the thousands of businesses dependent upon easy border transit. Billions of dollars would be lost if each and every Canadian needed a visa for each and every trip. U.S. ambassador Gordon Giffin argued that Section 110 contravened countless agreements and long-established policies and practices. In short, it would rupture all the realms of Upper North America's dispersed relations. Even INS and Customs officials protested. They could not handle the paperwork as it was, and simultaneously, as if in sympathy, their overloaded and aging computer system collapsed.

A flood of protests and petitions against Section 110 from border communities and businesses landed in Congress. Michigan Republican senator Spencer Abraham mobilized a congressional coalition, and in 1997 the House of Representatives voted to delay Section 110's implementation. Senior politicians assured Ambassador Chrétien that it was all a mistake. In Washington, however, legislation once enacted is difficult to amend or reverse. The Section 110 coalition had worked from the position that a pound of prevention was worth a ton of reaction, and it only obtained a reprieve.[21] U.S. border agents, meanwhile, continued to apply U.S. law. That included a "zero tolerance" policy on drug use that barred with no right of appeal anyone found with marijuana, who admitted to past use, or lied about it. Canadians bound for U.S. colleges and universities, trade shows, interviews, conferences, or jobs, even with full documentation, suffered close, at times menacing, interrogation. Canadian landed immigrants were in a limbo as not-yet citizens. In 1997–98, the INS seized nearly 1,000 automobiles from Canadians deemed to have attempted illegal entry into the United States. Canadians and Ottawa politicians protested, resenting being treated like the aliens they were in U.S. law. Meanwhile, frustrated expectations, bruised feelings, rights and wrongs, or wronged rights all compounded regular border management problems. National identities had been deeply ingrained, however, so the border retained both symbolic and practical power as a divider between the jurisdictions and their people.[22]

Canadian protests and organization along with Washington politics got Section 110 delayed, not expunged, so the stakeholder coalition maintained its pressure. The Council of Great Lakes Governors spoke out. Borderland politicians and business leaders escorted Lamar Smith and others around congested entry points where traffic already crawled through booths to show that Section 110 would cripple businesses and depress the U.S. part of the interdependent economy. Ottawa ordered new security measures, and officials shared immigrant information from computer databases so U.S. officials could check names. The Royal Canadian Mounted Police and other Canadian police forces investigated suspects, and Ottawa signed an International Convention to suppress terrorist financing.[23] Meanwhile, congestion worsened, so the lobbies maintained their pressure. The U.S. Senate attached repeal of Section 110 as a rider on a bill that passed Congress unanimously. Beginning on June 25, 2000, U.S. border agents were to gather information, but not visas, at entry ports along the Canadian border. The Upper North American coalition for an open border had triumphed.[24]

Nothing is certain in politics, and members of Congress still suspicious about Canadian policies and the northern border received an "I told you so" opportunity. In late December 1999, U.S. border officers at Port Angeles, Washington, arrested Ahmed Ressam when he drove off a ferry from Vancouver Island with a trunk full of explosive materials. His mission? To blow up the Los Angeles airport. His background? A shady life in Montreal's immigrant underground. This all emerged in testimony and documents at his trial. U.S. prosecutors easily portrayed Ressam as a dark angel of chaos and Ottawa as feckless about refugee and immigration control.[25] A spate of incidents, all reported in the U.S. media, reinforced this impression. Border Patrol officers at Beechers Falls, Vermont, detained Lucia Garofalo from Montreal and found an Algerian man in the trunk of her rented car. Investigation seemed to link Garofalo with arms sales suspects and Algerian terrorists. On the Pacific Coast, agents arrested for fraudulent entry a woman and five others who walked through Peace Arch Park without being cleared by border officers.[26]

Washington officials, and especially members of Congress, still lost confidence in Ottawa's political will and ability to secure its own country, let alone its neighbor, along the 5,000-mile border. Lamar Smith now argued that Canada's lax laws and slipshod procedures endangered all Americans. His new hearings made several points. For example, the FTA and NAFTA had increased economic integration and Upper North American cross-border travel to over 200 million people a year, with 15 million between New England and the Atlantic provinces alone. He also emphasized how wilderness, waterways, and isolated valleys lay between the major entry ports. Even remote surveillance was problematic. A collective fear of risk brushed aside Ottawa's protests about racial profiling, heavy security enforcement, hasty arrests, and allusions to the United States as a police state.[27]

Washington ignored such comments within the country, let alone from a foreign government. U.S. agencies reinforced the northern border, and Canada Customs and Revenue added staff on their side to demonstrate their appreciation of the situation and facilitate border crossings. Ottawa's February 2000 budget increased security funds. Basically, both governments relied upon bigger budgets and more border managers to expedite trade and transit and apply security regulations.[28] Public and political fears in the United States had altered the assumptions that drove border management. Given Upper North America's transnational economic integration and interdependence, Ottawa could do little except comply. Both governments acquired new technologies to read passports and identify people in transit. The Canadian Security and Intelligence Service collaborated with its U.S. counterparts, and Ottawa signed an international convention to suppress terrorism as aggressive border management extended and deepened.[29]

Section 110, the Ressam case, and other incidents spread along the border maintained a sense of urgency in both countries and deepened Ottawa-Washington collaboration to the point where calls for a "Binational Commission on North American Security" arose. At the same time, asymmetry meant that if events pushed Washington in one direction, Ottawa had to follow in a pas de deux, but neither ventured toward a shared management system, at least not yet. For all that, incremental reforms—such as transit controls at points of origin and audits of shipped goods before they reached ports of entry—accumulated to ameliorate crossing the border, or perhaps made it less awful than otherwise would have been the case.[30] The events of September 11, 2001, would therefore focus and intensify fears, entrench political positions, and speed changes already under way, but in an atmosphere of alarm and uncertainty with relentless reruns of the World Trade Center's twin towers collapsing into fiery rubble in Lower Manhattan.

Canadians never quite grasped that Washington and Americans believed themselves and their country at war, although this did not involve nation-states, or even organized political groups as Upper North Americans usually thought of them. This war was an inchoate struggle against little-understood, shadowy, pitiless, and fragmented organizations. The best historical analogy might have been the Thirty Years' War of the seventeenth century, which led to the concept of state sovereignty. Ottawa and Canadians now had to manage a dispersed Upper North American transnational system that they had taken largely for granted, if not lightly. Intense U.S. security checks congested, then congealed, vehicles, goods, and people into gridlocked masses. Major highway ports became parking lots. Just-in-time delivery became not in time, perhaps not at all, because trucks waited for up to nine hours. Detroit's health care system almost collapsed because staff could not get to work until improvised procedures bused them across the Ambassador Bridge from Windsor. Factories cancelled shifts, then closed.[31] Washington rebuffed Ottawa's pleas to reopen the border but reinforced its border staffs. Canadian nationalists feared that a Washington-directed integrated-perimeter policy would be the price for trade resumption.[32] Legislation shot through Congress on visas and entry/exit registration for even short-term visits. Ottawa again protested, wanting Washington to exempt Canadian citizens and landed immigrants; eventually, it got the former but not the latter. Most galling, Washington called on National Guard troops to reinforce U.S. border management. The undefended border cliché became nostalgia.[33]

Washington's focus on security swept aside calls from all realms of dispersed relations for more open borders. Canada was now very much alone in Upper North America with the United States. Asymmetry and U.S. fears about further terrorist attacks submerged historical traditions, personal relationships, and any ideas of binational friendship except in rhetoric. Canadian business leaders endorsed a perimeter policy to reduce costs and losses, while Foreign Secretary and Deputy Minister John Manley worked with former Pennsylvania governor Tom Ridge, President Bush's first secretary for the new Homeland Security Department. Ridge understood Upper North American interdependence, and together with Manley, crafted border management reform to sustain the integrated and interdependent economies.[34] Ottawa agreed to create secure travel documents, aligned visa requirements from other countries with Washington, and shared airline passenger lists. Manley and Ridge created the December 2001 Smart Border Accord with a thirty-point agenda to reform shared border management. Precleared traveler programs revived, first for the Blue Water Bridge at Sarnia–Port Huron, then elsewhere.[35] Frequent travelers applied for precleared electronic passes, and Washington negotiated special arrangements with transport companies such as CN Rail and large trucking firms. The Smart Border Accord balanced security and access within the climate of emergency and sustained dispersed asymmetrical transnational relations. Other agreements echoed what the Coalition for Secure and Trade Efficient Borders, with nearly fifty trade, business, transport, and service members, had promoted for some time. By the spring of 2002, congestion eased at the largest land crossing points while the new era of border management unfolded.[36] These measures applied more friction to the transit of goods and people, however, which increased the cost of preparation and passage. Canadians grumbled, but they had to accept it all. At the same time, ordinary borderlanders found it hard to forget when a whim and a wave were enough to spend an afternoon or a weekend across the line.[37]

Bureaucratic and electronic efficiencies only partly offset the increasingly costly and labor-intensive border management. Through 2002, the Windsor-Detroit corridor daily had eighteen-wheel trucks in five-mile lines. CN's trains took twenty-four to thirty-six hours to inspect, at the border or behind. A preclearance for trains and crews at least moved them across the line with minimal delays. The physical and psychological impact of traffic in border cities and towns continued, and worsened. Furthermore, the Canada–United States–Ontario–Michigan Border Transportation Partnership's very name suggested the cumbrous complexity of post–September 11 border management.[38] New security technology, such as iris and fingerprint scanners, and special attention to Middle East and South Asian peoples angered civil libertarians in both countries. They denounced the Smart Border Accord for personal intrusions and "racial profiling," but such charges in Canada had no more impact on U.S. policies and practices that the American Civil Liberties Union had in Washington.

The new border management could also be aggressive, as when U.S. officials arrested a man in the Madawaska region for unlawful entry. He drove into Maine to buy gasoline without reporting at the nearest entry port, several miles away. He spent time in a jail while a cause célèbre erupted and Ottawa bickered with Washington over his case, visa lists, and identity requirements. Any incident could provoke a crisis atmosphere that generated insults and further strained the social, economic, and political strands of the dispersed relations.[39]

At operational levels, border management improved as U.S. and Canadian officials adapted to changed conditions. Despite continued U.S. fears about the porous northern border, discussions resumed about shared facilities at small crossing points, such as on the Yukon/Alaska or Port Hill / Rykerts (Idaho/B.C.) line. Congress passed appropriations for shared facilities at a new bridge planned over the Saint Croix River upstream from Calais / Saint Stephen to ease congestion in the small towns. Proximity, asymmetry, and interdependence reshaped border management into new patterns as Upper North Americans learned how to deal with enhanced security. Binational organizations paid more attention to direct and public lobby efforts. For example, the Canadian Council of Chief Executive Officers held their spring 2003 meeting in Washington to establish contacts with

U.S. think-tank analysts, public policy researchers, and business and advocacy groups such as the Canada America Border Trade Alliance and the Canadian American Business Council. Staffers from the Canadian Embassy and various Washington departments ensured that the discussions at these meetings appeared in further talks and reports.[40]

These changes spread among government and private agencies and organizations embarked upon an incremental North American security perimeter. At airport, land border, and seaport stations, interlinked computer systems sped record keeping, data searches, and information sharing among agencies in both governments. Ottawa achieved small victories. The U.S. Visit Program—with its iris and face scans, electronic fingerprinting, and biometric identity cards—exempted Canadian citizens, although landed immigrants and noncitizens had to comply. When Ottawa resisted U.S. policies, compromise usually followed, because Washington would generally proceed with or without consent. Jean Chrétien's government had little choice but to adapt. More costs arrived when fees of transit rose for the 358 million 2003 border crossers. Canadians watched an increase in border militarization when in 2004 the first of several bases for Blackhawk helicopter surveillance teams became operational in Birch Bay, near Bellingham, Washington. Other bases appeared in northern Montana, North Dakota, Michigan, and New York, at Plattsburgh. Unmanned U.S. surveillance drones also appeared in the skies over the undefended border.[41]

Throughout, in U.S. minds, Ottawa failed to change Canada's image as a potential haven for terrorists. Embassy officials in Washington met with skittish politicians and corrected false reports or impressions when they could, but fears remained, and members of Congress, increasingly sensitive to both northern and southern border issues by 2007, lashed out at any sign, real or imagined, of terrorists in Canada. Each incident produced fresh strains in the political realm. Even when, in 2006, federal and provincial police and intelligence agencies thwarted a possible terrorist assault within Canada, a fresh outcry rose in the United States about the dangers of the porous northern border.[42] In terms of the Upper North American transnational economy, Canadian and U.S. interests stood in a common cause that cooperated and facilitated stringent border management to balance security and access, but at a price. A 2005 U.S. estimate put border congestion costs at over $4 billion annually, and rising.[43]

The Smart Border Action Plan had unleashed a flood of reform in Upper North American border management. A maritime liaison shared instruction teams and training, and exchange agreements put U.S. Coast Guard and

Royal Canadian Mounted Police officers on each other's patrol boats on the Great Lakes. North American Aerospace Defense become a maritime as well as an air security agreement. At two-thirds of the 147 one-person designated land stations and marinas, U.S. and Canadian officers worked together in liaison. The Conservative government elected in 2006 in Ottawa moved to arm Canadian border agents; and by then joint training occurred at large ports, so U.S. and Canadian officers understood one another's procedures better and built personal relationships.[44] Ottawa and Washington cooperated through dozens of bureaus and agencies to share instead of just manage the border from their respective sovereign territories. Throughout, while exasperation about U.S. policies flared occasionally, overt anti-Americanism muted in Ottawa and in the Canadian media after the Conservative government entered office in early 2006. Meanwhile, writers and academics who viewed the United States with jaundiced eyes began to redefine what the border meant for their country under these new and inescapable circumstances.[45]

Old and new routines blended as border agents sought criminals as well as potential terrorists. The much-dreaded and bureaucratic U.S. Visit Program arrived, and Ottawa gained a concession so that Canadians who lived within twenty-five miles of the border, or planned only three-day visits in the United States, would be exempt. The Western Hemisphere Travel Initiative (WHTI) proved another matter. This required passports or some approved identity card for the entry of foreigners or returning citizens to the United States. WHTI would apply first at airports, and later at all entry ports.[46] This had serious implications for interlinkages in the transnational cultural, social, and economic realms. Throughout the automobile age, a massive integrated and interdependent Upper North American travel and tourism industry had developed. Canadian and U.S. cities advertised themselves in each country, and planners of special events counted on visitors from the huge leisure and entertainment market next door. For example, Vancouver marketed its Expo 86 to Americans along the Pacific Coast with great success. British Columbia won the 2010 Olympic Games partly on the same grounds, a large market along the entire Pacific Coast. Professional associations rotated their annual conventions among U.S. and Canadian cities. In 2003, Canadians made 34.5 million visits to the United States and Americans made 22 million trips to Canada. In 2005, border crossings included thousands of snowbirds headed south for winter sojourns in the southern belt of states from Florida to California. Border statistics for that year also showed 22 million same-day trips and 1.3 million overnight stays.

Even these numbers were below 1990s levels, and the 31.8 million Americans who came to Canada were the fewest for fifteen years.[47] WHTI might reduce, but could never eliminate, the risk of terrorist incidents in the United States, as attacks and alleged plots in England and Ontario by second-generation immigrants in 2005 and 2006 demonstrated. WHTI guaranteed, conversely, greater friction on individuals, especially ordinary people. The costs of their travel within Upper North America rose, and they would perhaps reach the point where the major form of cross-border social mingling that remained—travel to visit friends, take vacations, or attend special events—would vanish. Canadians and Americans would grow apart from one another because of the bureaucratic fences implanted between them. Some took grim solace that Department of Homeland Security inefficiencies might delay WHTI from being applied until after its scheduled date, but few doubted the day would arrive.[48]

In the economic realm, the Canadian Council of Chief Executive Officers, the C. D. Howe Institute in Toronto, the Institute for Research on Public Policy, and the Council on Foreign Relations in New York all urged political agreements beyond NAFTA, such as a customs union, concurrent regulatory regimes, or mutual standards to harmonize the integrated and interdependent economies and reduce paperwork.[49] The added costs to transnational commerce sat in 2005 at between $8 and $16 billion (U.S.) annually. Border crossing delays cost Ontario $5.25 billion and Canada $8.3 billion by 2006. By 2030, the Detroit-Windsor corridor alone could see trade earnings reduced by $18 billion.[50] Such studies all but ignored the social impact on border communities and how even in Upper North American regions regular mingling of the two peoples waned. Washington, with Ottawa's reluctant connivance, ran roughshod over all Upper North American stakeholders for the sake of security, their interdependent economies, and revenues. In 2005, a trilateral program, the Security and Prosperity Partnership, accepted current conditions as given and probed for further efficiencies but offered no fundamental changes.[51] Two imperatives clashed: mutual access and security. Furthermore, domestic security legislation imperiled the inherited values of the civil liberties that Upper North Americans had come to prize and cherish. The events of September 11, 2001, and the forces they unleashed had assumed psychological, emotional, and policy command of over 200 years of Upper North America's mutual cultural attitudes, social mingling, economic exchange, and border management.

Chapter 12

Ottawa-Washington Axis

Media correspondents in the United States gave Canada's 2006 federal election more attention than usual. A testy tone at the coaxial axis core had fractured the public face of Washington-Ottawa relations over the six years George W. Bush served as president. The history of dispersed relations had seen only one previous occasion when Ottawa's and Washington's chief executives had equally dysfunctional relations: John F. Kennedy and John G. Diefenbaker in the early 1960s. The rhythms and results of electoral politics in Upper North America can always produce a mismatch, but modern political relations at the coaxial axis core seriously deteriorated after the events of September 11, 2001, as Washington took control of the northern border as a front of the "war on terror." The Liberal prime ministers Jean Chrétien, then Paul Martin, both slid into a morass of acrimony about Bush and his foreign policy. Tone-deaf ears on both sides derailed the central management of political dispersed relations. In Canada's 2006 winter election, Martin campaigned against Bush as much as against his opponent, the Conservative Party leader Stephen Harper. Many U.S. observers softly rooted for Harper, and held their breath, lest they produce a backlash in Canada against the Conservatives. When Harper won a minority, they cheered openly at the death of anti-Americanism. They had a point. Presidents and prime ministers can disagree but should not be deliberately disagreeable, so all sides expected a better tone at the core of the Washington-Ottawa axis.[1]

Pragmatism underlay Prime Minister Harper's choice of Michael Wilson to be his ambassador in Washington. Bush accepted Wilson's credentials the day he arrived, in almost unseemly haste, but domestic politics as well as protocol propelled relations at the coaxial axis core. Moreover, Wilson clearly had Harper's ear, just as David Wilkins could always get Bush on the telephone. Presidents in recent times had nominated political intimates to the Ottawa embassy, but until Martin chose Frank McKenna, prime ministers relied on senior Foreign Service officers. When problems arose, however, a direct link with a political confidant outweighed working through civil service channels.[2] Both Bush's ambassadors were seasoned Republican politicians who had helped to deliver their home states in presidential elections. Some Canadians chuckled at David Wilkins's unfamiliarity with their country, but that mattered far less than his ability to put Upper North American issues on the president's agenda.[3] The McKenna and Wilson appointments seemed to reflect belated recognition by Ottawa of advice that U.S. senator William Fulbright of Arkansas once gave Pierre Trudeau: Time spent on Capitol Hill was more useful than with the State Department because in Washington, politicians mattered, not bureaucrats. Provinces had also begun to develop a less diplomatic than quasi-lobbyist presence in the United States. Quebec had done so for decades, and Alberta sent down Murray Smith, who was well acquainted with energy matters. Ottawa managed to fold Smith into the Canadian Embassy Secretariat for congressional relations, but he promoted provincial rather than federal interests, just as Quebec's "tourism" office did.[4]

Domestic politics had always shaped president–prime minister relations. Their decisions guide, but do not create, transnational interlinkages in the realms. The broad base of Upper North American political relations limited the impact of ideological, moralistic, or personal perspectives, and at times even the tone of the conversation. In the 1950s, U.S. secretary of state Dean Acheson noted that Ottawa had a tendency to sound like the stern voice of the daughter of God when dealing with Washington. Acheson and others put up with that, but Bush had not. Chrétien's tone alienated the Bush White House and produced a paralytic relationship. The threads wrapped around the president–prime minister core sustained political and policy relations, but each issue or discussion became more difficult while Bush and his senior staff—and much of official Washington, in fact—waited for Chrétien to retire. Martin took office in the fall of 2003. At the January 2004 Summit of the Americas at Monterrey, Mexico, and in Washington three months later, a better tone emerged. Then anti-Americanism crept back into public political discourse in Canada over Bush's foreign policy and Ottawa's opposition to Washington's Ballistic Missile Defense (BMD) program and border management policies.

Martin and his Liberals openly hoped for a Democratic victory in the 2004 U.S. general elections, but Bush won a second term. Then the White

House launched an international diplomatic offensive to restore the tone of its international relations, and Canada was the first stop. As former U.S. ambassador to Canada James Blanchard noted: "I think the Europeans and Asians figure that if they [the Bush administration] can't get along with Canada, who can they get along with?"[5] Ottawa-Washington relations basked in Upper North American media attention for over a week, with broadcasts on major U.S. networks and cover stories in national newspapers and magazines. Once together, the two chief executives set a cordial public tone, although private conversations misfired, especially over security and the BMD issue. Martin then accompanied Bush to Halifax, where the president thanked Canadians for harboring thousands of U.S. air travelers stranded on September 11, 2001. He also quoted Canada's 1960s Social Credit leader Robert Thompson's remark that Canadians and Americans were best friends, whether they liked it or not. The finale of this episode in Upper North American political relations came when Martin did a feature interview with Wolf Blitzer on CNN's *Late Edition.*[6]

The Coaxial Axis Forms

For all the contemporary, albeit asymmetrical, attention on the president–prime minister core of the Washington-Ottawa coaxial axis, this part of Upper North American political relations dates back only to 1925. The political realm emerged, however, in the immediate aftermath of the American Revolution and the Treaty of Paris of 1783. London managed provincial relations with the United States, and even when the 1867 British North America Act created the Dominion of Canada, with John A. Macdonald as prime minister, he remained subordinate to London, the imperial overlord. In the economic realm, Ottawa became active almost at once, but the prime minister was de jure unable to manage the tone or much else in Upper North American political affairs. Canadian prime ministers visited Washington informally before they had full sovereign authority through the Statute of Westminster in 1931, but the political realm had more historical depth than seemed evident at first glance. The Ottawa-Washington core actually appeared in embryonic form in the 1860s.

Other threads of the coaxial axis were already in place. Consuls established the first links. Merchants and traders in the Upper North American borderland managed their own affairs (or evaded by smuggling), with customs officers at crossing points and water ports. After London and Philadelphia exchanged a formal agreement, British consuls handled provincial interests in the United States, but the first accredited U.S. consul in the provinces opened for business in Halifax in 1827, ten years after the office had operated informally. Other consuls and consular agents appeared in provincial ports throughout the Upper North American borderlands in the succeeding decades. Israel Andrews, a New Brunswick–born U.S. consul who worked in several provincial centers, reported not only trade data but also information on political events and local attitudes. Andrews opined (and seems to have hoped) that at some indeterminate future date, the provinces and states might merge into one country. Upper North American interdependence was not as advanced as Andrews imagined, but he became the major political actor behind the Elgin-Marcy, or Reciprocity, Treaty of 1854. The treaty dealt with commerce, but it would come into effect only for those provinces whose legislatures ratified it. All did, and the economic results were mixed, but profitable for those involved. When Congress invoked the year's notice to cancel the Reciprocity Treaty in 1865, an active lobby of businessmen and entrepreneurs in both countries, stakeholders in the first stages of the integrated and interdependent economy, lobbied to maintain the agreement in force. They lost that political battle but continued work to reinstate the treaty's provisions.[7]

The growth of transnational commerce put provincials in direct political contact with Washington politicians and officials. Alexander Galt became Ottawa's first unofficial agent/lobbyist. After Confederation in 1867, a federal government sat in Ottawa, and provincial interests began to lobby the way state politicians did in Washington. Prime Minister Macdonald hired George W. Brega to live in the U.S. capital and lobby members of Congress, an early strand in the political coaxial axis. Macdonald lobbied Congress himself from time to time, principally to renew reciprocity, but his office also made him a delegate for negotiation of the Treaty of Washington in 1871. He recognized that London's and Ottawa's interests diverged and signed the treaty under protest because it ceded provincial fishing interests. In the following decades, Washington and London developed bureaucratic governments of professional civil servants, some of whom acquired responsibilities for Upper North American affairs. Influential U.S. industrialists such as Andrew Carnegie began to view Canada less as a British province than as a North American industrial country with natural links to the United States.[8]

Lingering rhetoric about the annexation of Canada seemed alarming from a distance or when read in newspapers but had no domestic political support in the post–Civil War United States. Interests focused on western and industrial expansion, while Washington policymakers tended the long Anglo-American rapprochement. Canadian politicians often exploited public fears of amalgamation on the hustings, but business interests concentrated on Upper North American commercial development. Ordinary Canadians exploited proximity and open borders to mingle for jobs and land. Americans saw Canada as a market for investment and source of commodities and materials, such as wheat and timber. Republican protectionism deflected all provincial attempts to renew a reciprocity agreement, but Macdonald's national policy exploited proximity to draw north investment and branch plants of the U.S. industrial revolution. Private interests drove these developments, but by the 1890s Charles M. Pepper of the U.S. Bureau of Trade Relations believed Washington should draw Canada into a greater North American economic sphere and reduce Britain's influence in the Western Hemisphere.[9] When conflict, and even violence, arose in the Great Lakes Basin over pollution and fish stocks, Ottawa/London and Washington created a joint commission that recommended a treaty to resolve such issues then, and into the future manage the Great Lakes Basin. Political complexity defeated this proposal in 1892, but a recurrence of the issues in 1908 led to the Boundary Waters Treaty and International Joint Commission of 1909, the first permanent institution in the Ottawa-Washington coaxial axis. This, and what seemed London's betrayal in settlement of the Alaska Boundary, persuaded Canadian interests and Ottawa's politicians that Britain was more interested in rapprochement with Washington than its North American dominion. By that time, however, about three-quarters of London's Washington Embassy staff handled Upper North American affairs on Canada's behalf.

Ottawa governments began to find the triangular political structure cumbersome and inefficient. On any official matter that required a sovereign decision, Canadian prime ministers consulted the governor-general, who communicated with London's Privy Council. The appropriate British Cabinet minister(s) would take the issue under advisement and return recommendations to the Cabinet. The linkage then ran through the foreign minister to the British ambassador in Washington, whose staff members would deal with U.S. officials. A reverse flow transmitted disposition of the issue. Granted, by 1900 the transatlantic cable sped communication, and much could be done informally in the meantime, but provincial affairs with Washington were only a part of London's U.S. concerns. Expanding cross-border relations prompted Prime Minister Wilfrid Laurier to dispatch William Lyon Mackenzie King, who had business interests in the United

States, to report and consult informally with U.S. officials to expand Laurier's policy understanding for upcoming London Imperial conferences. In 1909, the governor-general advised Laurier to establish a Canadian Department of External Affairs to manage correspondence and conduct research about Ottawa-Washington business. At border crossing posts, meanwhile, officials inspected goods and collected duties and data on people in transit. The core of the coaxial axis formed in 1910, when President William Howard Taft's administration suggested a reciprocity agreement at an informal meeting with Canada's governor-general and finance minister. That indirect cross-border summit led to Laurier running in the 1911 election, in part on reciprocity with the United States. Informal political linkages occurred during World War I, when Robert Borden and Woodrow Wilson consulted at the Paris Peace Conference of 1919.[10]

Robert Borden, who succeeded Laurier as prime minister in 1911, pursued full Canadian sovereignty, which meant an independent foreign policy, formal Washington-Ottawa relations, and autonomy from London's Imperial policies. As a result, he established two important strands of the coaxial axis. First, he recruited Loring Christie—who had worked in the United States, learned much about its society and politics, and gained many well-placed contacts there—to transform Ottawa's modest External Affairs department into a foreign affairs ministry. Second, he approved that Ottawa finance officials work with New York bankers to manage Canada's fiscal affairs. When the guns of August thundered in 1914, Britain's declaration of war committed Canada. The struggle against German militarism seemed an Upper North American cause, but U.S. politicians and corporate leaders were apparently content to profit from war orders while Britons and Canadians died defending democracy and Anglo-Saxon civilization. President Woodrow Wilson's aversion to embroilment in European power politics had strong philosophical and historical roots from warnings in George Washington's Farewell Address onward, but that perspective escaped Canadians. When the United States became an associate ally in 1917, Sir George Foster, head of Ottawa's War Trade Board, dealt directly with Washington officials, and the Imperial Munitions Board opened a liaison with the U.S. Department of War's Ordnance Department.

By 1918, Canada's minister of munitions, J. W. Flavelle, worked with Washington more than London. His colleague, the finance minister, Sir Thomas White, coordinated cross-border fiscal relations directly with U.S. Treasury secretary William McAdoo. In February 1918, Borden paid an informal visit to Washington, calling on U.S. officials and Ottawa's War Mission, which he and Christie treated as a de facto legation. Borden also contacted Wilson about using Ottawa as an interlocutor with London. The November 11, 1918, armistice ended most of these informal Upper North American political and bureaucratic threads, but Borden's personal relationship with Wilson at Versailles in 1919 grew from a shared North American perspective on European political affairs that separated them from the other delegates. Wilson even seemed willing to recognize Canada as an independent country, but London wanted any Ottawa representative in Washington to be subordinate to the British ambassador. Poor health forced Borden out of public life, but his successors continued the campaign for Canada's full sovereignty and formal diplomatic relations with the United States.[11]

Upper North American interlinking in all realms, meanwhile, quickened throughout the 1920s. Canadians drew from U.S., rather than British, forms in policymaking. Provincial education planners, for example, adapted U.S. public education systems, although English boarding school models shaped elite Anglophile private institutions such as Upper Canada College in Toronto and later Saint George's in Vancouver. Labor unions and community service clubs also patterned themselves on U.S. models and developed Upper North American linkages, as Samuel Moffett had noted. The influence of conservative and Imperial-minded intellectuals remained strong in Anglo-elite political circles, but in 1922 Prime Minister William Lyon Mackenzie King headed for Washington to visit President Warren Harding and Secretary of State Charles Evans Hughes. After an informal summit, King and Harding agreed that their signatures alone on the Pacific Halibut Treaty of 1923 would make it the law of both lands. London accepted this as a de facto declaration of Canada's full sovereignty, released control of Ottawa's foreign policy, and at the 1925 Imperial Conference promised future de jure sovereignty.

King moved at once to create Ottawa's axis with Washington. He appointed the wealthy Vincent Massey as Canada's first minister to Washington, and agents worked to locate suitable quarters for the legation. Massey was in residence by the early fall of 1927. That November, King boarded a train for the official opening, and a U.S. diplomatic minister arrived in Ottawa the following year. Canada's legation was tiny, so much so that Lester Pearson, then a young Foreign Service officer, drove south in the sweltering summer of 1929 to manage everything on his own while the staff decamped for cooler climes. Ottawa's only Upper North American political problem grew out of U.S. Prohibition and rampant cross-border alcohol smuggling.

When a U.S. Coast Guard vessel fired on and sank the *I'm Alone,* a rum runner under Canadian colors on the high seas off the Florida coast, a minor crisis rumbled but then quieted. Throughout the 1920s and early 1930s, Washington officials observed Ottawa's foreign interests diverge from London's toward a North American outlook regarding European affairs.[12]

President–prime minister summits in this era had a leisurely, almost quaint character and tone compared with the bustling anxiety of modern times. Prime Minister R. B. Bennett sought, in an early example of special pleading, President Herbert Hoover's support to exempt Canada from the protective Fordney-McCumber Tariff of 1922, but the Republican Congress, which controlled trade legislation, would not agree, and Hoover could do nothing. The Great Crash and Depression ruined Republican political strength, and in 1932 Franklin Roosevelt and the Democrats entered office. Bennett and Mackenzie King both wanted Roosevelt to reduce the protective Smoot-Hawley Tariff of 1931 in Canada's favor, but over the next few years King maneuvered from the opposition through a complex negotiation so that the binational accord of 1935 appeared when he was in office. In 1936, the first summit on Canadian soil occurred when Roosevelt traveled to Quebec City. Two years later, as Britain faced the prospect of a war with Nazi Germany, U.S. and Canadian military and civilian officials began a series of talks about shared problems. King arranged an honorary degree for Roosevelt at Queen's University in Kingston as part of his bilateral strategy. While the president and prime minister made public appearances and speeches, senior staff conferred privately. The United States remained neutral when World War II began in September 1939, but the Washington-Ottawa coaxial axis thickened. In 1940, the two leaders met in Ogdensburg, New York, across the Saint Lawrence River from Prescott, Ontario, and announced the Permanent Joint Board on Defense while senior military officers met. The next year, King went to Roosevelt's Hyde Park estate overlooking the Hudson River, where a joint declaration drew Canada into an Upper North American economic arrangement. Canada also received war materials through Lend-Lease aid on a line of credit Washington never called in.[13]

Wars and Political Interaction

The Washington-Ottawa relationship expanded once the United States became a full belligerent following the December 7, 1941, Japanese attack on

Pearl Harbor. Pearson was at the Washington Embassy throughout the war and near the core of the thickening coaxial axis. He created an intelligence unit to work with U.S. counterparts, and military and civilian conferences occurred weekly. Ottawa-Washington linkages proliferated and interwove among bureaucracies, and officials often bypassed diplomatic protocol to work as binational groups. Asymmetry guaranteed Canada a perpetual junior status, however, because Pearson knew that leaders of the big powers in a major war made the big political and strategic decisions for everyone else. At the same time, the growth of dispersed political relations transformed Ottawa's Washington legation into an embassy by 1944.

Foreign observers noted that Canadians and Americans worked harmoniously because of shared cultural and social values and political systems. Both spoke the same language, were plainspoken Anglo-Saxon peoples, were economically integrated, and had a North American strategic outlook. Pearson and his small staff were everywhere they could be, and Canadians and Americans mingled on official and personal levels, notably at informal baseball games that Pearson organized to build relationships. An intimacy developed among senior bureaucrats, politicians, Cabinet officers, and their staffs. Roosevelt and King, political unequals in the Grand Alliance, maintained a personal rapport until the president died in 1945. This wartime Ottawa-Washington generation carried into the postwar years and created the "special relationship" that faded into legend after the later 1960s but lived on in Canadian nostalgia well into the 1980s to color expectations of how the Washington-Ottawa axis should work. Many analysts and commentators by then wondered, as Washington-Ottawa discord accumulated, what had happened to this "special relationship." The answer: The generation that created it came out of a particular time and set of circumstances. They left public life or died, and times changed. In external affairs, like politics, interests are the only permanent forces behind policymaking

Canada had severe fiscal and economic problems in 1945, and only Washington could help. Ambassador Hume Wrong's intimate connections with President Harry Truman's administration allayed congressional concerns over a proposal that Marshall Plan dollars be spent in Canada. Ottawa's first consulates general opened in Chicago in 1947 and in Boston in 1948, which reflected the focus on economic affairs at that time. Through the later 1940s and into the1950s, Canadian officials also learned how to deal with Congress and Washington's proliferating executive departments. Throughout this period, neither Canadians nor Americans saw one another as foreign in the sense that people in overseas countries were. Representatives and senators from northern borderland states regularly dealt with local cross-border issues, and personal relationships among Cabinet ministers, senior bureaucrats, and legislators continued. Canadians and Americans worked together and generally shared outlooks on the importance of bilateral and multilateral international commissions and legislative groups that planned and managed Upper North American affairs. Ottawa-Washington linkages enhanced Canada's work at the United Nations, the International Monetary Fund, and the ill-fated International Trade Organization and its successor, the General Agreement on Tariffs and Trade. All levels of government became involved.

By the 1970s, fourteen border states and provinces had signed nearly two-thirds of over seven hundred Upper North American agreements in force.[14] Pearson managed the political coaxial axis core after 1948 as secretary of state for external affairs during the early Cold War years, and then as prime minister in the 1960s. His extensive U.S. contacts included Dean Acheson and his Canadian family, many politicians and bureaucrats, and influential journalists such as James Reston of the *New York Times* and the columnist Walter Lippmann.[15] Pearson and Acheson personified the special relationship, and its golden glow shone while the wartime generation remained to engage in policymaking. While the coaxial axis thickened, however, domestic politics and partisanship developed increasingly national perspectives with less cross-border knowledge and fewer personal connections except from experience on the job. Domestic policymaking looked increasingly inward. In time, sensibilities chafed over particular issues, and that often put an edge on the Ottawa-Washington conversational tone.

The Liberals lost power to John Diefenbaker's Conservatives in 1957, and the new prime minister's suspicion of Washington generated the inaugural public short circuit at the core of the coaxial axis. Diefenbaker felt comfortable with President Dwight Eisenhower. They were of the same generation, and Eisenhower's avuncular style played to the prime minister's sensibilities. Ike gained Ottawa's support for U.S. policy toward Havana after Fidel Castro took power in Cuba, but in 1960, John F. Kennedy defeated Richard Nixon. Kennedy's youth, manner, style, glamour, and self-assurance grated on Diefenbaker. He complained to his cabinet about the new president, and at times he harangued U.S. ambassador Arnold Heeney about Kennedy and Washington politics in general. If upset, Diefenbaker reportedly waved letters that he claimed were from anti-American Canadians opposed to U.S. Cold War policies. Washington dismissed Diefenbaker as a demagogue, but during the October 1962 Cuban Missile Crisis, the prime minister refused to support the U.S. stance against the Soviet Union, or, as the crisis built into confrontation, put Canadian forces on alert as treaty and other agreements obliged him to do. Instead, he summoned Ambassador Charles Ritchie back from Washington for consultations, a form of extreme displeasure in international relations. At first Ritchie refused to come, and then he did but returned to Washington—to keep communications open, he claimed. Diefenbaker's Cabinet shattered as ministers went off to manage their own departments as they saw fit.

In Canada's 1963 election, Diefenbaker made the United States an issue, the first such occasion since 1911.[16] Throughout his time in office, he had ignored the principal axiom of Upper North American political asymmetry: Washington defined and managed North American security. Diefenbaker also allowed his personality with his acerbic tone, suited to the hustings but not diplomacy, to dominate his policy pronouncements. His government fell, and after elections, Pearson won a minority and brought a positive tone to Ottawa-Washington relations at the core. Even he, however, later trespassed on President Lyndon Johnson's sensibilities in a Temple University speech about U.S. bombing in Vietnam.[17] Such episodes illustrated that personality and tone could easily short-circuit the coaxial axis core, and a change in personnel could restore it just as quickly because so many strands carried on in the interim until personal pique dissipated or new chief executives appeared. The coaxial axis's increasing diameter thus limited the impact of any deterioration in tone at the core.

When Pierre Trudeau became prime minister in 1968, he followed Fulbright's advice to visit Capitol Hill as well as the White House and State Department when in Washington. Domestic and international threads interwove in Upper North America, and Canadian Embassy personnel turned increasing attention to Congress. They attended committee hearings, developed relationships with staff members in research and other congressional offices, and cultivated officials below the secretary level in U.S. Cabinet departments. For all that, electoral politics dominated many discussions over Washington-Ottawa relations, and headway in resolving disputes, difficult enough in the perpetual U.S. electoral cycles, slowed during general elections in either country. Partisan rhetoric on campaigns never resulted in any wholesale overturn of Ottawa or Washington policies, although a general evacuation of appointed political officers and staff occurred if parties changed in the White House because thousands of new advisers from senior to menial, and new Cabinet secretaries appeared. The two systems were quite different, so little of that happened below the Cabinet and caucus levels after Canadian general elections. All the same, Canada's episodic electoral rhythm, amplified when minority governments are in power, can disrupt continuity in many strands of the coaxial axis. Conversely, even what at first glance seem to be intellectually or temperamentally antagonistic presidents and prime ministers can work well together. Trudeau and Richard Nixon seemed opposites that way, yet they did business in a pragmatic way and developed mutual personal respect, perhaps because both external events and domestic politics intruded less forcefully on their time than later happened to Chrétien and Bush.[18]

Coaxial wrappings by the 1980s included senior and midrange bureaucrats, embassy and consular officials, advisers, military officers, and politicians. Asymmetry and proximity meant that U.S. affairs absorbed the lion's share of attention in Ottawa's Foreign Affairs Ministry, but the reverse was not true in the State Department. Cross-border matters dispersed through all Cabinet departments in both capitals but were diluted far more in Washington's enormous government with its global concerns than in Ottawa's leaner system with its more focused interests. Neither Canada nor the United States ever developed a coherent policy toward each other as a whole, largely because the transnational issues and interlinkages were so diffuse and dispersed in so many dimensions. U.S. relations could become a fixation in Parliament, but the reverse never happened. In the White House and Congress, Canadian affairs wove among a variety of themes, although commercial and border management affairs became central after September 11, 2001. Recently, informal caucuses from the northern border states and a "Friends of Canada" group were formed in Washington. Ottawa also has an informal border caucus group that confers on trade and other issues. Members of Congress from border states share interests and concerns with members of Parliament (MPs) in neighboring electoral ridings, and stakeholders in Upper North America's social and economic affairs often ally for coordinated offensives against their federal governments. Legislators also meet in a cross-border parliamentary group, and state and provincial politicians can also mutually lobby for shared interests.

The relative impact of border affairs differs in each country, because 80 percent of Canada's population lives within 100 miles of the border, compared with 12 to 15 percent of Americans in a comparable zone across the line.[19] One significant difference lies in the way every country and interest group on Earth competes for attention in Washington's cave of political winds. Ottawa competes with them all for attention, while the personal relationships of chief executives wax and wane. Withal, asymmetry abides.

Canadians inevitably must work harder at political dispersed relations in all the realms than Americans do, an obvious point not always obvious to politicians and commentators in either country.

As prime minister, Brian Mulroney revealed how concerted effort and compatible personalities at the core can under the right circumstances manage change. His terms (1984–92) coincided with the presidencies of the Republicans Ronald Reagan and George H. W. Bush (1981–93). They also reflected the North American version of the neoconservative revolution of that era. Reagan's and Mulroney's political instincts also focused on personal links to pursue agendas. Many Canadians cringed when at a 1985 Quebec City meeting, Mulroney drew Reagan and their wives into an impromptu public rendition of "When Irish Eyes Are Smiling." The conviviality was natural. In his private career, Mulroney had understood and worked with Americans, maintaining a circle of friends and associates who opened Washington doors for him. Of all modern prime ministers, he understood the importance of tone at the core and how to manage the coaxial axis to Canada's advantage. He came to know well both Reagan and his vice president and successor, George H. W. Bush. He urged his Cabinet officers to confer regularly with their Washington counterparts just to build a relationship against the day when they had to resolve a crisis. Mulroney's ambassadors, Allan Gotlieb and Derek Burney, behaved as lobbyists with Congress as well as diplomats with the State Department. After the Conservatives lost power in 1992, Mulroney maintained those associations on corporate boards, and on a personal level with the Reagan and Bush families. His relationships endured, and Mulroney was one of four invited eulogists at Reagan's state funeral in 2004.[20]

How much Mulroney's close relationship with U.S. presidents contributed to his party's debacle in 1992 is hard to isolate from the many other factors in that election. The new prime minister, Jean Chrétien, seemed in public to be businesslike about cross-border political affairs. Yet the interplay of personalities set a positive tone with President Bill Clinton, whose time in office (1993–2001) closely paced Chrétien's (1992–2003). Although Chrétien once joked audibly that Canadian prime ministers could not seem too cozy with U.S. presidents lest they lose domestic support, he and Clinton visibly liked each other and shared a passion for golf. They conducted business, such as the Open Skies Agreement, in an openly amicable spirit, and Chrétien made a cameo appearance one Christmas when Clinton escorted a U.S. TV crew around an otherwise empty West Wing of the White House.[21] The personal and political shaped policy when Clinton abandoned Washington's "no public comment" position on Quebec separatism. As Quebecers were about to vote on a referendum in 1996, he called Canadian correspondents in Washington together and praised their country's accomplishments and unity. They filed stories, as Clinton surely knew they would, that appeared in newspapers across Canada on voting day. How much that affected the outcome, a hair's breadth victory for federalism, is impossible to say. Some time later at a conference in Quebec, however, he abandoned a prepared text and argued ex tempore to visibly shocked separatist politicians that Quebecers could never justify their policy of independence because they had never been oppressed. Observers agreed that Clinton had done Canada an enormous political favor.[22] The amicable Chrétien-Clinton tone carried into other strands of the cross-border coaxial axis and pervaded the early exploration of binational border management in the Canada United States Partnership and the Committee on Our Shared Border. Their positive personal tone more than offset Secretary of State Madeleine Albright's irritation over Foreign Affairs Minister Lloyd Axworthy's insistent and somewhat anti-American multilateralism.[23]

Partisan politics soured the tone at the core of the coaxial axis after the 2000 U.S. election sustained Republican majorities in Congress and placed (after recounts and court decisions) George W. Bush in the White House. During the campaign, Raymond Chrétien, Canada's Washington ambassador and the prime minister's nephew, remarked in public that Canadians felt more comfortable with Democrats than Republicans. Republicans and Bush took that remark as a slur that reflected Ottawa's bias. Negative Canadian media and political reactions to Bush's victory set a discordant cross-border tone even before the new president took office. Civility faded from the public relationship. Polls revealed that Canadians disapproved of Republicans, Bush, and his policies.[24] Ottawa became increasingly critical of Washington, and Bush, and short circuits sparked at the coaxial axis' core. Meanwhile, the strands sustained the dispersed workaday relationship. Upper North America's economic interdependence touched many interests and had enormous momentum. The public gaze focused on the president–prime minister relationship, however, and ignored the rest. The political and bureaucratic musical chairs in Ottawa and Washington after each federal election notwithstanding, thousands of people in the coaxial axis focused on their jobs, not personal or ideological preferences. For example, Spencer Abraham as Bush's secretary of energy, Robert Zoellick as the U.S. trade representative, and Paul Cellucci, Bush's choice for U.S. ambassador, had long experience and knowledge of Upper North American issues and had worked closely on problems with Canadian colleagues.[25] The Canadian minister of foreign affairs, John Manley, declared Washington his top priority and worked well with Secretary of State Colin Powell. When Bush's first summit was with Mexico's president, Vincente Fox, and not with Chrétien, the Canadian press howled. Bush had broken tradition, they insisted, which was untrue for those with historical memories. But the incident remained a burr under the saddle for Canadians who carried a self-insistent sense of neglect about Washington's "failure" to pay appropriate attention to them.[26]

Era of Anxiety

Then the events of September 11, 2001, sent high-voltage surges through the axis from core to surface. Washington's reflexive border control clogged the open transit that the stakeholders in the integrated and interdependent economic realm relied upon. Manley sought out Tom Ridge, the former Pennsylvania governor and future secretary of homeland security. They established a professional rapport that proved crucial for the coaxial axis and led to the Smart Border Accord of December 2001, which balanced border management and security. Even so, contending partisan factions soon soured the tone of Ottawa's relations with Washington and in time infected the core of the axis.[27] Ottawa supported Bush's offensive against Afghanistan's Taliban government to subdue or crush those responsible for September 11, Osama bin Laden and his al Qaeda group. Canadian and U.S. armed forces worked together, but Chrétien, many Liberal MPs, and segments of Canadian public opinion seemed sullen about Bush's "war on terror."

The personal and the political clashed over the following months as partisan factions about any issue connected with the Bush administration emerged in Canada. Senior people in the business community and binational organizations, think-tank scholars, and conservative-minded politicians from both major parties argued for close political collaboration to sustain Upper North America's economy. This was vital for Canada's prosperity, jobs, and public income at all levels in the borderland regions.[28] A loose amalgam of antibusiness, civic action, nationalist and anti-American groups unhappy about economic integration, Republicans, and Bush and his foreign policy complained about cooperation with Washington. Some argued that U.S. corporate greed, militaristic foreign policies, and global meddling had drawn retribution from resentful overseas groups. Other insisted that

Canadians were peacekeepers, not war makers, so allied campaigns with Washington would transform Canada into a lackey. Chrétien became this faction's symbolic standard bearer, and his tolerance for anti-Americanism both inside and outside Parliament convinced analysts that he was behind subsequent short circuits at the coaxial axis core that threatened to derail Canada–United States relations.[29] Manley and Ridge, meanwhile, became surrogate chief executives and comanaged the border and the core while others held their strands in the coaxial axis together. Former prime minister Brian Mulroney conferred with U.S. friends and contacts, including the Bush family and Washington officials, to offset what some critics interpreted as Chrétien's failure of leadership.[30]

Many in Ottawa insisted that Canada should be Washington's conscience, as though the war in Afghanistan were a UN rather than a NATO operation. They misread both Bush's and American determination about the war on terror. The U.S. public expected their president to lead, not acquiesce in an international coalition that operated on consensus.[31] Chrétien's visible dislike and distrust of Bush and broad suspicion of the United States colored parliamentary discourse. MPs derided Bush and moralized over his policies, and none of this escaped U.S. officials and politicians, however little of it appeared in their media. Arguably most damaging was Chrétien's interview aired on September 11's first anniversary, in which he implied that U.S. wealth and power had generated Muslim anger and drawn the al Qaeda attack. Ottawa next opposed the Bush administration's campaign for UN support and allies to eject Saddam Hussein as ruler of Iraq.[32] Anti-Americanism and personal animus intertwined, and the tone at the core deteriorated further. Bush's focus on Iraq moved into, then out of, the United Nations. Chrétien aligned Canada with multilateralism, but he overestimated Ottawa's influence and misread the implications of asymmetry. In any foreign matter close to Washington's vital interests, the White House would act as it saw fit.

Moreover, Ottawa broke with its cousins, London and Canberra, over the Iraq invasion. For their part, Washington policymakers misread Chrétien's elliptical, meandering, at times even contradictory statements throughout the fall of 2002. They concluded that Canada would ultimately stand with the United States, even when the prime minister scolded Bush publicly before the Chicago Council on Foreign Relations, said the world did not trust the president, and later mocked his economic policies. More damaging, Chrétien tolerated open anti-Americanism in his caucus and Parliament. Washington officials understood parliamentary Cabinet solidarity, so when a government minister called Bush a failed statesman, they concluded that he spoke for Chrétien. U.S. officials and politicians believed that Ottawa refused to control refugee and immigrant groups in Canada for fear of losing political support at the next election. In short, Washington concluded that Canada was not a staunch and trusted ally after all.[33] How the prime minister managed himself during this period mattered at least as much as, and perhaps more than, his government's policies. Political tension built over Iraq, and the axis core blew a fuse and then shut down. It was up to the bundled strands wound about the president–prime minister core to keep the coaxial axis working. Canadian public opinion supported Ottawa over Iraq, and Upper North American cultural, social, economic, and even political interlinkages remained in operation because even a president–prime minister breakdown cannot disrupt dispersed relations.

A strange interlude followed in Canada. Many in Parliament believed that Bush would still, as previously scheduled, visit Ottawa that May. He did not. Premier Ralph Klein of Alberta publicly thanked Bush for his leadership against terrorists and Saddam Hussein, and demonstrations of support for the United States occurred in Toronto, Calgary, and other Canadian cities.[34] At the Economic Club of Toronto, U.S. ambassador Paul Cellucci cleared up any doubts about the White House's reaction to Chrétien's policy address. Washington was "disappointed," which meant serious displeasure. If Canada needed the United States, Cellucci insisted, Americans would be there, because Canada was "part of our family." He waved aside anti-American incidents in Montreal, such as a U.S. flag burning, as untypical of Canadian views he knew about.[35]

Meanwhile, at North American Aerospace Defense (NORAD) headquarters and the Pentagon, Canadian officers were barred from offices, desks, briefings, and scheduled duties. They were not allies at that moment, and hence were not privy to U.S. intelligence or consultation. Impatience grew for Paul Martin to take over as prime minister, but none knew when that would be. Bush cancelled his scheduled Ottawa visit and went to his Texas ranch near Waco, where he feted Australian prime minister John Howard, a visible ally in the invasion of Iraq. At the same time, nervous Canadian chief executives on a private diplomatic foray to Washington encountered no signs of American anger or resentment.[36] The Ridge-Manley bond over border management proved more important in the longer run for the coaxial axis than Chrétien-Bush relations. Officials negotiated security agreements and understandings, and tougher preclearance procedures for U.S.-bound flights were put in place at Canadian airports.[37] The coaxial threads compensated for the core's short circuit.

In December 2003, Paul Martin became prime minister and displayed a positive and moderate personal tone. Bush reciprocated. This restarted the coaxial axis core. Martin announced new staff for the Washington embassy, a Secretariat for congressional relations, and new consular offices to serve the integrated and interdependent economies. He denounced anti-Americanism in Ottawa and his party, and he supported amending the NORAD agreement so that it could link with BMD once that system became operational. His principal advisers met with their Washington counterparts.[38] Martin openly consulted with officials and MPs sympathetic to the United States, such as Jonathan Friedman and Anne McClellan, who assumed control of the Canada Border Security Agency. Martin displayed businesslike cordiality in Monterrey in January 2004, and he urged his senior staff to get to know their White House counterparts. He next went to Washington, where he spoke at the Woodrow Wilson International Center for Scholars and then met with Bush at the White House. Minister of Foreign Affairs Bill Graham insisted that rumors of a Washington-Ottawa split had been much exaggerated.[39] When Canadians reduced Martin's government to a minority in the June elections, he became cautious. Washington observers concluded that politics had turned him soft on security and the war on terror.[40]

These Washington doubts about Ottawa's reliability as an ally in the war on terror accumulated from three episodes. First, Ottawa had not accommodated Washington's concerns over the 1997 land mines convention's impact on U.S. Korean interests. Washington officials concluded that Ottawa was more interested in using the issue to curry domestic and international favor than in working with its principal security partner. Second, Ottawa's refusal to support Washington's Iraq invasion on grounds of Canadian values seemed a gratuitous rationale to U.S. policymakers. Third, by 2006 Washington officials believed they had accommodated all of Ottawa's expressed concerns over BMD because a series of preparatory agreements had been reached. Then Ottawa balked because of domestic political reasons. This came atop open Canadian favor in 2004 for Democratic presidential nominee John Kerry and dislike of Bush and the Republicans. On international and cross-border issues, little separated the two candidates, and had Kerry won, personal tone and language at the core might have softened, at least initially. But such speculation evaporated when U.S. voters returned Bush with increased popular majorities and Electoral College votes for a second term.[41]

Throughout these developments, the coaxial axis remained in operation, although U.S. news coverage revealed a hard truth for Canadians who believed that they had suffered a Washington attention deficit disorder. U.S. journalists and officials openly and in detail portrayed Canada as a minor ally, of little assistance or reliability in the war on terror. Ottawa could be useful, however, if it just secured the northern border and reformed its refugee and immigration policies.[42] Ottawa and Washington both knew that the cultural, social, economic, and hence political realms of Upper North American transnational relations were so interwoven and interdependent that neither could abandon the coaxial axis. So the strands around the core compensated as they had before when president–prime minister pairs blew personal fuses. Despite perceptions of where Ottawa and Washington sat on such scales as growing closer or father apart, being hot or cold, cozy or aloof, the texture and three-dimensional character of dispersed relations in all the realms compensated for a sagging president–prime minister relationship where a civil tone gave way to personal rancor in the service of domestic partisanship.[43]

The Conservative minority government elected in January 2006 offered a change of face and opportunity to burnish the tone. Washington at least had gained experience with Ottawa minority governments. Prime Minister Stephen Harper and his ministers set to work at once with their counterparts along the coaxial axis to restore a businesslike civility and tackle problems. This demonstrated that long-range trends in the realms, not short-term shifts of people in power, offered the better vantage point for understanding the Upper North American political realm. The border divided political structures, domestic policies, and patriotic identities, but those themes often seemed more variations on North American themes than stark distinctions. Even attitudes toward politics betrayed interdependence, because Canadians in modern times have never used Britain, France, or any other country as a comparator against which to measure themselves as political actors. External forces such as the events of September 11, 2001, revealed that the transnational North American political engine ran, if not quite on automatic, at least with sufficient inertia to push through disputes and rough ground.

In 2007, the North American Security and Prosperity Partnership stood as the overarching institutional agreement among the United States, Canada, and Mexico. It emerged in March 2005 from a summit meeting of the North American Free Trade Agreement leaders at Bush's Waco ranch. The sequence of the principal themes was deliberate: Without North American security, there would not be prosperity; and neither would be possible without a partnership.[44] From Ottawa's standpoint, in the post–September 11 era Washington judged everything in the political realm against the logic of the war on terror and public fears about further attacks in the U.S. homeland. It was fortunate that when the core of the axis sparked, the binational federal ministers, secretaries, and bureaucracies, private and public institutions, and states and provinces sustained the interests of personal and organizational stakeholders. Overall, the Ottawa-Washington political relationship remained stronger than shifting media coverage of spats and disagreement would have readers and viewers believe. Furthermore, by 2007, polls showed that at the basic stakeholder level of ordinary citizens, the deep reservoir of trust and regard between Canadians and Americans had rebounded.[45]

Epilogue: Unavoidable Interdependence

Contemporary interpretations of dispersed Upper North American relations have fallen into a pattern. U.S. and Canadian observers broadly agree that the two governments are searching for greater efficiencies to balance border security with access for goods and for travelers and to sustain the integrated economic interdependence obvious to all. Since September 11, 2001, this strategy has increased human, financial, and political costs for all involved and produced continuous Washington-Ottawa discussions, because border management has become a full-time occupation for thousands of bureaucrats and agents. Costs have risen for taxpayers in both countries, and for organizations, workers, and customers in the Upper North American system. Congestion at the five or six biggest crossing ports remains, and it will worsen once the Western Hemisphere Travel Initiative (WHTI) comes into force. National sovereignty remains an irreducible value, however, so no serious observer in either country expects or calls for a political amalgamation akin to what we see in Europe. Ottawa and Washington follow default policies of drift while they adapt and adjust in full knowledge that the border cannot be made truly secure, their best efforts notwithstanding.[1]

Commentators on the future of Upper North American relations in Canada sort into three main camps. *Reductionists* call for Ottawa to resist Washington's demands and, as they have for decades, transform Canada into an independent global actor. A subset of this camp agrees, laments Canada's lost virtue in global affairs, and insists that Ottawa distinguish itself from the United States in the war on terror.[2] *Resignationists* admit the trends, but they see no feasible alternative to interdependent integration and convergence in the economic realm. They also grudgingly accept a North American security perimeter and the perpetual U.S. initiative and dominance in border management. Perhaps an Upper North American political amalgamation of some kind might emerge, perhaps not. In the meantime, they place stock in the Security and Prosperity Partnership (SPP) of the North American Free Trade Agreement (NAFTA) member governments as a mechanism to sustain Canada's sovereign identity. *Engagers* argue for Ottawa's active cooperation with Washington to bring the perimeter policy out of the closet and to craft new policies, or even an overarching grand design. The Americas' Society and the Council on Foreign Relations have attempted to combine these three approaches, and the SPP calls for balancing economic integration with national sovereignty.[3] Finally, everyone has had to accept that Washington is basically driving the agenda.

This book argues that the Washington-Ottawa relationship is in transition from a long historical process whereby the four realms emerged and interwove. This interpretive framework offers a paradigm for understanding the modern structure of Upper North American transnationalism and eschews false dichotomies about integrating or diverging, so often captured in chiding commentary that a given president–prime minister pair is too cozy or cool, too close, or distant, and that national identities supersede all other considerations. The authors of such comments seem discomfited with the idea that Upper North Americans, whichever their country or region, have shared transnational development, and they see the U.S.-Canadian relationship as a historical zero-sum game.[4] These realms of dispersed relations suggest that government-to-government interaction took a traditional international course in some cases but not in others. Themes from one or more realms have also intertwined or become integrated over time. Some began with interdependence, and others ran on the parallel tracks that Seymour Martin Lipset used as an overall metaphor for Canadians and Americans in North America. Themes in the cultural realm have operated largely independent of the others, and over time have proven least vulnerable to national ideas or policies. The millions of stakeholders in this realm have always had independent control as creators or consumers. Contemporary analysts speak about global cultures in the same way, but folk culture and ethnic identities, religion, and especially language are far more significant in other regions of the world than in Upper North America.[5]

Themes in the social realm relate in part to the peoples who migrated and mingled. Mass mingling has ended, but a selective skill-based mingling continues on temporary, extended, and even permanent terms. There is still a transnational Upper North American market for highly educated and professional workers on many career paths. Ordinary people, local stakeholders in free movement, have been most affected by evolving border controls, but they doggedly work through their congressional and parliamentary representatives to gain exemptions from or assistance with new regulations, such as those that the WHTI promises to impose on their lives. These stakeholders have shared values, habits, and working languages that make them comfortable in either jurisdiction, for whom being a borderlander is a way or life. They are more at home with neighbors across the border than fellow citizens in other regions of their own country.

The economic realm has the deepest historical roots and has been the steadiest and most thoroughgoing force for Upper North American integration. At times, the region seems to be a single economy, with millions of stakeholders for whom political boundaries are ideologically and intellectually irrelevant, a bureaucratic nuisance that adds to costs. Countless associations, organizations, and corporations constitute this realm. They have considerable political influence through alliances for the commerce upon which their interests, profits, and livelihood depend. The Upper North American transnational economic realm comprises a dense, dispersed matrix wherein the concept of cross-border trade is a political and bureaucratic construct. This is clear in the chain of regional clusters along Upper North America's borderland belt from the Atlantic Northeast to the Pacific Northwest.[6]

The Atlantic Northeast has the deepest historical roots. Relics such as gravestones, architectural styles, and historic sites evoke eighteenth- and nineteenth-century regional foundations. For instance, Canadians and Americans have an equal share of the more than 3,000 names of fishermen lost at sea between 1716 and 1999 inscribed on a Gloucester monument. Displays in museums are often as much regional as local or national. When Boston organized a massive relief expedition to care for the wounded and homeless after the 1917 Halifax explosion, it became part of Nova Scotia's heritage. The government still sends Boston a giant fir tree every year, and after a ceremonial lighting of remembrance in Commonwealth Square, it becomes the city's official Christmas tree. Atlantic northeasterners welcomed NAFTA because they believed it restored the natural economic linkages that Confederation had severed. The New England–Canada Business Council is over a quarter century old. Governor Angus King easily raised funds for a Maine International Trade Center that served the Atlantic Northeast. Nova Scotia's and New Brunswick's common interests became so visible in the Bangor area that a local newspaper once welcomed visitors to the "province" of Maine. When Quebec separatists sniffed success in 1995, a Nova Scotia premier mused that the Atlantic provinces could not survive isolated from central Canada, and their only recourse would be union with the United States. "Atlantica," a regional coalition of academic, civic, and economic interests, has economic but not political ambitions.[7] Stringent border security after September 11, 2001, depressed traffic 4 percent by that December, and another 10 percent in 2002. Pre–September 11 levels returned in 2004. When Ottawa-Washington relations fractured during the Iraq War, the Nova Scotia premier met directly with the U.S. vice president to ensure that cross-border energy trade continued.[8] Cross-border agreements developed resources, created jobs, and drew provincial interests to New England, not west to Quebec or Ontario. Nova Scotia's Intergovernmental Affairs Office once dealt with other Atlantic provinces and Ottawa, but in 2006 devoted over half its work to the New England states.[9]

The next borderland region includes Quebec and upstate Vermont and New York, with fragmentary linkages to upper New Hampshire and Maine. The Franco-American heritage extends farther south, because millions of French left Quebec to resettle in the northeastern United States from the 1840s to the 1930s and created a cultural, social, and economic, transnational region. Linguistic assimilation with Americans transformed the Franco-American identity into a heritage, but at the political level Quebec City opened offices in Boston and other northeastern U.S. cities, even in Washington, after the 1960s' "Quiet Revolution."[10] Separatist premiers signed trade and other agreements with U.S. and state officials. Plattsburgh became a virtual Montreal suburb for shopping and health care. Mayors have learned French to accommodate relations with Quebec City, one part of a Quebec-Albany-Burlington triangle that promotes business and transportation projects, a regional customs union, and security arrangements.[11] After September 11, 2001, Washington focused on border security, but the three state governments were allies in federal lobbying in both capitals, and the common cultural and social heritage remained prominent where towns and villages straddled the border.[12]

The Great Lakes Basin borderland embraces that vast water system and the upper Saint Lawrence River. This has been the deepest historically and most complex and interdependent of all transnational borderlands. By 2000, U.S. trade with Ontario exceeded that with either Japan or the European Union. Commodities, goods, and people moved through a complex transportation system including a handful of major bridges and hundreds of vessels carrying millions of people and shipments every year. More millions were on the water in summer months. Before and after September 11, 2001, binational regional organizations such as the Canadian-American Business

Council and the Can-Am Border Trade Alliance lobbied Ottawa and Washington, and state and provincial governments, to improve efficiency. Politicians in this region dealt with one another as much as with Ottawa and Washington. A Great Lakes governors' and premiers' group handled regional issues long before their Atlantic northeastern and Quebec / New York counterparts. When Ontario officials and business leaders talked about becoming closer to the United States, they intended to use political relations to liberate and speed up the growth of their transnational economy.[13]

The Upper Great Plains region emerged in the 1880s from pioneer ranch, homestead, and wheat economies. Settlers shared frontier populist cultural, social, and political outlooks combined with a sense of alienation from eastern centers of economic and political power. Interlinkages went deep into the United States in modern times, because U.S. investment and expertise from as far south as Texas developed Alberta and Saskatchewan oil fields. Formal state-provincial links appeared in the 1990s when premiers and governors began to hold annual meetings. After September 11, 2001, Edmonton's political links with Washington in some respects overshadowed its links with Ottawa, in part because resentment over the National Energy Program of the 1980s festered in memories. The vast tar sands deposits became a viscous tie that bound Edmonton with Washington. Albertan premier Ralph Klein publicly rebuked Ottawa's refusal to support President George W. Bush's invasion of Iraq in March 2003, and he sent an open letter of support to U.S. ambassador Paul Cellucci. Klein conferred with Vice President Dick Cheney and announced that an Alberta office would open in Washington. Murray Smith, Alberta's first emissary, pursued provincial interests, and Saskatchewan also recently developed intergovernmental linkages of its own. In 2006, strong western support for the Conservative government under Stephen Harper revealed a third region in Canadian political affairs equal in power to Quebec or Ontario.[14]

Cascadia, or the Pacific Northwest transnational borderland, included the littoral from Alaska to Oregon and inland to the Rocky Mountains. Shared values in cultural and social realms, transnational economic interests a century old, and a sense of political self-sufficiency spread through this region in the 1980s. Private stakeholder delegates convened in Seattle in 1990 as a Pacific Northwest Legislative Leadership Forum. Concurrent state and provincial laws then created the Pacific Northwest Economic Region, with a Seattle-based secretariat. A Pacific Corridor Enterprise Council and other groups planned regional transnational economic integration under joint management.[15] A regional Open Skies agreement preceded the Ottawa-

Washington Open Skies covenant of 1995. Cascadian leaders promoted a high-speed rail line to reduce traffic and congestion on the B.C. 99–Interstate 5 "Main Street" between Vancouver and Portland. Ottawa and Washington finally delegated the rancorous Pacific salmon dispute to the province and states involved, and the subfederal governments created the final binational agreement.[16]

Cascadians gathered enough political strength in Congress to defeat proposed border-crossing fees, and they got approval for dedicated commuter lanes and smart cards to speed transit at the Peace Arch crossing. The Seattle Discovery Institute, Vancouver's Cascadia Institute, and the International Centre for Sustainable Cities planned regional policy integration and perhaps a pilot project for the "NAFTA Plus" that Washington and Ottawa had bruited. By June 2001, Cascadia fed into the 17 percent of Canadians who opined that the national economies would merge within a decade, and the 23 percent who believed that in 2020 Canada would no longer be a sovereign state.[17] Such prognostications misread the complexity of what was going on. Cascadians were only pursuing a quasi-political and jointly managed cultural, social, and economic regional system.

Global developments darkened regional borderland expectations. First came Ahmed Ressam, the Millennium Bomber. Then al Qaeda attacked the United States. Washington at once ran roughshod over all regional borderland sensibilities with a flurry of orders, legislation, and reinforcements to secure the U.S. homeland. In this atmosphere of crisis, a sea change in Washington's strategic thinking exposed the limited power of dispersed cultural, social, and economic relations to shape federal policy. Even so, governors and premiers reached many regional agreements within their constitutional jurisdictions to offset as best they could the draconian impact of Washington's power over their mutual border.[18] The interlinkages of dispersed relations survived, intensified, mitigated, and even offset Washington's efforts, because it could not control the northern border without regional cooperation. A dozen more states, meanwhile, established trade offices in Canadian cities to further regional business. Ontario and Quebec became associate members in the U.S. Council of State Governments, and the increasingly complex political management of dispersed cross-border relations in Upper North America continued.[19] The political realm embraced a bewildering variety of interlinkages at both local and regional levels that tempered and even limited Washington's and Ottawa's power over the border and national security.

At the federal level, Washington adapted and adjusted to the new geopolitical context of the war on terror, signed a blizzard of agreements with Ottawa, and renovated border management regimes to restore and sustain the integrated and interdependent economic realm that social elements operated. Think-tank scholars and policy analysts urged a customs union or common market to reduce border drag, but that would have to include common or mutually recognized refugee and immigration standards and regulations, which neither federal government seemed prepared to pursue. Conversely, new agreements emerged on shared interests, such as energy, transportation, and communications. No Ottawa government would accept Washington's standards on refugee policies, but not long after September 11, Ottawa agreed to an almost identical list of countries whose nationals needed visas for entry. John Manley and Tom Ridge produced many small changes that together constituted incremental border management reform. Their thorough and far-ranging omnibus Smart Border Accord became a charter for further Upper North American cooperation.[20] A gaggle of nationalists saw such agreements as nails in the coffin of Canada's sovereignty, but these rag-tag anti-Americans had a waning impact on the policies that reshaped the Ottawa-Washington approach to Upper North American transnationalism.[21] Business executives and other leaders along with rank-and-file stakeholders in the regional borderlands had sufficient political strength to offset the demands of U.S. politicians fearful of appearing weak on national security at election time.[22] Ottawa's exertion of political will to reduce U.S. vulnerability on its northern border was what Washington expected, and generally got, after September 11, 2001. That was sufficient to dilute the sometimes extreme attitudes of individual members of Congress toward border control.

These Upper North American forces appeared in several reports throughout the winter and spring of 2005 that sketched policy goals and guidelines for Upper North America's future. The American Assembly argued that Canadians and Americans were also North Americans. Ottawa and Washington shared responsibility for security and defense, trade, energy, border management, and the environment. Reforms, not drastic change, and incremental evolution of the integrated economies meant that transnationalism remained central to Upper North American relations. New York's Council on Foreign Relations had a panel that worked within a NAFTA framework. Mexico was therefore included in a similar set of recommendations for economic harmonization, an eventual common external tariff, and an investment fund projected for 2010. Meanwhile, the governments should enhance security along a common perimeter and shared borders, which was already well under way between Ottawa and Washington. Last, the three NAFTA heads announced the SPP in March 2005 to manage their integrated and interdependent economies at the federal levels.[23]

The impact of government decrees on stakeholders varied according to the realm and region. On culture, they had virtually no impact. Upper North American values and identity, the printed word, and mass entertainment responded to other imperatives—public attitudes and taste. Most cultural stakeholders did not have to move physically, so clogged borders had little impact on them. Film crews, once through, did their work as before. Electronic communications and networks released the results to the same audiences. Social realm stakeholders felt the impact of September 11, 2001, almost at once, by contrast, especially for border crossing and length of visit. Personal and business travel included tens of millions of people a year, most with specialized roles and interests. Transnational social groups had pressed their political representatives to defeat or amend the Illegal Immigrant Reform and Immigrant Responsibility Act's Section 110 on visa requirements, and they won concessions. By 2006, the illegal immigrant issue along the southern U.S. border and shifts in demographic and political centers of gravity southward and westward reduced the political power of such groups. Efforts to shape details and conditions of the WHTI, known in Canada as the passport issue, had limited impact.[24] Security remained Washington's polestar, especially in an election year. At the same time, the personal and institutional trust that developed among border and law enforcement agencies intensified. Some modification and delays (more from the U.S. Department of Homeland Security's inability to meet timetables than sympathy for those affected) reshaped the WHTI's provisions and postponed implementation dates.[25] People in adjacent borderland towns and cities still feared personal, social, and mutual economic disruption, so they maintained a concerted political campaign in the United States. In International Falls, Minnesota, and Plattsburgh, New York, tourism and convention managers and local chambers of commerce worked through members of Congress as well as state officials and politicians to alter or limit the effect of the WHTI on their transnational lives.[26] Their concerns became buried in the issues that shaped voting patterns in the 2006 U.S. midterm elections.

The currents in all realms of dispersed relations continued to pulse because geography, proximity, and historical intertwining defined the Upper North American neighborhood. The political will to manage or control that interaction ebbed and flowed over time, and often diluted, held back, or delayed the bureaucratic power of the two nation-states. Both peoples continued to hold broadly liberal democratic values, with English as their common language. Similar arguments about the clash between civil liberty and the need for security occurred in both countries as terrorist plots came to light and government agents searched for others. Fashion, habits of amusement, and forms of entertainment were all immune to state power, which paid them little if any heed. In the social realm, Upper North Americans on an individual basis retained freedom to move, associate, and live and work in either country. Polls revealed that mutual trust and positive regard had returned among the people of Upper North America. Stakeholder interests in transnational interaction on personal and broader social grounds pressed for open (albeit documented) access as a historical entitlement. Stakeholders in the economic realm, which produced Upper North American prosperity and government revenues, became better informed and organized to protect their interests. Networks of interlinkages dispersed further in all cross-border regions, and stakeholders joined forces across the border to coordinate work with their respective federal governments. Political power in dispersed relations became more federal in character as well as name. In combination, the organizations and governments in the borderland regions had through their integration gained considerable de facto freedom to act on their own while they pressed Washington and Ottawa to reshape policies they opposed, such as the WHTI.[27]

Stakeholders in these regions created their own transnational coaxial axes and organized studies and projects that increased their national as well as regional efficiency and political impact. The cumulative, mutually reinforcing threads and forces of the first three realms of dispersed relations fed from regions into the Upper North American political realm. While the two federal governments interrelated, so too did states and provinces, ameliorating (albeit not bypassing) security regulations. The events of September 11, 2001, hung over Upper North American relations in all the realms, and would for the foreseeable future. At the same time, allusions to false dichotomies—such as cozy or aloof, close or far—confused and muddied rather than clarified how dispersed relations worked because they put carts and horses in the wrong order. Since the Revolutionary War of 1776, Upper North American affairs have always involved much more than mere bilateralism. And in modern times, anyone who believes that Canadian-American relations are just about presidents and prime ministers has missed 98 percent of what goes on.

Notes

This section includes a guide to abbreviations used throughout the notes. Then the reader will find the notes, part by part and chapter by chapter.

Introduction

This book rests heavily on media, government, academic and private think-tank publications, interviews, and the extensive secondary literature in Upper North American history and current affairs. The Internet provided access to all media sources when printed copies or personal viewing was unavailable. Most interviewees, at their request, remain anonymous. The names of scholarly and research periodicals and a few other publications are abbreviated in the citations; their full names are listed below. Secondary studies not directly cited are listed in the bibliography.

Scholarly and Research Periodicals and Journals

AER	*American Economic Review*
AHR	*American Historical Review*
ARCS	*American Review of Canadian Studies*
CAPP	*Canadian-American Public Policy*
CHR	*Canadian Historical Review*
CWH	*Civil War History*
DH	*Diplomatic History*
DR	*Dalhousie Review*
FA	*Foreign Affairs*
FP	*Foreign Policy*
IJ	*International Journal*
JAH	*Journal of American History*
JCS	*Journal of Canadian Studies*
JEH	*Journal of Economic History*
LRC	*Literary Review of Canada*
NYH	*New York History*
PHR	*Pacific Historical Review*
PO	*Policy Options*
QQ	*Queens Quarterly*
WEA	*World Economic Association*
WQ	*Wilson Quarterly*

Newspapers and Magazines

BDN	*Bangor Daily News*	*NR*	*National Review*
BG	*Boston Globe*	*NYT*	*New York Times*
CH	*Chronicle Herald* (Halifax)	*OC*	*Ottawa Citizen*
CS	*Calgary Sun*	*SPI*	*Seattle Post-Intelligencer*
CT	*Chicago Tribune*	*SH*	*Sunday Herald* (Halifax)
DN	*Daily News* (Halifax)	*SN*	*Saturday Night*
EJ	*Edmonton Journal*	*ST*	*Seattle Times*
FP	*Financial Post*	*TS*	*Toronto Star*
G&M	*Globe & Mail*	*USAT*	*USA Today*
HH	*Halifax Herald*	*VS*	*Vancouver Sun*
MG	*Montreal Gazette*	*VTC*	*Victoria Times Colonist*
MS	*Mail Star* (Halifax)	*WP*	*Washington Post*
NP	*National Post*	*WT*	*Washington Times*

Notes

Prologue

1. "Upper North America" refers to Canadian provinces and U.S. states in a continental unit, the geographic stage where dispersed relations in the realms have played out over time. "Transnationalism" refers to themes that overrode or ignored political boundaries and established permanent patterns.

2. For the border as a divider, see Seymour Martin Lipset, *Continental Divide: The Values and Institutions of the United States and Canada* (Toronto and Washington: C. D: Howe Institute and the National Planning Association, 1989). Edward Grabb and James Curtis, *Regions Apart: The Four Societies of Canada and the United States* (Don Mills, Ont.: Oxford University Press, 2005), argue that transborder regional, not bordered national, identities evolved in Upper North America alongside divergent patriotic sensibilities.

3. See, as the best examples, Edelgard E. Mahant and Graeme S. Mount, *An Introduction to Canadian-American Relations,* 2nd ed. (Toronto: Nelson Canada, 1989); John Herd Thompson and Stephen J. Randall, *Canada and the United States: Ambivalent Allies,* 3rd ed. (Montreal and Kingston: McGill–Queen's University Press, 2002); and Norman Hillmer and J. L. Granatstein, *For Better or For Worse: Canada and the United States into the Twenty-First Century,* 2nd ed. (Toronto: Thompson Nelson, 2007).

4. David M. Thomas, ed., *Canada and the United States: Differences That Count* (Toronto: Broadview Press, 2000), 2nd ed.; William Watson, *Globalization and the Meaning of Canadian Life* (Toronto: University of Toronto Press, 1998); John N. McDougall, *Drifting Together: The Political Economy of Canada-US Integration* (Toronto: Broadview Press, 2006); Stephen Clarkson, *Uncle Sam and US: Globalization, Neoconservatism, and the Canadian State* (Washington and Toronto: Woodrow Wilson Center Press and University of Toronto Press, 2002); Katherine Morrison, *Canadians Are Not Americans: Myths and Literary Tradition* (Toronto: Second Story Press, 2003).

5. D. W. Meinig, *The Shaping of America: A Geographical Perspective on 500 Years of History,* 4 vols.: *Vol. I, Atlantic America 1492–1800; Vol. II, Continental Amer-*

ica 1800–1867; Vol. III, Transcontinental America 1850–1915; Vol. IV, Global America 1915–1992 (New Haven, Conn.: Yale University Press, 1985, 1993, 1999, 2004); Randy William Widdis, *With Scarcely a Ripple: Anglo-Canadian Migration into the United States and Western Canada 1880–1920* (Montreal and Kingston: McGill–Queen's University Press, 1998); Randy William Widdis, "The Historical Geography of the Canadian-American Borderlands: Conceptual and Methodological Challenges," paper delivered at ACSUS Colloquium in Canada, Vancouver, October 7, 2004, copy courtesy of the author. Historical geography as a discipline is little more than a half century old.

6. See the Borderland Project Pamphlets of the Canadian-American Center, University of Maine, Orono: No. 1, Lauren McKinsey and Victor Konrad, *Borderland Reflections: The United States and Canada* (1989); No. 2, Roger Gribbins, *Canada as a Borderlands Society* (1989); No. 3, Seymour Martin Lipset, *North American Cultural Values and Institutions in Canada and the United States* (1990); No. 4, Clark Blaise, *The Border as Fiction,* and Russell Brown, *Borderlines and Borderlands in English Canada* (1990); No. 5, Patrick McGreevy, *The Wall of Mirrors: Nationalism and Perceptions at Niagara Falls,* and Chris Merrit, *Crossing the Border: The Canada–United States Boundary* (1991). Also see Robert Lecker, ed., *Borderlands: Essays in Canadian-American Relations* (Toronto: ECW Press, 1991); and Claudia Sadowski-Smith and Claire F. Fox, "Theorizing the Hemisphere: Inter-Americas Work at the Intersection of American, Canadian, and Latin-American Studies," *Comparative American Studies: An International Journal* 2, no. 1 (Spring 2002): 14–20.

7. John J. Bukowcyzk et al., *Permeable Border: The Great Lakes Basin as a Transnational Region, 1650–1990* (Calgary and Pittsburgh: University of Calgary Press and University of Pittsburgh Press, 2005); Claire Puccia Parham, *From Great Wilderness to Seaway Towns: A Comparative History of Cornwall, Ontario, and Massena, New York, 1784–2001* (Albany: State University of New York Press, 2004).

8. Lewis Hanke, ed., *Do the Americas Have A Common History? A Critique of the Bolton Thesis* (New York: Alfred A. Knopf, 1964); Joel Garreau, *The Nine Nations of North America* (Boston: Houghton Mifflin, 1981); Anthony DePalma, *Here: A Biography of the New American Continent* (New York: PublicAffairs, 2001); Reginald C. Stuart, "First & Further Drafts: Reappraisals of North American Identities," *Canadian Journal of History* 37, no. 1 (April 2002): 95–101.

9. W. H. New, *Borderlands: How We Talk about Canada* (Vancouver: University of British Columbia Press, 1969); James Laxer, *The Border: Canada, the U.S. and Dispatches from the 49th Parallel* (Toronto: Random House of Canada, 2003); Daniel Drache, *Borders Matter: Homeland Security and the Search for North America* (Halifax: Fernwood, 2004).

10. The Carnegie scholars' work was funded by the Carnegie Endowment for International Peace. See John Bartlet Brebner, *North Atlantic Triangle: The Interplay of Canada, the United States, and Great Britain* (New Haven, Conn.: Yale University Press, 1945); Carl Berger, "Internationalism, Continentalism, and the Writing of History: Comments on the Carnegie Series on the Relations of Canada and the United States," in *The Influence of the United States on Canadian Development: Eleven Case Studies,* ed. R. A. Preston (Durham, N.C.: Duke University Press, 1972), 32–54; and Edward P. Kohn, *This Kindred People: Canadian-American Relations and the Anglo-Saxon Idea, 1895–1903* (Montreal and Kingston: McGill–Queen's University Press, 2005).

11. William Redman Duggan, *Our Neighbors Upstairs: The Canadians* (Chicago: Nelson Hall, 1979); Andrew H. Malcolm, *The Canadians* (New York: Times Books,

1985); Clarence Page, "Greetings from the United States of Canada," *WT,* November 16, 2004; Steven Pearlstein, "O Canada! A National Swan Song?" *WP,* September 5, 2000; notes of author's conversation with Steven Pearlstein, February, 2004, Washington.

12. Ian Lumsden, ed., *Close the 49th Parallel, Etc.* (Toronto: University of Toronto Press: 1970); Stephen Clarkson, ed., *An Independent Foreign Policy for Canada?* (Toronto: McClelland & Stewart, 1968); Philip Resnick, *The European Roots of Canadian Identity* (Toronto: Broadview Press, 2005).

13. Michael S. Cross, ed., "Introduction," *The Frontier Thesis and the Canadas: The Debate on the Impact of the Canadian Environment* (Toronto: Copp Clark, 1970), 1–7; Randy William Widdis, "Where Is Here? The Problem of Identity," in *With Scarcely a Ripple: Anglo-Canadian Migration into the United States and Western Canada, 1880–1920,* by Randy William Widdis (Montreal and Kingston: McGill–Queen's University Press, 1998), 9–43; Sheila McManus, *The Line which Separates: Race, Gender and the Making of the Alberta-Montana Borderlands* (Lincoln: University of Nebraska Press, 2005); Warren M. Elofson, *Frontier Cattle Ranching in the Land and Times of Charlie Russell* (Montreal and Kingston: McGill–Queen's University Press, 2004.

14. In political science terms, "stakeholder" refers to how people can link with policy makers in democratic societies . In Upper North America, mobility, shared cultural and social views, and economic interests made the vast majority of people stakeholders in open interaction.

15. Stephen Hornsby, ed., *The Northeastern Borderlands: Four Centuries of Interaction* (Fredericton, N.B.: Acadiensis Press and Canadian-American Center, University of Maine, 1989); John Reid and Hornsby, eds., *New England and Atlantic Canada* (Montreal and Kingston: McGill–Queen's University Press, 2005).

16. See Michael Adams, *Fire and Ice: The United States, Canada and the Myth of Converging Values* (Toronto: Penguin Canada, 2003); Noah Richler, "Taking Measure of Our Country," *NP,* July 3, 2003; and Alan Gregg, "Bumpy Ride," *Maclean's,* December 29, 2003. See the December–January editions of *Maclean's* from 1985 to 2002 (annual surveys), where questions of identity vis-à-vis Americans has been part of the questionnaires. Also see Alan S. Alexandroff and Don Guy, *What Canadians Have to Say about Relations with the United States,* Border Paper 73 (Toronto: C. D. Howe Institute, 2003).

17. Pearlstein, "O Canada!"; Charlie Gillis, "Luminaries Cast Canada as 51st State," *NP,* September 6, 2000; "Portrait of Two Nations: Should the Two Countries Become One?" *Maclean's,* June 26, 1990, 37–58; Richard Gwyn, "The 51st State? Never," editorial, *NP,* September 9, 2000; Andrew Cohen, "OK Canada, Let's Bury the U.S. Obsession," *G&M,* September 11, 2000. See the essays in Maureen Appel Molot and Fen Osler Hampson, eds., *Vanishing Borders: Canada among Nations* (Toronto: Oxford University Press, 2000).

18. Charlie Gillis, Joseph Brean, and Heather Skolkoff, "Border Debate Picking Up Speed" and "Erasing the Frontier," *NP,* August 18, 2001; William Watson, "Drawing the Line," *NP,* August 18, 2001; Bill Cameron, "So Sure, Just Blow It Up," *NP,* August 18, 2001.

19. Tyler Cowen, *The Promise of Global Culture* (Cambridge, Mass.: Harvard University Press, 2000); Thomas Friedman, *The Lexus and the Olive Tree: Understanding Globalization* (New York: Anchor Books, 2000); Joel Swerdlow, "Global Culture," *National Geographic* 196, no. 2 (1999): 4–89. See the early-twentieth-century expectations

of Samuel Moffett, *The Americanization of Canada* (Toronto: University of Toronto Press, 1972; orig. pub. 1907); and William T. Stead, *The Americanization of the World, or The Trend of the Twentieth Century* (New York: Garland, 1972, orig. pub. in *Review of Reviews,* London, 1902).

20. George Hoberg, ed., *Capacity for Choice: Canada in a New North America* (Toronto: University of Toronto Press, 2002), has a broad sample of views.

21. Michael Kluckner, *Vanishing Vancouver* (Vancouver: Whitecap Books, 1990), 22–29.

22. Washington's insistence upon biometric identification to enter the United States for its own citizens, as well as foreign nationals, has met sufficient transnational resistance to effect delays and modifications along the Canada–United States border because of local, state, and provincial political action. See, e.g., Jacob Resnick, "McHugh Has Hard Words for Border Reforms," *Adirondack Daily Enterprise,* May 23, 2006, http://www.adirondackdailyenterprise.com/news/articles; and Tim Harper, "Ottawa Scores on Export Front," *TS,* May 18, 2006.

23. "Portrait of Two Nations: Should the Two Countries Become One?" *Maclean's,* June 25, 1990, 37–53; Rae Corelli, "How Very Different We Are," *Maclean's,* November 4, 1996, 36–40; Chris Wood, "The Vanishing Border," *Maclean's,* December 20, 1999, 20–29; Robert Sheppard, "We Are Canadian," *Maclean's,* December 25–January 1, 2000–1, 26–32; EKOS, *Rethinking North American Integration: Marketplace May Not Equal Community—Not "Here" Yet* (Toronto: EKOS, 2002); Daniel Schwanen, *Deeper, Broader: A Roadmap for a Treaty of North America, No. 4 of Thinking North America* (Montreal: Institute for Research on Public Policy, 2004).

Part I: Cultural Realm

1. Lippmann is cited in *American Culture American Tastes: Social Change and the 20th Century,* by Michael Kammen (New York: Alfred A. Knopf, 1999), xvii, 26. Also see Gilbert Gagne, "North American Integration and Canadian Culture," in *Capacity for Choice: Canada in a New North America,* ed. George Hoberg (Toronto: University of Toronto Press, 2002), 159–83.

2. Seymour Martin Lipset, *Continental Divide: The Values and Institutions of the United States and Canada* (Toronto and Washington: C. D. Howe Institute and National Planning Association, 1989); Edward Grabb and James Curtis, *Regions Apart: The Four Societies of Canada and the United States* (Don Mills, Ont.: Oxford University Press, 2005). See David M. Thomas, ed., *Canada and the United States: Differences That Count,* 2nd ed. (Toronto: Broadview Press, 2000); Keith Banting, George Hoberg, and Richard Simeon, eds., *Degrees of Freedom: Canada and the United States in a Changing World* (Montreal and Kingston: Montreal–Queen's University Press, 1997); Neil Nevitte, Miquel Basanez, and Ronald Inglehart, "Directions of Value Change in North America," in *NAFTA in Transition,* ed. Stephen J. Randall and Herman W. Konrad (Calgary: University of Calgary Press, 1995), 329–43; John D. Wirth, "Advancing the North American Community," *ARCS* 26, no. 2 (Summer 1996): 261–73.

3. Patricia Wood, "Borders and Identities among Italian Immigrants in the Pacific Northwest, 1880–1938," in *Parallel Destinies: Canadian-American Relations West of the Rockies,* ed. John M. Findlay and Ken S. Coates (Seattle: University of Washington

Press, 2002), 104–22; Eric R. Crouse, *Revival in the City: The Impact of American Evangelists in Canada, 1884–1914* (Montreal and Kingston: McGill–Queen's University Press, 2005).

4. Stephen Vail, *Canadians' Values and Attitudes on Canada's Health Care System* (Ottawa: Conference Board of Canada, 2001); Stephen Vail, "Canadian Values in Flux," *Insidedge,* Winter 2001, 7.

Chapter 1: Cultural Identities

1. Andrew and Judith Kleinfield, "Two Miles Apart, or a World Away," *NP,* July 13, 2004; Kevin Newman, "Love It *and* Leave It," *Maclean's,* July 1, 2001, 76.

2. Robert MacNeil and William Cran, *Do You Speak American?* (New York: Nan A. Talese, 2004).

3. David Frum, "We Are Alike, Eh?" *EnRoute,* October 1995, 17–19; Peter Jennings, "Moose Jaw, U.S.A.? Never! Jamais!" *Maclean's,* June 25, 1990, 86–87.

4. Kelly Shiers, "You Are What You Say, Eh?" *SH,* May 6, 2001; Associated Press, "Canadians Love Show about Ignorance," *NYT,* May 25, 2001; Linda Williamson, "Canada—Love It or Leave It," *CS,* March 12, 2002; Scott Reid, "Portrait of a Canadian," *NP,* March 10, 1999; Michael Adams and Amy Langstaff, ". . . and I Say Relax," *G&M,* July 1, 2000.

5. Marc Pachler, "American Identity: A Political Compact," in *Identities in North America: The Search for Community,* ed. Robert L. Earle and John D. Wirth (Stanford, Calif.: Stanford University Press, 1995), 29–39; Seymour Martin Lipset, "Metaphor and Nationality in North America," in *Continental Divide: The Values and Institutions of the United States and Canada,* by Seymour Martin Lipset (Toronto and Washington: C. D. Howe Institute and National Planning Association, 1989), chap 3.

6. Allan Smith, *Canada: An American Nation? Essays on Continentalism, Identity, and the Canadian Frame of Mind* (Montreal and Kingston: McGill–Queen's University Press, 1994), chaps. 6, 7; Editorial, "The Truths We Hold about Americans," *G&M,* April 7, 1994; Graeme Wynn, "New England's Outpost in the Nineteenth Century," in *The Northeastern Borderlands: Four Centuries of Interaction,* ed. Stephen Hornsby (Fredericton, N.B.: Acadiensis Press and Canadian-American Center, University of Maine), 1989, 65–93.

7. William T. Stead, *The Americanization of the World, or The Trend of the Twentieth Century* (New York: Garland, 1972, orig. pub. in *Review of Reviews,* London, 1902), 39–51.

8. Samuel Moffett, *The Americanization of Canada* (Toronto: University of Toronto Press, 1972; orig. pub. 1907), 114; Paul Rutherford, *A Victorian Authority: The Daily Press in Late Nineteenth-Century Canada* (Toronto: University of Toronto Press, 1982), on how Canadian editors adopted U.S. styles and organization for their papers.

9. Frederick Gibson and Jonathan Rossie, *The Road to "Ogdensburg: The Queen's–St. Lawrence Conferences on Canadian-American Affairs* (East Lansing: Michigan State University Press, 1993); Damien Claude Bélanger, "Pride and Prejudice: Canadians Intellectuals Confront the United States," Ph.D. thesis, Department of History, McGill University, 2005, chaps. 9–11.

10. Sir Robert Falconer, *The United States as a Neighbour from a Canadian Point of View* (Cambridge: Cambridge University Press, 1925), 237–38.

11. Hugh MacLennan, "How We Differ from Americans," *Maclean's,* December 15, 1946, 9, 49–55; Clyde H. Farnsworth, "Davies Looks South—Sourly," *MS,* December 17, 1994; Robertson Davies, *Murther & Walking Spirits* (Toronto: Viking Penguin, 1991).

12. Lipset, *Continental Divide,* passim; Douglas Baer, Edward Grabb, and William A. Johnston, "The Values of Canadians and Americans: A Critical analysis and Reassessment," *Social Forces* 68 (1990): 693–713; George Perlin, "The Constraints of Public Opinion: Diverging or Converging Paths?" in *Degrees of Freedom: Canada and the United States in a Changing World,* ed. Keith Banting, George Hoberg, and Richard Simeon (Montreal and Kingston: McGill–Queen's University Press, 1997), 71–74.

13. Charles Doran, ed., *Forgotten Partnership: U.S. Canada Relations Today* (Toronto: Fitzhenry & Whiteside, 1981), 97–108 (quotation on 100).

14. George Rawlyk, "The Federalist-Loyalist Alliance in New Brunswick, 1874–1815," *Humanities Association Review* 27 (1976): 142–60; Graeme Wynn, "New England's Outpost in the Nineteenth Century," in *Northeastern Borderlands,* ed. Hornsby, 64–90; John Reid and Stephen Hornsby, eds., *New England and Atlantic Canada* (Montreal and Kingston: McGill–Queens University Press, 2005); Douglas Baer, Edward Grabb, and William A. Johnston, "Defining Moments and Recurring Myths: Comparing Canadians and Americans after the American Revolution," *Canadian Review of Sociology and Anthropology* 37 (2000): 373–419.

15. S. F. Wise, "Colonial Attitudes from the Era of the War of 1812 to the Rebellion of 1837," and "The Annexation Movement and its Effect on Canadian Opinion, 1837–67," in *Canada Views the United States: Nineteenth-Century Political Attitudes,* ed. S. F. Wise and Robert Craig Brown (Toronto: Macmillan of Canada, 1967), respectively 16–43 and 44–97; Allan Smith, "The Continental Dimension in the Evolution of the English-Canadian Mind," in *Canada: An American Nation?* chap. 3.

16. Reginald C. Stuart, *United States Expansionism and British North America, 1775–1871* (Chapel Hill: University of North Carolina Press, 1988), chap. 6; David M. Potter, "Canadian Views of the United States as a Reflection of American Values," in *Canada Views the United States,* ed. Wise and Brown, 121–30.

17. See Ian Lumsden, ed., *Close the 49th Parallel Etc.* (Toronto: University of Toronto Press, 1970).

18. "Joe's Rant," printed on T-shirts with a Molson (brewery) logo; Jonathan Gatehouse, "With Glowing Hearts, We See Thee Advertise," *NP,* April 12, 2000.

19. Patrick Allossery, "It's Canadian from Eh to Zed," *FP,* April 17, 2000; Linda Frum, "My Name Is Jeff, and I Am an Actor," *Weekend Post,* June 10, 2000, 3; DeNeen Brown, "'Joe Canada' Crosses the Line," *WP,* January 17, 2001; Tony Lofaro, "I Am Canadian, Heading to U.S. to Look for Work," *NP,* January 12, 2001; Bill Cameron, "Joe Canadian Takes L.A.," *NP,* January 20, 2001.

20. Jonathan Kay, "I Am . . . Nationalistic," *NP,* April 14, 2000; Jonathan Kay, "Molson Ads as Canadian as, Um . . . Montana?" *FP,* April 17, 2000; Lee-Anne Goodman, "Most Americans Oblivious to Canadian Ad Targeting Them," *CH,* April 19, 2000; Jeff Jacoby, "My Name Is Joe, and I'm Not American," *NP,* April 24, 2000 (from *BG*); Steven Pearlstein, "Beer Ad Fires Canadian Pride," *BDN,* April 29–30, 2000, from *WP;* Andrew Coyne, "I Am Canadian, Hear Me Whine," *NP,* May 3, 2000; Mark Steyn, "I Am Canadian, You Nationalist Yankee Nitwit," *NP,* May 8, 2000.

21. Adam Bryant, "Message in a Beer," *Newsweek,* May 29, 2000; Val Ross, "Monkeying Around with the Canadian Identity," *G&M,* June 27, 1998; Sonia Arrison, "Try-

ing to Package a Unique Canadian Identity," *TS,* May 24, 1999; David Rider, "CBC Hires U.S. Firm to Package Canadian Identity," *NP,* April 20, 2001.

22. Allan Smith, "Conservatism, Nationalism, and Imperialism: The Thought of George Grant," in *Canada: An American Nation?* chap. 13; Clyde Farnsworth, "Don't Tread on Me, Either," *G&M,* September 28, 1996; Peter C. Newman, "Who Stands on Guard?" *VS,* September 21, 1996; Tara Brautigam, "Canadians Becoming Somewhat Pushy," *CH,* August 1, 2005.

23. Andrew Coyne, "Let This Please Be the Last Essay on the Canadian Identity," *Saturday Night,* July 1989, 25–30; Christopher Sands, "The God That Failed Canadians," *Canada Focus* (Center for Strategic and International Studies) 1 (June 2000); Steve Maich, "Closer Than You Think," *Maclean's,* October 17, 2005, 16–17.

24. Allan Fotheringham, "Learning to Love the American Bully Next Door," *Maclean's,* April 13, 1998, 68; David Crane, "The Line between U.S., Canada Getting Blurrier," *CH,* October 17, 1999; David M. Shribman, "Damn Yankees," *SH,* August 27, 2000 (from *BG*); Harry Bruce, "All They Need Is Love," *CH,* October 14, 2000; James Laxer, *Stalking the Elephant: My Discovery of America* (Toronto: Viking, 2000).

25. Andrew H. Malcolm, *The Canadians* (New York: Times Books, 1985), 154; James Baxter, "U.S. Still Thinks of Canada as Family: Ambassador," *NP,* June 3, 2002; Jeanne Morouney, "Pots, Kettles and Dark Accusations," *G&M,* May 8, 1992; Charles Truehart, "Strangers in a Not-So-Strange Land," *G&M,* October 5, 1996; Alex Beam, "The Endearing Foibles of the Peaceable Kingdom," *SH,* August 9, 1999; Kathleen Kenna, "Canada Gives Americans 'Warm and Fuzzy' Feeling," *TS,* May 12, 1999; Jonathan Gatehouse, " 'We're Almost the Same Country,' " *Maclean's,* May 6, 2002, 33, 35; John Ibbitson, "Americans Aren't More Libertarian, Just More Local," *G&M,* February 11, 2002.

26. Dan Brown, "Canada: A Quaint Outpost for U.S. Newspapers," *NP,* April 28, 1999; Chris Cobb, "The Ignorant Americans," *OC,* August 4, 1999; Andrew Phillips, "Benign Neglect," *Maclean's,* December 20, 1999, 24–25; Steven Pearlstein, "O Canada! A National Swan Song," *WP,* September 5, 2000; Steven Pearlstein, "Canada's Political Life Adrift amid Doldrums," *WP,* July 2, 1999.

27. Chris Wood, "A Different Kind of 'North-South' Dialogue: Canadians and Americans Size Each Other Up (and Down)," *World Press Review,* August 1989, 36–38; "Portrait of Two Nations: Should the Two Countries Become One?" *Maclean's,* June 25, 1990, 37–58; Rae Corelli, "How Very Different We Are," *Maclean's,* November 4, 1996, 35n40; Chris Wood et al., "The Vanishing Border," *Maclean's,* December 20, 1999, 20–49; Robert Sheppard, "We Are Canadian," *Maclean's,* December 25, 2000–January 1, 2001, 26–35; Wayne Norman, "Shared Values Do Not a Country Make," *NP,* June 24, 2000; Andrew Cohen, "OK Canada, Let's Bury the U.S. Obsession," *G&M,* September 11, 2000; David Akin, "We're Becoming Less Like Americans: Poll," *NP,* June 21, 2001.

28. Robert Fulford, "U.S. Bashing No Longer a Game," *NP,* September 14, 2001; Margaret Wente, "They Had It Coming?" *G&M,* September 15, 2001; Robert Fulford, "Anti-American Cant a Self-Inflicted Wound, *NP,* September 22, 2001; Allan Gotlieb, "We're Talking to One Another, Not the U.S., *NP,* September 25, 2001; Andrew Coyne, "We Are All Americans Now," *NP,* October 3, 2001; William Watson, "We Like Freedom More Than We Think," *FP,* October 13, 2001; J. L. Granatstein and Norman Hillmer, "Those Damn Yankees," *Maclean's,* October 2, 2001, 58–59; Marcus Gee, "Anti-Semitism and Anti-Americanism: Blood Brothers of Hate," *G&M,* December 1, 2001; Allan R. Gregg, "Scary New World," *Maclean's,* December 31, 2001–January 7,

2002, 22–30; Robert Sheppard, "In Search of Our Role," *Maclean's,* December 31, 2001–January 7, 2002, 37–38.

29. Richard Gwyn, "Do We Really Want to Be American Flunkies?" *SH,* January 27, 2002; Linda McQuaig, "The Suburb of Canada," *FP,* February 4, 2002.

30. Stephen Handelman, "Going Our Own Separate Way," *Time,* November 6, 2000, 53; Andrew Duffy, "Support for Social Programs Waning, New Report Says," *NP,* December 21, 2000; Neil Nevitte, Miguel Basanez, and Ronald Inglehart, "Directions of Value Change in North America," in *NAFTA in Transition,* ed. Stephen J. Randall and Herman W. Konrad (Calgary: University of Calgary Press, 1995), 329–43; George Perlin, "The Constraints of Public Opinion," in *Degrees of Freedom,* ed. Banting, Hoberg, and Simeon, 71–149; Richard Simeon, George Hoberg, and Keith Banting, "Globalization, Fragmentation, and the Social Contract," in *Degrees of Freedom,* ed. Banting, Hoberg, and Simeon, 389–416; George Hoberg, ed., *Capacity for Choice: Canada in a New North America* (Toronto: University of Toronto Press, 2002); Andrew Coyne, "Memo to Canada: Get Over Yourself," *NP,* September 9, 2000; Jennifer M. Welsh, "Is a North American Generation Emerging?" *Isuma* 1 (Spring 2000): 86–92; Peter Foster, "Canadians Losing Their Liberal Ways," *FP,* December 27, 2000.

31. Jack McLeod, "Canada's Other Revolution," *G&M,* December 27, 1991; Stephen LeDrew, "Think Strategically about Sovereignty," *NP,* January 23, 2002; Yves Fortier, "Time to Grow Up," *NP,* January 25, 2002; Richard Gwyn, "Canadians Are the Global North Americans," *SH,* May 12, 2002; Richard Gwyn, "Closer U.S. Ties Make Us More and Less Canadian," *SH,* June 30, 2002.

32. Bernard Yack, "The Myth of Civic Nationalism," *NP,* January 7, 2000; Conrad Black, "Out of Uncle Sam's Shadow," *NP,* January 11, 2000; Anthony Wilson-Smith, "A New Kind of Patriotism," *Maclean's,* August 28, 2000, 48; John Herd Thompson, "History for Dummies," *NP,* March 31, 2001; Richard Gwyn, *Nationalism without Walls: The Unbearable Lightness of Being Canadian* (Toronto: McClelland & Stewart, 1995), 47–48, 147–49, 155–59, 239–73.

Chapter 2: Print and Culture

1. Richard Siklos, "New York Diary: Sheila's Protection Racket," *NP,* March 27, 2000.

2. Samuel Moffett, *The Americanization of Canada* (Toronto: University of Toronto Press, 1972; orig. pub. 1907), chap. 9; Nick Mount, "Introduction," in *When Canadian Literature Moved to New York* (Toronto: University of Toronto Press, 2005), shows how the lack of opportunity drew Canadian writers into New York to find jobs.

3. Jane Errington, "Friends and Foes: The Kingston Elite and the War of 1812—A Case Study," *JCS* 20 (1985): 58–79.

4. Paul Rutherford, *A Victorian Authority: The Daily Press in Late Nineteenth Century Canada* (Toronto: University of Toronto Press, 1982), 34, 59–60, 184–85; John Warnock, "All the News It Pays to Print," in *Close the 49th Parallel, Etc.,* ed. Ian Lumsden (Toronto: University of Toronto Press, 1970), 117–34; Richard Keshenard and Kent MacAskill, "I Told You So: Newspaper Ownership in Canada and the Kent Commission Twenty Years Later," *ARCS* 30 (2000): 315–26; Dallas W. Smythe, *Dependency Road: Communications, Capitalism, Consciousness, and Canada* (Norwood, N.J.: Ablex,

1981), 105–11; Paul Rutherford, "Made in America: The Problem of Mass Culture in Canada," in *The Beaver Bites Back: American Popular Culture in Canada,* ed. David H. Flaherty and Frank E. Manning (Montreal and Kingston: McGill–Queen's University Press, 1993), 260–65.

5. John H. Thompson, with Allen Seager, "The Conundrum of Culture," in *Canada 1922–1939: Decades of Discord* (Toronto: McClelland and Stewart, 1985), by John H. Thompson and Allen Seager, chap. 8; Mary Vipond, "Canadian Nationalism and the Plight of Canadian Magazines in the 1920s," *CHR* 53 (1972): 125–48.

6. Lionel Shapiro, "The Myth That's Muffling Canada's Voice," in *Canada in the Fifties: From the Archives of Maclean's* (Toronto: Viking, 1999), 174–83; Andrew Purvis, "Canada 2005, Marquee," *Time,* August 6, 1999, 49–51, 54–58; Charles Pullen, "Culture, Free Trade, and Two Nations," *QQ* 95 (1988): 881–91; Ann Marie Owens, "Am-Lit's Appropriation of Atwood," *G&M,* January 13, 2001; Tyler Cowen, "Cashing In on Cultural Free Trade," *NP,* April 24, 1999.

7. See Kenneth J. Harvey, "Who Is Reading Canadian?" *NP,* July 1, 2000. See also Val Ross, "Gathered Together in Literature's Name," *G&M,* January 14, 1995; Elizabeth Renzetti, "Canadian Booksellers Pray to Oprah," *G&M,* September 19, 1998; Lori Culbert and George Jonas, "The Trouble with Arts Handouts," *G&M,* February 13, 1999; John Metcalf, "Canada's Successful Writers Must Rely on Blessings from the U.S. First," *NP,* June 17, 2000; Douglas M. Gibson, "Canadian Literature Strong and Free," *NP,* June 24, 2000; Francine Dubet, "Crime (Writing) Pays," *NP,* June 2, 2000; and Dan Francine Dubet and Mary Vallis, "Young, Hip and Out in the Cold," *NP,* November 11, 2000.

8. Justin Smallbridge, "Fiction's Ringmaster," *Maclean's,* September 5, 1994, 54–55; Jason Cowley, "American Novel Conquers All," *SH* [orig. in (London) *Sunday Times*], August 30, 1998; "American Novelist Has His Own Ideas of North," *G&M,* October 24, 1998; Jeanette Lynes, "Anne Heads West," *SH,* October 25, 1998; Frank Moher, "Back to the Present," *NP,* November 19, 1999; Rosemary McCracken, "Interview with a Vampire Lover," *NP,* December 18, 2000; Jeet Heer, "Following Faulkner," *NP,* December 30, 2000; Anne Marie Owens, "Am-Lit's Appropriation of Atwood," *NP,* January 13, 2001.

9. Pamela Cuthbert, "Reborn in the U.S.A.," *G&M,* June 5, 1997; Pamela Cuthbert, "Graydon Carter: The World He Left behind Him," *G&M,* June 14, 1997; Anthony Wilson-Smith, "The Man Who Loves to Write," *Maclean's,* August 17, 1998, 11; Gord McLaughlin, "Home Is Where the Rejection Is," *NP,* November 24, 2000.

10. Seymour Martin Lipset, *Continental Divide: The Values and Institutions of the United States and Canada* (Toronto and Washington: C. D. Howe Institute and National Planning Association, 1989), chap. 4.

11. Don Hutchinson, *The Great Pulp Heroes* (Toronto: Mosaic Press, 1996); Carolyn Strange and Tina Loo, *True Crime, True North: The Golden Age of Canadian Pulp Magazines* (Vancouver: Raincoats Cooks, 2004); John Herd Thompson, "Comic Relief," *Horizon Canada* (Centre for the Study of Teaching Canada) 8 (1987): 2174–79; Rebecca Caldwell, "Nancy Drew's New Assignment," *G&M,* February 11, 2004.

12. The definitive study is Paul Litt, *The Muses, the Masses, and the Massey Commission* (Toronto: University of Toronto Press, 1992).

13. Paul Audley, *Canada's Cultural Industries: Broadcasting, Publishing, Records and Film* (Toronto: James Lorimer, 1983), 118–36; Paul Litt, "The Massey Commission, Americanization, and Canadian Cultural Nationalism," *QQ* 98 (1991): 375–87; Gilbert

Gagne, "North American Integration and Canadian Culture," in *Capacity for Choice: Canada in a New North America,* ed. George Hoberg (Toronto: University of Toronto Press, 2002), 59–83.

14. Val Ross, "Stylish Publishing Team Looking Forward to a Quiet, Warm Winter," *G&M,* October 2, 1993.

15. Simon Houpt, "Back from the Shark Pond," *G&M,* May 6, 2004.

16. Diane Turbide, "Sell-Off or Sellout?" *Maclean's,* March 7, 1994, 62–63; Hugh Winsor, "Ginn Fizzle," *G&M,* March 17, 1992; Jennifer Prittie and Paul Waldie, "McClelland & Stewart Gift Sparks Fear in Book World," *NP,* June 2, 2000; Editorial, "Free Trade in Books," *NP,* June 28, 2000; Gordon Ritchie, *Wrestling with the Elephant: The Inside Story of the Canada-US Trade Wars* (Toronto: Macfarlane Walter & Ross, 1997), 220–21.

17. See Jennifer Pike, "Canada's Book Business Inefficient, Obsolete, Absurd," *FP,* June 21, 2001; Peter Kuitenbrouner and Kate MacNamara, "Ottawa's Role in the Collapse of Stoddart," *FP,* May 13, 2002; and Kate MacNamara, "Selling Assets by the Book," *FP,* May 14, 2002. James Laxer, "Turn the Page on Publishing," *G&M,* May 22, 2002, called for a state-run book publishing system.

18. Val Ross, "Why U.S. Book Giants May Spell Disaster: Is the Canadian Book Trade Crying Wolf?" *G&M,* December 2, 1995. In the Tom Hanks and Meg Ryan film *You've Got Mail*" (1998), a New York megabookstore owner drove a little bookshop around the corner out of business, but the movie was about romance, not print culture.

19. Margaret Feldstein, "Bookish Indignation," *Time,* September 29, 1997, 40; Peter Foster, "Scary Chapters in Canadian Bookselling History," *FP,* March 3, 2000; George Bragues, "Bookstore Protectionism," *FP,* March 31, 2000.

20. William Stanbury, "A Cancon Scary Tale," *FP,* May 15, 1999; Eric Reguly, "The Bookstore Blues," *Time,* December 11, 2000, 53; Paul Waldie and Zena Olijnyk, "Former Premier to Lobby Ottawa for Amazon.com," *NP,* June 23, 2000; Paul Waldie and Zena Olijnyk, "New Chapter Could Open for Booksellers in Canada, *NP,* June 24, 2000.

21. Kate MacNamara, "Amazon Poised to Set Up Shop in Canada," *FP,* April 19, 2002; Noah Richler, "Indigo, You Had Your Chance," *NP,* June 27, 2002; Hollie Shaw, "Indigo Meddling Says Amazon," *FP,* June 27, 2002.

22. See Theodore Peterson, *Magazines in the Twentieth Century* (Urbana: University of Illinois Press, 1964), 92–93, 109–11, 359–60; for circulation aggregates, see 59.

23. Mary Vipond, "Canadian Nationalism and Magazines," *Saturday Night,* February 27, 1926; C. W. Stokes, "Our Americanized Newsstands," *Saturday Night,* February 27, 1926; Thompson and Seager, *Canada 1922–1939,* 183–84. This theme weaves through Damien-Claude Bélanger, "Pride and Prejudice: Canadian Intellectuals Confront the United States, 1890–1945," Ph.D. dissertation, McGill University, 2006.

24. See Peterson, *Magazines,* 359–60, for bans; also see Thompson, "Comic Relief."

25. Ramsay Cook, "Cultural Nationalism in Canada: An Historical Perspective," in *Canadian Cultural Nationalism: The Fourth Lester B. Pearson Conference on the Canada–United States Relationship,* ed. Janice L. Murray (New York: New York University Press, 1977), 15–44.

26. Audley, *Canada's Cultural Industries,* 55–75; Isaiah A. Litvak and Christopher J. Maule, "Bill C-58 and the Regulation of Periodicals in Canada," *IJ* 36 (1980–81): 70–90; Keith Acheson and Christopher J. Maule, "No Bark, No Bite: The Mystery of Magazine Policy," paper prepared for meeting of Society for Historians of American Foreign Relations Conference, Toronto, June 22, 2000, courtesy of the authors.

27. Stephen Azzi, "Magazines and the Canadian Dream: The Struggle to Protect Canadian Periodicals 1955–1965," *IJ* 54 (1999): 502–23; Isaiah Litvak and Christopher Maule, *Cultural Sovereignty: The* Time *and* Reader's Digest *Case in Canada* (New York: Praeger, 1974); Ted Magder, "Franchising the Candy Store: Split-Run Magazines and a New International Regime for Trade in Culture," *CAPP* 34 (April 1998). Williams is quoted by Gagne, "North American Integration," 90.

28. Val Ross, "Bonnie's Miracle Makeover," *G&M,* June 8, 1996; Jeanne Beker, "Revenge of the Fashionistas," *NP,* May 30, 2001; Simon Houpt, "Star-Gazed Editor Abducted by *Enquirer,*" *G&M,* June 28, 2003; Anne Kingston, "Talking Trash," *Saturday Post,* July 12, 2003, 1, 5.

29. Dan Brown, "The Editor as Chameleon," *NP,* February 25, 1999.

30. NAFTA Articles 2005–2007; Barrie McKenna, *G&M,* January 18, 1999; Jeffrey Simpson, *G&M,* February 10, 1999; Robert Russo *MS,* February 24, 1999; Stephen Pederson, "Canada's House Votes to Curb Ad Sales to Foreign Magazines," *WP,* March 16, 1999; James Baxter, "Magazine Protectionism Called Threat to U.S. Policy," *NP,* April 19, 1999; Matthew Fraser, "Telemedia's Conversion to Continental Culture," *FP,* October 15, 1999.

31. Serena French, "This Might Explain the Frontier Gear on the Runways," *NP,* September 16, 1999; Leanne DeLap, "The Great Canadian Style Drain," *G&M,* September 30, 1999.

32. Murray Whyte, "Playing with the Big Boys," *NP,* June 23, 1999; "The Selling of *Shift* Magazine," *NP,* October 4, 1999; Simon Houpt, "Award-Winning *Shift* Magazine Awaits Fate after Finances Dry Up," *G&M,* June 22, 2000; Whyte, "*Shift* Magazine Gives Up on American Market," *G&M,* October 10, 2000; Robert Collison, "*Shift* Changes Gears," *Weekend Post,* November 25, 2000, 6–7.

33. Rod Dobell, "A Social Charter for a North American Community," *Isuma* 1 (Spring 2000): 52–56.

34. Keith Acheson and Christopher Maule, "Canadian Magazine Policy: International Conflict and Domestic Stagnation," draft, August 10, 1999, http://www.carleton.ca/~kacheson/atlanta5; Keith Acheson and Christopher Maule, "Rethinking Canadian Magazine Policy," draft, September 24, 1999, http://www.carleton.ca/atcheson/holland.

35. Marci McDonald, "A Blow to Magazines," *Maclean's,* January 27, 1997, 58–59; George Russell, "The WTO Takes Issue," *Time,* January 27, 1997, 29; Marci McDonald, "Menacing Magazines," *Maclean's,* March 24, 1997, 54; Robert Lewis, "When Culture Is Attacked," *Maclean's,* March 24, 1997, 4; Laura Eggerton, "Cultural 'Assault' by U.S. Feared," *G&M,* January 18, 1997; Laura Eggerton, "Ottawa Plans New Strategy in Campaign to Save Magazines," *G&M,* May 13, 1997; Ritchie, *Wrestling with the Elephant,* 225–27, 230–31.

36. John Schofield, "Subscribing to Rules," *Maclean's,* August 10, 1998, 38; Heather Schofield, "U.S. Assails Ottawa's Magazine Bill," *G&M,* October 10, 1998; Heather Schofield, "U.S. Ambassador Optimistic for Changes to Magazine Bill," *G&M,* November 3, 1998; Paul Brent, "Advertisers Blast Copps for Protecting 'Special' Publishers, *NP,* November 18, 1998; Ian Jack, "Magazine War Fallout May Hit Textile and Steel Producers," *NP,* November 25, 1998; Robert Fife, "Marchi Rebukes Copps for Major Bilateral Feud," *NP,* November 28, 1998; Fife and Peter Morton, "Congress Backs Threat of Sanctions over Magazine Bill, *NP,* February 25, 1999.

37. Joel-Denis Bellavance and Robert Fife, "Copps Offers to Talk with U.S. Am-

bassador about Magazine Bill," *NP*, January 24, 1999; Graham Fraser, "Copps Challenges U.S. Envoy over C-55," *G&M*, January 23, 1999; James Baxter, "A Trade War Mostly of Words," *NP*, February 6, 1999; Hugh Winsor, "Dog Failed to Bark in the Magazine Dispute," *G&M*, March 17, 1999; Barrie McKenna, "Opinions Split on Magazine Legislation," *G&M*, February 13, 1999; John Geddes, "Mad about Magazines," *Maclean's*, May 10, 1999, 25.

38. Giles Gherson, "Ottawa Willing to Drop Demand for Canadian Content in Magazines," *NP*, May 14, 1999; Robert Fife, "Copps' Deputy Takes Fall for Retreat on Bill C-55," *NP*, May 19, 1999; Shawn McCarthy, "Ottawa Sweetens Offer in Bid to Avert U.S. Trade War," *G&M*, May 21, 1999; Shawn McCarthy, "Magazine Deal Closer as Officials Scurry to Avert Trade War," *G&M*, May 22, 1999; Ian Jack, "Copps, Marchi Battle over C-55," *NP*, May 21, 1999.

39. Peter Morton, "Magazine Dispute Deadlocked over Content," *NP*, April 8, 1999; "Ottawa and Washington Agree on Access to the Canadian Advertising Services Market," May 26, 1999, available at http://www.pch.gc.ca; Office of the United States Trade Representative, Executive Office of the President, "United States and Canada Resolve 'Periodical' Differences," May 26, 1999, available at http://www.ustr.gov/releases; Steven Pearlstein, "U.S., Canada Resolve Dispute," *WP*, May 27, 1999; Ian Jack, "Deal with U.S. averts trade war over magazines," *NP*, May 26, 1999; Heather Schofield and Shawn McCarthy, "U.S. Magazines Win Access," *G&M*, May 26, 1999; Christopher Sands, "This Pregnant Pause: The Future of Cultural Trade Conflict between Canada and the United States," paper presented to Society for Historians of American Foreign Relations Annual Conference, Toronto, June 22, 2000, courtesy of the author.

40. Heather Schofield, "Publishers Greet Split-Run Deal with Dismay," *G&M*, May 27, 1999; Heather Schofield, "'Canada Won,' Copps Insists," *G&M*, May 27, 1999; Shawn McCarthy, "PM Moved to Stop a Trade War," *G&M*, May 27, 1999; Ian Jack and Peter Morton, "Proposed Concessions on Magazine Bill Anger Canadian Publishers," *NP*, May 22, 1999; Giles Gherson, "Better Than Nothing, but Not by Much," *NP*, May 31, 1999; Canadian Press, "Profits Up, but Fewer Periodicals," *MS*, September 17, 1998.

41. John Geddes, "A Run for the Money," *Maclean's*, June 7, 1999, 54–56; Val Ross, "Maclean's, Time, the First Split-Run War," *G&M*, June 6, 1977; William Watson, "Magazine Deal: Did We Win by Losing or Lose by Winning?" *FP*, June 2, 1999; Peter Morton, "Hearst Sees Canadian Edition of *Cosmo*," *NP*, June 2, 1999; Ian Jack, "Magazines Get $50M Annual Infusion," *NP*, December 17, 1999; Chris Tenove, "*Equinox* a Casualty of Magazine Law, Executive Says," *NP*, August 7, 2000.

42. James Baxter, "$5.7 Million for French-Language Magazines," *NP*, May 5, 2002; William Watson, "Get Ottawa Out of the Magazine Biz," *FP*, May 22, 2002; Sean Silicoff, "Ottawa Cuts Magazine Subsidy," *NP*, July 9, 2003; Sean Silicoff, "U.S. Magazine Threat Never Materialized," *FP*, February 10, 2003.

43. Barbara Shecter, "CIBC Takes a Stake in *Village Voice*," *FP*, January 6, 2000; Michael Raphael, "Punk Finally Gets Paid," *NP*, April 28, 1999; Paul Brent, "Upstart Publisher Brunico to Launch Another Magazine," *FP*, August 2, 1999; Sheryl Ubelacker, "Looking for a Good Old Read?" *NP*, April 5, 2000; Murray White, "But Is It a Magazine?" *NP*, October 6, 1999; Murray White, "Last-Resort Marketing," *NP*, December 21, 2000.

44. Alex Kuczynski, "Giant Moves In on Crowded Internet Business," *FP*, June 6, 2000; Alex Kuczynski, "The Decline and Fall of the American Magazine," *NP*, August 11, 1999; Shannon Karl, "Why You Can Judge a Magazine by Its Cover," *NP*, August

11, 1999; John Fraser, "That Was the *Newsweek* That Was," *NP,* January 17, 2001; Finbarr O'Reilly, "*Books in Canada* Brought Back to Life by Amazon," *NP,* January 17, 2001.

45. Katrina Onstad, "Can the Image Be Changed but Integrity Kept?" *NP,* July 21, 1999; John Fraser, "Maclean's Needs a Brave New Focus," *NP,* March 29, 2000; Dan Brown, "What Would Tina Like?" *NP,* February 8, 2000; Murray Whyte, "What Still Matters," *NP,* May 31, 2000; Charlotte Gray, "Issues Mattered, Once," *NP,* December 30, 2000.

46. See Bruce Wallace, "What Makes a Canadian?" *Maclean's,* December 20, 1999, 32–34, 36; Michael Adams, *Fire and Ice: The United States, Canada and the Myth of Converging Values* (Toronto: Penguin Canada, 2003), 48–49; and Kevin Mulcahy, "Cultural Imperialism and Cultural Sovereignty in U.S.-Canadian Relations," *ARCS* 30 (2000): 181–206. See also Dennis Browne, "Canada's Cultural Trade Quandary," *International Affairs* 54 (1999): 363–74.

Chapter 3: Mass Entertainment

1. Andrew Philips, "Elvis the Immortal," *Maclean's,* August 18, 1997, 54–57; Frank McEnany, "The King and I," *G&M,* August 16, 1997.

2. See Geoff Pevere and Greig Dymond, *Mondo Canuck: A Canadian Pop Culture Odyssey* (Scarborough, Ont.: Prentice Hall, 1996). David Flaherty and Frank E. Manning, eds., *The Beaver Bites Back: American Popular Culture in Canada* (Montreal and Kingston: McGill–Queen's University Press, 1993), surveys various media and genre in North America.

3. Paul Rutherford, "Made in America: The Problem of Mass Culture in Canada," in *Beaver Bites Back,* ed. Flaherty and Manning, 260–80.

4. "The Newly Arrived Elephants," *NYT,* July 22, 1871; "Barnum's Success in Brooklyn," *NYT,* April 20, 1873; "Attacked by Tigers," *NYT,* October 9, 1884; "Empress, the Old and Gentle Elephant, Retires to a Home," *WP,* July 8, 1906; Mary Malone, "Fun and Games," *Horizon Canada* (Centre for the Study of Teaching Canada) 3 (1987): 848–53; "The Art of the Circus," *Guide to the Performing Arts,* http://www.theartofperforming.com.circus.

5. Bruce Lenton, "The Development and Nature of Vaudeville in Toronto: From 1899 to 1915," Ph.D. dissertation, University of Toronto, 1983; Hilary Russell, *All That Glitters: A Memorial to Ottawa's Capitol Theatre and Its Predecessors,* Canadian Historical Sites 13, Occasional Papers in Archeology and History (Ottawa: Indian and Northern Affairs, 1975).

6. "Vaudeville Managers Combine," *WP,* November 24, 1894; Tina Loo and Carolyn Strange, "The Traveling Show Menace: Contested Regulation in Turn-of-the-Century Ontario," *Law Society Review* 29 (1995): 639–67; "French Canadian Stage," *NYT,* August 2, 1903; Anthony Slide, *The Vaudevillians: A Dictionary of Vaudeville Performers* (Westport, Conn.: Arlington House, 1981), xi–xiv; John E. Dimeglio, *"Vaudeville U.S.A"* (Bowling Green, Ohio: Bowling Green University Press, 1973), 166–67, 192–202; "Bob Hope and American Variety," exhibit, Library of Congress, Washington, 2002.

7. Yves Theriault, "Merchants of Happiness: The Cirque du Soleil Plays to Win in Vegas," *EnRoute,* October 1995, 44–48; Kate Taylor, "Stratford Festival Antes Up for

Gamble on Broadway," *G&M,* November 7, 1998; Suzan Sherman, "Daniel Goldfarb and the Jew Play," *Weekend Post,* November 13, 1999; Frank Moher, "Why New York Tells Canadian Theatre 'Don't Call Us . . .' " *NP,* March 27, 2000.

8. John Bemrose, "The Rag to Riches," *Maclean's,* January 15, 1999, 70, 72; Michael Posner, "Garth Goes to Broadway: A Mogul Is Born," *G&M,* January 17, 1998; Gayle MacDonald and Michael Posner, "Garth Dabrinsky's Curtain Call," *G&M,* May 30, 1998.

9. Seth Feldman, "And Always Will Be: The Canadian Film Industry," in *Seeing Ourselves: Media Power and Policy in Canada,* ed. Helen Holmes and David Taras (Toronto: Harcourt Brace, 1992), 99–115; Henry Garrity, "Book Review Essay: Searching for Identity in Canadian Film . . . Again," *ARCS* 33, no. 3 (Autumn 2003): 415–18.

10. Kerry Seagrave, *American Films Abroad: Hollywood's Domination of the World's Movie Screens* (London: McFarland & Company, 1997), 2–12.

11. "Loew's Legacy: 100 Years of Escape and Memories," *WP,* May 7, 2004.

12. Seagrave, *American Films Abroad,* 2, 19 (quotation), 12, 19–27, 57–58; 103; Ted Magder, *Canada's Hollywood: The Canadian State and Feature Films* (Toronto: University of Toronto Press, 1993), chaps. 1, 2.

13. Doug Owram, *Born at the Right Time: A History of the Baby Boom Generation* (Toronto: University of Toronto Press, 1996), 143–52.

14. See reminiscences in *Signing On: The Birth of Radio in Canada,* ed. Bill McNeill and Morris Wolfe (Garden City, N.Y.: Doubleday, 1982); and Frederick Lewis Allen, *Only Yesterday* (New York: Harper, 1931), 116.

15. See Michele Hilmes, *Hollywood and Broadcasting: From Radio to Cable* (Urbana: University of Illinois Press, 1990).

16. Margaret Prang, "The Origins of Public Broadcasting in Canada," *CHR* 46 (1965): 1–25; Frank Peers, *The Politics of Canadian Broadcasting, 1920–1951* (Toronto: University of Toronto Press, 1969), 4–12, 19–40, 228–29, 276–84; Anthony Smith, ed., *Television: An International History* (New York: Oxford University Press, 1995), 89–91.

17. *The War of the Worlds: Mars' Invasion of Earth, Inciting Panic and Inspiring Terror* (Naperville, Ill.: Sourcebooks, 2001), 3–75.

18. Owram, *Born at the Right Time,* 155.

19. John Clare, "The Scramble for the Teenage Dollar" (orig. pub. in *Maclean's,* September 14, 1957), in *Canada in the Fifties: Canada's Golden Decade,* ed. the Editors of *Maclean's* (Toronto: Penguin Books, 1999), 184–91; Martin Laba, "No Borders, No Problems: Mixed Media, Cultures of Youth, and Music in the Marketplace," in *Seeing Ourselves,* ed. Holmes and Taras, 73–83; Peter Fornatale and Joshua E. Mills, "The Emerging Teen Culture," in *Radio in the Television Age* (Woodstock, N.Y.: Overlook Press, 1980), chap. 3.

20. Litt, "Americanization, and Canadian Cultural Nationalism," *QQ* 98 (1991): 375–87; Robert Fulford, "How Massey Smothered the Arts," *NP,* December 22, 2001; Ramsay Cook, "Cultural Nationalism in Canada: An Historical Perspective," in *Canadian Cultural Nationalism: The Fourth Lester B. Pearson Conference on the Canada–United States Relationship,* ed. Janice L. Murray (New York: New York University Press, 1977), 15–44; Roger Frank Swanson, "Canadian Cultural Nationalism and the Public Interest," in *Canadian Cultural Nationalism,* ed. Murray, 55–82; Gilmour's movie ratings in *Maclean's,* January 1, 1951, 38–39, and *Maclean's,* January 7, 1961, 40, 41.

21. Dwight Macdonald, "A Theory of Mass Culture," in *Mass Culture: The Popular Arts in America,* ed. Bernard Rosenberg and David White (New York: Free Press,

1987), 59–73; Feldman, "And Always Will Be," 105–8; Seagrave, *American Films Abroad,* 187–89, 226–27, 262–63; McDonald, "The Paramount Connection," *Maclean's,* April 25, 1994, 17–18; Peter Birnie, "Bordering on Hollywood," *VS,* October 2, 1996; Robin Mathews, "Canadian Culture and the Liberal Ideology," in *Canada Ltd.: The Political Economy of Dependency,* ed. Robert Laxer (Toronto: McClelland & Stewart, 1973), 213–31; Sinclair Stewart, "Do Tax Payers Belong in Showbiz?" *FP,* June 7, 2000.

22. Brenda Bouw, "Of Mice and (Bronf)man," *NP Business,* September 1999, 74–78; Daryl-Lynn Carlson, "Turning the Silver Screen into Gold," *The Wealthy Boomer* 2, no. 1 (2000): 68–70; Mike King, "Montreal Becoming a Famous 'Player' as Hollywood of the North," *NP,* October 2, 1999; Michael Posner, "A Really Big Show," *Maclean's,* August 11, 1997, 38–39; Brian D. Johnson, "Austen Powers," *Maclean's,* November 22, 1999, 106–8; Cori Howard, "Canadians of the Academy," *NP,* March 23, 2000; Brian Steinberg, "Lions Gate Finds Own Territory in Hollywood Jungle," *NP,* July 30, 2002; Mark Anderson, "Selling Toronto," *Financial Post Magazine,* March 1996, 31–33, 36, 61; Stephen Handelman, "Will Canada Be Reeling," *Time,* September 30, 2002, 33.

23. Chris Wood, "Canadian Made," *Maclean's,* June 24, 1996, 38–43; Joe Chidey, "Dawn of *Spawn,*" *Maclean's,* August 11, 1997, 52–53; Doug Saunders, "Canadians Take on Toon Town," *G&M,* May 30, 1998; Jonathan Gatehouse, "Cartoon Time for Canuckleheads," *NP,* February 19, 2000; "Oscars to Include Musical Jab at Canada," *MS,* March 1, 2000.

24. Brian Johnson, "The Canadian Patient," *Maclean's,* March 24, 1997, 42–46; Scott Burnside, "A Canadian Story Goes Hollywood," *NP,* October 2, 1999; Cori Howard, "Canadian Films Suffer from Being Canadian," *NP,* April 3, 2000; Terence Corcoran, "Now Bombing at Cinema Canada," *G&M,* March 28, 1998; Doug Saunders, "Planet America," *G&M,* October 17, 2000.

25. Ron Graham, "Born Again in Babylon," *Saturday Night* 98 (June 1983): 23–39; Matthew Fraser, "Canada's Cultural Joan of Arc," *NP,* November 18, 1999; Michael McKinley, "The $5000 Cup Of Coffee," *Weekend Post Entertainment,* April 3, 1999, 6–7; Matthew Fraser, "Movie Industry a Chronic Failure," *NP,* September 3, 2002; David Weaver, "It's Time the Big Guys Left the Public Trough," *G&M,* April 10, 2000.

26. Robert Remington, "Canada Warned Tax Hikes on Actors Jeopardize Industry," *NP,* December 27, 2000; Brenda Bouw, "Striking U.S. Actors Seek Canadian Help," *FP,* May 31, 2000; Sinclair Stewart, "U.S. Actors Strike Keeps Canadian Studios Hopping," *FP,* July 8, 2000; Cori Howard, "Action Heats Up in Hollywood North," *NP,* February 12, 2001.

27. Ian Bailey, "U.S. Unions Target 'Runaway' Film and Television Production," *MS,* July 5, 1999; Robert Russo, "Canada Stealing U.S. Film Jobs, Gore Report Says, "*NP,* February 19, 2001; Jeffrey Simpson, "Hollywood's Case against Canada," *G&M,* December 4, 2001; Alexander Burroughs, "New Border Skirmish Pits Alberta against Montana," *NP,* August 6, 2005.

28. These statistics are found in *The Measured Century: An Illustrated Guide to Trends in America, 1900–2000,* ed. Theodore Caplow, Louis Hicks, and Ben J. Wattenberg (Washington, D.C.: AEI Press, 2001), 100–1; Paul Rutherford, *When Television Was Young: Primetime Canada 1952–1967* (Toronto: University of Toronto Press, 1990); Pamela Young, " 'Deadly Drivel' Plagued TV Screens More Than 50 Years Ago," *Maclean's,* September 12, 2005, 5.

29. Owram, *Born at the Right Time,* 88–93.

30. Jeffrey Simpson, *Star-Spangled Canadians: Canadians Living the American Dream* (Toronto: HarperCollins, 2000), 317–21; J. Kelly Nestruck, "Kicking Kirk," *NP,* September 2, 2003; two TV documentaries, *Trekkies* and *Trekkies 2,* broadcast several times after *Star Trek*'s enduring global appeal was documented in 2000.

31. Mark Stokes, "Canada and the Direct Broadcast Satellite: Issues in the Global Communications Flow," *JCS* 27 (1992): 82–96; John Meisel, "Escaping Extinction: Cultural Defence of an Undefended Border," in *Southern Exposure: Canadian Perspectives on the United States,* ed. David Flaherty and William McKercher (Toronto: McGraw-Hill Ryerson, 1986), 152–68; Gordon Ritchie, *Wrestling with the Elephant: The Inside Story of the Canada-U.S. Trade* Wars (Toronto: Macfarlane, Walter & Ross, 1997), 217–22, 230–34.

32. Doug Saunders, "Chaos in the Culture Industry," *G&M,* April 25, 1998; John Geddes, "Canada's Culture Clash," *Maclean's,* July 13, 1998, 26–27; Doug Saunders, "Why Canadian TV will Soon Be More Canadian," *G&M,* July 25, 1998; John Geddes, "Tussling Over the Tube," *Maclean's,* October 5, 1998, 70–71.

33. Martin Knelman, "Made for TV Moves," *Report on Business Magazine,* May 1994, 63–68; Barbara Wickens, "Romancing the Small Screen," *Maclean's,* August 22, 1994, 54–55; Knelman, "Mickey on the Road to Avonlea," *Financial Post Magazine,* March 1996, 22–28; Doug Saunders, "Exporting Canada's Culture," *G&M,* January 25, 1997; Anthony Keller, "Have Can-Con, Will Travel," *G&M,* September 13, 1997; Ellen Vanstone, "Cops, Christians and Conspiracy Theorists," *G&M,* September 30, 1997; Matthew Fraser, "Is CBC relevant? Not to Young Canadians," *FP,* May 25, 1999; Simpson, *Star-Spangled Canadians,* 217–30; Shirley Won, "Movie Makes Rolling Back into Canada," *G&M,* March 3, 2006.

34. Peter Morton, "Bell Canada to Be Part of Biggest Phone Firm in U.S.," *NP,* March 25, 1999; Matthew Fraser, "Telecom Deal Sounds Bell for U.S. Cable Invasion," *NP,* March 26, 1999; Ross Laver, "America on the Line," *MacLean's,* April 5, 1999, 38–41; David Akin, "U.S. Politicians Angry as Canadians Elected to Internet Board," *FP,* November 9, 1999; Peter Morton, "U.S. Telecoms Want Rules Overhauled in Canada," *FP,* April 5, 2000.

35. Caplow, Hicks, and Wattenberg, *Measured Century,* 276–77; Graeme Hamilton, "Reality TV Storms Quebec," *NP,* November 7, 2003.

36. Nicholas Jennings, "Cross-Border Shopping," *TV Times,* August 26–September 2, 1994, 1; Chris Dafoe, "TV Hopefuls Go Due South," *G&M,* March 7, 1998.

37. Sean B. Pasternak. "iCrave to Offer Canadian TV in the U.S.," *FP,* January 1, 2000; Peter Morton and Barbara Shecter, "Hollywood Seeks to Crush iCrave TV," *FP,* January 21, 2000; Matthew Fraser, "Enforcer Valenti Takes on Net Fight," *FP,* January 21, 2000; Peter Morton, "U.S. Court Order Keeps iCrave TV Off the Internet," *FP,* February 9, 2000; Barbara Schecter, "Ottawa Takes Aim at TV Piracy, *FP,* September 6, 2003; Scott Adams, "Canadian Dithering Led to Sale of DocSpace to U.S.," *FP,* December 27, 1999; Barry Brown, "Despite Some Success, E-Commerce to Canada Faces Particular Hurdles," *NYT,* April 7, 2000; Matthew Fraser, "Media Giants Still Don't 'Get' the Net," *FP,* April 10, 2000.

38. *Maclean's* polls since 1984; EKOS, "Canadian Attitudes towards the Upcoming U.S. Election for *Time Magazine,* October 25, 2004, available at http://www.ekos.com.

39. Stephen Cole, "Perhaps Canadians Understand the Jokes," *NP,* October 7, 1999; Tony Atherton, "Our Taste in TV—from Ridiculous to Sublime," *NP,* January 10, 2000;

Jeffrey Simpson, "Watching the Bigger Picture through U.S. Eyes," *G&M,* February 26, 2002; Kate McNamara, "Off the Dial," *FP,* June 25, 2002. For a thorough analysis see Jason Bristow, "Symbolic Tokenism in Canada: U.S. Cultural Sector Trade Relations," *CAPP* 55 (November 2003).

40. Brenda Bouw, "Star Light, Star Bright," *FP,* August 14, 1999; Brenda Bouw, "Princess Diana and the Cult of Fame," *G&M,* September 13, 1997; Daniel Boorstin, *The Image: A Guide to Pseudo Events in America* (New York: Vintage Books, 1961); Tyler Cowen, "The Gift of Fame," *NP,* May 27, 2000. Quebec has a closed celebrity world because of language; see Ingrid Peritz, "Quelle Horreur! Celebrity Mags Wage War!" *G&M,* February 17, 2005.

41. Kate Taylor, "Shooting Stars," *G&M,* May 22, 1993; Gina Mallet, "Starved for Stars," *G&M,* January 17, 1998; Rae Corelli, "Desert Isle Desires," *Maclean's,* June 25, 1990, 72–73; Rae Corelli, "True North Strong and Geeky," *NP,* December 28, 2000.

42. Christopher Harris, "But Can We Walk the Walk?" *G&M,* June 20, 1998; Shiovan Govani, "The End of Shame, but Not of Fame," *NP,* September 23, 2000; Rebecca Eckler, "Inside Canada's Star Chamber," *NP,* January 17, 2001; Kamel Al-Sobyee, "The Star Recycling Machine," *G&M,* July 17, 2003; Shiovan Govani, ""An Impressive Group of Hosers,'" *NP,* June 25, 2004.

43. Robert A. Wright, "'Dream, Comfort, Memory, Despair': Canadian Popular Musicians and the Dilemma of Nationalism, 1968–1972," *JCS* 22 (1987–88): 27–43, citation on 30; Patrick Dillon, "'Let Life Live Me,'" *G&M,* April 26, 1997; Konrad Yakabuski, "A Tin Flute Goes Platinum," *G&M,* May 24, 1997; Sean Flinn, "Canadians Invaded U.S. in 1997," *G&M,* December 27, 1997; Edna Gunderson, "Celine Dion," *USAT,* August 21, 1998; Elio Jannacci, "Grammy's Glamour Clause," *Weekend Post,* February 20, 1999, 13–14; Colleen McEdwards, "From Celine to Shania, Canada perfecting the export," http://www.cnn.com/showbiz/music/9903/17canada.music.wb; Brenda Bouw, "Getting Soaked in Beer Worth It for Exposure in the U.S.," *NP,* October 11, 1999; "Krall's Musical Catharsis," *WP Express,* May 6, 2004; David Segal, "Avril and Alanis: Blame Canada," *WP,* May 19, 2004; Geoff Pevere and Greig Dymond, "Paul Anka: Highway to My Way," "Rock of Ages: The Endurables," "Another *Fine* Messer: The Down-Home Tradition That Will Not Die," and "A Great Broad: Anne Murray," in *Mondo Canuck: A Canadian Pop Culture Odyssey,* by Pevere and Dymond (Scarborough, Ont.: Prentice Hall, 1966), respectively 8–11, 46–49, 136–41, and 146–47.

44. Beverley Rasporich, "Canadian Humor in the Media: Exporting John Candy and Importing Homer Simpson," in *Seeing Ourselves,* ed. Holmes and Taras, 84–98; Liam Lacey, "The Yucks of the Canucks," *G&M,* August 8, 1995; Rick Moranis, "It Is to Laugh," *Weekend Post,* November 20, 1999, 1–3; Siobhan Roberts, "Science of Mirth," *NP,* August 13, 2001.

45. Rasporich, "Canadian Humor," 333–34; "Culture and Communications," http://tv.cbc.ca/national/pgminfo/border/culture/html; Pevere and Dymond, "TV Nation: SCTV," "Mr. Michaels Takes Manhattan: Saturday Night Live," and "No Joke: The Canadian Sitcom Paradox," in *Mondo Canuck,* ed. Pevere and Dymond, respectively 188–93, 194–99, and 204–8; Morton Ritts, "Boobs on the Tube," *Maclean's,* December 23, 1996, 77, 79.

46. Michael Posner, "There's Something Funny Going on Here," *G&M,* October 31, 1998; Andrew Clark, "The Land of Laughs," *Maclean's,* February 1, 1999, 66, 68; Simpson, *Star-Spangled Canadians,* 309–17.

47. "Come Alive in Canada," *NYT,* May 4, 1997; Jill Mahoney, "Luxury on the

Cheap: Tourists Love 67¢ Dollar," *G&M,* July 18, 1998; Anthony DePalma, "U.S. Travelers Feast on Canadian Exchange Rate," *SH,* August 30, 1998; Jon Bricker, "U.S. Tourists Back to Pre-9/11 Numbers," *NP,* August 29, 2002.

48. Lowry W. McNeil, ed., *Arts and Public Policy in the United States* (Englewood Cliffs, N.J.: Prentice Hall, 1984), 1–22; Andrew Purvis, "Marquee," *Maclean's,* August 9, 1999, 49–55; Tyler Cowen, "Cashing In on Cultural Free Trade," *NP,* April 24, 1999; James B. Twitchell, *Branded Nation: The Marketing of Megachurch, College, Inc., and Museum World* (New York: Simon & Schuster, 2004), 193–273.

49. Charles Gordon, "The New Challenge Threatening Culture," *Maclean's,* February 1, 1999, 13. Chris Cobb, "Pop Icons Bring Wealth into Canada," *NP,* June 21, 2001; Michelle MacAfee, "Canadians Feel Culture Threatened by Americans: Poll," *CH,* July 1, 2002.

50. P. Wills, "What's Canadian? What's Culture?' *NP,* April 6, 1999; Purvis, "Marquee"; Micheline Charest and Ronald A. Weinberg, "Youthful Vision," *Time,* August 9, 1999, 64–66.

Part II: Social Realm

1. Steven Pearlstein, "O Canada! A National Swan Song," *WP,* September 5, 2000; conversation between Steven Pearlstein and the author, February 29, 2004.

2. "Americans and Canadians: The North American Not-So-Odd Couple," *Commentary,* Pew Center for People and the Press, January 14, 2004, available at http://people-press.org/commentary.

3. David Montgomery, "Whoa! Canada! Legal Marijuana. Gay Marriage. Peace. What the Heck's Going On Up North, Eh?" *WP,* July 1, 2003; Kevin J. Critiano, "Woe Canada? Things Not So Bad: There's Nothing for Americans to Fear," *CT,* November 11, 2003, http://www.nd.edu/~prinfo/news/2003; Robert Fulford, "Two Neighbours, Growing Apart," *NP,* December 27, 2003.

4. "Statistical Comparisons," in *Canada and the United States: Differences That Count,* 2nd edition, ed., David M. Thomas (Toronto: Broadview Press, 2000), 387–90; Stuart Banner, "The Death Penalty's Strange Career," *WQ* 26 (Spring 2004): 70–82.

5. Tamara Palmer Seiler, "Melting Pot and Mosaic: Images and Realities," in *Canada and United States,* ed. Thomas, 97–120; Barry Came, "Accents of Conflict," *Maclean's,* June 25, 1990, 77, 79; Hilary Mackenzie, "The Racist Underside," *Maclean's,* June 25, 1990, 82–83; Jeffrey Simpson, "Trans-America, the Beautiful," *G&M,* August 26, 1995; Gina Malley, "Has Diversity Gone Too Far?" *G&M,* March 15, 1997; Sherry Cooper, "Inevitable integration," *G&M,* March 15, 2002; Irving Abella, "A Hostile Time and Place," *Literary Review of Canada,* March 2004, 23; Michael Bliss, "The Multicultural North American Hotel," "The End of English Canada," and "Deux Nations in the Socialist North," *NP,* January 13–15, 2003; Andrew Parkin and Matthew Mendelsohn, *A New Canada: An Identity Shaped by Diversity* (Ottawa: Centre for Research and Information on Canada, 2003), available at http://www.cris.ca; Tamara Jacoby, "Rainbow's End," *WP Book World,* May 16, 2004; David Frum, "America the Just," *NP,* November 14, 2005.

6. Jack Mintz, "A Textbook Case of success," *G&M,* February 6, 2004; Henry Srebrnik, "Football, Frats and Fun vs. Commerce, Cold, and Carping: The Social and Psychological Context of Higher Education in Canada and the United States," in *Canada*

and United States, ed. Thomas, 165–91; Julie Smyth, "57% Back School Vouchers," *NP,* September 4, 2001.

7. Clifford Krauss, "Canada's View on Social Issues Is Opening Rifts with the U.S.," *NYT,* December 1, 2003, http://www.independent-media.tv/itemprint.cfm?; Allan R. Gregg, "Bumpy Ride," *Maclean's,* December 29, 2003; Ishrad Manji, "The Strange Case of Liberal Canada," *Time,* December 29, 2003.

Chapter 4: North American Mingling

1. Michael Kane, "Covering Those Snowbirds," *VS,* October 23, 1995; Prior Smith, "The Saga of Canadian Newspapers in Florida," *MS,* October 28, 1995; Patricia Chisholm, "A Southern Longing," *Maclean's,* October 26, 1998, 44–45; Réjean Lachapelle, "Population Exchange between Quebec and the United States over the Last Two Decades," in *Problems and Opportunities in U.S.-Quebec Relations,* ed. Alfred O. Hero and Marcel Daneau (Boulder, Colo.: Westview Press, 1984), 64–79.

2. Richard G. Lowe, "Massachusetts and the Acadians," *William & Mary Quarterly* 3rd series, 25 (April 1968): 212–29; Louis R. Genticore, ed., *The Historical Atlas of Canada: From the Beginning to 1800* (Toronto: University of Toronto Press, 1993), vol. 1, plate 30; R. A. LeBlanc, "The Acadian Migration," *Cahiers de Geographie du Quebec* 23, no. 58 (April 1979): 99–124.

3. Graeme Wynn and Debra McNabb, "Pre-Loyalist Nova Scotia," in *Historical Atlas of Canada,* ed. Genticore, vol. 1, plate 31; Ministry of Supply and Services, *The New England Planters in Nova Scotia* (Ottawa: Ministry of Supply and Services, 1986).

4. See Neil MacKinnon, *This Unfriendly Soil: The Loyalist Experience in Nova Scotia, 1783–1791* (Montreal and Kingston: McGill–Queen's University Press, 1986); James St. G. Walker, *The Black Loyalists: The Search for a Promised Land in Scotia and Sierra Leone 1783–1870* (Toronto: University of Toronto Press, 1992).

5. J. T. Bukowcyzk et al., eds., *Permeable Border: The Great Lakes Basin as a Transnational Region, 1650–1990* (Calgary and Pittsburgh: University of Calgary Press and University of Pittsburgh Press, 2005), chaps. 2, 3.

6. See George W. Brown, "Do the Americas Have a Common History? A Canadian View," in *Do the Americas Have a Common History? A Critique of the Bolton Thesis,* ed. Lewis Hanke (New York: Alfred A. Knopf, 1964), 119–27. See also Fred Landon, *Western Ontario and the American Frontier* (Toronto and New Haven, Conn.: Ryerson Press and Yale University Press, 1941).

7. George Sheppard, *Plunder, Profit, and Paroles: A Social History of the War of 1812 in Upper Canada* (Montreal and Kingston: McGill–Queen's University Press, 1994), chaps. 8–9; J. L. Granatstein, *Yankee Go Home? Canadians and Anti-Americanism* (Toronto: HarperCollins, 1996), 25–27.

8. Graeme Hamilton, "Slave's Graves Marked for Historic Site," *NP,* May 17, 2002; Daniel G. Hill, "Black History in Early Toronto," *Polyphony,* Summer 1984, 28–30; "Address to Black History Conference," University of Toronto, February 18, 1978, http://collections.ic.gc.ca/magic/mt4o.html.

9. Examples are G. M. Davidson, *The Fashionable Tour: A Guide to Travelers Visiting the Middle and Northern States and the Provinces of Canada* (Saratoga Springs, N.Y.: G. M. Davidson, 1830); O. J. Holley, ed., *The Picturesque Tourist: Being a Guide through the Northern and Eastern States and Canada* (New York: Disturnell, 1844); and

Reginald C. Stuart, *United States Expansionism and British North America, 1775–1871* (Chapel Hill: University of North Carolina Press, 1988), chap. 7.

10. James Walker offers an overview in *Identity: The Black Experience in Canada* (Toronto: Gage Educational Press, 1979).

11. Robin W. Winks, "The Creation of a Myth: Canadian Enlistments in Northern Armies during the American Civil War," *CHR* 39 (March 1958): 24–41; Damien-Claude Bélanger, "Canada, French Canadians and Franco-Americans in the Civil War," *Franco-American History,* Marianopolis College, Montreal, 2001, http://www2.marianopo...ry/frncdns/studies/deb/default.htm; Greg Marquis, *In Armageddon's Shadow: The Civil War and Canada's Maritime Provinces* (Toronto: University of Toronto Press, 2000), chaps. 3–5; Damien-Claude Bélanger, "America's Forgotten French Canadians Rise Again," *G&M,* May 14, 2002.

12. Patricia A. Thornton, Ronald H. Walder, and Elizabeth Buchanan, "The Exodus Migrations, 1860–1900," in *Historical Atlas of Canada,* ed. Genticore, vol. 1, plate 31; Patricia A. Thornton, "The Problems of Out-Migration from Atlantic Canada, 1871–1921," *Acadiensis* 15 (1985): 3–24; Ben Levine, "Reveil . . . Waking Up French: The Repression and Renaissance of the French in New England," available at http://wakingupfrench.com; Gary Burrill, "Part One: Massachusetts," in *Away: Maritimers in Massachusetts, Ontario, and Alberta* (Montreal and Kingston: McGill–Queen's University Press, 1992); Armand B. Chartier, "Franco-Americans and Quebec: Linkages and Potential in the Northeast," in *Problems and Opportunities,* ed. Hero and Daneau, 151–68.

13. Randy William Widdis, "'We Breathe the Same Air': Eastern Ontario Migration to Watertown, New York," *NYH* 68 (1987): 261–80; David Harvey, *Americans in Canada: Migration and Settlement since the 1840s* (Queenston: Edwin Mellen Press, 1991), 35–77, 199–243.

14. Randy William Widdis, "Red River Bound: Canadian Migration to Eastern North Dakota," in *With Scarcely a Ripple: Anglo-Canadian Migration into the United States and Western Canada 1880–1920,* by Randy William Widdis (Montreal and Kingston: McGill–Queen's University Press, 1998), 255–89; Randy William Widdis, "The Last Best West? Return and Interprovincial Migration to Saskatchewan," in *With Scarcely a Ripple,* by Widdis, 290–336.

15. Jim Beatty, "Tribunal to Hear Bountiful case," *NP,* September 4, 2002; Fabian Dawson, "U.S. Probe into Young Brides Eyes B.C. Sect," *CH,* September 25, 2002.

16. John W. Bennett and Seena B. Kohl, *Settling the Canadian-American West, 1890–1915: Pioneer Adaptation and Community Building* (Lincoln: University of Nebraska Press, 1995), chaps 8–10, 12–13; Shepard R. Bruce, "Diplomatic Racism: Canadian Government and Black Migration from Oklahoma," *Great Plains Quarterly* 3 (1983): 12–13.

17. Marvin McInnis, "The Move to the West, 1891–1914, and "Immigration, 1896–1914," in *The Historical Atlas of Canada: Addressing the Twentieth Century,* ed. Donald Kerr and Deryck Holdsworth (Toronto: University of Toronto Press, 1990), vol. 3, plate 27; Beth LaDow, "'We Can Play Baseball on the Other Side': The Limits of Nationalist History on a U.S.-Canada Borderland," in *American Public Life and the Historical Imagination,* ed. Wendy Gamber, Michael Grossberg, and Hendrik Hartog (Notre Dame, Ind.: University of Notre Dame Press, 2003), 163–82.

18. Claude Bélanger, ed., "Canadians in the United States: Documents on Franco-American History-Quebec History," 2001, http://www2.marianopolis.edu/quebechistory/frcdns.

19. John Herd Thompson and Stephen J. Randall, *Canada and the United States: Ambivalent Allies,* 3rd ed. (Montreal and Kingston: McGill–Queen's University Press, 2002), 51–56; Samuel Moffett, *The Americanization of Canada* (Toronto: University of Toronto Press, 1972; orig. pub. 1907), chap. 1.

20. Nora Faires, "Leaving the Land of the Second Chance: Migration from Ontario to the Upper Midwest in the Nineteenth and Early Twentieth Centuries," in *Permeable Border,* ed. Bukowcyzk et al., 78–119; Ninette Kelly and Michael Trebilock, *The Making of the Mosaic: A History of Canadian Immigration* (Toronto: ECW Press, 1998), 118–20, 188; Harvey, *Americans in Canada,* 1–33, 79–127, 245–75; Thompson and Randall, *Canada and the United States,* 17–18, 79–81; Jeffrey Simpson, *Star-Spangled Canadians: Canadians Living the American Dream* (Toronto: HarperCollins, 2000), 16–21, 27–34.

21. Adrian Wilshire, "'Where Are the Roads?' Tourism and Promotion Films of Nova Scotia, 1945–1970," master's thesis, Department of History, Dalhousie University, 1996.

22. Bruno Ramirez, *Crossing the 49th Parallel: Migration from Canada to the United States, 1900–1930* (Ithaca, N.Y.: Cornell University Press, 2001), 70–72, 104–6, 143.

23. John Higham, *Strangers in the Land: Patterns of American Nativism 1860–1925* (New York: Athenaeum, 1971), 2nd ed., chaps. 9–11; Simpson, *Star-Spangled Canadians,* 20–28; Howard Palmer, "Nativism in Alberta, 1925–1930," *Historical Papers* (Canadian Historical Association), 1974, 183–212; Alvin Finkel, "Canadian Immigration Policy and the Cold War, 1945–1950," *JCS* 21 (1986): 53–70.

24. Carl Berger, "The Conferences on Canadian-American Affairs, 1935–1941: An Overview," in *The Road to Ogdensburg: The Queen's / St. Lawrence Conferences on Canadian-American Affairs,* ed. Frederick W. Gibson and Jonathan Rossie (East Lansing: Michigan State University Press, 1933), 17–18; Thompson and Randall, *Canada and the United States,* 114n15, 122–23, 129.

25. Wallace Immen, "Border Shopping Becomes a Habit," *G&M,* August 9, 1993; Ken Becker, "Exchange Rate Keeping Canadians Away from U.S.," *MS,* October 16, 1999; Kelly Shiers, Statistics Canada, *The Daily,* May 17, 2001, available at http://www.statcan.ca/Daily/English; Felicia R. Lee, "The Rise and Fall of Vacations," from *NYT* in *NP,* August 17, 1999.

26. Jenny Carson, "Riding the Rails: Black Railroad Workers in Canada and the United States," *Labour,* no. 50 (Fall 2002): 1–20, http://www.historycooperative.org/llt/50/carson.html; conversations with a black civil rights leader in Nova Scotia.

27. Sue Ferguson, "A Torn Divide," *Maclean's,* September 10, 2001, 42–43; Howard Palmer, "Mosaic versus Melting Pot? Immigration and Ethnicity in Canada and the United States," *IJ* (1976); Morton Weinfeld, "North American Integration and the Issue of Immigration: Canadian Perspectives," in *NAFTA in Transition,* ed. Stephen J. Randall and Herman W. Konrad (Calgary: University of Calgary Press, 1995), 236–50; Bradley Miller, "60 Years of Canadian Citizenship," *NP,* May 11, 2006; Sally Ito, "Exiled," *G&M,* May 27, 2006.

28. Granatstein, *Yankee Go Home?* 192–216; James Steele and Robin Mathews, "The Universities: Takeover of the Mind," in *Close the 49th Parallel, Etc.,* ed. Ian Lumsden (Toronto: University of Toronto Press, 1970), 169–78.

29. Tamera Palmer Seiler, "Melting Pot and Mosaic: Images and Realities," in *Canada and the United States: Differences That Count,* 2nd edition, ed. David M.

Thomas (Toronto: Broadview Press, 2000), 97–120; Graham Fraser, "What an African Canadian Is," *G&M,* August 30, 1997; David Schribman, "Continent Faces Challenge of Diversity," *SH,* August 23, 1998; Jan Cienski, "New Voters with Clout," *NP,* June 23, 1999; Simon Avery, "Minorities to Comprise the Majority in California," *NP,* July 6, 2000.

30. Simpson, *Star-Spangled Canadians,* 28–32; Stanley R. Tupper and Douglas L. Bailey, *Canada and the United States: The Second Hundred Years* (New York: Hawthorn Books, 1967), 153–55; Herbert D. Grubel and Anthony D. Scott, "The Immigration of Scientists and Engineers to the United States, 1949–1961," *Canadian Journal of Economics* 2 (1976); K. V. Pankhurst, "Migration between Canada and the United States," *Annals of the American Academy of Political and Social Science,* September 1996; Harvey, *Americans in Canada,* 277–317.

31. See Robert Fulford, "Those American Strangers Among Us," *NP,* June 26, 2001; and Granatstein, *Yankee Go Home?* 182–85. See also Myrna Kostash, *Long War from Home: The Story of the Sixties Generation in Canada* (Toronto: Lorimer, 1980); and James Dickerson, *North to Canada: Men and Women against the Vietnam War* (Westport, Conn.: Praeger, 1999).

32. Janice Paskey, "The Extraordinary Route to a Green Card," *NP,* May 22, 1995; Deborah Jones, "Why David Left Canada," *G&M,* December 7, 1996; Paul Kennedy, "NAFTA Helping Canadians Get U.S. Jobs," *NP,* July 3, 1999; Richard Siklos, "A Man with *Time* on His Side," *NP Business,* December 2000, 81–82; Thomas Alcock, "Go South, Young Lawyer," *NP,* September 1, 2001; Simpson, *Star-Spangled Canadians,* 142–47.

33. David Stonehouse, "Canadian Snowbirds Face New Restrictions," *OC,* May 11, 2002; Graeme Smith, "Canadians Win Exemption to Tougher U.S. Visa Rules," *G&M,* May 17, 2002; James W. Ziglar to Ellen K. White, July 5, 2002, available at http://www.usembassy.org.

34. Ron Graham, "Born Again in Babylon," in *Our American Cousins: The United States Through Canadian* Eyes, ed. Thomas S. Axworthy (Toronto: James Lorimer, 1987), 181–205; Lisa Granatstein, "America's Invisible Snowbacks," *G&M,* August 12, 1995; Tim Cesnick, "Look Before You Leave," *G&M,* June 14, 1997; Norma Greenway, "Only 15% of Us Think Life in U.S. Would Be Better," *NP,* June 23, 2001; Jeannie Marshall, "The Coffee Crisp Club," *NP,* January 25, 2000; John Ibbitson, "Meet the Brain Drain Dinner Club," *NP,* January 13, 2001.

35. Shirley Brady, "The New Nomads," *Time,* June 28, 1999, 48–49; William Watson, "The Brain Drain Is a Myth; Too Bad," *NP,* May 19, 2000, summarizes the data. Also see Diane Lu-Hovasse, "Clogging the Brain Drain at the Border," *NP,* October 16, 2000.

36. Paul Wadie, "Best Brains Most Likely to Drain: Statscan," *NP,* August 28, 1999; Jeffrey Frank and Eric Belair, "Are We Losing Our Best and Brightest to the U.S.?" *Isuma* 1 (Spring 2000): 111–13; C. D. Howe Institute, *Putting the Brain Drain in Context: Canada and the Global Competition for Scientists and Engineers* (Toronto: C. D. Howe Institute, 2000); Tim O'Neill, "Trends in Canada-U.S. Migration: Where's the Flood," *Economic Analysis* (Economics Department, Bank of Montreal), March 24, 1999.

37. Michael Friscolanti et al., "U.S. Abruptly Alters Canadian Student Rules," *NP,* May 30, 2002; Norma Greenway, "Emigration to United States Takes Giant Leap," *NP,* December 7, 2002.

38. "Hands across the Border: Working Together at Our Shared Border and Abroad to Ensure Safety, Security and Efficiency," Standing Committee on Citizenship and Immigration, December 2001, available at http://www.gc.ca; Stephen Handelman, "The New Immigration Dilemma," *Time,* March 10, 2003, 28; "Canada and U.S. Negotiators Agree to Final Draft Text of Safe Third Country Agreement," available at http://www.cic.gc.ca.

39. Data are from the Migration Policy Institute, Washington, available at http://migration/immigration.org; Deborah Myers, "Security at US Borders: A Move Away from Unilateralism," *Migration Information Source,* Migration Policy Institute, August 1, 2003; and Ninette Kelly and Michael Trebilock, *The Making of the Mosaic: A History of Canadian Immigration* (Toronto: EVW Press, 1998), 100–10. See also Michael R. Haines and Richard H. Steckel, *A Population History of North America* (Cambridge: Cambridge University Press, 2000), passim.

40. Marina Jimenez, "Disaffected Americans Look North to 'Better Government,'" *G&M,* November 4, 2004; Richard Starnes, "Immigration Web Site Is Still a 'Hit' with Americans," *NP,* November 10, 2004; Richard Harris et al., *Brains on the Move: Essays on Human Capital Mobility in a Globalizing World and Implications for the Canadian Economy,* Policy Study 42 (Toronto: C. D. Howe Institute, 2005).

Chapter 5: Negative Vibrations

1. "U.S. Flag Booed in School Parade," *G&M,* March 20, 2004; Guy Quenneville, "Cross-Border Cold Shoulders," *SH,* April 24, 2005; "Canadians to Bush: Hope You Lose, Eh," *Maclean's,* February 9, 2004; Jonathan Gatehouse, "The Know-It-All Neighbour," *Maclean's,* May 3, 2004; Claire Hoy, "Canadian Bush-Bashers Should Stay Home," *NP,* September 1, 2004; Norman Spector, "It's a Shame, but Anti-Americanism Is on the Rise," *G&M,* November 29, 2000.

2. Richard Foot, "Goodwill Gone Bad: What's to Blame? Bush, the War in Iraq, Maybe It's the Imperious Self-Interest," *EJ,* September 11, 2004; Steven Frank, "Our Take on America," *Time,* November 1, 2004, 17n18; "Canadian Attitudes toward Americans," GPC Public Affairs, November 26, 2004; "Friends of America," http://www.friendsofamerica.ca; Pew Research, *Global Opinion: The Spread of Anti-Americans* (New York: Pew Research, 2005), 105–19; "The View from Abroad," *The Economist,* February 19, 2005, 24–26.

3. "Lexington: The Old Slur," *The Economist,* February 19, 2005, 34; Andrew M. Johnson, "Beyond Anti-Americanism: A Balanced Look at Canadian-American Relations," address at Windsor-Detroit Alumni Reception, October 18, 2004, http://www.alumni.uwo.ca/branches/windsor.htm; Reginald C. Stuart, "Review Essay: Anti-Americanism in Canadian History," *ARCS* 27 (1997): 293–310; Damien Claude Bélanger, "Pride and Prejudice: Canadian Intellectuals Confront the United States, 1891–1945," Ph.D. dissertation, Department of History, McGill University, 2006.

4. S. F. Wise, "The Origins of Anti-Americanism in Canada," Fourth Seminar on Canadian-American Relations, Assumption University of Windsor, 1962; Seymour Martin Lipset, *Continental Divide: The Values and Institutions of the United States and Canada* (Toronto and Washington: C. D. Howe Institute and National Planning Association, 1989), chaps. 1, 12; Richard Gwyn, *The 49th Paradox: Canada in North America* (Toronto: McClelland & Stewart, 1985), chap 1.

5. George Rawlyk, "The Federalist-Loyalist Alliance in New Brunswick, 1784–1815," *Humanities Association Review* 27 (1976): 142–60; Jane Errington, "Friends and Foes: The Kingston Elite and the War of 1812—A Case Study in Ambivalence," *JCS* 20 (1985): 58–79; Edward Grabb and James Curtis, *Regions Apart: The Four Societies of Canada and the United States* (Don Mills, Ont.: Oxford University Press, 2005), chaps. 2, 4, 5.

6. Allen Smith, "The Continental Dimension in the Evolution of the English-Canadian Mind," in *Canada an American Nation? Essays on Continentalism, Identity, and the Canadian Frame of Mind,* ed. Allen Smith (Montreal and Kingston: McGill–Queen's University Press, 1994), chap. 3; Allen Smith, "Samuel Moffett and the Americanization of Canada," in *Canada an American Nation?* ed. Smith, chap. 4.

7. Reginald C. Stuart, *United States Expansionism and British North America, 1775–1871* (Chapel Hill: University of North Carolina Press, 1988), chaps. 2–5.

8. Samuel J. Watson IV, "Army Officers Fight the 'Patriot War': Responses to Filibustering on the Canadian Border, 1837–1839," *Journal of the Early Republic* 18 (1998): 487–521; Robert E. May, *Manifest Destiny's Underworld: Filibustering in Antebellum America* (Chapel Hill: University of North Carolina Press, 2002), chap. 1.

9. See Lester B. Shippee, *Canadian-American Relations, 1849–1874* (New Haven, Conn.: Yale University Press, 1939), for a detailed treatment; see also Donald F. Warner, *The Idea of Continental Union: Agitation for the Annexation of Canada to the United States* (Lexington: University Press of Kentucky, 1960).

10. "Coming Home from the Fair" (orig. pub. in *Canadian Illustrated News,* 1876), in *Canada and the United States: Ambivalent Allies,* 3rd ed., by John Herd Thompson and Stephen J. Randall (Montreal and Kingston: McGill–Queen's University Press, 2002), 43; Patricia Wood, "Defining 'Canadian': Anti-Americanism and Identity in Sir John A. Macdonald's Nationalism," *JCS* 36 (2001), 49–69; James Marsh, "Sir John's Last Stand," *NP,* December 10, 2005; Gordon T. Stewart, *The American Response to Canada since 1776* (East Lansing: Michigan State University Press, 1992), chaps. 2, 3.

11. William M. Baker, "A Case Study of Anti-Americanism in English-Speaking Canada: The Election Campaign of 1911," *CHR* 51 (1970): 426–49; "The Anti-American Ingredient in Canadian History," *DR* 53 (1970): 57–77; J. L. Granatstein, *Yankee Go Home? Canadians and Anti-Americanism* (Toronto: HarperCollins, 1996), chap. 2; P. E. Corbett, "Anti-Americanism," *DR* 10 (1930): 295–300; Stewart, *American Response,* chap. 4.

12. Damien-Claude Bélanger, "Lionel Groulx and Franco-America," *ARCS* 33 (Winter 2003): 373–89; Yvan Lamonde, "American Cultural Influence in Quebec," in *Problems and Opportunities in U.S.-Quebec Relations,* ed. Alfred O. Hero Jr. and Marcel Daneau (Boulder, Colo.: Westview Press, 1984), 106–26.

13. Thompson and Randall, *Canada and the United States,* 94–98.

14. Spry cited in *Listening In: The First Decade of Canadian Broadcasting, 1922–1932,* by Mary Vipond (Montreal and Kingston: McGill–Queen's University Press, 1992), 228; Mary Vipond, "Canadian Nationalism and the Plight of Canadian Magazines in the 1920s," *CHR* 58 (1977): 43–64; Stephen T. Moore, "Defending the Undefended: Canadians, Americans, and the Multiple Meanings of Border during Prohibition," *ARCS* 34 (Spring 2004): 3–32; Bélanger, "Pride and Prejudice," part III.

15. Paul Litt, "Massey Commission, Americanization, and Canadian Cultural Nationalism," *QQ* 98 (1991): 375–87.

16. Knowlton Nash, *Kennedy and Diefenbaker: Fear and Loathing across the Un-*

defended Border (Toronto: McClelland & Stewart, 1990), 13–14; 52–59; John Hilliker and Donald Barry, *Canada's Department of External Affairs: Coming of Age, 1946–1968* (Montreal and Kingston: McGill–Queen's University Press, 1995), vol. 2, 237–46; Granatstein, *Yankee Go Home?* 121–45.

17. David S. Surrey, *Choice of Conscience: Vietnam Era Military and Draft Resisters in Canada* (New York: Praeger, 1982), 113–16.

18. Underhill is quoted in Granatstein, *Yankee Go Home?* 8, 146–89.

19. Michael Fellman, "Sam I Am," *Saturday Night,* October 1996, 43–46; and see the letters in response, *Saturday Night,* December 1996, 9; James Steele and Robin Mathews, "The Universities: Takeover of the Mind," in *Close the 49th Parallel, Etc.,* ed. Ian Lumsden (Toronto: University of Toronto Press, 1970), 169–78. See also Karel D. Bicha, "Five Canadian Historians and the USA," *ARCS* 29 (1999): 195–210; Theodore Plantinga, "Anti-Americanism and the Canadian Identity," *Myodicy* 3 (April 1997), http://www.redeemer.on.ca/~tplanti.

20. Colin Campbell and William Christian, *Parties, Leaders and Ideologies in Canada* (Toronto: McGraw-Hill Ryerson, 1996), 27–28, 100–1, 155–92.

21. George Grant, *Lament for a Nation: The Defeat of Canadian Nationalism* (Toronto: McClelland & Stewart, 1965); Stephen Clarkson, *Canada and the Reagan Challenge: Crisis and Adjustment* (Toronto: University of Toronto Press, 1985), chaps. 1, 12–13; Granatstein, *Yankee Go Home?* 251 ff.

22. Alan Toulin, "Chrétien Signals Returning Party to Productivity Agenda," *NP,* March 20, 2000; James Blanchard, *Behind the Embassy Door: Canada, Clinton and Quebec* (Toronto: McClelland & Stewart, 1998), chaps. 1, 2.

23. The quotation is in Diane Francis, "The U.S. Is Hated for Its Success," *NP,* September 11, 2002; Margaret Wente, "They Had It Coming?" *G&M,* September 15, 2001; "Discussion: Canadian Reaction to WTC Disaster," *Argosy,* September 20, 2001, http://argosy.mta.ca/archives; Rene Biberstein, "Upping the Anti: Does Being Young in Canada Mean Being Anti-American?" http://www.tgmag.ca/tgof97/rene2/htm; Shawn McCarthy, "Majority Thinks U.S. Partly to Blame for Sept. 11," *G&M,* October 7, 2002; John O'Sullivan, "Their Amerika," *NR,* October 15, 2001; J. L. Granatstein and Norman Hillmer, "Those Damn Yankees," *Maclean's,* October 22, 2001, 58–59; conference speaker Renata Thobani, cited in Granatstein, "Our Best Friend—Whether We Like It or Not," *NP,* October 23, 2002; "Ugly Anti-Americanism," *NP,* March 28, 2003; "Letters," *NP,* March 29, 2003.

24. "The Hot Issues," *Canadian Alliance,* September 24, 2001, http://www.canadian alliance.ca.hot; Robert Fulford, "Anti-American Cant a Self-Inflicted Wound," *NP,* September 14, 2001; "U.S. Bashing No Longer a Game," *NP,* September 22, 2001; Allan Gotleib, "We're Talking to One Another, Not the U.S., *NP,* September 25, 2001; Terrence Corcoran, "Keeping Up with Intellectual Cranks," *NP,* September 21, 2001; Claire Hoy, "More Than Borderline Friends," *NP,* December 10, 2002.

25. Joan Bryden, "Liberal MPs Grow Tired of Unity with U.S., *NP,* January 24, 2002; Richard Gwyn, "Do We Really Want to Be American Flunkies?" *SH,* January 27, 2002; Linda McQuaig, "The Suburb of Canada," *NP,* February 4, 2002; "Security, Sovereignty and Continentalism: Canadian Perspectives on September 11," EKOS poll, September 27, 2001, and Ipsos Reid poll, September 2002, both at http://www.cric.ca/en_html/sondages/ekos.html.

26. Jay Banjeree, "That Most Canadian Virtue: Anti-Americanism," *G&M,* May 1,

1999; Sheldon Alberts, "Liberal MPs Liken Bush to WW2 Villains," *NP,* October 3, 2002; Jim Meek, "Border Blues and Ugly Canadianism," *CH,* November 8, 2002.

27. Robert Fife and Sheldon Alberts, "PM Calls Bush Friend, 'Not Moron,'" *NP,* November 22, 2002; Christie Blatchford, "She [Ducros] Spoke for Many, Unfortunately," *NP,* November 23, 2002; DeNeen Brown, "Aide to Chrétien Quits in Flap over Gibe about Bush," *WP,* November 27, 2002; Campbell Clark, "Opposition, U.S. Media Fan Sparks over Insult," *G&M,* November 28, 2002; Sheldon Alberts, "Manley Criticizes Smug Attitudes toward U.S.," *NP,* December 4, 2002; Glenn Woiceshyn to the Editor, "Media Link," September 28, 2001, available at http://www.aynrand.org.

28. DeNeen L. Brown, "Canadian Apologizes for Expletive about U.S.," *WP,* February 28, 2003; Sheldon Alberts, "Liberals Distance Themselves from Parrish," *NP,* February 28, 2003; "Anti-War Liberals Vow to Oppose PM," *G&M,* March 15, 2003.

29. L. Ian MacDonald, "Our Only Best Friends?" *Maclean's,* March 3, 2003, 52; John Ibbitson, "Insulting the U.S. with Impunity," *G&M,* March 19, 2003; Brian Tobin, "Grow Up and Stop Pulling the Eagle's Tail Feathers," *G&M,* March 20, 2003; John Ibbitson, "Our MPs Should Take Their Feet Out of Their Mouths," *G&M,* March 20, 2003; Jane Taber, "Ottawa Is Not Anti-American, Martin Maintains," *G&M,* March 27, 2003; Jane Taber, "Stop Criticizing U.S., Manley Says," *G&M,* March 28, 2003; Jane Taber, "Treat Bush Like a War Criminal: Robinson," *G&M,* March 20, 2003.

30. Diane Francis, "The Plight of the Invisible Immigrant," *NP,* October 23, 2004; Siri Agrell, "Expats Face Anti-U.S. Bias," *NP,* October 23, 2004; Nora Jacobson, "Before You Flee to Canada, Can We Talk?" *WP,* November 28, 2004.

31. Sheldon Alberts, "End the U.S. bashing, Businesses Tell PM," *NP,* March 5, 2003; Shawn McCarthy, "No Official Apology for Anti-U.S. Talk, *NP,* April 4, 2003; Taber, "Ottawa Is Not Anti-American"; Taber, "Stop Criticizing U.S."; Ian Bailey, "Dhaliwal Says Bush Remarks Misconstrued," *NP,* March 29, 2003.

32. Christopher Sands, "The Eavesdropping Problem," *Canada Focus* (Center for Strategic and International Studies) 3, no. 1 (January 2002).

33. Jeffrey Simpson, "Why Canada Gets No Respect in Washington," *G&M,* January 29, 2003; Walter Russell Mead, "Analyzing Uncle Sam," *Time,* February 3, 2003, 35; Mike Blanchfield, "U.S. Sees Canada as 'Weak, Socialist,'" *OC,* September 10, 2002; Sheldon Alberts, "Parrish's Irrelevance Not Discerned in U.S.," *NP,* November 19, 2004; Randy Boswell, "'Shifty' Canada Mocked on CNN," *OC,* November 26, 2002.

34. Arnold Beichman, "Canada's Cold Shoulder to U.S.," *WT,* September 20, 2004; David Jones, "Yo Canada! A Wake-Up Call for Y'All Up There," *PO,* February 2003, 45–48; Jackson Murphy, "Jonah Goldberg versus the Wimps," November 18, 2002, available at http://www.enterstageright.com/archive; Jackson Murphy, "The Curious Case of the Disappearing Nation," May 26, 2003, available at http://www.enterstageright.com/archive; "Canada Was Purposely Cut from 2001 Speech, Frum Says," *G&M,* January 8, 2003; David Frum, *The Right Man: The Surprise Presidency of George W. Bush* (New York: Random House, 2003), 149–50.

35. Sheldon Alberts, "U.S. Losing Faith in Northern Neighbor," *NP,* February 8, 2003; Norman Spector, "Insults Are Our Chief Export," *G&M,* February 4, 2003; author's conversations with U.S. officials over several years; Clifford Krauss, "Was Canada Just too Good to Be True?" *NYT,* May 25, 2005.

36. Jonah Goldberg, "Anti-American Attitude? Blame Canada," *Jewish World Review,* November 15, 2002, http://www.jewishworldreview.com/cols/jonah111502;

Goldberg File, "'Soviet Canuckistan': Such a Rare Country," *NR,* November 8, 2002, available at http://www.nationalreview.com; "'Shocked and Dismayed' by Canada," *FP,* October 28, 2005; Beth Gorham, "Canadians Too Big for Their Britches, Fox News Says," *CH,* December 20, 2005; Bennet G. Kelley, "Carlson, Coulter, and Canada," *Democratic Underground,* December 10, 2004, http://www.democraticunderground.ocm/articles/04/12/10_canada.html; "In Their Own Words," http://www.tranquileye.com/stockwell/rightoncanada.html.

37. George Szamuely, "'Anti-Americanism,' Pose and Reality," April 12, 2000, http://www.antiwar.com/szamuely/pf/p-sz041200.html; David Shribman, "Damn Yankees," *SH,* August 27, 2000; William Paff, "The U.S. Misreads the Causes of Anti-Americanism," *The Nation,* April 4, 2001, available at http://www.nation-online.com; "Anti-Americanism: The 'Anti-Imperialism' of Fools," *World Socialist Web,* September 22 and October 1, 2001, available at http://www.businessweekmagazine/content; Editorial, "America-Hating: A Badge of Identity," *NP,* February 8, 2002; Lee Harris, "The Intellectual Origins of America-Bashing," *Policy Review* 116 (December 2002–January 2003); Ellen Hale, "The Return of Anti-Americanism," *USAT,* August 14, 2002; *Canadian Dimension,* available at http://www.canadiandimension.mb.ca.

38. "Notes for an Address by the Honourable Lloyd Axworthy, "Liberals at the Border: We Stand on Guard for Whom?" Sixth Annual Keith Davey Lecture, Liu Centre for the Study of Global Issues, Victoria University, March 11, 2002, available at http://www.liucentre.ubc.ca; Lloyd Axworthy, "A Human Approach Will Defeat Terrorism," *OC,* November 21, 2002, available at http://www.canada.com.network; Lloyd Axworthy, "Missile Counter-Attack," *Winnipeg Free Press,* March 3, 2005, available at http://www.truthout.org.

39. Andrew J. Bacevich, "The Real World War IV," *WQ,* Winter 2005, 36–61.

40. Chrétien's speech was reported in "Don't Act Alone," and "You're Not Trusted: PM to U.S.," *G&M,* February 14, 2003. Also see DeNeen L. Brown, "Will Canada Support War, or Not?" *WP,* January 30, 2003; Barry Cooper and Ted Morton, "Chrétien Has Put Party Ahead of Country," *NP,* March 3, 2003; Norman Hillmer and Maureen Appel Molot, "The Diplomacy of Decline," in *A Fading Power: Canada among Nations 2002,* ed. Norman Hillmer and Maureen Appel Molot (Toronto: Oxford University Press, 2002), 1–33; and Christopher Sands, "Fading Power or Rising Power: 11 September and Lessons from the Section 110 Experience," in *Fading Power,* ed. Hillmer and Molot, 49–73.

41. David Orchard, "Conservatives Can Win If Only They Remember Their History," *TS,* June 29, 1998, available at http://www.davidorchard.com; David Crane, "U.S. Inroads Threaten Canada, Ex-PM Warns," *MS,* July 2, 1999; "The Line between U.S.-Canada Getting Blurrier," *MS,* October 15, 1999; Ed Janzen, "Stars and Gripes: Our Patriotic Duty," *Manitoban,* January 9, 2002; Judy Rebick, "There's a War to Be Stopped," *G&M,* March 13, 2003, http://www.flora.org/nowar/forum/402; Paul Wells, "Why the NDP Can't Rise," *NP,* January 18, 2003; Jay Banerjee, "That Most Canadian Virtue: Anti-Americanism," *G&M,* May 1, 1999; Stephen Clarkson, "What Uncle Sam Wants . . . Is Good for Corporate America, but Not Necessarily His Neighbours," *G&M,* December 2, 2002.

42. Ted Byfield, "We Need to Know Who's Running [the] Country," *CS,* March 13, 2005, http://www.canoe.ca/NewsStand/Columnists/Calgary; Salim Mansur, "Saying 'No' to U.S. Was Very Liberal," *Toronto Sun,* March 7, 2005; Monique Gagnon-Tremblay,

minister of international relations for Quebec, "Quebec and America," *NP,* March 14, 2005; Earl Fry, "Quebec Relations with the United States," *ARCS* 32 (2002): 323–41; Jacqueline Swartz, "Toronto the Intolerant," *TS,* October 15, 2003; Lydia Miljan and Barry Cooper, "The Canadian 'Garrison Mentality' and Anti-Americanism at the CBC," *Studies in Defence & Foreign Policy* (Fraser Institute) 4 (May 2005).

43. Granatstein, *Yankee Go Home?* 167–68, 272–75; Diane Pacom, "Being French in North America: Quebec Culture and Globalization," *ARCS* 31 (2001): 441–48; Sheldon Alberts, "End the U.S. Bashing, Businesses Tell PM," *NP,* March 5, 2003.

44. "Five Facets of the Collective Canadian Mindset," *Opinion Canada* 4, no. 42 (November 21, 2002), available at http://www.cric.ca; Barrie McKenna, "Friendly Canadians Buck Anti-U.S. Trend," *G&M,* December 5, 2002; "CRIC Survey on International Affairs," Environics, March 7–27, 2003, http://www.cric.ca/pwp/international affairs/2003/Canada; "A Special Report: Attacking Iraq," Ipsos Reid, January 17, 2003, available at http://www.cric.ca; "Canada Fears 'Biggest Risk to World Peace' on Its Doorstep," *Financial Times,* January 23, 2003; "Lonely America: Little Global Support for U.S. Government Policies," February 5, 2003, Ipsos Public Affairs, available at http://www.ipsospa.com; Robert Fulford, "Bashing the U.S. Makes Us Feel Good All Over," *NP,* September 20, 2003; Laura Macdonald, "Civil Society and North American Integration," *PO,* June/July 2004, 54–57.

45. Patrick Buchanan in *National Review,* November 25, 2002, 30–32; "Letters," *NR,* December 23, 2002; "Blame Canada: Interview with Pat Buchanan," CBC News: Disclosure, February 27, 2003; Jonah Goldberg, "Bomb Canada: The Case for War," *NR,* November 25, 2002, http://www.findarticles.com; Ann Coulter, "Canada Is Lucky . . . ," *Media Matters for America,* April 12, 2004, http://mediamatters.org/items/printable; "The American Right Talks about Canada," *In Their Own Words,* available at http://www.intheirownwords.ca; Bennet G. Kelly, "Carlson, Coulter, and Canada," December 10, 2004, http://www.democraticunderground.com; Matt Stearns, "Times Are Tough for U.S.-Canada Relations," *Kansas City Star,* March 9, 2005, available at http://www.freerepublic.com; comment string on "Lucianne.com," March 13, 2005, http://lucianne.com/threatds2.asp?; "Denouncing Canadian 'Free Riders,'" *NP,* March 2, 2005, reprinted U.S. editorials on Ottawa's rejection of BMD; Matthew Scully, "Canada's Season of Shame Is Upon Us," *NP,* March 28, 2005.

46. Matt Labash, "Welcome to Canada: The Great White Waste of Time," *Weekly Standard,* March 21, 2005, 23–29; Christin Schmitz, "'The Great White Waste of Time," *NP,* March 28, 2005.

47. Jamie Glazov, "The Sickness of Canadian Anti-Americanism," *FrontPage Magazine.com,* March 7, 2003, http://www.frontpagemag.com/Articles; Sheldon Alberts, "Bad Guys Come in Red and Blue," *NP,* March 4, 2005; Canadian Press, "Canada a Tiny Blip on U.S. Radar, Envoy Says," *G&M,* February 27, 2005; Stephen Handelman, "Who Are Canada's American Enemies?" *Time,* March 21, 2005.

48. Sheldon Alberts, "U.S. an Easy Target during Federal Vote," *NP,* December 1, 2005; Tony Keller, "Damn Americans," *Maclean's,* December 26, 2005, 22; Dan Dunsky, "Self-Righteous Anti-Americanism as a Poor Excuse for a Foreign Policy," *G&M,* December 27, 2005; Anna Morgan, "Northern Ire: Canadian Politics Are All About America," *WP,* January 8, 2006; Editorial, "A Defeat for Anti-Americanism," *WP,* January 28, 2006.

49. Dan Dunsky, "Why We Bash America," *NP,* December 21, 2005; Adrian Humphreys, "Bush Disliked by 73% in Canada, but 68% Like Americans," *NP,* De-

cember 11, 2005; Robert Fulford, "Anti-Americanism, Bred in the Bone," *NP,* November 17, 2005.

50. Jack Aubrey, "Canadians too Patriotic, Americans Say in Study," Canwest News Service, December 8, 2003, available at http://www.canada.com; Roy McGregor, "Why It Takes $49,543 to Find Out Our Neighbours to the South Think We're Slightly Annoying," *G&M,* December 9, 2003; Richard Gwyn, "Anti-Americanism, 'the New Ideology'—Shame," *SH,* April 16, 2003; Jeffrey Simpson, "Choose Your Side: Puerile or Servile?" *SH,* April 4, 2003; James Bissett, "Hating Bush Is Unhealthy," *NP,* December 2, 2004.

51. Steven Frank, "Our Take on America," *Time,* November 1, 2004, 16–23; GPC Public Affairs, "Canadian Attitudes toward Americans," November 29, 2004, available at http://www.friendsofamerica.ca; Editorial, "Un-Happy Birthday, Canada," *Maclean's,* July 1, 2005, 25; response by John Moore, "'America-Bashers'? Not Us," *NP,* July 12, 2005; John C. Page and Philip Guirlando in "Letters of the Day," *NP,* July 13, 2005.

Chapter 6: Transnational Societies

1. Beth Gorham, "Americans Flood Liberal MPs with Letter in Gay Marriage Debate," *CH,* February 23, 2005; Elizabeth Thompson, "Same-Sex Debate Gets U.S. Infusion," *NP,* February 7, 2004; Marina Jiminez, "Dispirited U.S. Gays Choosing Canada," *G&M,* November 10, 2004.

2. Jacqueline Thorpe, "Canada Still Autonomous Despite U.S. Links: Study," *FP,* September 8, 2004; Keith Banting and Richard Simeon, "Changing Economies, Changing Societies," in *Degrees of Freedom: Canada and the United States in a Changing World,* ed. Keith Banting, George Hoberg, and Richard Simeon (Montreal and Kingston: McGill–Queen's University Press, 1997), 23–70; Christopher Clausen, *Faded Mosaic: The Emergence of Post-Cultural America* (Chicago: Ivan R. Dee, 2000), 55–62, 102–3, 157–59.

3. David Thalen, "The Nation and Beyond: Transnational Perspectives on United States History," *JAH* 86 (1999): 965–67; Reginald C. Stuart and M. Brook Taylor, "The Epic of Greater North America: Themes and Periodization in North American History," in *New England and Atlantic Canada,* ed. John Reid and Stephen Hornsby (Montreal and Kingston: McGill–Queens University Press, 2005), 280–94.

4. Justice R. P. Kerans, "Two Nations under Law," in *Canada and the United States: Differences That Count,* 2nd edition, ed. David M. Thomas (Toronto: Broadview Press, 2000), 359–76; and Christopher Manfredi, "Rights and the Judicialization of Politics in Canada and the Untied States," in *Canada and the United States,* ed. Thomas, 301–18.

5. George Bain, "Cross-Border Journalism," *Maclean's,* January 24, 1994, 16–17; Rae Corelli, "North versus South," *Maclean's,* May 29, 1995, 19–20; Kirk Martin, "Men, Trials, Countries," *G&M,* September 24, 1994; John Jaffey, "Litigation Television," *National Post Business,* April 2001, 51; Luiza Chwialkowska, "Ottawa Ready to Cede Legal Powers," *NP,* December 28, 2001; "International Netforce Launches Law Enforcement Effort," April 2, 2003, U.S. Embassy, http://www.usembassye..._usa&document=internetfraud.

6. Sean Fine, "Eagleton Forces U.S. to Request Extradition," *NP,* March 12, 1994;

Brian Bethune, "Cross-Border Fugitive," *Maclean's,* October 14, 2002, 76–77; Roman J. Zorn, "Criminal Extradition Menaces the Canadian Haven for Fugitive Slaves, 1841–1861," *CHR* 38 (1957): 284–94; Ian Bailey, "No Death Penalty for Canadians: U.S. Prosecutor," *NP,* March 10, 2001, A 2.

7. Jeff Lee, "U.S.-Canada Investigators Team Up to Combat Fraud," *VS,* October 3, 1996; Gary Fields, "Seniors Lose Millions in Sweeps Scam," *USAT,* January 8, 1999; John Nicol, "Phone Scams," *Maclean's,* October 19, 1998, 24–29, 32; Stewart Bell, "Ottawa Boosts Security at Airports to Fight Organized Crime," *NP,* June 18, 1999.

8. Marci McDonald et al., "The Enemy Within," *Maclean's,* May 8, 1995, 34–40, 42–43; Jim Bronskill, "RCMP Eyes Extremists," *SDN,* July 20, 1997.

9. See Gordon Stewart and George Rawlyk, *A People Highly Favoured of God: The Nova Scotia Yankees and the American Revolution* (Toronto: Macmillan of Canada, 1972); and Fred Landon. *Western Ontario and the American Frontier* (Toronto: Ryerson Press, 1941), chaps. 6–8. A later transnational theme is developed in Eric R. Crouse, *Revival in the City: The Impact of American Evangelists in Canada 1884–1914* (Montreal and Kingston: McGill–Queen's University Press, 2001).

10. See Theodore Caplow, Louis Hicks, and Ben J. Wattenberg, eds., *The Measured Century: An Illustrated Guide to Trends in America, 1900–2000* (Washington, D.C.: AEI Press, 2001), 1–20, for a statistical analysis and charts on the modern U.S. demographic matrix. Also see Howard Palmer, "Reluctant Hosts: Anglo-Canadian Views of Multiculturalism in the Twentieth Century," in *Readings in Canadian History: Post Confederation,* ed. R. Douglas Francis and Donald B. Smith (Toronto: Holt, Rinehart and Winston, 1986), 185–201.

11. Tamera Palmer Seiler, "Melting Pot and Mosaic: Images and Realities," in *Canada and the United States,* ed. Thomas, 97–120; Jeffrey G. Reitz and Raymond Breton, *The Illusion of Difference: Realities of Ethnicity in Canada and the United States* (Toronto: C. D. Howe Institute, 1994); Nancy L. Green, "*Le Melting-Pot:* Made in America, Produced in France," *JAH* 86 (1999): 1188–1208; Bill Curry and Maria Jiminez, "Canadian Attitudes Harden on Immigration," *G&M,* August 12, 2005; John C. Harles, "Immigrant Integration in Canada and the United States," *ARCS* 34 (2004): 233–58.

12. Ingrid Peritz, "Teacher Wants a Town in Quebec to Remember the Slaves Lying Buried Beneath It," *G&M,* May 20, 2002; Jenny Carson, "Riding the Rails: Black Railroad Workers in Canada and the United States," *Labour* 50 (Fall 2002), http://www.historycooperative.org/llt/50/carson.html.

13. Wendy Cox, "Canadians Just as Racist as Americans—Study," *MS,* June 9, 1994; Alan MacEachern, "Why Martin Luther King Didn't Spend His Summer Vacation in Canada," *G&M,* January 14, 1995; Sue Ferguson, "A Town Divided," *Maclean's,* September 10, 2001, 42–43; DeNeen L. Brown, "A Whitewashing of History," *WP,* February 17, 2002; Constance Backhouse, *Colour-Coded: A Legal History of Racism in Canada, 1900–1950* (Toronto: Osgoode Society for Canadian Legal History and University of Toronto Press, 1999).

14. Patricia E. Roy, "'The Wholesome Sea Is at Her Gates / Her Gates Both East and West': Canada's Selective and Restrictive Immigration Policies in the First Half of the Twentieth Century," in *Canada, 1900–1950: A Country Comes of Age,* ed. Serge Bernier and John MacFarlane (Ottawa: Organization for the History of Canada, 2003), 33–49; "Pioneer Asian Indian Immigration to the Pacific Coast," http://www.lib.ucdavis.edu/punjab; Brian Laghi, "PM Offers $20,000 and Apology to Survivors of Chines Head Tax," *G&M,* June 22, 2006.

15. Sally Ito, "Exiled," *G&M,* May 27, 2006.

16. See James E. St. G. Walker, *"Race," Rights and the Law in the Supreme Court of Canada: Historical Case Studies* (Waterloo: Wilfrid Laurier University Press for Osgoode Society for Canadian Legal History, 1997); Irving Abella and Harold Troper, *None Is Too Many: Canada and the Jews of Europe 1933–1948* (New York: Random House, 1983); Peter Li, *Ethnic Inequality in a Class Society* (Toronto: Thompson Educational Publishing, 1988); Stewart Bell, "Klansman Turns Back on Hatred," *NP,* July 15, 2002; Abraham McLaughlin and Tim Regan, "Suddenly, America Has a Brash Neighbor Up North," *Christian Science Monitor,* June 27, 2003.

17. Stephen T. Moore, "Defining the Undefended: Canadians, Americans, and the Multiple Meanings of Border during Prohibition," *ARCS* 34, no. 1, (2004): 3–32; Richard Kottman, "Volstead Violated: Prohibition as a Factor in Canadian-American Relations," *CHR* 43 (1962): 114–23; M. Paul Holsinger, "The *I'm Alone* Controversy: A Study in Inter-American Diplomacy, 1919–1935," *Mid-America* 50 (1968): 305–13; James Laxer, *The Border: Canada, the U.S. and Dispatches from the 49th Parallel* (Toronto: Random House of Canada, 2003), 142–46.

18. Manon Tremblay, "Gender and Society: Rights and Realities—A Reappraisal," in *Canada and the United States,* ed. Thomas, 319–37.

19. Raymond Tatalovich, "The Abortion Controversy in Canada and the United States," *CAPP* 25 (February 1996).

20. Karen Balcom, "Of Babies and Black Markets: Transnational Social Welfare Policy and History Across the Border," paper presented at American Studies Association meeting, Montreal, October 28, 1999, courtesy of the author; Susan Gilmore, "Baby-Selling Ring Used B.C. as Conduit, U.S. Alleges," *NP,* October 7, 1999.

21. See Joe Chidlet, "The New Burbs," *Macleans,* July 27, 1997, 16–21; and Andrew Phillips, "The Disney Dream," *Macleans,* July 27, 1997, 24–25. Also see Dolores Hayden, *Building Suburbia: Green Fields and Urban Growth 1820–2000* (New York: Pantheon Books, 2003).

22. Richard Gilbert, "Can Cities Survive the Car?" *G&M,* August 16, 1997; Witold Rybczynski, "Urban All Over," *Maclean's,* September 14, 1998, 48–50, 52; Victoria Griffith, "The De-Malling of America," *FP,* October 19, 1999.

23. Ray Conlogue, "A Crisis of Culture," *G&M,* June 19–22, 2000; Francine Dube, "Big Cities Push for More Power, U.S.-Style Taxing," *NP,* February 26, 2001; David Crombie, "Grow Smart or Grow Worse," *G&M,* April 4, 2001.

24. Keith Banting, "The Social Policy Divide: The Welfare State in Canada and the United States," in *Degrees of Freedom,* ed. Banting, Hoberg, and Simeon, 267–309.

25. Centers for Medicare and Medicaid Services, http://www.cms.hhs.gov/about/history; Daniel Kraker, "The Canadian Cure," http://www.inmotionmagazine.com/hcare/canadahc.html; Canada Health Act, http://www.hc-sc.gc.ca/datapcb/datahins.htm.

26. Antonia Maioni, "Parting at the Crossroads: The Development of Health Insurance in Canada and the United States, 1940–1965," *Comparative Politics* 29 (July 1997): 411–31.

27. Robert G. Evans, "Two Systems in Restraint: Contrasting Experiences with Cost Control in the 1990s," in *Canada and the United States,* ed. Thomas, 21–51. See Robert Chernomas and Ardeshir Sepehri, eds., *How to Choose? A Comparison of the U.S. and Canadian Health Care Systems* (Amityville, N.Y.: Bywood, 1998).

28. James Frogue, "A High Price for Patients: An Update on Government Health

Care in Britain and Canada," Backgrounder, Heritage Foundation, Washington, D.C., September 2000.

29. Canadian Press, "U.S. Doctors Scan Canada for Potential Patients," *MS,* December 6, 1999; Stephen Handelman, "What Alan Rock Isn't Saying," *Time,* February 14, 2000, 40; Theodore R. Marmor, "U.S. Media, Corporate Interests Paint False Caricature of Canadian Health Care System," *G&M,* May 15, 2000; Colleen Fuller, *Caring for Profit: How Corporations Are Taking over Canada's Health System* (New York: New Star Books, 1998); Don Harrison, "Overcrowded B.C. Hospitals Force Patients to Head South," *NP,* October 16, 2000; Anne Marie Owens, "'Solid Base' of Canadians Accept Private Care: Survey," *NP,* December 18, 2000; Theodore R. Marmor et al., "Whither Health Care Policy? U.S., Canadian, and European Perspectives," *NP,* November 12, 2002.

30. Tom Koch, "Organ Transplants without Borders," *NP,* April 30, 2001; Tom Arnold, "The Dawn of Cross-Border Medicare," *NP,* June 13, 2001; Tom Arnold, "Cross-Border Health Care OK: Ottawa," *NP,* June 14, 2001; Lisa Priest, "Provinces Spend Millions on U.S. Care for Patients," *G&M,* October 5, 2002; Stephen Vail, *Canadians' Values and Attitudes on Canada's Health Care System: A Synthesis of Survey Results* (Ottawa: Conference Board of Canada, 2001); James Frogue, David Gratzer, Timothy Evans, and Richard Teske, "Buyer Beware: The Failure of Single-Payer Health Care," *Heritage Lectures* 702 (May 4, 2001), available at http://www.americanheritage.com; Kirstin Downey, "A Heftier Dose to Swallow," *WP,* March 4, 2004; Brian Lee Crowley, "The Top Ten Things People Believe about Canadian Health Care, but Shouldn't," 2004, http://www.aims.ca/commentary/top10.html.

31. Andrew Phillips, "America's Bitter Pills," *Maclean's,* December 20, 1999, 98; Barry Brown, "Quebec, Vermont Seek Cross-Border Health Deal," *NP,* February 12, 2000; Peter Morton, "U.S. Senator's Drug Crusade Could End Up Costing Canadians," *NP,* April 12, 2000.

32. Brad Evenson, "True Patriot Love? Not in Health Care Ads," *NP,* September 27, 2000; Morley Safer, narrator, "Prescriptions and Profits," *CBS 60 Minutes,* March 12, 2004, http://www.cbsnews/stories/2004/03/12/60minutes.

33. Canadian Press, "Manitoba Entrepreneurs Cash In on High U.S. Pharmacy Costs," *CH,* January 16, 2002; Helen Dewar, "Senate Votes to Allow Drug Reimportation," *WP,* July 17, 2002; Joseph Brean, "U.S. City Buys Its Medicine from Canada," *NP,* August 30, 2003; Tom Blackwell, "MDs Prescribe for Unseen U.S. Patients," *NP,* October 31, 2003; William M. Welch, "States Continue Push for Canadian Drugs," *USAT,* December 31, 2003; Tim Craig, "[Maryland] Senate Wants Permission to Buy Prescription Drugs From Canada," *WP,* March 31, 2004.

34. Beth Gorham, "U.S. Takes Aim at Mail-Order Drugs from Canada," *SH,* October 2, 2003; Mark Kaufman, "FDA Warns 3 Firms to Stop Importing Drugs from Canada," *WP,* January 23, 2004; Ceci Connolly, "Pfizer Cuts Supplies to Canadian Drugstores," *WP,* February 19, 2004; Shawn McCarthy and Brian Lagh, "N.Y. Mayor Seeks Boycott of Canada by Drug Firms," *G&M,* October 30, 2003; DeNeen Brown, "U.S. and Canada Sign Accord to Regulate Internet Drug Sales," *WP,* November 19, 2003.

35. Ceci Connolly, "Illinois Couple Sues Over U.S. Drug Import Ban," *WP,* February 26, 2004; Associated Press, "U.S. Governors to Press Cross-Border Pill Trade," February 24, 2004, http://www.ctv.ca/servlet/ArticleNews/story.com; Al Swanson, "Analysis: Govs Taking Initiative on Drugs," *WT,* March 1, 2004; Beth Gorham, "White House,

FDA Blasted for Blocking Prescription Drug Imports from Canada," February 24, 2004, available at http://www.canada.com; "Prescriptions and Profit," *60 Minutes,* March 14, 2004, available at http://www.cbsnews.com; Canadian Press, "New Hampshire Governor Unveils State Internet Link to Canadian Pharmacy," April 6, 2004, available at http://www.canada.com.

36. Graeme Smith, "Internet Pharmacy Sales to U.S. More than Double, Study Shows," *G&M,* March 26, 2004; Daniel Girard, "War on Drug Costs Waged on Web," *TS,* April 10, 2004; Cameron Barr, "Montgomery Considers Canadian Drug Plan," *WP,* April 18, 2004; Ceci Connolly, "Drug Re-importation Plan Saves City $2.5 Million," *WP,* July 15, 2004; Bruce Constantineau, "Vancouver Firm Reaps Benefits of U.S. State-Sanctioned Online Drug Sales," *VS,* October 28, 2004.

37. Mark Kennedy, "Prescription Drug Worries to Bring Tighter Regulation," *NP,* March 14, 2005; Gloria Galloway, "Ottawa Warned Over U.S. Plans to Import Drugs," *G&M,* May 11, 2005; Brian Ferguson, "Contraindicated," *FP,* May 12, 2005; Doug Struck, "Canada to Restrict Exports to U.S. of Prescription Drugs, *WP,* June 30, 2005.

38. Tom Blackwell, "Canada Mulls Joint Drug Reviews with U.S. Regulator," *NP,* February 28, 2006; Tom Blackwell, "Faster Drug Approval Good for All: Report," *NP,* March 8, 2006.

39. Miro Cernetig, "Mounties Swamped by Ocean of Drugs," *G&M,* November 19, 1994; Steven Edwards, "UN Labels Canada a Haven for Drug Trade," *G&M,* February 23, 2000; Jan Cienski and Carl Hanlon, "U.S. Fears Drug Spillover from Canada," *NP,* May 17, 2002; Erin Anderssen, "Would Softer Pot Law Stir Wrath of U.S.?" *G&M,* July 13, 2002; David Crary, "Americans Eye Canada as Liberal Haven," *SH,* July 20, 2003.

40. Thom Cohen, "Canada's Pot Proposal Worries U.S.," *WP,* October 15, 2002; David Montgomery, "Whoa! Canada! Legal Marijuana. Gay Marriage. Peace. What the Heck's Going On Up North, eh?" *WP,* July 1, 2003.

41. Clayton E. Cramer, "Confiscating Guns from America's Past," *The Freeman: Ideas on Liberty,* January 2001, http://www.fee.org/vnews.php?; W. T. Stanbury and Allan Smithies, "A Brief History of 'Gun Control' in Canada, 1867–1995," March 17, 2003, http://www.garrybreitkreuz.com; Leslie Pal, "Between the Sights: Gun Control in Canada and the United States," in *Canada and the United States,* ed. Thomas, 68–93.

42. Los Angeles anecdote from conversation with Canada's Washington Embassy staff. Caitlin Kelly, "Ladies, Get a Gun," *G&M,* September 29, 1996.

43. Charles Gillis, "Ontario Man Charged with Sneaking Guns into U.S.," *NP,* February 7, 2001; Betsy Powell, "Police Get New Ally in Gun Fight," *TS,* May 18, 2003; Charlie Gillis, "American Guns, Canadian Violence," *Maclean's,* August 15, 2005, 18–26; Campbell Clark and Oliver Moore, "PM Says U.S. Partly to Blame for Gun Crime Proliferating in Canadian Communities," *G&M,* October 25, 2005; John R. Lott, "Don't Blame American Guns," *NP,* October 28, 2005.

44. Eoin Kenny, "Canadians React to Alberta Death 'with Disbelief,'" *SH,* May 2, 1999; Ian Bailey, "Test to Identify Potential School Shooters Deemed Impossible," *NP,* January 12, 2000; Michael Moore, *Bowling for Columbine.*

45. Richard Foot, "'Reclaim Your God-Given Right' to Guns, Heston Urges Canadians," *NP,* April 14, 2000.

46. Mark Stevenson, "U.S. in a Lather Over Gay Boy Scout Leaders," *NP,* October 28, 1999; Andrew Phillips, "Working the System," *Maclean's,* June 5, 2000, 42–44; Jeet Heer, "The Conservative Closet," *NP,* June 10, 2000; Bob Harvey, "Canadian, U.S. Uni-

tarians Stage 'Friendly' Split Over Gay Rights," *OC,* May 18, 2002; Jeremy Rifkin, "Canada and the Blue States: A New Romance," *The Walrus,* March 2005, 36–41.

47. DeNeen Brown, "Hundreds of Gay Couples Make Their Way to Ontario to Say 'I Do,'" *WP,* June 22, 2003; Cheryl Wetzstein, "Gay 'Marriages' Ahead," *WT,* July 13, 2003; Associated Press, "Nova Scotia Becomes Sixth Canadian Province, Territory to Allow Gay Marriages," *San Francisco Chronicle,* September 24, 2004, available at http://www.sfgate.com.; Clifford Kraus, "Gay Couples Follow a Trail North Blazed by Slaves and War Resisters," *NYT,* November 23, 2003.

48. DeNeen Brown, "For Toronto Family, Gay Marriage Fortifies 'Normal,'" *WP,* March 3, 2004; Gary Lee, "For Gays, Toronto Is the Marrying Kind," *WP,* March 14, 2004; Ken MacQueen, "Mr. and Mrs. in Gay Mecca," *Maclean's,* March 29, 2004; John Geddes, "Tell It to the Court," *Maclean's,* March 29, 2004; Danylo Hawaleshka, "Honeymoon Heaven," *Maclean's,* March 29, 2004; Jonathan Gatehouse, "Across the Great Divide," *Maclean's,* March 29, 2004; "By the Numbers," *Maclean's,* March 29, 2004; Doug Struck, "Same-Sex Marriage Advances in Canada," *WP,* June 29, 2005.

49. Gerard Boychuk, "Are Canadian and U.S. Social Assistance Policies Converging?" *CAPP,* July 1997; Banting, "Social Policy Divide."

Part III: Economic Realm

1. Earl H. Fry, "North American Economic Integration: Policy Options," *Policy Papers on the Americas* (Center for Strategic and International Studies) 14, no. 8 (July 2003); Stephen Blank, Stephanie Golub, and Guy Stanley, *Mapping the New North American Reality: Introduction,* Mapping the New North American Reality Series IRPP Working Paper 2004-09 (Montreal: Institute for Research on Public Policy, 2004), http://www.irpp.org/wp/archive/NA_integ/wp2004-09.pdf; Stephen Blank, Stephanie Golub, and Guy Stanley, *Mapping the New North American Reality: Conclusion,* Mapping the New North American Reality Series, IRPP Working Paper 2004-09q (Montreal: Institute for Research on Public Policy, 2004), http://www.irpp.org/wp/archive/NA_integ/wp2004-09q.pdf; Danielle Goldfarb, *U.S. Bilateral Free Trade Accords: Why Canada Should Be Cautious about Going the Same Route,* Commentary: Border Paper 214 (Toronto: C. D. Howe Institute, 2005), 2–3; Robert O. Keohane and Joseph S. Nye, *Power and Interdependence,* 3rd ed. (New York: Longman, 2001), 143–90. The General Motors slogan referred only to the United States.

2. The Carnegie scholars produced several seminal studies that probed this development. See, e.g., Herbert Marshall et al., *Canadian-American Industry: A Study in International Investment* (New York: Russell & Russell, 1970; orig. pub. 1936). See also Robin Neill, "The Making of the Third National Policy: Canada, 1900–1920" and "The Canadian Quandary: Continentalization, Regionalization, 1950–1970," both available at http://www.upei.ca/rneill/canechist.

3. Michael Hart, *A Trading Nation: Canadian Trade Policy from Colonialism to Globalization* (Vancouver: University of British Columbia Press, 2002), 41–84; Margaret Beattie Bogue, "To Save the Fish: Canada, the United States, the Great Lakes, and the Joint Commission of 1892," *JAH* 79 (March 1993): 1429–54; Stephen Handelman, "Dealing with Devils Lake," *Time,* August 22, 2005, 32.

4. David Massell, "'As Though There Was No Boundary': The Shipshaw Project and Continental Integration," *ARCS* 34 (Summer 2004): 187–222.

5. Upper North American trade themes are found in "Bush Administration Submits Annual Trade Report to Congress," Office of the United States Trade Representative, March 31, 2006, http://www.ustr.gov/document_library/press_releases/2006/march/bush_administration, 68–81; Paul Boothe and Douglas Purvis, "Macroeconomic Policy in Canada and the United States: Independence, Transmission and Effectiveness," in *Degrees of Freedom: Canada and the United States in a Changing World,* ed. Keith Banting, George Hoberg, and Richard Simeon (Montreal and Kingston: McGill–Queen's University Press, 1997), 189–230; and Robert Howse and Marsha Chandler, "Industrial Policy in Canada and the United States," in *Degrees of Freedom,* ed. Banting, Hoberg, and Simeon, 230–66.

Chapter 7: Markets and Consumers

1. Miro Cernetig, "Canada Isn't Working," *G&M,* April 27, 2001; James B. Twitchell, *Branded Nation: The Marketing of Megachurch, College Inc., and Museum World* (New York: Simon & Schuster, 2004), chap. 1.

2. See James E. Vance Jr., *The North American Railroad: Its Origin, Evolution, and Geography* (Baltimore: Johns Hopkins University Press, 1995); D. W. Meinig, *The Shaping of America: A Geographical Perspective on 500 Years of History, Vol. 2, Continental America 1800–1867* (New Haven, Conn.: Yale University Press, 1993), 331–99, 533–46; D. W. Meinig, *The Shaping of America: A Geographical Perspective on 500 Years of History, Vol. 3, Transcontinental America 1850–1915* (New Haven, Conn.: Yale University Press, 1985), 245–65, 327–47; John J. Burkowczyk, "Migration, Transportation, Capital and the State in the Great Lakes Basin, 1815–1890," in *Permeable Border: The Great Lakes Basin as a Transnational Region, 1650–1990,* ed. John J. Burkowczyk et al. (Calgary and Pittsburgh: University of Calgary Press and University of Pittsburgh Press, 2005), chap. 3.

3. Michael Bliss, "Canadianizing American Business: the Roots of the Branch Plant," in *Close the 49th Parallel, Etc.,* ed. Ian Lumsden (Toronto: University of Toronto Press, 1970), 27–42; Herbert Marshall et al., *Canadian-American Industry: A Study in International Investment* (New York: Russell & Russell, 1970; orig. pub. 1936), chap. 1.

4. Daniel J. Boorstin, *The Americans: The Democratic Experience* (New York: Random House, 1974), 89–164, 411–48; Dale Hrabi, "The Ads of Our Lives," *Saturday Post,* March 30, 2002, 1, 3.

5. David Monod, *Store Wars: Shopkeepers and the Culture of Mass Marketing, 1890–1939* (Toronto: University of Toronto Press, 1996), 340–50.

6. Mary Bellis, "Shopping Innovations," available at http://www.inventors.about.com. This chapter draws on David M. Potter, *People of Plenty: Economic Abundance and the American Character* (Chicago: University of Chicago Press, 1954); Richard S. Tedlow, *New and Improved: The Story of Mass Marketing in America* (New York: Basic Books, 1990); Joy L. Santink, *Timothy Eaton and the Rise of His Department Store* (Toronto: University of Toronto Press, 1990); and "Money," in *The Measured Century: An Illustrated Guide to Trends in America, 1900–2000,* ed. Theodore Caplow, Louis Hicks, and Ben J. Wattenberg (Washington, D.C.: AEI Press, 2001), 160–79.

7. John M. Dobson, *A History of American Enterprise* (Englewood Cliffs, N.J.: Prentice Hall, 1988), 167–70, 190–201, 225–38, 300–9, 311–17, 333–42, 356–60; Boorstin, *The Americans,* 307–60, 411–48; Peter Morton, "Sears Going Back to Simpler Times," *FP,* October 26, 2001, 16.

8. Donald F. Davis, "Dependent Motorization: Canada and the Automobile to the 1930s," *JCS* 21 (1991): 106–31; Marshall, *Canadian-American Industry,* 63, 65, 69, 164, 276; Boorstin, *The Americans,* 116, 422–30, 546–55; Robin Neill, "Remaking National Policy: Canada," http://www.upei.ca/~rneill/canechist/topic_21.html.

9. Adrian Wilshire, " 'Where Are the Roads?' Tourist and Promotion Films of Nova Scotia, 1945–1970," master's thesis, Dalhousie University, 2000.

10. John Herd Thompson and Stephen J. Randall, *Canada and the United States: Ambivalent Allies,* 3rd ed. (Montreal and Kingston: McGill–Queen's University Press, 2002), chaps. 4, 5.

11. Dimitry Anastakis, *Auto Pact: Creating a Borderless North American Auto Industry* (Toronto: University of Toronto Press, 2005), chaps. 1–2.

12. Andrew Axline et al., *Continental Community? Independence and Integration in North America* (Toronto: McClelland & Stewart, 1974), argues the theories about economic forces and social integration.

13. Greg Donaghy, *Tolerant Allies: Canada & the United States 1963–1968* (Montreal and Kingston: McGill–Queen's University Press, 2003), explores Gordon's frustrations.

14. Maureen Appel Molot, ed., *Driving Continentally: National Policies and the North American Auto Industry* (Ottawa: Carleton University Press, 1993); Daphne Bramham, "Car Sales Drive Export Figures Up," *VS,* June 22, 1999; Steve Erwin, "Post-Auto Pact Strategy Pondered for Canada," *CH,* February 19, 2001; Isabel Studer, *The North American Auto Industry,* Mapping the New North American Reality Series, IRPP Working Paper 2004-09o (Montreal: Institute for Research on Public Policy, 2004), http://www.irpp.org/wp/archive/NA_integ/wp2004-09o.pdf; Anastakis, *Auto Pact,* 172–83.

15. David H. Bradley, "Trucking's Advantage," *FP,* January 8, 2002; Mary Klinkenberg, "Big Wheels Hope for a Smarter Border," *FP,* March 1, 2002; Greg Keenan, "Consumer Fatigue Cited as Car Sales Plummet," *G&M,* February 4, 2004.

16. Steve Merti, "Historic Mail Flight Marked," *MS,* March 1, 1999; Marshall, *Canadian-American Industry,* 135–37, 173, 266, 282; "Fact Sheet: U.S.-Canada Civil Aviation Negotiations: Transborder Air Services," Backgrounder, U.S. Embassy, Ottawa, March 11, 1991; Terence Corcoran, "Open Skies and the Power of 'the Big Idea,'" *G&M,* February 24, 1995; Andrew Willis, "Open Season in the Air," *Maclean's,* March 6, 1995, 38.

17. Terence Corcoran, "We Don't Need National Airlines," *FP,* June 3, 1999; Alan Toulin, "Extend NAFTA to the Skies, Panel Says," *FP,* August 19, 2001; Alan Toulin, "U.S. Raises Prospect of Wider Sky Pact," *FP,* July 20, 2001.

18. Peter Fitzpatrick, "Air Canada Seeks Open Skies," *FP,* December 7, 2001; Don Carty, "Freedom in the Air," *FP,* July 4, 2002; Peter Shawn Taylor, "Taking a Step toward Open Skies," *NP,* November 4, 2004; "Remarks by the Honorable Norman Y. Mineta, Secretary of Transportation, at the Canadian Open skies Forum," Ottawa, February 24, 2005, available at http://www.usembassycanada.gov; Canadian Press, "Talks Slated on Liberalized Canada-U.S. Air Travel," *Business,* October 29, 2005, available at http://www.chroniclejournal.com.

19. Felicia R. Lee, "The Rise and Fall of Vacations," *NP,* August 17, 1999.

20. "Come Alive in Canada," *NYT,* Special Advertising Supplement, May 1997; David Thomas, "Canada's Travel Deficit Tumbles," *NP,* November 28, 1998; Christopher Michael, " 'They Love Our Dollar, Not Us,' " *NP,* July 23, 1999; Patricia Chisholm, "A Southern Longing," *Maclean's,* October 26, 1988, 44–45; International Travel Ac-

count, *The Daily,* May 28, 2001, Statistics Canada, http://www.statcan.ca/Daily/English; Jon Bricker, "U.S. Tourists Back to Pre-9/11 Numbers," *NP,* August 29, 2002.

21. Kenneth T. Jackson, "All the World's a Mall: Reflections on the Social and Economic Consequences of the American Shopping Center," *AHR* 101 (1996): 1111–21; Lizabeth Cohen, "From Town Center to Shopping Center: The Reconfiguration of Community Marketplaces in Postwar America," *AHR* 101 (1996): 1050–81.

22. "Evolution of the Shopping Center," *History of the Shopping Center and Mall,* http://www.history.samdiego.edu.gen/soci/shoppingcenter.html; Robert J. Samuelson, Paco Underhill, and Daniel Akst, "Shopping and the American Way of Life," *WQ* 28 (Winter 2004): 21–47."Retail Sales," Statistics Canada, series V 35-52, available at http://www.statscan.ca; "Shopping Centers in Canada by Type," Statistics Canada, series V 1, available at http://www.statscan.ca.

23. Gillian Livingston, "Big Retailers Face Turmoil, Challenges," *MS,* May 25, 1999; David Thomas, "'Affluenza' Gives U.S., Canada a Shot in the Arm," *NP,* January 30, 1999; Rod McQueen, "A Second Visit to Canadian Retailing," *FP,* April 21, 2000.

24. Kelly Shiers, "Border Shopping," *MS,* June 11, 1991; Gigi Suhanic and Sandra E. Martin, "Cross-Border Shopping Is Back," *FP,* November 6, 2004.

25. Melanie Collison, "Small Shops Must Stress Service," *CH,* June 17, 1994; David Estok, "Attention Shoppers," *Maclean's,* May 6, 1996, 34–36; Rod McQueen, "We're Grim, Grey and Cheap," *NP,* November 9, 1999; Marina Strauss, "Bay Adds More U.S. Brands," *G&M,* September 23, 2003; Peter Brieger, "Top Canadian Retailing Chains Slowly Dying Off," *FP,* October 29, 2005; John Greenwood, "A Legacy Lost," *FP,* January 27, 2006.

26. Ric Dolphin, "Been Shoppertained Lately?" *NP,* September 18, 1999; Zena Olijnyk, "U.S. Names to Form Core of Vaughan Mills Project," *FP,* September 8, 1999; Paul Brent, "Big-Box Stores Thump Retailers Downtown," *FP,* August 8, 2000; Gillian Livingston, "U.S. Retailers Move into Canada Seen as Part of Globalization," *CH,* August 16, 2001.

27. Andrew Poon and Dawn Walton, "Tables Turning on Fast Food," *G&M,* July 5, 1997; Eric Reguly, "Why Molson Needed to Merge," *Maclean's,* August 2, 2004, 25; Kim Hanson and Theresa Tedesco, "Seattle Coffee Co. Eyeing Second Cup," *FP,* December 23, 1999.

28. Wendy Evans et al., *Border Crossings: Doing Business in the U.S.* (Scarborough, Ont.: Prentice Hall, 1992), 302–32; Zena Olijnyk, "Plan to Quit U.S. Lists Future Shop Stock 24%," *FP,* March 10, 1999; Paul Brent, "It's Tough to Make It South of the Border," *FP,* March 10, 1999; Robert Steiner, "D.O.A. in the U.S.A," *National Post Business,* October 1999, 70–77.

29. Bernard Simon, "In Men's Clothing, More and More Say 'Made in Canada,'" *NYT,* March 23, 2002; Sheldon Gordon, "How to Succeed in the U.S. Market by Really Really Trying," *Financial Post 500,* June 1999, 76–84; Constance Droganes, "Canadian Roots—New York Branches," *Weekend Post Style,* April 17, 1999, 18; Zena Olijnyk, "Canadian Retailers Bite at the Big Apple: Courting the New York Crowd," *G&M,* June 3, 2000; Hollie Shaw, "Kelsey's Moves Montana's South of the Border," *G&M,* March 14, 2001; Hollie Shaw, "Roots Ponders Massive U.S. Expansion," *FP,* February 21, 2002.

30. Patrick Allosary, "M&A Fever Strikes Ad Industry," *FP,* May 28, 1999; Patrick Allosary, "Canadian Agencies Eye U.S. Ad Market," *FP,* August 6, 1999; Paul Brent,

"David Carson Targets Canada," *FP,* October 11, 1999; Sinclair Stewart, "Cossette Still Hunts for U.S. Beachhead," *FP,* March 1, 2001.

31. Peter Morton, "In U.S., a Dizzying Flood of New Entrants," *FP,* November 13, 1999; Zena Olijnyk, "Merchants Race to the Net, Like It or Not," *FP,* November 13, 1999; "Internet Erases Borders for IT firms," *NP,* December 20, 1999; Patrick Allossery, "AOL Canada Building Brand," *FP,* December 20, 1999; Matthew Fraser, "U.S. Pulls the Plug on Asper's Invasion Plan," *FP,* August 17, 1999; Sandra Rubin, "Foreign Firms Will Dominate Telco Market: Business Leaders," *FP,* August 16, 2001.

32. David Akin, "'The Next Internet Revolution,'" *FP,* January 11, 2000; David Crane, "AOL, Time Warner Mega-Merger May Bode Ill for Canada," *MS,* January 14, 2000; Livio Di Matteo, "The Internet Express," *MS,* April 1, 2000; Andrew Phillips, "Unsung Hero," *Maclean's,* October 2, 2000, 60–64; Chris Turner, "Silicon Circuits," *Time,* June 11, 2001, 58–61.

33. Zack Fuerstenberg and Jordan Worth, "Canadian E-Commerce Faces Death of a Thousand Clicks," *FP,* May 11, 1999; Marina Strauss, "U.S. Web Sites Click with Canadian Shoppers," *G&M,* June 22, 1999; "Business Cover," *Maclean's,* July 12, 1999, 32–34.

34. Susan Yellin, "Canadian Firms Eye U.S. Acquisitions, Shun EC," *MS,* April 17, 1999; Michael Lewis, "GSW Snaps Up U.S. Water Heater Company from Southcorp," *MS,* June 14, 2002; Canadian Press, "CP, Fairmont Linkup Forms Giant Hotel Operator," *MS,* October 13, 1999; Robert Giddens, "Great-West Life on Prowl in U.S.," *MS,* May 19, 2000; W. Evans and P. Barbiero, "Foreign Retailers in Canada," November 1999, http://www.csra.ryerson.ca/Publications/1999-11.html.

35. John Greenwood, "Making It Big in E-Town," *FP,* October 9, 1999; John Greenwood, "The Internet Tycoon from Moose Jaw," *FP,* October 9, 1999; John Greenwood, "Where Bragging Rights Are Measured by Size of Construction Sites," *FP,* October 9, 1999; Susan Heinrich, "E-Shoppers Rap Lack of Canadian Retail Web sites," *FP,* December 28, 1999; David Akin, "Passage to the North," *FP,* May 23, 2000; Jacqueline Thorpe, "E-Commerce North," *FP,* April 26, 2002.

36. Rod McQueen, "Fast Fade at the Bay," *NP,* March 13, 1999; Hollie Shaw, "Patriotic Pitch Waste of Money for Retailers," *NP,* July 12, 2001; Eric Reguly, "U.S. Giant Seeks to Buy the Bay," *G&M,* August 13, 2004; Steve Maich, "Flag-Waving Isn't Enough," *Maclean's,* August 30, 2004, 37.

37. Ross Laver, "Canada: Who Needs It?" *Maclean's,* January 11, 1999, 40–41; Terence Corcoran, "Maybe Canada Is for Sale," *FP,* March 11, 1999; John Barber, "Is Canada a Lost Cause?" *G&M,* June 26, 1999; James Stevenson, "Scotiabank's Godsoe Says It's Time for Ottawa to Take a Stand on U.S. Takeovers," *FP,* October 13, 1999; William Thorsell, "'Canada Has Very Little Time to Act,'" *G&M,* October 30, 1999; Jeffrey Simpson, "Hey, Canada, Wake Up," *G&M,* November 5, 1999.

38. Peter C. Newman, "The Year of Living Dangerously," *Maclean's,* December 20, 1999, 53–56; Silver Donald Cameron, "Told You So . . . ," *SH,* January 9, 2000; "They Leave, We Lose," *NP Business,* February 2000, 74; Sandra Rubin, "Bay Street Worries as Takeovers Accelerate," *FP,* May 22, 2002; A. E. Safarian's arguments—in "Some Myths about Foreign Business Investment in Canada," *JCS* 6 (August 1971): 3–21—still apply.

39. Paul Vieira, "Focus on U.S. Trade, Think Tank Tells Feds," *FP,* August 17, 2005.

40. Neville Nankivell, "They're Not 'Branch Plants' Any More," *FP,* 30 September 1999; William Watson, "Well, Maybe Don't Sell the Whole Country," *FP,* December 15,

1999; Thomas d'Aquino, "Make Canada Competitive, Don't Blame the U.S.," *FP,* December 17, 1999; George A. Carver Jr. et al., *The View From the South: A U.S. Perspective on Key Bilateral Issues Affecting U.S.-Canadian Relations* (Washington, D.C.: Georgetown University and Center for Strategic and International Studies, 1985); Christopher Sands, "One Economy, Two Systems," *Canada Focus* (Center for Strategic and International Studies) 1, no. 3 (November 2000), available at http://www.csis.org ,americas/canada/focus; Canadian-American Business Council, "U.S.-Canada Business Dialogue," March 31, 2004, on the post-9/11 era; Steven Chase, "Ottawa Moving to Slash Red Tape," *G&M,* March 21, 2005; Jacquie McNish, "Running Canada Inc. by Remote Control," *G&M,* September 14, 1998.

Chapter 8: Upper North American Commerce

1. John Greenwood, "U.S. Senator Plays Hardball over Softwood," *FP,* November 18, 2004; Michael Jamison, "Baucus Reaches Out to Canada over Water Quality Concerns," *Missoulian,* March 3, 2005, available at http://www.missoulian.com; Stephen Handelman, "Who Are Canada's American Enemies?" *Time,* March 21, 2005, 28–29.

2. The following two papers were prepared to hand out when lobbying the U.S. Congress (copies courtesy Canadian Embassy, Washington): "Canada–United States: The World's Largest Trading Relationship," Department of Foreign Affairs and International Trade, Ottawa, 2005; and "Canada-United States Trade and Security Partnership Map: A State-by-State Look," Department of Foreign Affairs and International Trade, Ottawa, 2005. Also see R. Neill, "The Canadian Quandary: Continentalization, Regionalization, 1950–1970," http://www.upei/~rneill/canechist/topic_24.html.

3. Office of U.S. Trade Representative, "National Trade Estimate Reports on Foreign Trade Barriers," March 31, 2006, http://www.ustrgov/Document_Library/Reports_Publications/2006, 68–81; Kathleen Miller et al., "The 1999 Pacific Salmon Agreement: A Sustainable Solution?" *CAPP* 47 (2001); Paul Veira, "Focus on U.S. Trade, Think Tank Tells Feds," *FP,* August 17, 2005; Danielle Goldfarb, *U.S. Bilateral Free Trade Accords: Why Canada Should Be Cautious about Going the Same Route,* Border Paper 214 (Toronto: C. D. Howe Institute, 2005); Barrie McKenna, "'Hardy Perennials' of Trade Wars Will Never Die," *G&M,* February 22, 2002.

4. Reginald C. Stuart, *United States Expansionism and British North America, 1775–1871* (Chapel Hill: University of North Carolina Press, 1988), chaps. 2–3; John Boileau, *Half-Hearted Enemies: Nova Scotia, New England and the War of 1812* (Halifax: Formac Publishing, 2005), chaps. 1, 3, 6; Chilton Williamson, "New York's Struggle for Champlain Valley Trade," *NYH* 22 (October 1941): 426–36; Joshua Smith, "Humbert's Paradox: The Global Context of Smuggling in the Bay of Fundy," in *New England and the Maritime Provinces: Connections and Comparisons,* ed. Stephen J. Hornsby and John G. Reid (Montreal and Kingston: McGill–Queen's University Press, 2005), 109–24.

5. Dorothy Kendall Cleaveland, "The Trade and Trade Routes of Northern New York from the Beginning of Settlement to the Coming of the Railroad," *Quarterly Journal* 4 (October 1923): 205–31; Michael Hart, *A Trading Nation: Canadian Trade Policy from Colonialism to Globalization* (Vancouver: University of British Columbia Press, 2002), 29–44.

6. Israel Andrews, *Report upon the Trade and Commerce of the British North American Colonies and upon the Trade of the Great Lakes and Rivers* (Washington,

D.C.: U.S. Government Printing Office, 1854); D. C. Masters, *The Reciprocity Treaty of 1854* (Toronto: McClelland & Stewart, 1963; orig. pub. 1937); Laurence Officer and Lawrence B. Smith, "The Canadian-American Reciprocity Treaty of 1854–1866," *JEH* 28 (1968): 598–623; John J. Burkowczyk, "Migration, Transportation, Capital and the State in the Great Lakes Basin," in *Permeable Border: The Great Lakes Basin as a Transnational Region, 1650–1990,* ed. J. T., Bukowcyzk et al. (Calgary and Pittsburgh: University of Calgary Press and University of Pittsburgh Press, 2005), 47–65; Louis Genticore, ed., *The Historical Atlas of Canada: The Land Transformed, 1800–1891* (Toronto: University of Toronto Press, 1993), plates 11, 38.

7. Paul F. Sharp, "When Our West Moved North," *AHR* 55 (1950): 286–300; Arthur H. DeRosier, "American Annexation Sentiment toward Canada, 1865–1871," M.A. thesis, Mississippi Southern College, 1955; John C. Everitt, "The Borderlands and the Early Canadian Grain Trade," in *Borderlands: Essays in Canadian-American Relations,* ed. Robert Lecker (Toronto: ECW Press, 1991), 147–72.

8. Burkowczyk, "Migration, Transportation," 29–77; Hart, *Trading Nation,* 29–68.

9. Israel T. Hatch, *Report upon the Commercial Relations of the United States with the Dominion of Canada* (Washington, D.C.: U.S. Government Printing Office, 1869); Gordon T. Stewart, *The American Response to Canada since 1776* (East Lansing: Michigan State University Press, 1992), chap. 3; Michael Bliss, "Canadianizing American Business," in *Close the 49th Parallel, Etc.,* ed. Ian Lumsden (Toronto: University of Toronto Press, 1970), 27–42; Walter LaFeber, *The New Empire: An Interpretation of American Expansion 1860–1898* (Ithaca, N.Y.: Cornell University Press,1963), 32–24, 41, 107, 114, 201.

10. Good studies are H. V. Nelles, *The Politics of Development: Forests, Mines and Hydro Electric Power in Ontario 1849–1941* (Toronto: Macmillan, 1965); and Gordon Hak, *Turning Trees into Dollars: The British Columbia Coastal Lumber Industry, 1858–1913* (Toronto: University of Toronto Press, 2000).

11. Hart, *Trading Nation,* 61–84.

12. Robert E. Hannigan, "Reciprocity 1911: Continentalism and American *Weltpolitik,*" *DH* 4 (Winter 1980): 1–18; Stewart, *American Response,* chap. 4.

13. L. E. Ellis, *Reciprocity 1911: A Study in Canadian-American Relations* (New Haven, Conn.: Yale University Press, 1939); W. M. Baker, "A Case Study of Anti-Americanism in English Canada: The Election Campaign of 1911," *CHR* 51 (1970): 432–35; John Bartlett Brebner, *North Atlantic Triangle: The Interplay of Canada, the United States, and Great Britain* (New Haven, Conn.: Yale University Press, 1945), 225–43, 308–26.

14. R. D. Cuff and J. L. Granatstein, *Ties That Bind: Canadian-American Relations in Wartime from the Great War to the Cold War,* 2nd ed. (Toronto: Samuel Stevens Hakkert, 1977), chaps. 1–3; Hart, *Trading Nation,* chap. 4.

15. Randall White, *Fur Trade to Free Trade: Putting the Canada-U.S. Trade Agreement in Historical Perspective* (Toronto: Dundurn Press, 1988), 100–14; Richard N. Kottman, "Herbert Hoover and the Smoot-Hawley Tariff: Canada, A Case Study," *JAH* 62 (1975): 609–35; Peter Kresl, "Before the Deluge: Canadians on Foreign Ownership, 1920–1955," *ARCS* 6 (1976): 93–96; Marc Boucher, "The Politics of Economic Depression: Canadian-American Relations in the Mid-1930s," *IJ* 41 (1985–86): 3–36.

16. J. L. Granatstein, *How Britain's Weakness Forced Canada into the Arms of the United States* (Toronto: University of Toronto Press, 1989); Hart, *Trading Nation,* 125–44; Brebner, *North Atlantic Triangle,* 308–26.

17. Bruce Muirhead, "Trials and Tribulations: The Decline of Anglo-American Trade, 1945–50," *JCS* 24 (1989): 50–65; J. L. Granatstein and R. D. Cuff, "Canada and the Marshall Plan, June–December 1947," *Historical Papers* (Canadian Historical Association), 1977, 196–213; J. L. Granatstein and R. D. Cuff, "The Rise and Fall of Canadian-American Free Trade, 1947–1948," *CHR* 57 (1977): 469–73; John Kirton, "The Consequences of Integration: The Case of the Defence Production Sharing Agreements," in *Continental Community? Independence and Integration in North America,* ed. Andrew Axline et al. (Toronto: McClelland & Stewart, 1974), 116–36; Robert O. Keohane and Joseph S. Nye, *Power and Interdependence,* 3rd ed. (New York: Longmans, 2001), chap. 7.

18. J. L. Granatstein, *Yankee Go Home? Canadians and Anti-Americanism* (Toronto: HarperCollins, 1996), chaps. 4–6; Lydia Miljan and Barry Cooper, *The Canadian "Garrison Mentality" and Anti-Americanism at the CBC,* Studies in Defence and Foreign Policy 4 (Calgary: Fraser Institute, 2005), 3–8.

19. See John Holmes, "From Three Industries to One: Towards an Integrated North American Automobile Industry," in *Driving Continentally: National Policies and the North American Auto Industry,* ed. Maureen Appel Molot (Ottawa: Carleton University Press, 1993), 1–22; and Paul Wonnacott, *U.S. and Canadian Auto Policies in a Changing World Environment* (Toronto: C. D. Howe Institute, 1987). The best work on the topic is Dimitry Anastakis, *Auto Pact: Creating a Borderless North American Auto Industry, 1960–1971* (Toronto: University of Toronto Press, 2005).

20. Joseph M. Dukert, "The Quiet Reality of North American Energy Interdependence," *PO* 25, no. 6 (June–July 2004): 40–44; Joseph M. Dukert, "The Evolution of the North American Energy Market: Implications of Continentalization for a Strategic Sector of the Canadian Economy," *ARCS* 30 (Autumn 2000): 349–59; Shawn McCarthy, "Oil Sands Helping to Quench U.S. Thirst for Energy, PM Says," *G&M,* April 7, 2001; Colin Nickerson, "U.S. Looks to Canada as Savior on Energy," *BG,* April 27, 2001; Claudia Cattaneo, "Alberta MLAs in U.S. Energy Talks," *FP,* February 2, 2001; Jill Mahoney, "Alberta Aims to Boost Trade Ties by Opening Washington Office," *G&M,* February 18, 2004; Brian Bergman, " Energized," *Maclean's,* June 11, 2001, 16–20; Ipsos Reid, "Continental Views on Energy, Summary Presentation," February 2004, available at http://www.ipsos.ca/reid; "Canadians and Americans Give Their Views on North American Energy Issues," Canada Institute at Woodrow Wilson International Center for Scholars, March 1, 2004.

21. David Massell, "'As Though There Was No Boundary': The Shipshaw Project and Continental Integration," *ARCS* 34 (Summer 2004): 187–222.

22. Alan Toulin, "U.S. Predicts Energy Pact with Canada," *NP,* February 23, 2001; Richard Gwyn, "How U.S. Energy Policy Becomes Canada's Energy Policy," *SH,* May 13, 2001; Paul Cellucci, "Bush's Energy Report Is Not Just about Supply," *NP,* June 26, 2001.

23. Brent Jang, "TransAlta Snares U.S. Power Plant," *G&M,* May 11, 1999; Joseph M. Dukert, *The Evolution of the North American Energy Market,* Policy Papers on the Americas, X Study 6 (Washington, D.C.: Center for Strategic and International Studies, 1999), 24–33; Barrie McKenna, "Canada Plugs in to U.S. Energy Bill," *G&M,* August 25, 2003; Barrie McKenna, "U.S. Opening the Taps on Energy Alternatives," *G&M,* October 20, 2003; Kate Jaymet, "Alberta Joins North American Agreement on Transmission Lines," April 16, 2004, http://www.canada.com; Judy Myrden, "Powerful Line Keeps Maine, Maritimes in Electrical Game," *CH,* August 20, 2004; Alan Freeman,

"What Weighs 800 Pounds and Sits Just North of Montana," *G&M,* October 18, 2005; Patrice Hill, "Looking North for Power," *WT,* November 27, 2005; Richard Pierce, Michael Trebilock, and Evan Thomas, *Beyond Gridlock: The Case for Greater Integration of Regional Electricity Markets,* Commentary: Border Paper 223 (Toronto: C. D. Howe Institute, 2006).

24. Andrew F. Cooper, *Canadian Foreign Policy: Old Habits and New Directions* (Scarborough, Ont.: Prentice Hall Allyn Bacon, 1997), 252–73; Richard G. Lipsey, "Canada and the United States: The Economic Dimension," in *Canada and the United States: Enduring Friendship, Persistent Stress,* ed. Charles F. Doran and John H. Sigler (Englewood Cliffs, N.J.: Prentice Hall, 1985), 69–108; J. L. Granatstein and Robert Bothwell, *Pirouette: Pierre Trudeau and Canadian Foreign Policy* (Toronto: University of Toronto Press, 1990), 158–77.

25. David Leyton-Brown, "Canadianizing Oil and Gas: The National Energy Program, 1980–1983," in *Canadian Foreign Policy: Selected Cases,* ed. Don Munton and John Kirton (Scarborough, Ont.: Prentice Hall, 1992), 199–210; Ron Graham, *One-Eyed Kings: Promise and Illusion in Canadian Politics* (Toronto: Collins, 1986), 371–86; William Diebold, "Change and Continuity in Canada-U.S. Economic Relations," *CAPP* 5 (1991); Stephen Clarkson, *Uncle Sam and US: Globalization, Neoconservatism, and the Canadian State* (Washington and Toronto: Woodrow Wilson Center Press and University of Toronto Press, 2002), 47–48, 262–66; Stephen Clarkson, *Canada and the Reagan Challenge: Crisis and Adjustment,* 2nd ed. (Toronto: Lorimer, 1985), 55–82.

26. For details of the negotiation, see Michael Hart with Bill Dymond and Colin Robertson, *Decision at Midnight: Inside the Canada-U.S. Free Trade Negotiations* (Vancouver: University of British Columbia Press, 1994); and Mordechai E. Kreinin, ed., *Building a Partnership: The Canada–United States Free Trade Agreement* (East Lansing and Calgary: Michigan State University Press and University of Calgary Press, 2000).

27. See Daniel Glenday, "Canada, the Left, and Free Trade," *QQ* 95 (1988): 251–84. Duncan Cameron, ed., *The Free Trade Papers* (Toronto: James Lorimer, 1986), contains a broad selection from Canadian printed statements and analysts about the topic. For details of the negotiations, see also Allan Gotlieb, *The Washington Diaries 1981–1989* (Toronto: McClelland & Stewart, 2006).

28. See Ann Walmsley, "Free Trade's Sour Taste," *Maclean's,* June 25, 1990, 62–64; Murray Smith, "The Future Evolution of the Canada-U.S. Free Trade Agreement: Opportunities and Risks," *ARCS* 21 (1991): 295–403; James Blanchard, *Behind the Embassy Door: Canada, Clinton and Quebec* (Toronto: McClelland & Stewart, 1998), chap 2; Stephen Blank, "The Emerging Architecture of North America," in *The North-South Agenda* (Coral Gables, Fla.: North-South Center, University of Miami, 1993); and Chris Morris, "NAFTA Blueprint for the Americas—Chrétien," *G&M,* December 10, 1994. Stephen Clarkson evaluated such proposals in "Fearful Asymmetries: The Challenge of Analyzing Continental Systems in a Globalizing World," *CAPP* 35 (1998); also see Darren Prokof, "NAFTA Freed Trade: Now Let's Free Transport," *NP,* June 18, 1999; Jacqueline Thorpe, "NAFTA Cuts U.S. Impact on Neighbours," *FP,* November 19, 2001; Rafael Gomez and Morley Gunderson, "The Integration of Labour Markets in North America," in *Capacity for Choice: Canada in a New North America,* ed. George Hoberg (Toronto: University of Toronto Press, 2002), 104–27; Tom McFeat, "Summit of the Americas: Canada's Trade with the Americas," CBC News Online, January 7, 2004, http://www.cbc.ca/printablestory.jsp.

29. John McCallum, *Two Cheers for the FTA: Tenth-Year Review of the Canada-U.S. Free Trade Agreement* (Toronto: Royal Bank of Canada Economics Department, 1999); *WEA* 3 (Autumn 1999): 19–52; Matthew Stevenson, "Bias and the NAFTA Dispute Panels: Controversies and Counter-Evidence," *ARCS* 30 (Spring 2000): 19–33; John Ibbitson, "Trading with the 'Schoolyard Bully,'" *G&M,* August 20, 2005.

30. See Stephen Blank and Jerry Haar, *Making NAFTA Work: U.S. Firms and the New North American Business Environment* (Coral Gables, Fla.: North-South Center Press, 1998); Statistics Canada data in *What Border? The Americanization of Canada,* CBC National Production, 1996, http://www.tv.cbc.ca/national/pgminfo/border/trade; and Thomas J. Courchene, "NAFTA, the Information Revolution, and Canada-U.S. Relations: An Ontario Perspective," *ARCS* 30 (2000): 159–80; "Canada–United States Trade and Security Partnership Map," and other embassy fact sheets.

31. John McCallum, "National Borders Matter: Canada-U.S. Regional Trade Patterns," *AER,* July 1995, 615–23; Charles Engel and John Rogers, "How Wide Is the Border? *AER,* December 1996, 1112–15; John Helliwell, *How Much Do National Borders Matter?* (Washington, D.C.: Brookings Institution Press, 1998); Richard Lipsey, "Free Trade: Real Results Versus Unreal Expectations," *WEA* 3 (April 1999): 29–32; Robin Neill, "Free Trade, Globalization, Continentalization, and Atlantica," updated January 14, 2005, http://www.upei.ca/~rneill/canecpro/pro/topic2.html.

32. Sidney Weintraub, "NAFTA Evaluation," *Issues in International Political Economy* 8 (August 2000), http://www.csis.org/americas/pubs; Terence Corcoran, "The Wal-Mart Gap," *FP,* October 16, 2001; Shawn McCarthy, "Canada Slips [to Eighth] in Competitiveness," *G&M,* October 13, 2004; World Economic Forum, *Global Competitiveness Report,* availalable at http://www.weforum.org/en/initiatives/gcp/Global%20 Competitiveness%20Report/index.htm.

33. Ian Jack, "U.S. Takes Aim at Drug, Fish Rules," *FP,* May 1, 1999; Peter Morton, "Barshevsky Issues Her Hit List Concerning Trade with Canada," *FP,* April 1, 2000.

34. John Geddes, "The Politics of Trade," *Maclean's,* March 22, 1999, 24–28; Ian Jack, "Trade War Looms in Peace Garden," *FP,* April 2, 1999; Jack Aubry, "U.S. Customs Confiscates 20 Tons of Farmer's Hemp Bird Feed," *NP,* October 5, 1999, A 10; Neville Nankivell, "To Help Shipbuilders Target Trade Barriers," *FP,* May 13, 2000; Peter Morton, "New Dairy War Looms with U.S. Industry," *FP,* February 4, 2000; Steve Erwin, "Canada Urged to Piggyback on U.S. Moves to Stop Dumping of Steel," *FP,* June 6, 2001; Drew Hasselback, "Growers Accuse U.S. Rivals of Dumping Tomatoes," *FP,* June 29, 2001; Drew Fagan, "When It Comes to Open Borders, Canada Often Just Talks the Talk," *G&M,* June 1, 2002; Jeffrey Simpson, "The American Way of Trading," *G&M,* January 22, 2003; Peter Morton, "U.S. Hammers Canadian Wheat with New Duty," *FP,* May 3, 2003.

35. Margaret Beattie Bogue, "To Save the Fish: Canada, the United States, the Great Lakes, and the Joint Commission of 1892," *JAH* 79 (March 1993): 1429–54; John Herd Thompson and Stephen J. Randall, *Canada and the United States: Ambivalent Allies,* 3rd ed., revised (Montreal and Kingston: McGill–Queen's University Press, 2002), 33, 73, 130–34, 212–13, 231–32; John Geddes, "Water Wars," *Maclean's,* March 6, 2000, 20–24; Mathew Ingram, "Flag-Waving Hindering a Serious Debate on Water Exports," *Maclean's,* June 1, 2001, 12; Jim Olson and Ralph Pentland, "Decision Time: Water Diversion Policy in the Great Lakes Basin," One Issue, Two Voices Series, Canada Institute at Woodrow Wilson International Center for Scholars, Washington, 2004, http://www.wilsoncenter.org/topics/pubs/ACF1D93.pdf; Dennis Bueckert, "Pressure to Ex-

port Water to U.S. Likely to Grow," Canadian Press, January 1, 2006, available at http://www.canada.com.

36. Barry Cooper, "The Mythic Cowboy West Is Alive and Well," *NP,* October 27, 2004.

37. Dawn Walton, "Two Countries, One Market for Cattle Trade," *G&M,* January 2, 2004; Marc Kaufman and Cindy Skrycki, "USDA Rescinds Policy Allowing Sale of Canadian Beef," *WP,* May 6, 2004; Beth Gorham, "Cattle to Cross Border March 7," *CH,* February 10, 2005; Beth Gorham, "Ruling: Judge Wrong to Bar Canadian Cattle," *CH,* July 2, 2005.

38. DeNeen L. Brown, "Canada Bristles at U.S. Tariffs on Lumber," *WP,* February 28, 2001; Barrie McKenna, "Lawyers, Lobbyists Gear Up for Battle in Lumber War," *G&M,* March 7, 2001; Barrie McKenna, "Lumber Dispute Heads for Full-Scale Trade War," *G&M,* March 8, 2001; Andrew Phillips, "Duelling Chainsaws," *Maclean's,* March 26, 2001, 32–33; Hilary MacKenzie, "Millworkers Heap Blame on 'Socialist' Canadians," *VTC,* April 1, 2001; Russ Gorte and Jeanne Grimmett, "Lumber Imports from Canada: Issues and Events," Congressional Research Service, Library of Congress, May 21, 2001, courtesy of staff member; Stephen Thorne, "U.S. Groups Line Up against Their Own Government in Canada-U.S. Lumber Dispute," *CH,* July 19, 2001; Carl Ek, "Canada-U.S. Relations," in *Report for Congress* (Washington, D.C.: Congressional Research Service, Library of Congress, 2003), 49–51. See also Thomas R. Waggener, "Forests, Timber, and Trade: Emerging Canadian and U.S. Relations under the Free Trade Agreement," *CAPP* 4 (1990); and Benjamin Cashore, "Flights of the Phoenix: Explaining the Durability of the Canada-U.S. Softwood Lumber Dispute," *CAPP* 32 (1997).

39. W. J. "Rusty" Wood, "Let the Markets Set the Price," *FP,* March 10, 2000; Peter Morton, "U.S. Lobby Group a Front for Lumber Producers," *FP,* June 6, 2000; Allan Swift, "Ottawa to Spend $20M to Lobby U.S. on Lumber," *CH,* May 28, 2002.

40. Steve Merti, "Forest Industry in Civil War over Softwood," *CH,* October 12, 1999; Gordon Hamilton, "Put All Trade Issues on the Table: B.C. Industry," *VS,* April 3, 2001; Shawn McCarthy and Steven Chase, "Trade War Explodes in Storm of Insults," *G&M,* March 23, 2002; Madelaine Drohan, "United We Stand, Divided We Fall," *G&M,* February 28, 2001; Ian Jack, "Eastern Firms Vow Court Battle over Lumber Deal," *G&M,* March 6, 2002; "Text: USTR on Lumber Dispute with Canada," February 13, 2002, available at http://www.usembassycanada.gov; Christin Schmitz, "Softwood Legal Battle Costs Ottawa $10.9M," *NP,* May 21, 2002.

41. Jason Kirby et al., "Softwood Deal Reached," *NP,* April 28, 2006; Barrie McKenna and Stephen Chase, "Softwood Deal Was Brewing for Year or More," *G&M,* April 29, 2006.

42. Paul Vieria, "Negotiated Softwood Deal Sought: [Jim] Peterson," *FP,* August 12, 2005; Ibbitson, "Trading with the 'Schoolyard Bully'"; Editorial, *Wall Street Journal,* August 17, 2005, quoted in *NP,* August 19, 2005; Stephen Chase and Peter Kennedy, "Fuming Canada Won't Talk Softwood," *G&M,* August 17, 2005; Gordon Ritchie, "Pick One: Bad or Worse," *G&M,* January 6, 2004; Barrie McKenna, "Looming U.S. Vote Poses Trade Dilemma for Canada," *G&M,* May 10, 2004; Peter Morton, "U.S. Threat Aimed at NAFTA," *NP,* January 26, 2000.

43. "UPS Suing Ottawa for $230 M," *FP,* April 22, 2000; Peter Morton, "$1B Methanol Battle Fires Up This Week," *FP,* May 9, 2000; "NAFTA's Silent Suit," *WT,* March 13, 2002; Ezra Levant, "NAFTA Ruling Sends a Message to Canada Post," *NP,* August 8, 2003; Anthony DePalma, "NAFTA's Powerful Little Secret," *NYT,* March 11,

2001; Heather Scoffield, "Trade Officials Put NAFTA Secrecy Issues on Agenda," *G&M,* September 26, 1998; Pierre Pettigrew, "We Need to Clarify NAFTA to Fix Tribunal 'Errors,' *FP,* March 23, 2001; Jan Cienski, "NAFTA Chapter 11 Facing Closer Public Scrutiny," *FP,* August 1, 2001.

44. Zussman quoted in Alan Toulin, "Union with U.S. on Table: PM's Advisor," *NP,* June 29, 2001; Robert Fife and Alan Toulin, "U.S. Hopes to Erase Borders," *NP,* June 30, 2001; John M. Weekes, "Why Canada Needs the WTO," *Time,* November 29, 1999, 32–33; Kathryn Leger, "Mapping Future Trade Deals," *NP,* April 12, 2001; Office of U.S. Trade Representative, "National Trade Estimate Reports on Foreign Trade Barriers."

45. Weekes, "Why Canada Needs the WTO"; Greg Corne, "Battle over Free Trade One of Ideology, D'Aquino Says," *Time,* November 2, 1999, 6; Leger, "Mapping Future Trade Deals"; Sean Silcoff, "Benefits of NAFTA Far Outweigh the Drawbacks, Study Concludes," *NP,* June 5, 2001; David Zussman, "What's after NAFTA?" *NP,* June 29, 2001; Barrie McKenna, "U.S. Turns Deaf Ear to Canadian Talk of Trade Reform," *G&M,* November 2, 2002; Ipsos Reid, "On the 10th Anniversary of NAFTA," December 8, 2002, available at http://www.ipsos.ca/reid/; "Rethinking North American Integration: Marketplace May Not Equal Community: Not "Here" Yet?" EKOS, Ottawa, 2002; Danielle Goldfarb and William B. P. Robson, *Risky Business: U.S. Border Security and the Threat to Canadian Exports,* Border Paper 177 (Toronto: C. D. Howe Institute, 2003); Perrin Beatty, "Overcoming Potholes and Roadblocks and the Border," in paper prepared for a "A Dynamic Partnership for Changing Times: Canada-U.S. Trade Relations Summit," conference sponsored by Canadian Manufacturers and Exporters, Winnipeg, 2004 (author's personal copy); Stephen J. Weber, "In Mexico, US and Canada, Public Support for NAFTA Surprisingly Strong, Given Each Country Sees Grass Greener on the Other Side," March 29, 2006, available at http://www.worldpublicopinion.org; Greg Anderson, "Protection(ism)," *North American Integration Monitor* (Center for Strategic and International Studies) 2, issue 1 (March 2004); Paul Boothe and Douglas Purvis, "Macroeconomic Policy in Canada and the Untied States: Independence, Transmission and Effectiveness," in *Degrees of Freedom: Canada and the United States in a Changing World,* ed. Keith Banting, George Hoberg, and Richard Simeon (Montreal and Kingston: McGill–Queen's University Press, 1997), 189–230; Robert Howse and Marsha Chandler, "Industrial Policy in Canada and the United States," in *Degrees of Freedom,* ed. Banting, Hoberg, and Simeon, 230–66.

46. Stephanie R. Golob, "North America Beyond NAFTA? Sovereignty, Identity, and Security in Canada-U.S. Relations," *CAPP* 52 (2002); Gary C. Hufbauer and Jeffrey J. Schott, *The Prospects for Deeper North American Economic Integration: A U.S. Perspective,* Commentary: Border Paper 195 (Toronto: C. D. Howe Institute, 2004); Council on Foreign Relations, Press Release, "Council Joins Leading Canadians and Mexicans to Launch Independent Task Force on the Future of North America," available at http://www.cfa.com; Robert Fife, " 'NAFTA-Plus' Talks Aim for Security Pact," *NP,* October 16, 2004, A 1, 6; Greg Anderson, "NAFTA at 10: Still Weathering the Storm," *North American Integration Monitor* 2, issue 2 (November 2004).

47. "NAFTA Partners Continue to Liberalize Rules of Origin," News Release, January 11, 2005, International Trade Canada, http://www.international.gc.ca/nafta-alena/ann-401; Thomas D'Aquino, "Beyond Missiles," *FP,* March 4, 2005; Steven Chase, "MPs Told U.S. Aims to Erode NAFTA Power," *G&M,* March 9, 2005; Peter Morton, "Common Duty Urged for NAFTA," *FP,* March 15, 2005; Bill Dymond and Michael

Hart, *Policy Implications of a Canada-US Customs Union,* Discussion Paper, PRI Project North American Linkages (Ottawa: Centre for Trade Policy and Law, 2005).

Chapter 9: Fiscal Integration

1. The nickname "loonie" began to be used for the Canadian dollar in 1987, the year the dollar coin was issued, because this coin has an image of a common loon on one side. See Heather Scoffield and Bertrand Marotte, "Time Is Right for a Stronger Dollar: Dodge," *G&M,* February 12, 2004; Irene Marushko, "Dodge Won't Rule Our Common Currency," *G&M,* January 31, 2002; Jacqueline Thorpe, "Common Currency Good for Canada, Economists Argue," *FP,* November 10, 2004.

2. Yvan Guillamette, David Laidlaw, and William Robson, "The Real Reasons for the Dollar's Power Trip—and What Not to Do about It," e-brief, C. D. Howe Institute, December 7, 2004, available at http://www.cdhowe.org; Martin Coiteaux, *Monetary Convergence between Canada and the United States: A Critique of the Official View,* Mapping the New North American Reality Series, IRPP Working Paper 2004-09m (Montreal: Institute for Research on Public Policy, 2004), http://www.irpp.org/wp/archive/NA_integ/wp2004-09m.pdf.

3. See Bray Hammond, *Banks and Politics in America, from the Revolution to the Civil War* (Princeton, N.J.: Princeton University Press, 1957); Peter Baskerville, "Banking in Pre-Confederation Canada," *Horizon Canada* (Centre for the Study of Teaching Canada) 10 (1987): 2672–77; Eric Helleiner, "North American Monetary Union? A Mid-Nineteenth-Century Prelude," *Common-Place* 6, no. 3 (April 2006), http://www.common-place.org/vol6/no-03/helleiner.

4. Ken Polsson, "Chronology of Canadian Coins, 1842–1911," available at http://www.islandnet.com; Bank of Canada, *A History of the Canadian Dollar* (Ottawa: Bank of Canada, 2001); Bureau of Engraving and Printing, U.S. Treasury Department, "U.S. Money History," available at http://www.bep.treas.gov.

5. John Bartlett Brebner, *North Atlantic Triangle: The Interplay of Canada, the United States, and Great Britain* (New Haven, Conn.: Yale University Press, 1945), 238; Christopher J. Mailander, *Reshaping North American Banking: The Transforming Effects of Regional Markets and Policy Shifts,* Policy Papers on the Americas, vol. 1, study 5 (Washington, D.C.: Center for Strategic and International Studies, 1999).

6. "Understanding How Glass-Steagall Act Impacts Investment Banking and the Role of Commercial Banks," http://www.cftech.com/BrainBank/specialreports/GlassSteagal; Carlos D. Ramirez, "The Decline and Fall of the Glass-Steagall Act: The Role of PAC Contributions," http://www.pubchoice.org/papers/remirez.

7. Herbert Marshall et al, *Canadian-American Industry: A Study in International Investment* (New York: Russell & Russell, 1970; orig. pub. 1936), 165–66, 175, 266; J. L. Granatstein and R. D. Cuff, "Canada and the Marshall Plan, June–December 1947," *Historical Papers* (Canadian Historical Association), 1977, 196–213; CBC, "What Border? The Americanization of Canada," http://www.cbc.ca/national/pgminfo/border/.

8. Edelgard Mahant and Graeme S. Mount, *Invisible and Inaudible in Washington: American Policies toward Canada* (Vancouver: University of British Columbia Press, 1990), 136–61; Dimitry Anastakis, *Auto Pact: Creating a Borderless North American Auto Industry, 1960–1971* (Toronto: University of Toronto Press, 2005), chap. 3; George

Haynal, "Interdependence, Globalization and North American Borders," *PO,* September 2002, 20–26.

9. Robert Bothwell, " 'Small Problems': Trudeau and the Americans," in *Trudeau's Shadow: The Life and Legacy of Pierre Elliott Trudeau,* ed. Andrew Cohen and J. L. Granatstein (Toronto: Random House of Canada, 1998), 207–22.

10. Gordon Thiessen, "Remarks," December 4, 2000, available at http://www.bankofcanada.org: Jane Little, "Mapping the Economy," *Regional Review* (Federal Reserve Bank of Boston) 10, no. 1 (Quarter 1, 2000); Robert Mundell, "Currency Areas, Exchange Rate Systems and International Monetary Reform," paper delivered at Universidad del CEMA, Buenos Aires, April 17, 2000, http://www.3/jjcong/jjwc0925.htm.

11. Richard Simeon, George Hoberg, and Keith Banting, "Globalization, Fragmentation, and the Social Contract," in *Degrees of Freedom: Canada and the United States in a Changing World,* ed. Keith Banting, George Hoberg, and Richard Simeon (Montreal and Kingston: McGill–Queen's University Press, 1997), 398–416.

12. Michael Hart, with Bill Dymond and Colin Robertson, *Decision at Midnight: Inside the Canada-U.S. Free Trade Negotiations* (Vancouver: University of British Columbia Press, 1994), 213–25, 335–46; A. E. Safarian, "Harmonizing Investment Policies in Canada, the United States, and Mexico: Is Liberalization Possible?" Centre for International Studies, University of Toronto and Fraser Institute, 1991, available at http://www.fraserinstitute.org; John Chant, "Free Trade in the Financial Sector: Expectations and Experience," Centre for International Studies, University of Toronto and Fraser Institute, 1991, available at http://www.fraserinstitute.org; Alan Rugman and Michael Gestrin, "The Investment Provisions of NAFTA," in *Assessing NAFTA: A Trinational Analysis,* ed. Steven Globerman and Michael Walker (Vancouver: Fraser Institute, 1992), 271–92; information from North American Securities Administrators Association, Washington, http://www.nasaa.org.

13. John McCallum, "Will Canada Matter in 2020?" *NP,* February 19, 2000; Alan Toulin, "Canada's Sliding to Ruin: Royal Bank," *NP,* February 18, 2000; Daniel Schwanen, "Catching Up Is Hard to Do: Thinking about the Canada-U.S. Productivity Gap," in *Vanishing Borders: Canada among Nations,* ed. Maureen Appel Molot and Fen Osler Hampson (Toronto: Oxford University Press, 2000), 117–44.

14. Robert Evans, "Two Systems in Restraint: Contrasting Experience with Cost Control in the 1990s," in *Canada and the United States: Differences That Count,* 2nd edition, ed. David M. Thomas (Toronto: Broadview Press, 2000), 21–51; Jack Carr, "The Lessons of the '90s," *FP,* February 8, 2000.

15. Industry Canada, *Challenges of Rapid Technological Change: Catching Up with the Jetsons* (Toronto: Industry Canada, 2000); Alan Toulin, "Canadian Industry Faces 'Extinction,' " *NP,* August 16, 2001.

16. Douglas Goold and Ellen Roseman, "Dollar Daze," *G&M,* January 14, 1995; Reuven Brenner, "The Case for a World Dollar," *FP,* March 15, 1999; Ralph Sultan, "The Case for Dollarization," *FP,* May 17, 1999; Thomas Courchene, "Towards a North American Common Currency: An Optimal Currency Analysis," in *Room to Manoeuver,* ed. Thomas Courchene (Kingston: John Deutch Institute, Queen's University, 1999); Terence Corcoran, "From Solid Gold to 63 cents," *FP,* January 1, 2000; Luiza Chwialkowska, "Dollar's Disappointing and Perplexing Decline," *NP,* November 3, 2000.

17. Alan Freeman, "Nobel Economist Tying Loonie to U.S. Greenback," *G&M,* October 14, 1999; Richard G. Harris, "The Case for North American Monetary Union," *Isuma* 1 (Spring 2000): 93–96; Rod McQueen, "A New Dollar Proposal, Interview with

Robert Mundell," *FP,* September 29, 2000; "Friedman v. Mundell," *FP,* December 11, 2000; Sherry Cooper, "The Inevitable Demise of the Loonie," *FP,* December 7, 2001; Herbert Grubel, "It's Time to Create the 'Amero,'" *FP,* August 9, 2002; Robert Gibbins, "CN's Tellier Says Monetary Union Is Inevitable," *CH,* January 25, 2002; DeNeen L. Brown, "Canada's 'Loonie' Heading South," *WP,* February 1, 2002.

18. Jacqueline Thorpe and Alan Toulin, "Does the Dollar Matter?" *NP,* January 28, 2002; Eric Beauchesne, "Canadians Worried about the Loonie: Poll," *NP,* February 2, 2002.

19. George Bragues, "We Need an 'Open Sky' Policy for Canadian Investors," *FP,* June 1, 1999; Joel Fried and Ron Wirick, "RRSP Foreign Property Rule Benefits Neither Governments nor Investors," *FP,* February 7, 2002; Paul Brent, "Foreign Flight," *FP,* April 7, 2005; David Berman, "Absence of RRSP Cap to Spur Shake-Out," *FP,* April 10, 2005. Ottawa removed all limits on RRSP foreign investment in the 2005 budget.

20. Robert Gibbens, "Single Exchange Forecast for North America, *FP,* June 5, 1999; Eric Reguly, "Overstocked with Watchdogs," *Time,* January 21, 2002, 40; Kathryn Leger, "Quebec Strikes nasdaq Deal," *FP,* April 27, 2000; Katherine Macklem, "Nightmare on Bay Street," *NP Business Magazine,* May 2000, 52–63; A. Douglas Harris, "Exchange Murder a Mistake," *FP,* March 27, 2001.

21. Patrick Allossery, "We Hold Our Own in Merger Market," *FP,* March 26, 1999; Peter Kuitenbrouwer, "U.S. Takeover of Economy Fails to Occur," *FP,* June 1, 2000; Barbara Stymiest, "Corporate Myths," *FP,* May 10, 2002.

22. Joel-Denis Bellivance, "Canada, U.S. Need Common Currency: PQ," *NP,* June 8, 1999; Thomas J. Courchene and Richard Harris, "Down the Slippery Slope of Market Dollarization," *NP,* June 23, 1999; William Watson, "Keep Studying the Currency Union," *NP,* June 30, 1999; Murray Campbell, "Canadians Expect Loonie to Disappear," *G&M,* August 3, 1999; Joel-Denis Bellevance, "U.S. Senate Report Touts Single Currency," *NP,* August 27, 1999; Robert Fife, "U.S. Senator Pushing for Monetary Union," *NP,* November 17, 1999.

23. Jacqueline Thorpe, "Bank of Canada Backs Flexible Loonie," *NP,* May 11, 2001; TD Economics, "Ten Common Misconceptions about the Canadian Dollar," http://www.td.com/economics/special/in1013002.html.

24. John Murray, "Why Canada Needs a Flexible Exchange Rate," Bank of Canada working paper for Western Washington University Conference, April 30, 2000; Mary Janigan, "Plight of the Loonie," *Maclean's,* August 13, 2001, 32.

25. Sherry Cooper, "The Canadian Dollar's Still Going Down . . . ," *FP,* July 23, 1999; Marian Stinson, "Global Gloom Hammers Dollar," *G&M,* March 17, 2001.

26. Jacqueline Thorpe, "Raging Greenback Tramples Loonie, Euro, and Yen," *G&M,* November 17, 2000; Jacqueline Thorpe, "Canadians Bulk Up on Foreign Securities," *NP,* November 24, 2000; Pierre Lemieux, "Dollarization by Default," *FP,* July 17, 2001; Jacqueline Thorpe, "Tired Loonie Headed Lower, Analysts Say"; Terence Corcoran, "Why Is Canada an Unsafe Haven?" *FP,* November 1, 2001; Richard Harris, "Symbol of Weakness," *FP,* November 1, 2001; Eric Beauchesne and Reuven Brenner, "Does the Dollar Matter?" *FP,* January 28, 2002; Paul Vieira, "U.S. Influence Beginning to Wane, Annual Report Says," *FP,* June 21, 2005.

27. Chris Wattie, "Bank of Montreal Buys Up 54 Branches in the United States," *CH/MS,* May 15, 1994; Sandra Cordon, "Royal Bank Buys into U.S. Market," *CH/MS,* March 10, 1998; Derek DeCloet, "Banks Well Sheltered from Free-Trade Storm," *NP,* April 20, 2001; Stephen Clarkson, *Uncle Sam and US: Globalization, Neoconservatism,*

and the Canadian State (Washington and Toronto: Woodrow Wilson Center Press and University of Toronto Press, 2002), 138–61; Mailander, *Reshaping North American Banking,* 1–10. Also see Norman Hillmer et al., "Canadians Abroad," in *The Historical Atlas of Canada: Addressing the Twentieth Century,* ed. Donald Kerr and Deryck Holdsworth (Toronto: University of Toronto Press, 1990), vol. 3, plate 57.

28. Rod McQueen, "Unfinished Business," *FP,* January 23, 1999; Caroline Van Hasselt, "Amex Bank to Compete for Canadians' Deposits," *FP,* June 3, 1999; Alan Toulin, "Reform Plan 'Will Force Banks to Look South for Growth,'" *FP,* June 26, 1999; Derek DeCloet, "Wall Street, Meet Bay Street," *FP,* February 28, 2000.

29. "Bank of Montreal Buys U.S. Discount Brokerage," *FP,* September 23, 1999; Katherine Macklem, "Bank of Montreal Looks South for Growth," *FP,* February 26, 1999; "Harris Bank Looking to Grow in the Sun Belt," *FP,* January 20, 2000; Paul Bagnell, "BMO Looking to Make Chicago Its Kind of Town," *FP,* March 3, 2001; John Partridge, "BMO Adds to U.S. Expansion," *G&M,* September 28, 2002.

30. Katherine Macklem, "Royal Shopping for U.S. Retail Bank," *FP,* October 5, 1999; Shannon Kari, "Incoming Royal Bank CEO Pushes for Growth in the U.S.," *FP,* April 11, 2001; "Southern Exposure," *R.O.B. Magazine,* March 2002, 45–46, 48, 88–89; RBC Financial Group, *First Principles: 2004 Corporate Responsibility Report and Public Accountability Statement* (Toronto: RBC Financial Group, 2004), 22.

31. Katherine Macklem, "TD Bank Aims at U.S. Market," *FP,* November 18, 1999; Derek deCloet, "TD Secures Beachhead in U.S. Wal-Marts," *FP,* September 11, 2001; Keith Kalawsky, "TD Has List of U.S. Targets for Acquisition," *FP,* April 12, 2002.

32. Theresa Tedesco, "CIBC in Talks to Offer Banking in U.S. Groceries," *FP,* June 3, 1999; Katherine Macklem, "CIBC, Safeway Sign Banking Kiosk Deal," *FP,* June 27, 2000; David Steinhart, "CIBC Gets a New York Home," *G&M,* March 13, 2001; Gillian Livingston, "CIBC to Shut Its U.S. Electronic Operations," *FP,* November 15, 2002; Barbara Schecter, "Stick to Your Knitting, Canadian Banks Told," *FP,* February 15, 2005.

33. Eric Reguly, "Banks May Have No Choice but to Go Due South," *G&M,* July 15, 2003; Clarkson, *Uncle Sam and US,* 152–67; Duncan Mavin, "Ohio Bank Sees Commercial Branch Niche in Canada," *FP,* March 1, 2006; Jon Harding, "BMO to Double Branch Count in U.S. Midwest," *FP,* March 3, 2006; Duncan Mavin, "McKenna Joins TD Bank as Deputy Chairman," *NP,* April 7, 2006; Keith McArthur and Sinclair Stewart, "The Unknown Canadian: TD Spends Big on U.S. Marketing Push," *G&M,* April 18, 2006.

34. Terence Corcoran, "U.S. Banks Get Bigger, Canada's Get Smaller," *FP,* October 26, 1999; Katherine Macklem, "Can Bay Street Survive?" *Maclean's,* May 14, 2001, 46–48; John Cleghorn, "Canadian Banks Bound for the Minors," *FP,* May 25, 2000; Eric Reguly, "Feds Beware: Nortelization of the Banks Has Begun," *G&M,* June 22, 2000.

35. John Southerst, "U.S. Franchise Lenders Look to Crack Canadian Market," *G&M,* October 23, 1999; Katherine Macklem, "ING Direct Moves South of the Border," *FP,* December 1, 1999; Paul Bagnell, "Banks Reaping Rewards of Moves to U.S.," *FP,* September 10, 2000; Stephen Handelman, "Vaulting to the South," *Time,* March 26, 2001, 37; Sandra Rubin, "The Vaporizing Border," *FP,* February 27, 2002; Paul Brent, "Foreign Flight," *FP,* April 7, 2005; David Berman, "Absence of RRSP Cap to Spur Shakeout," *FP,* April 8, 2005.

36. John Chant, "A Third Way for Banking," *FP,* May 30, 2001; Keith Kalawsky, "Royal Posts Record Earnings," *FP,* February 23, 2002; Barrie McKenna, "Unlike Canada, U.S. Likes Bank Mergers," Canadian Press; Derek DeCloet, "Bank Scouting

Parties in U.S. Should Come Home," *G&M,* October 28, 2003; Sinclair Stewart, "Fleet Boston Deal Could Stall Canadian Banks' U.S. Plans, " *G&M,* October 28, 2003; Eric Reguly, "U.S. Deal Puts Heat on Martin," *G&M,* October 28, 2003; "Bank of Montreal Buys Chicago-Based New Lennox State Bank for $306M Cdn," February 4, 2004, available at http://www.canada.com.

37. Theresa Tedesco and Keith Kalawsky, "Banks Review Expansion Plans in U.S.," *FP,* September 28, 2001; Keith Kalawsky and Derek DeCloet, "U.S. Federal Reserve Sets Aside Money for Canadian Banks," *CH,* September 15, 2001; Derek DeCloet, "U.S. Fund Giant to Come North," *FP,* November 2, 2001; Keith Kalawsky, "CIBC to Issue New Amex Cards," *FP,* January 10, 2002.

38. Brian Milner, "U.S. Growth Pressures Canada," *G&M,* January 28, 1995; Canadian Press, "Canada Hostage to U.S. Rates: OECD," *CH/MS,* May 19, 1999; "Thiessen Raises Interest Rates to 'Avoid Accident,'" *FP,* November 18, 1999; Bank of Canada, "A New System of Fixed Dates for Announcing Changes to the Bank Rate: Summary of Consultation Results," February 8, 2002, available at http://www.bankofcanada.ca; Bank of Canada, "Bank of Canada releases 2002 schedule of dates for policy interest announcement," October 1, 2002, available at http://www.bankofcanada.ca.

39. Robyn Meredith, "Dollar Makes Canada Land of the Spree," *NYT,* August 1, 1999; Eric Beauchesne, "Canadian Companies Rapidly Increase Use of the Greenback," *NP,* June 29, 1999; Janet McFarland, "Reporting Results the American Way a Growing Trend," *G&M,* July 22, 1999.

40. Rob Ferguson, "Low Canadian Dollar Fuels Foreign Takeovers," *CH/MS,* March 3, 1999; Terence Corcoran, "Spending Our Way to a Low Dollar," *FP,* May 10, 2000, and related articles, *FP,* March 21 and 22, 2001; David Frum, "The Jig Is Up for Our Cheap Dollar," *NP,* December 23, 2000; Michael Walker, "Lost Standard of Value," *NP,* April 4, 2001; Michael LeGault, "The High Costs of a Low Dollar," *FP,* April 10, 2001.

41. Eric Beauchesne, "U.S. Dollar Will Be Ours by 2030: Economist [Thomas Courchene]," *NP,* July 10, 2000; Heather Scoffield, "Finance Ministers Duck Common Currency Topic," *G&M,* April 9, 2001; Don Drummond, Marc Levesque, and Craig Alexander, *The Penny Drops* (Toronto: TD Economics, 2001), available at http://www.td.com/economics.

42. Ross Laver, "Lament for the Loonie," *Maclean's,* July 5, 1999, 14–18; Jacqueline Thorpe, "Creeping Dollarization a Myth, Study Says," *FP,* May 17, 2001; Canwest News Service, "Common Currency Only after Common Markets: Bank of Canada Says Link with U.S. Means Much More Than Cash," *VTC,* August 8, 2003.

43. Paul Vieira, "Majority of Americans Don't Want to Share Dollar," *FP,* June 4, 2002; Jacqueline Thorpe, "Low Dollar Has to Stay: Think Tank," *NP,* October 9, 2002; Sidney Weintraub and Christopher Sands, "Why Dollarization Is a Canadian Affair," Americas Program Canada Project, March 2002, http://www.csis.org/americas/canada; Richard Harris, "A United Dollar," *FP,* May 17, 2003.

44. Terry Weber, "Rising Loonie, U.S. Growth," *G&M,* December 21, 2003; David Frum, "The Perils of a Rising Loonie," *NP,* November 9, 2004.

45. Industry Canada, *Challenges of Rapid Technological Change;* Ian Jack, "Ottawa to Focus Attention on Productivity Gap," *NP,* May 15, 2000; Terence Corcoran, "Flotsam and Jetsons," *NP,* July 25, 2000; Terence Corcoran, "Bigger Gap Needs Bigger Solutions," *NP,* June 26, 2001.

46. Examples include the Council of Canadians leaders Mel Hurtig and Maude Barlow, and writers such as James Laxer and Linda McQuaig.

47. Eric Beauchesne, "Canada Must Cut Taxes to Keep Up with the United States, OECD Says," *NP,* September 9, 1999; Jacqueline Thorpe, "Canada's Tax Structure Moves Closer to That of U.S.," *NP,* October 19 2000; Eric Beauchesne, "Productivity Gap Widens: Study," *NP,* May 7, 2001.

48. Thurow is quoted in "There Is No BCNI," by Terence Corcoran, *NP,* April 8, 2000; Rod McQueen, "So Many Voices, So Little to Say," *NP,* May 2, 2000.

49. Don Drummond, "What It Will Take to Be Number One," *NP,* September 7, 2002; Bruce Little, "Keeping Up with the Americans Could Be Getting Harder," *G&M,* August 25, 2003; Michael Bliss, "The Fate of the U.S.'s Northern Suburb," *NP,* January 29, 2002; Michael Bliss, "Has Canada Failed?" *LRC* 14, no. 2 (March 2006): 3–5.

50. Jan Cienski, "Canada-U.S. Comparisons Always Tricky," *NP,* February 9, 2001; Terence Corcoran, "Scotiabank Brings You the Socialist Mob," *FP,* April 14, 2001.

51. Sonita Horvitch, "Stress on Stocks with U.S. Links," *FP,* December 30, 1998; Anthony Di Meo and Dexter Robinson, "99 Index Chart for Canadian Investors," Windsor-Andex Associates Inc., 1999; Diane Francis, "Investors' Loonies Flying South in Increasing Numbers," *FP,* October 14, 1999; Garry Marr, "U.S. Regulator Eyes Changes Affecting Snowbirds' RRSPs," *FP,* February 11, 2000; Robert Kerr, "Moving Stateside and RRSP Worries," *FP,* September 22, 2000.

52. Peter Kuitenbrouer, "South: Where the Money Is," *FP,* March 27, 1999; Gary Marr, "High Taxes Curb New IPOs: Poll," *FP,* August 28, 1999; Diane Lu-Hovasse, "Dot-Coms Wait for Funding, Look to U.S.," *FP,* June 19, 2000; Km Hanson and Jill Vardy, "U.S. Investor Cash May Flow Back South," *FP,* May 10, 2001.

53. Margaret Philip, "Debt-Rating Giants Stomp North," *G&M,* September 4, 1993; Bruce Little, "Ottawa, Provinces Told to Cut Deficits," *G&M,* January 15, 1994; Rob Carrick, "S&P Goes to War against Canadian Ratings Agencies," *G&M,* March 18, 1998; Katherine Macklem, "Moody's Upgrades Canada's Debt Rating," *FP,* June 22, 2000.

54. Brenda Dalgleish, "Common Interest," *Maclean's,* November 28, 1994, 54–55; Terence Corcoran, "Gold, Greenspan and Our Dollar," *FP,* July 22, 1999; Sandra Rubin and Joel-Denis Bellavance, "Central Bank Facing Pressure to Raise Rates," *NP,* March 3, 2001; Thomson Macdonald, *The Activity of American Centure Capital Funds in the Ontario Market: Issues, Trends and Prospects,* prepared for the Institute for Competitiveness and Prosperity (Toronto: Thomson Macdonald, 2005); Compas Inc., "Moderately Bullish on the Economy, Confident in U.S. Federal Reserve and Bank of Canada, Concerned about Fate of Canadian Manufacturing," Toronto, February 20, 2006, available at http://www.compas.ca.

55. Kathleen Day, "Banker Charged in Mutual Fund Scandal," *WP,* February 4, 2004; Sinclair Stewart, "Ex-CIBC Executive Arrested," *G&M,* February 4, 2004; Eric Reguly, "How CIBC Got Roughed Up in the U.S.," *G&M,* February 13, 2004.

56. Leonard Quigley, as quoted by Katherine Macklem, "Securities Disclosure Deal under Review," *FP,* February 10, 2000.

57. Katherine Macklem, "Securities Disclosure Deal under Review," *FP,* February 11, 2000; "Cross-Border Finance Pact Preserved," *FP,* May 30, 2000; Neville Nankiwell, "Canada Faces Choice over Global Accounting Rules," *FP,* January 5, 2000; Monique West, "SEC Investigation into IPOs Grows More Serious," *FP,* May 1, 2001.

58. John Kazanjian, "U.S. Reforms Hit Bay St.," *FP,* August 2, 2002; Sinclair Stewart, "U.S. May Put OSC in Back Seat," *FP,* August 12, 2002; Eric Reguly, "Rules of the

Capitalist Road," *Time,* December 11, 2002, 53; Theresa Tedesco and Wojtek Debrowski, "Ottawa Set to Push On with National Regulator," *FP,* February 25, 2005; Peter Morton, "New U.S. Accounting Rules Costly for Canadian Firms," *FP,* April 14, 2005; Cameron French, "Canadian Accountants Align with Europe," *FP,* May 15, 2005. Also see Jay Lorsch and Edward Waitzer, "Corporate Governance in Canada and the United States: A Comparative View," *One Issue, Two Voices* (Canada Institute at Woodrow Wilson International Center for Scholars), issue 5, April 2006, http://www.wilsoncenter.org/topics/pubs/OneIssueTwoVoices_5.pdf.

59. Theresa Tedesco, "Sarbanes Oxley Act Working: Donaldson," *FP,* April 13, 2006; Peter Morton, "TSX Welcomes Move toward Consolidation," *FP,* April 5, 2006.

Part IV: Political Realm

1. James Morrison, "Embassy Row," *WT,* March 15, 2006; Alan Freeman, "U.S. Envoy Wilson Predicts 'a Change in Tone,'" *G&M,* March 14, 2006; Beth Gorham, "'I Bear No Ill Will"—Bush," *CH,* March 29, 2006.

2. Fred McMahon, "The Problem with Sovereignty," *Fraser Forum,* March 2005, 5–6; Joseph S. Nye Jr., *The Paradox of American Power: Why the World's Only Superpower Can't Go It Alone* (New York: Oxford University Press, 2002), 53–62, 163–71.

3. Christopher Manfredi, "Rights and the Judicialization of Politics in Canada and the United States," in *Canada and the United States: Differences That Count,* 2nd edition, ed. David M. Thomas (Toronto: Broadview Press, 2000), 301–18; James Gillies, "Thinking the Unthinkable: The Republic of Canada," *G&M,* June 28, 1997.

4. Chris Cobb, "A Soft Side to the Hard Sell," *OC,* September 4, 1993; Carl Mollins, "Newt's Axis," *Maclean's,* March 27, 1995, 30–31; Jeffrey Simpson, "Conservatism by Any Other Name," *G&M,* March 29, 1997; William Walker, "Outcry over Americanization of Our Politics," *TS,* May 30, 1999; Jane Taber, "Liberals Bring in American Organizer," *G&M,* March 21, 2003.

5. Richard Gwyn, "Canada's Little Voice in the Back of America's Head," *SH,* October 31, 1999; Adrian Humphreys, "US Thinks Little of Canada: Poll," *NP,* May 7, 2002; Scott Feschuk et al., "One Nation, Invisible," *NP,* May 11, 2002; William Thorsell, "The Americans' New View of Us: The Ugly Canadian," *G&M,* May 12, 2003.

6. Peter Morton, "Institute Aims to Give Canada More Visibility," *NP,* April 26, 2002; *The Canada Institute at the Woodrow Wilson Center* (Washington, D.C.: Woodrow Wilson International Center for Scholars, 2002); *Canada Institute Annual Report, 2003* (Washington, D.C.: Woodrow Wilson International Center for Scholars, 2003); Leon Panetta, "Talking with Americans," *G&M,* February 5, 2004.

7. Scotty Greenwood, "Advice to a Friend: It's Time for a New Mantra," *G&M,* November 29, 2004; Christopher Sands, "Canada and the Bush Challenge," *Canada Focus* (Center for Strategic and International Studies) 2, no. 1 (January 2001), http://www.csis.org/americas/canada0101.html.

8. See Frank P. Harvey, "Canada's Addiction to American Security: The Illusion of Choice in the War on Terrorism," *ARCS* 35, no. 2 (Summer 2005): 265–94. Stéphane Roussel, *The North American Democratic Peace: Absence of War and Security Institution-Building in Canada-US Relations, 1867–1958* (Montreal and Kingston: McGill–Queen's University Press, 2004), blends political ideology and security themes.

Chapter 10: North American Security

1. David Pugliese, "U.S. to Install Missile Shield at NORAD Base," *NP,* March 2, 2002; Paul Wells, "Incoming, Incoming!" *Maclean's,* December 13, 2004, 33; CTV, "Norad Pact Amended to Reflect U.S. Missile Plan," August 5, 2004; National Defence [Canada], "Canada and United States Commit to Renewed Defence Cooperation," NR-04.093, November 29, 2004, http://www.forces.gc.ca/site/newsroom; Francis Kofi-Abiew, *Canadian Defence and the Canada-U.S. Strategic Partnership,* NPSIA Occasional Paper 29 (Ottawa: Carleton University Centre for Security and Defence Studies, 2002), http://www.carleton.ca/csds/occasional_papers; Colonel M. W. Haché, "The Illusion of Choice: Options for Canadian Security," Canadian Forces College, 2003, http://www.cfc.forces.gc.ca/papers/nssc5/hache.htm; Finn Poschmann and Jack Granatstein, "Missile Defence—Then and Now," *WP,* November 29, 2004.

2. John Ibbitson, "Why Ottawa Won't Join Bush's Missile Plan," *G&M,* February 10, 2005; Chantel Herbert, "PM's Leadership Called into Question, Again," *TS,* 25 February 2005; Doug Struck, "Canada Rejects Missile Shield Plan," *WP,* February 25, 2005; Clifford Krauss, "Divergent Paths: Canada Breaks with U.S. Over Missile Shield," *NYT,* February 27, 2005; Ann Crearan (Associated Press), "Canada's Missile Stance Disappoints Rice," March 1, 2005, http://www.boston.com/news/world/canada; CTV, "Bush Ignored Martin's Call on Missile Issue," March 2, 2005, http://www.ctv.ca; Dwight Mason, "A Flight from Responsibility: Canada and the Missile Defense of North America," Center for Strategic and International Studies, March 2005, available at http://www.csis.org.

3. Desmond Morton, "America: Our Neighbour, Our Shield," *G&M,* October 12, 2004; Joel Sokolsky, "The U.S. Is Not Taking Advice," *Maclean's,* December 6, 2004, 34; Dwight Mason, "The Canadian-North American Defence Alliance in 2005," *IJ,* Spring 2005, 385–96; Luiza Savage, "All For One?" *Maclean's,* September 2, 2005, 36–39; Innovative Research Group, "Two Fifths of Canadians Feel We Have Been Free Riding on National Defence in Post-WWII Era," Dominion Institute / CDFA survey, November 12, 2005, available at http://www.dominioninstitute.ca.

4. Samuel Flagg Bemis, *Jay's Treaty: A Study in Commerce and Diplomacy,* 2nd ed., revised (New Haven, Conn.: Yale University Press, 1962; orig. pub 1923), 453–88; See also Reginald C. Stuart, *United States Expansionism and British North America, 1775–1871* (Chapel Hill: University of North Carolina Press, 1988), chaps. 2–4.

5. C. P. Stacey, "The Myth of the Unguarded Frontier 1815–1871," *AHR* 56 (October 1950): 1–18; Randy Boswell, "Great Lakes Gun Upgrade," *NP,* March 16, 2006; Bradley Miller, "Our 'Undefended' Border, Then and Now," *NP,* March 22, 2006.

6. Stuart D. Scott, "The Patriot Game: New Yorkers and the Canadian Rebellion of 1837–1838," *NYH* 68, no. 3 (July 1987): 281–96; Stuart, *United States Expansionism,* 127–47, 234–36; Samuel T. Jackson, "Army Officers Fight the 'Patriot War': Responses to Filibustering," *Journal of the Early Republic* 18 (Fall 1998): 487–521.

7. Robin Winks, *Canada and the United States: The Civil War Years* (Baltimore: Johns Hopkins University Press, 1960), chaps. 13–17; Alvin C. Gluek, *Minnesota and the Manifest Destiny of the Canadian Northwest* (Toronto: University of Toronto Press, 1965), chap. 9; Stuart, *United States Expansionism,* 238–61.

8. Richard A. Preston, *The Defence of the Undefended Border: Planning for War in North America 1867–1939* (Montreal and Kingston: McGill–Queens University Press, 1977), chaps. 1–2.

9. Stéphane Roussel, *North American Democratic Peace: Absence of War and Security Institution-Building in Canada-U.S. Relations, 1867–1958* (Montreal and Kingston: McGill–Queen's University Press, 2004), chap. 5; Edward P. Kohn, *This Kindred People: Canadian-American Relations & the Anglo-Saxon Idea, 1895–1903* (Montreal and Kingston: McGill–Queen's University Press, 2005), 13–21, 145–46, 198.

10. Jean-Sebastien Rioux, "Two Solitudes: Quebecers' Attitudes Regarding Canadian Security and Defence Policy," Canadian Defence and Foreign Affairs Institute, Level University, February 23, 2005; "Mr. [Henri] Bourassa's Reply to Capt. Talbot Papineau's Letter," August 2, 1916, R. Douglas Francis and Donald B. Smith, eds., *Readings in Canadian History: Post Confederation* (Toronto: Holt, Rinehart & Winston, 1986), 357–63.

11. R. D. Cuff and J. L. Granatstein, *Ties That Bind: Canadian-American Relations in Wartime from the Great War to the Cold War* (Toronto: Samuel Stevens Hakkert, 1997), chaps 1–3.

12. John Hilliker and Donald Barry, *Canada's Department of External Affairs: Volume II, Coming of Age, 1946–1968* (Montreal and Kingston: McGill–Queen's University Press, 1995), vol. 1, chaps 4–7; Roussel, *North American Democratic Peace,* 151–58.

13. Carl Berger, "The Conferences on Canadian-American Affairs, 1935–1941: An Overview," in *The Road to Ogdensburg: The Queen's / St. Lawrence Conferences on Canadian-American Affairs,* ed. Frederick W. Gibson and Jonathan Rossie (East Lansing: Michigan State University Press, 1933), 11–32; and Edward Meade Earle, "Inter-American Factors in Security," in *Road to Ogdensburg,* ed. Gibson and Rossie, 334–45.

14. C. P. Stacey, "The Canadian-American Permanent Joint Board on Defence, 1940–1945,"*CHR* 9 (Spring 1954): 105–24; Joel J. Sokolsky and Joseph T. Jockel, "The Road from Ogdensburg," in *The Road from Ogdensburg: Fifty Years of Defense Cooperation,* ed. Joel Sokolsky and Joseph Jockel (Lewiston, Maine: Edwin Mellen Press, 1992), 1–6; J. L. Granatstein, "Mackenzie King and Canada at Ogdensburg, August 1940," in *Road from Ogdensburg,* 9–29; W. A. B. Douglas, "Democratic Spirit and Purpose: Problems in Canadian-American Relations, 1934–1945," in *Road from Ogdensburg,* 31–37.

15. Ron Purver, "The Arctic in Canadian Security Policy, 1945 to the Present," in *Canada's International Security Policy,* ed. David B. Dewitt and David Leyton-Brown (Scarborough, Ont.: Prentice Hall, 1995), 81–110.

16. Richard A. Preston, *The Defence of the Undefended Border: Planning for War in North America 1867–1939* (Montreal and Kingston: McGill–Queen's University Press, 1977), 220 ff; Lester B. Pearson, *Mike: The Memoirs of the Right Honourable Lester B. Pearson* (Toronto: University of Toronto Press, 1948), vol. 1, chaps. 8–14; Roussel, *North American Democratic Peace,* chaps. 6–7.

17. Hilliker and Barry, *Canada's Department of External Affairs,* 33–35, 75–78.

18. Joseph T. Jockel, "The Canada-United States Military Co-operation Committee and Continental Air Defence, 1946," *CHR* 64 (1983): 352–77; Edelgard E. Mahant and Graeme S. Mount, *Invisible and Inaudible in Washington: American Policies Toward Canada* (Vancouver: University of British Columbia Press, 1999), 16–22; David Leyton-Brown, "Managing Canada-United States Relations in the Context of Multilateral Alliances," in *America's Alliances and Canadian-American Relations,* ed. Lauren McKinsey and Kim Nossal (Toronto: Summerhill Press, 1988), 162–79.

19. Danford Middlemiss, "Economic Defence Co-operation with the United States 1948–63," in *An Acceptance of Paradox: Essays in Honour of John W. Holmes,* ed. Kim Richard Nossal (Toronto: Canadian Institute of International Affairs, 1982), 86–114.

20. Mahant and Mount, *Invisible and Inaudible,* 22–34; Colin S. Gray, *Canadian Defence Priorities: A Question of Relevance* (Toronto: Clarke, Irwin, 1972), 132–33; Hilliker and Barry, *Canada's Department of External Affairs,* 108–10, 235–37.

21. Greg Marquis, "The Cold War on Our Shore," *SH,* November 1, 1998; Robert Russo, "Report Details U.S. Nukes in Canada," *MS,* October 20, 1999; Charlie Gillis, "Pearson 'Signed Away' Right to Decide against War," *NP,* January 31, 2000; Andrew Phillips, "The Nuclear Legacy," *Maclean's,* March 17, 2001, 46–47; John Ward, "Admiral Dyer Dies," *CH,* November 10, 2002; Gray, *Canadian Defence Priorities,* 127–63.

22. Jeff Sallot, "Canada Refuses to Back U.S. on Nuclear Arms," *G&M,* November 12, 1998; Anthony DePalma, "Rubbing America the Wrong Way," *SH,* January 10. 1999 (first published in *NYT*); Mike Blanchfield, "U.S. Envoy Belittles Axworthy Arms Idea," *NP,* February 7, 2000; Mahant and Mount, *Invisible and Inaudible,* chap. 3.

23. Joseph T. Jockel, *Security to the North: Canada-U. S. Defense Relations in the 1990s* (East Lansing: Michigan State University Press, 1991), 96–138; Joel J. Sokolsky, "The Future of North American Defence Co-operation," *IJ* 46 (Winter 1990–91): 27–57.

24. Douglas Murray, "NORAD and US Nuclear Options," in *Fifty Years of Defense Cooperation,* ed. Sokolsky and Jockel, 209–38; David Cox, "Canada and Ballistic Missile Defence," in *Fifty Years of Defense Cooperation,* ed. Sokolsky and Jockel, 239–62.

25. Douglas Ross, "SDI and Canadian-American Relations: Managing Strategic Doctrinal Incompatibilities," in *America's Alliances,* ed. McKinsey and Nossal, 137–161.

26. Joel Sokolsky and David DeTomasi, "Canadian Defense Policy and the Future of Canada–United States Security Relations," *ARCS* 24 (Winter 1994): 537–56; Joseph T. Jockel and Joel J. Sokolsky, "The End of the Canada–United States Defense Relationship," in *Creating the Peaceable Kingdom: And Other Essays on Canada,* ed. Victor Howard (East Lansing: Michigan State University Press, 1998), 197–219; Jean-Philippe Racicot, "Canadian Perspectives on North American Defense," *Isuma* 1 (Spring 2000): 113–18; Joel J. Sokolsky, "The Bilateral Defence Relationship with the United States," in *Canada's International Security Policy,* ed. Dewitt and Leyton-Brown, 180–93; Alexander Rose, "'Americans Are from Mars, Europeans from Venus,'" *G&M,* January 1, 2003.

27. Graham Allison and Gregory F. Treverton, "Introduction and Overview," in *Rethinking America's Security* (New York: W. W. Norton, 1992), ed. Graham Allison and Gregory F. Treverton, 15–31; David C. Hendrickson, "The End of American History: American Security, the National Purpose, and the New World Order," in *Rethinking America's Security,* 386–406, and Gregory F. Treverton and Barbara Bicksler, "Conclusion: Getting from Here to Where?" in *Rethinking America's Security,* 407–33.

28. Dewitt and Leyton Brown, "Canada's International Security," in *Canada's International Security Policy,* ed. Dewitt and Leyton-Brown, 1–27.

29. See Michael Ignatieff, *Virtual War: Kosovo and Beyond* (Toronto: Viking, 2000); and *The 9/11 Commission Report: Final Report of the National Commission on Terrorist Attacks Upon the United States* (New York: W. W. Norton, 2004), chaps. 2–6.

30. Gordon Giffin, "The Challenges of Shared Security," January 11, 1999, U.S. Embassy, Ottawa; Jonathan N. Winer, "Defending the Indefensible? U.S.-Canada Cooperation on New Global Security Issues," address to the Canadian Council for International Peace and Security, February 24, 2000, U.S. Embassy, Ottawa; Lawrence MacAulay, "Statement on National Security," House of Commons, December 16, 1999, available at http://www.sgc.gc.ca/speeches.

31. Peter Morton, "Ottawa Pushes Compromise in Defense Fight with U.S.," *NP,*

June 11, 1999; Peter Morton and Heather Scoffield, "U.S. Security Crackdown Could Ground Canadian Satellite," *G&M,* June 29, 1999; Peter Morton and Joel-Denis Bellivance, "Canada, U.S. Resolve Defense Security Row," *NP,* October 8, 1999.

32. David Pugliese, "Defense Puts $10M into U.S. Stealth Fighter Project," *NP,* November 25, 1999; Thomas Watson, "GM Canada Will Give U.S. Military $4B Ticket to Ride," *FP,* November 18, 2000; Stephen Handelman, "Ottawa's Naval Engagement," *Time,* June 7, 1999, 25; Alistair Edgar, "Let's Get a Continental Market Treaty," *PO,* April 2002, 50–56; David A. Baldwin, "Security Studies and the End of the Cold War," *WP* 48, no. 1 (1996): 117–41.

34. Danielle Goldfarb, *Thinking the Unthinkable: Security Threats, Cross-Border Implications, and Canada's Long-term Strategies,* Border Papers: Backgrounder (Toronto: C. D. Howe Institute, 2004); Joel Sokolsky, "Realism Canadian Style: The Chrétien Legacy in National Security Policy and the Lessons for Canada-U.S. Relations," Woodrow Wilson International Center, Washington, January 14, 2004, copy courtesy of the author.

35. "Next Canadian PM Vows Role in Security," *USAT,* November 15, 2003; Wesley Wark, "Martin's New Security Agenda: Feeling Safe Yet?" *G&M,* December 18. 2003; Scot Robertson, "Finding a War: National Security and Defence Policy for a New Liberal Leadership," *PO,* December 2003–January 2004, 56–61.

36. For the unintended consequences theory, see Chalmers Johnson, "Blowback," *The Nation,* October 15, 2001, http://www.thenation.com/docprint.

37. Stephen Flynn, "Bolstering the Maritime Weak Link," statement presented before the U.S. Senate Committee on Governmental Affairs, December 6, 2001; and Stephen Flynn, "America the Vulnerable: The Fragile State of Container Security," testimony to the U.S. Senate Governmental Affairs Committee, March 20, 2003; Chris Sands, "Terrorism, Border Reform, and Canada–United States Relations: Learning the Lessons of Section 110," keynote address, Linkages Across the Border: The Great Lakes Economy Conference, April 4, 2002, available at http://www.csis.org; CBS News, "North of the Border."

38. Robert Fife, "Manley to Manage Security Sweep," *NP,* October 2, 2001; "U.S. Praises Intelligence Gathering," *NP,* October 4, 2001.

39. Christopher Sands, "Canada and the War on Terrorism: The U.S. Challenge on the North American Front," *Canada Focus* 2, no. 3 (October 2001), available at http://www.csis.org/americas; David Pratt, "State of Readiness of the Canadian Forces: Response to the Terrorist Threat," Interim Report of the Standing Committee on National Defence and Veterans Affairs [House of Commons] (November 2001), courtesy of the author; Sheldon Alberts, "Ottawa Seeks 'Widest Possible' Integration with U.S. Defence, *NP,* November 22, 2001; Colin Nickerson, "US Wary of 'Time Bombs' Waiting to Strike from North," *BG,* February 4, 2002; Clifford Kraus, "Canada Alters Security Policies to Ease Concerns," *NYT,* February 18, 2002; J. L. Granatstein, "Now as Then, Defense Must Be Continental;" Bill Graham (member of Parliament), "Canada and the North American Challenge: Managing Relations in Light of the New Security Environment," *NP,* January 31, 2002; J. L. Granatstein, "Carrying Our Fair Share of the Defence Burden," *NP,* June 11, 2002; *A Friendly Agreement in Advance: Canada-U.S. Defence Relations Past, Present, and Future* (Toronto: C. D. Howe Institute, 2002).

40. Tom Ridge (secretary, U.S. Department of Homeland Security), "Two If by Sea: The Need for a Multi-Layered Approach to North American Maritime Defence and Port Security," *Canadian American Strategic Review,* April 2004, available at http://

www.sft.ca.casr; and Colin Kenny, "Port Security: Which Agencies, National and Local, Civilian and Military, Provide Security for Canadian Ports?" *Canadian American Strategic Review,* June 2004, available at http://www.sft.ca.casr; Shawn McCarthy, "U.S. Plays Down Northcom Threat," *G&M,* April 19, 2002; Paul Knox, "Are We Being Integrated in the U.S. without Having Any Real Public Debate?" *G&M,* April 20, 2002.

41. Bradley Graham, "Pentagon Plans New Command for U.S.," *WP,* January 27, 2002; Graham and Bill Miller, "Pentagon Debates Homeland Defense Role," *WP,* February 11, 2002; Paul Cellucci, "North American Security," speech at Canadian Defence Industries Association Dinner, February 14, 2002, http://www.usembassycanada.gov; "Special Briefing on the Unified Command Plan," U.S. Department of Defense, April 17, 2002, http://www.defense link.mil.news/Apr2002; "U.S. Northern Command," *Global Security,* April 17, 2002, http://www.globalsecurity.org/military; Michael Byers, "On Guard for Uncle Sam?" *G&M,* April 18, 2002; [Senator] Colin Kenny, "Let's Warm Up to This Idea," *G&M,* April 29, 2002; "State of Readiness of the Canadian Forces: Response to the Terrorist Threat," Interim Report of the Standing Committee on National Defence and Veterans Affairs, House of Commons, Ottawa, November 2001; Brad W. Gladman, "Strengthening the Relationship: NORAD and Canada Command," *Journal of Military and Strategic Studies* 9, no. 2 (Winter 2006–7), available at http://www.jmss.org.

42. Flynn, "America the Vulnerable"; Rick Mofina and Jim Bronskill, "Senate Group Worried about Coastal Threats," *NP,* August 30, 2002; Steven Chase, "Port Security Tops Transport Agenda," *NP,* January 16, 2004; Murray Brewster, "U.S. Coast Guard Presence after 9/11 Worried Canada," *CH,* January 19, 2004.

43. Drew Fagan, "Canada Should Captain Push for More Secure Maritime Shipping," *G&M,* April 10, 2002; Department of National Defense Backgrounder, "Canada Joins the Inter-American Defense Board," November 20, 2002, http://www.forces.gc.ca/site/Newsroom; DeNeen L. Brown, "U.S., Canada Reach Agreement to Let Troops Cross Border," *WP,* December 10, 2002; Geoffrey York, "Canada Part of Ship-Intercept Plan," *WP,* February 16, 2004; Jim Bronskill, "Canada-U.S. Exercise Reveals Flaws in Terrorism Response," *G&M,* November 17, 2003; David Pugliese, "Special Forces Prepare for Al-Qaeda Attack on B.C. Coast," March 18, 2004, available at http://www.canada.com; "Joint Statement by Canada and the United States on Common Security, Common Prosperity: A New Partnership in North America, November 30, 2004, http://www.usembassy.ca.gov; Canada-U.S. Security Cooperation Agreement, http://www.canadianembassy.org/defence/text-en.asp; Dwight Mason, "Canada and the Future of Continental Defense: A View from Washington," *Policy Papers on the Americas* (Center for Strategic and International Studies) 14, no. 10 (September 2003): 8–12.

44. Michael Friscolanti, "NYPD Moves to Post Detectives in Toronto," *NP,* July 16, 2002; Barrie McKenna, "The Long Arm of the New U.S. Security Agency Will Reach Far into Our Sphere," *G&M,* November 26, 2002; Sheldon Alberts, "U.S. Orders Foreign Airlines to Add Guards," *NP,* December 30, 2003.

45. James Baxter et al., "22 Canadian Sites on U.S. Warning List," *NP,* November 11, 2002; Michael Friscolanti, "Ottawa Is Warned of Terrorism Loophole," *NP,* January 20, 2004; Beth Gorham, "U.S. Not Sold on Canada's Anti-Terrorism Fight—Easter," *CH,* July 15, 2003; Stewart Bell, "Ottawa Impedes War on Terror, U.S. Report Says," *NP,* May 1, 2003.

46. DeNeen Brown, "Canadians Sense Climate of Fear," *WP,* October 24, 2001; Stephen Handelman, "Are Canada's Defenses All at Sea?" *Time,* November 4, 2002, 33; Joseph S. Nye Jr., "Geopolitics in 3-D," *Time,* November 4, 2002, 36; Matthew Fisher, "U.S. Forces Losing Faith in Canada," *NP,* January 8, 2003; Aaron Brown, "Canadian Security Issues," "Canadian Jihad," and "Report from Canada on Terrorism," CNN Newsnight, October 12 and 13, 2004; Joel Sokolsky, *The "Away Game": Canada–United States Security Relations from Outside North America,* Mapping the New North American Reality Series, IRPP Working Paper 2004-091 (Montreal: Institute for Research on Public Policy, 2004), http://www.irpp.org/wp/archive/NA_integ/wp2004-091.pdf.

47. Stephen Handelman, "The Division of Labor," *Time,* January 21, 2002, 23; [General] George A. MacLean, "Redefining Continental Defence: The Hemispheric Multilateral Dimension," *PO,* April 2002, 46–49; Donna Miles, "Planning Group Weighs Value of 'Maritime NORAD,'" Defense Link, U.S. Department of Defense, American Forces Press Service, November 4, 2004, http://www.canadiandimension.mb.ca/extra; Bill Curry, "Liberals Support Expanding NORAD to Coastal Defence," *G&M,* May 1, 2006.

48. Steven Frank and Stephen Handelman, "War Footing," *Time,* October 1, 2001, 30–32; Chris Wattie, "Closer Partnership with U.S. Urged;" *NP,* November 9, 2001; Jonathan Gatehouse, "In Search of Our Role," *Maclean's,* December 31, 2001; Rioux, "Two Solitudes"; Steven Chase and Krista Foss, "Joint Defense Talks Come under Fire," *G&M,* January 30, 2002; DeNeen L. Brown, "Canada Wary of U.S. Anti-Terror Plan," *WP,* February 24, 2002; Campbell Clark, "Canadians Want Strict Security, Poll Finds," *G&M,* August 11, 2005.

49. Danford Middlemiss and Denis Stairs, "The Canadian Forces and the Doctrine of Interoperability: The Issues," *Policy Matters* 3, no. 7 (June 2002); Joel Sokolsky, "Clausewitz, Canadian Style," *Canadian Military Journal,* Autumn 2002, 3–10; Sean M. Maloney, *Are We Really Just Peacekeepers? The Perception Versus the Reality of Canadian Military Involvement in the Iraq War,* IRPP Working Paper 2003–02 (Montreal: Institute for Research on Public Policy, 2003); Ben Rowswell, "Ogdensburg Revisited: Adapting Canada-U.S. Security Cooperation to the New International Era," *Policy Papers on the Americas* (Center for Strategic and International Studies) 15, study 5, May 2004; Joel Sokolsky, "Walking the Line: Canada-U.S. Security Relations and the Global War on Terrorism," *Breakthroughs* 15, no. 1 (Spring 2006): 29–41.

50. Tom Blackwell, "9/11 Changed Canadian Lives, Study Finds," *NP,* July 31, 2004; Stewart Bell, "Blind to Terror," *Time,* March 15, 2004; Mike Blanchfield, "Terror via Canada 'Inevitable': Cellucci," *Time,* October 21, 2004; Tara Brautigam, "Canada Ripe Spot for Terror, Ex-FBI Agent Says," *CH,* July 3, 2005; Clark, "Canadians Want Strict Security"; Joe Friesen, "The Allegations: Shocking Revelations as Terror Suspects Appear in Court," and other stories, *G&M,* June 7, 2006; Paul Koring, "Canadian Catch Leads to American Anxiety," *G&M,* June 5, 2006; Don Butler "Security Trumps Civil Liberties for Many Canadians," *OC,* June 24, 2006.

51. Barry Cooper and Mercedes Stephenson, "Ballistic Missile Defence and the Future of Canada-U.S. Cooperation," *Fraser Forum,* March 2005, 9–11; Joseph T. Jockel and Joel Sokolsky, "A New Continental Consensus? The Bush Doctrine, the War on Terrorism and the Future of U.S.-Canada Security Relations," in *Split Images: Canada Among Nations 2005,* ed. Andrew F. Cooper and Dane Rowlands (Montreal and Kingston: McGill–Queen's University Press, 2005), 63–78.

Chapter 11: Border Management

1. See Don Martin, "The Undecided Border" (five parts), *NP,* August 5–9, 2003; Jerry Seper, "Guarding America's Border" (three parts), *WT,* December 8–10, 2003; and Associated Press, "Parts of U.S.-Canadian Border Disappear in Brush," *NYT,* April 4, 2004. Compare with Marian Botsford Fraser, *Walking the Line: Travels along the Canadian/American Border* (Vancouver: Douglas & McIntyre, 1958).

2. Deborah Waller Meyers and Demetrious G. Papademetriou, "Self-Governance along the U.S.-Canada Border: A View from Three Regions," in *Caught in the Middle: Border Communities in an Era of Globalization,* ed. Demetrious G. Papademetriou and Deborah Waller Meyers (Washington, D.C.: Carnegie Endowment for International Peace, 2001), chap 1; Public Policy Forum, "Canada's Policy Choices: Managing Our Border with the United States, November 28, 29, 2001, http://www.publicpolicyforum.org.

3. William E. Lass, "How the Forty-Ninth Parallel Became the International Boundary," *Minnesota History* 44 (1975): 209–19; Ken S. Coates, "Border Crossings: Pattern and Processes along the Canada-United States Boundary West of the Rockies," in *Parallel Destinies: Canadian-American Relations West of the Rockies,* ed. John M. Findlay and Kenneth S. Coates (Seattle: University of Washington Press, 2002), 3–30; and Carl Abbott, "That Long Western Border: Canada, the United States, and a Century of Economic Change," in *Parallel Destinies,* ed. Findlay and Coates, 203–20; Sheila McManus, *The Line Which Separates: Race, Gender and the Making of the Alberta-Montana Borderlands* (Lincoln: University of Nebraska Press, 2005), chaps. 1, 2; Edward P. Kohn, *This Kindred People: Canadian-American Relations and the Anglo-Saxon Idea, 1895–1903* (Montreal and Kingston: McGill–Queen's University Press, 2005), chaps. 4, 5.

4. Stacey, "Myth of the Unguarded Frontier"; Reginald C. Stuart, *United States Expansionism and British North America, 1775–1871* (Chapel Hill: University of North Carolina Press, 1988), chaps. 4–6; Stéphane Roussel, *North American Democratic Peace: Absence of War and Security Institution-Building in Canada-U.S. Relations, 1867–1958* (Montreal and Kingston: McGill–Queen's University Press, 2004), chap. 5.

5. Homer Calkin, "St. Albans in Reverse: The Fenian Raid of 1866," *VH* 35 (1967): 19–34.

6. Richard A. Preston, *The Defence of the Undefended Border: Planning for War in North America 1867–1939* (Montreal and Kingston: McGill–Queen's University Press, 1977), chap. 1; Herbert M. Hart, *Old Forts of the Northwest* (New York: Bonanza Books, 1963), 177; Edward P. Kohn, *This Kindred People: Canadian-American Relations and the Anglo-Saxon Idea, 1895–1903* (Montreal and Kingston: McGill–Queen's University Press, 2005), chaps. 4, 5.

7. Alvin C. Gluek, "The Passamaquoddy Bay Treaty, 1910," *CHR* 47 (1966): 1–21; Peter Neary, "Lord Grey and the Settlement of Canadian-American Differences, 1905–1911," *CHR* 49 (1968): 357–80; Elizabeth B. Elliot-Mazel, "Still Unresolved after Fifty Years: The Northwest Passage in Canadian-American Relations, 1946–1998," *ARCS* 29 (1999): 407–30; Dean Beeby, "Canada, U.S. Both Claim Tiny Bay of Fundy Island," *CH,* August 7, 1996.

8. CAA Ontario, "History," http://www.caaontario.net/history.html.

9. This information is from http://www.ambassadorbridge.com/history.

10. Stephen Handelman, "When Smoke Gets in Your Lives," *Time,* August 27, 2001,

35; Charlie Gillis, Joseph Brean, and Heather Sokolof, "Erasing the Frontier," *NP,* August 18, 2001; Bill Cameron, "'So Sure, Just Blow It Up,'" *NP,* August 18, 2001; William Watson, "Drawing the Line," *NP,* August 18, 2001.

11. See the articles in *MS,* October 4–6, 1999, and July 17–18, 2000; and Stephen Frank, "Oceans of Opportunity," *Time,* July 10, 2000, 28–29.

12. Adam Killick, "Western Premiers to Join U.S. Governors to Improve Relations," *NP,* June 14, 1999; Martin O'Hanlon, "Premiers, Governors Meet to Talk Trade," *SH,* June 13, 1999; Stephen Handelman, "The Ties That Really Bind," *Time,* November 15, 1999, 39; John Ibbitson, "Ontario Growing Closer to U.S.," *G&M,* October 19, 2000; Patrick J. Smith and Arthur M. Goddard, "Globalist Governance in Cascadia: The Pacific Northwest as a Subnational, Binational, International Region," paper prepared for On Brotherly Terms: Canadian-American Relations West of the Rockies Conference, Center for the Study of the Pacific Northwest / Canadian Studies Center, University of Washington, Seattle, September 11–14, 1996; Policy Research Institute, *The Emergence of Cross-Border Regions* (Ottawa: Policy Research Institute, 2005).

13. "Officials Seek Open Border," *MS/CH,* May 14, 1997; Lawrence Martin, "Erasing the U.S. Border," *DN,* May 13, 1999; Mike Trickey, "Open Border with U.S. Not Imminent, Ambassador Says," *NP,* July 13, 1999; "First Meeting of the Canada-U.S. Partnership (CUSP) Niagara-on-the-Lake, Buffalo, NY," April 11–12, 2000, and Department of Foreign Affairs and International Trade, "Canada-U.S. Cooperation: Transportation, Customs & Immigration, Crime and Terrorism," http://www.dfait-maeci.gc.ca/geo/usa/cusp; Jan Cienski, "Canada-U.S. Border Will Disappear, Study Says," *NP,* June 17, 2000; Alan Toulin, "Canadian Agency Calls for Open Border," *NP,* July 17, 2001.

14. Speech by Lawrence Macaulay, solicitor general of Canada, to the Canada-U.S. Cross Border Crime Forum, Charlottetown, June 17, 1999, available at http://www.sgc.ca/Speeches; Attorney General John Ashcroft to Cross-Border Crime Forum, June 20, 2000, available at http://www.usembassy.ca; Madeleine K. Albright and John Manley to President William J. Clinton and Prime Minister Jean Chrétien, "Canada-U.S. Partnership Forum Report: Building a Border for the 21st Century," December 2000, http://www.state.gov.http://www/regions; Government of Canada, *Canada–United States Accord on Our Shared Border: Update 2000* (Ottawa: Minister of Public Works and Government Services, 2000).

15. Andrew Duffy, "Ottawa Urges U.S. to Adopt Continental Security Ring," *NP,* January 29, 2000; Andrew Duffy and Jim Bronskill, "Official Denies Ottawa Is Snoozing over Terror, Migrants," *NP,* January 29, 2000; Stewart Bell, " Mauritanian Suspected of Plotting Attack Detained," *NP,* January 29, 2000.

16. James P. Rubin, U.S. Department of State, "Joint Statement on Border Cooperation and the Canada-U.S. Partnership Forum," http://www.usembassycanada.gov/cusp; Peter Romero, Remarks on the Occasion of the First Meeting of the Canada–U.S. Partnership Forum, April 12, 2000, http://www.state.gov/policy_remarks/2000; Lauren Monsen, "Strong U.S.-Canada Relations Fuel Cooperation on Border Issues, April 19 2000, available at http://www.usinfo.state.gov; John Nicol, "Hands across the Border," *MacLean's,* July 31, 2000, 16–24.

17. John D. Worth, "Advancing the North American Community," *ARCS* 26 (1996): 261–73; Deborah Myers and Demetrious Papademetriou, "Law Enforcement Problems of the U.S.-Canada Border: Testimony before the Subcommittee on Immigration and Claims of the Committee on the Judiciary," U.S. House of Representatives, April 14,

1999, available at http://www.carnegieendowment.org/publications; Joel-Denis Bellavance, "Canada Ready to Open Up U.S. Border," *NP,* April 2, 2001; Alan Toulin, "BCNI Urges Extension of Free Trade," *FP,* May 30, 2001; Robert Fife and Alan Toulin, "U.S. Hopes to Erase Borders," *SH,* July 29, 2001; Robert Fife and Alan Toulin, "Canada-U.S. Border Soon May Be Gone," *SH,* July 29, 2001.

18. Chris Wood, "The Vanishing Border," *MacLean's,* December 20, 1999, 20–23; David Crane, "North American Integration Raises Some Serious Questions," *CH/MS,* August 3, 2001; "Rethinking the Line: The Canada-US Border," *Horizons,* March 2001; Alan Toulin, "Canadian Agency Calls for Open Border," *NP,* July 17, 2001; Laura Bogomolny, "The Future of the Canadian-U.S. Border," *CSIS Prospectus* 2, no. 3 (Fall 2001).

19. Kathleen Kenna, "'Smart Pass' to Speed Up Crossings," *TS,* May 20, 1999; Robert Fife, "Minister Pushes Swipe Card to Reduce U.S. Border Checks," *NP,* May 21, 1999; Stewart Bell, "Customs to Offer Quick Lanes for Pre-Screened Travelers," *NP,* April 8, 2000; Stephen Handelman, "Two Nations, Indivisible," *Time,* July 12, 2000, 22–23.

20. Susan Brunette, "Firms Gird for U.S. Border Crossing," *G&M,* March 28, 1998; Andrew Phillips, "Trouble on the Border," *MacLean's,* August 3, 1998, 30–33; Laura Ramsay, "State the Purpose of Your Visit," *FP,* August 16, 1999; Peter Morton, "U.S. Lawmakers Slam Canada over 'Porous Border,'" *NP,* April 16, 1999; Marina Jiminez, "Canada Seen as Soft Touch," *NP,* June 26, 1999; Theodore H. Cohn, "Cross-Border Travel in North America: The Challenge of U.S. Section 110 Legislation," *CAPP* 4 (October 1999): 7–8.

21. Dean Fischer, "Good-Neighbor Gridlock," *Time,* September 29, 1997, 32; Robert Russo, "Border Battle Gets Postponed," *CH,* November 11, 1997; Ron Anderson, "Law Could Make It a Long Wait to Cross into Canada," *ST,* September 16, 1998; Robert Russo, "New Border Law Unenforceable, Say U.S. Officials," *NP,* October 1, 1998; "Fact Sheet on Illegal Immigration Reform and Immigration Responsibility Act," December 6, 2001, available at http://www.usembassycanada.gov.

22. Sean Fine, "U.S. Border Crackdown Keeping Canadians Out," *G&M,* March 14, 1998; Laura Ramsay, "U.S. Bans 200 under New Immigration Law," *CH,* March 24, 1998; Susan Bourette, "Firms Gird for U.S. Border Crossing," *G&M,* March 28, 1998; Timothy Appleby, "Driving into the U.S.? Be Prepared for a Shock," *G&M,* June 12, 1999; Martin Loney, "Porous Borders Make Mean Streets," *NP,* January 3, 2000.

23. Jan Cienski, "U.S. Sends 300 Extra Inspectors to Border," *NP,* December 22, 1999; Peter Morton, "U.S. Congress in Talks on Border Delays," *NP,* March 23, 2000; "Canadian Visitors to the U.S.A. to Be Put on Cop Database under New Border Law," *OC,* May 26, 2000; Stewart Bell, "Canada to Outlaw Fund Raising for World Terrorism," *NP,* December 30, 1999; Paul Waldie, "Papers Describe Elaborate Hezbollah Support Ring," *NP,* July 25, 2000.

24. Robert Russo, "Border Battle Gets Postponed," *CH,* November 11, 1997; Bronwyn Lance, "Bordering on Insanity," *NP,* July 16, 1999; "Immigration and Naturalization Service Data Management Improvement Act of 2000," http://www.ins.usdoj.gov/graphics/lawenfor.

25. Rick Ouston, "FBI Terrorism Unit Probes Man Held at Border," *NP,* December 18, 1999; "Ottawa Ups Security at Border Crossings, Airports," *CH/MS,* December 23, 1999; Robert Russo, "Bombing Trial Could Embarrass Canada," *CH,* March 12, 2001; William Booth, "Focus Narrow as Ressam Trial Begins," *WP,* March 13, 2001; Robert

Russo, "Ressam Repeatedly Flouted Canadian Immigration Laws, Trial Told," *VS,* March 20, 2001; Stewart Bell, "CSIS Watched Ressam for Years before Arrest," *NP,* April 7, 2001; Stewart Bell, "Jury Convicts Montrealer at Bomb Trial," *NP,* July 14 2001.

26. Campbell Clark, "Canadian Woman Has Ties to Terrorist Group, Court Told," *NP,* December 31, 1999; Stewart Bell, " 'Routine' Alien Incident Sets of Border Alarms," *NP,* December 28, 1999; "Border Security Tightened," *SH,* December 19, 1999.

27. Barrie McKenna, "U.S. Congressman Issues Warning on Border Security," *G&M,* April 30, 1998; Morton, "U.S. Lawmakers Slam Canada"; Stewart Bell et al., "Canada Is a 'Sieve' Leaking Terrorists, Critics Charge," *NP,* December 21, 1999; Ronald Noble, "Canadian Border: Proceed with Caution," *NYT,* December 26, 1999; statement of the Honorable Lamar Smith, Chairman, Subcommittee on Immigration and Claims, House Committee of the Judiciary, "Hearing on Terrorist Threats to the United States," January 25, 2000, http://www.usembassycanada.gov/canadahearings.htm; statement of Steven Emerson, Executive Director, Terrorism Newswire, Inc., http://www.usembassycanada.gov/canadahearings.htm; David B. Harris, former chief of strategic planning, Canadian Security Intelligence Service, http://www.usembassycanada.gov/canadahearings.htm; statement of John C. Thompson, director, Mackenzie Institute, Toronto, http://www.usembassycanada.gov/canadahearings.htm; statement of Chris Sands, director of Canada Project, Center for Strategic and International Studies, http://www.usembassycanada.gov/canadahearings.htm; Scott Allen, "Terrorist Scare Focuses Attention on Tiny Border Posts," *SH,* January 2, 2000; Mike Blanchfield, "Governor Downplays Criticism of Canada as Haven for Terrorists," *NP,* January 25, 2000.

28. Barrie McKenna, "Do More to Right Terrorism, U.S. Security Expert Tells Canada," *G&M,* February 11, 2000; James V. Grimaldi, "Lawmakers Push to Plug Holes in U.S.-Canada border," *ST,* January 26, 2000; Testimony of Michael A. Pearson, executive associate commissioner for field operations, U.S. Immigration and Naturalization Service, before Subcommittee on Immigration of the Senate Judiciary Committee Regarding Border Security Issues, February 10, 2000, 4–7, http://www.senate/gov~judiciary/210200mp.htm.

29. Bell, "Canada to Outlaw Fund Raising"; "Canadian Visitors to the U.S.A. to Be Put on Cop Database"; Stewart Bell and Jan Cienski, "Canada Agrees to Outlaw Terrorist Fund Raising," *NP,* February 11, 2000.

30. Testimony before Subcommittee, February 10, 2000, 4–7; Stephen E. Flynn, "Beyond Border Control," *FA* 79, no. 6 (November/December 2000): 57–68; Jan Cienski, "Crackdown at Canada–U.S. Border to Be Permanent," *NP,* January 8, 2000.

31. "Ambassador Cellucci Press Conference," Ottawa, September 12, 2001, available at http://www.usembassycanada.gov; Ian Jack and Robert Benzie, "Trucks Wait at Border for Up to Nine Hours," *NP,* September 13, 2001; Peter Brieger et al., "Choked Border Threatens Economy," *NP,* September 14, 2001; James Stevenson, "CP Chief Calls for Common Standards at U.S. Border," *G&M,* September 15, 2001; Alan Toulin, "Make U.S. Border a Top Priority, CTA Urges Ottawa," *G&M,* October 15, 2001.

32. "Testimony of the Customs Commissioner Robert C. Bonner and INS Commissioner James Ziglar at the Treasury General Government Appropriations Subcommittee hearing to discuss Northern Border Security issues," October 3, 2001, available at http://appropriations.senate.gov/releases; "U.S. Looks to Beef Up 'Crummy' Security on Maine-Canada Border," *CH/MS,* September 24, 2001; Jan Cienski, "U.S. Approves Beefed-Up Border Patrols," *NP,* October 10, 2001; Alan Toulin, "U.S. Border Plan Forces All Visitors to Register," *NP,* October 23, 2001; Associated Press, "Ashcroft

Seeks to Strengthen Border," *NYT,* December 3, 2001; Sheldon Alberts, "Military at the Border," *G&M,* December 4, 2001.

33. Gloria Galloway, "New Canadians Alienated by U.S. Travel Indignities," *G&M,* January 2, 2003; Amran Abocar, "U.S. Security Measures Drive Asylum Seekers to Canada," *WP,* March 31, 2003; Robert Russo, "U.S. Wants All Canadian Visitors to Have Passports," *WP,* September 15, 2003.

34. Barrie McKenna, "Delays at Border Excessive, U.S. Told," *G&M,* October 25, 2001; "Canada's Policy Choices: Managing Our Border with the United States," Public Policy Forum Conference, Toronto, November 28–29, 2001, available at http://www.publicpolicy.org; Barrie McKenna, "Plans for a 'Modernized' Border Will Hit Canada Like a Freight Train," *G&M,* March 22, 2002.

35. Luiza Chwialkowska, "Bordering on Harmonization: Why Canada Faces Pressure," *NP,* October 1, 2001; "Joint Statement on Cooperation on Border Security and Regional Migration Issues," December 3, 2001, U.S. Embassy, Ottawa; Ashcroft Announces Canada Agreement," *NYT,* December 3, 2001; "Canada and the United States Sign Smart Border Declaration," December 12, 2001, available at http://www.usembassycanada.gov; Eric Pianin and DeNeen L. Brown, "U.S., Canada Agree to Tighten Border," *WP,* December 13, 2001; Norman Hillmer and J. L. Granatstein, "Sharing a Continent with Americans Is an Exercise in Tension Management," *Maclean's,* December 31, 2002, 45–46.

36. Liza Chwialkowska, "U.S. Seeks Common Immigration Rules," *NP,* September 20, 2001; Julian Beltrame, "Fortress North America: How Our World Will Change," *Maclean's,* October 15, 2001, 23–27; Anthony de Palma, "Canada Altering Its System of Vigilance against Terror," *NYT,* December 3, 2001; "U.S. Attorney General John Ashcroft and Solicitor General of Canada Lawrence Macaulay Expand Integrated Border Enforcement Program," December 3, 2001, available at http://www.sgc.gc.ca; Bill Miller, "Firms, U.S. in Border Bargain," *WP,* April 16, 2002; Barrie McKenna, "Companies Enlist in U.S. War against Terrorism," *G&M,* April 16, 2002; Drew Fagan, "U.S. Learning Value of Open Border," *G&M,* April 23, 2002; "U.S., Canadian Officials Discuss Ways to Stop Terrorists," transcript of McClellan-Ridge press conference, U.S. Embassy, Ottawa, January 30, 2004; "White House Hails Progress with Canada on Smart Border Action Plan," March 8, 2002, U.S. Embassy, Ottawa.

37. Camille Bains, "U.S. Officers to Staff Ports," *CH,* January 17, 2002; Robert C. Bonner, "Speech before the Center for Strategic and International Studies, Washington," January 17, 2002, available at http://www.customs.ustreas.gov/about/speeches; author's conversation with Halifax Port authority official and Bonner; Alan Toulin, "U.S. Vows to Improve Traffic Flow," *NP,* November 17, 2001; Department of Foreign Affairs and International Trade, "Notes for an Address by . . . John Manley," November 28, 2001, http://dfait-maeci.gc.ca/mx; Edward Greenspan, "When the 800-Pound Gorilla Shifts Position," *G&M,* December 1, 2001.

38. Alan Toulin, "Railways Hike Security at U.S. Border," *FP,* October 13, 2001; Coalition for Secure and Trade-Efficient Borders, *Rethinking Our Borders: A Plan for Action,* December 3, 2001, http://www.-cm-mec-ca/coalition (includes 1995 Canada-U.S. Shared Border Accord); Scott Roberts, "Border Security Initiatives and the North American Railroad Industry," Halifax meeting of Borderlines: Canada in North America: A National Consultation, November 23, 2002, available at http://www.aims.ca; "The Border," *NP Business,* June 2003, 24–31.

39. Jeff Sallot and Shawn McCarthy, "Tougher Border Checks Anger Ottawa,"

G&M, November 1, 2002; David Ljunggren, "Canada in New Dispute with U.S. over Travel Rules," *WP,* November 4, 2002; Sheldon Alberts, "Cabinet Split on U.S. Plan," *NP,* November 5, 2002; Campbell Clark, "A Town Where Buying Gas Can Get You in Real Trouble . . . ," *G&M,* November 12, 2002.

40. Bill Miller, "Plugging a Very Porous Northern Border," *WP,* April 8, 2002; Lisa M. Seghetti, "Border Security: U.S.-Canada Border Issues," CRS Report for Congress, Domestic Social Policy Division, July 8, 2002; Office of Press Secretary, White House, "United States–Canada Free and Secure Trade Program," http://www.whitehouse.gov/news/releases/2002/09; Office of Press Secretary, White House, "Summary of Smart Border Action Plan Status," http://www.whitehouse.gov/news/releases/2002/09; Office of Press Secretary, White House, "United States–Canada Nexus Program," September 9, 2002, http://www.whitehouse.gov/news/releases/2002/09; U.S. Department of State, "U.S., Canada Release Update on Border Security Initiatives," December 6, 2002, http://www.usinfo.state.gov.topical/pol/terror; *The Bar-Code Border* 2, no. 3 (February 17, 2002); *The Bar-Code Border* 2, no. 7 (October 1, 2002); *The Bar-Code Border* 3, no. 4 (March 2003); Chris Sands, "The Border after September 11: Learning the Lessons of the Section 110 Experience," in *A Fading Power: Canada among Nations 2002,* ed. Norman Hillmer and Maureen Appel Molot (Toronto: Oxford University Press, 2002), 49–73; Standing Senate Committee on Banking, Trade, and Commerce, "Our Shared Border: Facilitating the Movement of Goods and People in a Security Environment," Interim Report, 2002, available at http://www.gc.ca/senate; Tom Ridge, secretary of homeland security, testimony to U.S. Senate Committee on Commerce, Science, and Transportation, April 9, 2003.

41. Hugh Winsor, "Dispelling the Myth about Canada as Terrorist Portal," *G&M,* December 4, 2001; John Sullivan, "U.S. and Canada United to Secure Open Portal," *NYT,* March 11, 2002; "Progress Report on the Smart border Deal," June 28, 2002, available at http://www.can-am.gc.ca/menu; "Canada-U.S. Immigration Cooperation," available at http://www.canadianembassy.org/border/immigration; "Canada-U.S. Customs Cooperation," available at http://www.canadianembassy.org/border/immigration; Associated Press, "Officials Dedicate Border Base," *WP,* August 21, 2004; Paul Vieira, "Border a Mess: Business," *NP,* July 26, 2005.

42. [Ambassador] Michael Kergin, "Stop Blaming Canada," *WT,* January 26, 2003; CBS News, "North of the Border," September 7, 2003, available at http://www.cbsnews.com; CBC, "Terror Groups Flourish in Canada: U.S. Report," February 15, 2004, http://www.cbc.ca/cgi-bin/templates/print.cgi; PBS, "Frontline: Is Canada a Safe Haven for Terrorists?" http://www.pbs.org/wgb...ntline/shows/trail/etc/canada.html; Ronald Irwin, "U.S.-Canada Border Security Is No Hoax," *BDN,* January 15 2003; "Aaron Brown's Nightline," CNN, November 1 and 2, 2004; Paul Koring, "Canadian Catch Leads to American Anxiety," *G&M,* June 5, 2006; Beth Gorham, "U.S. Congressman Blasts Canada on Terrorism: Supports Immigration Ban," Canadian Press, June 9, 2006.

43. "U.S.-Canada Business Dialogue," U. S. Chamber of Commerce, Washington, March 31, 2004, author's notes; John Ibbitson, "Police Our Borders, or Else," *G&M,* March 24, 2003; Wesley Wark, "Terrorism: It's Time to Grow Up," *G&M,* April 1, 2004; Beth Gorham, "Americans Won't Admonish Canada for Security Lapses, Says Official," Canadian Press, April 1, 2004, http://www.canada.com; Adrian Humphreys, "Trouble at Border," "Computer Glitch Creates Border Danger," *NP,* April 11, 2005; and "American 'Patience Running Out' over Border," *NP,* April 12, 2005; Sheldon Alberts, "Choked

Border Crossings Cost U.S. Economy $4B a Year," *NP,* April 21, 2005; Simon Tuck, "Paid $800 Extra for Car? Blame Border," *G&M,* July 26, 2005.

44. Department of Foreign Affairs and International Trade, "Smart Border Action Plan Status Report," December 17, 2004, Canadian Embassy, Washington, available at http://www.dfait-maeci.gc.ca/embassies/United States; Brian Hutchinson, "Lone Officer Guards Most Borders," *NP,* November 6, 2004; Mike Blanchfield, "Small Border Posts Face Congestion: MP," *NP,* December 16, 2004; "Welcome to U.S. Customs and Border Protection," available at http://www.customs.gov; Adrian Humphreys, "Call for Guns at Border," *NP,* June 15, 2005.

45. James Laxer, *The Border: Canada, the U.S. and Dispatches from the 49th Parallel* (Toronto: Random House of Canada, 2003), 314–28; Daniel Drache, "'Friends at a Distance': Reframing Canada's Strategic Priorities after the Bush Revolution in Foreign Policy," in *Split Images: Canada Among Nations 2005,* ed. Andrew F. Cooper and Dane Rowlands (Montreal and Kingston: McGill–Queen's University Press, 2005), 115–36.

46. U.S. Immigration and Naturalization Service, "Public Information Sheet on National Security Entry Exit Registration System," September 26, 2002, available at http://www.usembassycanada.org; Tom Blackwell and Anne Dawson, "Two-Hour Waits Common at Border," *NP,* March 19, 2003; Clifford Kraus, "A Nation at War: The Canadian Border: Concerns about Commerce as Borders Tighten," *NYT,* March 23, 2003; Kevin McGran, "Alert Levels and Border Management," presentation at briefing, Center for Strategic and International Studies, Washington, February 9, 2004, author's notes; "Border Policy and U.S. Visit," Smart Border North, working group meetings, Center for Strategic and International Studies, Washington, April 9, 2004, author's notes; Associated Press, "Neighbors Will Need Papers to Enter U.S., *WP,* September 2, 2005; Stephen Handelman, "May I Please See Your Passport?" *Time,* October 10, 2005, 28; Department of Foreign Affairs and International Trade, "Canada–United States: The Secure Flow of People at the Canada-U.S. Border," available at http://www.dfait-maeci.gc.ca.

47. Eric Beauchesne, "Tighter Border Security to Take Toll on Tourism: Study," *FP,* February 16, 2006; Conference Board of Canada, "Border Tightening Will Weaken Tourist Profits Next Year," February 15, 2006, http://www.conferenceboard.ca/press/2006/Tourism; Ian Austen, "Passport Rule 'War on Tourism,'" *CH,* April 4, 2006 (first published in *NYT*); Beth Gorham, "Canadians Enjoying Higher Dollar in U.S.," Canadian Press, February 15, 2006.

48. "Borderlines: Canada in North America, A National Consultation," *Ideas That Matter* 2, no. 4 (2003); Christopher Sands, "Canada as a Minor Ally: Optional Considerations for Relations with the United States," presentation at 2003 Canadian Crude Oil Conference, Kananaskis, Alberta, September 5, 2003, courtesy of author; Andre Belelieu, "The Smart Border Process at Two: Losing Momentum?" *Hemisphere Focus* (Center for Strategic and International Studies) 11, issue 31 (December 10, 2004); Doug Struck, "Canada Holds 17 in Alleged Bomb Plot," *WP,* June 4, 2006.

49. Allison Dunfield, "Customs Union Proposes Fix for Border Delays," *G&M,* October 25, 2001; Fred McMahon, "Perimeter Puzzle," *Fraser Forum,* December 2001, 31–32; International Trade Canada, "NAFTA Partners Continue to Liberalize Rules of Origin," January 11, 2005, http://www.international.gc.ca/nafta-alena/ann-401-en.asp; Danielle Goldfarb, *Thinking the Unthinkable: Security Treats, Cross-Border Implications, and Canada's Long-Term Strategies,* Border Paper 77 (Toronto: C. D. Howe In-

stitute, 2004); John C. Taylor and Associates, "The U.S.-Canada Border: Border Economic Costs, Their Costs, Their Causes, and Alternative Border Management Strategies," November 4, 2003, available at http://www.occ.on.ca; James D. Phillips, "Improving Border Management," *IJ,* Spring 2005, 407–15.

50. Sidney Weintraub, "North American Integration: Migration, Trade, and Security —Big Issues Come in Combinations," Spring 2004, available at http://www.csis.org; Rey Koslowski, "International Cooperation to Create Smart Borders," North American Integration: Migration, Trade and Security," IIRP Conference, Ottawa, April 1–2, 2004, courtesy of the author; CSIS Canada Project, "Canada-U.S. Border Security in the Next Four Years: What Can We Expect?" Conference, Montreal, November 12, 2004; Melissa Long, "U.S. to Require New ID to Cross Border by 2008," *NP,* July 30, 2005.

51. U.S. Department of Homeland Security, "Security and Prosperity Partnership: Implementation Report—Security Agenda," June 27, 2005, available at http://www.usembassycanada.gov; U.S. Department of Homeland Security, "Fact Sheet: Security and Prosperity Partnership of North America," updated June 27, 2005, available at http://www.usembassycanada.gov; Peter Morton, "NAFTA Partners Move to Slice Up Red Tape," *FP,* June 28, 2005.

Chapter 12: Ottawa-Washington Axis

1. "Paul Martin's Shifting Rhetoric on Canada-U.S. Relations," *G&M,* December 15, 2005; Paul Koring, "Canadian Vote a Chance to End 'Petty Rancour' with Bush Team," *G&M,* December 28, 2005; Helle Hale, "A Warming Trend from the North: Canadian Conservatives Back in Power," Heritage Foundation, January 27, 2006, http://www.heritage.org/Press/Commentary; "A Defeat for Anti-Americanism," editorial, *WP,* January 28, 2006; Beth Gordon, "'Disagree without Being Disagreeable,'" *CH,* January 28, 2006.

2. Allan Woods, "'Could Be a Match Made in Heaven," *NP,* February 16, 2006; Brian Laghi, "Michael Wilson Gets Envoy's Job," *G&M,* February 15, 2006.

3. Sheldon Alberts, "South Carolinian Named New Ambassador to Canada," *NP,* April 28, 2005; David H. Wilkins, "Remarks to U.S. Senate Foreign Relations Committee," May 25, 2005, available at http://www.usembassycanada.gov; Louisa Savage, "Not What He Seems," *Maclean's,* July 1, 2005, 22, 24.

4. Fred Chartrand, "Mending Fences on the 49th Parallel," *Nova Scotian,* March 5, 2006; Allan Freeman, "Ambassador Has 'Hill to Climb,' to Get Washington's Attention," *G&M,* January 15, 2005; Sheldon Alberts, "Keeping Us on the Map," *NP,* February 11, 2006; Derek H. Burney, *Getting It Done: A Memoir* (Montreal and Kingston: McGill–Queen's University Press, 2005), 65–191.

5. Brian Laghi and Alan Freeman, "Grateful Bush Set to Visit Halifax," *G&M,* November 25, 2004; Blanchard, cited in Alan Freeman, "U.S. Sets About Mending Fences," *G&M,* November 27, 2004.

6. Doug Struck, "Forecast Frosty for U.S.-Canadian Ties," *WP,* November 27, 2004; White House, "President Discusses Strong Relationship with Canada," December 1, 2004, http://www.whitehouse.gov/news/releases; Rick Klein, "Bush Tries to Mend Ties to Canada," December 1, 2004, http://www.boston.com/news/nation/articles; Brian Laghi et al., "The Cozy Summit," *G&M,* December 1, 2004; John Ibbitson, "Tensions Are Easing, and That's a Good Thing," *G&M,* December 1, 2004; Anne

Dawson and Mike Blanchfield, "Bush and Martin Mend the Fences," *NP,* December 1, 2004; George W. Bush, "Remarks at Pier 21," December 1, 2004, available at http://www.esembassycanada.gov; Elisabeth Miller, "Bush in Canada, Declares He'll 'Reach Out' to Friends," *NYT,* December 2, 2004; Dominic Pattern, "One Big Family," *WP,* December 1, 2004; "Late Edition with Wolf Blitzer," CNN, December 5, 2004.

7. Reginald C. Stuart, *United States Expansionism and British North America, 1775–1871* (Chapel Hill: University of North Carolina Press, 1988), chap. 9.

8. James G. Snell, "A Foreign Agent in Washington: George W. Brega, Canada's Lobbyist 1867–1870," *CWH* 26 (March 1980): 53–70; Joe Patterson Smith, "American Republican Leadership and the Movement for the Annexation of Canada in the 1860s," Canadian Historical Association, *Annual Report* (1935), 67–75; David Shi, "Seward's Attempt to Annex British Columbia, 1856–1869," *PHR* 47 (May 1978): 217–38; Donald Marquand Dozer, "Anti-Expansionism during the Johnson Administration," *PHR* 12 (September 1943): 253–75; Doris Dashew, "The Story of an Illusion: The Plan to Trade the *Alabama* Claims for Canada," *CWH* 15 (December 1969): 332–48; S. F. Wise and Robert Craig Brown, *Canada Views the United States: Nineteenth-Century Political Attitudes* (Toronto: Macmillan of Canada, 1967), 98–120.

9. Edward P. Kohn, *This Kindred People: Canadian-American Relations & the Anglo-Saxon Idea, 1895–1903* (Montreal and Kingston: McGill–Queen's University Press, 2005), 37–38, 124, 165–70, 202–3; Gordon T. Stewart, *The American Response to Canada since 1776* (East Lansing: Michigan State University Press, 1992), chaps. 2, 3; Robert L. Beisner, *From the Old Diplomacy to the New, 1865–1900* (New York: Thomas Y. Crowell, 1975), 11, 23–25, 40–42, 125–26; Margaret Beattie Bogue, "To Save the Fish: Canada, the United States, the Great Lakes, and the Joint Commission of 1892," *JAH* 79 (March 1993): 1429–54; Walter LaFeber, *The New Empire: An Interpretation of American Expansion 1860–1898* (Ithaca, N.Y.: Cornell University Press, 1963), 28–41, 112–14, 143–45, 201–8; Robert E. Hannigan, "Reciprocity 1911: Continentalism and American *Weltpolitik,*" *DH* 4 (Winter 1980): 1–18.

10. John Bartlett Brebner, *North Atlantic Triangle: The Interplay of Canada, the United States, and Great Britain* (New Haven, Conn.: Yale University Press, 1945), chap. 14; John Hilliker, *Canada's Department of External Affairs: Volume I, The Early Years, 1909–1946* (Montreal and Kingston: McGill–Queen's University Press, 1990), chaps. 2, 3; R. C. Brown, "Sir Robert Borden: The Great War and Anglo-Canadian Relations," in *Character and Circumstances: Essays in Honor of Donald Creighton,* ed. J. S. Moir (Toronto: Macmillan, 1970), 201–24.

11. Hilliker, *Canada's Department of External Affairs,* chaps. 3, 4; R. D. Cuff and J. L. Granatstein, *Ties That Bind: Canadian-American Relations in Wartime from the Great War to the Cold War* (Toronto: Samuel Stevens Hakkert, 1997), chaps. 1–3; Lawrence Martin, *The Presidents and the Prime Ministers: Washington and Ottawa Face to Face: The Myth of Bilateral Bliss 1867–1982* (Toronto: Doubleday, 1982), 82–90.

12. Roger Frank Swanson, ed., *Canadian-American Summit Diplomacy, 1923–1973: Selected Speeches and Documents* (Toronto: McClelland & Stewart, 1975), 23–28; Moore, "Defining the Undefended;" Hilliker, *Canada's Department of External Affairs,* 93–95.

13. Brebner, *North Atlantic Triangle,* chaps. 15, 16; Swanson, *Canadian-American Summit Diplomacy,* 84–105; Boucher, "Politics of Economic Depression;" Hilliker, *Canada's Department of External Affairs,* chaps. 4–7; Granatstein and Cuff, "The Hyde Park Declaration, 1941: Origins and Significance," *Ties that Bind,* 69–92.

14. John Hilliker and Donald Barry, *Canada's Department of External Affairs: Volume II, Coming of Age, 1946–1968* (Montreal and Kingston: McGill–Queen's University Press, 1995), 3–130; Swanson, *Canadian-American Summit Diplomacy,* 67–94.

15. Cuff and Granatstein, "Corporal Pearson, General Acheson, and the Cold War," in *Ties That Bind,* 113–30; Pearson, Lester B. *Mike: The Memoirs of the Right Honourable Lester B. Pearson.* 2 vols. Toronto: University of Toronto Press, 1948, vol. 1, 244–63, and vol. 2, 25–29; Greg Donaghy, *Tolerant Allies: Canada and the United States 1963–1968* (Montreal and Kingston: McGill–Queen's University Press, 2003), chaps. 9–11.

16. Knowlton Nash, *Kennedy and Diefenbaker: Fear and Loathing across the Undefended Border* (Toronto: McClelland & Stewart, 1990), passim; Swanson, *Canadian-American Summit Diplomacy,* 165–215; Donaghy, *Tolerate Allies,* chap. 1; Mark Kennedy, "Great Friend Theory of Politics," *NP,* November 27, 2004; Norman Hillmer, "Populism Unleashed," *NP,* December 31, 2005.

17. Martin, *Presidents and Prime Ministers,* 240–61; Donaghy, *Tolerant Allies,* chap. 5; Swanson, *Canadian-American Summit Diplomacy,* 165–215.

18. Robert Bothwell, "'Small Problems': Trudeau and the Americans," in *Trudeau's Shadow: The Life and Legacy of Pierre Elliott Trudeau,* ed. Andrew Cohen and J. L. Granatstein (Toronto: Random House of Canada, 1998), 209–21.

19. John Holmes, in Stanley R. TUpper and Douglas Bailey, *Canada and the United States: The Second Hundred Years* (New York: Hawthorn Books, 1967), 8, 134–42; Annette Baker Fox and Alfred O. Hero Jr., "Canada and the United States: Their Binding Frontier," *IO* 28, no. 4 (Autumn 1974): 99–114; Bogdan Kipling, "Border Insecurity: Interview with Chárles Doran," *SH,* June 2, 2002; Canadian Press, "Canada a Tiny Blip on U.S. Radar, Envoy Says," *G&M,* February 27, 2005; "Revisiting Canada's Contribution to Resolving the Iranian Hostage Crisis: On the 25th Anniversary of the Awarding of the Congressional Gold Medal to Former Canadian Ambassador to Iran, Kenneth Taylor," Woodrow Wilson International Center for Scholars, Washington, March 1, 2005, available at http://www.wilsoncenter.org; Canadian Press, "U.S. Legislators Kick Off 'Friends of Canada' Group to Bolster Ties," June 22, 2006, available at http://www.canada.com.

20. Lawrence Martin, "U.S. Sang the Praises of Mulroney," *NP,* August 17, 1999; Lawrence Martin, "The Gipper and His Vision," *NP,* February 5, 2001; Stephen Handelman, "The Rise of North America Inc.: A Perspective from the United States," *Isuma* 1, no. 1 (Spring 2000): 17–33; Richard Gwyn, "Mr. Canuck Goes to Washington," in *The Forty-Ninth Paradox: Canada in North America,* by Richard Gwyn (Toronto: McClelland & Stewart, 1985), 249–66; Drew Fagan, "Martin Won't Go to Reagan's Funeral," *G&M,* June 8, 2004. Reagan's funeral telecast, July 2004; Derek Burney, "Canada-U.S. Relations: The Risk of Complacency, the Need for Engagement," *PO,* December 2003–January 2004, 46–51.

21. Stephen Handelman, "When Clinton Comes Calling," *Time,* October 11, 1999, 29; Canadian Press, "Clinton Cheers Canadian Clarity, Shares Round of Golf with Chrétien," *SH,* December 13, 2000; "Address by William Clinton to the Canadian Parliament," February 23, 1995, "Official Transcripts," State Visit to Canada of President William J. Clinton, February 23 and 24, 1995, Public Affairs Office, Consul General of the United States, Montreal; Kennedy, "Great Friend Theory of Politics."

22. John Gray and Jeff Sallot, "Their Man in Ottawa," *G&M,* October 21, 1995; Robert Russo, "Diplomats Often Had Sympathy for Canada," *MS,* October 15, 1997;

Jim Brinskill, "PM's Strategy Almost Cost Referendum: U.S. Envoy," *NP,* October 30, 2001; James Blanchard, *Behind the Embassy Door: Canada, Clinton and Quebec* (Toronto: McClelland & Stewart, 1998), 225–73.

23. Paul Koring, "Arm's-Length Friends," *Time,* April 7, 1997, 36–38; Andrew Phillips, "The 'Just Right' Summit," *Maclean's,* April 21, 1997, 22–24; Robert Fife, "America's Man Tells It Like It Is," *NP,* January 12, 1999; Sheldon Alberts, "'I'm Not Lloyd Axworthy,' Manley," *NP,* April 12, 2001; Robert Bothwell, "Lloyd Axworthy: Man of Principle," *NP,* September 19, 2000.

24. Raymond Chrétien, "America's Partner for the New Millennium," speech at the Woodrow Wilson International Center for Scholars, April 29, 1999, http://wwics.si.edu/whatsnew/nenews/canam.htm; Allan Gotlieb, "Should Canadians Care Who Wins?" *NP,* November 17, 2000; Christopher Sands, "Canada and the Bush Challenge," *Canada Focus* (Center for Strategic and International Studies) 2, no. 1 (January 2001); Thomas Axworthy, "How to Win Friends and Influence Washington," *G&M,* January 22, 2001; Andrew Phillips, "No More Touchy-Feely," *Maclean's,* January 29, 2001, 26; Andrew Phillips, "A New Cast of Powerful Players," *Maclean's,* February 19, 2001, 32–43.

25. Alexander Rose, "Time Canada Moved Past Axworthyism," *NP,* February 5, 2001; Andrew Malcolm, "A Texan Looks South," *Maclean's,* February 12, 2001, 34; Steven Handelman, "Trading Power for Influence," *Time,* February 19, 2001, 24; Paul Wells, "Bushwacked," *Saturday Night,* June 9, 2001, 25–30; Robert Wolfe, "See You in Washington? A Pluralist Perspective on North American Institutions," *Choices* (Institute for Research on Public Policy) 9, no. 4 (April 2003); Dierdoon Moouafo, Nadia Ponce Moralles, and Jeff Heynen, *Building Cross-Border Links: A Compendium of Canada–U.S. Government Collaboration* (Ottawa: Canada School of Public Service, 2004); Department of Foreign Affairs and International Trade, "Canada's International Policy Statement," April 19, 2005, http://www.dfait-maeci.gc.ca.cip/ips/overview; David Frum, "Returning to the Fold," *NP,* December 7, 2004.

26. John Ward, "John Manley: Self-Described Pragmatist Settles in at Foreign Affairs," *OC,* April 9, 2001; Stephen Handelman, "Colin Powell and Canada," *Time,* February 5, 2001, 2, 27; DeNeen Brown, "And the Winner is . . . Chrétien First to Visit Bush," *WP,* February 4, 2001.

27. "Transcript: Secretary Powell, Canadian Foreign Minister Address Reporters," September 24, 2001, available at http://www.usembassycanada.gov; John Geddes, "Canada's Point Man," *Maclean's,* October 1, 2001, 38, 40; John Geddes, "The Most Important Job," *Maclean's,* December 31, 2001–January 7, 2002, 40, 68–70, 73.

28. John Ibbitson, "Manley's Manoeuvres Keep Canada in Line to Join U.S. 'Club,'" *G&M,* January 16, 2002; Drew Fagan, "Manley's 'Intermestic' World Blends National and Continental," *G&M,* June 5, 2002; Peter Morton, "Martin Strengthened 'Wobbly' Relationship between Bush, PM," *FP,* June 4, 2002.

29. Lawrence Martin, "Grow Up, Mr. Manley: It's Okay to Question the Policies of a U.S. Government," *G&M,* September 7, 2002; Tom Nichols, Chrétien's State of Denial Is Dangerous," *NP,* September 25, 2002; David Crane, "Manley Must Succeed in Keeping Border with U.S. Open," *CH,* February 14, 2003; Shawn McCarthy and Brian Laghi, "Chrétien Jab Stirs Criticism in Ottawa and U.S.," *CH,* May 2, 2003; Diane Francis, "After Chrétien: Let the Healing Begin," *NP,* May 13, 2003.

30. Sheldon Alberts, "PMO Finds No Cash for Canada-U.S.-U.S. Task Force," *NP,* December 3, 2002; Allan Gotlieb, "No Access, No Influence," *NP,* December 3, 2002; Robert Russo, "Manley's Friendship with U.S. Seems Warmer Than PM's," *CH,* De-

cember 6, 2002; Robert Fife, "Bush Gives Mulroney Red-Carpet Treatment," *NP,* December 12, 2002; Sheldon Alberts, "Ottawa Looks to Tighten Relations with U.S.," *NP,* December 13, 2002; Bernard Patry, Chair, *Partners in North America: Advancing Canada's Relations with the United States and Mexico* (Ottawa: Public Works and Government Services, 2002), 281.

31. Walter Russell Mead, "Analyzing Uncle Sam," *Time,* February 3, 2003, 35; Sean M. Maloney, *Are We Really Just Peacekeepers? The Perception versus the Reality of Canadian Involvement in the Iraq War,* Working Paper 2-2003 (Montreal: Institute for Research on Public Policy, 2003).

32. John Ibbitson, "Don't Look Now, but Canadian Nationalism Is Back," *G&M,* September 9, 2003; Mike Allen and Jim VandeHei, "Canada Rejects Strike on Iraq," *WP,* September 10, 2002; David Pugliese and Mike Trickey, "PM's Comments May Damage Relationship," *NP,* September 13, 2002.

33. DeNeen Brown, "Will Canada Support War or Not?" *WP,* January 30, 2003; Mark Hume, "U.S. Expects Canada to Back Action on Iraq," *NP,* February 16, 2003; Julian Beltrame, "Washington Is Watching," *Maclean's,* March 31, 2003, 36–37.

34. Barrie McKenna, "Canada Turns on the Charm to Woo U.S.," *G&M,* February 3, 2003; Jeff Sallot, "Chrétien Faces Caucus Revolt over Iraq," *G&M,* February 11, 2003; Stephen Handelman, "Ottawa's P.R. Blitz," *Time,* February 10, 2003, 38; Drew Fagan, "Image and Substance: Canada South of the Border," *G&M,* March 4, 2003; Les Leyne, "Resentment Mitigates Canada's Instincts to Help a Friend," *SPI,* March 20, 2003; Sheldon Alberts, "Klein Thanks Bush for Going to War against Tyranny," *NP,* March 22, 2004.

35. Paul Cellucci to Economic Club of Toronto, March 25, 2003, available at http://www.usembassy.ca; Joseph Brean and Sheldon Alberts, "U.S. Loses Faith in Canada," *NP,* March 26, 2003; Shawn McCarthy, "White House Consulted Cellucci on Rebuke," *G&M,* March 27, 2003; Robert Fife, "Bush Advisor: Canadians Will Rue PM's Stand," *NP,* April 12, 2003; David M. Malone, "A Question of Style," *LRC* 12, no. 2 (March 2004): 3–5.

36. Robert Fife, "Bush Cancels Visit to Canada," *NP,* April 12, 2003; Brian Russell, "Canada Better Smarten Up—and Quick," *CH,* March 30, 2003; Brian Laghi, "U.S. Backlash Seen Growing," *G&M,* March 27, 2003; Robert Fife, "White House Rebukes Prime Minister," *NP,* May 29, 2003; Robert Fife, "Only Chrétien's Departure Will Normalize Relations with U.S. Liberal MP Says," *NP,* March 29, 2003; Michael Friscolanti, "It's Business as Usual, Promises [U.S.] Commerce Head," *NP,* April 4, 2003; Paul Wells, "Waiting for Him to Go," *Time,* April 7, 2003, 76; Sheldon Alberts, "Left and Right Attack PM for Criticizing Bush," *FP,* May 26, 2003.

37. Drew Fagan, "How to Stay the Slippery Slide of Canada-U.S. Relations," *G&M,* April 1, 2003; Irwin Block, "'Squall' Will Blow Over, Says Ambassador to U.S.," *Canada.comNews,* April 1, 2003; Sinclair Stewart, "Warm U.S. Welcome Cheers CEOs," *G&M,* April 8, 2003; Drew Fagan, "U.S. Fears Unstable Canada," *G&M,* June 9, 2003.

38. Robert Fife, "Repair Canada-U.S. Rift, Think Tank Tells Martin," *FP,* October 30, 2003; Sheldon Alberts, "U.S. Expects 'Rejuvenated Ties' under Martin," *NP,* November 19, 2003; Sandra Cordon, "Martin too Cosy with Americans: Axworthy," October 11, 2003, available at http://cnews.canoe.ca; James Ferrabee, "Prime Minister Martin Gets His First Lesson in U.S.-Canada Relations and Learns We Are Not among the Favoured Nations in Washington," December 15, 2003, http://www.irpp.org/ferrabee; Drew Fagan, "Martin Hails Capture as Ottawa's Tone Shifts," *G&M,* Decem-

ber 15, 2003; "Remarks by President Bush and Prime Minister Martin, in a Photo Opportunity," January 13, 2004, available at http://www.usembassycanada.gov; James Travers, "A Fine First Impression," *TS,* January 14, 2004; Mark Blanchard, "New Canadian Leader Signals Thaw in Ties with U.S.," *WT,* January 15, 2004.

39. Jonathan Gatehouse, "Border Blues," *Maclean's,* December 22, 2003–January 19, 2004; Blanchard, "New Canadian Leader Signals Thaw"; "Notes for an Address by the Honourable Bill Graham, Minister of Foreign Affairs, Kroeger Leadership Forum," February 10, 2004, available at http://webapps.dfait-maeci.gc.ca; "Address by Prime Minister Paul Martin on . . . His Visit to Washington, D.C.," April 29, 2004, available at http://www.pm.gc.ca/eng; Stephen Handelman, "Wooing the Neighbours," *Time,* May 3, 2004; John Manley, "Memo to Martin: Engage Canada-U.S. Relations as One of PM's 'Overriding Responsibilities,'" *PO,* May 2004, 5–9.

40. Arnold Beichman, "Shifting Northern Winds," *WT,* June 18, 2004; Danielle Goldfarb, "Note to the Prime Minister: Put Canada-U.S. Relations First," *Howe Report,* July 2004.

41. Jeffrey Simpson, "On Foreign Policy, Kerry Is Not Far from Bush," *G&M,* March 3, 2004; Jonathan Gatehouse, "The Know-It-All Neighbour," *Maclean's,* May 3, 2004; Jonathan Gatehouse, "Taking the Pulse," *Maclean's,* May 3, 2004; Graeme Hamilton, "Howard Dean Greeted as Hero in Anti-Bush Quebec, *NP,* October 27, 2004; Mike Blanchfield, "Canadians Would Give Kerry a Clear Victory," *VS,* October 30, 2004; Keith Leslie, "PM Downplays Importance of U.S. Elections to Canadians," *SH,* October 31, 2004; Jonathan Gatehouse, "Are We Having Fun Yet? Why It's Time to Be Friends Again," *Maclean's,* December 6, 2004; John Geddes, "Hard Truths," *Maclean's,* December 6, 2004, 24–30.

42. Doug Struck, "U.S.-Canada Relations Seen Growing Chilly," *WP,* March 4, 2005; Sheldon Alberts, "Bush Won't Call PM," *NP,* March 2, 2005; Andrew Cohen, "The U.S. Is in No Mood for This Nonsense," *NP,* March 2, 2005; Christopher Sands, "Canada as a Minor Ally: Operational Considerations for Relations with the United States," paper prepared for Canadian Crude Oil Conference, Center for Strategic and International Studies, Washington, September 5, 2003.

43. Jeff Heynen and John Higginbotham, *Advancing Canadian Interests in the United States: A Practical Guide for Canadian Public Officials* (Ottawa: Canada School of Public Services, 2004); David Zussman, "Canada-U.S. Ties Are More Binding than We Thought," *OC,* January 31, 2005; conversations with Christopher Sands of the Institute for Strategic and International Studies, Washington.

44. Jennifer Loven, "U.S. Unveils New Pact with Canada, Mexico," *WP,* March 23, 2005; Peter Baker, "U.S., Mexico, Canada Agree to Increase Cooperation," *WP,* March 24, 2005; Brian Laghi, "Martin, Bush Stand Together," *G&M,* March 24, 2005; B. Peschard-Sverdurp, "North American Cooperative Security Act (NACSA) Was Proposed in the U.S. Congress," *America's Program Newsletter* (Center for Security and International Studies) 4, no. 5 (May 2004): 4; James M. Lindsay, *The End of the American Century,* Foundation Occasional Paper Series, vol. 1, ed. Michael K. Hawes (Ottawa: Foundation for Educational Exchange between Canada and United States of America, 2004); Christopher Sands, "Different Paths Leading from Cancún," *North American Integration Monitor* (Center for Strategic and International Studies) 3, no. 2 (May 2006).

45. Ipsos Reid, "A Public Opinion Survey of Canadians and Americans," prepared for Canada Institute at Woodrow Wilson International Center for Scholars and Canada

Institute on North American Issues, October 2006, available at http://www.wilson center.org and http://thecanadainstitute.ca.

Epilogue: Unavoidable Interdependence

1. Emily Heard, ed., *Toward a North American Community?* Conference Report (Washington, D.C.: Woodrow Wilson International Center for Scholars, 2002), available at http://www.wilsoncenter.org; Council on Foreign Relations, *NAFTA: What Next? Council Joins Leading Canadians and Mexicans to Launch Independent Task Force on the Future of North America* (New York: Council on Foreign Relations, 2004), available at http://www.cfr.org; Americas Society, "Policy Resources," in *Building North America,* available at http://www.americassociety.org.

2. Denis Trevor Adams; "Best Friends and 'Bastards,'" *Business Voice,* June 2003, 10–13; Thomas S. Axworthy, "On Being an Ally: Why Virtue Is Not Reward Enough," paper presented at North American Integration Conference, Ottawa, April 1, 2004, available at http://www.irpp.org; Hugh Segal, "The Politics of Enhanced Canada-U.S. Relations," paper presented at Canada-US Relations Project Conference, Centre for Global Studies, University of Victoria, Victoria, November 27, 2004.

3.. EKOS, "Presentation to Media Partners," Ottawa, February 21, 2003; EKOS, "Bushwacking and Other Ingredients of Canadian Outlook on the USA," *Time,* October 25, 2004; EKOS, "Canada and the New American Empire," Centre for Global Studies, University of Victoria, Victoria, November 27, 2004; Luiza Ch. Savage, "All for One?" *Maclean's,* September 12, 2005, 36–39; Ken Alexander, with Michael Adams, Stephen Handelman, Linda McQuaig, and Pamela Wallin, "Is Canada Disappearing from the World Stage?" *Walrus Online Debate,* October 28, 2004, available at http://www.walrus magazine.com.

4. Department of Foreign Affairs and International Trade, "The Challenge of Communicating Canada's Message in the USA," issue paper, 2002, available at http://www.dfait-maeci.gc.ca; Allan Gotlieb, "Why Not a Grand Bargain with the U.S.?" *NP,* September 11, 2002; Perrin Beatty, "North American Partnership Inevitable," *FP,* September 12, 2002; Terry Colli, "Canada-U.S. Relations—A 21st Century Partnership (and What It Means for U.S.)," paper presented at Ottawa Public Policy Forum, Ottawa, May 27, 2003, courtesy of the author.

5. Joel Swerdlow, "Global Culture," *National Geographic,* August 1999, 4–89; Reginald C. Stuart, "Death of the Nation-State? Global Mass Culture in the Twenty-First Century: A Roundtable Discussion," *ARCS* 31 (Autumn 2001): 427–40.

6. Randy William Widdis, "The Historical Geography of the Canadian-American Borderlands, 1784–1090: Conceptual and Methodological Challenges," paper presented at ACSUS Colloquium in Canada, Vancouver, October 7, 2004, courtesy of the author.

7. Robert Russo, "New England States Fear Crisis in Canada," *MS,* June 5, 1997; Chris Morris, "Governor Backs Border Stance," *CH,* October 5, 1999; Amy Smith and David Jackson, "Premiers, Governors Stress Unity," *CH,* July 18–19, 2000.

8. "Canadian, U.S. Families Gather to Remember Lost Fishermen," *CH,* May 9, 2003; Associated Press, "Maine Governor to Lead March Trade Mission to Nova Scotia," *CH,* January 13, 1999; Roger Taylor, "Tapping into the Massachusetts Connection," *SH,* May 16, 1999; Richard Foot, "Premiers Aim to Bypass PM on U.S.," *NP,* July 8, 2003; "Welcome to the Province of Maine," *Maine Times,* October 5–11, 2000, 4–6;

Steven Frank, "Oceans of Opportunity," *Time,* July 10, 2000, 28–29; "New England Atlantic Canada Business Council," available at http://www.necbc.org; Theresa M. Maggio, "Up the St. Croix, with a Paddle," *NYT,* August 8, 1999; Katherine Ashenburg, "What's Doing in St. John's," *NYT,* August 8, 1999; Jan Matthews, ed., "Atlantica: Two Countries, One Region," *Ideas Matter* (Fall 2004).

9. Andrea Mandel-Campbell, "U.S. Market Called Maritimes' Best Hope," *FP,* April 9, 2002; Trevor J. Adams, "What Now?" *Business Voice,* November 2001, 8–11; Canadian Press, "Terror Attacks Could Cost Atlantic Region 23,000 Jobs, Report Says," *CH,* October 25, 2001; Janice Stuckless, "Border Patrol," *Atlantic Business Magazine* 15, no. 6 (2004): 36–39; CBC, "Borderline," October 19, 2004, 22–26, http://halifax2.cbc.ca/features/borderline; Shawna Richer, "Canadians with That Long-Distance Feeling," *G&M,* June 21, 2004.

10. Dean R. Louder, "Le Quebec et la Franco-Americaine: A Mother Country in the Making," in *The Northeastern Borderlands: Four Centuries of Interaction,* ed. Stephen Hornsby (Fredericton, N.B.: Acadiensis Press and Canadian-American Center, University of Maine, 1989), 127–36; Ben Levine, "Waking Up French: The Repression and Renaissance of the French in New England," http://wakingupfrench.com; Earl H. Fry, "Quebec's Relations with the United States," *ARCS* 32, no. 2 (2002): 323–42; Robert Russo, "Documents Reveal PQ Pondered U.S. Option," *MS,* October 14, 1997; Graham Fraser, "Mr. Bouchard Comes to Washington," *G&M,* March 5, 1998; Robert Russo, "Bouchard Gets Support from Massachusetts," *MS,* May 19, 1998; Doug Saunders, "Quebec Expanding Missions in the U.S.," *G&M,* May 20, 2002.

11. Lise Bissonette, "Washington Only Plays Dumb about Canada," *G&M,* April 21, 1990; Jeffrey Simpson, "In and Out of the Mind of the U.S. Eagle, *G&M,* May 5, 1990; Christopher Odgen, "Crossed-Fingers Policy," *Time,* June 18, 1990, 21; Charles Doran, "Will Canada Unravel," *FA* 75, no. 5 (September–October 1996): 97–109; Robert Russo, "Quebec Separation Threat Ho-Hum for U.S. Politicians, *VS,* September 26, 1996; "Congressional Hearings on Canadian Unity," September 1996, http://www.uni.ca/congress.html; Peter Morici, "A Sovereign Quebec and U.S. National Interests," *ARCS* 27, no. 1 (Spring 1997): 143–49; Joan Bryden, "Quebec's U.S. Ad Campaign Falls on Deaf Ears," *NP,* January 12, 2000; Bogdan Kipling, "Sagging Quebec Separatism Brings Comfort in Washington," *CH,* April 3, 2001.

12. Stephen Handelman, "Menage a Deux," *Time,* August 5, 2002, 29; James Christie and Rheal SeGuin, "Quebec, New York Plot Joint Bid for Olympics," *G&M,* January 9, 2003; Alison Gregor, "Charest Courts U.S. Audience," *CH,* October 3, 2003; Ross Marowits, "Cross-Border Business Connections Bind Quebec and Upstate New York," March 13, 2004, available at http://www.canada.com; Albert Juneau, "Quebec–New York Trade Corridors Initiatives," in *New North American Reality,* no. 2004-09p.

13. Michael Bliss, "Heartland dynasties," *NP,* June 5, 1999; John Ibbitson, "Ontario Growing Closer to U.S.," *G&M,* October 19, 1999; Stephen Handelman, "The Ties That Really Bind," *Time,* November 15, 1999, 39; Council of Great Lakes Governors, "Overview," http://www.cgig/overview.html; Robert Benzie, "Harris, Landry Sign Great Lakes Water Accord," *NP,* June 19, 2001; "Two Nations," *Time,* July 10, 2003, 20–29; Jim Olson and Ralph Pentland, "Decision Time: Water Diversion Policy in the Great Lakes Basin," One Issue, Two Voices Series, Canada Institute at Woodrow Wilson International Center for Scholars, Washington, 2004, http://www.wilsoncenter.org/topics/pubs/ACF1D93.pdf.

14. Adam Killick, "Western Premiers Join U.S. Governors to Improve Relations," *NP,* June 14, 1999; Peter Morton, "Klein Takes Campaign to U.S. Senators," *NP,* June 14, 2001; Charlie Gillis, "Albertans Plan Rallies to Show Support for U.S.-Led War," *NP,* March 29, 2003; Tom Olsen, "Alberta MLAs Speak Out on Iraq," *Calgary Herald,* April 5, 2003; Don Martin, "Klein in Washington: A Sight to Behold," *Calgary Herald,* June 26, 2003; Stephen Handelman, "Whose Calling the Shots?" *Time,* June 11, 2001, 55; Colin Robertson, "Alberta in America: A Perspective from California," Notes for Remarks to the Calgary Chamber of Commerce, May 14, 2004, courtesy of the author; Paul Koring, "PM No Help in Border Spat, Klein Says in Washington," *G&M,* March 23, 2005.

15. Miro Cernetig, "Cascadia: A Western State of Mind," *G&M,* January 25, 1992; Miro Cernetig, "The Cascadia Solution," *Report on Business Magazine,* January 1995, 32–34; Paul Schell and John Hamer, "Cascadia: The New Binationalism of Western Canada and the U.S. Pacific Northwest," in *Identities in North America: The Search for Community,* ed. Robert D. Earle and John D. Wirth (Stanford, Calif.: Stanford University Press, 1995), 133–56, 242–43; Alan J. Artibise, "Cascadian Adventures: Shared Visions, Strategic Alliances, and Ingrained Barriers in a Transborder Region" and "On Brotherly Terms: Canadian-American Relations West of the Rockies," papers presented at symposium, University of Washington, Seattle, September 12–14, 1996, courtesy of the authors; "The International Mobility and Trade Corridor Project," 1997 http://www.wcog.Org/imtcbriefing.html.

16. Robert D. Kaplan, "Travels into America's Future," *Atlantic Monthly,* August 1998, 37–61; Elizabeth Nickson, "The Last Best Place," *NP,* July 7, 2001; Discovery Institute, "Cascadia," 1999, http://www.cascadiaproject.org.background.html; Susan E. Clarke, "Regional and Transnational Discourse: The Politics of Ideas and Economic Development in Cascadia, available at http://www.spaef.com; useful summary in Lawrence Douglas Taylor Hansen, "The Character of Non-Governmental Transborder Organizations in the Cascadia Region of North America," *Revista Mexicana de Estudios Canadiansis* 2 (2002): 11–37; "What Exactly Is Cascadia," http://www.geocities.com/rinfingers/cascadia2.html; Matthew S. Mingus, "Transnationalism and Subnational Paradiplomacy: Is This Perforated Sovereignty or Are Democracy and Civil Society Just Reaching across Borders?" paper presented to Sixteenth Annual Conference of the Public Administration theory Network, Anchorage, June 20, 2003, http://www.patnet2003 alaska.edu/pdf/papers/mingus.

17. "What Border?" *Time,* July 10, 2000, 20–27; Tom Arnold, "Almost Half Foresee Canada, U.S. in Union within a Decade," *NP,* June 4, 2001; Richard Simeon, George Hoberg, and Keith Banting, "Globalization, Fragmentation, and the Social Contract," in *Degrees of Freedom: Canada and the United States in a Changing World,* ed. Keith Banting, George Hoberg, and Richard Simeon (Montreal and Kingston: McGill–Queen's University Press, 1997), 389–416.

18. Associated Press, "A Border Town's Isolation after 9/11," MSNBC News, October 30, 2002, available at http://www.msnbc.com.news; April Lingen and Robert Benzie, "Canada-U.S. Ties Still Strong, Pataki Says," *FP,* April 10, 2003; Stephen Handelman, "Side-Door Diplomats," *Time,* April 21, 2003, 38; John Higginbotham and Jeffrey Heynen, "Managing through Networks: The State of Canada–US Relations," in *Setting Priorities Straight: Canada among Nations 2004,* ed. David Carment, Fen Osler Hampson, and Norman Hillmer (Montreal and Kingston: McGill–Queen's University Press, 2005), 123–40; Americas Society, "Building North America," available at http://www

.theamericassociety.org; Roy MacGregor, "Town Is a Toy America That's Only Reachable by Going through Canada," *G&M,* February 9, 2004; Robert McClure, "Throttle on Northwest Power Use Wide Open," *SPI,* March 10, 2004, available at http://seattlepi.nwsource.com.

19. Stephen de Boer, "Canadian Provinces, US States and North American Integration: Bench Warmers or Key Players," *Choices: Canada's Options in North America* (Institute for Research on Public Policy) 8, no. 4 (November 2002); Earl Fry, "The Role of Subnational Governments in North American Integration," in *New North American Reality,* no. 2004-09d.

20. Michael Bliss, "Attacks Hasten the End of Our Border," *NP,* September 29, 2001; Stephen E. Flynn, "Inside the Perimeter," *FP,* October 3, 2001; Drew Fagan, "It's the Year 2025. There Is No U.S. Border. Has Canada Become the 51st State?" *G&M,* March 16, 2002; Wendy Dobson, *Shaping the Future of the North American Economic Space: A Framework for Action,* Border Paper 166 (Toronto: C. D. Howe Institute, (June 2002); James Baxter, "Integration with U.S. Inevitable, Beatty Says," *NP,* March 7, 2003; Policy Research Initiative, "Strengthening the North American Partnership: Scenarios for the Future," Conferences Summary, May 12–13, 2001, available at http://www.policyresearch.gc.ca; Allan Gotlieb, "Foremost Partner: The Conduct of Canada-US Relations," in *Canada among Nations: Coping with the American Colossus,* ed. David Carment et al. (Toronto: Oxford University Press, 2003), 19–31; EKOS, "Rethinking North American Integration: Marketplace May Not Equal Community: Not 'Here' Yet?" April 3, 2002, available at http://www.ekos.com; John N. McDougall, *Drifting Together: The Political Economy of Canada-US Integration* (Toronto: Broadview, 2006), 299–320; Higginbotham and Heynen, "Managing through Networks"; Robert Bothwell, "Canadian-American Relations: Old Fire, New Ice?" in *Setting Priorities Straight,* ed. Carment, Hampson, and Hillmer, 123–40, 141–54.

21. Robert Wolfe, "See You in Washington? A Pluralist Perspective on North American Institutions," *Choices* 9, no. 4 (April 2003); Drew Fagan, "North America's Remarkable Reluctance to Build a Community," *G&M,* May 27, 2003; Andre Downs, "The North American Linkages Project: Focusing the Research Agenda," paper presented to Association for Canadian Studies in the United States 17th Biennial Conference, Portland, November 2003; Gary C. Hufbauer and Jeffrey J. Scott, *The Prospects for Deeper North American Economic Integration: A U.S. Perspective,* Border Paper 195 (Toronto: C. D. Howe Institute, 2004); John J. Noble, "Fortress America or Fortress North America?" paper for Institute for Research on Public Policy Conference, North American Integration: Migration, Trade and Security, Ottawa, April 1–2, 2004; Stephen Blank et al., "Mapping the New North American Reality Project," in "North-American Integration" issue of *PO* 25, no. 6 (June/July 2004): 28–61. Nationalist views include Richard Gwyn, "Anyone Notice? We Become More American Every Day," *SH,* January 6, 2002; Lawrence Martin, "We Always Stood Up to Them," *G&M,* February 20, 2003; James Laxer, "Where Have All the Tories Gone?" *G&M,* April 9, 2002; Mel Hurtig, "'The Big Idea,' the 'Grand Bargain,' Our Next PM and the Vanishing Country," speech to 72nd Annual Couchiching Conference, August 8, 2002, available at http://www.canadiandimension.mh.ca/extra; Mac Lee, "Why a Canada-US Customs Union Is a Bad Idea," *Canadian Dimension,* January/February 2005, available at http://www.canadiandimension.mh.ca/extra.

22. J. L. Granatstein, "The Importance of Being Less Earnest: Promoting Canada's National Interests through Tighter Ties with the U.S.," C. D. Howe Institute Benefac-

tors Lecture, Toronto, 2003; Donald Barry, "Managing Canada-U.S. Relations in the Post–9/11 Era: Do We Need a Big Idea?" *Policy Papers on the Americas* (Center for Strategic and International Studies) 14, no. 11 (November 2003); Robert Pastor, "North America's Second Decade," *FA* 83 (January/February 2004): 124–35; Daniel Schwanen, "Deeper, Broader: A Roadmap for a Treaty of North America," in *The Art of the State,* ed. Thomas Courchene, Donald J. Savoie, and Daniel Schwanen (Montreal: Institute for Research on Public Policy, 2004), vol. 2.

23. The 105th American Assembly, "Renewing the U.S.-Canada Relationship," February 5–6, 2005, http://www.americanassembly.org/programs.dir/prog; John P. Manley, Pedro Aspe, and William F. Weld, *Creating a North American Community;* Chairmen's Statement, Independent Task Force on the Future of North America (New York: Council on Foreign Relations, 2005), available at http://www.cfr.org; Office of the Prime Minister, Canada, "Security and Prosperity Partnership Established," March 23, 2005, available at http://www.pmgc.ca.eng/news; "Security and Prosperity of North America," Office of the Press Secretary, White House, Washington, March 23, 2005, http://www.spp.gov/spp/factsheet.asp; John Ibbitson, "Can This Friendship Be Fixed? Should It Be?" *G&M,* December 26, 2005; Dwight Mason, "The Canada–United States Relationship: Is There a View from Washington?" *Commentary: A Publication of the Royal Canadian Military Institute,* December 2005, available at http://www.rcmi.org.

24. "Canada–United States: The Secure Flow of People at the Canada-U.S. Border," August 2005, available at http://www.dfait-maeci.gc.ca; Canadian Press, "Wilson Warns of Passport 'Wedge,'" *CH,* May 16, 2006; Steven Edwards, "Mexican Border Crackdown Could Affect Canada," CanWest News Service, May 16, 2006, available at http://www.canada.com; Stephen Handelman, "May I See Your Passport?" *Time,* October 10, 2005, 28; Associated Press, "Neighbors Will Need Papers to Enter U.S.," *WP,* September 2, 2005.

25. Beth Gorham, "U.S. Passport Plan Ditched," CNEWS, January 17, 2006, available at http://cnews.canoe.ca.cnews/canada; Ian Austin, "Passport Rule 'War on Tourism,'" *CH,* April 15, 2006 (from *NYT*); Terry Pedwell, "Ottawa to Address New Travel-Security Law in Meeting with U.S.," *G&M,* April 18, 2006.

26. Jacob Resnick, "McHugh Has Harsh Words for Border Reforms," *Adirondack Daily Enterprise,* May 23, 2006; Tom Robertson, "Border Towns Want Changes to 2008 Passport Requirements," Minnesota Public Radio, June 2, 2006, http://minnesota publicradio.org...passports; Beth Gorham, "U.S. Congressman Blasts Canada on Terrorism: Supports Immigrant Ban," Canadian Press, June 9, 2006, available at http://www .canada.com.

27. Policy Research Institute, *North American Linkages: The Emergence of Cross-Border Regions between Canada and the United States: Roundtable Synthesis Report* (Ottawa: Government of Canada, 2006), available at http://policyresearch.gc.ca. This report is a summary synthesis of conferences in Canadian cities.

Bibliography

Abella, Irving, and Harold Troper. *None Is Too Many: Canada and the Jews of Europe 1933–1948.* New York: Random House, 1983.

Adams, Michael. *Fire and Ice: The United States, Canada and the Myth of Converging Values.* Toronto: Penguin Canada, 2003.

Aitken, Hugh. *American Capital and Canadian Resources.* Cambridge, Mass.: Harvard University Press, 1961.

Allen, Frederick Lewis. *Only Yesterday.* New York: Harper, 1931.

Anastakis, Dimitry. *Auto Pact: Creating a Borderless North American Auto Industry, 1960–1971.* Toronto: University of Toronto Press, 2005.

Angus, Henry F., ed. *British Columbia and the United States: The North Pacific Slope from Fur Trade to Aviation.* New York: Russell & Russell, 1970.

Audley, Paul. *Canada's Cultural Industries: Broadcasting, Publishing, Records and Film.* Toronto: James Lorimer & Company, 1983.

Axline, Andrew, et al. *Continental Community? Independence and Integration in North America.* Toronto: McClelland & Stewart, 1974.

Axworthy, Thomas S., ed. *Our American Cousins: The United States through Canadian Eyes.* Toronto: James Lorimer, 1987.

Ayers, Jeffrey. *Defying Conventional Wisdom: Political Movements and Popular Contention against North American Free Trade.* Toronto: University of Toronto Press, 1988.

Azzi, Stephen. *Walter Gordon and the Rise of Canadian Nationalism.* Toronto: Macmillan, 1971.

Backhouse, Constance, and David Flaherty, eds. *Challenging Times: The Women's Movement in Canada and the United States.* Montreal and Kingston: McGill–Queen's University Press, 1992.

Banting, Keith, George Hoberg, and Richard Simeon, eds. *Degrees of Freedom: Canada and the United States in a Changing World.* Montreal and Kingston: McGill–Queen's University Press, 1997.

Barlow, Maude, and Bruce Campbell, *Take Back the Nation: Meeting the Threat of NAFTA.* Toronto: Key Porter, 1993.

Beisner, Robert. *From the Old Diplomacy to the New, 1865–1900*. New York: Thomas Y. Crowell, 1975.

Bemis, Samuel Flagg. *Jay's Treaty: A Study in Commerce and Diplomacy,* 2nd ed. New Haven, Conn.: Yale University Press, 1962 (orig. pub. 1923).

Bennett, John W., and Seena B. Kohl. *Settling the Canadian-American West, 1890–1915: Pioneer Adaptation and Community Building.* Lincoln: University of Nebraska Press, 1995.

Berton, Pierre. *Hollywood's Canada: The Americanization of Our National Image.* Toronto: McClelland & Stewart, 1975.

Bircha, Karel Denis. *The American Farmer and the Canadian West 1896–1941.* Lawrence: University Press of Kansas, 1968.

Blanchard, James. *Behind the Embassy Door: Canada, Clinton and Quebec.* Toronto: McClelland & Stewart, 1998.

Blank, Stephen, and Jerry Haar. *Making NAFTA Work: U.S. Firms and the New North American Business Environment.* Coral Gables, Fla.: North-South Center Press, 1998.

Bloomfield, Maxwell. *Alarm and Diversion: The American Mind through American Magazines.* New York: Basic Books, 1967.

Brown, Robert Craig. *Canada's National Policy 1883–1900.* Princeton, N.J.: Princeton University Press, 1964.

Boileau, John. *Half-Hearted Enemies: Nova Scotia, New England and the War of 1812.* Halifax: Formac Publishing, 2005.

Boorstin, Daniel J. *The Americans: The Democratic Experience.* New York: Random House, 1974.

———. *The Image: A Guide to Pseudo Events in America.* New York: Vintage Books, 1961.

Bourne, Kenneth. *Britain and the Balance of Power in North America, 1815–1908.* Berkeley: University of California Press, 1967.

Bowlby, Rachel. *Carried Away: The Invention of Modern Shopping.* New York: Columbia University Press, 1999.

Brault, Gerard. *The French-Canadian Heritage in New England.* Hanover, N.H.: University Press of New England, 1986.

Brebner, John Bartlett. *North Atlantic Triangle: The Interplay of Canada, the United States, and Great Britain.* New Haven, Conn.: Yale University Press, 1945.

Breen, David. *The Canadian Ranching Frontier and the Prairie West.* Toronto: University of Toronto Press, 1983.

Brison, Jeffrey D. *Rockefeller, Carnegie & Canada: American Philanthropy and the Arts & Letters in Canada.* Montreal and Kingston: McGill–Queen's University Press, 2005.

Brown, Dona, *Inventing New England: Regional Tourism in the Nineteenth Century.* Washington, D.C.: Smithsonian Institution Press, 1995.

Brown, Robert C. *Canada's National Policy 1883–1900: A Study in Canadian-American Relations.* Princeton, N.J.: Princeton University Press, 1964.

Bukowcyzk, J. T., et al., eds. *Permeable Border: The Great Lakes Basin as a Transnational Region, 1650–1990.* Calgary and Pittsburgh: University of Calgary Press and University of Pittsburgh Press, 2005.

Burrill, Gary. *Away: Maritimers in Massachusetts, Ontario, and Alberta.* Montreal and Kingston: McGill–Queen's University Press, 1992.

Campbell, Colin, and William Christian. *Parties, Leaders and Ideologies in Canada.* Toronto: McGraw Hill Ryerson, 1996.

Campbell, William A. B., and Richard K. Melchin. *Western Security and the Strategic Defence Initiative.* Vancouver: Canadian Conservative Centre, 1986.

Carroll, Francis M. *A Good and Wise Measure: The Search for the Canadian-American Boundary, 1783–1842.* Toronto: University of Toronto Press, 2001.

Carver, George A., Jr., et al. *The View From the South: A U.S. Perspective on Key Bilateral Issues Affecting U.S.-Canadian Relations.* Washington, D.C.: Georgetown University and Center for Strategic and International Studies, 1985.

Chernomas, Robert, and Ardeshir Sepehri, eds. *How to Choose? A Comparison of US and Canadian Health Care Systems.* Amityville, N.Y.: Byword, 1998.

Clarkson, Stephen. *An Independent Foreign Policy for Canada?* Toronto: McClelland & Stewart, 1968.

———. *Uncle Sam and US: Globalization, Neoconservatism, and the Canadian State.* Washington and Toronto: Woodrow Wilson Center Press and University of Toronto Press, 2002.

Classen, George H. *Thrust and Counterthrust: The Genesis of the Canada–United States Boundary, 1783–1842.* Toronto: University of Toronto Press, 2001.

Clausen, Christopher. *Faded Mosaic: The Emergence of Post-Cultural America.* Chicago: Ivan R. Dee, 2000.

Coates, Kenneth, and William R. Morrison. *The Alaska Highway in World War II: The U.S. Army of Occupation in Canada's Northwest.* Toronto: University of Toronto Press, 1992.

Cohen, Andrew. *While Canada Slept: How We Lost Our Place in the World.* Toronto: McClelland & Stewart, 2003.

Cohen, Andrew and J. L. Granatstein, eds. *Trudeau's Shadow: The Life and Legacy of Pierre Elliott Trudeau.* Toronto: Random House of Canada, 1998.

Collins, Richard. *Culture, Communications & National Identity: The Case of Canadian Television.* Toronto: University of Toronto Press, 1990.

Cook, Ramsay. *The Maple Leaf Forever: Essays on Nationalism and Politics in Canada.* Toronto: Macmillan, 1971.

Cooper, Andrew F. *Canadian Foreign Policy: Old Habits and New Directions.* Scarborough: Prentice Hall Allyn Bacon, 1997.

Corbett, P. E. *The Settlement of Canadian-American Disputes: A Critical Study of Methods and Results.* New Haven, Conn.: Yale University Press, 1937.

Corey, Albert B. *The Crisis of 1830–1842 in Canadian American Relations.* New Haven, Conn.: Yale University Press, 1941.

Cowen, Tyler. *The Promise of Global Culture.* Cambridge, Mass.: Harvard University Press, 2000.

Crouse, Eric R. *Revival in the City: The Impact of American Evangelists in Canada 1884–1914.* Montreal and Kingston: McGill–Queen's University Press, 2005.

Cuff, R. D., and J. L. Granatstein. *Ties That Bind: Canadian-American Relations in Wartime from the Great War to the Cold War.* Toronto: Samuel Stevens Hakkert, 1997.

Dale, Stephen. *Lost in the Suburbs: A Political Travelogue.* Toronto: Stoddart Books, 1999.

Damon-Moore, Helen, *Magazines for the Millions: Gender and Commerce in the "Ladies Home Journal" and the "Saturday Evening Post."* Albany: State University of New York Press, 1994.

Daniels, Roger. *Asian America: Chinese and Japanese in the United States Since 1850.* Seattle: University of Washington Press, 1990.

———. *Concentration Camps North America: Japanese in the United States and Canada during World War II.* Malabar: Krieger Publishing, 1993.
———. *The Politics of Prejudice: Anti-Japanese Movement in California and the Struggle for Japanese Exclusion.* Los Angeles: University of California Press, 1970.
Davies, Christie. *Jokes and Their Relation to Society.* Berlin: Mouton de Gruyer, 1998.
———. *The Mirth of Nations.* New Brunswick, N.J.: Transaction, 2002.
Davies, Harold. *An International Community on the St. Croix 1640–1930.* Orono: University of Maine Press, 1950.
Davies, Robertson. *Murther & Walking Spirits.* Toronto: Viking Penguin, 1991.
DePalma, Anthony. *Here: A Biography of the New American Continent.* New York: Public Affairs, 2001.
Dimeglio, John E. "*Vaudeville U.S.A.*" Bowling Green: University Press of Kentucky, 1973.
Dobson, John M. *A History of American Enterprise.* Englewood Cliffs, N.J.: Prentice Hall, 1988.
Doern, Bruce, and Brian Tomlin. *Faith and Fear: The Free Trade Story.* Toronto: University of Toronto Press, 1991.
Donaghy, Greg. *Tolerant Allies: Canada and the United States 1963–1968.* Montreal and Kingston: McGill–Queen's University Press, 2003.
Doran, Charles F. *Why Canadian Unity Matters and Why Americans Care: Democratic Pluralism at Risk.* Toronto: University of Toronto Press, 2001.
———, ed. *Forgotten Partnership: U.S.-Canada Relations Today.* Toronto: Fitzhenry and Whiteside, 1984.
Doyle, James. *North of America: Images of Canada in the Literature of the United States 1775–1900.* Toronto: ECW Press, 1983.
———, ed. *Yankees in Canada: A Collection of 19th Century Travel Narratives.* Toronto: ECW Press, 1980.
Drache, Daniel. *Borders Matter: Homeland Security and the Search for North America.* Halifax: Fernwood Publishing, 2004.
Duggan, William Redman. *Our Neighbors Upstairs: The Canadians.* Chicago: Nelson Hall, 1979.
Dziuban, Stanley. *Military Relations Between the United States and Canada, 1939–1945.* Washington, D.C.: Office of the Chief of Military History, Department of the Army, 1959.
Earle, Robert D., and John D. Wirth, eds. *Identities in North America: The Search for Community.* Stanford, Calif.: Stanford University Press, 1995.
Eayrs, James. *In Defence of Canada: From the Great War to the Great Depression.* Toronto: University of Toronto Press, 1967.
Edgar, Alastair D., and David G. Haglund. *The Canadian Defence Industry in the New Global Environment.* Montreal and Kingston: McGill–Queen's University Press, 1995.
Egnal, Marc. *Divergent Paths: How Culture and Institutions Have Shaped North American Growth.* New York: Oxford University Press, 1996.
Ellis, L. E. *Reciprocity 1911: A Study in Canadian-American Relations.* New Haven, Conn.: Yale University Press, 1939.
Elofson, Warren M. *Frontier Cattle Ranching in the Land and Times of Charlie Russell.* Montreal and Kingston: McGill–Queen's University Press, 2004.

Emerick, K. F. *War Resisters Canada: The World of American Political-Military Refugees.* New York: Free Press, 1995.

Errington, Jane. *The Lion, the Eagle, and Upper Canada: A Developing Colonial Ideology.* Montreal and Kingston: McGill–Queen's University Press, 1987.

Evans, Wendy, Rochelle J. Lipsitz, and Harry Lane. *Border Crossings: Doing Business in the US.* Scarborough, Ont.: Prentice Hall, 1992.

Falconer, Sir Robert. *The United States as a Neighbour from a Canadian Point of View.* Cambridge: Cambridge University Press, 1925.

Ferguson, Ted. *A White Man's Country: An Exercise in Racial Prejudice.* Garden City, N.Y.: Doubleday, 1975.

Findlay, John M., and Kenneth S. Coates, eds. *Parallel Destinies: Canadian-American Relations West of the Rockies.* Seattle: University of Washington Press, 2002.

Fiske, John. *Understanding Popular Culture.* Boston: Unwin Hyman, 1989.

Flaherty, David, and Frank E. Manning, eds. *The Beaver Bites Back: American Popular Culture in Canada.* Montreal and Kingston: McGill–Queen's University Press, 1993.

Flaherty, David, and William McKercher, eds. *Southern Exposure: Canadian Perspectives on the United States.* Toronto: McGraw-Hill Ryerson, 1986.

Fornatale, Pete, and Josh Mills. *Radio in the Television Age.* Woodstock: Overlook Press, 1980.

Foster, Charles. *Once Upon a Time in Paradise: Canadians in the Golden Age of Hollywood.* Toronto: Dundurn, 2003.

Fox, Richard Wrightman, and T. J. Jackson Lears. *Culture of Consumption.* New York: Pantheon, 1983.

Fraser, Marian Botsford. *Walking the Line: Travels Along the Canadian-American Border.* Vancouver: Douglas & McIntyre, 1958.

Fraser, Matthew. *Weapons of Mass Distraction: Soft Power and American Empire.* Toronto: Key Porter Books, 2003.

Friedman, Thomas. *The Lexus and the Olive Tree: Understanding Globalization.* New York: Anchor Books, 2000.

Gaffen, Fred. *Cross Border Warriors: Canadians in American Forces, Americans in Canadian Forces: From the Civil War to the Gulf.* Toronto: Dundurn Press, 1995.

Galbraith, John S. *The Establishment of Canadian Diplomatic Status in Washington.* Berkeley: University of California Press, 1951.

Gamber, Wendy, Michael Grossberg, and Hendrick Hartog, eds. *American Public Life and the Historical Imagination.* Notre Dame, Ind.: University of Notre Dame Press, 2003.

Garreau, Joel. *Edge City: Life on the New Frontier.* New York: Doubleday, 1991.

———. *The Nine Nations of North America.* Boston: Houghton Mifflin, 1981.

Gasher, Mike. *Hollywood North: The Feature Film Industry in British Columbia.* Vancouver: University of British Columbia Press, 2002.

Genticore, Louis, ed. *The Historical Atlas of Canada: The Land Transformed, 1800–1891.* Toronto: University of Toronto Press, 1993.

Gibson, Frederick W., and Jonathan Rossie, eds. *The Road to Ogdensburg: The Queen's / St. Lawrence Conferences on Canadian-American Affairs.* East Lansing: Michigan State University Press, 1933.

Glazer, Nathan, and Daniel Patrick Moynihan. *Beyond the Melting Pot.* Cambridge, Mass.: Harvard University Press, 1963.

Globerman, Steven, and Michael Walker, eds. *Assessing NAFTA: A Trinational Analysis.* Vancouver: Fraser Institute, 1992.

Gluek, Alvin C. *Minnesota and the Manifest Destiny of the Canadian Northwest.* Toronto: University of Toronto Press, 1965.

Gottlieb, Allan, *"I'll Be with You in a Minute, Mr. Ambassador": The Education of a Canadian Diplomat in Washington.* Toronto: University of Toronto Press, 1991.

Grabb, Edward, and James Curtis. *Regions Apart: The Four Societies of Canada and the United States.* Don Mills, Ont.: Oxford University Press, 2005.

Graham, Ron. *One-Eyed Kings: Promise and Illusion in Canadian Politics.* Toronto: Collins, 1986.

Granatstein, J. L. *How Britain's Weakness Forced Canada into the Arms of the United States.* Toronto: University of Toronto Press, 1989.

———. *Yankee Go Home? Canadians and Anti-Americanism.* Toronto: HarperCollins, 1996.

Granatstein, J. L., and Robert Bothwell. *Pirouette: Pierre Trudeau and Canadian Foreign Policy.* Toronto: University of Toronto Press, 1990.

Gray, Colin. *Canadian Defence Priorities: A Question of Relevance.* Toronto: Clarke Irwin, 1972.

Gray, Douglas. *The Canadian Snowbird Guide.* Toronto: McGraw-Hill Ryerson, 1999 (and subsequent annual editions).

Gray, John. *Lost in America: The Imaginary Canadian in the American Dream.* Toronto: Talon Books, 1997.

Green, Lewis. *The Boundary Hunters: Surveying the 141st Meridian and the Alaska Panhandle.* Vancouver: University of British Columbia Press, 1982.

Gwyn, Richard. *The Forty-Ninth Paradox: Canada in North America.* Toronto: McClelland & Stewart, 1985.

———. *Nationalism without Walls: The Unbearable Lightness of Being Canadian.* Toronto: McClelland & Stewart, 1995.

Haig-Brown, Alan. *Hell No, We Won't Go: Vietnam Draft Resisters in Canada.* Toronto: Raincoast Books, 1995.

Haines, Michael R., and Richard H. Steckel. *A Population History of North America.* Cambridge: Cambridge University Press, 2000.

Hak, Gordon. *Turning Trees into Dollars: The British Columbia Coastal Lumber Industry, 1858–1913.* Toronto: University of Toronto Press, 2000.

Hammond, Bray. *Banks and Politics in America, from the Revolution to the Civil War.* Princeton, N.J.: Princeton University Press, 1957.

Hanke, Lewis, ed. *Do the Americas Have a Common History? A Critique of the Bolton Thesis.* New York: Alfred A. Knopf, 1964.

Hart, Michael. *A Trading Nation: Canadian Trade Policy from Colonialism to Globalization.* Vancouver: University of British Columbia Press, 2002.

Hart, Michael, and William Dymond. *Common Borders, Shared Destinies: Canada, the United States, and Deepening Integration.* Ottawa: Center for Trade Policy and Law, 2001.

Hart, Michael, with Bill Dymond and Colin Robertson. *Decision at Midnight: Inside the Canada-U.S. Free Trade Negotiations.* Vancouver: University of British Columbia Press, 1994.

Harvey, David. *Americans in Canada: Migration and Settlement Since the 1840s.* Queenston: Edwin Mellen Press, 1991.

Harvey, Frank. *Smoke & Mirrors: Globalized Terrorism and the Illusion of Multilateral Security.* Toronto: University of Toronto Press, 2004.

Hayden, Dolores. *Building Suburbia: Green Fields and Urban Growth, 1820–2000.* New York: Pantheon Books, 2003.

Helliwell, John. *How Much Do National Borders Matter?* Washington, D.C.: Brookings Institution Press, 1998.

Helmes-Hayes, Richard, and James Curtis, eds. *The Vertical Mosaic Revisited.* Toronto: University of Toronto Press, 1998.

Hero, Alfred Olivier, Jr. *Louisiana and Quebec: Bilateral Relations and Comparative Socio-Political Evolution, 1763–1993.* Lanham, Md.: University Press of America, 1995.

Hero, Alfred Olivier, Jr., and Marcel Deneau, eds. *Problems and Opportunities in U.S.-Quebec Relations.* Boulder, Colo.: Westview Press, 1984.

Hewitt, David B., and David Leyton Brown. *Canada's International Security Policy.* Scarborough, Ont.: Prentice Hall, 1995.

High, Steven. *Industrial Sunset: The Making of North America's Rust Belt, 1969–1984.* Toronto: University of Toronto Press, 2003.

Higham, John. *Strangers in the Land: Patterns of American Nativism 1860-1925.* New York: Athaneum, 1971, second edition.

Hilliker, John. *Canada's Department of External Affairs: Volume I, The Early Years, 1909–1946.* Montreal and Kingston: McGill–Queen's University Press, 1990.

Hilliker, John, and Donald Barry. *Canada's Department of External Affairs: Volume II, Coming of Age, 1946–1968.* Montreal and Kingston: McGill–Queen's University Press, 1995.

Hillmer, Norman, and J. L. Granatstein. *For Better or For Worse: Canada and the United States into the Twenty-First Century,* 2nd ed. Toronto: Thompson Nelson, 2007.

Hilmes, Michele. *Hollywood and Broadcasting: from Radio to Cable.* Urbana: University of Illinois Press, 1990.

Hoberg, George, ed. *Capacity for Choice: Canada in a New North America.* Toronto: University of Toronto Press, 2002.

Holmes, Helen, and David Taras. *Seeing Ourselves: Media Power and Policy in Canada.* Toronto: Harcourt Brace, 1996.

Hornsby, Stephen, ed. *The Northeastern Borderlands: Four Centuries of Interaction.* Fredericton, N.B.: Acadiensis Press and Canadian-American Center, University of Maine, 1989.

Hornsby, Stephen, and John G. Reid. *New England and the Maritime Provinces: Connections and Comparisons.* Montreal and Kingston: McGill–Queen's University Press, 2005.

Horowitz, Daniel. *The Morality of Spending: Attitudes toward the Consumer Society, 1875–1940.* Baltimore: Johns Hopkins University Press, 1985.

Howard, Victor, ed. *Creating the Peaceable Kingdom: And Other Essays on Canada.* East Lansing: Michigan State University Press, 1998.

Huntington, Samuel P. *The Clash of Civilizations and the Remaking of World Order.* New York: Simon & Schuster, 1996.

———. *Who Are We? The Challenge to America's National Identity.* New York: Simon & Schuster, 2003.

Hurtig, Mel. *The Vanishing Country: Is It Too Late to Save Canada?* Toronto: McClelland & Stewart, 2002.

Hutchinson, Bruce. *Struggle for the Border.* Toronto: Longmans Green, 1955.
Hutchinson, Don. *The Great Pulp Heroes.* Toronto: Mosaic Press, 1996.
Ignatieff, Michael. *Virtual War: Kosovo and Beyond.* Toronto: Viking, 2000.
Innis, Harold. *The Cod Fisheries: The History of an International Economy.* Toronto: University of Toronto Press, 1954.
Jenkins, Brian. *Fenians and Anglo-American Relations during Reconstruction.* Ithaca, N.Y.: Cornell University Press, 1969.
Jockel, Joseph T. *Security to the North: Canada-U.S. Defense Relations in the 1990s.* East Lansing: Michigan State University Press, 1991.
Kammen, Michael. *American Culture, American Tastes: Social Change and the 20th Century.* New York: Alfred A. Knopf, 1999.
Keats, Robert. *The Border Guide: A Canadian's Guide to Investment, Immigration, and Retirement Planning in the United States.* Windsor: Ontario Motorist Publishing Company, 1994.
Kelly, Ninette, and Michael Trebilock. *The Making of the Mosaic: A History of Canadian Immigration.* Toronto: EVW Press, 1998.
Keohane, Robert O., and Joseph S. Nye. *Power and Interdependence,* 3rd ed. New York: Longmans, 2001.
Kerr, Donald, and Deryck Holdsworth, eds. *The Historical Atlas of Canada: Addressing the Twentieth Century.* Toronto: University of Toronto Press, 1990.
Knowles, Valerie. *Strangers at Our Gates: Canadian Immigration and Immigration Policy, 1540–1990.* Toronto: Dundurn Press, 1992.
Kohn, Edward P. *This Kindred People: Canadian-American Relations and the Anglo-Saxon Idea, 1895–1903.* Montreal and Kingston: McGill–Queen's University Press, 2005.
Kostash, Myrna. *Long Way from Home: The Story of the Sixties Generation in Canada.* Toronto: Lorimer, 1980.
Kreinen, Mordechai, ed. *Building a Partnership: The Canada-U.S. Free Trade Agreement.* East Lansing and Calgary: Michigan State University Press and University of Calgary Press, 2000.
LaDow, Beth. *The Medicine Line: Life and Death on a North American Borderland.* New York: Routledge, 2001.
LaFeber, Walter. *The New Empire: An Interpretation of American Expansion 1860–1898.* Ithaca, N.Y.: Cornell University Press, 1963.
Lamont, Lansing. *Breakup: The Coming End of Canada and the Stakes for America.* New York: W. W. Norton, 1994.
Landon, Fred. *Western Ontario and the American Frontier.* Toronto: Ryerson Press, 1941.
LaPierre, Laurier, ed. *If You Love This Country: Facts and Feelings on Free Trade.* Toronto: McClelland & Stewart, 1987.
Laxer, James. *The Border: Canada, the U.S. and Dispatches from the 49th Parallel.* Toronto: Random House of Canada, 2003.
———. *Stalking the Elephant: My Discovery of America.* Toronto: Viking, 2000.
Laxer, Robert, ed. *Canada Ltd.: The Political Economy of Dependency.* Toronto: McClelland & Stewart, 1973.
Leach, William. *Land of Desire: Merchants, Power, and the Rise of a New American Culture.* New York: Random House, 1995.

Lecker, Robert, ed. *Borderlands: Essays in Canadian-American Relations.* Toronto: ECW Press, 1991.

Li, Peter. *Ethnic Inequality in a Class Society.* Toronto: Thompson Educational Publishing, 1988.

Lind, Michael. *American Nation: The New Nationalism and the Fourth American Revolution.* New York: Free Press, 1995.

Lipset, Seymour Martin. *Continental Divide: The Values and Institutions of the United States and Canada.* Toronto and Washington: C. D. Howe Institute and National Planning Association, 1989.

Lisee, Jean François. *In the Eye of the Eagle.* Montreal: Boreal, 1990.

Litt, Paul. *The Muses, the Masses, and the Massey Commission.* Toronto: University of Toronto Press, 1992.

Litvak, Isaiah, and Christopher Maule. *Cultural Sovereignty: The* Time *and* Reader's Digest *Case in Canada.* New York: Praeger, 1974.

Lower, A. R. M., W. A. Carrothers, and S. A. Saunders. *The North American Assault on the Forest: A History of the Lumber Trade between Canada and the United States.* Toronto: Ryerson Press, 1938.

Lumsden, Ian, ed. *Close the 49th Parallel, Etc.* Toronto: University of Toronto Press, 1970.

Maclean's. Canada in the Fifties: From the Archives of Maclean's. Toronto: Viking, 1999.

MacKinnon, Neil. *This Unfriendly Soil: The Loyalist Experience in Nova Scotia, 1783–1791.* Montreal and Kingston: McGill–Queen's University Press, 1986.

MacNeil, Robert. *Looking for My Country: Finding Myself in America.* New York: Doubleday, 2003.

MacNeil, Robert, and William Cran. *Do You Speak American?* New York: Nan A. Talese, 2004.

Magder, Ted. *Canada's Hollywood: The Canadian State and Feature Films.* Toronto: University of Toronto Press, 1993.

Mahant, Edelgard E., and Graeme S. Mount. *An Introduction to Canadian-American Relations.* Toronto: Nelson Canada, 1989.

———. *Invisible and Inaudible in Washington: American Policies toward Canada.* Vancouver: University of British Columbia Press, 1999.

Marquis, Greg. *In Armageddon's Shadow: The Civil War and Canada's Maritime Provinces.* Montreal and Kingston: McGill–Queen's University Press, 1998.

Marshall, Herbert, Frank Southard Jr., and Kenneth W. Taylor. *Canadian-American Industry: A Study in International Investment.* New York: Russell & Russell, 1970 (orig. pub. 1936).

Martin, Lawrence. *Pledge of Allegiance: The Americanization of Canada in the Mulroney Years.* Toronto: McClelland & Stewart, 1993.

———. *The Presidents and the Prime Ministers: Washington and Ottawa Face to Face: The Myth of Bilateral Bliss 1867–1982.* Garden City, N.Y.: Doubleday, 1982.

Masters, D. C. *The Reciprocity Treaty of 1854.* Toronto: McClelland & Stewart, 1963 (orig. pub. 1937).

Mathews, Robin, and James Steele, eds. *The Struggle for Canadian Universities.* Toronto: New Press, 1969.

May, Robert E. *Manifest Destiny's Underworld: Filibustering in Antebellum America.* Chapel Hill: University of North Carolina Press, 2002.

Mazurkewich, Karen. *Cartoon Capers: The History of Canadian Animators.* Toronto: MacArthur, 2000.

McCall, Bruce. *Thin Ice: Coming of Age in Canada.* Toronto: Random House, 1997.

McDougall, John N. *Drifting Together: The Political Economy of Canada-U.S. Integration.* Toronto: Broadview, 2006.

McKercher, B. J. C., and Lawrence Aronsen, eds. *The North Atlantic Triangle in a Changing World: Anglo-American-Canadian Relations, 1902–1956.* Toronto: University of Toronto Press, 1996.

McKinsey, Lauren, and Kim Nossal. *America's Alliances and Canadian-American Relations.* Toronto: Summerhill Press, 1988.

McManus, Sheila. *The Line which Separates: Race, Gender and the Making of the Alberta-Montana Borderlands.* Lincoln: University of Nebraska Press, 2005.

McNeil, Lowry, ed. *Arts and Public Policy in the United States.* Englewood Cliffs, N.J.: Prentice Hall, 1984.

McNeill, Bill, and Morris Wolfe, eds. *Signing On: The Birth of Radio in Canada.* Garden City, N.Y.: Doubleday, 1982.

Meinig, D.W. *The Shaping of America: A Geographical Perspective on 500 Years of History, Vol. 1, Atlantic America, 1492–1800.* New Haven, Conn.: Yale University Press, 1985.

———. *The Shaping of America: A Geographical Perspective on 500 Years of History, Vol. 2, Continental America 1800–1867.* New Haven, Conn.: Yale University Press, 1993.

———. *The Shaping of America: A Geographical Perspective on 500 Years of History, Vol. 3, Transcontinental America 1850–1915.* New Haven, Conn.: Yale University Press, 1985.

———. *The Shaping of America: A Geographical Perspective on 500 Years of History, Vol. 4, Global America 1915–1992.* New Haven, Conn.: Yale University Press, 2004.

Middlemiss, D. W., and J. J. Sokolsky. *Canadian Defence: Decisions and Determinants.* Toronto: Harcourt Brace Jovanovich, 1989.

Miller, Mary Jane. *Rewind and Search: Conversations with the Makers and Decision-Makers of CBC Television Drama.* Montreal and Kingston: McGill–Queen's University Press, 1996.

Molot, Maureen Appel, ed. *Driving Continentally: National Policies and the North American Auto Industry.* Ottawa: Carleton University Press, 1993.

Molot, Maureen Appel, and Fen Osler Hampson, eds. *Vanishing Borders: Canada among Nations.* Toronto: Oxford University Press, 2000.

Monod, David. *Store Wars: Shopkeepers and the Culture of Mass Marketing, 1890–1939.* Toronto: University of Toronto Press, 1996.

Morris, Peter. *Embattled Shadows: A History of Canadian Cinema 1895-1936.* Kingston: McGill-Queen's University Press, 1978.

Morrison, Katherine. *Canadians Are Not Americans: Myths and Literary Traditions.* Toronto: Second Story Press, 2003.

Morton, Desmond. *Understanding Canadian Defence.* Toronto: Menguin / McGill Institute, 2003.

Mount, Nick. *When Canadian Literature Moved to New York.* Toronto: University of Toronto Press, 2005.

Mulcahy, Kevin V., and Richard Swain, eds. *Public Policy and the Arts.* Boulder, Colo.: Westview Press, 1982.

Munro, John A., ed. *The Alaska Boundary Dispute.* Toronto: Copp Clark, 1970.
Munton, Don, and John Kirton, eds. *Canadian Foreign Policy: Selected Cases.* Scarborough, Ont.: Prentice Hall, 1992.
Murray, Janice L., ed. *Canadian Cultural Nationalism: The Fourth Lester B. Pearson Conference on the Canada–United States Relationship.* New York: New York University Press, 1977.
Nash, Knowlton. *Kennedy & Diefenbaker: Fear and Loathing Across the Undefended Border.* Toronto: McClelland & Stewart, 1990.
Nelles, H. V. *The Politics of Development: Forest, Mines and Hydro Electric Power in Ontario 1849–1941.* Toronto: Macmillan, 1965.
New, W. H. *Borderlands: How We Talk about Canada.* Vancouver: University of British Columbia Press, 1969.
Nicol, Eric, and Dave Moore. *The U.S. or US: What's the Difference, Eh?* Edmonton: Hurtig, 1986.
Nichols, M. E. *The Story of the Canadian Press.* Toronto: Ryerson Press, 1948.
Nye, Joseph S., Jr. *The Paradox of American Power: Why the World's Only Superpower Can't Go It Alone.* New York: Oxford University Press, 2002.
Owram, Doug. *Born at the Right Time: A History of the Baby Boom Generation.* Toronto: University of Toronto Press, 1996.
Parham, Claire Puccia. *From Great Wilderness to Seaway Towns: A Comparative History of Cornwall, Ontario, and Massena, New York, 1784–2001.* Albany: State University of New York Press, 2005.
Pearson, Lester B. *Mike: The Memoirs of the Right Honourable Lester B. Pearson.* 2 vols. Toronto: University of Toronto Press, 1948.
Peers, Frank. *The Politics of Canadian Broadcasting, 1920–1951.* Toronto: University of Toronto Press, 1969.
Penlington, Norman. *The Alaska Boundary Dispute: A Critical Reappraisal.* Toronto: McGraw-Hill Ryerson, 1972.
Peterson, Theodore. *Magazines in the Twentieth Century.* Urbana: University of Illinois Press, 1964.
Pevere, Geoff, and Greig Dymond. *Mondo Canuck: A Canadian Pop Culture Odyssey.* Scarborough, Ont.: Prentice Hall, 1966.
Porter, John. *The Vertical Mosaic: An Analysis of Social Class and Power in Canada.* Toronto: University of Toronto Press, 1965.
Potter, David M. *People of Plenty: Economic Abundance and the American Character.* Chicago: University of Chicago Press, 1954.
Preston, Richard A. *The Defence of the Undefended Border: Planning for War in North America 1867–1939.* Montreal and Kingston: McGill–Queen's University Press, 1977.
———, ed. *The Influence of the United States on Canadian Development: Eleven Case Studies.* Durham, N.C.: Duke University Press, 1972.
Ramirez, Bruno. *Crossing the 49th Parallel: Migration from Canada to the United States, 1900–1930.* Ithaca, N.Y.: Cornell University Press, 2001.
———. *On the Move: French Canadian and Italian Migrants in the North Atlantic Economy.* Toronto: McClelland & Stewart, 1991.
Randall, Stephen J., and Herman W. Konrad, eds. *NAFTA in Transition.* Calgary: University of Calgary Press, 1995.
Reitz, Jeffrey G., and Raymond Breton. *The Illusion of Difference: Realities of Ethnicity in Canada and the United States.* Toronto: C. D. Howe Institute, 1994.

Resnick, Philip. *The European Roots of the Canadian Identity.* Toronto: Broadview Press, 2005.

Ritchie, Gordon. *Wrestling with the Elephant: The Inside Story of the Canada-U.S. Trade* Wars. Toronto: Macfarlane, Walter & Ross, 1997.

Rosenberg, Bernard, and David White, eds. *Mass Culture: The Popular Arts in America.* New York: Free Press, 1987.

Rosenberg, Emily. *Spreading the American Dream: American Economic and Cultural Expansion 1890–1945.* New York: Hill & Wang, 1982.

Roussel, Stéphane. *North American Democratic Peace: Absence of War and Security Institution-Building in Canada-U.S. Relations, 1867–1958.* Montreal and Kingston: McGill–Queen's University Press, 2004.

Roy, Patricia E. *White Man's Province: British Columbia Politicians and Chinese and Japanese Immigrants 1854–1914.* Vancouver: University of British Columbia Press, 1989.

Rutherford, Paul. *A Victorian Authority: The Daily Press in Late Nineteenth Century Canada.* Toronto: University of Toronto Press, 1982.

———. *When Television Was Young: Primetime Canada 1952–1967.* Toronto: University of Toronto Press, 1990.

Rybczynski, Witold. *City Life: Urban Expectations in a New World.* Toronto: HarperCollins, 1995.

Safdie, Moshe. *The City After the Automobile.* Toronto: Stoddart, 1997.

Santink, Joy. *Timothy Eaton and the Rise of His Department Store.* Toronto: University of Toronto Press, 1990.

Schneirov, Matthew. *The Dream of a New Social Order: Popular Magazines in America, 1893–1914.* New York: Columbia University Press, 1995.

Seagrave, Kelly. *American Films Abroad: Hollywood's Domination of the World's Movie Screens.* North Carolina and London: McFarland & Company, 1997.

Senior, Hereward. *The Last Invasion of Canada: The Fenian Raids, 1866–1870.* Toronto: University of Toronto Press, 1991.

Shaffer, ed. *Canada's Oil and the American Empire.* Edmonton: Hurtig, 1983.

Sharp, Paul. *Whoop Up Country: The Canadian-American West 1865–1885.* Norman: University of Oklahoma Press, 1978.

Sheppard, George. *Plunder, Profit, and Paroles: A Social History of the War of 1812 in Upper Canada.* Montreal and Kingston: McGill–Queen's University Press, 1994.

Shippee, Lester B. *Canadian-American Relations, 1849–1874.* New Haven, Conn.: Yale University Press, 1939.

Simpson, Jeffrey. *Star-Spangled Canadians: Canadians Living the American Dream.* Toronto: HarperCollins, 2000.

Sklar, Robert. *Movie Made America: A Cultural History of the American Movies.* New York: Random House, 1994.

Slide, Anthony. *The Vaudevillians: A Dictionary of Vaudeville Performers.* Westport, Conn.: Arlington House, 1981.

Slotkin, Richard. *Gunfighter Nation: The Myth of the Frontier in 20th Century America.* New York: Athaneum, 1992.

Smelyan, Susan. *Selling Radio: The Commercialization of American Broadcasting 1920–1934.* Washington, D.C.: Smithsonian Press, 1994.

Smith, Allen. *Canada: An American Nation? Essays on Continentalism, Identity, and the Canadian Frame of Mind.* Montreal and Kingston: McGill–Queen's University Press, 1994.

Smith, Anthony, and Richard Patterson, eds. *Television: An International Industry,* 2nd ed. New York: Oxford University Press, 1998.

Smith, Denis. *Gentle Patriot: A Political Biography of Walter Gordon.* Edmonton: University of Alberta Press, 1973.

Smythe, Dallas W. *Dependency Road: Communications, Capitalism, Consciousness, and Canada.* Norwood, N.J.: Ablex, 1981.

Stairs, Denis, and Gilbert Winham, eds. *The Politics of Canada's Economic Relationship with the United States.* Toronto: University of Toronto Press, 1985.

Stewart, Gordon T. *The American Response to Canada since 1776.* East Lansing: Michigan State University Press, 1992.

Strange, Carolyn, and Tina Loo. *True Crime, True North: The Golden Age of Canadian Pulp Magazines.* Vancouver: Raincoast Books, 2004.

Strasser, Susan. *Satisfaction Guaranteed: The Making of the American Mass Market.* New York: Pantheon Books, 1989.

Stuart, Reginald C. *United States Expansionism and British North America, 1775–1871.* Chapel Hill: University of North Carolina Press, 1988.

Surrey, David S. *Choice of Conscience: Vietnam Era Military and Draft Resisters in Canada.* New York: Praeger, 1982.

Swanson, Roger Frank. *Intergovernmental Perspectives on the Canada-U.S. Relationship.* New York: New York University Press, 1978.

———, ed. *Canadian-American Summit Diplomacy, 1923–1973: Selected Speeches and Documents.* Toronto: McClelland & Stewart, 1975.

Tansill, Charles C. *The Canadian Reciprocity Treaty of 1854.* Baltimore: Johns Hopkins Press, 1922.

Taras, David. *Seeing Ourselves: Media Power and Policy in Canada.* Toronto: Harcourt Brace, 1996.

Tedlow, Richard. *New and Improved: The Story of Mass Marketing in America.* New York: Basic Books, 1990.

Thomas, David M., ed. *Canada and the United States: Differences That Count,* 2nd ed. Toronto: Broadview Press, 2000.

Thompson, John Herd, and Stephen J. Randall. *Canada and the United States: Ambivalent Allies,* 3rd ed. Montreal and Kingston: McGill–Queen's University Press, 2002.

Thompson, John Herd, and Allen Seager. *Canada, 1922–1939: Decades of Discord.* Toronto: McClelland & Stewart, 1985.

Troper, Harold. *Only Farmers Need Apply: Official Canadian Government Encouragement of Immigration from the United States, 1896–1911.* Toronto: Griffin House, 1972.

Truesdell, Leon. *The Canadian Born in the United States: An Analysis of the Statistics of the Canadian Element in the Population of the United States, 1850–1930.* New Haven, Conn.: Yale University Press, 1943.

Tupper, Stanley R., and Douglas Bailey. *Canada and the United States: The Second Hundred Years.* New York: Hawthorn Books, 1967.

Twitchell, James B. *Branded Nation: The Marketing of Megachurch, College Inc., and Museum World.* New York: Simon & Schuster, 2004.

Vance, James E., Jr. *The North American Railroad: Its Origin, Evolution, and Geography.* Baltimore: Johns Hopkins University Press, 1995.

Vipond, Mary. *Listening In: The First Decade of Canadian Broadcasting, 1922–1932.* Montreal and Kingston: McGill–Queen's University Press, 1992.

Walker, James E. St. G. *The Black Loyalists: The Search for a Promised Land in Nova Scotia and Sierra Leone 1783–1870.* Toronto: University of Toronto Press, 1992.

———. *Identity: The Black Experience in Canada.* Toronto: Gage Educational Press, 1979.

———. *Race, Rights and Law in the Supreme Court of Canada: Historical Case Studies.* Waterloo: Wilfrid Laurier University Press for Osgoode Society for Canadian Legal History, 1997.

Ward, Peter. *White Canada Forever: Popular Attitudes and Public Policy toward Orientals in British Columbia.* Montreal and Kingston: McGill–Queen's University Press, 1978.

Warner, Donald F. *The Idea of Continental Union: Agitation for the Annexation of Canada to the United States, 1849–1893.* Lexington: University of Kentucky Press, 1960.

Watson, William. *Globalization and the Meaning of Canadian Life.* Toronto: University of Toronto Press, 1998.

Welsh, Jennifer. *At Home in the World: Canada's Global Vision.* Toronto: HarperCollins, 2004.

White, Randall. *Fur Trade to Free Trade: Putting the Canada-U.S. Trade Agreement in Historical Perspective.* Toronto: Dundurn Press, 1988.

Widdis, Randy William. *With Scarcely a Ripple: Anglo-Canadian Migration into the United States and Western Canada, 1880–1920.* Montreal and Kingston: McGill–Queen's University Press, 1998.

Winks, Robin. *The Blacks in Canada.* Montreal and Kingston: McGill–Queen's University Press, 1971.

———. *Canada and the United States: The Civil War Years.* Baltimore: Johns Hopkins Press, 1960.

Wise, S. F., and Robert Craig Brown. *Canada Views the United States: Nineteenth-Century Political Attitudes.* Toronto: Macmillan of Canada, 1967.

About the Author

Reginald C. Stuart is professor of history and political and Canadian studies at Mount Saint Vincent University in Halifax. He was born in Vancouver, and he studied at the University of British Columbia and earned his doctorate at the University of Florida in 1974. He taught at the University of Prince Edward Island from 1968 to 1988. He was dean of arts and sciences at Mount Saint Vincent University from 1988 to 1996, when he returned to teaching and research.

His books include *The Half-Way Pacifist: Thomas Jefferson's View of War* (University of Toronto Press, 1978); *War and American Thought: From the Revolution to the Monroe Doctrine* (Kent State University Press, 1982); the texts *The Enlightenment in America* (1985) and *Readings in the American Enlightenment* (Open Learning Institute, 1985); and *The First Seventy-Five Years: A History of the Certified General Accountants Association of Canada* (Certified General Accountants Association, 1988). His book *United States Expansionism and British North America, 1775–1871* (University of North Carolina Press, 1988) won the Canadian and American historical associations' Albert Corey Prize in 1990.

In 2003, he won a Canada–United States Fulbright Fellowship and became the Fulbright–Woodrow Wilson Center Distinguished Chair in Canada-U.S. Relations attached to the Canada Institute at the Woodrow Wilson International Center for Scholars from January to May 2004. He is currently a coeditor of *Shared and Separate Histories: Canada and the United States Since 1800* (forthcoming).

Index